Successes in African Agriculture

**Other Books Published in Cooperation with
the International Food Policy Research Institute**

IFPRI

Successes in African Agriculture

Lessons for the Future

EDITED BY STEVEN HAGGBLADE
AND PETER B. R. HAZELL

Published for the International Food Policy Research Institute

The Johns Hopkins University Press
Baltimore

The Johns Hopkins University Press
2715 North Charles Street
Baltimore, Maryland 21218-4363
www.press.jhu.edu

International Food Policy Research Institute
2033 K Street, NW
Washington, DC 20006
(202) 862-5600
www.ifpri.org

IFPRI's research, capacity strengthening, and communications work is made possible by its financial contributors and partners. IFPRI gratefully acknowledges the generous unrestricted funding from Australia, Canada, China, Finland, France, Germany, India, Ireland, Italy, Japan, the Netherlands, Norway, the Philippines, Sweden, Switzerland, the United Kingdom, the United States, and the World Bank.

LIBRARY OF CONGRESS CATALOGING-IN-PUBLICATION DATA

Successes in African agriculture : lessons for the future / edited by Steven Haggblade and Peter B. R. Hazell.
    p.   cm.
  Includes bibliographical references and index.
  ISBN-13: 978-0-8018-9502-9 (hardcover : alk. paper)
  ISBN-10: 0-8018-9502-2 (hardcover : alk. paper)
  ISBN-13: 978-0-8018-9503-6 (pbk. : alk. paper)
  ISBN-10: 0-8018-9503-0 (pbk. : alk. paper)
  1. Agricultural development projects—Africa, Sub-Saharan—Case studies.
2. Agricultural productivity—Africa, Sub-Saharan—Case studies.   3. Agricultural assistance—Africa, Sub-Saharan—Case studies.   I. Haggblade, Steven.
II. Hazell, P. B. R.
  HD2117.S84   2010
  338.1′867—dc22   2009035572

A catalog record for this book is available from the British Library.

Special discounts are available for bulk purchases of this book. For more information, please contact Special Sales at 410-516-6936 or specialsales@press.jhu.edu.

The Johns Hopkins University Press uses environmentally friendly book materials, including recycled text paper that is composed of at least 30 percent post-consumer waste, whenever possible. All of our book papers are acid-free, and our jackets and covers are printed on paper with recycled content.

Contents

Figures

Tables

Boxes

Foreword

Africa stands at the dawn of a new era. In spite of the global financial meltdown and spiraling food prices, the continent has shown remarkable resilience. On the economic front, Africa has achieved remarkable progress in recent years. Reforms have opened up political and economic space for the private sector, including traders and farmers, and have allowed civil-society organizations to actively participate in national agriculture development. Eighteen countries in the region have maintained average economic growth of 5.5 percent per year during the past decade, while more than half of the continent's countries have recorded agricultural growth exceeding 4 percent during the past five years. Africa is moving toward social and political stability, albeit slowly.

Africa's impressive gains, however, were not enough to compensate for more than two decades of economic stagnation and decline before the recent recovery. As a result, many African countries are still facing high levels of poverty and malnutrition. Increasingly volatile world markets, coupled with global environmental change and increased population pressure on arable land, will increase the challenges for rural communities in Africa.

To successfully combat hunger in the region, future efforts must focus more on agriculture. More than two-thirds of Africa's poor work primarily in agriculture, yet agricultural productivity in Africa remains the lowest in the world. Clearly, agricultural productivity must increase if Africa is to improve the welfare of the majority of its citizens. Only increased agricultural productivity can simultaneously reduce food prices—which govern real incomes and poverty in urban areas—and increase the incomes of the majority of Africa's poor. For this reason, agricultural growth provides a central thrust around which the battle against African poverty must be waged. In recognition of this fact, Africa's leaders adopted the Comprehensive African Agricultural Development Programme (CAADP) in 2003 and agreed to raise budget allocations for agriculture to a minimum of 10 percent of public spending.

To help translate this new financial commitment into more effective action on the ground, the International Food Policy Research Institute (IFPRI) and the New Partnership for Africa's Development (NEPAD) Secretariat have collaborated with a host of other partners to systematically examine past episodes of successful agricultural development in Africa. Indeed, in the past, African agriculture has seen moments of great promise. In 1960, maize breeders in Africa released the first commercially grown single-cross hybrids in the world. In 1977, cassava breeders in Nigeria released the first of the Tropical Manioc Selection (TMS) varieties that have subsequently revolutionized breeding lines and cassava productivity across the tropical midsection of Africa. Additionally, West African farmers have increased cotton production and exports at a compound annual rate of 9 percent per year for more than four decades. This book explores these case studies, as well as others, in an effort to identify key elements driving successful agricultural growth in Africa. By identifying the institutions, investments, processes, and policies that have made past successes possible, the authors provide a basis for fostering partnerships and an enabling environment in which African farmers can raise their productivity and welfare more consistently in the future.

Given newfound commitment to agriculture by African leaders and the community of development partners, we believe that the time is ripe to review, reflect, and build upon what has worked well in the past. We hope this book will contribute to these ongoing efforts to invigorate and accelerate growth in African agriculture.

Joachim von Braun   Richard Mkandawire
Director General, IFPRI Agriculture Advisor, NEPAD Secretariat

Acknowledgments

This volume covers a broad geographic and historical landscape. Given the complexity and diversity of African farming systems, a review of this sort would not have been possible without strong support from a variety of sources.

In launching this work, we are grateful to Per Pinstrup-Andersen, who strongly supported this major review effort while director general of the International Food Policy Research Institute (IFPRI) and allocated core IFPRI funding to finance it. His successor, Joachim von Braun, has likewise proven highly supportive, particularly in facilitating IFPRI support for the series of stakeholder consultations and coordination with the New Partnership for Africa's Development (NEPAD) Secretariat. Eleni Gabre-Madhin served as one of the two original research coordinators. In that capacity, she played a key role in helping to execute the expert survey, develop the analytical framework, launch the case study teams, and organize the case study workshop.

Our distinguished external advisory group included Michel Benoit-Cattin, Josué Dione, Simeon Ehui, Carl Eicher, and Wilberforce Kisamba-Mugerwa. We are grateful to all of them for the thoughtful, constructive guidance they provided throughout this effort. Their broad experience proved particularly helpful in guiding the selection of a portfolio of case studies that would offer both contrast and illumination.

The empirical foundations of this research have depended largely on accessing and analyzing existing data sources, published material, and a large gray literature. In this effort, the case study authors proved highly entrepreneurial. Ghada Shields likewise provided exceptionally able backstopping and reference support to the field teams. In assembling aggregate data of various sorts, the analytical team acknowledges critical assistance from Ming Chen, Michael Johnson, Stanley Wood, and Ulrike Wood-Sichra.

To solicit feedback and practical insights from policymakers, farmers, agribusiness, and other stakeholder groups, the analytical team has worked closely with Richard Mkandawire, Agriculture Advisor at the NEPAD Secretariat, in conducting a series of three major stakeholder consultations. He and his colleagues at the Secretariat, Ingrid Kirsten and Augustin Wambo, demonstrated extraordinary organizational skills, an exceptional capacity for hard work, and a high degree of diplomacy and congeniality in managing these workshops. Jergen Richter and his colleagues at Internationale Weiterbildung und Entwicklung (InWEnt) provided outstanding professional facilitators for the three stakeholder workshops. They ensured that all participants' viewpoints were expressed in the professionally facilitated small-group break-out sessions that formed the backbone of these workshops. The team is grateful to InWEnt, the Technical Centre for Agricultural and Rural Cooperation (CTA), the International Fund for Agricultural Development, Centre de Coopération Internationale en Recherche Agronomique pour le Développement, and the host governments of Kenya and South Africa for material and financial support in running the three stakeholder consultations in Pretoria, Nairobi, and Somerset West.

Finally, we thank the conference participants—the government policymakers, farmers, private agribusiness groups, agricultural researchers, donors, and operational project personnel—who took the time to review our preliminary research findings and help us distill the key lessons emerging from this work.

Acronyms and Abbreviations

AADI	Addis Ababa Dairy Industry
ACP	African, Caribbean, and Pacific
ACU	Acceleration of Cassava Utilization Task Force
ADMARC	Agricultural Development and Marketing Corporation
ADPs	agricultural development programmes
AER	agroecological region
AI	artificial insemination
AR	African Reserve
ASARECA	Association for Strengthening Agricultural Research in Eastern and Central Africa
AU	African Union
AVs	*associations villageoises*
Bt	*Bacillus thuringiensis*
CAADP	Comprehensive African Agricultural Development Programme
CAIS	Central Artificial Insemination Service
CF	conservation farming
CFA	Communauté Financière Africaine
CFAF	CFA franc
CFDT	Compagnie Française de Développement des Textiles
CFU	Conservation Farming Unit
CGM	cassava green mite
CIMMYT	Centro Internacional de Mejoramiento de Maíz y Trigo
CIRAD	Centre de Coopération Internationale en Recherche Agronomique pour le Développement
CLUSA	Cooperative League of the USA
CM	cassava mealybug
CMDT	Compagnie Malienne pour le Développement des Textiles
CMV	cassava mosaic virus

COMESA	Common Market for Eastern and Southern Africa
COPACO	Compagnie Cotonnière
CORFRUITEL	Coopérative de Producteurs pour la Commercialization des Fruits et Légumes de la Côte d'Ivoire
COSCA	Collaborative Study of Cassava in Africa
CTA	Technical Centre for Agricultural and Rural Cooperation
DDA	Dairy Development Agency
DDE	Dairy Development Enterprise
DE-A-R framework	Decisionmaking Environment (DE)–Action (A)–Results (R) framework
DFCS	Dairy Farmer Cooperative Societies
DRC	Democratic Republic of Congo
DRSK	Dairy Record Service of Kenya
EAC	East African Community
EPAs	Economic Partnership Agreements
FAO	Food and Agriculture Organization of the United Nations
FARA	Forum for Agricultural Research in Africa
FPEAK	Fresh Produce Exporters Association
GART	Golden Valley Agricultural Research Trust
GATT	General Agreement on Trade and Tariffs
GDP	gross domestic product
GMB	Grain Marketing Board
GMOs	genetically modified organisms
HCDA	Horticultural Crops Development Authority
HYV	high-yielding variety
ICAC	International Cotton Advisory Council
ICRAF	World Agroforestry Centre
ICRISAT	International Crops Research Institute for the Semi-Arid Tropics
IER	Institut d'Économie Rurale
IFPRI	International Food Policy Research Institute
IITA	International Institute of Tropical Agriculture
InWEnt	Internationale Weiterbildung und Entwicklung GmbH, or Capacity Building International
IOPVs	improved open-pollinated varieties
IP	intellectual property
IPM	integrated pest management
IRCT	Institut de Recherche Cotonnière et des Fibres Textiles Exotiques
ISI	import-substituting industrialization
KAIS	Kenya Artificial Insemination Service

KARI	Kenya Agricultural Research Institute
KCC	Kenya Cooperative Creameries
KDB	Kenya Dairy Board
KEFRI	Kenya Forestry Research Institute
KFP	Kenya Fruit Processing
KNAIS	Kenya National Artificial Insemination
KSB	Kenya Stud Book
LPA	Lagos Plan of Action
LRC	Livestock Recording Centre
MCB	Maize Control Board
MDG	Millennium Development Goal
MK	Malawi kwacha
NAMBOARD	National Agricultural Marketing Board
NEPAD	New Partnership for Africa's Development
NGOs	nongovernmental organizations
NRM	natural resource management
NSCM	National Seed Company of Malawi
OCAB	Office Centrale des Producteurs-Exportateurs d'Ananas et de Bananes
OECD	Organisation for Economic Co-operation and Development
PICPE	Presidential Initiative on Cassava Production and Export
R&D	research and development
RTIP	Root and Tuber Improvement Programme
SACCAR	Southern African Centre for Cooperation in Agricultural Research and Training
SAP	structural adjustment program
SCAER	Société de Crédit Agricole et d'Equipement Rural
SDFs	small-scale dairy farmers
SFC	State Farms Corporation
Shell-BP	Shell BP Petroleum Company of Nigeria
SIDA	Swedish International Development Cooperation Agency
SP	Starter Pack
SRDP	Smallholder Rehabilitation and Development Programme
SSA	Sub-Saharan Africa
SWC	soil and water conservation
SYCOV	Union of Cotton and Food Crop Producers
TIP	Targeted Input Program
TMS	Tropical Manioc Selection
ULV	ultra-low-volume

UNICEF	United Nations Children's Fund
USAID	United States Agency for International Development
WECARD/CORAF	West and Central African Council for Agricultural Research and Development
WFP	World Food Programme
WTO	World Trade Organization
ZIAP	Zambia Integrated Agroforestry Project
ZNFU	Zambia National Farmers Union

PART I

Overview

1 Challenges for African Agriculture

STEVEN HAGGBLADE, PETER B. R. HAZELL,
AND ELENI GABRE-MADHIN

Motivation

Needs

Sub-Saharan Africa faces critical challenges.[1] More than 40 percent of all Africans live on less than US$1 per day, and a staggering one out of three is undernourished (Table 1.1). Yet 70 percent of the continent's poor work in agriculture.[2] Clearly, Africa's agriculture has underperformed. Under "business-as-usual" projections for agriculture, Africa will increasingly depend on food imports to meet its basic consumption requirements. Only in Africa, among all developing regions, are the numbers of malnourished children projected to increase over the next two decades (Rosegrant et al. 2001, 2005).

Although many factors contribute to Africa's persistent hunger and poverty, poor agricultural performance lies at the heart of the problem. On average, agriculture accounts for 65 percent of full-time employment in Africa, 25–30 percent of gross domestic product (GDP), and over half of total export earnings (IFPRI 2004; World Bank 2007b).[3] It underpins the livelihoods of over two-thirds of Africa's poor and assumes even greater importance in the continent's poorest countries, such as Burundi, Ethiopia, Malawi, and Tanzania. Yet Africa's agricultural performance over the past 45 years has ranked worst in the world according to most conventional measures. Given low levels of land and labor productivity, African farmers produce output per capita valued at only half

---

1. For brevity, the discussion hereafter will use *Africa* when referring to Sub-Saharan Africa.

2. Complete data on the sectoral composition of poor households' income do not exist for all of Sub-Saharan Africa. This estimate relies on work by Ravallion, Chen, and Sangraula (2007), who project the percentage of poor households residing in rural and urban parts of Sub-Saharan Africa; by Valdés et al. (2009), who provide breakdowns of the sectoral composition of income among poor rural households; and Garret (2004) and others, who provide evidence on the prevalence of urban agriculture among poor African households.

3. Weighting by GDP for all countries outside of South Africa (which alone accounts for 40 percent of Sub-Saharan Africa's aggregate GDP) produces an agricultural share of 25 percent. Weighting by population produces an agricultural GDP share of 30 percent.

3

TABLE 1.1 Indicators of agricultural performance and welfare

	Sub-Saharan Africa	South Asia	East Asia	Latin America
Agriculture				
Cereal yields, 2005 (tons/ha)	0.9	2.8		3.0
Value of agricultural production per farm population, 2005 (US$)	$225	$446		$2,105
Food aid cereals, 2000–03 (kg/capita)	4.6	1.1		1.1
Welfare				
Poverty headcount, 2004 (% living on less than US$1 per day)	41	31	9	9
Undernourishment, 2004 (% of population)	32	21	12	10
Malnutrition, 2004 (% children under 5 underweight for age)	29	45	15	7
Per capita income, 2005 (US$)	$746	$692	$1,630	$4,045
Aid per capita, 2005 (US$)	$44	$6	$5	$11
Population				
Population growth rate, 2006 (% per year)	2.3	1.5	0.8	1.3
Population, 2005 (millions)	743	1,470	1,886	551

SOURCES: World Bank (2007b), FAOSTAT (2008).

NOTE: The agricultural data for South Asia and East Asia refer to developing Asia.

the level achieved in developing Asia, while cereal yields in Africa attain only one-third of the level prevailing in developing Asia and Latin America (see Table 1.1). Africa likewise remains the only developing region where per capita agricultural production has fallen over the past four and a half decades (Figure 1.1). Today, in comparison with other developing regions of the world, Africa lays claim to the world's lowest agricultural productivity, its highest incidence of poverty, and per capita food aid quadruple that of other developing regions (see Table 1.1).

Opportunities

Increased agricultural productivity offers a potentially powerful tool for spearheading broad-based income gains among Africa's poor (see World Bank 2007a; Diao et al. 2008). On a continent where 70 percent of the poor work in

FIGURE 1.1 Trends in the value of agricultural production per capita, 1961–2006

Index (1961 = 100)

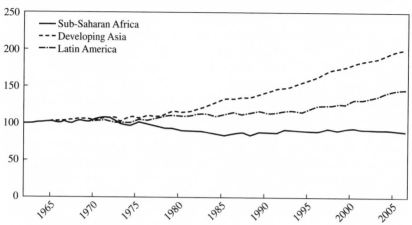

SOURCE: FAOSTAT (2008).

agriculture, an upsurge in farm productivity contributes directly to raising rural living standards. In addition, a prosperous agriculture generates powerful growth linkages to the rest of the economy, providing cheap food, raw materials, and a growing demand for nascent processing and service industries (Mellor 1976; Haggblade, Hazell, and Brown 1989; Haggblade, Hazell, and Dorosh 2007). Even the urban poor, who spend the majority of their income on food, see their real incomes rise when growing agricultural productivity and output enable reductions in staple food prices. Likewise, the many rural households that remain net purchasers of food—a majority in many locations—benefit from rising farm productivity and falling food prices (Jayne, Mather, and Mghenyi 2006). Consequently, growing agricultural productivity attacks poverty from three different directions. It increases the productivity and incomes of the majority of Africa's poor, who work primarily in agriculture. It reduces food prices, which govern real incomes and poverty in urban areas. And it generates important spillovers to the rest of the economy.

Despite Africa's weak past performance, many agricultural specialists see significant potential for agricultural growth in Africa.[4] The continent is blessed with abundant natural resources, 12 times the land area of India with only two-thirds as many people to feed. Growing urbanization, from currently low levels, coupled with high rates of overall population growth, portends rapidly growing domestic and regional food markets. With few exceptions, African

---

4. See, for example, InterAcademy Council (2004), FAO (2005), and World Bank (2009).

land distribution is still equitable by international standards (Valdés et al. 2009). Small farms, efficient but poor, dominate the continent. Agricultural proponents likewise take heart from recent improvements in Africa's policy environment. The structural adjustment programs of the 1980s and 1990s have removed the worst of the previous biases against agriculture and have improved incentives for agricultural investments (Binswanger-Mkhize and McCalla 2008; Anderson and Masters 2009). Agricultural specialists similarly see opportunities for raising Africa's currently low yields through technological change. Some of the required technologies are already available, and modern science is opening up new opportunities to increase agricultural productivity, even in countries and regions that have not benefited significantly from new technologies in the past. The recent surge in world food prices, at least partly sustained by the biofuels policies of the United States and the European Union, seems likely to create new market opportunities for African farmers while at the same time adding urgency to the imperative for more rapid agricultural growth.

Recognizing these potential gains, a growing contingent of African leaders and technical specialists has become convinced that enhanced agricultural performance will constitute a necessary centerpiece for broad-based poverty reduction efforts. African leaders, through the African Union's (AU's) New Partnership for Africa's Development (NEPAD), have highlighted the critical importance of accelerating agricultural growth in Africa. In 2003 they launched a Comprehensive African Agricultural Development Programme (CAADP) to spearhead agricultural development efforts at a continental level (AU/NEPAD 2003a). Many donors and Africa specialists, likewise, consider agriculture fundamental to broad-based economic growth and poverty reduction in Africa.[5]

Impediments

But past lackluster performance in African agriculture has discouraged some professionals, even those who remain convinced of agriculture's potential importance as a poverty fighter. They question whether African agriculture can grow as rapidly as required, given a variety of historical, geographic, epidemiological, political, and world market handicaps.[6]

Geography and natural resource endowments give rise to a series of concerns. Africa's old and weathered soils, primarily kaolinitic clay, provide poor nutrient and water retention capacity. Its tropical climate precludes freezing winter temperatures that in temperate latitudes help to control pests and fracture soil clods and plow pans to facilitate plant root development (Lowe 1986;

---

5. Borlaug (1996), Partnership to Cut Hunger (2002), AU/NEPAD (2003a), InterAcademy Council (2004), FAO (2005), Valdés and Foster (2005), World Bank (2007a, 2009), Alliance for a Green Revolution in Africa (AGRA 2009).

6. See, for example, Bloom and Sachs (1998), Diamond (1998), Maxwell, Urey, and Ashley (2001), and Ellis (2005).

Masters and McMillan 2001). Endowed with a paucity of domesticable plant and animal species, African farmers operated for many millennia with a restricted agricultural genetic base (Diamond 1998). Given the continent's limited irrigation potential, most farmers depend on rainfed cultivation under difficult climatic conditions. Endemic diseases such as malaria, yellow fever, and HIV/AIDS have weakened Africa's labor force, while debilitating livestock diseases such as trypanosomiasis have severely limited livestock rearing, animal traction, and mixed cropping in the tropical zones (Bloom and Sachs 1998; Sachs 2001). Africa's land surplus and its consequently low population density have limited incentives for agricultural intensification, raised transport costs, and made it more difficult for viable input, output, and credit markets to emerge (Hyami and Platteau 1997).

Small countries pose problems of scale and market access. With a welter of political boundaries, many delineated in Berlin in 1885, independent Africa inherited a continent of nearly 50 independent states yet a population two-thirds the size of India's. For agricultural research and technology development, small countries imply high fixed costs. Africa, with the same cultivable area as the United States, operates eight times as many public agricultural research institutes. The resulting small size of Africa's nearly 400 public research agencies limits prospects for achieving economies of scale and spillovers in agricultural research (Pardey et al. 2007). A constellation of small countries, coupled with disease-ridden coasts and temperate inland plateaus, has led to an unusually high concentration of inland population and landlocked countries in Africa (Collier and Gunning 1999). This spatial configuration results in long distances to world markets and high transport costs. Yet coastal countries have limited incentives to invest in the road and transit infrastructure needed to serve their inland neighbors (Bloom and Sachs 1998; Chigunta, Herbert, and Mkandawire 2003; Collier 2007).

Weak institutions, poor governance, and bad policies also give pause. Skeptics highlight Africa's weak rural development institutions and poor rural infrastructure, with road densities today even lower than in India during the 1950s (Spencer 1994). Weak states, regional conflicts, and poor governance compromise the efficiency of public interventions in agriculture as well as in other sectors of the economy (Chigunta, Herbert, and Mkandawire 2003; Collier 2007).

The skeptics likewise point to volatile and generally falling commodity prices for Africa's major agricultural exports. Until the world commodity boom of 2007 and 2008, they note that slumping international prices posed long-term disincentives for African farmers. They further argue that Africa's low agricultural productivity, coupled with high transport costs and growing world market liberalization, make it increasingly difficult for African farmers to compete in global markets. Instead of focusing on what they see as slow-growth, low-return agriculture, some development specialists see urban-based manufacturing and services as more likely to stimulate broad-based economic growth in many African settings (Maxwell 2003; Ellis 2005; Collier 2009). In short, the skeptics see attempts to develop African agriculture as too expensive and too late. They consider the prospects for success to be bleak.

Objectives

These concerns, coupled with the substantial benefits anticipated should agricultural growth accelerate, motivate interest in exploring the conditions under which African agricultural performance might improve. To do so, the following chapters examine a series of instances in which African policymakers and farmers have succeeded in sustaining agricultural growth over long periods of time.

This book explores the conditions under which Africa can successfully accelerate agricultural growth and thereby contribute to broad-based economic expansion and poverty reduction. A welter of past reviews has focused on Africa's failures and asked why African agriculture has performed poorly.[7] This book asks the opposite question. Instead of cataloging failures and constraints, it identifies episodes of successful agricultural growth, a series of region- and commodity-specific booms, many of which have lasted for decades. By examining a series of instances in which important advances have occurred in the past in African agriculture, this book aims to identify promising avenues for achieving success more consistently in the future.

Past Performance

Early Developments

Agricultural production across the continent has changed considerably since the beginning of domesticated agriculture in Africa 7,000 years ago. Today, imported plant species—such as maize, cassava, groundnuts, bananas, cocoa, potatoes, sweet potatoes, tea, and imported varieties of cotton and rice—account for over two-thirds of the value of Africa's gross agricultural output (Gabre-Madhin and Haggblade 2003). Even more striking, the continent's 600 million head of livestock and 700 million head of poultry descend almost exclusively from imported species, with the lone exception of the guinea fowl (Diamond 1998). Despite a virtual absence of indigenous domesticable livestock species, and with a limited range of indigenous plants, African farmers have built up diverse agricultural systems based largely on imported plant and animal species. This transformation has taken place in spite of the formidable ecological constraints imposed by Africa's old and weathered soils, limited irrigation potential, and debilitating endemic diseases such as malaria, tapeworm, and yellow fever. Livestock diseases, such as trypanosomiasis, have likewise severely limited livestock rearing, animal traction, and mixed cropping in the tropical zones (Bloom and Sachs 1998).

---

7. Berg (1981), World Bank (1989, 2000), Bloom and Sachs (1998).

The first half of the 20th century brought with it profound changes in smallholder agriculture all across Africa. Migrant smallholder farmers spread cocoa across much of West Africa (Hill 1963). Others introduced cassava to replace cocoyams, receiving important assistance from rural artisans who developed the necessary processing equipment along the way (Nweke 2004). Maize, cassava, and sweet potatoes gradually replaced sorghum and millets, leading to productivity gains across much of Africa (Jones 1957; Miracle 1966; McCann 2005). Tree crops and growing population pressure led farmers to abandon shifting cultivation and reduce fallow periods. Outside the endemic trypanosomiasis zones of Central Africa, ox plowing took root among many small farmers and commercial settler farmers. As Carr (2001, 331) has observed, "A striking feature of these developments was the speed at which many of these major innovations were adopted by large numbers of smallholders."

Sluggish Recent Performance

Since the middle of the 20th century, however, aggregate performance in Africa has lagged behind that of other developing regions. Over the past 45 years, the value of aggregate agricultural output has increased by 2.4 percent annually in Sub-Saharan Africa compared to 2.8 percent in Latin America and 3.6 percent in developing Asia (FAOSTAT 2008). Both labor and land productivity have stagnated, remaining far below levels achieved in other developing regions (Figure 1.2). African farmers apply an average of 8 kilograms of fertilizer per hectare compared to between 80 and 100 kilograms in developing Asia and Latin America (Morris et al. 2007). Given stagnant productivity, Africa's meager output gains have come mainly from area expansion. This extensification, coupled with shortened fallow periods and minimal input use, has led to nutrient mining and declining soil fertility (Cleaver and Schreiber 1994; Smaling, Nandwa, and Janssen 1997). In international markets, Africa has lost market share in all of its traditional export crops (World Bank 2007a; Hazell and Wood 2008). Since 1960, Africa's share of the value of world agricultural commodity exports has fallen from 5.0 percent to 1.3 percent (FAOSTAT 2008).

Africa's aggregate performance has lagged at the same time it confronts the most daunting demographic challenge of any developing region. Since 1960, Africa has contended with population growth rates of 2.6 percent per year, 0.5–0.7 percent greater than in Latin America and developing Asia (FAOSTAT 2008). Consequently, comparisons of per capita production performance across continents over the past 45 years reveal deteriorating agricultural performance in Africa alone (see Figure 1.1). As per capita food production has fallen, Africa has turned from a food exporter to a net food importer.

Equally worrisome are signs of decapitalization of Africa's key agricultural resources—its soils, human talent, and support institutions. Nearly half of Africa's farmland suffers from erosion and nutrient depletion (Cleaver and Schreiber 1994; AU/NEPAD 2003a). HIV/AIDS, with over 70 percent of known

FIGURE 1.2 Trends in agricultural factor productivity, 1961–2003

Land productivity
(value of agricultural output per hectare in constant 2005 US$)

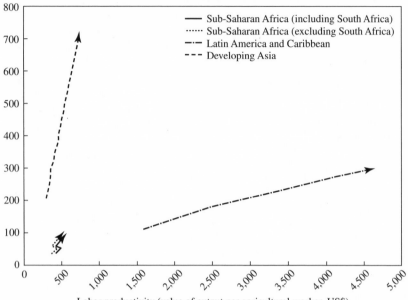

Labor productivity (value of output per agricultural worker, US$)

SOURCE: FAOSTAT (2008).
NOTE: The arrows at the tip of each time series indicate the value in 2003.

cases concentrated in Africa, has likewise extracted a heavy toll on Africa's human capital. Eroding civil service salaries and anemic recurrent budgets have immobilized agricultural extension and research staff, diminished staff incentives, and fueled an exodus of senior scientists from public research institutions (Pardey, Roseboom, and Beintema 1997; InterAcademy Council 2004). These disconcerting trends place Africa's natural, human, and institutional capital under pressure and threaten Africa's capacity to sustain agricultural productivity growth in the future.

Bright Spots

This bleak aggregate picture contrasts with periodic bursts of more promising region- and commodity-specific performance. A review of 26 village studies in Africa documents a series of impressive achievements, a collection of "small and not so small booms in production of food crops for the national and subnational markets" (Wiggins 2000, 635). Since 2000, half a dozen different groups have set out to identify and explore instances of superior performance in African agriculture.[8] Several wonder aloud if a green revolution is already taking place in various parts of Africa (Wiggins 2007; Zachary 2008).

Indeed, African farmers and agricultural policymakers have achieved a series of substantial successes in agricultural development, although in recent decades these have proven inadequate in number and scale to counter Sub-Saharan Africa's heavy demographic pressure. Despite their temporal and regional dispersion, many have endured for decades, as the following thumbnail sketches suggest.

BANANAS IN AFRICA'S CENTRAL HIGHLANDS.   For over 800 years, beginning about A.D. 500, farmers in the Great Lakes region experimented intensively with imported bananas. Through assiduous selection of cultivars, farmers bred a wide range of varieties suitable for human consumption, launching an extraordinary agricultural and demographic revolution in the Central African Highlands, a region that today supports one of the highest population densities in Africa (Schoenbrun 1993; de Langhe, Swennen and Vuysteke 1996; Reader 1997).

MAIZE IN EAST AND SOUTHERN AFRICA.   The development and diffusion of modern, high-yielding varieties of maize have transformed this imported cereal from a minor crop in the early 1900s into the continent's major source of calories today. Maize breeding in Zimbabwe and Kenya launched the first major breakthroughs during the 1960s, when Africa's breeders produced the first commercially grown single-cross hybrids in the world. These breeding breakthroughs have improved the productivity of millions of small and large farms throughout Africa while moderating food prices for tens of millions of urban consumers (Smale and Jayne 2003).

CASSAVA.   Cassava breeding and pest control efforts over the past three decades have triggered broad productivity gains for producers of Africa's number-two staple food. A stream of improved cassava varieties—the Tropical Manioc Selection series released beginning in 1977—has invigorated breeding programs across Africa, increasing on-farm yield gains by over 40 percent without purchased inputs, and permitting rapid responses to recurring viral attacks. Given the improved cassava's high productivity, low purchased input requirements, and well-recognized drought tolerance, Nweke, Spencer, and Lynam (2002) have dubbed this cassava transformation "Africa's best-kept secret."

COTTON IN WEST AFRICA.   Since independence in the 1960s, West African cotton production and exports have both grown rapidly, at a compound annual rate of over 8 percent per year over the ensuing four and a half decades. As a result, francophone Africa's share in world exports has grown from near zero

---

8. In addition to Wiggins (2000), see the recent reviews by Pretty and Hine (2001), Reij and Waters-Bayer (2001), Gabre-Madhin and Haggblade (2004), Noble et al. (2004), FAO (2005), and Reij and Smaling (2007), as well as earlier work by Leonard (1991).

to 14 percent, making it the world's third-largest cotton-exporting block after the United States and the former Soviet Union (Tefft 2003).

HORTICULTURE EXPORTS FROM EAST AFRICA.   From the early 1970s onward, Kenya's private traders have steadily expanded high-value exports of fruits and vegetables from Kenya. Over the past 30 years, horticultural exports have increased fivefold in real terms to become the country's third-largest source of foreign exchange after tourism and tea (Minot and Ngigi 2003).

DAIRY PRODUCTION IN KENYA.   In recent decades, Kenya's dairy production has grown rapidly, resulting in per capita production double the levels found elsewhere on the continent. Today 600,000 small farmers operating with one to three dairy cows each produce 80 percent of Kenya's milk. By the year 2000, nearly 70 percent of Kenyan smallholders produced milk and it had become their fastest-growing income source, with net earnings from milk averaging US$370 per year (Ahmed, Ehui, and Asseva 2003; Ngigi 2005). As a result, dairy marketing offers an important pathway out of poverty for farms of all size (Burke et al. 2007).

RICE PRODUCTION IN MALI.   Policy reform in rice milling and marketing has radically altered opportunities and incentives for Mali's rice producers over the past two decades. Price deregulation, together with the dismantling of public monopolies on paddy assembly, milling, and rice marketing, led to the emergence of small private dehuller mills operating at one-fourth the milling cost of the large state mills. The subsequent 50 percent devaluation of the Communauté Financière Africaine (CFA) franc (CFAF), in January 1994, further boosted producer incentives. Producers responded rapidly to these new options and incentives. As a result, Malian rice production more than tripled after 1985, growing by 9 percent annually over the ensuing 20 years (Diarra et al. 2000; FAOSTAT 2008).

The Disconnect

Why have these impressive individual episodes not added up to rapid aggregate growth? In part, sluggish aggregate statistics may understate Africa's agricultural accomplishments, particularly in cassava, bananas, and other difficult-to-measure perennial crops. Agricultural sample frames, often geared to measuring major grain staples, prove unreliable for tracking dairy, livestock, cassava, beans, and other minor food crops. Likewise, large countries such as Nigeria weigh heavily in continental aggregations, despite the questionable reliability of their statistical projections (Jaeger 1992; Wiggins 2000).

More fundamentally, Africa's high population growth rates impose the largest demographic challenge of any developing region. Given its high fertility rates, Africa will have to run faster than the rest of the developing world just to keep pace with its growing population. Because of Africa's belated demographic transition, dependency ratios remain higher and growth of the prime age workforce more limited than elsewhere. Past successes, impressive but episodic, have proven insufficient to keep pace with Africa's daunting demographic challenge.

Although episodes of robust agricultural performance have occurred too infrequently in the past to counter Africa's demographic pressures, their occurrence suggests a possible diagnostic for improving future performance. By examining a series of cases in which important advances have occurred in the past, it may be possible to identify promising avenues for achieving success more consistently in the future.

Learning from Past Successes

Goals

Sometimes, things go right. And when they do, we may benefit from asking why. This book summarizes efforts by the International Food Policy Research Institute (IFPRI) to systematically identify instances of superior agricultural performance in Africa, to study them, and to learn from them. In doing so, the book aims to identify processes, practices, and policies that have successfully stimulated agricultural growth in Africa.

Our goal is to learn from what has gone right in the past. We begin with the premise that performance in some periods and locations has proven superior to that in others and that by comparing them it will prove possible to identify the causes of this variation. Using a comparative case study approach, the individual case studies that follow, in Part II of this book, attempt to contrast instances of superior performance with similar cases in which results have proven lackluster. The resulting method resembles a positive deviance study, in which instances of superior agricultural performance become the role models to be understood and emulated. Historically, this work most closely resembles the detailed case studies of African agriculture assembled by de Wilde (1967) and colleagues over 40 years ago.[9]

Research Methods

To identify common ingredients and processes that underlie agricultural "success," the research team first identified episodes of strong performance in African agriculture along with contrasting instances, over time or space, in which performance had lagged. They then recruited specialists to study these contrasting cases using a common research protocol. In a final stage, the analytical team brought the individual case study results together before groups of experienced African agricultural specialists to enlist their expertise in helping

---

9. Methodologically, the focus on detailed case studies of positive deviance resembles the approach adopted by Leonard (1991) in his study of successful rural development managers in Kenya.

to extract cross-cutting general lessons emerging from this body of collective case study experience (Table 1.2).

To identify a broad range of successful episodes in African agriculture, the team first launched an expert survey targeting IFPRI's extensive contact list of African and Africanist agricultural specialists. A one-page questionnaire posed the following single question: "What do you consider the most successful instances of improved agricultural performance in Sub-Saharan Africa?" To encourage the respondents to think broadly, the questionnaire deliberately left the criteria for success, as well as the time and geographic scope, unconfined. For each success story nominated, the survey form asked respondents to provide both their selection criteria and the factors they considered crucial in determining the favorable outcome.

In response, the team received over 250 nominations ranging broadly in geographic and historical scope. Some highlighted recent cutting-edge technical breakthroughs, while others went back thousands of years. Table 1.3 provides an overview of the nominations received, while Gabre-Madhin and Haggblade (2003, 2004) provide greater detail on the methods and findings.

In order to select instructive case studies and to help focus the analytical work, the team required a clear definition of "success." For purposes of this work, the Successes in African Agriculture team defined "success" as "a significant, durable change in agriculture resulting in an increase in agriculturally derived aggregate income, together with reduced poverty and/or improved environmental quality" (Haggblade 2004, 4). This definition retained the three vertices of the "critical triangle"—income, equity, and sustainability. Given the importance ascribed to aggregate income growth, the definition calls for a significant increase in income coupled with improvement in either sustainability or equity, or both.

With this definition in hand, the research coordinators and an external advisory group reviewed the expert survey success nominations in order to select a dozen cases for in-depth review (Table 1.4). The resulting selection provides a series of important contrasts among private and public instigators of change, a variety of intervention points, differing levels of subsidy, a mix of food and export crops, regional diversity, and impacts of variable duration and scale. Geographically, the case studies covered 11 countries in West, Eastern, and Southern Africa (Figure 1.3). In total, the analytical team produced 11 case study reports as well as an additional half dozen background and synthesis papers. These provide the substance on which the remaining chapters of this book are based.

To provide an appropriate counterfactual comparison, the team attempted to identify paired comparisons of successful and unsuccessful efforts for each of the case study selections. This proved relatively straightforward with the dairy, horticulture, cassava, and cotton case studies.[10] The other case studies—

---

10. Due to a debilitating illness suffered by one of the co-authors of the cotton sector study, only the "successful" Malian case study was completed.

TABLE 1.2 The successes in African agriculture research process

Activity	Purpose	Participants	Venue	Timing
1. Identify successes				
Expert survey	Inventory African successes Define *success*	Research coordinators (RCs)		June–November, 2000
Advisory group (AG) meeting	Select case study topics	AG and RCs AG	Washington, D.C.	November 20–21, 2000
2. Scrutinize selected cases				
Recruitment of the analytical team				
Analytical team inception workshop	Develop analytical framework Design standard case study protocol	RCs Analytical team (AT)	Washington, D.C.	October 1–5, 2001
Case studies	Share information	AT RCs	Lusaka	June 10–12, 2002
Case study workshop	Provide team feedback to all authors	AT		
3. Generalize across case studies				
Stakeholder input	Synthesize and generalize	African policymakers AG, RCs One AT member per case study	Pretoria	December 1–3, 2003
Validation	Validate and refine findings Gain regional perspective	African policymakers RCs	Nairobi	November 22–25, 2004
Policy summary	Summarize case studies and policy implications Explore agricultural budgeting issues with parliamentarians	African parliamentarians RCs	Somerset West, South Africa	May 15–18, 2006

NOTES: RCs—During the first half of the Successes in African Agriculture (SAA) review, Eleni Gabre-Madhin and Steven Haggblade served as IFPRI's research coordinators. During the second half of the review, Haggblade and Peter Hazell served in this role. AG—The external advisory group for the SAA review included Michel Benoit-Cattin, Josué Dione, Simeon Ehui, Carl Eicher, and Wilberforce Kisamba-Mugerwa. AT—The analytical team includes the case study authors: Mohamed A. M. Ahmed, Oluyede C. Ajayi, Yemesrach Assefa, Simeon Ehui, Steven Franzel, Steven Haggblade, Bashir Jama, Thomas Jayne, Daniel Kaboré, Freddie Kwesiga, Paramu Mafangoya, Nicholas Minot, Margaret Ngigi, Quereish Noordin, Felix Nweke, Frank Place, Chris Reij, Melinda Smale, James Tefft, Gelson Tembo, and Ballard Zulu.

TABLE 1.3 Expert survey success nominations

| | African agricultural successes identified (%) | | |
Category	Total	Africa-wide	Region-specific[a]
Commodity-specific			
Maize	10.3	11.1	10.0
Cassava	6.7	15.3	3.3
Horticulture	6.6	1.4	8.6
Livestock	6.2	9.7	4.8
Cotton	4.5	1.4	5.7
Coffee	4.3	5.6	3.8
Dairy	3.4	0.0	4.8
Rice	3.3	5.6	2.4
Cocoa	2.5	2.8	2.4
Bananas	2.5	1.4	2.9
Beans	1.8	1.4	1.9
Other	9.5	6.9	10.5
Subtotal	**61.6**	**62.5**	**61.2**
Activity-specific			
Soil fertility enhancement[b]	7.1	5.6	7.7
Policy reform			
Agricultural markets	2.0	0.0	2.7
Macro policy	1.6	0.0	2.2
Irrigation development	2.4	1.4	2.7
Specific technology development[c]	1.6	1.4	1.6
Other	6.7	6.9	6.6
Subtotal	**21.2**	**15.3**	**23.5**
Institution building			
Agricultural research	5.5	12.5	2.7
Farmer organizations	3.1	1.4	3.8
Market institutions	2.4	1.4	2.7
Human capacity building[d]	1.6	5.6	0.0
Other institutions	3.5	1.4	4.4
Subtotal	**16.1**	**22.2**	**13.7**
Countries			
Ethiopia, 1990s	0.4		0.5
Ghana, 1990s	0.4		0.5
Ivory Coast, 1960s and 1970s	0.4		0.5
Subtotal	**1.2**		**1.6**
Total			
Share	**100.0**	**100.0**	**100.0**
Number of nominations	**253**	**71**	**182**

SOURCE: Gabre-Madhin and Haggblade (2004).

[a]Specific to East, Southern, Central, or West Africa or to a specific country.

[b]Includes improved fallows, crop rotations, conservation farming.

[c]Biotechnology applications, vaccines.

[d]Finance, management, business.

TABLE 1.4 Case study selections

Paper no.	Topic	Countries covered	Regional applicability	Authors
1	Cassava	Nigeria, Ghana	West Africa	Nweke
2	Cassava	Zambia, Malawi	Southern Africa	Haggblade and Zulu
3	Cotton	Mali	Francophone West Africa	Tefft
4	Dairy	Kenya, Uganda	East Africa	Ngigi
5	Dairy	Ethiopia	Horn of Africa	Ahmed, Ehui, and Assefa
6	Horticulture	Kenya, Côte d'Ivoire	Africa	Minot and Ngigi
7	Maize	Kenya, Malawi, Zambia, Zimbabwe	East and Southern Africa	Smale and Jayne
8	SSFM: planting basins	Burkina Faso	Semiarid Africa	Kaboure and Reij
9	SSFM: planting basins	Zambia	Semiarid Africa	Haggblade and Tembo
10	SSFM: improved fallows	Kenya	Africa	Place, Franzel, Noordin, and Jama
11	SSFM: improved fallows	Zambia	Africa	Kwesiga, Franzel, Ajayi, and Mafangoya

NOTE: SSFM, sustainable soil fertility management.

including those for maize, cotton, and sustainable soil fertility management technologies—have instead relied on temporal comparisons within the selected case study countries. In both sets of case studies, periods of sluggish performance provide a contrasting scenario against which to compare periods of rapid growth. For this reason, the turning points and the forces driving change at those junctures become central to helping us understand what instruments have proven effective in turning around agricultural performance in a variety of African settings.

Analytical Framework

Eleven case studies provide the empirical foundation for this analytical work. In order to produce comparable narratives, the analytical team developed a common framework for guiding each of the case studies. As a first step, the an-

FIGURE 1.3 Case study countries

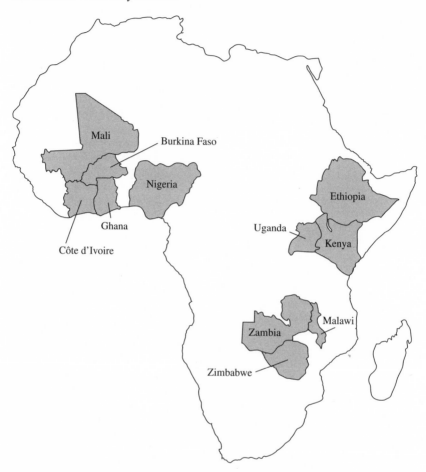

alytical team—a group of subject-matter specialists recruited to conduct each of the case studies—convened in Washington, D.C., for one week to develop a common analytical framework and to plan the case study work.

They sought an analytical framework that would help them track sources of change in agricultural trajectories. Given the long lead times required in technology development and the ongoing continuous evolution in biological systems, the framework needed to track interactions between human and biological systems over time. In constructing such a framework, the analytical team has drawn key features from a number of different conceptual paradigms ranging across a wide spectrum of disciplines. The umbrella framework and core dynamic processes draw heavily on the co-evolution paradigm developed in the anthropological and archaeological literature to study the emergence and long-term evolution of agriculture.[11] This literature focuses broadly on the inter-dependence between biological systems and the human institutions governing agriculture. To help refine and operationalize that core dynamic framework, a related body of work in the biological and social sciences has likewise proven useful.[12] Figure 1.4 summarizes the resulting analytical framework, which the analytical team refers to as the Decisionmaking Environment (DE)–Action (A)–Results (R) framework (the DE-A-R framework).

DECISIONMAKING ENVIRONMENT. Because future growth in African agri-culture will depend on improved performance by millions of individual farm-ers, the analytical framework places farmer decisionmaking at its core (see Fig-ure 1.4). It focuses on the decisionmaking environment that shapes incentives and opportunities available to farm households. Farmers' productive capacity, or opportunity sets, are determined at any given time by household assets as well as a set of public and collective goods, including available technology, roads, and community land management systems. Biophysical features of the agroecological zone—such as rainfall, soil fertility, and the incidence of pests and disease—also clearly affect productive capacity. The second major com-ponent of the decisionmaking environment, the existing incentive structure, de-pends on prevailing prices, local values and culture, and institutions governing the marketing and processing of farm products. Public actors such as govern-ments, donors, and nongovernmental organizations (NGOs) influence the farm-ers' decisionmaking environment through investments in public goods, such as infrastructure and research, through support institutions and through policies that shape the incentives to which farmers respond.

ACTIONS. Farmers act, motivated by the prevailing incentive structure and constrained by their productive capacity. They allocate land, labor, draft power, and financial capital across a portfolio of farm and nonfarm activities. Within each, they select a given technology and level of input use. They ex-periment, monitor, and compare outcomes. At the end of each production cy-cle, they decide to market some of their farm output, process a portion, and con-sume or store the remainder.

The natural biological environment likewise responds to changes in agri-cultural systems. Farm technologies and input use influence soil fertility, soil

---

11. See Rindos (1980, 1984) and Price and Gebauer (1995).

12. On crop evolution, see, for example, Harlan (1992, 1995), Smith (1995), Evans (1996), and Diamond (1998). On nutrient monitoring, see Stoorvogel and Smaling (1990), Smaling, Nandwa, and Janssen (1997), de Jager, Nandwa, and Okoth (1998), and van den Bosch, de Jager, and Vlaming (1998). On induced innovations, see, for example, Boserup (1965), Hyami and Rut-tan (1971), and Binswanger and Ruttan (1978). On institutions and institutional innovation, see Binswanger and McIntyre (1987), Nabli and Nugent (1989), North (1990), and Hayami and Ot-suka (1993). On development pathways, see Pender, Scherr, and Duron (2001) and Pender et al. (2004). For the related literature on economic livelihoods, see, for example, Ellis (2000), Pretty (2000, 2005), and Pretty and Hine (2001).

FIGURE 1.4 The DE-A-R framework

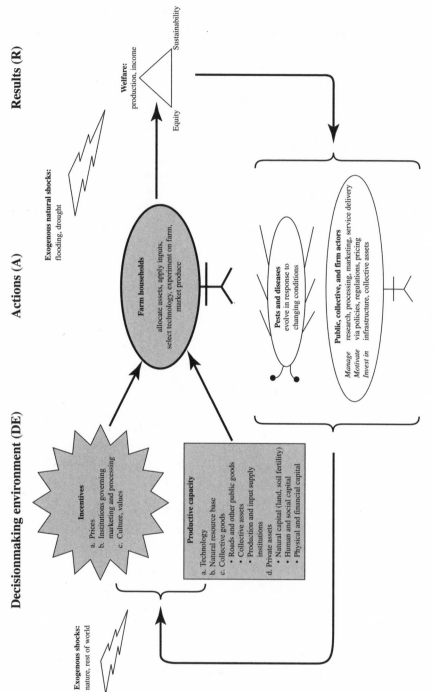

SOURCE: IFPRI (2003).

organic matter, and biotic activity. Plant and animal viruses evolve continuously as they adapt to changing agronomic practices, plant populations, input applications, and weather. Pests, diseases, and weed species change over time in response to human agricultural practices.

RESULTS. These actions, together with natural variations in weather, generate a set of results for individual households and, in aggregate, for the rural community. The results indicators adopted by the analytical team include empirical measures for each component of agricultural "success" (Table 1.5). The case study teams agreed that they would attempt to measure indicators along each dimension of success. While recognizing that this would not always be possible with available primary and secondary data, team members helped each other to identify possible sources of microdata necessary for making these calculations.

FEEDBACK AND INTERACTION. In a giant dynamic feedback loop, outcomes in each period influence both dimensions of the decisionmaking environment in the next season. Agricultural output and income influence farmers' capacity and inclination to finance productive investments. Asset accumulation in any one period increases farm households' productive capacity in the next. Marketed volumes likewise influence market price incentives as well as consumption and future production. Outcomes from one period affect soil fertility and other household assets as well as the behavior of external actors such as agribusiness firms, farm organizations, government, donors, NGOs, and nonfarm consumers. The resulting responses by these actors, external to the farm household, alter the decisionmaking environment facing farm households in the following period.

Pests, weed populations, and diseases likewise respond and adapt to changing circumstances. Over time, these adaptations lead to periodic violent

TABLE 1.5 Measuring results

Success indicator	Measure

1. Improved welfare	a. Income
	   Number of households adopting change (small, medium, large)
	   Increased average income per household
	b. Assets
	c. Consumption
	d. Nutrition

2. Equity	a. Smallholder participation in production growth b. Income change for smallholders c. Poverty reduction

3. Sustainability
  a. Ecological
  b. Financial
	a. Net nutrient flows
	b. Financial viability, with and without subsidies

upsurges in pest and disease infestation. The case studies in Part II of this book routinely demonstrate the recurring difficulties posed by mutating diseases, viruses, pests, and weed populations. The case studies explore how these adaptations in the biological system trigger corresponding responses on the part of farm managers and researchers on whom farmers rely for a steady infusion of new genetic and phytosanitary material.

CASE STUDY PROTOCOL. The standard case study protocol emerging from the DE-A-R framework is described in Table 1.6. This standard protocol begins by defining the scope of the case study and explaining why agricultural specialists generally considered it a success. The team then summarizes historical dynamics in order to define key turning points and phases in each given commodity case study. Within each period, discussion and analyses focus on key shocks to the decisionmaking environment, the ensuing changes in farm household actions, and key results in terms of income, equity, and sustainability. Each case study concludes with a discussion of policy implications.

To provide some specificity and microeconomic grounding to these broad case study overviews, the analytical team agreed to prepare a series of short farmer case histories exploring how changing opportunities and incentives affected individual farm families in practice. Summarized in short boxes in the case study chapters, these profiles aim to help illustrate key dimensions of the changes under way. They likewise serve to focus attention on individual farm families, whose improved performance and welfare lie at the heart of agricultural development efforts.

Key Policy Issues

WHAT INTERVENTIONS? Two key structural features of the agricultural decisionmaking environment govern human responses at any given point in time (see Figure 1.4). First, productive capacity places bounds on the scope of

TABLE 1.6 Case study protocol

---

1. Scope of the case study
   Commodity, time period, and location of the study
   Scale and scope of the "success"
   Why is this considered a success?
2. Historical turning points
   Change in aggregate production trends (output, yield, area)
   Identification of key turning points
   Definition of key phases
3. Dynamics and drivers of change during each phase
   Key shocks to the farmer decisionmaking environment
   Actions and responses by farm households and others
   Results: income, equity, sustainability
4. Policy implications

---

action available to farmers. These opportunity sets depend on the available quantity, productivity, and distribution of key productive assets such as land, labor, capital, and water; on the stock of available biological and agronomic technology; on the state of physical infrastructure; and on supporting institutions for resource management, input supply, and marketing. Second, prevailing incentive structures govern which of the available options farmers will select from within their available opportunity sets. Incentives such as enhanced food security, social solidarity, or risk reduction influence individual and household decisionmaking, while market prices affect input supply as well as the production, storage, processing, and marketing of outputs.

Levers available for initiating change thus fall into two broad categories. Interveners can elect to expand productive capacity through development of new agricultural technology, provision of public and collective goods (roads, institutions governing production and input supply), or investment in private assets such as soil fertility, human capital, and physical and financial capital. Alternatively, they can focus on improving farmer incentives. Common tools include exchange rates, tariffs, subsidies, and taxes that influence market prices as well as investment in institutions governing output marketing and processing.

WHO INTERVENES? The case studies that follow identify key actors and agents of change. Who has taken the key initiatives? Given rapidly changing agricultural technology and the privatization of gains from biotechnology and genetic engineering, private and public roles may differ in the future. Trends toward agricultural market liberalization have opened up large agricultural markets to private investment and trade. From a policy perspective, it becomes critical to determine when and where public intervention is required and, conversely, where the private sector can most usefully take the lead. Chapters 8 and 9 return to these key questions.

Generalizing across the Case Studies

To generalize from a dozen individual, historical case studies, the analytical team first compared the findings from all the case studies in order to identify general determinants of success. What, they asked, has driven past successes in African agriculture? What investments, technologies, policies, institutions, organizational structures, and processes have proven key to enabling success in each of the case studies under review? How have public and private actions shaped these opportunities? Second, they explicitly asked how the future environment facing African agriculture might differ from that of the past. What principal changes are under way—in technology, communications, world markets, and local institutions—that might influence future prospects for African farmers? Finally they asked, given these changes, how can farmers and policymakers best apply the lessons of the past going forward?

To answer each of these questions requires considerable judgment and collateral knowledge. Therefore the analytical team, in collaboration with the NEPAD Secretariat, convened a series of three groups of experienced agricultural specialists and political leaders from across Africa to provide input into this synthesis effort. Participants included a broad spectrum of farmers, government officials, and private sector agribusiness operators. The first workshop, held in Pretoria in December 2003, involved roughly 70 senior African agricultural policy and technical specialists.[13] The second, focusing exclusively on East and Southern Africa, took place in Nairobi in November 2004.[14] The third, drawing African parliamentarians from all across Africa, took place in Somerset West, South Africa, in May 2006.[15] In all three settings, following brief plenary presentations by the case study teams, the participants spent the bulk of their time interacting in a series of professionally facilitated small-group working sessions.

Through the facilitated small group sessions, participants worked together to complete a series of specific tasks: (1) summarize key lessons learned from past successes in African agriculture, (2) realistically assess the domestic and international policy environment within which African decisionmakers currently operate, and (3) identify priorities for future policy action necessary to trigger sustained agricultural growth in Africa. Part III of this book, which summarizes key lessons for the future, has drawn heavily on these successive dialogues with African agricultural stakeholders and policymakers.

Organization of the Book

Part I of this book has described the objectives, methods, and analytical framework used in reviewing agricultural successes in Africa. Part II, the core of the book, reports in detail on the individual case studies selected for review. Chapter 2 begins by examining the cassava production surge that has occurred across much of Africa since the 1980s using case study material from Nigeria, Ghana, Zambia, and Malawi. Chapter 3 then reviews the causes and consequences of hybrid maize development and diffusion in eastern and southern Africa by examining four contrasting country case studies from Zimbabwe, Kenya, Malawi, and Zambia. Given the long-term investments that underpin these productivity gains, this discussion covers roughly a 100-year period, from the early 1900s to 2005. Chapter 4 details the origins and impact of francophone West Africa's long-term cotton expansion over the four and a half decades following independence, focusing on evidence and experience from Mali. Chapter 5, in turn,

---

13. The full conference program, proceedings, participant list, and all background papers are available at <www.ifpri.org/event/successes-african-agriculture>.

14. Titled "Agricultural Successes for the Greater Horn of Africa," these results are summarized by Haggblade (2005). A full set of conference materials is available at <www.ifpri.org/event/nepadigad-regional-conference-agricultural-successes-greater-horn-africa>.

15. The outcomes of this conference, Championing Agricultural Successes for Africa's Future: A Parliamentarians' Dialogue on NEPAD, are summarized in NEPAD (2010) and at <www.ifpri.org/sites/default/files/publications/if15.pdf>.

explores two contrasting experiences with horticultural export development, one in Kenya and the other in Côte d'Ivoire, focusing on the years since 1970. Chapter 6 reviews the East African dairy experience, contrasting the century-long expansion and modernization in Kenya with the less impressive performance in neighboring Ethiopia and Uganda. To wind up the case study reviews, Chapter 7 describes the development and impact of two pairs of sustainable soil fertility management technologies. The first pair contrasts systems of minimum-tillage planting basins developed independently in Burkina Faso and in Zambia, while the second compares the development of improved fallow systems in Western Kenya and in Eastern Zambia.

Part III of the book generalizes and looks forward. Chapter 8 begins that effort by summarizing, comparing, and contrasting the six case study chapters. In so doing, it aims to distill the general policy lessons that emerge and to separate out actionable items from idiosyncratic factors responsible for superior agricultural performance. Chapter 9 looks forward by examining several key questions. Why has Africa not experienced more frequent agricultural successes in the past? How will recent rapid changes in technology, global markets, and agricultural institutions affect future strategies for stimulating agricultural growth? What needs to change to get African agriculture growing more rapidly? The book sums up by examining how lessons from the past can help governments, farm leaders, and agribusinesses shape future strategies for successful agricultural development in Africa.

PART II

Success Stories

2   The Cassava Transformation in West and Southern Africa

FELIX NWEKE AND STEVEN HAGGBLADE

There was once a king of Bushongo who was called Samba Mikepe who was the wisest man who had ever lived. Before he mounted the throne, he made long voyages toward the west; no one knows to what distance to the other side of the Kasai River he went, and it was from this that he acquired his wisdom. . . . During one season of his reign the harvests of the Bushongo were completely destroyed by locusts and the people were in imminent danger of perishing from hunger. But they were saved by Samba Mikepe who showed them the use of manioc which could not be destroyed by any amount of locusts.[1]

Torday and Joyce (1911, 249)

Scope of the Study

Cassava production has grown rapidly in Africa in recent decades. In the early 1960s, Africa accounted for roughly 40 percent of world cassava production. Forty-five years later, by the mid-2000s, Africa's share had risen to 50 percent of world output. In the process, Nigeria has surpassed Brazil as the world's leading cassava producer. As a result of these gains, cassava now provides Africa's second-most-important calorie source, after maize, and one-third of all Africans consume cassava as a food staple.

Nigeria has led Africa's cassava surge. Production tripled there in less than a decade, beginning in the mid-1980s, as improved cassava varieties, successful pest control efforts, and strong producer incentives unleashed a pent-up surge in productive potential. Subsequently, advances in plant breeding, pest control, and cassava processing technology have spilled over from Nigeria to stimulate production surges across much of the rest of the African cassava belt (Figure 2.1).

Cassava, a tropical root crop, possesses several key properties that make its recent expansion significant. Because of cassava's well-known drought tolerance and because farmers can harvest cassava as they need it, any time over

---

1. Manioc is another name for cassava. Brazilians refer to the crop as mandioca, while Mexicans and Central Americans know it as yuca.

FIGURE 2.1 Africa's cassava belt, 1980

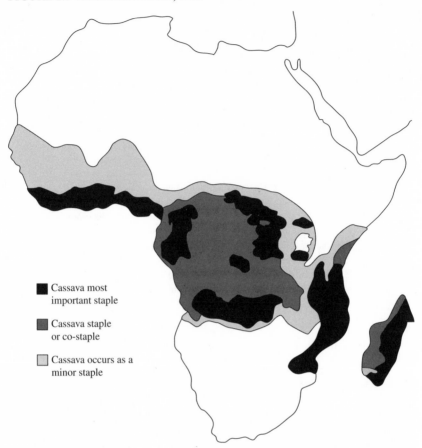

■ Cassava most
   important staple

■ Cassava staple
   or co-staple

□ Cassava occurs as a
   minor staple

SOURCE: Okigbo (1980).

a two to three year period, cassava provides an important food security buffer, allowing farmers to compensate for cereal production shortfalls in drought years. Similarly, because farmers can harvest cassava throughout the year, in many settings cassava remains the only food staple available for harvest during the lean season, when cereal prices and on-farm labor demands peak, caloric intake falls, and undernutrition among vulnerable households becomes most acute. Expansion of cassava production, therefore, can potentially improve food security significantly both during the lean season and during drought years. Moreover, because new varieties have proven so highly productive, cassava offers a low-cost source of carbohydrates not only for human consumption but also for use in animal feeds and industrial processing.[2] So increasing productivity among cassava producers offers potential gains in farm income, food security, and industrial processing.

This chapter examines the causes and consequences of Africa's unfolding cassava transformation. It begins by focusing on performance in Nigeria, the continental leader in these efforts and catalyst for many of the technological changes that have subsequently enabled productivity-led surges elsewhere in Africa. Ghana provides a contrasting example from West Africa, while Zambia and Malawi offer a Southern African perspective, highlighting potential differences in the dynamics of cassava production and commercialization across regions and agroecological zones. Data for these reviews come from the Collaborative Study of Cassava in Africa (COSCA), conducted between 1989 and 1997 in six different African countries, including Nigeria and Ghana, as well as from national farm-level surveys in Zambia and Malawi.[3]

The Nigerian Cassava Transformation

Over the past century, a series of changes in the farmer decisionmaking environment have propelled several waves of cassava-led growth in Nigeria. Intermittent drought, insect attacks, wars, and the sudden emergence of major plant and human diseases have triggered short-run surges in cassava production, both upward and downward (Figure 2.2). Over the long run, new breeding and processing technologies, together with favorable government policy, have propelled several long waves of productivity-led growth. Key actors have included Portuguese traders, several cohorts of emancipated Sierra Leonean slaves, local artisans who have developed low-cost processing technology, oil companies that have supported cassava research and promotion, and researchers who have generated a stream of highly productive new cassava varieties, particularly over the past 40 years. In responding to evolving opportunities and threats,

---

2. As Jones (1959, 255, 281) puts it, "Manioc's outstanding characteristic, from an economic standpoint, is its capacity for producing large amounts of food calories per hectare. . . . To say that manioc is a low-cost calorie source is also to say that cultivation of manioc increases a community's productivity, either because more calories can be produced with the same land and labor, or because the same amount of calories can be produced by smaller inputs, thus freeing resources to be used in producing other things."

3. Data on cassava production are subject to a wide margin of error, for two principal reasons. First, because cassava farmers can harvest any time over a 2- to 3-year period and because farmers typically maintain a portfolio of cassava plots of differing maturity, total cropped area does not provide a reliable barometer of annual cassava production. Second, because farmers typically harvest their mature plots throughout the year, and often over multiple years, yield estimates based on recall data are notoriously suspect. Even where researchers conduct crops cuts, uncertainties about harvested area complicate output projections. In recognition of these difficulties, this chapter has preferred to use COSCA data where they are available, because these come from crop cuts and individual plot measurements.

FIGURE 2.2 Cassava production trends in Nigeria and Ghana, 1961–2006

a. **National cassava production**

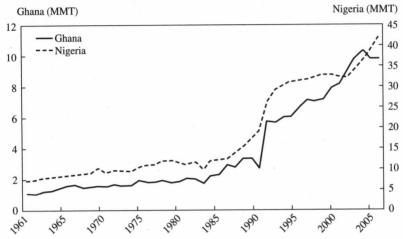

b. **Per capita cassava production**

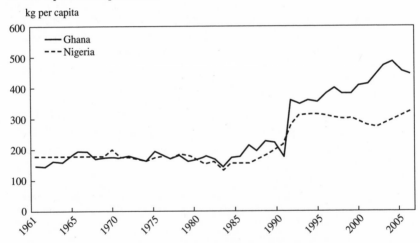

SOURCE: FAOSTAT (2008); for summary of raw data, see Appendix Table 2A.1.

these actors have traced out five distinct phases in Nigeria's ongoing cassava transformation (Table 2.1).

Phase 1: Cassava as a Food Staple, 1910–45

In the late 16th century, Portuguese traders introduced cassava to the west coast of Africa from South America. By 1700, cassava had become an important food crop in Sao Tome, in Fernando Po, and at Warri (Jones 1959). But cassava did not spread much farther until early in the 20th century, because the people of West Africa enjoyed a comfortable food security based on indigenous root crops, such as yams and cocoyams.

Early in the 20th century, several factors spurred a rapid diffusion of cassava in different parts of Nigeria. A war of resistance against the British, from 1899 to 1914, followed by the First World War, from 1914 to 1918, and then the influenza epidemic of 1918 all contributed to sharply constricted labor availability in the lower Niger Delta. The resulting labor shortage precipitated a major shift among farm families from cultivation of labor-intensive yams to less labor-intensive cassava. During wartime, cassava's flexible harvesting calendar and long-term in-ground storage also offered considerable attraction for intermittently displaced villagers. By the late 1920s, cassava production had spread to most parts of the lower Niger (Ohadike 1981; Chiwona-Karltun 2001).

The dissemination of cassava processing technology further accelerated the adoption and marketing of cassava-based products in the Niger Delta. In 1916, pastors of the Niger Delta Pastorate, mostly emancipated slaves from Sierra Leone and Western Nigeria, brought *gari* processing technology, along with Christianity, to Ngwa land in Eastern Nigeria.[4] Transformation of cassava into *gari,* by pressing out the water after grating and fermenting the roots, reduces transport and handling costs by over 60 percent. Further processing, by drying and toasting the *gari,* extends the shelf life of cassava from 2 days for fresh roots to several months for *gari.* By lowering transport costs and improving shelf life, this new processing technology proved vital to the development of cassava as a staple food as well as a cash crop.

Between 1930 and 1939 in Oyo and Ondo provinces, north of Lagos, an invasion of locusts inflicted considerable damage on the yam crop. During this period, many farmers turned to more insect-tolerant cassava. Cassava's drought tolerance likewise contributed to its steady inroads in the yam belt. In 1945 and 1946 in Ondo province, farmers planted cassava in areas where yams had failed to sprout because of the long dry season (Agboola 1968).

Phase 2: Cassava as a Cash Crop, 1946–77

The period around World War II marked a turning point in Nigerian cassava development, when the confluence of several major forces combined to stimulate the rapid expansion of cassava as a cash crop. Growing urban markets increased the demand for *gari,* while the introduction of new cassava varieties

---

4. *Gari* is a granulated, precooked cassava-based convenience food. It is especially popular in West Africa, where customers appreciate its convenience as a ready-to-eat food. Processing involves grating, fermenting, drying, and toasting. After purchasing, consumers merely need to add hot or cold water to the *gari* granules to produce a thick porridge.

TABLE 2.1 Dynamics and drivers of change in Nigeria's cassava transformation

	Phase 1: Cassava becomes a food staple	Phase 2: Cassava becomes a cash crop	Phase 3: Mealybug invasion	Phase 4: The cassava surge	Phase 5: New markets and new challenges
Timing	1910–45	1946–77	1978–83	1984–94	1995–present
Key actors	Immigrants Farmers	Rural artisans International Institute of Tropical Agriculture (IITA) Private oil companies	IITA	Government National Root Crop Research Institute Private oil companies	Government Presidential Cassava Marketing Commission Private millers
Motors of change	Severe rural labor shortages (due to wars and the influenza epidemic of 1918) induce a move out of labor-demanding cocoyam and into cassava	Mechanized cassava graters developed by local artisans Graters spread, relieving processing bottlenecks Tropical Manioc Selection varieties are developed (1971–77) but	Mealybug invasion attacks the cassava crop	Biological control of mealybugs (1981 on) takes effect Policy changes stifle food imports: • Rice import subsidies dropped • Cereal imports banned	Rising wage rates lead to labor constraints in harvesting and processing Requirement of 10% cassava flour in bread spurs industrial processing

	Emancipated slaves from Sierra Leone introduce *gari* processing technology Immigrants bring in new, bitter varieties of cassava	initially fail to spread		• Devaluation of the naira, which raises food import prices Government includes cassava in extension programs Oil companies help finance cassava promotion	Ethanol subsidies in developed countries raise world maize prices, open potential opportunities for cassava substitution
Beneficiaries	Small farmers Urban *gari* consumers	Small farmers Urban consumers	Farmers and consumers both lose	Small farmers Urban consumers	Small farmers Cassava millers
Production gains	Rapid growth from a very low base	Annual growth of 2.5% per year	Production falls by roughly 20%, a decline of 3.1% per year	Annual growth of 11% per year	Growth slows to 2.7% per year
Impact	Cassava becomes established as a rural food staple	Growing urban markets attract *gari* trade	Massive mobilization for biological control of mealybugs across Africa	Real *gari* prices fall The *gari*/yam price ratio falls by 50% The *gari*/rice price ratio falls by 25%	Consumer *gari* prices trend upward

and mechanical small-scale processing technology combined to increase the productivity and profitability of cassava.

GROWING URBAN DEMAND. During the late 1800s, cassava products began appearing regularly on the Lagos market (Agboola 1968). By the eve of the Second World War, trade in *gari* began to grow in other urban centers such as Aba and Umuahia (Martin 1988). A long-distance trade in *gari* emerged as the people of Eastern Nigeria exchanged *gari* for cattle produced in northern Nigeria. The early *gari* trade initially developed along growing road networks, particularly following the opening of the Benue River bridge in 1931. By 1944, the railway had also become an important means of transporting *gari* from Eastern to Northern Nigeria. Growing urban populations, rising income, and strongly positive expenditure elasticities all contributed to increasing demand for *gari* (Table 2.2). Throughout the 1940s and 1950s, Nigerian cassava production expanded because of the growing urban demand for *gari*.

MECHANICAL GRATERS. Cassava processing requires peeling, grating, soaking, pressing, and toasting, all labor-intensive operations originally carried out by hand, primarily by women. To help relieve this labor constraint, local artisans and government technical institutes experimented with mechanical cassava graters to develop prototypes that would reduce emerging labor bottlenecks in cassava processing. These efforts built on prototypes introduced during the 1930s by the French into the Republic of Benin (formally Dahomey) to teach farmers how to prepare *gari* and tapioca for export markets (Jones 1959). During that same decade in Nigeria, local artisans introduced and mod-

TABLE 2.2 Income elasticity of demand for cassava and other food staples in Nigeria and Ghana

| | Nigeria | | | Ghana | |
	All households	Low-income households	High-income households	Rural households	Urban households
All cassava	0.78	0.84	0.76	0.73	1.46
Fresh roots	1.24	1.28	1.21	—	—
Gari	0.85	0.85	0.77	—	—
Dried roots	0.55	0.57	0.53	—	—
Maize	0.71	0.74	0.65	0.84	0.83
Rice	1.12	1.13	1.13	1.00	1.50
Pulses	1.02	1.01	1.02	—	—
Plantains	2.06	1.97	1.69	1.13	1.10
Yams	0.91	0.90	0.92	—	—

SOURCES: Alderman (1990); Nweke, Spencer, and Lynam (2002).

NOTE: —, not available.

ified these mechanical graters (Adegboye and Akinwumi 1990; Adjebeng-Asem 1990). Beginning in the 1940s, mechanical graters began to spread, albeit slowly at first. By the end of the 1970s, the mechanical grater was available in one-third (22 of 65) of the COSCA villages. And by the end of the 1980s, over one-half (34 of 65) reported the operation of mechanical graters (Nweke et al. 1999b).

NEW CASSAVA VARIETIES.   In the early decades of the 20th century, Nigerian farmers planted mostly sweet varieties of cassava. They could consume these varieties without processing, although the sweet varieties produced low yields and proved susceptible to pests and diseases. As the cassava transformation progressed and cassava increasingly became a cash crop for rural and urban consumption, farmers began to replace several of the sweet cassava varieties with higher-yielding bitter varieties (Nweke et al. 1994). As a result, from 1941 to 1950 the number of cassava varieties introduced in Nigeria's cassava-growing villages began to accelerate, offering testament to the growing farmer interest in cassava as a cash crop (Figure 2.3). Varietal selection and distribution during this period depended primarily on farmer observation and informal farmer-to-farmer transfer of preferred varieties.

In parallel with these informal efforts, scientists at the International Institute of Tropical Agriculture (IITA) launched a scientific cassava breeding program in 1971. Led by S. K. Hahn, the IITA team built on a stream of cassava research first begun 35 years earlier, in 1935, at the Amani Research Station in Tanzania. The Amani cassava breeders had produced a critical breakthrough; by crossing cassava with several wild rubber species (relatives of the cassava plant), they produced cassava hybrids resistant to the cassava mosaic virus (Storey and Nichols 1938; Nichols 1947; Jennings 1976). From the Amani crosses, Hahn and his team members combined the genes for resistance to mosaic virus with genes for high-yielding varieties with good root quality, low cyanogens, and resistance to lodging by crossing them with high-yielding varieties from West Africa and Brazil. Then, in partnership with national researchers, the IITA team selected and tested clones at the farm level in different agroecological zones (Hahn, Howland, and Terry 1980; Otoo et al. 1994; Mba and Dixon 1998). They likewise established a partnership with the Shell BP Petroleum Company of Nigeria (Shell-BP) to conduct on-farm testing of the IITA's clones in the delta areas of Nigeria where Shell-BP operated.

In 1977, the IITA team released the first of the Tropical Manioc Selection (TMS) cassava varieties, a series of new, high-yielding, mosaic-resistant varieties that would subsequently provide an adrenaline jolt to cassava breeding programs throughout Africa.[5] Adoption by farmers and national breeding systems proceeded in waves over the ensuing 30 years, although with a lag that varied across countries for a variety of reasons.

---

5. The early TMS released included varieties 50395, 63397, 30555, 4(2)1425, and 30572.

FIGURE 2.3 Technology adoption in Nigeria's 65 COSCA villages

a. Number of cassava varieties introduced per decade

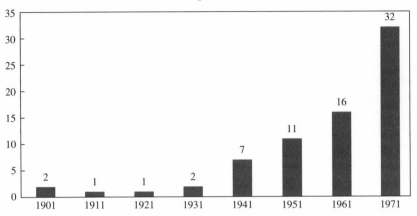

b. Number of villages in which mechanical grater was introduced in each decade

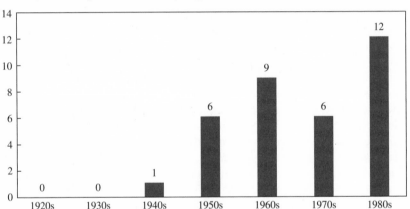

SOURCES: COSCA data analysis and Nweke et al. (1999b).

PERFORMANCE.   As a result of growing demand for cassava and growing productivity in both on-farm production and postharvest processing, production grew rapidly in the years after World War II. Within a decade, between the late 1940s and the late 1950s, the area planted in cassava nearly doubled, increasing from 382,000 hectares per year to 635,000 hectares (FAO 1951–1960). During the 1960s and 1970s, growth in cassava production leveled off to about the same rate as population growth (see Figure 2.2b), leading to roughly constant per capita production of about 180 kilograms per person per year (see Appendix Table 2A.1). By the end of the 1970s, cassava had become well established as a rural and urban food staple.

Phase 3: Mealybug Invasion, 1978–83

The cassava mealybug, an exotic pest from South America, was accidentally introduced into Africa during the early 1970s. It penetrated rapidly throughout the cassava-growing areas of Africa, spread by wind and through the exchange of infested planting material. Because affected plants suffer yield losses of up to 60 percent of their root mass and 100 percent of their leaves, this infestation posed a serious threat to cassava farmers across the continent (Herren 1981).

Arriving in Nigeria in about 1978, the cassava mealybug precipitated a roughly 20 percent fall in cassava production by the early 1980s (IITA 1992). Given the seriousness of the mealybug threat to the continent's number-two food staple, the IITA led a large-scale biological control campaign starting in 1979. The team identified a natural predator wasp that feeds on the mealybug in its home habitat in South America. They then transferred specimens to research stations in Africa for mass rearing and subsequent release over the major cassava-growing areas (IITA 1992). Nigerian researchers first released the wasp by airplane over cassava-growing zones in 1981 (Herren et al. 1987; Norgaard 1988). Within three years, these efforts had succeeded in reducing the mealybug population to a new, lower-level equilibrium.

Phase 4: The Cassava Surge, 1984–94

CHANGING POLICY INCENTIVES.   In 1977, S. K. Hahn's research team at IITA released the first wave of TMS cassava varieties. Yet farmers did not adopt the TMS varieties on a wide scale until seven years later, because the policy environment of the oil boom years favored imported cereals at the expense of local food staples such as cassava. From the 1970s through the early 1980s, Nigeria's oil exports grew dramatically as oil's share in the Nigerian economy increased from negligible levels to over 30 percent of gross domestic product in 1980. Sparking a rapid appreciation of the naira and a now-classic case of "Dutch disease," rising oil exports triggered an abrupt fall in traditional agricultural exports, rapidly rising urban wages, large-scale rural-to-urban migration, and rapid increases in cheap rice and wheat imports to meet this growing urban demand (Oyejide 1986; Bienen 1988; Akande 2000). The resulting surge in low-cost rice and wheat imports artificially depressed the price of *gari* and acted as a constraint to the spread of the TMS varieties from the late 1970s to 1984. Undoubtedly, the Nigerian government's policy of cheap grain imports contributed to the lackluster growth in cassava production from 1971 to 1983.

By the early 1980s, rapid petroleum-led economic growth had slowed significantly. The government adopted a structural adjustment program (SAP), imposing a devaluation of the naira and strict public spending controls that required the removal of subsidies on fertilizer and cereals (Oyejide 1986; Akande 2000). The SAP and the currency devaluation resulted in dramatically improved incentives for cassava growers, triggering a belated but rapid uptake of the TMS varieties.

TMS VARIETIES ADOPTED.   Starting about 1984, the Nigerian government resumed active promotion of domestic food staple production. The government established agricultural development programmes (ADPs) in the cassava-producing states and began active distribution of the high-yielding TMS varieties, including free distribution of planting material to farmers (Nweke, Hahn, and Ugwu 1994). As a result of improved cassava productivity and rapidly rising consumer demand, the TMS vareties spread rapidly and cassava production soared (Figure 2.2). By 1989, nearly 90 percent of Nigeria's cassava-growing villages reported availability of TMS varieties. Nearly 60 percent reported that many or most farmers were growing the new varieties (Nweke et al. 1999b).

The ensuing dramatic increase in cassava output per capita from 1984 to 1994 arose from a combination of increased yield and area expansion. At the farm level, TMS varieties in Nigeria yielded 40 percent more than local varieties, even when grown without fertilizer. At 16- to 24-ton yields per hectare (equivalent to 5- to 7-ton cereal yields), the TMS cassava varieties attained yields comparable to those achieved by green revolution wheat and rice varieties in Asia during the 1960s and 1970s (Ruttan 2001).

Phase 5: New Markets and New Challenges, 1995–Present

After the surge, cassava production continued to grow in Nigeria, though at a slower rate than before (Figure 2.2). In the decade ending in 1994, a combination of productivity gains on the supply side and rapidly growing markets on the demand side fueled rapid growth in cassava production. Since the mid-1990s, new markets and new sources of productivity growth have governed the pace of growth.

INDUSTRIAL PROCESSING AND EXPORT MARKETS.   Over the past century, Nigerian cassava producers have served primarily domestic food markets. By the early 2000s, available estimates suggest that food consumption still accounted for about 84 percent of cassava utilization (Phillips et al. 2004). Of the cassava consumed as human food, roughly 80 percent is prepared as *gari* and other processed foods, while households consume the remaining 20 percent in fresh form (Nweke et al. 1999b).

Given already high levels of cassava consumption, most market observers believe that the next phase of growth in Nigerian cassava production will require expanded industrial and export markets (Balagopalan et al. 1988; Bamikole and Bokanga 2000). Of the cassava production currently processed for industrial use, the livestock feed industry absorbs the majority, while industrial sweeteners, high-quality starches, and confectionary flours account for the remainder (Phillips et al. 2004).

In July 2002, in order to accelerate the market growth of cassava-based products, Nigeria's President Olusegun Obasanjo established a Presidential Initiative on Cassava Production and Export (PICPE). He tasked the commission to find ways of ramping up cassava production, processing, and exports in order to take production from 32 million to 150 million metric tons. In the process, he aimed to raise the value added in cassava-based products from US$1 to US$5 billion (Nigeriafirst 2005). Under PICPE auspices, members of Nigeria's private sector have visited major cassava-exporting countries such as Thailand, major European importers and feed manufacturers, and major production and processing facilities in Brazil (Anga 2003a,b). To encourage domestic industrial processing, the Nigerian government mandated a 10 percent mixture of cassava with wheat flour in bread starting in June 2006 (Africa Research Bulletin 2006).

SECOND-GENERATION LABOR CONSTRAINTS. Labor productivity gains from the adoption of mechanical graters and manually operated hydraulic presses accelerated the rapid diffusion of cassava as a cash crop for urban consumption in Nigeria. By 1990, the mechanical grater was available in over half of Nigeria's cassava-producing villages, and that percentage has continued to grow. As grating has become increasingly mechanized, peeling has emerged as the most labor-intensive processing task, followed by the toasting required in *gari* preparation and the rising labor required for harvesting high-yielding varieties.

Progressive farmers who achieve high yields by growing TMS varieties face new labor bottlenecks during harvesting and processing. Yet rural wages continue to rise. In 1991, cassava farmers in Nigeria paid wage labor the equivalent of US$1.24 per manday. Ten years later, in 2001, wages had nearly tripled to US$3.50 per manday. Over the same period, the price of *gari* increased by less than 40 percent, from an average of US$185.00 per ton in 1991 to an equivalent of US$255.00 per ton in 1998.[6] Clearly, significant gains in labor productivity will be necessary to maintain the profitability of cassava production and processing.

Motors of Change

Cassava production in Nigeria has ebbed and surged over time, as the preceding chronology has emphasized. Turning points and trends within each period can be explained by several driving forces. Productivity changed radically at several junctures: with the introduction and diffusion of the mechanized cassava grater, with the arrival of the cassava mealybug and subsequent biological control efforts, and with the development and diffusion of new high-yielding TMS cassava varieties. Incentives have likewise shifted over time, gradually in the case of growing urban markets and rising rural wage rates, abruptly in the

---

6. Government of Nigeria, Ministry of Finance and Economic Development, Benin City.

case of policy-induced changes in exchange rates, trade regulations, and subsidies that affect the price of cassava and competing food products. Nigerian cassava farmers and processors have responded decisively as opportunities and incentives in their decisionmaking environment have changed, sometimes gradually and sometimes abruptly, over time.

Results

FARM INCOME.   From the mid-1980s to the early 1990s, during the period of rapid diffusion of TMS varieties in Nigeria, cassava production per capita increased and cassava prices to consumers fell (Figure 2.4). The productivity boost from TMS cassava varieties combined with the productivity gains from mechanical grating to significantly raise farm income, even in the face of productivity-led falling prices. The mechanical cassava grater reduced post-harvest processing labor by about 50 percent, while TMS varieties increased yields by 40 percent. As a result, farmers who plant local varieties and grate manually earn a modest net profit of 42 naira (about US$3.50) per ton of *gari,* while those with access to mechanical grating earn over 10 times as much, about US$40.00 per ton of *gari.* Access to TMS varieties has increased profits a further 60 percent, to US$65.00 per ton of *gari.* Given these productivity gains, returns to labor increased by over 60 percent, from US$1.75 per day under manual processing of local varieties to US$2.82 per day for mechanical processing of TMS varieties (Table 2.3).

Clearly, labor-saving grating technology has improved incentives for farmer adoption of TMS varieties. Conversely, the productivity gains resulting from TMS cassava cultivation have enabled faster development of commercial surpluses and encouraged private sector investment in mechanical cassava graters. In fact, TMS adoption increases the likelihood of subsequent mechanization by 75 percent (Johnson and Masters 2004).

PRICES.   During the period of rapid diffusion of TMS cassava varieties in Nigeria, from 1984 to 1994, cassava prices fell sharply, as shown by *gari*-to-yam and *gari*-to-rice price ratios (Nweke 2004). The average inflation-adjusted *gari* price during this period (18,000 naira per ton) was 40 percent lower than the price (29,000 naira per ton) that had prevailed in the prior period, from 1971 to 1983, before the TMS diffusion (Figure 2.4). This dramatic reduction in the *gari* price represents a significant increase in the real income of millions of rural and urban households who consume cassava as their most important staple food.

NUTRITION AND FOOD SAFETY.   High productivity in cassava production and processing has led to low cassava prices, providing consumers with their cheapest available source of calories (Table 2.4). Falling cassava prices, by further reducing the cost of their principal food staple, has conferred a nutritional benefit, particularly on low-income consumers. Some critics complain that cassava is a nutritionally deficient food because of its low protein and vitamin con-

TABLE 2.3 Returns to cassava production and processing in Nigeria, 1991

	Production and processing technologies			
	Local varieties		Tropical manioc selection varieties	
	Manual processing	Mechanized processing	Manual processing	Mechanized processing
Labor inputs				
Farm production and harvesting	208	208	234	234
Processing	180	74	261	107
Total labor (person-days/ha)	388	282	495	341
Outputs				
Root yield (tons/ha)	13.4	13.4	19.4	19.4
Usable root yield (80% of root yield)	10.7	10.7	15.6	15.6
Root/*gari* conversion ratio	0.3	0.3	0.3	0.3
Gari yield (tons/ha)	3.5	3.5	5.1	5.1
Village market price of *gari* (naira/ton of *gari*)	3,140	3,140	3,140	3,140
Nonlabor costs (naira/ha)				
Transport	2,065	2,065	2,995	2,995
Other	1,023	1,184	1,482	1,715
Total nonlabor costs	3,088	3,249	4,477	4,710
Performance measures (naira)				
Revenue/ha	11,116	11,116	16,108	16,108
Gross margin/ha	8,028	7,867	11,631	11,398
Returns to labor (naira/day)	21	28	23	33
Returns to labor (US$/day)[a]	1.75	2.35	1.98	2.82
Net profit per ton of *gari* (naira/ton)	42	478	339	776
Net profit per ton of *gari* (US$/ton)[a]	3.54	40.32	28.59	65.45

SOURCE: Nweke, Spencer, and Lynam (2002).

[a]Dollars converted to 2005 values.

tent (Nicol 1954; Brock 1955; Latham 1979). On similar grounds, one could declare beef a nutritionally deficient food because of its low and highly expensive carbohydrate content. Clearly, no single food can provide a balanced diet. Nigeria's cassava transformation, by reducing the cost of cassava-based carbohydrates, has enabled improved nutritional outcomes among the poor by lowering the cost of their principal staple food.

Some cassava varieties contain high levels of cyanogenic glucosides that, if not removed during processing, can be lethal (Osuntokun 1973, 1981;

FIGURE 2.4 Inflation-adjusted price of *gari* in Edo State, Nigeria, 1971–98

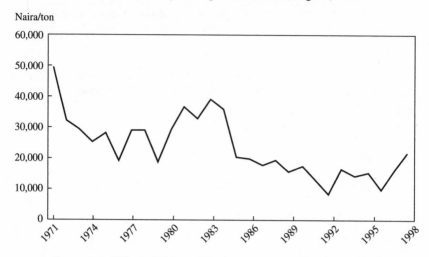

SOURCE: Government of Nigeria, Ministry of Finance and Economic Development, Benin City.

TABLE 2.4 Retail price of 1,000 calories from fresh cassava roots and maize in rural market centers of Nigeria and Ghana, 1992

Rural market	Fresh cassava	Maize	Cassava price/ maize price (%)
Nigeria	(Naira per 1,000 calories)		
Busanfung	0.71	3.20	22
Donga	0.36	0.95	38
Ofabe	0.24	0.60	40
Garbabi	0.38	0.85	45
Guyuki	0.85	1.60	53
Yaburawa	0.63	1.11	57
Namtaringure	0.80	1.20	67
Wuse	0.81	1.07	76
Suwabarki	1.09	1.37	80
Ghana	(Cedis per 1,000 calories)		
Koluedor	32	83	39
Nkurakan	44	71	62
Tafiano	35	53	66
Sagboi	34	49	69

SOURCE: Nweke, Spencer, and Lynam (2002).

Nartey 1977).[7] In general, though not always, sweet varieties contain nonlethal doses, while bitter varieties require processing—usually soaking and sun drying —to remove the cyanogens (Brimer 2000; Chiwona Karltun et al. 2004). In Nigeria, where households consume 20 percent of their cassava in fresh form, marketers and households ensure food safety by consuming only sweet varieties fresh (Nweke, Spencer, and Lynam 2002). For this reason, farmers in peri-urban centers plant primarily sweet cassava varieties for sale as fresh roots for snack food in urban centers. The remaining 80 percent they consume as *gari,* generally made using bitter varieties. Many farmers prefer bitter varieties because they prove most resistant to human, insect, and animal pests.[8] Standard *gari* processing removes cyanogens by soaking, pressing, drying, and toasting, thus ensuring consumer safety.

EQUITY.   In Nigeria, cassava provides a major source of cash income for farm households. During the COSCA surveys in 1992, food crops contributed 55 percent of cash income for study households. Cassava, the most important single cash income source, accounted for 11.6 percent of total cash income per farm household compared to 8.3 percent for yams, 7.7 percent for maize, and 6.1 percent for rice (Nweke, Spencer, and Lynam 2002).

Cassava sales likewise proved more egalitarian than the alternative staples, such as yams and maize. Cassava cash income accrued to more households than did earnings from these other major staples. Among rural households, 40 percent earned cash income from cassava, while 35 percent sold maize and 24 percent earned income from selling yams. Although food sales typically remain highly concentrated among an upper stratum of smallholder farmers (see Jayne, Mather, and Mghenyi 2006), cassava sales accrue to a broader spectrum of farm households than do sales of other food staples. The top 10 percent of cash-earning households from the COSCA villages earned 50 percent of all cassava cash income, 60 percent of yam earnings, and 70 percent of total income from maize sales (Nweke, Spencer, and Lynam 2002).

GENDER.   Cassava income accrues to both men and women in Nigeria, despite a strongly held view that cassava is primarily a "women's crop" (World Bank 2000). Both men and women work in cassava fields, although they specialize by task. In Nigeria and Ghana, men provide the bulk of labor for land clearing and plowing, while both men and women participate in planting, weed-

---

7. Several other crops—including yams, taro, plantains, beans, and peas—can also be lethal if eaten without proper preparation.

8. In most of the COSCA study countries, sweet cassava varieties predominated in the forest zone (70 percent sweet and 30 percent bitter), whereas bitter varieties proved more popular in the savanna zone (30 percent sweet and 70 percent bitter). Farmers in the savanna zone processed bitter cassava as dried roots by peeling and soaking the roots and drying them in the sun. But because sun drying is difficult in the forest zone, farmers plant sweet varieties that they can eat without soaking, drying, or fear of cyanide poisoning (Nweke, Spencer, and Lynam 2002).

ing, and harvesting. During transport and processing, particularly peeling, women's labor predominates (Table 2.5). As cassava becomes commercialized, the men's role typically increases at all stages of cassava production and processing. A comparison between Congo and Nigeria reveals this distinction most starkly. In Congo, where cassava remains a rural food staple and marketed volumes remain low, women dominate at all stages of cassava production except land preparation. But in Nigeria, where urban cassava markets are well developed and where *gari* sales account for 80 percent of human cassava consumption, men's role in cassava production and processing increases perceptibly (see Table 2.5). As the cassava transformation has unfolded in Africa, cassava has also become a "man's crop" (Nweke, Spencer, and Lynam 2002).

Dissemination of improved technology has likewise cut across genders. Despite an extension service staffed with 95 percent male officers, both men and women have gained access to the new TMS varieties. Adoption studies carried out during the COSCA fieldwork in Nigeria found TMS varieties planted in 55 percent of women's cassava fields, roughly the same as in men's fields (60 percent) (Nweke, Spencer, and Lynam 2002). The absence of recurrent input purchases for cassava clearly favors broad-based technology diffusion and continued utilization of improved cassava varieties over time by households at all income levels. In this respect, TMS cassava contrasts starkly with hybrid maize and cotton, which require annual cash purchases of improved seeds, fertilizer, and (in the case of cotton) pesticides (see Chapters 3 and 4).

SUSTAINABILITY.   Unlike other food crops, such as maize, cassava requires little in the way of purchased seed, fertilizer, or chemical inputs. The high productivity of the TMS varieties, combined with an absence of purchased inputs, ensure the financial sustainability of smallholder cassava production in Nigeria.

Environmental sustainability seems likewise established. Because cassava can grow on marginal soils better than most food crops, farmers frequently plant it in unfavorable locations. Observing this association between infertile soils and cassava production, some scholars and agriculturalists have assumed that cassava depletes the soil. But a 20-year trial conducted by S. K. Hahn on a single, continuously cultivated cassava plot at the IITA research station in Ibadan suggests otherwise. Without fertilizer or externally administered soil amendments other than natural recycling of cassava leaves, Hahn found that although production dropped from 40 tons per year during the first 4 years of production, it stabilized at about 20 tons per hectare for the remaining 16 years (Nweke, Spencer, and Lynam 2002). He concluded that recycled cassava leaves replenished the soil sufficiently to sustain yields, even under continuous cultivation.

THE BOTTOM LINE.   In terms of broad-based income creation, equity, and sustainability—the three performance criteria laid out by the Decisionmaking Environment–Action–Results (DE-A-R) framework—Nigeria's cassava transformation constitutes an unambiguous success. Not only has it improved the welfare of rural farmers and urban consumers, but it has generated significant

TABLE 2.5 Percentage of cassava fields in which women and men provide the bulk of each kind of labor

	Land clearing	Plowing	Planting	Weeding	Harvesting	Transporting	Processing[a]
Congo							
Women	27	75	85	84	85	92	—
Men	68	9	5	6	2	1	—
Both equally	5	16	10	10	13	7	—
Total	100	100	100	100	100	100	—
Ghana							
Women	1	1	25	10	24	78	68
Men	97	94	52	70	48	1	2
Both equally	2	5	23	20	28	21	30
Total	100	100	100	100	100	100	100
Nigeria							
Women	4	4	24	34	30	83	49
Men	94	95	71	62	66	10	11
Both equally	2	1	5	4	4	7	40
Total	100	100	100	100	100	100	100

SOURCES: Nweke et al. (1999a,b); Nweke, Spencer, and Lynam (2002).

NOTE: —, not available.

[a]Percentage of villages; all other columns list percentage of cassava fields.

technology spillovers. These have contributed to cassava surges across the African cassava belt, as the following examples reveal.

Cassava Spillovers in Ghana

In Ghana, the cassava transformation benefited from technologies developed in Nigeria. The spread of both TMS cassava varieties and mechanical graters built on early research and development efforts in Nigeria. Yet, for many years government policy in Ghana focused on rapid industrialization. And within agriculture, they favored grain production on large public farms. As a result, Ghana invested comparatively late in research and development for small farmers and for root crops. Though later than in Nigeria, cassava production in Ghana has grown rapidly over the past two decades, largely due to spillovers from the earlier efforts in Nigeria.

Phase 1: Introduction and Early Diffusion of Cassava, 1750–1956

In the mid-18th century in Ghana, cassava was the most widely grown crop on the coastal plains (Adams 1957). But its spread from the coast into the hinterland proceeded slowly. Cassava reached the interior settlements in Ashanti and Tamale only in 1930 (Ghana, Ministry of Food and Agriculture 2005). By 1955, cassava remained a minor crop in Ghana, with only 66,000 hectares planted (FAO 1960).

Phase 2: Cassava Marginalization, 1957–81

For nearly 25 years after Ghana achieved independence, from 1957 to 1981, Ghanaian agricultural policy marginalized root crops in favor of grains. The government encouraged production of grains with a price support program provided through the Grains Marketing Board and the Food Distribution Corporation and through subsidized irrigation water, farm mechanization, and agricultural credit (Nweke 1978a,b, 1979).[9] Similarly, most agricultural bank credit for food crops focused on maize and rice (Nweke 1978b).

In 1962, Ghana's government established the State Farms Corporation (SFC) to apply modern farming methods in order to expand the production of food crops and agricultural raw materials on a commercial scale (Agricultural Committee of the National Liberation Council 1966). The SFC absorbed proportionately more resources than it farmed land, and it focused on mechanized farming of cereal and export crops. In spite of a token expression of interest in cassava during the First Five-Year Development Plan (1975–1980), "policy still favored the cereals, rice and maize, the long time favorites" (Ghana, Ministry of Food and Agriculture 2005, 22).

---

9. The mechanical technologies available for seedbed preparation are designed for plowing, harrowing, and ridging. They are not relevant for no-till seedbeds and are not designed for mound making, which predominates among cassava farmers, the former in well-drained soils and the latter in poorly drained soils.

Phase 3: Drought as a Wake-Up Call, 1982–85

A severe drought in 1982–83 served as a wake-up call for Ghana's agricultural policymakers, highlighting the importance of cassava in ensuring national food security. The drought imposed severe consequences: crop failure, skyrocketing food prices, and a mass exodus of Ghanaians attempting to escape famine by relocating to other countries in West Africa. Cassava, the only crop that did not fail, helped Ghana cope with the drought. This experience and the key role played by cassava in preventing famine led Ghanaian agricultural policy circles to question the wisdom of reliance on maize for national food security. This recognition ultimately led to a significant reordering of commodity priorities within the Ministry of Agriculture.

On the heels of the drought, the cassava mealybug outbreak of 1983 resulted in heavy on-farm cassava losses and a doubling of *gari* prices (Norgaard 1988). In response, in 1984 the Ghanaian authorities launched a biological control program with assistance from the IITA and the Food and Agriculture Organization of the United Nations. They released two batches of natural predators, in March 1984 and again in March 1985, in order to bring mealybugs under control (Ghana, Ministry of Food and Agriculture 2005).

In 1984, Ghana's commissioner (minister) for Agriculture visited the IITA in Ibadan and met with Dr. S. K. Hahn, head of the IITA's cassava breeding program. The crisis had awakened Ghanaian government interest in cassava.

Phase 4: Government Investment in Cassava, 1986–Present

In 1988, Ghana launched a National Root and Tuber Crops Improvement Project as a component of the Ghana Smallholder Rehabilitation and Development Programme (SRDP) sponsored by the International Fund for Agricultural Development. As a result, 11 years after the TMS varieties were released in Nigeria, Ghana officially imported TMS stem cuttings from the IITA and turned them over to Ghanaian researchers for field testing. From 1988 to 1992, Ghanaian researchers, with backstopping from the IITA, evaluated TMS varieties in farmer fields. In 1993, the SRDP team released three improved cassava varieties to farmers. In on-farm trials, these new releases—Afisiafi, Gblemo Duade, and Abasa Fitaa—produced yields roughly double those of local varieties (Ghana, Ministry of Food and Agriculture 2005).

In subsequent years, Ghanaian policymakers have begun to explore export market potential as well as prospects for industrial processing (Daily Graphic 2001). Several private firms have exported cassava chips to the European Union. In 1996, Ghana exported about 20,000 tons of cassava to the European Union for use in livestock feed (Ghana, Ministry of Food and Agriculture 2005). As in Nigeria, future growth will depend on the development of industrial and livestock markets (Graffham et al. 1998).

Results

Since 1961, performance in Ghana's cassava sector has varied, as in Nigeria, depending on the technologies and government policies in force during different periods. From 1961 to 1985, the Ghanaian government's neglect of cassava in agricultural promotion efforts led to sluggish performance and stagnant cassava production per capita (Figure 2.2).

From 1986 onward, however, performance improved dramatically as the government recognized the importance of cassava and began to support on-farm research, technology transfer, and testing. The spread of TMS varieties, mealybug control efforts, and diffusion of the mechanical grater resulted in rapid cassava growth. Between 1986 and 2006, cassava production increased at 7 percent per year. As a result, per capita output grew rapidly (Figure 2.2b); the real price of *gari* fell, as did the *gari*-to-maize price ratio (Nweke 2004); and Ghana moved from sixth-largest cassava producer in Africa to fourth (FAOSTAT 2008).

In Ghana, as in Nigeria, cassava provides a key source of cash income for rural households producing cassava and other crops. Among the COSCA study households in Ghana, food crop production provided the main source of cash income, and cassava tied with maize as the most important cash earner among food crops (Nweke et al. 1999a).

The Cassava Surge in Zambia and Malawi

Cassava and maize, the two principal food staples in Zambia and Malawi, both came to southern Africa from the Americas. Over time, these two imported food crops revolutionized agriculture in central and southern Africa, displacing sorghum and millets as the principal food staples. From the beginning, the histories of cassava and maize have remained inextricably intertwined, with gains in one frequently coming at the expense of the other.

Throughout most of the independence years, government policies in Zambia and Malawi have overwhelmingly favored maize. However, during the 1980s and 1990s a series of sudden changes in the natural and human environment triggered an astonishing renaissance in cassava production in both countries. Since the early 1990s, cassava production in Zambia and Malawi has grown rapidly, at roughly 6 percent per year in Zambia and, according to official figures, as much as 20 percent per year during the surge in Malawi (Figure 2.5).[10]

---

10. The high cassava growth rates reported for Malawi since the mid-1990s stem, in part, from heavy mealybug damage during the 1980s, which depressed the base from which the production rebound is measured. In addition, changes in methods for estimating cassava output likely account for some of Malawi's remarkable gain in reported cassava output. While official figures probably overstate national cassava growth rates, observations on the ground confirm rapid growth in cassava production and marketing since the mid-1990s.

FIGURE 2.5 Trends in cassava production in Malawi and Zambia, 1961–2006

a. National cassava production

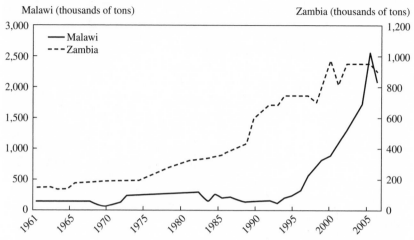

Malawi (thousands of tons)

Zambia (thousands of tons)

b. Per capita cassava production

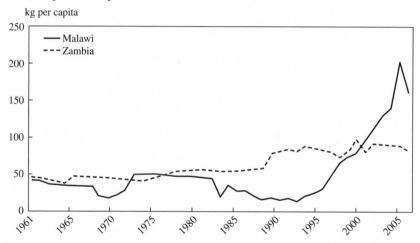

kg per capita

SOURCE: FAOSTAT (2008). See Appendix Table 2A.1.

To understand why cassava production in Zambia and Malawi has grown rapidly, the following review traces out four clear phases in the evolution of cassava production and policy. In both countries, the forces driving change and their timing closely mirrored one another. Although the dates given below refer specifically to Zambia, the trends and turning points in Malawi track those of its neighbor within a handful of years (Table 2.6).

TABLE 2.6 Dynamics and drivers of change in Zambian cassava

	Phase 1: Introduction of Cassava	Phase 2: Cassava as a famine reserve crop	Phase 3: Maize as "king of crops"	Phase 4: The cassava crises	Phase 5: Cassava's take-off
Timing	1830–1929	1930–63	1964–81	1982–90	1991–present
Key actors	Traders Farmers Village leaders	Colonial authorities	Government	Mealybug Root and Tuber Improvement Programme (RTIP) International Institute of Tropical Agriculture	RTIP Private nurseries Nongovernmental organizations
Motors of change	Cassava cuttings become available Drought and pest attacks encourage adoption	Colonial orders requiring farmers to plant cassava plots as insurance against famine	Heavy input and marketing subsidies favoring maize production	Mealybug invasion threatens 60% to 100% of the cassava crop Mass rearing and distribution of natural predators to counter this threat Breeding program begins in earnest	New varieties released Maize subsidies withdrawn Drought HIV/AIDS?

Beneficiaries	Small farmers	Small farmers	Small and commercial maize farmers	Small farmers in northern and western cassava zones	Small farmers
Production gains	Cassava becomes established in northern and western Zambia	Small production gains in non-traditional zones (central and southern areas)	Cassava production stalls	Negative growth reversed by the end of the period	Production growth of about 6% per year
Impact	Food security improves	Cassava remains dominant in northern and western zones / Small plots appear in central and southern areas	Maize production grows rapidly, even in northern cassava zones, due to heavy subsidies	Mealybug threatens the food security of 300,000 farm households	Maize area falls by 20% / Cassava area expands by 50% / 20% of cassava area planted in new varieties / Cassava begins to spread to eastern, central, and southern Zambia

Phase 1: Introduction of Cassava to the Region, 1830–1929

Introduced to coastal areas of Africa by Portuguese traders, cassava spread inland at varying rates along the Zambezi and Congo rivers and via long-distance trade routes (Jones 1959). Traders, travelers, and farmers carried it from village to village, where it spread, often as part of efforts by tribal leaders to ensure food supplies in the face of various natural threats (Jones 1959). Based on fragmentary historical records, it appears that cassava came to what is now northern Zambia, via the Congo, around the 1830s. Cassava likely arrived in Malawi during the 1860s, transiting from the East African coast via inland trading routes (Carter et al. 1992).

Phase 2: Cassava as a Famine Reserve Crop, 1930–63

The British Colonial Office, which took over the direct administration of Northern Rhodesia in 1924, largely ignored agriculture except insofar as it could contribute to cheap urban food supplies for the mines. For this purpose, they encouraged white settlers to establish farms along the line of rail leading north to the copper mines. In 1936, the colonial authorities established a Maize Control Board (MCB) to control food prices and facilitate bulk procurement for the urban mining centers. The MCB also became the government's primary instrument for providing subsidized support to white settler farmers through differential pricing and favorable allocation of sales quotas (Wood et al. 1990). In urban areas and for white farmers, maize was king.

Cassava held interest only as a famine reserve crop in the African farming zones. As elsewhere in British Africa, colonial authorities encouraged, and sometimes required, farmers to produce cassava as a precaution against periodic famines (Jones 1959). Under the Laws of Northern Rhodesia, the Native Authority Ordinance of 1936 authorized provincial commissioners, through the paramount chiefs, to mandate the cultivation of cassava and other drought-tolerant crops as a means of preventing food shortages.[11] Farmers failing to comply faced sanctions of up to 3 months in prison, a fine of 5 pounds, or both (Laws of Northern Rhodesia 1952, CAP 157).[12] Because of this imposition, farmers often regard cassava as a "colonial" crop (Marter 1978).[13]

---

11. Farmers remember these edicts well. During our field interviews in northern Zambia, old farmers described how district officers would come to inspect their cassava fields armed only with a stone. Standing in one corner of a farmer's cassava field, the inspecting officer would throw the stone as far as he could. If he could launch it out of the plot, the field was too small, and the farmer was liable to sanctions.

12. See Moore and Vaughan (1994) for several accounts of the application of Native Authority rules on cassava production.

13. Because of their prior experience growing cassava during the 1950s and 1960s, older farmers have proven the most ready adopters of cassava in southern Zambia over the past decade, as government and NGOs have introduced improved cassava planting material in response to recurrent drought (Pongolani and Kalonge 1999).

Phase 3: Maize as "King of Crops," 1964–81

When Zambia and Malawi achieved independence, government orders on growing cassava fell into disuse, along with a host of other colonial edicts. Maize, the reigning king of crops among settler commercial farmers in Zambia, came to rule of all of Zambian and Malawian agricultural policy. Via a growing network of farmer cooperatives and a pair of parastatal marketing boards, the Zambian and Malawian governments provided subsidized inputs to maize farmers and ensured a guaranteed market for maize at a fixed panterritorial price (see Chapter 3).

As a result, maize area, yields, and production all soared, even in regions where farmers had traditionally grown cassava, millet, and sorghum. In the face of substantial maize input subsidies and a guaranteed market outlet, even farmers in the cassava zones of Zambia and Malawi put land into maize cultivation (Kokwe 1997). With heavy maize subsidies and omnipresent government marketing boards, maize became preeminent as both a food staple and a cash crop. Cassava, like sorghum and millet, languished under this maize-centric policy regime.

Phase 4: The Cassava Crises, 1982–1990

THE MEALYBUG INVASION. Beginning in 1981, a pair of lethal cassava pests, the cassava mealybug (CM) and the cassava green mite (CGM), threatened Zambia's cassava crop at the same time that maize production faltered in the face of a sequence of drought years (Malambo et al. 1999). As the pests spread, yield losses under CM infestation rose to between 60 percent and 100 percent, while the CGM infestation resulted in 10–30 percent losses in root production (Herren 1987; Ministry of Agriculture 1989).

Five years later, in 1986, a similar scenario played out in Malawi when the CM entered the country across the northern shores of Lake Malawi from Tanzania (Sauti et al. 1994). A subsequent drought in central Malawi threatened the country's maize crop as well. With its two principal food staples threatened, the government of Malawi declared a national food emergency from January to August 1988 (Pelletier and Msukwa 1990). Pest damage had compromised the cassava crop in the northern zones of both Zambia and Malawi, where it serves as the principal food staple.

BIOLOGICAL CONTROL EFFORTS. The seriousness of this threat forced both governments to take an active interest in cassava. They turned for support to the IITA-led consortium, which helped them develop programs for the mass rearing of predator wasps, followed by aerial and ground release. Releases over a period of three to four seasons resulted in a significant decline in the CM population and in the establishment of a pest–predator equilibrium (Ministry of Agriculture 1989; Malambo et al. 1999). In both Zambia and Malawi, this sudden threat to the cassava crop propelled cassava from virtual anonymity to center stage in food policy debates (see Minde, Ewell, and Teri 1999).

RECOGNITION OF CASSAVA AS A KEY FOOD SECURITY CROP.   Simultaneous threats to the maize and cassava crops forced cassava into the limelight for the first time since independence. Meanwhile, budgetary shortfalls and donor pressure forced a critical rethinking of governments' large-scale maize subsidies. During the late 1980s and early 1990s, both governments scaled back their expensive maize input and marketing subsidies (see Chapter 3 for details). Though maize remained king, its virtual monopoly on government agricultural resources had been broken. In November 1994, Malawi's new agricultural plan announced: "Production of maize in areas that are not suited to its production, largely as a result of low rainfall, will be discontinued to give room for more drought-resistant crops such as cassava and sweet potato to improve household food security" (Akoroda 1999, 10). As a result of this series of natural disasters, cassava emerged with a place at the food policy table.

THE RESEARCH RESPONSE.   In response to these food crises, both Zambia and Malawi established highly productive cassava research programs beginning in the early to mid-1980s. With donor support from German assistance followed by 10 years of funding from the Swedish International Development Cooperation Agency, Zambia's Root and Tuber Improvement Programme (RTIP) cataloged many hundreds of local and exotic cassava varieties, launched a series of mass selection trials, and screened their accessions systematically for yield, earliness of bulking, and resistance to cassava mosaic virus (CMV). The program identified five recommended clones that went into on-farm trials in 1991/92. Then, in 1993/94, the RTIP released three improved local varieties, Bangweulu, Kapumba, and Nalumino (Table 2.7).[14] They yielded 20–30 tons per hectare, compared to an average of 6 tons from local varieties; bulked 12 months earlier; and provided superior resistance to CMV and major pests in both research and on-farm trials. These recommended local varieties came on stream just as the new government agricultural policy withdrew subsidies for maize, making cassava more attractive than at any other time in a generation.

As in Zambia, Malawi's cassava breeding efforts initially focused on identification of the most resistant local varieties and rapid distribution of cleaned, improved cuttings.[15] In response to the drought of 1991/92, Malawian breeders began an accelerated program of multiplication and distribution of cassava planting material with support from the Malawian government, the U.S. Agency for International Development, and the Southern African Root Crops Research Network. This three-year program launched a first wave of large-scale distri-

---

14. This summary of cassava breeding and multiplication efforts draws on Engelmeyer (1987), Zambia, Department of Agriculture (1992), Chitundu and Soenarjo (1997), Chitundu (1999), Ngoma, Miti, and Mbunji (1999), and interviews with staff of the RTIP.

15. This summary of Malawian cassava research draws on Sauti (1982), SARRNET (1994), Sauti et al. (1994), Akoroda (1999), Benesi et al. (1999), Mahungu (1999), Terri et al. (2000), and Mkumbira (2002), as well as discussions with Southern African Root Crops Research Network staff.

TABLE 2.7 Release of improved cassava varieties in Malawi and Zambia

Variety name	Date released	Type[a]	Taste
Malawi			
Gomani	1989	CRLV	Bitter
Mbundumali/Manyokola[b]	1989	CRLV	Sweet
Chitembwere	1989	CRLV	Sweet
Mkondezi	1999	IV	Bitter
Silira	1999	IV	Bitter
Maunjili	1999	IV	Bitter
Sauti (CH 92/077)[c]	2002	IV	Bitter
Yizaro (CH 92/100)[c]	2002	IV	Bitter
Zambia			
Bangweulu	1993	CRLV	Bitter
Kapumba	1993	CRLV	Sweet
Nalumino	1993	CRLV	Sweet
Mweru	2000	IV	Sweet
Chila	2000	IV	Bitter
Kampolombo	2000	IV	Sweet
Tanganyika	2000	IV	Sweet

SOURCES: Root and Tuber Improvement Programme and Southern African Root Crops Research Network.

[a]CRLV, clean recommended local variety; IV, improved varieties bred from Tropical Manioc Selection and local crosses.

[b]The Malawian variety, Manyokola, is also grown in Zambia under the name of Manyopola.

[c]Variety numbers are listed in parentheses.

bution of cleaned local cassava varieties selected for CMV tolerance and early bulking. The distributed varieties included Gomani, Mbundumali, and Manyokola. These concerted efforts at seed multiplication resulted in the rapid resuscitation of cassava production throughout Malawi (Figure 2.5).

Phase 5: Cassava's Take-Off, 1991–Present

PRODUCTION GROWTH.   In Zambia, government withdrawal of maize subsidies began in the late 1980s, just at the moment when Zambia's cassava research team had identified and cleaned three superior local cassava varieties for distribution. The combination of improved cassava productivity and depressed maize markets produced startling results (Figure 2.5). Without subsidized maize seeds and fertilizer and with the public maize marketing apparatus in disrepair, farmers in the traditional cassava-, sorghum-, and millet-producing regions rapidly reduced the area they planted to maize (Box 2.1). The total cropped area devoted to maize fell from nearly 80 percent in 1982 to around 60 percent in 2004, while the corresponding share for cassava and sweet potatoes increased from 20 percent to 30 percent (Zulu et al. 2000; Jayne et al. 2007).

BOX 2.1 A small farmer tests the new cassava varieties

John Tilimba supports a family of 12 in the district of Samfya in Luapula province of northern Zambia. He has been farming since 1975, though he supplements his farm income with piece work as a painter.

When he began in 1975, Mr. Tilimba initially farmed 1.5 limas of land (1 lima is 0.25 hectare). Like most farmers in Luapula province, he devoted most of his land to cassava, supplementing his 1 lima of local cassava with 0.5 lima of groundnuts and cabbage. In 1980, with the advent of the government-sponsored Lima Pack program supplying subsidized maize seeds and fertilizer to farmers, Tilimba added a lima of maize to his cropping system alongside his 1 lima of cassava and small plot of groundnuts.

After the Zambian government withdrew its maize subsidies, in the early 1990s, Mr. Tilimba was forced to reduce his maize production. He could not afford hybrid seeds or fertilizer at the free market price. So he reduced his maize production from 1 lima to 0.25 lima. And because he has limited cash, he plants only local maize varieties without fertilizer. As a result, his maize yields have fallen drastically.

To fill the gap left by his diminished maize production, Mr. Tilimba turned once again to cassava. His neighbors told him of an improved cassava variety, called Bangweulu, that yielded more than double what his local varieties could achieve. And instead of waiting 30 months to harvest, he could begin eating roots after only 12–16 months. In 1999, Mr. Tilimba was able to obtain Bangweulu cuttings from one of his neighbors. He has added 1 lima per year since then. By 2003, he was farming 3 limas of cassava, which he intercropped with groundnuts the first year. He has also added half a lima of rice in the *dambo* (low-lying wet area) nearby.

Mr. Tilimba's family consumes half of his annual cassava production. He uses one-fourth to pay in-kind wages to laborers he hires to help with his weeding, and one-fourth he sells for cash. Mr. Tilimba wonders how he would feed his family without the improved cassava. "Cassava is now a cash crop," he marvels, "and I can harvest after only 12 months."

Rapid expansion of cassava area, together with the gradual availability of improved clones, resulted in a double boost that propelled growth in cassava production to roughly 6 percent per year over the ensuing decade and a half (Appendix Table 2A.1). About three-fourths of the increase in cassava output has come from area expansion, with the remainder coming from rising yields due to improved varieties.

Malawian cassava growth has proven even more spectacular, though it began about five years later, in the mid-1990s (Figure 2.5). Given changes in data collection methodology, some of this remarkable gain seems likely to have been overstated. Even so, other indicators suggest that cassava production has indeed grown very rapidly there (Box 2.2). Crop budgets suggest that in some years cassava has been two to three times more profitable than tobacco, groundnuts, or maize as a cash crop in central Malawi (Akoroda and Mwabumba 2000). Unlike in Zambia, where the most rapid growth occurred in the northern cassava-producing zones, in Malawi cassava production has grown rapidly in all regions of the country (Haggblade and Zulu 2003). Cassava expansion in central and southern Malawi has occurred primarily at the expense of maize and tobacco, while in the less densely populated northern regions it has come from cassava expansion onto virgin land (Phiri et al. 2001).

COMMERCIALIZATION.   Since the early 1990s, cassava marketing has grown more rapidly in Malawi than in Zambia. High population density, coupled with rising maize and wheat prices, has led to the rapid emergence of an urban fast-food market for prepared cassava in central Malawi, a traditionally maize-consuming region (Moyo, Benesi, and Sandifolo 1998; Phiri et al. 2001). As a result, cassava has emerged as a highly profitable cash crop for the urban

---

BOX 2.2 Commercial cassava production in central Malawi

Wilson Masoambeta has become a serious commercial cassava farmer since he retired from his butchery business and began farming in 1994. Living only 50 kilometers from Lilongwe, in central Malawi, he has ridden a dramatic wave of increasing urban demand for boiled cassava roots as a morning meal and midday snack food. With the demise of maize subsidies in Malawi and the liberalization of foreign exchange markets, both mealie meal and bread (produced from imported wheat flour) have grown far more expensive than cassava. So urban demand for cassava has literally exploded over the past decade, as Mr. Masoambeta will readily attest.

From 2 acres in 1995, he has steadily increased his cassava holdings to 14 acres in 2002. Because he rents his cassava land and sells the entire crop, he treats his cassava holdings like a business. Including land rental and labor costs, he figures that 1 acre of cassava costs him 10,000 kwacha to produce. He sells the roots for 30,000, netting him 20,000 kwacha per acre in profits. And his cuttings are valuable as well. Because he plants improved, high-yielding, disease-resistant varieties, his neighbors line up for cuttings when he is ready to harvest. Not only do they pay him 11,000 kwacha for 1 acre's worth of cuttings; they provide harvesting labor in order to obtain first rights to the cuttings.

By Mr. Masambeta's reckoning, cassava has become a far more profitable cash crop than maize, cotton, or even tobacco. The regular stream of boys who visit the cassava fields on bicycles, with specially fitted racks for carrying cassava into neighboring towns, attests to the ease of marketing this newfound cash crop.

market (see Box 2.2). According to one recent study, "The cassava revolution in the central region has been driven by the growth in the fresh cassava market" (Phiri et al. 2001, 8). Small distances permit large-scale trade in fresh cassava transported primarily by bicycle. The marketed share of cassava production in central Malawi now reaches 75–90 percent of total cassava production (Moyo, Benesi, and Sandifolo 1998; Phiri et al. 2001). However, in the cassava-consuming regions of northern Malawi, farmers market a much smaller fraction of their output. Overall, farmers market about 25 percent of national cassava production in Malawi, 80 percent of it in fresh form for use as an urban snack food (Kambewa and Nyembe 2008). Industrial manufacturers have begun to experiment with composite flour (cassava blended with wheat) in baked goods and with cassava-based starch (Nthonyiwa et al. 2005; Siyeni et al. 2005; Kambewa and Nyembe 2008).

The situation in Zambia differs considerably, given the large distances between production centers and urban agglomerations. Zambian farmers market between 8 and 10 percent of total production (van Otterdijk 1996; Haggblade and Nyembe 2007), though this share appears to be growing. Long a staple in northern and western Zambia, marketed cassava flour, toasted roots, and boiled fresh varieties have made inroads in urban markets in the central, southern, and eastern parts of the country (Langmead and Baker 2003; Hichaambwa 2005). While production has grown at about 6 percent per year during the 2000s, marketed volumes have increased at a compound annual rate of about 13 percent. Given the long distances between Zambia's major producing zones and its urban centers, a majority of traded cassava takes the form of dried chips (Haggblade and Nyembe 2007). Northern Zambia exports dried cassava to the Democratic Republic of Congo and to the Zambian copper belt for use in household porridge and by several manufacturers as an industrial glue. In 2007, Zambia's largest feed company began to buy cassava for its feed rations on a trial basis (Chitundu, Droppelmann, and Haggblade 2009).

Industry observers generally agree that continued growth in cassava production in both Zambia and Malawi will depend on growing commercial markets for prepared foods, livestock feeds, and industrial uses. For this reason, in mid-2005 a group of Zambian stakeholders launched an Acceleration of Cassava Utilization (ACU) Task Force to help stimulate cassava processing and commercialization. Unlike the presidential initiative in Nigeria, Zambia's efforts at stimulating cassava commercialization were spearheaded by a group of private sector and nongovernmental stakeholders, with modest involvement by government. In spite of its very different origins, the ACU Task Force has drawn inspiration and technical input from the Nigerian experience through ongoing interaction between individual task force members and cassava specialists elsewhere in Africa (Chitundu, Droppelmann, and Haggblade 2009).

Motors of Change

Farmers in Zambia and Malawi have responded to radical changes in productive capacity and policy incentives that, together, shape their decisionmaking environment (see Chapter 1, Figure 1.4). As in Nigeria, the arrival of higher-productivity varieties of cassava has coincided with improved incentives—reduced maize subsidies, rising fertilizer prices, and prominent droughts. Some cassava specialists also hypothesize that the epidemic outbreak of HIV/AIDS in both countries may have induced a move to labor-saving, low-input crops like cassava (Chiwona-Karltun 2001). They recall historical evidence of a similar shift during the 1918 influenza epidemic in Nigeria (Ohadike 1981). The following discussion examines each of these potential driving forces in turn.

DECLINING MAIZE SUBSIDIES. Both Zambia and Malawi dismantled large maize subsidy systems at the end of the 1980s (see Chapter 3). In Zambia, the withdrawal of subsidies for fertilizer and maize resulted in a 33 percent decline in maize profitability (Bangwe 1998). In Malawi, returns to high-input maize production appear to have turned negative, at least in some years (see Chapter 3, Table 3.5), while cassava has become a profitable cash crop (Akoroda and Mwabumba 2000). Rising cassava yields, together with steep increases in fertilizer and maize seed prices, have led to clear financial incentives to switch from maize to cassava (Table 2.8).

IMPROVED CASSAVA VARIETIES. The improved cassava varieties released over the past decade in Zambia and Malawi roughly double cassava yields on the farm. As a result, they double returns to both labor and land (see Table 2.8). In addition, they bulk early and enable harvesting 6–18 months earlier than do traditional varieties (Mkumbira 2002). More resistant to pests and diseases, the new varieties likewise reduce risk and variability in cassava production (Box 2.3)

Fragmentary studies of cassava adoption in central Malawi suggest that about 44 percent of cassava farmers now plant improved varieties (Akoroda and Mwabumba 2000). As a result, time series data suggest that yields roughly doubled between 2000 and 2005, from 7 to 16 tons per hectare (see Appendix Table 2A.1). In Zambia, about 22 percent of cassava farmers grow improved and cleaned recommended local varieties of cassava, roughly doubling on-farm yields (van Otterdijk 1996; MAFF 2000). Though cassava yields are notoriously difficult to measure (Akoroda 1999), Malawi's tight land constraints, coupled with available adoption studies, suggest that yield increases probably account for a majority of the production increase there. In contrast, area gains have predominated in Zambia.

DROUGHT. The Malawian drought of 1991/92 triggered government investment in rapid cassava and sweet potato multiplication, which continued throughout the 1990s. Similarly, in Zambia the droughts of the early 1980s were instrumental in convincing policymakers to invest in cassava research. The

TABLE 2.8 Changing incentives for cassava producers in Zambia

	Preliberalization (1985)		Post-liberalization (2002)			
	Cassava + groundnuts	Maize, HYV	Cassava + groundnuts	Cassava	Maize	
					HYV	Local
Output						
Production (tons/ha)	6	2.5	12	20	2.5	1
Years to harvest	3	1	2	2	1	1
Value (US$/ha)[a]	407	451	760	1,086	339	136
Input costs (US$/ha)[a]	0	84	0	0	116	0
Labor (person-days/ha)	151	175	159	159	175	157
Gross margin (US$/ha)[a]	407	367	760	1,086	224	136
Financial returns						
Returns to labor (US$/person/day)[a]	2.70	2.10	4.78	6.83	1.28	0.86
Returns to land (US$/ha/year)[a]	136	367	380	543	224	136
Calorie returns						
Returns to labor (cal/person/day)	44	44	83	138	44	20
Returns to land (cal/ha/year)	2,197	7,678	6,591	10,985	7,678	3,071

SOURCES: Marter (1978), Kokwe (1997), Ngoliya (1999), MAFF (2000), Tembo and Chitundu (2001), Haggblade and Zulu (2003), Barratt et al. (2006).

NOTE: HYV, high-yielding variety.

[a]Valued in 2005 dollars.

drought of 2002, following the RTIP's release of two waves of improved cassava varieties, further spurred the interest of farmers, the government, and donors in cassava production in the southern, more drought-prone, zones of the country, where it now figures as a key component of food security packs distributed by the Programme Against Malnutrition.

HIV/AIDS.   Cassava has long held a reputation as a less labor-using crop than maize and other food crops (Marter 1978; Ohadike 1981). Though cassava and maize require comparable labor inputs during land preparation, many cassava farmers weed only once or twice in the first year and not at all in the second (Soenarjo 1993). They likewise avoid the labor required to apply fertilizer and other inputs used primarily on maize and export crops. Based on an 18-month cropping calendar and given two weedings in the first year, rough estimates suggest that cassava production requires about 10 percent less labor per hectare per year than does maize.[16] Possibly more important is cassava's flex-

---

16. Note that cassava processing can be highly labor intensive. The earlier discussion on

---

BOX 2.3 Hedging against cassava mosaic virus

George Chipendano of Mwense district in northern Zambia began farming in
1990. In his early years, he grew equal areas of cassava and maize, 3 limas (0.75
hectare) each. But a decade later, as maize subsidies disappeared and both seeds
and fertilizer became more expensive, he cut his maize area from 3 limas to 1.

To compensate, he drastically increased his cassava production. From 3
limas of local varieties in 1990, he expanded to 2.5 hectares (10 limas) of cassava
in 2002. He consumes half his cassava crop to feed his six family members, but
he sells the other half.

Mr. Chipendano devotes 1 hectare of his cassava land to the improved Bangweulu variety. But the remaining 1.5 hectares he plants with a mix of local cassava varieties, including Chiliber, Sailise, and Nakasone. Asked why, he explains
that the mixture of varieties serves as a hedge against the cassava mosaic disease
that periodically infests his fields.

---

ibility in the timing of certain labor operations. Where peak-season labor bottlenecks constrain output, as they do among most rainfed smallholder farms in
Zambia, cassava offers the considerable advantage of a flexible planting and
harvesting calendar.

With national HIV prevalence rates above 25 percent among prime-age
adults in urban areas of Zambia and Malawi and roughly half that level in rural areas, both governments and farmers worry about potential labor shortages
in agriculture (Ministry of Health 1999). Indeed, HIV/AIDS could potentially
affect farm labor supply in two ways. First, by increasing mortality rates, it
could decrease the adult labor available for farm work. Second, HIV/AIDS–
affected adults are normally weaker and less productive than healthy adults,
thus leading households to seek less labor-using activities.

An empirical test of these hypotheses using data from Zambian farm
households affirms these two possible links between the growing prevalence of
HIV/AIDS and increased cassava production (Table 2.9). To the extent that
HIV/AIDS reduces a household's adult labor supply, households respond by increasing their cassava area and reducing the area farmed in maize. Thus, lower
adult labor supply in any given household (adults per capita) appears to induce
farm households to move out of maize and into cassava production. In addition,
a higher HIV/AIDS prevalence (as measured by the proxy of chronic illness for

---

Nigeria, where the bulk of cassava production has become commercialized and where thousands
of rural processing plants convert cassava roots into dried convenience food, has emphasized the
labor constraints that have emerged requiring new, less labor-intensive processing technologies.
This may account for the prevalence of marketing fresh rather than processed cassava in Malawi.

TABLE 2.9 Impact of household labor availability and HIV/AIDS on cassava and maize production

Explanatory variable	Cassava		Maize	
	Share of cropped area	Hectares per capita	Share of cropped area	Hectares per capita
Agroecological region (base = AER3, high-rainfall)				
AER 1. Low-rainfall zones	-0.629***	-0.372***	0.669***	0.296***
	(-28.0)	(-23.7)	(50.7)	(34.4)
AER 2a. Moderate-rainfall, heavy soils	-0.380***	-0.216***	0.536***	0.261***
	(-39.0)	(-35.4)	(43.6)	(32.5)
AER 2b. Moderate-rainfall, sandy soils	-0.204***	-0.093***	0.304***	0.151***
	(-21.1)	(-15.3)	(19.7)	(14.9)
Land cropped (ha per capita)	0.048***	0.202***	-0.080***	0.395***
	(7.0)	(73.5)	(-7.0)	(106)
Household income (million kwacha per capita)	-0.100***	-0.051***	0.130***	0.053***
	(-6.7)	(-5.4)	(9.3)	(5.9)
Livestock ownership (million kwacha per capita)	-0.088***	-0.126***	0.059***	0.152***
	(-3.8)	(-8.6)	(2.9)	(12.0)
Household labor availability				
Adults per capita	-0.035**	-0.033***	0.054**	0.045***
	(-2.1)	(-3.2)	(2.3)	(2.9)
AIDS "prevalence" per capita	0.050*	0.017	-0.116***	-0.101***
	(1.8)	(1.0)	(-2.5)	(-3.3)
Constant	0.160	-0.003	0.098***	-0.224***
	(16.2)	(-0.4)	(6.3)	(21.8)
Sample size				
Total sample	6,732	6,732	6,732	6,732
Zero observations on dependent variable	4,253	4,253	1,559	1,559
Pseudo R-squared	0.63	1.17	0.29	0.66

SOURCE: Tobit estimates based on Zambia's Post Harvest Survey 1999/2000.

NOTES: t-ratios are listed in parentheses under regression coefficients; *, **, and *** indicate significance at the 90 percent, 95 percent, and 99 percent confidence levels, respectively. AIDS "prevalence" is estimated as the number of adults chronically ill for the previous 3 months.

the previous 3 months) is associated with statistically significant increases in the area devoted to cassava and decreases in the area devoted to maize. Thus, households with weaker laborers gravitate toward cassava. These results suggest that HIV/AIDS may have indeed contributed to the observed growth of area planted to cassava in Zambia.

Results of the Cassava Surge in Zambia and Malawi

INCOME. Farmer income has increased as a result of the rapid growth of improved cassava varieties in Zambia and Malawi. With identical inputs of labor and land, farmers roughly double their output. Subsistence farmers can ensure their food security with fewer resources, while farmers who market their crop more than double their cash returns (see Table 2.8). Given low marketed shares of cassava in Zambia and in the northern lakeshore districts of Malawi, gains in these regions have accrued mainly in the form of improved household food security. But in central and southern Malawi, where farmers sell the majority of their cassava crop, cash returns have grown dramatically, making cassava a highly profitable cash crop.

EQUITY. In both Zambia and Malawi, small farms dominate cassava production. Though a handful of commercial farmers have begun to experiment with large-scale cassava production, cultivating 100 hectares or more, the vast majority of cassava producers are small, hand-hoe farmers. Cassava plots under half a hectare account for 79 percent of the area farmed in cassava in Malawi, while farmers planting under 1 hectare account for 96 percent of the cassava area (Table 2.10). In Zambia, where larger farm sizes alter these figures slightly, farms growing less than half a hectare in cassava account for 61 percent of the total area cropped in cassava, while allocations under 1 hectare account for 89 percent of all the cassava area.

In Malawi, gender influences cassava cropping patterns as well. Female-headed farm households, poorer on average than their male counterparts, farm about 25 percent less land per household but devote a greater share to cassava. While female-headed households allocate 14.4 percent of their land area to cassava, male-headed households devote 9.7 percent to cassava (Table 2.11).

SUSTAINABILITY. Because farmers apply virtually no purchased inputs to their cassava plots, they can continue to grow cassava without depending on credit or input markets. They need not rely on seed suppliers, fertilizer distributors, or rural credit programs to continue growing high-yielding cassava.

Environmentally, unlike fertilizer-intensive maize production, low-input cassava production does not contribute to soil acidification. Nor does it generate the pesticide residues that sometimes occur in cash crop production. Although all crops withdraw nutrients from the soil as they grow, cassava seems to be more efficient than most other food crops in converting carbon dioxide from the air into edible biomass. Despite the crop's relative efficiency and lack of polluting inputs, cassava farmers, like others, must find crop rotations, fal-

TABLE 2.10 Size distribution of cassava area in Malawi and Zambia (percent)

Region	Cassava area cultivated (ha per household)					
	0.0	< 0.5	0.5–0.99	1.00–1.99	2.00–4.99	Total
Malawi						
Northern	30.6	45.5	18.0	4.8	1.2	100
Central	85.6	10.9	2.4	1.1	0.0	100
Southern	59.5	34.1	5.6	0.6	0.2	100
All Malawi	66.5	26.2	5.7	1.3	0.2	100
All Malawi, growers only	0.0	78.5	17.1	3.8	0.6	100
Zambia						
Northern (AER 3)	22.6	44.8	23.5	7.5	1.4	100
Western (AER 2b)	67.2	22.8	7.4	1.8	0.8	100
Central (AER 2a)	89.2	8.4	1.7	0.8	0.0	100
Southern (AER 1)	99.6	0.4	0.0	0.0	0.0	100
All Zambia	64.9	21.4	9.9	3.2	0.6	100
All Zambia, growers only	0.0	61.0	28.2	9.1	1.7	100

SOURCES: Malawi, International Food Policy Research Institute / Malawian Agricultural Policy Research Unit Smallholder Farm Survey, 1998; Zambia, Post Harvest Survey, 1999/2000.

NOTES: See Table 2.9 for definitions of AERs. AER, agroecological region.

TABLE 2.11 Gender distribution of cassava production in Malawi, 1998

	Gender of household head		
	Male	Female	Both
Total cropped area (ha/household)	1.59	1.15	1.43
Expenditure quintiles (percent)			
Lowest	17.3	27.8	20.0
2nd	18.8	21.8	20.0
3rd	21.6	13.7	20.0
4th	21.1	20.5	20.0
Highest	21.1	16.2	20.0
Cassava			
Households growing cassava (percent)	31.8	36.6	33.4
Average cassava area (ha per capita)	0.09	0.11	0.09
As a share of total cropped area (percent)	9.7	14.4	11.4

SOURCE: International Food Policy Research Institute / Malawian Agricultural Policy Research Unit Smallholder Farm Survey, 1998.

lows, or some combination of soil restoration strategies that will enable them to maintain long-term soil fertility (see Chapter 7).

Policy Implications

The Impact of the Cassava Surge across Africa

Across the entire breadth of Africa's cassava belt, a substantial majority of Africa's many millions of cassava farmers have benefited from the large-scale investment of public resources in cassava breeding and pest control programs. The rapid outbreak and spread of the CM across Africa in the late 1970s motivated a largely successful continental effort at biological pest control (Norgaard 1988; Herren and Neuenschwander 1991). The case studies in this chapter illustrate the importance of these efforts in four different countries. A classic public good, these pest control efforts have clearly benefited Africa's 200 million cassava consumers.

Similarly, the breeding breakthroughs by the IITA's cassava team and their successive waves of TMS varietal releases to national breeding programs have launched a generation of highly productive new cassava varieties across the continent (Jennings 1976; Thresh et al. 1997; Legg et al. 1999; Nweke, Spencer and Lynam 2002). Continentwide estimates suggest that African cassava farmers now plant more than 20 percent of cassava area in improved varieties, with average yield gains of roughly 50 percent over local varieties (Manyong et al. 2000). In the country case studies reviewed in this chapter, improved cassava varieties and processing technologies have resulted in 60–80 percent increases in returns to labor for adopting households.

On equity grounds, microeconomic evidence overwhelmingly suggests that these productivity gains have accrued to small farmers, who dominate cassava production across Africa. Urban cassava consumers have likewise benefited, as growing urban cassava sales in Ghana, Malawi, and Nigeria attest. The productivity-led price fall in cassava-based food products in Ghana and Nigeria suggests that urban consumers have gained from the new cassava varieties and processing technologies. Thus, Africa's broad-based cassava surge has contributed to higher real incomes and improved food security for Africa's rural and urban poor alike.

In terms of the DE-A-R framework's performance criteria—aggregate income, equity, and sustainability—Africa's cassava transformation has proven an unambiguous success. No wonder Nweke and colleagues refer to it as "Africa's best-kept secret" (Nweke, Spencer, and Lynam 2002, i).

The Public Sector's Role

Public actors have played two major roles in making these cassava developments possible. First, they invested heavily in cassava breeding and pest control programs. Given strong externalities and nonexcludability, both are public goods. Unlike hybrid maize, from which seed companies can earn money by selling seed year after year to the same farmer, a vegetatively propagated crop like cassava does not generate a similar annual revenue stream for seed suppliers. Farmers simply root cuttings from existing plants to expand their production in ensuing years. Following an initial distribution of improved cuttings, farmers need never return to the supplier for more planting material. Because cassava cuttings reproduce exact genetic clones of the parent plant, seed companies cannot recover their investment costs through annual sales of planting material. Hence, vegetatively propagated crops such as cassava rarely attract research and development investments from the private sector.[17]

Second, policy has played a critical role in driving change in all of the four case study countries. Throughout most of the past 50 years, African government policies have penalized cassava by subsidizing other food staples. The removal of these subsidies—for maize in Southern Africa and for rice and wheat in Nigeria—radically altered farmer incentives. When paired with the improved productive potential of TMS varieties, these new incentives triggered rapid booms in cassava production across the continent. Where both key components of the farmers' decisionmaking environment improve together—increasing productive capacity along with market incentives—production has surged. The Nigerian case suggests that one without the other (TMS varieties without the policy incentives, from 1977 to 1984) proved far less successful. As all four country case studies suggest, cassava has fared well in neutral policy environments but less well when governments have heavily subsidized production of maize or other food staples.[18]

In the past, domestic agricultural policies dominated incentives for Africa's cassava farmers and processors. But in the future, international incentives may play a significant role. Rising oil prices and interest in biofuels, evidenced by the introduction of ethanol subsidies in the United States and elsewhere, promise rising maize prices worldwide. In turn, rising maize prices will stimulate demand for cassava, both as a food crop and as a carbohydrate substitute in feeds, starches, and industrial applications.

Private Sector Contributions

Early adaptation and diffusion of the mechanical grater by West African artisans played a crucial role in alleviating labor bottlenecks and in launching the

---

17. Private sector tissue culture labs have emerged in Africa to multiply and distribute vegetatively propagated crops such as bananas. But they have not financed the breeding research necessary to produce new varieties.

18. In Nigeria, recent policy has promoted cassava through restrictions on competing cornstarch and ethanol imports as well as a mandated inclusion of 10 percent cassava flour in bread products (Nigeriafirst 2005).

widespread commercialization of *gari* and prepared cassava-based foods. Although the public sector played an important supporting role by introducing early prototype technologies, most of the public models proved overbuilt. The key to commercially viable adaptation lay in the simplification and cost cutting imposed by private sector artisans.

In the future, processing technologies, packaging, and the development of industrial applications will be crucial to the sustained commercial expansion of cassava production and marketing. In each of the four countries reviewed, on-farm production surges led the initial rounds of cassava-led growth. Processing and marketing development have proven essential to sustaining production incentives and to subsequent growth in each case. Throughout Africa, the private sector has historically dominated cassava marketing and processing. Given that future growth in cassava production will increasingly rely on the development of new commercial and industrial markets, private traders will continue to play a vital role in linking farmers with growing markets in food, feed, and industrial uses. While past growth in cassava production has focused on markets for human foods, future gains will likely require further expansion into convenience foods, livestock feeds, sweeteners, and industrial starches. In these efforts private sector innovation in processing and marketing will play a crucial role in sustaining further rounds of cassava-led growth.

Appendix 2A

TABLE 2A.1 Trends in cassava production (5-year trailing averages)

	1965	1970	1975	1980	1985	1990	1995	2000	2005
Ghana									
Production (million tons)	1.2	1.5	1.7	1.8	2.1	3.0	6.0	7.4	9.7
Production per capita (kg)	159	183	176	174	169	208	361	396	461
Yield (tons/ha)	7.9	8.0	7.2	7.9	8.7	7.5	11.1	12.0	12.4
Area (thousand ha)	150	190	233	233	238	398	538	622	779
Nigeria									
Production (million tons)	7.8	9.0	9.7	11.5	11.3	15.6	29.5	32.2	36.6
Production per capita (kg)	181	185	173	178	153	185	309	296	297
Yield (tons/ha)	9.4	10.0	9.9	10.2	9.6	11.2	10.5	10.5	10.4
Area (thousand ha)	829	907	976	1,126	1,177	1,401	2,804	3,078	3,518
Malawi									
Production, adjusted[a] (thousand tons)	140	118	200	280	241	164	218	817	1,847
Production, unadjusted (thousand tons)	140	118	200	280	241	164	218	1,146	2,245
Production per capita, adjusted[a] (kg)	38	28	40	48	34	19	21	73	148
Yield (tons/ha)	7.0	6.6	6.1	6.2	3.8	2.5	2.8	7.3	16.3
Area (thousand ha)	20	18	32	45	66	67	76	148	137
Zambia									
Production (million tons)	145	185	199	278	343	497	719	810	943
Production per capita (kg)	41	46	43	52	54	66	84	83	88
Yield (tons/ha)	6.3	6.2	6.2	6.2	6.2	6.2	6.2	5.8	5.6
Area (thousand ha)	23	30	32	45	55	80	116	140	168

SOURCE: FAOSTAT (2008).

[a]Data for Malawi's high-side outliers in 2000 and 2001 have been adjusted downward by interpolating between 1999 and 2002.

3 "Seeds of Success" in Retrospect: Hybrid Maize in Eastern and Southern Africa

MELINDA SMALE AND THOMAS S. JAYNE

> Inability to pay for seed and inability to sell product in a stable (and honest) market is the chief impediment to adoption of improved (and properly adapted) varieties, either private or public, in many developing countries. . . . In Africa I fear that what was happening yesterday may not be a good predictor of what is happening today.
>
> D. H. Duvick, late Pioneer Company maize breeder

Scope of the Case Study

Maize, like cassava, arrived comparatively recently in Africa. During the 1500s, traders introduced both of these New World crops into Africa, where they supplemented indigenous staples such as sorghum, millet, and yams. Traveling inland at varying speeds in different locations, maize became widely cultivated as a secondary food crop by the end of the 19th century (Miracle 1966). Since the second half of the 20th century, with the advent of modern breeding breakthroughs and a heavy policy emphasis on maize, production has grown rapidly. In the process, maize has become Africa's number-one food staple.

Agricultural stakeholders frequently cite maize research and development in Africa as one of the continent's major agricultural successes (see Chapter 1, Table 1.3). Certainly maize productivity and output have grown rapidly in some locations and over specific time periods. Yet performance has varied both spatially and temporally, as have the sometimes heavy costs associated with maize input supply and marketing. As a result, specialists who have examined the performance of maize seed research and development in Sub-Saharan Africa have described the outcomes variously as a "maize revolution" (Byerlee and Eicher 1997), a "qualified success story" (Eicher 1995), a "stop-and-go revolution"

The authors acknowledge significant contributions from staff of the national Ministries of Agriculture in the case study countries, as well as from Centro Internacional de Mejoramiento de Maíz y Trigo, the International Food Policy Research Institute, the Rockefeller Foundation, Egerton University / Tegemeo Institute, and Michigan State University's activities in East and Southern Africa, including the Food Security Cooperative Agreement.

(Howard and Mungoma 1996), a "delayed green revolution" (Smale 1995), an "obscured revolution" (Gilbert et al. 1993), a "failure" (Kydd 1989), and a "cause of peasant impoverishment" (Page and Chonyera 1994). Each label refers to a specific time, location, and dimension of performance.

Modern research and maize seed technical change have clearly contributed to the growth of maize production in Africa. Widespread evidence suggests that African commercial and smallholder farmers have readily adopted well-adapted modern maize germplasm (Byerlee and Eicher 1997). By the late 1990s, the most recent period for which comprehensive continental data are available, African farmers were planting 47 percent of all maize area in Sub-Saharan Africa with hybrids or improved open-pollinated varieties of maize (Morris 2001). For Eastern and Southern Africa, more recent data suggest that in 2006 farmers planted 44 percent of maize area with modern seeds (Langyintuo et al. 2008) and as much as 70 percent among smallholder farmers in Kenya (Ariga et al. 2008).[1]

This chapter reviews the origins and impact of maize research and development in East and Southern Africa. Discussion centers on the four heavily maize-consuming countries of Kenya, Malawi, Zambia, and Zimbabwe, where maize occupies 75 percent of the area cropped in cereals, annual per capita maize consumption exceeds 85 kilograms, and the available documentation permits a broadly comparable review (Table 3.1).[2] The following narrative traces key actors, innovations, and policies that have promoted maize production in these countries over time. The discussion aims to synthesize a vast published literature on maize seed technical change, institutional development, and policy change in the region, although it is selective in its geographic focus on the areas where technology adoption proceeded most rapidly. Viewing these changes from a perspective that spans much of the 20th century, this chapter seeks to identify the factors that have contributed to episodes of rapid production growth as well as those that may have provoked periods of uncertainty and decline.

Our discussion focuses on maize developments in the 20th century, particularly the second half, when the establishment of formal plant breeding institutions on the continent resulted in the systematic release of improved open-pollinated varieties (IOPVs) of maize and maize hybrids. For purposes of analysis and exposition, we have defined three key historical phases (Table 3.2). During the first phase, the period between 1900 and 1965, maize became the dominant food crop in the four case study countries. In a second period, running from the time of these countries' independence through the late 1980s,

---

1. In this chapter *modern maize seeds* refers to cultivars generated through adaptive on-station research, including either improved open-pollinated varieties or hybrids.

2. Prior to the transition to majority rule in 1966 and 1980, respectively, Zambia and Zimbabwe were known as Northern and Southern Rhodesia, respectively. Malawi was known as Nyasaland. For simplicity, this chapter refers to these areas by their current names.

TABLE 3.1 Selected production and consumption statistics for the maize case study countries, 2000–2005

Country	Production (thousands of tons)	Maize area as a percentage of total cereal area	Average per capita consumption of maize as food (kg/yr)	Average percentage of maize used in human consumption
Kenya	2,597	79	86	96
Malawi	1,770	95	121	79
Zambia	868	82	86	94
Zimbabwe	1,076	80	89	72

SOURCE: FAOSTAT (2008).

smallholder maize production expanded significantly in each of the study countries, though the rates varied, as did the precise timing, given differing political and institutional histories. The third phase, from 1990 to 2005, we have labeled the "uncertain period."[3] This period witnessed a combination of unfavorable weather conditions, declining public investments in agricultural research, subsidy reductions, and erratic policies, which appear to have precipitated a decline in national maize yields and production in some case study countries.

The Challenge of Maize

Several properties of maize influence the nature of seed genetic change and therefore the likelihood of improving the welfare of African smallholder farmers through yield increases. Before reviewing the record of maize technology development in these case study countries, the following short summary highlights key technical challenges affecting maize production, research, and promotion.[4]

---

3. This review ends in 2005. From this point onward, country policies increasingly diverged, and the policy and performance differences became as important as the parallels. While Kenya's maize marketing and trade policy has become more stable and conducive to growth, at least up to 2007, the policy environment in other countries covered by our analysis, such as Malawi and Zambia, have become more unpredictable and erratic. Zambia's reconstituted Food Reserve Agency has resumed large-scale maize marketing since 2005. In both Malawi and Zambia, a return to periodic government control over imports and exports has impeded the role of regional trade in reducing price instability. Malawi and Zambia have witnessed a resurgence of fertilizer subsidies, while Kenya has pursued a more market-oriented input promotion strategy. The impact and cost-effectiveness of these policies remain hotly debated and the subjects of ongoing empirical work. A definitive assessment of the post-2005 period will therefore require ongoing detailed empirical analysis and individual country narratives. For that reason, we have elected to truncate this collective review, ending it in 2005.

4. The following summary draws heavily on Morris (1998, 2001) and Pandey (1998).

TABLE 3.2 Dynamics and drivers of change in maize production in Eastern and Southern Africa

	Phase 1: Dominance of maize as a food crop	Phase 2: Expansion of smallholder maize	Phase 3: Period of uncertainty
Timing	1900–1965	1965–89	1990–2005
Key actors	1920s—commercial farmers lobby for public research and policy protection Colonial legislatures fund maize research, institute marketing controls Maize breeders develop hybrids Large millers emerge to control urban markets Private seed companies emerge	National research programs continue to develop a stream of hybrid lines Extension staff focus on small farmers Seed companies expand State marketing corporations established: the National Cereal and Produce Board, Agricultural Development and Marketing Corporation, National Agricultural Marketing Board, Grain Marketing Board	Private seed companies Private input suppliers Government policymakers State marketing corporations
Motors of change	Maize breeding breakthroughs: 1960—SR52 released in Zimbabwe 1964—H611 released in Kenya	New germplasm: R2000 series in Zimbabwe, semiflint hybrids in Malawi, an array of hybrids and improved open-pollinated maize varieties in Zambia	Withdrawal of state subsidies and marketing support Falling funding for agricultural research Drought

Beneficiaries	Commercial farmers receive favorable prices, above export parity	Extension support Institutions to coordinate marketing, seed and fertilizer, credit Smallholders increase hybrid use: Malawi—to 14–37% Kenya—to 70% Zambia—to 77% Zimbabwe—96%	
Production growth per year		Kenya (1965–80): 3.3% Malawi (1983–93): 3.1% Zambia (1970–89): 1.9% Zimbabwe (1980–89): 1.8%	Kenya: 0.8% Malawi: 1.4% Zambia: –2.4% Zimbabwe: –7.0%
Impact	Commercial farm yields double from 1950 to 1960	Smallholder production surges (doubling in Zimbabwe between 1980 and 1989)	Area and production in maize fall by 10 to 30% Secular decline in soil fertility aggravated by diminished fertilizer use

Maize is predominantly a cross-pollinating species. When rates of cross-pollination are high in a crop, genetic material is exchanged when pollen flows among neighboring plants. Unless pollination is carefully controlled, all of the maize plants in a given field will differ from the preceding generation and from each other. When maize self-fertilizes, the progeny often have undesirable traits, but when it cross-fertilizes, some demonstrate significant yield advantages relative to their parents (termed "hybrid vigor"). Maize is the world's most widely grown cereal, cultivated across a range of latitudes, altitudes, moisture regimes, slopes, and soil types using the simplest to the most mechanized production technologies.

High rates of cross-pollination mean that the attribution of yield increases in farmers' fields in response to specific introductions of improved seed (either of IOPVs or of hybrids) is more difficult than it is for other major cereals such as rice or wheat. The yield advantages of F1 hybrid maize seeds can degenerate rapidly when farmers save seed and replant it, though evidence suggests that in some cases advanced-generation hybrids significantly outperform the variety that the farmer was growing previously, depending on the type of hybrid and the control that serves as the basis for comparison (Morris, Risopolous, and Beck 1999). Due to market imperfections and cash constraints, African smallholders often "recycle" F1 seed.

Hybrid vigor in maize means three very important things for African smallholder farmers. First, it means that to sustain the yield increases they seek, they are reliant on a seed industry in a way that neither the rice nor wheat farmers of Asia's green revolution ever have been. On the other hand, a hybrid-based maize sector also requires large-scale commercial seed enterprises whose profits can be sustained only by strong seasonal demand by farmers for renewing their seed (Tripp 2001). Furthermore, temperate maize germplasm is not easily adapted to the nontemperate environments of the developing world, so the gains achieved by private companies in the United States, Europe, and some parts of China are not easily transferred to many of the smallholder farmers who produce in the wide range of microclimates and technologies found in the developing world (Morris 2001).

Phase 1: Dominance of Maize as a Food Crop, 1900–1965

The earliest written records of maize cultivation in Africa report production in close proximity to trading posts along Africa's west and east coasts during the 1500s as a result of introduction by Portuguese and other European traders. Linguistic evidence suggests a possible second transmission route into Africa from the Americas via Europe, down the Nile Valley, and across the desert into Sub-Saharan Africa (Miracle 1966; McCann 2005). Traders' accounts indicate that maize regularly supplied rations at slave trading posts and on trans-Atlantic slave ships during the 18th century. Yet the penetration of maize cultivation into the African interior proceeded at variable rates across the continent. By 1600, maize cultivation had become well established as much as 600 miles inland in the Congo Basin, while in Uganda maize production began only in the latter half of the 1800s (Miracle 1966). Initially, most African farmers adopted maize as a niche vegetable crop tucked within complex farming systems (McCann 2005). After the shift to maize monocropping during the second half of the 20th century, maize significantly changed African farming systems.

In the four case study countries, sorghum and millet remained the dominant cereal crops until the 20th century. In Zambia, Miracle (1966, 156) indicated that "there are no large areas where maize was more than a minor food at the beginning of this century," although Howard (1994) suggested that maize was a staple in Zambia's Luapula province by the end of the 1700s. In Zimbabwe, white settlers began producing maize as early as the 1890s (Byerlee and Heisey 1997). Maize's transition to a major crop in Kenya occurred during World War I, when disease in millet led to famine and millet seed was consumed rather than planted. Williamson (1956) reports that maize did not dominate as a staple food crop in Malawi until well into this century.

Before 1965, the rise of maize production in all of the case study countries was propelled, to a greater or lesser extent, by five driving factors: (1) the agronomic suitability of maize, (2) the British starch market, (3) milling technology, (4) the integration of Africans into the settler wage economy, and (5) market and trade policies promoted by settler farmer lobbies.

The Agronomic Suitability of Maize

Millet and sorghum remained the primary staple cereals of East and Southern Africa until about the 20th century.[5] Even so, agriculturalists regarded maize as "eminently suitable" (Anthony 1988) for mixed farming by settlers because (1) it required less capital investment and technical skill than did cotton and tobacco (and could therefore be produced by newly arrived novices) and (2) it gave higher returns to land than did other indigenous cereals under reasonably favorable conditions, though not throughout the entire range of ecological conditions (Harrison 1970; Weinmann 1972). Long-term weather patterns and soils maps suggest that much of Malawi's growing environment has long been favorable for rainfed maize (Heisey and Smale 1995, 5), as are a number of environments in Kenya, Zambia, and Zimbabwe. Returns to labor are likely to have been higher for maize. Maize is protected from bird damage by its leafy covering, while the exposed grain of sorghum and millet requires labor time for scaring away birds. When off-farm wage employment became important for

---

5. In the case of West Africa, however, McCann (2005, 24) cites reports by French scholars indicating that maize had replaced millet and sorghum on the West African coast by the early 17th century.

Africans, these agronomic features of maize provided further advantages compared to sorghum and millet (Low 1986).

The British Starch Market

Until the 1920s, export volumes exceeded human consumption of the maize produced by settlers in Kenya and Zimbabwe. Ironically, the preferences of today's African consumers for white as opposed to yellow grain began with the influence of the British starch market during these years.

As early as 1911, increasing demand and price premiums were evident for white maize in the British starch market, apparently because North American producers of yellow maize had a decisive transportation cost advantage in supplying Britain (Masters 1994). Because the British starch market provided a premium for white maize, local legislation was passed in some parts of the region requiring that only white maize be accepted for export. Though both white and yellow maize varieties were grown, settler farmers were informed by the secretary of the London Corn Exchange that exports required better grading and uniformity (Weinmann 1972, 19–20). Farmers discovered that when yellow and white maize were grown in close proximity and cross-pollinated, the grain of the progeny was mixed in color, rendering it unsuitable for export. The Rhodesian Maize Authority passed a resolution in 1923 stating that the introduction of yellow maize varieties into the territory posed "a vital danger to the maize growing industry." In Zimbabwe, the Maize Act (1925–70), enabled growers to petition the government to restrict the growing of maize in their area to a specific variety and color (Jayne et al. 1995).

Emphasis was also given to the soft dent-type maize favored by the British starch market, for this was easier to process and less injurious to industrial roller mills (Kydd 1989). By 1920, both smallholder and commercial farmers in Zambia and Zimbabwe had largely replaced their white flint cultivars with improved white dents, though these may also have been higher-yielding varieties (Jayne et al. 1995).[6]

The Integration of Africans into the Settler Wage Economy

The grafting of mines, plantations, and cattle enterprises onto the local economy expanded the demand for food in the country. Eventually the domestic demand for maize grew as Africans left their farms to work on settler farms, in

---

6. Denty grains have a higher density of hard starch granules and a higher proportion of usable endosperm that can be converted into white flour compared to flinty grains. Flinty maize, in contrast, is more resistant to weevils in storage. Malawian women prepare maize flour in multiple steps consisting of hand pounding, lactic fermentation, drying, and, more recently, hammer milling in the final stage. When processed in this way, flinty maize has a higher flour-to-grain extraction rate. Both denty and flinty maize can be milled to produce a whole-grain flour, but this flour is not preferred in Malawi (Ellis 1954).

mines, or in industrial plants, particularly in Kenya, Zambia, and Zimbabwe (Jansen 1977; Mosley 1983). Food consumption preferences were influenced by the rations that employers used as in-kind payments. Diets adapted in a self-generative process as "people got used to what they consumed" (Shopo 1985).

By the 1920s, maize accounted for approximately 80 and 60 percent of the settler-cropped area in Zimbabwe and Zambia, respectively, and provided in-kind payments for the rapidly increasing African labor force. By contrast, Malawi had the smallest extent of land in the former British Central Africa but the largest concentration of peoples (Pachai 1973). An exporter of African labor to the mines of the Rand and the farms of Zambia and Zimbabwe (Tindall 1968), Malawi had few areas with elevations high enough to attract a European population easily decimated by malaria (in contrast to Zimbabwe) and had no rich mineral deposits (in contrast to Zambia). Consequently, Malawi never developed an organized settler constituency, a distinction that has led to a different trajectory in maize research and maize consumption preferences.

Settler Lobbies, Market Control, and Trade

The threat of competition from African farmers led colonial administrations to design and implement controlled marketing systems from the 1930s. Evidence from Kenya, Zambia, and Zimbabwe indicates that African farmers were capable of generating maize surpluses at prices below the production costs for most settler farms and that settler farmers successfully lobbied colonial legislatures for protection (Jayne et al. 1995). Initially, in both Kenya and Zimbabwe, settler consumer interest groups such as animal feeders, mine owners, and plantation farmers strongly opposed protection for settler maize farmers on the grounds that it would raise the cost of maize (Keyter 1975; Mosley 1975). Over time, however, settler maize producers' interests were increasingly well represented in the colonial legislatures.

Catalyzed by slumping world agricultural markets during the depression of the 1930s, the colonial governments passed the Maize Control Acts of the 1930s in Zambia and Zimbabwe and the Native Produce Ordinance in Kenya in 1935. These marketing acts (1) created state crop-buying stations in European farming areas without parallel investments in African farming areas, (2) enforced a two-tiered pricing scheme with higher prices for settler farmers than for native Africans, and (3) established restrictions on grain movement from African areas to towns, mines, and other demand centers. From 1935 on, the combination of maize legislation, land evictions, and fiscal policies weakened Africans' position in food marketing relative to that of settler farmers in Kenya, Zambia, and Zimbabwe (see Figure 3.1 for evidence in Zimbabwe; see also Mosley 1983; Jayne et al. 1995).

The rise of centralized state maize marketing boards also encouraged the development of large-scale concentrated grain milling industries using roller mill technology first employed on a large scale in Kenya, South Africa, and

FIGURE 3.1 Per capita grain production in Zimbabwean communal lands, 1914–94

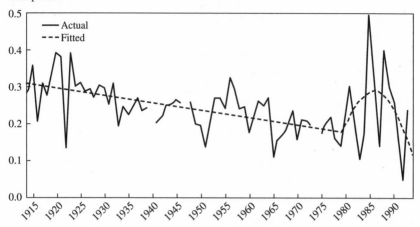

Tons/person

SOURCES: Computed from data in Annual Reports of the Chief Native Commissioner presented by Mosley (1983); Zimbabwe, Ministry of Agriculture (1995).

NOTES: This trend line was fitted by using the regression coefficients from the following spline function:

$$Y_t = b + b_1(TREND_t) + b_3D(TREND_t - I) + b_4D(TREND_t - I)^2 + v_t,$$

where Y_t is grain output per capita in Zimbabwe's communal lands in year t, $TREND$ is a time trend, I is a constant equaling the value of the time trend variable at independence in 1980, D is a dummy variable taking on a value of 0 before independence in 1980 and 1 otherwise. The term t is assumed to be independent and identically normally distributed with a mean of 0 and constant variance. The estimated average annual change in per capita grain output was b_1 from 1914 to 1979 and $b_1 + b_3$ + $2b_4(TREND - I)$ from 1980 to 1994. This specification allows for nonlinearity in the trend after independence. F-test results rejected the assumption of linearity at the 0.001 significance level. Model estimation produced the following results (t-statistics in parentheses; DW = Durbin-Watson statistic):

$$Y_t = 308.7 - 1.85(TREND_t) + 32.8(TREND_t - I) - 2.21(TREND_t - I)^2$$
$${(18.3)}{(-4.32)}{(3.99)}{(-3.77)}$$

$$R^2 = 0.23$$
$$F = 8.99$$
$$DW = 2.21$$

The results indicate that the average annual change in grain production per capita was −1.85 kg from 1914 to 1979 and −1.12 kg when evaluated at the midpoint of the postindependence period (1987).

Zimbabwe in the 1950s. Controls on private maize movement provided the licensed roller millers (which produced a refined and more expensive type of meal) with a de facto monopoly on maize meal sales to cities and grain-deficit rural areas once local supplies were exhausted (Jayne et al. 1995).

  This system of market regulation was effective in achieving its principal objectives. Settler maize production expanded, and producers earned prices that generally exceeded export parity. Kenya and Zimbabwe remained reliably self-sufficient in maize (except during World War II). Through discriminatory pricing made feasible by controls on marketing, the cost of supporting settler maize production was paid largely by African farmers and consumers rather than European taxpayers, making the system fiscally sustainable (Jayne and Jones 1997). Opposition to agricultural price supports was accommodated by selective consumer subsidies. The stability of the policy and pricing environment (and the limited competition faced by industrial mills) contributed to the rapid growth in commercial agriculture, the demand for maize research, and later the adoption by commercial farmers of hybrid maize varieties developed by national research systems.

The Introduction of Milling Technology

African maize production received a boost with the introduction of the hammer mill in the 1920s (Shopo 1985). Hammer mills gave a processing cost advantage to maize over small grains, because maize could be dumped into the hopper for grinding, while millet and sorghum required dehulling first.

The prevalence of large-scale industrial maize processors in Kenya, Zambia, and Zimbabwe contributed to preferences, particularly in urban areas, for dent types. The removal of the germ and pericarp makes refined meal look whiter, last longer, and taste sweeter than whole meal. Hammer-milled whole meal remains the primary staple food in the grain-self-sufficient rural areas of these countries. Though they also consume whole meal in rural areas, Malawi's population has long expressed a strong preference for maize porridge made from *ufa woyera* (white, almost iridescent, flour). The fact that Malawi's population remained predominantly—and densely—rural may explain the persistence of other processing methods.[7] In rural areas of Malawi, maize flour is processed with a combination of hammer-mill technology and several stages of pounding by hand, soaking, washing, and drying (Ellis 1962; Kydd 1989).

Early Maize Research

The investments by colonial government and settlers themselves in the maize research that radically transformed maize production in Kenya and Zimbabwe began as early as the 1930s, "soon after the news of the great success of hybrid breeding in the USA began to be widely known" (Harrison 1970, 28). In 1919, commercial farmers in Zimbabwe founded the Maize Breeders Association (Rusike 1998). Zimbabwe's maize breeding program, initiated by H. C. Arnold in 1932, was the first outside of the United States to produce double-cross hybrids for commercial use, releasing Southern Rhodesia-1 (SR1) in 1949. The

---

7. The appropriate technology depends in part on the opportunity cost of women's labor, because grain processing has been viewed as a woman's task in most of Southern Africa (Bagachwa 1992).

team then turned their attention to single-cross hybrids, which have a greater yield advantage and are more uniform in the F1 generation, though their seed is more costly to produce. In 1960 they released the first commercially grown single-cross hybrid in the world, SR52 (Rusike 1998, 306).[8] "The combination of SR52 seed, fertilizer and improved agronomic practices increased maize yields 46% over Southern Cross, the most common improved local variety" (Eicher 1995, 807). SR52 was diffused rapidly and widely among commercial farmers, becoming one of the most popular hybrids in the region and a parent of many others.

Before it achieved independence, Zambia relied on its federation partner Zimbabwe for improved maize germplasm, and the importation and use of SR52 (as well as other hybrids) is said to have doubled commercial farmer yields from 1949–53 levels of 1.3 tons per hectare to 2.7 tons per hectare in 1959–63 (Howard 1994). The preferences of Malawi's smallholder farmers and the superior on-farm processing rates of Malawi's flint maize types relative to dents were recognized by Malawi's first maize breeder, R. T. Ellis (1954, 1962), who developed several synthetics as well as flint hybrid LH11 before his resignation in 1959.

The first scientific maize research program in Kenya began in 1955 in Kitale, the center of maize production in the White Highlands. The first modern maize type released in Kenya, Kitale Synthetic II (an IOPV released in 1961), was based on inbred lines developed from the Kenya Flat White complex of farmers' selections. M. N. Harrison, chief Kenyan maize breeder, felt "the need to widen the genetic base of the Kitale program," and thought that although "nothing of value" had come from earlier testing of U.S. Corn Belt, European, South African, Rhodesian, and Australian materials, "the great diversity of center-of-origin material from similar ecological conditions to those of East Africa, close to the Equator with a wide range of altitude, had never been tried" (Harrison 1970, 38). In 1958 he returned from a trip to Colombia and Mexico funded by the Rockefeller Foundation with exotic breeding material (Anthony 1988). After screening 124 test top-crosses of these materials with Kitale Synthetic II, the outstanding result was a cross with an unimproved Ecuadorian landrace (Ecuador 573). Released in 1964, the varietal hybrid (Hybrid 611) made from Kitale Synthetic II and Ecuador 573 was the basis of all hybrids developed since by the national breeding program (Hassan et al. 1998). The yield advantage of this unique varietal hybrid over Kitale Synthetic II was 40 percent (Gerhart 1975, 5). Varietal hybrids have lower seed costs than conventional hybrids, with less loss of yield advantages when recycled. Released on the eve of Kenya's independence, H611 was diffused among large- and small-scale farm-

---

8. Breeding records indicate that Pioneer first released single crosses as named hybrids in 1961, though small U.S. companies most likely released them before 1960 (D. H. Duvick, pers. comm., March 13, 2002).

ers in the high-potential areas of western Kenya "at rates as fast or faster than among farmers in the U.S. Corn Belt during the 1930s–40s" (Gerhart 1975, 51).

Phase 2: Expansion of Smallholder Maize, 1965–89

By the time of the transition to majority rule in Eastern and Southern Africa, maize had become the cornerstone of a "social contract" that the postindependence governments made with the African majority to redress the neglect of smallholder agriculture during the former colonial period (Jayne et al. 1999). The controlled marketing systems inherited by the new governments at independence were viewed as the ideal vehicle to implement these objectives.

The benefits of controls for settler farmers during the colonial period generated the belief that the same system could also promote the welfare of millions of smallholders if it were simply expanded (Jenkins 1997). The social contract meant that governments were responsible for ensuring food self-sufficiency in white maize at a cheap price. Because the world market for white maize was thin during this period, domestic production shortfalls often necessitated imports of yellow maize, an inferior substitute that connotes agricultural policy failure (Jayne and Rukuni 1993).

Each of the case study countries achieved impressive episodes of growth in maize production driven by interacting innovations in technology, policies, and institutions. We mark these growth episodes as 1965–80 in Kenya, 1970–89 in Zambia, 1980–89 in Zimbabwe, and 1983–93 in Malawi. Some of the ingredients of these episodic growth periods retain continued importance, while others could not be sustained and may have contributed to the uncertainty of the 1990s.

Good germplasm achieved through innovative breeding was the essential ingredient during each period of sustained production growth. Though each period had other, unique ingredients, all shared: (1) complementary investments in agronomic research, extension, seed distribution systems, and rural infrastructure and (2) institutions to coordinate grain marketing with seed, fertilizer, and credit delivery. This second ingredient, however, was implemented through controlled pricing and marketing systems that incurred large subsidies and treasury costs and eventually contributed to fiscal crises. The points reported in the following paragraphs synthesize findings from a set of detailed theses and studies analyzing the causes of seed technical change in smallholder maize production during the relevant time periods in Kenya (Gerhart 1975; Karanja 1990; Hassan 1998), Zimbabwe (Rohrbach 1988; Rusike 1995; Eicher and Kupfuma 1997), Zambia (Howard 1994; Howard and Mungoma 1996), and Malawi (Smale 1992; Heisey and Smale 1995).

Maize Germplasm

There is little doubt about the quality of the germplasm products released by Kenya's maize research program in the early years. Research breakthroughs were accomplished first and foremost because of the capacity and continuity of the Kenya maize program staff, which, according to Gerhart (1975), was unmatched in any national research program in Africa. From its inception in 1955 to 1973, the maize breeding program had only two directors, M. N. Harrison and F. Ogada. During those initial years, the Rockefeller Foundation and the United States Agency for International Development (USAID) facilitated the exchange of germplasm between continents as well as the sharing of new research experience concerning hybrid genetics (Harrison 1970; Gerhart 1975; Anthony 1988). The four Kenyan maize programs (Embu, Katumani, Kitale, and Mwtapa) have since released a succession of hybrids and IOPVs, and one of the greatest achievements has been the release of a range of materials to suit the nation's diverse agroclimatic conditions (Karanja 1990; Hassan 1998).

Similarly, in Zimbabwe "small teams of highly motivated and well-paid local scientists" devoted their entire careers to maize research (Eicher and Kupfuma 1997, 35–37), backed by the revenues earned and contributed by commercial farmers. The second major episode of maize seed technical change in Zimbabwe occurred following the country's independence in 1980 among smallholder farmers of the previously "communal" areas, largely based on R200, R201, and R215. Suitable for production on sandy soils in low-rainfall areas, these short-season maize hybrids were bred by Nelson for settler farmers seeking to diversify from tobacco exports when the Unilateral Declaration of Independence was declared in 1965. Though three-way crosses are in general relatively uniform and intended for annual purchase and higher levels of management, they may still perform well relative to unimproved types when grown with fairly low levels of management. Like SR52, the R200 series was later popular among smallholders in neighboring countries. Not until the change to majority rule in 1980, however, did smallholders acquire widespread access to the germplasm and complementary inputs. Earlier, smallholder use of modern maize would have occurred spontaneously as a result of native Africans' interaction with commercial settler farmers but not as part of a systematic nationwide effort. Estimates in the literature suggest that between 20 and 40 percent of Zimbabwe's smallholders in communal areas grew maize hybrids during the 1970s (Rohrbach 1988; Kupfuma 1994).

The germplasm produced by the Zambian maize program from the mid-1970s through the early 1990s included an impressive array of 10 double and three-way crosses bred by Ristanovic and 2 flint-type, early-maturing, IOPVs bred by Gibson (Howard 1994; Howard and Mungoma 1996). In all but the most difficult growing environments, the hybrids outyielded local (and improved) open-pollinated varieties even without fertilizer. Unlike the single-cross SR52, they were double- and three-way crosses, so the yield advantages they lost with recycling were not so great. Meanwhile, the ears of very early-maturing, drought-tolerant, flinty IOPVs were consumed green as a source of food during the hungry period preceding harvest (Howard 1994). As in Kenya and Malawi and to a far lesser extent as in Zimbabwe, the advances depended on access to both international breeding expertise and germplasm collections.

Malawian smallholders waited much longer for suitable hybrids. One reason was discontinuity in staffing and funding accompanied by shifts in emphasis between hybrids and IOPVs (Kydd 1989). Another constraint was scientific; local flint materials were too tall, regional breeding had focused on dents, and exotic flint germplasm with suitable characteristics was not easy to identify. Malawi did not have the dense urban populations to feed that preoccupied Zambian leaders, and neither the settler farmers nor Malawian smallholders had a political voice (Smale 1995). In 1990, B. T. Zambezi, E. M. Sibale, and W. G. Nhlane released the national program's first adapted semiflint hybrids, MH17 and MH18. These were top-crosses of Malawian lines and flint populations from Centro Internacional de Mejoramiento de Maíz y Trigo (CIMMYT). Three aspects of the semiflint top-crosses made them a success. First, semiflint, top-cross hybrids were well suited to production by smallholders, who process and consume their grain on farm and recycle their hybrid seeds (Zambezi et al. 1997; Benson 1999). Farmer evaluations (Smale et al. 1993) and experimental results demonstrated that these semiflint hybrids could be processed on the farm just as were local flint types (Box 3.1). Second, trial and demonstration results showed that there were only minor differences in yield among the various Malawi hybrids, so yield was not sacrificed for grain texture. Third, analysis of trial results and extensive demonstration data for three of the major maize-producing zones (representing 70 percent of Malawi's maize area) during the 1989/90–1991/92 seasons showed that unfertilized hybrid maize yields were higher than those of unfertilized local maize, even during the worst drought year in decades (Heisey and Smale 1995).

Complementary Investments

In Kenya, Harrison (1970) and Gerhart (1975) both attributed successful diffusion of improved maize seed not only to good maize germplasm but to sound agronomic research, effective linkages of research to extension, a strong commercial seed enterprise, and the coordination of input and maize marketing. The Kenya Seed Company was formed by large-scale farmers in 1956 but entered into an agreement with the Kenyan government to produce and distribute maize seed in 1963 (Karanja 1990), employing stockists who were "small-scale African storekeepers selected for their location, reputation, and interest." The approach, modeled on the marketing of Wilkinson razor blades, was "every stockist an extension agent" (Gerhart 1975, 9). Credit was used only at the discretion of individual stockists. Like Harrison, Gerhart (1975) emphasized that the Kenya Maize Research Program had never been isolated from the other components of a national maize program. These included, as early as the 1960–70s, a relatively dense transport network, crop research, marketing boards

BOX 3.1 Farmers' perceptions

At the outset of the 1991/92 season, the Malawi Ministry of Agriculture, Centro Internacional de Mejoramiento de Maíz y Trigo (CIMMYT), and the National Seed Company of Malawi (NSCM) undertook a farmer evaluation survey in which 150 farmers in clusters of villages located in Central Mzimba, Kasungu, and Blantyre districts compared the yield, maturity, processing, and storage quality of newly released semiflint hybrids MH17 and MH18 to those of their own local maize and the previously released dent hybrids MH12 and NSCM41. Each participating farmer was provided with a 5-kilogram sample of two hybrids and asked to grow them with their usual practices. Enumerators laid yield subplots to measure their yields and interviewed them later in the season regarding their perceptions.

In the drought year that followed, farmers harvested the highest yields with MH18 even when they applied no fertilizer to either the hybrid or their own local maize variety. Their statements conveyed their surprise about the new hybrids. MH18 was often called "the local seed you gave us" compared to the "real" dent hybrids, NSCM41 and MH12. One farmer said, "You have given us back the local maize we used to grow." Because flint type and pounding efficiency were long associated with local maize, farmers called seed that satisfied those conditions "local." Others insisted that the semiflint hybrids were local maize and that they would keep the seed (Smale et al. 1993).

Several of the participating farmers later traveled to Lilongwe to discuss their experiences on the radio with Ministry of Agriculture field staff, with Dr. B. T. Zambezi of the Department of Agriculture Research, who bred the hybrids, and with representatives from NSCM, who sold them. Alesi Matope, from Chiradzulu in Blantyre district, reported:

I have been farming for a long time and I used to plant local maize and NSCM41. In 1989, the field technicians brought MH17 and MH18, which I planted. Although there was little rainfall, I had good yields compared to local maize and the hybrid matured earlier. When I harvested this maize, the advisor came and told me that I should store a little of each because a visitor would come from Lilongwe to see me, and to see the yield, storage and poundability of these hybrids, and to see which seed produced more bran. I did not apply any chemical to prevent weevils. NSCM41 was the first to be attacked by weevils. When pounded, MH17, MH18 and local maize produced little bran. The *nsima* made from this type of hybrid is very tasty and its colour is pure white. The roasted green maize is even better, and of course when shelling from the cob, it shells very easily and one does not have to struggle with the task.

Jaleki Kapinga from Kasungu reported: "When setting off on my visit to Lilongwe I was told to tell the truth about the MH17 and MH18 hybrid seed by all other farmers in my area. 'They should breed plenty of seed.' That is what my fellow farmers told me to tell you. . . . We do not want to find problems in buying MH17 and MH18 hybrid seed in our markets." Lyson Mbewe from Central Mzimba said that his wife insisted on keeping the seed from the harvest, even though he told her it was only an introduction. A photo of Mayi Jumbe, another farmer from Thyolo in Blantyre district, seated on the top of her maize harvest after the drought year was later displayed on one of the annual reports of the Maize Commodity Team.

offering guaranteed prices, and an extension service. In 1965 the extension services reputedly planted 5,000 demonstrations, followed by hundreds of fertilizer demonstrations. Gerhart's survey revealed that extension agents were the first source of information about hybrid seed, followed by other farmers.

The second major phase in Zimbabwe's maize revolution (Eicher 1995) occurred from 1980 to 1988 following the end of the civil war in 1980. Much of the institutional foundation that fueled the smallholder growth episode in the 1980s was inherited from the colonial period. Private sector maize seed production began in 1940 when settler farmers established the Seed Maize Association of Southern Rhodesia, which successfully met the needs of its clients (Rusike 1995). In 1979, the Seed Maize Association was converted to the Seed Maize Cooperative, administered by the powerful Commercial Farmers Union and organized as a cooperative in order to transfer monitoring and inspection costs from the government to members as well as to avoid taxes and profit distributions (Rusike 1995). Seed Co-op was created in 1983 and continued to enjoy autonomy from the government at the same time that it benefited from tax breaks, exclusive rights to some seed types, and access to subsidized credit (Rusike 1998). When the civil war ended in Zimbabwe, the new government attempted to expand the input delivery, credit, and marketing programs that had previously served only large-scale producers (Rohrbach 1988; Blackie 1990). Rohrbach (1988) attributes the tripling in smallholder maize production that occurred from 1980 to 1988 to five factors: (1) the ending of the war for independence in 1979; (2) an increase in the use of hybrid maize seeds from about 40 percent in 1979 to 98 percent by 1985; (3) an increase in state crop-buying stations serving smallholder areas from 5 in 1980 to 148 in 1985, thus reducing the costs and risks associated with producing maize for the market; (4) an eightfold rise in in-kind credit allocated to smallholders between 1979 and 1986, which stimulated fertilizer use and maize yields; and (5) an associated response by private input suppliers to the increased demand for farm inputs.

In addition to improved maize germplasm, Zambia's land surplus, favorable weather, and the heavily subsidized state-led system of credit, input, and maize marketing support to smallholders combined to drive growth in smallholder maize production (Howard 1994; Howard and Mungoma 1996). The

Swedish International Development Cooperation Agency (SIDA), which funded maize research from the 1980s on, also funded the establishment of a seed industry, including Zamseed and the Seed Control and Certification Institute. Zamseed produced all seeds as a commercial company, though the government and SIDA owned large shares (Cromwell 1996).

In Malawi, several structural factors other than germplasm contributed to sharply rising smallholder maize adoption rates from the mid-1980s until 1993, as indicated by the fact that use of hybrids with dent grain texture rose in the years preceding the release of the semiflint top-crosses. Primary among them was a supply of quality commercial seed, which had been a binding constraint in the early years of Malawi's maize-breeding program. The National Seed Company of Malawi (NSCM) took responsibility from the Agricultural Development and Marketing Corporation (ADMARC) in 1978, and Cargill acquired most of the equity of NSCM in 1988, taking a more aggressive approach to seed production, procurement, and marketing. Price ratios were also favorable for the use of hybrid seed and fertilizer during the late 1980s in Malawi (Smale and Heisey 1994, 699). Seed prices also dipped in that period, likely in response to large inventories held by NSCM after years of low use of hybrid seed.

Coordinated Input and Grain Markets

All four case study countries adopted similar mechanisms to address their postindependence objectives (summarized earlier). These mechanisms enhanced the profitability of growing maize for smallholders, stabilized net returns in a variable rainfed growing environment, and encouraged maize consumption by urban and rural consumers.

First, the expansion of state marketing infrastructure in smallholder areas facilitated the disbursement of credit and subsidized inputs to smallholders by state agencies designed to recoup loans through farmer sales to the marketing boards (Jabara 1984; Rohrbach 1988; Kaluwa 1992; Smale 1992; Howard 1994). Second, both direct and indirect input and credit subsidies supported maize production. For example, fertilizer subsidies in Zambia averaged 60 percent of landed cost by 1982, with 90 percent of fertilizer used on maize (Williams and Allgood 1990). In addition to the direct subsidy, an expanded network of cooperative marketing depots reduced the transaction costs of selling maize in remote areas. In Malawi, ADMARC assumed an all-encompassing responsibility for delivering inputs for the production of the staple food, marketing maize output, stabilizing maize prices through maintaining storage facilities, and transporting maize into food-deficit areas during the hungry season. Third, panterritorial pricing brought smallholders in remote areas into production for state markets and ensured a national crop but distorted regional advantages. Finally, in some cases and periods, as in Zimbabwe from 1980 through 1998, maize producer prices were guaranteed by the state at well above export parity prices.[9] At the same time, most governments subsidized the retail price of industrial maize meal to consumers, thereby raising the demand for domestic production under a policy of maize self-sufficiency.

However, in all four countries, marketing board costs escalated as the scale and complexity of their activities increased. Losses were of two types: those that government forced on the board by mandating it to carry out activities that were unprofitable but fulfilled "social" functions, such as buying maize at above-market prices in remote areas (which encouraged maize production expansion), and those related to operational inefficiency (which probably had little effect on smallholder maize production). Panterritorial pricing was particularly burdensome in Zambia and Zimbabwe because it raised the share of grain delivered to the boards by smallholders in remote (but often agronomically high-potential) areas where transport costs were high (GMB 1991; Bryceson 1993). Stockpiling white maize, a consequence of government preoccupation with maize self-sufficiency, was also costly (Buccola and Sukume 1988; Pinckney 1993). Operational inefficiency varied across countries, though it appears to have been greatest in Kenya and Zambia (Bates 1989; Amani and Maro 1992; Scott 1995). Allegations of corruption were widespread, even in Zimbabwe's relatively efficient Grain Marketing Board (GMB) (CSM 1986). In some cases, the treasury costs of state marketing operations were so high that they affected rates of inflation, interest, and currency exchange, especially in Zambia during the 1980s (Jansen and Muir 1994).[10]

Other distortions resulted on farms. Packages were often of fixed size and input in proportions that were not optimal for all farmers. Farmers had little choice concerning seed source or type and grew what was available in a given year from a single source, while often seed was effectively rationed because certain quantities were reserved for credit club members (Smale et al. 1991; Cromwell and Zambezi 1993). Farmers near urban demand centers who were implicitly taxed through panterritorial pricing resorted to parallel markets. Declining volumes through the state marketing channels further exacerbated the boards' trading losses. In turn, the increasing proportion of maize sales by smallholder farmers, generally on poorer land with less reliable rainfall, increased the instability of marketing board purchases and sales and hence of the fiscal demands made by the marketing system. Controls on private grain movement imposed by the earlier colonial governments were continued in all countries, even after independence. These controls also prevented grain from flow-

---

9. This conclusion flows from the GMB's annual maize trading account statements showing losses on maize exports to regional neighbors during this period.

10. For example, Kenya's National Cereals and Produce Board accumulated losses equal to 5 percent of GDP in the 1980s, and the operating losses of Zambia's National Agricultural Marketing Board were roughly 17 percent of total government budgets in the late 1980s (Howard and Mungoma 1996).

ing directly from surplus to deficit rural areas (Odhiambo and Wilcock 1990; Jayne and Chisvo 1991). Official restrictions on private trade and weak market infrastructure often made it easier for surplus farmers to sell to the boards rather than to their deficit neighbors a few kilometers away (Jayne and Chisvo 1991). Finally, a growing body of empirical evidence pointed to the controlled marketing systems as suppressing or imposing additional costs on parallel trading and processing channels that often served the interests of both producers and consumers more effectively than did the official state apparatus (Amani and Maro 1992; Rubey 1995).

A major difference in the implementation of pre- and postindependence maize policy was the method of financing food production growth. The colonial governments in Zimbabwe and Kenya, in particular, drew the resources to support a relatively small, privileged group of settler farmers largely from consumers and African farmers through discriminatory pricing schemes. By contrast, the postindependence governments drew the resources primarily from the treasury when they attempted to lavish the same level of support on a much wider African farmer and consumer constituency. In most cases, the treasury and aid donors bore most of the cost of expanding marketing services to smallholders, and the system was not fiscally sustainable.[11]

Phase 3: Period of Uncertainty, 1990–2005

We have identified four major factors that contributed to lower rates of growth in maize production and maize yields during the 1990s: (1) weather instability, (2) the contraction of state subsidies and market support, (3) declining investment in public agricultural research combined with uneven progress in liberalizing the maize seed industry, and (4) erratic and crisis-motivated maize policies.

Although the first factor constituted an "exogenous shock" for all actors involved, the remaining three could be interpreted as evidence that governments "reneged" on the social contract of the postindependence period, choosing short-term politically expedient measures over longer-term policy solutions. The 1990s brought much tighter fiscal constraints on government social activities, largely due to the treasury deficits accumulated during the maize boom periods and to donors' unwillingness to continue supporting them. As is explained further later, tighter fiscal constraints during the 1990s led to a new series of government and donor programs that still served important political ends but provided less commitment to the long-term public investments needed to sustain rural productivity over time.

---

11. During this phase of marketing policy, donors helped cover the operating losses of the state marketing system, as in Malawi. Donors also provided extensive support to the expansion of government bulk grain-handling facilities, which yielded little direct benefit to smallholders but added substantially to the marketing board costs (Jones 1994).

Weather

Maize yields are considerably more variable in southern Africa, particularly in Zimbabwe, than in other parts of the world (Byerlee and Heisey 1996). But since 1990 the weather has probably accentuated yield instability. Meteorological data from 1914/15 to 2000/01 in Zimbabwe indicates that five of seven stations received at least 15 percent lower cumulative seasonal rainfall during the 1990s than in the previous eight decades. Drought beset the country in 1992/93, 1994/95, and 1997/98. The early 1990s in Malawi were characterized by frequent droughts or midseason dry spells, with the 1991/92, 1993/94, and 1994/95 seasons all poor for maize. In particular, the drought in 1991–92 devastated maize production in Malawi, Zambia, and Zimbabwe. A decade later, successive droughts, coupled with political dislocation in Zimbabwe, produced the regional food crisis of 2002/03 affecting Malawi, Zambia, and Zimbabwe.

Contraction of State Marketing Systems

Fiscal crises and increased donor leverage over policy pushed the grain marketing systems of Eastern and Southern Africa toward liberalization in the mid-1980s. After first trying to strengthen the performance of state marketing boards in the 1960s and 1970s, donors and international lending agencies began promoting the reform of food marketing and pricing as a central component of structural adjustment programs in Africa. Donors had lost patience with phased and partial reform programs, which were increasingly seen as propping up costly and otherwise unsustainable pricing and marketing policies rather than facilitating reforms (Jones 1994). Political economy models (e.g., Bates 1981) further suggested that state interventions in agricultural markets, while ostensibly designed for rural development or to correct for market failures, were in fact designed to serve the interests of a dominant elite composed of bureaucrats, urban consumers, and industry.[12] The framework of policy-based lending within which market reforms have occurred in each of these countries has strongly influenced the path of reforms and has expanded external leverage over domestic agricultural policy through aid conditionality.

In Zimbabwe, a major reason for the stagnation in smallholder maize production was that the costly marketing policies—for credit, inputs, and maize—could not be financially sustained from the tax base. Zimbabwe's GMB maize operations required government subsidies of US$30–90 million annually in the mid-1980s, roughly 5 percent of gross domestic product (GDP). By 1990, almost 80 percent of smallholder recipients of state credit were in arrears

---

12. Later political economy analyses (e.g., Toye 1992) also highlighted the importance of dominant rural elites. These rural elites have continued to reap income transfer benefits from input and output marketing policies even as these state marketing programs have contracted (Jayne et al. 2002a).

(Chimedza 1994). The maintenance of high maize prices to sustain surplus production also put pressure on government to cushion the impact on consumers by subsidizing the price of maize meal. Unable to tackle its mounting fiscal crisis, the Government of Zimbabwe reluctantly approached international lenders for financial support. The terms of these agreements involved a cutback in the activities that contributed to the fiscal deficit, maize marketing and credit policies among them. As a result, GMB buying stations in smallholder areas were reduced. Even though 20 additional depots were established between 1985 and 1991, the number of rural collection points in smallholder areas declined from 135 in 1985 to 42 in 1989 to 9 in 1991. The real value of the seasonal Agricultural Finance Corporation credit disbursed to smallholders declined steadily beginning in 1986. By 1999, the state was allocating less credit to smallholders than at independence in 1980. Smallholder use of fertilizer in the 1990s became more volatile than in the 1980s, although it has not declined on average. Yet smallholder maize production has not exceeded the levels reached in 1985 (Figure 3.2). Since the early 2000s, Zimbabwe's political crisis has made it difficult to evaluate the effects of maize policies on smallholder welfare, for such effects are likely to have been overwhelmed by broader macroeconomic and civil instability.

Kenya's Cereal Sector Reform Program began in 1988 and entailed a similar cutback in state grain depots. Because of the small size and dispersion of such maize sales, small traders tend to be more efficient and cost-effective in handling smallholder sales than is the National Cereal and Produce Board, whose activities are largely concentrated in maize-surplus, large farm areas (Karanja 1990, 34). Surveys of rural households conducted in 22 districts in 1997 and 2000 indicate that there is generally broad support for the liberalization process, except in the several districts where government policies traditionally have been designed to support maize prices (Jayne et al. 2002b). The broad rural support for maize market reform appears to be mainly driven by the majority of rural farm households that reside in maize-deficit areas, which were directly hurt by the former controls that restricted direct interdistrict trade in maize and therefore made them dependent on the more expensive industrial maize meal offered through the official marketing system to satisfy their residual grain consumption requirements (Argwings-Kodhek et al. 1999). Lower risks and costs of maize in the post-reform period have facilitated shifts in cropping patterns to other crops that provide higher returns to land and labor. Smallholder dairy, horticulture, and tea production have grown impressively during this period, and overall agricultural production growth was double that of maize during 1990–2005. The relatively slow growth of maize has been due to improved marketing systems for these alternative crops as well as the reduction over time in the real price offered by the state marketing board for maize, the reduction in the marketing board budget for purchasing maize, and continued policy uncertainty in the maize market. The Kenyan government has several

FIGURE 3.2 Public expenditures supporting smallholder maize yields in Zimbabwe during episodes of success and decline, 1970–2000

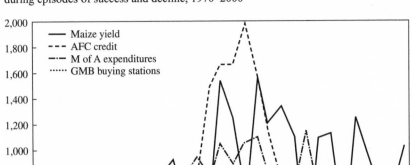

SOURCES: Agricultural Finance Corporation, Agricultural and Economic Review and Board papers, Harare office; Ministry of Lands, Agriculture, and Rural Resettlement, 2001; Agricultural Sector of Zimbabwe, Statistical Bulletin, 2001, Harare.

NOTES: Maize yield is measured in kg per hectare; AFC credit, the value of seasonal credit disbursed by the Agricultural Finance Corporation, is measured in millions of Zimbabwe dollars; Ministry of Agriculture (M of A) expenditures, which include research and development, extension services, and allied services, are measured in tens of millions of Zimbabwe dollars; Grain Marketing Board (GMB) buying stations include main depots and collection points. Monetary values are in constant 2000 Zimbabwe dollars.

times reversed its course in the liberalization process and has since 1999 resumed limited marketing board purchase of grain in politically important areas at fixed support prices, coupled with frequently changing tariff rates on maize imports. However, since the harmonization of trade policies within the East African Community in 2005, the policy environment for regional maize trade has become more stable.

In Zambia, reforms did not begin in earnest until 1993 (Howard and Mungoma 1996). Price controls were removed on all commodities with the exception of maize meal, and some restrictions on foreign exchange, imports, and exports were lifted. From 1991 to 1995, interest rates rose from 50 to 120 percent over 4 months. Throughout the 1990s, the volume of fertilizer distributed on credit through government programs declined as donors withdrew their earlier support. The National Agricultural Marketing Board (NAMBOARD) was abolished in 1990 and replaced by a combination of private trading networks and a government-organized cooperative system of crop marketing. Neither of these successor marketing networks had the ability to continue subsidizing maize production in remote areas through panterritorial pricing. The private sector has apparently responded vigorously to liberalization in areas of reasonably well-developed infrastructure, particularly in cotton zones, according to surveys in districts of the central and eastern provinces (Kähkönen and Leathers 1999). Yet for maize, the price ratios of fertilizer nutrients to maize grain rose sharply after the decline of NAMBOARD, particularly in the areas that had formerly benefited from the transport subsidies inherent in panterritorial pricing. Farmers were caught between rising input and financial costs, lower producer prices, and a contraction of market support in remote areas. As a result, there was a discernible shift in cultivated area from maize to crops such as cassava, groundnuts, and sweet potatoes (in the more remote northern and northwestern areas of the country) and to cotton (in the more commercialized areas). Maize remains the main food crop in most parts of the country, but its role as a commercial cash crop has been sharply diminished (Figure 3.3). As in Kenya, government maize purchases have increased in Zambia through the newly constituted Food Reserve Agency, particulary since 2005.

In Malawi, despite liberalization efforts during the late 1980s, the former parastatal ADMARC continued to enjoy a monopsonist/monopolist status given that Asian traders were restricted from selling in rural areas and the weak economies of neighboring countries limited cross-border trade opportunities (Christiansen and Southworth 1988), and producer–consumer price margins were often so narrow that it was not worthwhile for large traders to participate (Kandoole and Msukwa 1992). As part of the donors' structural adjustment program in the 1980s, fertilizer subsidies were gradually reduced, but when internal strife in Mozambique blocked the cheapest transport route, the subsidy removal plan was abandoned. Subsidies were again removed after the change in government. In 1995, nitrogen-to-grain price ratios rose by four times their earlier levels, though the fertilizer subsidy at its highest never exceeded 20 percent of the fertilizer cost (Mann 1998). This was the case for several reasons: (1) subsidies were removed, (2) the devaluation of the Malawi kwacha boosted fertilizer prices disproportionately to maize prices, (3) world fertilizer prices rose, and (4) private fertilizer dealers were requiring substantial risk premiums to hold and transport fertilizer in an inflationary economy with uncertain demand (Benson 1997; Conroy 1997; Diagne and Zeller 2001). Maize prices followed export parity, while fertilizer prices reflected full import costs, even though Malawi often imports maize. Because most fertilizer in Malawi is used on maize (and the remainder on tobacco), the removal of implicit subsidies in the form of overvalued exchange rates had a strong negative effect on fertilizer use. Depreciation of the real exchange rate also raised nitrogen-to-grain price ratios because fertilizer is imported (Heisey and Smale 1995; Minot, Kheral-

FIGURE 3.3 Maize area and maize marketed by the Zambian small-scale and medium-scale farming sector, 1984–2005

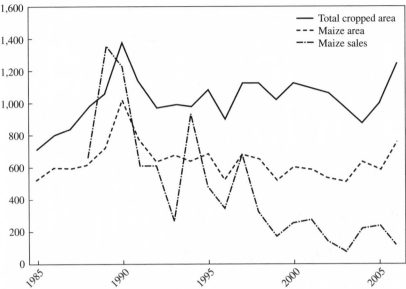

SOURCE: Crop Forecast Surveys, Central Statistics Office, Lusaka.
NOTES: Total cropped area and maize area are measured in thousands of hectares; maize sales are measured in thousands of tons marketed.

lah, and Berry 2000). These factors, along with shifts in relative prices of competing crops, may have contributed to the moderate decline from 1990 through 2000 in the percentage of cropped area devoted to maize by small-scale farmers (Figure 3.4).

None of the governments of the African countries in this study were able to find an internal solution to the large deficits to which their agricultural policies in the 1970s and 1980s contributed. Nor would external donors agree to make loans without redressing the sources of states' treasury deficits. Fiscal crises were the driving force behind the acceptance of structural adjustment. Yet despite the conventional perception that food markets have been "liberalized," many African governments, particularly in eastern and southern Africa, have continued to intervene heavily in food markets throughout their reform processes (Toye 1992; Jayne et al. 2002a; Harrigan 2003). These interventions have taken two main forms: (1) marketing board operations and (2) discretionary trade policy instruments, such as periodic export and import bans. A defining feature of the marketing environment in the "liberalization period" in countries such as Kenya, Malawi, Zambia, and Zimbabwe has been the tremen-

FIGURE 3.4 Changes in area distribution among maize and competing major crops in Malawi, 1982–2005

Percent

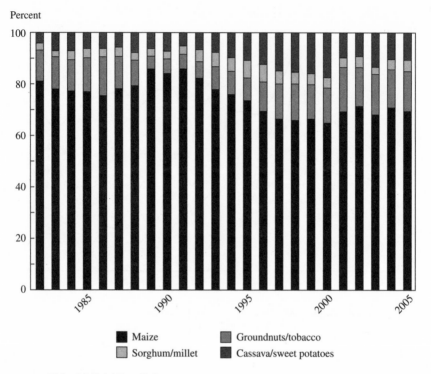

■ Maize   ■ Groundnuts/tobacco
▨ Sorghum/millet   ■ Cassava/sweet potatoes

SOURCE: Malawi Official Crop Estimates.

dous unpredictability and frequent change of direction in governments' role in the market (Mwanaumo et al. 2005; Govereh, Jayne, and Chapoto 2008). In this shifting policy environment, the private sector's response has naturally been muted, especially at the critical wholesaling stage. There have been few initiatives to support private trading activity and to develop the institutions—the legal and regulatory framework, transparent and rules-based policies, market information systems—and the public goods investments required for a privatized marketing system to function effectively (Jayne and Jones 1997; Kherallah et al. 2002).[13]

---

13. However, in spite of limited state support for the development of maize markets, in certain respects there have been remarkable benefits. For example, the lower grain processing costs made possible through liberalization have reduced the wedge between producer maize prices and consumer maize meal prices (Rubey 1995; Jayne and Argwings-Kodhek 1997). In some cases, price spreads between surplus and deficit regions have declined (Nyoro, Kiiru, and Jayne 1999). Evi-

Thus, in the mid-2000s, two decades after market reform programs were initiated in eastern and southern Africa, maize marketing policies in many countries have retained fundamental similarities to those used by the controlled marketing systems of their earlier histories. Though the quantities they trade are smaller than during the controlled market era, marketing boards in these countries still exert a dominant presence in the maize markets, handling between 10 and 60 percent of marketed volumes. Some aspects of policy reform have been implemented, primarily the legalization of private trading. And marketing board operations have been downsized, primarily due to fiscal constraints. Instead of purchasing the entire marketed surplus, as was the goal during the former control period, these boards now attempt to influence market prices through their purchase and sale operations, ostensibly for food security and/or price stabilization purposes. Many countries in eastern and southern Africa have continued food price stabilization along with subsidy programs of various types, and hence an empirical assessment of these countries' market performance since the 1990s reflects not the impacts of unfettered market forces but rather the mixed policy environment of legalized private trade within the context of continued strong government operations in food markets. There is a general consensus that this approach has largely failed to stabilize farm prices, provide adequate seasonal finance for small farmers' purchase of cash inputs, or stimulate private investment in the assembly and wholesaling stages of the value chain, and therefore it has been unable to provide smallholders with incentives to use improved farm technology in a sustainable manner (Govereh, Jayne, and Chapoto 2008).

The Maize Seed Industry

The genetic advances needed to sustain or enhance maize yields depend on past investments in maize research, with lagged effects. In Kenya, public maize research expenditure declined in real terms from 1980 through 1990. USAID withdrew its technical assistance in 1977, but in 1987 the government asked it to resume support. The scientific and institutional cooperation that created the maize success story of the 1960s and 1970s collapsed in the 1980s as a combination of fiscal crises and donor pressure weakened public financial support for research, extension, and credit (Hassan and Karanja 1997). In Zimbabwe, Eicher (1995) warned of declining government commitment to maintaining the continuity of research funding and scientific leadership based on a declining real budget for agricultural research from 1987. Public sector funding of agri-

---

dence indicates that the number of private traders serving smallholders has increased, especially in high-potential areas, within several years after the initiation of partial food market reform (Amani and Maro 1992; Kaluwa 1992; Nyoro, Kiiru, and Jayne 1999). However, in contrast to other regions in Africa where liberalization helped to dismantle agricultural taxation, the main effect of policy shifts in Eastern and Southern Africa was to reduce state expenditures on agricultural marketing investments and subsidies.

cultural research declined by 39 percent in real terms between 1975–1985 and 1990–2000.

Karanja (1990) has contended that the yield potential of successive maize seed releases in Kenya continued to rise, but the rate of increase declined. In plant breeding, yield breakthroughs of the type obtained when Kitale Synthetic II was crossed with Ecuador 573 are periodic rather than routine; according to Harrison, "The yield advantages offered by early releases were the cream to be skimmed off the milk" (by Gilbert et al. 1993, 29). In all case study countries, a more disturbing problem is that smallholders are likely to be even further from realizing yield potential, for reasons not confined to weather. One reason is that the genetic advances offered by breeding research have not been matched by agronomic practices and efficient support services for smallholders, many of whom are located in marginal areas (Rusike and Eicher 1997; Hassan et al. 1998; J. Ransom, pers. comm., 2002). As adoption of improved maize moves into more marginal areas, the effects on national yield levels are also numerically marginal (Byerlee and Heisey 1996). Simply put, Ransom believes that "there is little to no advantage of using a hybrid if the yield potential of your soil is less than 1 ton" (pers. comm., 2002). The secular decline in soil fertility in the intensive maize systems of this region has been aggravated by slackened fertilizer use and the abandonment of traditional methods of soil regeneration as populations increase (Lynam and Hassan 1998).[14] With the removal of subsidies, high nutrient-grain price ratios linked to high transportation costs have eroded the profitability of fertilizer use (Heisey and Mwangi 1996; Morris, Tripp, and Dankyi 1999; Minot, Kherallah, and Berry 2000; Morris et al. 2007). In addition, pest and disease problems have worsened with intensification of production. Advances in yield maintenance rather than yield potential may hold the greatest promise for this region (Lynam and Hassan 1998; De Vries and Toenniessen 2001), though the costs of resistance breeding are relatively high and yield "savings" from this type of breeding are not always perceptible to farmers.

At the farm level, seed supply problems have accompanied the patchy, incomplete process of seed market liberalization. On one hand, it is reasonable to ask why public sector companies in eastern and southern Africa persist in emphasizing hybrid maize, which could be provided as well or better by private companies (Tripp 2001). On the other hand, growth in seed sales in Kenya slackened considerably in the 1980s and has recently declined (Karanja 1996; de Groote, pers. comm., 2002), apparently provoked by inefficiencies and seed quality problems. More recent publicly bred releases have been diffused more slowly than their predecessors (Karanja 1990; Hassan et al. 1998; Bourdillon et al. 2002). In Zimbabwe, a number of private companies compete in the seed market, but the government maintains a firm grip on variety release and seed importation, which can be counterproductive (Tripp 2001; M. Banziger, pers.

---

14. Chapter 7 pursues these soil fertility issues in some detail.

comm., 2002). Seed Co-op has remained an important actor due to its research capacity, a diversified asset base, and collaborative technical agreements with a range of multinational companies (Rusike 1998). Though private investment may be compensating for the declining public research budget and there is no apparent slowdown in the rate of variety release, companies do not target the specific needs of marginal areas in Zimbabwe, such as IOPVs and stress tolerance (M. Banziger, pers. comm., 2002).

Liberalizing the market in Malawi only exposed its deficiencies, especially in the maize surplus–producing areas of the north, where population densities are low. Because the most common hybrids in Malawi yielded more than local maize without fertilizer at the seed prices that prevailed through the early 1990s, it made economic sense for farmers to grow hybrids even if they could not apply fertilizer (Heisey and Smale 1995; Benson 1999). However, the seed-to-grain price ratio nearly tripled between 1989 and 1997, and even if farmers could have gained access to the cash necessary to purchase a hectare of hybrid maize seed, it is unlikely that smallholders in many environments would have enjoyed the yield advantage required to pay the seed costs (Benson 1999). Furthermore, official price ratios in no way incorporated the transactions difficulties experienced by smallholders. Though a number of key steps were taken, in a 1995 report on the retail trade in agricultural inputs, Tsoka concluded that policy, legislative, and regulatory frameworks were not conducive to retailers' participation in the marketing of agricultural inputs. In 1997 compared to 1990, farmers purchased their seed from a range of retail sources, though ADMARC remained the major source of seed (Smale and Phiri et al. 1998). In 1998, Monsanto bought the controlling share of NSCM. Recent studies in the Central Region suggest that while the use of agents in maize seed distribution has extended coverage, smallholders pay almost 20 percent more in retail outlets than at the depot (Nakhumwa 2002). Although there are several companies operating in Malawi, many of the Monsanto–Malawi seed sales have been marketed through the supplementary inputs programs, just as Cargill–Malawi's were previously channeled through the smallholder credit system. All company representatives interviewed by Nakhumwa (2002) reported that seed sales are constrained by the low disposable income of farmers, an unpredictable growing environment, and a stagnating market. Likewise, the erratic upscaling and downscaling of donor-subsidized input distribution programs in Malawi have further restricted long-term private sector investment in support of smallholder maize productivity.

Crisis-Motivated Maize Policies

Malawi provides an illustrative example of the erratic policies of the 1990s that have directly affected the maize germplasm supplied to smallholders and, consequently, yields (Figure 3.5). Disruptive policy initiatives, sometimes pushed by donors, appear to have exacerbated the deepening poverty that has resulted

FIGURE 3.5 Maize production (left scale), hybrid maize diffusion (right scale), exogenous shocks, and policy changes in Malawi, 1981–2001

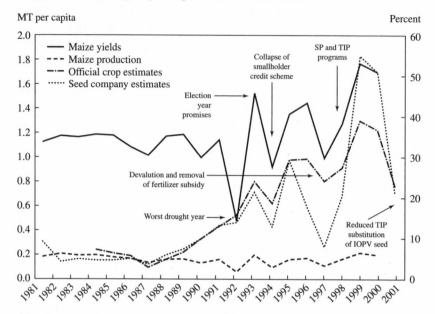

SOURCES: FAOSTAT (various years); Nakhumwa (2002); National Seed and Cotton Milling, Malawi Ministry of Agriculture (unpublished data).

NOTES: SP, Starter Pack; TIP, Targeted Input Program; IOPV, improved open-pollinated maize varieties.

from failure to redress the long-term structural problems in the economy (Kydd and Christiansen 1982; Lele 1990; Sahn and Arulpragasam 1991) and those factors more specific to the 1990s, described earlier.

In June 1993, Malawians voted to change their government to a multiparty system from an oppressive single-party dictatorship. Following this historic decision, many other changes occurred in the organization and delivery of inputs. While it became obvious that the promise of technical change in maize seed production would require addressing long-term structural factors—investing in physical infrastructure to reduce transfer costs, strengthening institutions to mobilize rural financial systems, continuing to invest in agricultural research and extension, and creating a stable agricultural policy environment—much of the cumulative learning from years of maize research in Malawi appears to have been discarded in favor of short-term, crisis-motivated solutions. Initiated during a food crisis in 1996–97, though originally conceived as a technology-based plan that was cheaper than importing maize, the Starter Pack (SP) and Targeted Input Program (TIP) initiatives have functioned as a relief effort, because the research input into the package they extend is minimal. In effect, a farm input subsidy system with controlled maize prices seems to have been replaced by in-kind transfers with full price liberalization, though the social welfare implications of the switch are unclear (Levy, Barahona, and Wilson 2000; Levy and Barahona 2001; Sibale et al. 2001; Levy 2005). Similar crisis-motivated approaches have substituted for long-term investments in public goods in both Zambia and Zimbabwe (Rohrbach, Minde, and Howard 2003).

Results

Cumulative Adoption

The cumulative adoption rates of modern maize types are higher in Kenya, Zambia, and Zimbabwe (over 70 percent) than in Malawi, where adoption stands at less than half that level (22 percent) (Table 3.3). Ranges in the data shown for 1996 reflect differences between national program and seed sales estimates. As a result of continued infusion of these materials through farmer purchases and seed distribution schemes and the involuntary mixture of germplasm types through cross-pollination in farmers' fields, it is difficult to reliably estimate the areas under improved seed.

National Maize Productivity

During the episodes of broad-based growth in smallholder maize production, growth rates in maize yields were positive in all case study countries, and a sizable component of the positive growth in maize production was attributable to yield (Table 3.4). However, growth rates in maize yield turned negative from 1990 through the mid-2000s in each country. Maize production likewise fell in both Zambia and Zimbabwe. Although output growth remained positive in Kenya and particularly in Malawi, where a few years of favorable weather and continued infusions of improved maize seed and fertilizer through free input distributions seems to have had an impact, growth rates fell to between one-fourth and one-half of their prior levels, well below the rate of population growth.[15] However, estimated growth rates mean little when coefficients of variation are so high. Maize yields are most variable in Zimbabwe and consid-

---

15. In Malawi, advanced-generation hybrid seed is likely to have gradually replaced local maize and F1 hybrid seed. Survey estimates suggest that in the major maize-producing zones, between 1990 and 1997 local maize as a percentage of the total estimated maize area declined from 85 to 60 percent, while the percentage planted to F1 seed was similar (12 and 10 percent, respectively). From 1990 to 1997, however, only a scant 7 percent of farmers were able to grow F1 seed in each season (Smale and Phiri et al. 1998). The estimated area in recycled hybrid seed rose from 2 to 30 percent, however, with IOPVs still representing only 1 percent. This pattern is likely to have become generalized for the nation from 1998 to 2001 with the subsequent annual infusions of small quantities of hybrid seed with SP and TIP schemes.

TABLE 3.3 Percentage of national maize area in improved maize for the case study countries, 1990–2007

	Open-pollinating varieties	Hybrids	All modern varieties
Kenya			
1990	8	62	70
1996	7.5–9.5	62–64	71–73
1999	2	85	87
2007	4	67	71
Malawi			
1990	3	11	14
1996	1.0–4.4	13–33	14–37
1999	4	39	43
2007	15	7	22
Zambia			
1990	5	72	77
1996	0.6–0.7	18–22	19–23
1999	3	62	65
2007	4	69	73
Zimbabwe			
1990	0	96	96
1996	0.0–4.5	82–91	82–96
1999	9	91	100
2007	6	74	80

SOURCES: López-Pereira and Morris (1994); Smale and Phiri et al. (1998); CIMMYT (2001); Hassan, Mekuria, and Mwangi (2001); Manyong et al. (2003); Malawi Ministry of Agriculture (unpublished data, 1990, 1996, 1999; ministry files, Lilongwe, Malawi); Langyintou et al. (2008).

erably more stable in Kenya than in any of the other countries. Furthermore, changes in actual aggregate maize yields underestimate the true achievements in maintaining yields against a naturally deteriorating germplasm and soil resource base (Gilbert et al. 1993). In none of the case study countries has actual maize production per capita kept pace with population growth over the past 40 years (FAOSTAT 2008). Even so, seed technical change clearly promoted these countries' ability to supply maize to consumers at a lower cost than otherwise would have been the case.[16]

Farmer Income

Net farm income from using maize hybrids and fertilizer depended not only on stable input-output price ratios (particularly the nitrogen-to-grain price ratio)

16. Other food crops, such as cassava or sweet potatoes, may offer prospects for supplying calories at lower cost than maize. However, assessment of these alternative food crops remains beyond the scope of this chapter.

TABLE 3.4 National maize area, yield, and production growth rates during and after periods of rapid production growth

	Area		Maize performance Yield			Production		Index of all agriculture production: Growth rate (%)
	Average area (thousands of ha)	Growth rate (%)	Average area (mt/ha)	Growth rate (%)	Coefficient of variation	Average area (thousands of mt)	Growth rate (%)	
Periods of growth								
Kenya (1965–80)	1,330	1.86	1.31	1.44	0.09	1,758	3.30	3.30
Malawi (1983–93)	1,253	1.92	1.10	1.18	0.23	1,380	3.10	1.41
Zimbabwe (1980–89)	1,293	–0.43	1.47	2.21	0.38	1,906	1.77	0.47
Zambia (1970–89)	774	–3.07	1.59	4.92	0.18	1,168	1.85	2.05
Periods of decline								
Kenya (1990–2005)	1,496	1.26	1.66	–0.42	0.11	2,482	0.84	1.95
Malawi (1994–2005)	1,372	2.84	1.25	–1.43	0.25	1,716	1.40	3.08
Zimbabwe (1990–2005)	1,336	0.52	1.14	–7.51	0.31	1,528	–6.99	–0.11
Zambia (1990–2005)	591	–2.11	1.63	–0.26	0.21	972	–2.37	1.10

SOURCE: FAOSTAT data used for purposes of internal consistency.

NOTES: Variation in the coefficient of yield adjusted for trend (Cuddy and Della Valle 1978). Data for 1992 excluded for Malawi, Zambia, and Zimbabwe because of extreme values. The authors note that estimated yield trends may be inaccurate and possibly downwardly biased due to a shift over time in the maize area from monocrop to intercrop.

but also on direct and hidden subsidies that reduced the transaction costs faced by smallholders. The illustrative partial budgets shown in Table 3.5 suggest that the returns to land in maize cultivation declined dramatically between the period of broad-based maize production growth and the subsequent period, considering the costs of credit, seed, and fertilizer after the collapse of the smallholder credit scheme, subsidy removal, and devaluation. After subsidies on seed, fertilizer, and especially those on credit were removed, and in a year that real nitrogen and seed prices reached their zenith relative to the real output price, returns to land and labor were in the negative range for fertilized hybrids and incentives shifted toward the cultivation of unfertilized local maize. For many smallholders, these figures in no way capture the sheer physical difficulty of obtaining the inputs when the marketing system changed.

Static, partial budgets reveal only a snapshot in time, however. Smale et al. (1991), Heisey and Smale (1995), Benson (1997), and Diagne and Zeller (2001) reported partial budgets and probability distributions of net returns constructed over a period of a decade in Malawi, with large numbers of yield observations from farmer surveys, on-farm trials, and demonstrations. The relative profitability of fertilized and unfertilized hybrid seed compared to the local benchmark varied by the growing season, whether or not subsidies were in effect and whether the household was a net buyer or consumer of maize. Detailed analysis of more than 1,900 trials conducted nationwide in 1995/96 demonstrated that in that season the most profitable recommendation for farmers in most areas of Malawi was to apply *no* fertilizer at all; fertilizer use at any level made economic sense only when maize was produced for home consumption (because of wide price bands) *and* the household had other cash-earning activities to finance the purchase of fertilizer (Benson 1997). Practically speaking, because maize is a food crop, smallholder credit has not been available for use in purchasing maize seed and fertilizer since the mid-1990s. In Malawi at least, instability in input-output price ratios also seems to have wreaked havoc with smallholder farm incomes.

Equity

On one hand, detailed adoption studies in the case study countries demonstrated that during the episodes of rapid production growth, maize hybrids and fertilizer were adopted by some of the poorest, smallest maize producers in the world, turning on its head the stereotype of the commercial hybrid grower (Gerhart 1975; Smale 1992; Howard 1994; Hassan et al. 1998). For example, in the major maize-producing regions of Malawi, in 1990 an estimated 36 percent of farmers with an average farm size of 1.2 hectares planted F1 maize hybrids. As is commonly demonstrated in microeconomic models of adoption, the likelihood of using hybrid seed differed by household assets such as total landholding, human capital variables such as farming experience and past extension contact, and physical factors such as the agroecological zone. Access to extension

TABLE 3.5 Illustrative partial budget for smallholder maize producers in Malawi, during and after the periods of maize growth

	1991		1996	
	Fertilized hybrid maize	Unfertilized local maize	Fertilized hybrid maize	Unfertilized local maize
Yield (kg/ha)	2,774	745	2,774	745
Producer price[a] (MK/kg)[b]	0.27	0.27	0.24	0.24
Transport and harvesting costs	0.04	0.04	0.04	0.04
Gross returns (MK/ha)	638	171	562	151
Variable cost				
Seed costs[c] (MK/ha)	38	7	77	11
Fertilizer[d]	196	0	359	0
Credit charges[e]	28	0	175	0
Total variable cost	262	7	611	11
Returns to land (MK/ha)				
MK/ha	376	165	−49	140
US$/ha[f]	197	86	−22	64
Returns to labor (MK/day)[g]				
MK/day	6.07	3.23	−0.79	2.75
US$/day[f]	3.17	1.69	−0.36	1.25

SOURCES: Yield, harvesting, labor, and wages from the survey data summarized by Smale et al. (1991) for 420 farmers in major maize-producing regions of Malawi; 1996 seed prices from the survey data summarized by Smale and Phiri et al. (1998). Fertilizer cost per hectare from Benson (1997).

[a]All values are in constant 1991 Malawi kwacha (MK).

[b]The producer price is used here, although the consumer price is relevant for most Malawian smallholder farmers, who are deficit producers of maize. Using the consumer price would increase the estimated returns to land and labor.

[c]At a constant seeding rate of 25 kg/ha.

[d]At the recommended rates for nitrogen, phosphorus, and potassium (96:40 nutrient kg/ha).

[e]Credit was virtually unavailable for smallholder maize production during the 1996 survey, and the interest rates charged by the Malawi Rural Finance Corporation ranged from 40 to 54 percent.

[f]Converted to 2005 US$.

[g]Calculated on the basis of 6-hour days, 62 person-days for hybrid maize, 51 person-days for unfertilized local maize. The modal rural wage of MK1.3/day in 1991 is assumed not to have changed in real terms in 1996.

and credit linked to input use and output markets, often through club membership, was a major explanatory factor. Access to oxen was significant in areas where farmers used animal traction, such as Zimbabwe and large parts of Zambia (less so in Kenya and Malawi).

In their 1995–96 survey of 400 households in five districts of Malawi where microcredit schemes operated after the collapse of the smallholder credit program, Diagne and Zeller (2001) found that when households chose to borrow they realized lower net crop incomes than did nonborrowers. Most explanations for this finding related to growing hybrid maize with high rates of fertilizer applications. The authors' conclusion that fertilized hybrid maize carried greater downside risk (higher cumulative probabilities of negative net margins) is consistent with some of those reported earlier for major maize-producing areas of the country (Smale et al. 1991).

By 1991–92, 60 percent of the total small- to medium-sized maize areas were planted with Zambian improved maize types (Howard 1994), with adoption rates differing by agroecological zone. Adopters were, as expected, those with larger farm sizes, those with larger household sizes (labor stocks), and those who used animals or machinery rather than hoes. They had more formal education and had been visited by extension agents. The majority lived close to service centers or roads, received credit for maize and sold maize output, and were dependent on local rather than regional depots.

In Zimbabwe, as in Kenya, the largest gains in smallholder maize production and sales were concentrated among farmers in areas with better rainfall and those owning more land and livestock. Based on detailed GMB data on maize purchases from 1985 to 1991, Jayne and Rukuni (1993) reported that 10 percent of the smallholder farmers accounted for 90 percent of the maize sold to the GMB during this period by smallholder farmers. Recent analysis using nationally representative survey data in Kenya and Zambia has shown that in 2000/2001, 2 percent of farmers defined as small- and medium-scale farmers (with farms under 25 hectares) accounted for 50 percent of the maize marketed by the smallholder sector (Table 3.6). As a result, the expensive marketing subsidies disbursed by state grain marketing agencies appear to have been concentrated among a relatively small segment of smallholder farmers. The relatively commercialized smallholders tend to hold more assets and earn higher incomes than do households that do not sell maize (see Table 3.6). The main attributes distinguishing these farmers are (1) location in "high-potential" areas with long growing seasons suited to the long-maturing hybrid maize varieties released in the 1970s and (2) relatively large farms by smallholder standards (in the range of over 5 hectares).

In Malawi, the greatest problem affecting the use of improved maize seed and fertilizer since 1993 has not been the input-output ratio or the profitability of the technology (because most farmers are net consumers) but cash flow and the continued erosion in the effective purchasing power of rural households with successive devaluations, inflation, and other macroeconomic changes. Until the purchasing power of the 60 percent of households in Malawi that are maize-deficit is raised, Benson says, "higher maize prices translate into increased misery" (1997, 20). Based on her longitudinal research in the Shire Highlands of southern Malawi, Peters (1996) argued that market liberalization provided new opportunities (through tobacco and maize sales) that have disproportionately benefited the better-off households, while the poorest 25 percent experienced a relative worsening in income and food security. By retain-

TABLE 3.6 Concentration of maize sales among smallholder farm households in Kenya (1999/2000), Malawi (2003/04), and Zambia (2000/2001)

	Maize sellers		
	Farms accounting for the top 50% of total smallholder maize sales	Rest of maize sellers	Households not selling maize
Percentage of households			
Kenya (unweighted)	1.7	37	61
Malawi (unweighted)	0.5	11	88
Zambia (weighted)	2.2	23	75
Landholding size (ha)			
Kenya	8.1	2.8	1.6
Malawi	3.8	1.3	1.0
Zambia	6.0	3.9	2.8
Value of farm assets (US$)			
Kenya	4,081	1,107	617
Malawi	1,336	186	154
Zambia	1,558	541	373
Total household income (US$)			
Kenya	8,849	2,357	1,565
Malawi	2,601	458	308
Zambia	2,282	629	291

SOURCE: Jayne (2008).

ing more maize, selling more labor, and increasing the budget share of purchased maize, the poorest quartile of the households suffered a decline in food security.

Changes in the marketing system had shifted the spatial locus of hybrid maize production, given the relative land abundance and lower road density of the Northern Region of Malawi. Between 1990 and 1997, the percentage of farmers growing F1 hybrid seed dropped from 40 to 18 percent in the villages of the Northern Region, where farmers had previously produced a surplus and grown the crop for cash (Smale and Phiri et al. 1998). Although the farmers in the villages of Blantyre district, Southern Region, were using F1 seed, they farmed such small areas and used such small amounts that they could not market a surplus. The farmers most consistently growing hybrid maize over the intervening years from 1990 to 1997 were found in the villages of Kasungu district in the Central Region, where tobacco and other cash crop opportunities were consistently better.

In Zambia, following price liberalization, Howard and Mungoma (1996, 27) report that "nearly full regional and seasonal differentiation of maize and other crop prices occurred" to reflect market conditions and transactions costs. The national maize area contracted relative to the expansion of the 1980s, particularly in the drier and more remote regions. Crop mixes have become diversified according to agroecological endowments and distances from transport infrastructure. Exports have doubled in value and become more diversified, including sugar, cut flowers, and specialty crops. Cassava, groundnut, cotton, and livestock production have grown impressively (Jayne et al. 2007). On the other hand, the incentives to grow maize commercially have declined for farmers in remote areas.

Gender Issues

In maize-based systems, maize is neither a men's nor a women's crop. Some studies suggest that gender-linked differences in the adoption of modern maize seeds and chemical fertilizer result from gender-linked differences in access to complementary inputs—land, labor, and extension services (Gladwin 1992; Smale and Heisey 1994; Doss and Morris 2001). If that is indeed the case, ensuring women's access to these inputs would increase adoption rates among women farmers. Gladwin (1992), for example, concludes that gender does not matter when one holds constant access to credit and cash. But where differential access to credit emerges, hybrids may become men's cash crops. Smale and Heisey (1994), for example, show that female-headed households were equally likely to apply fertilizer and similar amounts of nitrogen per hectare as male-headed households but were significantly less likely to grow hybrid maize because they did not have access to the resources necessary to qualify for credit or to be members of credit clubs. The distinction between men's and women's crops, different varieties, and subsistence and cash crops can be blurred, as in Malawi, where researchers developed high-yielding maize to meet the consumption and on-farm processing preferences of smallholder farmers.

Doss (2001) is critical of arguments that agricultural technologies should be developed particularly to meet the needs of women, arguing that the impacts of most are complex, dynamic, and indirect. Technologies related to "women's tasks," such as weeding, on-farm processing, and food preparation, have direct effects. Paradoxically, because on-farm processing of the flinty varieties of maize preferred for consumption was very time-consuming in Malawi, the adoption of semiflint hybrids is unlikely to have saved processing time for women. Considering the heterogeneity among different categories of female-headed households (widows, wives of long-term migrants, young mothers), Doss also notes that simple comparisons of adoption rates and characteristics between female- and male-headed households tells us little about gender-related impacts (Peters 1995). Given a dearth of data on intrahousehold differences among family members, it is difficult to generalize about the impact of new maize seed varieties on women.

Consumption

During the production "boom" period, there were undoubtedly widespread benefits to maize consumers in Kenya, Zambia, and Zimbabwe. Rapid rates of population growth would have resulted in a costly import bill had there been no expansion of maize production during this period—which would have added to the nation's external debt (Gilbert et al. 1993, 34). However, the controlled marketing systems during the boom period did not always allow the decline in real producer prices during the late 1980s to translate into lower consumer prices (Jayne and Jones 1997). In fact, real prices of packaged maize meal during the late 1980s in Zimbabwe remained relatively constant, despite falling real producer prices, as industrial millers benefited from their regulated oligopolistic position in the official marketing system (Jayne et al. 1995). Moreover, detailed farm-level studies in Malawi and Zambia were unable to demonstrate a link between adoption of hybrid maize and improved nutritional status of household members (e.g., Siandwazi, Bhattarai, and Kumar 1991; Diagne and Zeller 2001). How state promotion of maize relative to alternative food crops may have affected consumers is an unstudied question.

Fiscal Sustainability

In Kenya, Malawi, and Zimbabwe, published analyses suggested that public investment in maize research paid off (with returns ranging from 43 to 64 percent, depending on assumptions and time periods), even when curtailed by a small market, as in Malawi (Kupfuma 1994; Smale and Heisey 1994; Karanja 1996). However, these findings overestimate returns because they do not account for the allied investment costs in market infrastructure, credit and input distribution programs, and panterritorial pricing policies that encouraged the uptake of this technology. Costs were indeed high. Both the National Cereal and Produce Board in Kenya and the GMB in Zimbabwe incurred losses equivalent to 5 percent of their countries' GDP during parts of the 1980s (Jayne and Jones 1997). Zambia's input and output marketing subsidies were equivalent to 17 percent of the total government budget in the late 1980s (Howard and Mungoma 1996).

Only Howard's (1994) analysis for Zambia explicitly includes the costs of a full range of investments leading to hybrid maize adoption by smallholder farmers. Marketing costs accounted for roughly 59 percent of the total costs of all investments, in contrast with the seed research investments, which were only 3 percent of the total. Programs for extension and other service provision accounted for the remaining 38 percent. The rate of return on maize research was highly favorable when the costs of marketing were not included. Yet after including all investments (research, extension, seeds, and marketing), the average rate of return to maize research in Zambia was negative during 1987–91.

Policy Implications

We have argued that white maize became the dominant food staple in the case study countries between 1900 and 1965 and has become the preferred staple of today's African consumers because of (1) the agronomic suitability of the crop, (2) the British starch market, (3) milling technology, (4) the integration of Africans into the settler economy, and (5) market and trade policies established through agricultural settler lobbies. Furthermore, many of the institutions established during the colonial period, as well as colonial investments, generated benefits for smallholder maize production in the postindependence period. They spurred the maize breeding successes in Kenya and Zimbabwe before 1965. Of the two, however, only Kenya's was a smallholder maize revolution. Zimbabwe's brief smallholder maize revolution followed about 20 years later.

We conclude that in our case study countries, the maize "seeds" developed —that is, the quality of plant breeding and agronomic research that accompanied the adoption of maize—were an unquestionable success. Yet the broader marketing and input subsidy programs that supported maize uptake have proven fiscally unsustainable. In retrospect, the maize production surges were largely a phenomenon of the 1970s and 1980s. In later years, between 1990 and 2005, maize yields fell in all four countries. Production growth rates likewise declined dramatically, turning negative in both Zambia and Zimbabwe and falling to between one-half and one-fourth of their prior levels in Kenya and Malawi. We conclude, as did Byerlee and Eicher (1997, 251), that seed genetic change is a necessary but insufficient condition for improving the welfare of African smallholders. Since the 1990s, the necessary investments in germplasm have declined, while the investments in the institutions and market infrastructure required to translate germplasm advances into greater food security and incomes have also faltered. Public investments in state-controlled, coordinated maize input and output markets have proven fiscally unsustainable. At the same time, they have generated social costs by directing more resources to maize production and improved maize technologies in areas where farmers may not have chosen to grow it otherwise. Budget reviews suggest that these expensive maize marketing and input subsidy programs can easily consume the majority of individual countries' agricultural budgets, direct subsidies to a small group of commercial smallholders, and at the same time reduce the funds available for essential public goods such as breeding and agronomic research, agricultural extension, rural roads, and education (Govereh et al. 2006). Thus, the opportunity cost of these publicly subsidized marketing systems may be very high. The dismantling of the government marketing and input supply systems that supported maize production growth across the region and their replacement with an unstable and constantly changing mix of quasi-liberalization accompanied by sporadic government interventions have generated an uncertain decision-making environment for farmers who were already beset by unfavorable weather conditions.

Maize successes in the future will continue to depend on strategic crop improvements such as those targeted to relieve specific environmental and disease problems and enhance the stability of net returns to farmers, but also on enabling these advances to release land for alternative uses and diversify the income sources of farmers, regions, and nations. Renewed public investments in agronomic research and agricultural extension can complement breeding research by providing farmers with management tools for improving the productivity of the available inputs. Less intensive input packages, such as open-pollinating varieties of maize and management practices that improve the timeliness of planting and weeding, likewise offer prospects for increasing maize output in semiarid areas while at the same time relieving cash input constraints (see Chapter 7). Public action remains critical for restoring the growth of maize productivity. Key market institutions—such as legal and regulatory frameworks—remain fluid works in progress in most of our case study countries. Resolution of the widespread distrust between government and private traders requires transparency, dialogue, and goodwill on both sides. In addition to renewed investments in agricultural research and extension, public investment in rural road and rail systems, functional rural credit systems, and reliable crop forecasting and market information systems will be essential.

A third, vital, point concerns whether states will make the investments needed to support more efficient private systems of input delivery, finance, and commodity marketing, not only for maize but also for a range of crops that may offer higher returns to farming in the changing environment of Africa's rural areas. Because most parts of Africa are experiencing increased land pressure and limited potential for area expansion, population growth is causing a decline in land-labor ratios and farm sizes are declining. According to national surveys, about 50 percent of the small-scale agricultural households in Kenya, Malawi, Mozambique, Rwanda, and Zambia own less than 1.5 hectares of land (Jayne, Mather, and Mghenyi 2006). Maize is a relatively low value-to-bulk crop. It can provide consistently high returns per unit of land in only a relatively small proportion of smallholder farming areas in the region. Given reasonable assumptions about future productivity improvements, it is unlikely that maize can provide the net revenue on the millions of farms that are 0.5–1.0 hectare or smaller to generate substantial crop income growth, especially in the semiarid areas. Overcoming rural poverty will require achieving much higher returns on small farm sizes. This will require the same type of sustained support of institutional, policy, and technology systems for a wide range of other crops, for example, sugar in the lowlands of western Kenya, tea in the highlands, cotton in semiarid parts of Kenya, Zambia, and Zimbabwe, and horticulture where water control is possible and infrastructure for transport to export markets can be developed. Allied investments in education and skill development, market infrastructure, and agricultural research programs for a more diversified set of crops will all be critical.

However, even if successes are achieved in moving toward higher-return cropping patterns, maize will remain a crucial part of the food security equation, first, as a purchased commodity for satisfying the food requirements of a more diversified rural economy and second, as a cash crop in areas where it is agroecologically suited to provide high returns (e.g., Kenya's North Rift, parts of Zambia's central and southern provinces, and Zimbabwe's Mashonaland maize belt). Overall, however, rising land constraints will progressively encourage farmers to shift toward crops providing high returns to scarce land—provided that the marketing and institutional infrastructure allows them to do so. This shift will be manifested by a shift from the strategy of food self-sufficiency to a strategy based on comparative advantage.

Although such a shift will be crucial for poverty alleviation for millions of small farms in these countries, particularly in semiarid areas, this outcome is not ensured. Governments have an important role to play in building the institutions to reduce the transaction costs and physical costs of trade; supporting agricultural research and development, education, and extension; and investing in the development of reliable and low-cost food, finance, and input marketing systems to serve rural areas so that households can benefit from the higher incomes afforded by a well-functioning commercialized agricultural sector while ensuring their access to food (Dorward, Kydd, and Poulton 1998).

Finally, can a local constituency be formed to successfully stake a claim on public resources over the long run to support agricultural research, marketing institutions, and other kinds of growth-promoting public goods? These issues underscore the strong connection between agricultural development and governance. The early success of the maize industry in Kenya and Zimbabwe can be largely attributed to the strength of the institutions built by settler farmers, who provided a constituency to encourage sustained public and private support for the sector. Today, farm lobbies are generally weaker and more fragmented and reflective mainly of large-scale farmer interests. Representation has always been weak for smallholder farmers, particularly in semiarid regions where their welfare is closely tied to the reliability and efficiency of maize markets where they purchase maize as consumers. A crucial question is how can the key growth- and equity-promoting investments in agricultural research, infrastructure, and market institutions be financed? Perhaps most important, where will the domestic political pressure for these public investments come from?

4 Mali's White Revolution: Smallholder Cotton, 1960–2006

JAMES TEFFT

Scope of the Case Study

In 1960, cotton production in the CFAF zone of West and Central Africa accounted for only 1 percent of cotton fiber produced worldwide and 11 percent of total cotton output in Sub-Saharan Africa.[1] Over the next four decades, cotton production in the CFA zone grew at a compound rate of 9 percent per year, so rapidly that by 2000 francophone Africa accounted for roughly 70 percent of all cotton lint produced in Sub-Saharan Africa and 4.4 percent of total world production (Table 4.1). As a share of international cotton fiber trade, exports from the CFA countries increased from 2 percent in 1960 to between 12 and 14 percent of world totals in 2005 and 2006, making the CFA zone the world's third-largest cotton exporter after the United States and Uzbekistan (USDA 2007).

The impact of this rapid growth has impressed both farmers and policymakers. Roughly 1 million smallholder farm households account for all of the cotton produced in francophone Africa. They handpick their cotton crop and grow it exclusively under rainfed conditions in rotation with coarse grains. Given the scale of this activity, at a macroeconomic level the cotton sector has proven highly successful in generating foreign exchange and fiscal revenues. At the farm level, cotton earnings have financed agricultural investments and cereal crop inputs, such as high-yielding seeds and fertilizer, generating increased cereal production, higher incomes, and farm asset accumulation among cotton-farming households. High rates of capital accumulation and reinvestment by these smallholder cotton farmers have contributed directly to improved farm household productivity and welfare. Indirectly, they have spurred highly visible growth linkages in the nonfarm sector in cotton zones. Revenues from the cotton support institutions have helped finance roads, health clinics, and

---

1. Among the 13 countries comprising the CFAF zone, the following nine produce cotton: Benin, Burkina Faso, Cameroon, Central African Republic, Chad, Côte d'Ivoire, Mali, Senegal, Togo. This chapter refers to these countries as the CFA zone or the franc zone.

TABLE 4.1 Share of francophone Africa in world cotton production and trade (percent)

	Fiber production		Cotton exports	
	World	Sub-Saharan Africa	World	Sub-Saharan Africa
1960	1	11	2	13
1970	1	17	3	20
1980	1	42	4	45
1990	3	61	10	75
2000	4	69	13	75

SOURCES: Béroud (1999), ICAC (2002b), Goreux and Macrae (2003).

schools in the production zones, thereby increasing welfare and productivity more broadly throughout the cotton zone. The cotton companies, particularly in Mali, have sponsored functional literacy and numeracy programs, which have enabled village associations to take on new economic activities, including primary assembly of the cotton crop during the first stage of marketing. Because of these many beneficial direct and indirect effects on rural development, policymakers view cotton as a strategic subsector in most of the franc zone countries.

In order to delve into these dynamics and identify key drivers of cotton growth in the CFA zone, this chapter examines the historical development of cotton production in Mali. The largest producer and exporter in the franc zone, Mali provides generally good documentation and thus offers a window into the broad changes under way in francophone West and Central Africa. Through detailed examination of the Malian case, this chapter aims to identify the factors governing past success in cotton production as well as those helping to define its future.

To begin this effort, the following section provides some basic historical background. It briefly describes the historical development of cotton production in francophone Africa and then provides a review of world production trends and the world cotton market. The next sections dissect the Malian case in detail, dividing discussion into four historical phases marked by variable performance and a variety of key driving forces over the past 45 years. The final section highlights the policy implications of this experience for other African countries.[2]

---

2. The chapter draws on a large body of analyses conducted by a variety of authors working on different dimensions of cotton development in francopohone Africa, including the following: farmer organizations (Bingen), historical development (Compagnie Française de Développement des Textiles [CFDT]/Dagris, Coopération Française, Dioné), farm-level issues (Dioné, Giraudy, Kébé, Raymond), sector analysis (Badiane, CFDT/Dagris, Deveze, Goreux, McCrae), the world

Historical Background

The Origins of Cotton Production in Mali

Historians trace the origins of cotton production in Mali to Arab influence in the 11th century (Kergna and Kébé 2001). Its modern development originated with French efforts in the early 20th century to develop an independent supply of raw material for their textile industry (Dioné 1989; Fok 1997; Dequecker 1999).

The French colonial administration opened its first experimental farm in 1919 to test imported seed varieties and perfect cropping practices destined for use in the irrigated perimeter under development by the Compagnie de Culture Cotonnière du Niger (later the Office du Niger). Under coercive settlement and organizational schemes, cotton production reached 8,000 hectares before the scheme converted to irrigated rice production (Dioné 1989).

Following the difficulties and high cost of developing irrigated cotton production, the French government turned its focus to rainfed areas of the French Sudan. This led to a concentration of cotton production in the more reliable rainfall areas of southern Mali, where rainfall averages between 700 and 1,200 millimeters per year (Figure 4.1). Although several cotton gins operated in central and southern Mali in 1936, it was only after the Second World War that French cotton efforts began to accelerate appreciably. In 1946, the French government established a research institute (the Institut de Recherche Cotonnière et des Fibres Textiles Exotiques, or IRCT) followed by a cotton development company (Compagnie Française de Développement des Textiles, or CFDT) in 1949. Shortly after its establishment in 1946, IRCT opened up the N'Tarla experiment station and farm school in Mali to breed new varieties, carry out agronomic research, and train extension agents (Dioné 1989; Fok 1997; de Carbon Ferrière 1999; Kergna and Kébé 2001). As the majority shareholder and director of CFDT activities, the French government viewed this cotton company as a specialized technical assistance vehicle for promoting rainfed cotton production and assisting in the implementation of France's development cooperation efforts in West and Central Africa (Dioné 1989; Vinay 1999).[3]

The Structure of the CFA Zone's Cotton Sector

Today, the corporate and institutional successors of these colonial organizations manage the cotton industry in francophone Africa. As a result, the CFA zone has largely adopted a vertically integrated model for managing production, ginning, and marketing. Given the propensity for direct state intervention and the

---

market (Baffes, International Cotton Advisory Committe, USDA), and research (Bingen, Kébé, Dembélé).

3. French development agencies included, consecutively, the Caisse de la France Libre (1941), Caisse Centrale de la France d'Outre-Mer (1941), Caisse Centrale de Coopération Économique (1958), and Caisse Française de Développement (1992) prior to Agénce Française de Développement (1998).

FIGURE 4.1 Cotton zones of Mali, 2003

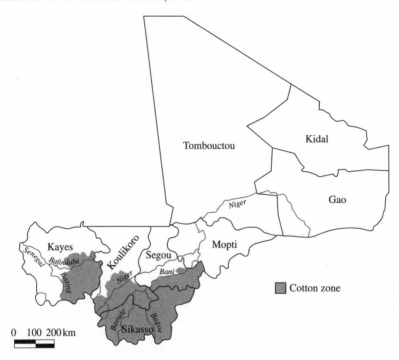

SOURCE: Marian Mitchell, Geography Department, Michigan State University, East Lansing, 2003.

anti-merchant bias prevailing in Sahelian political circles, coupled with the French colonial legacy of centralized planning, most of these integrated cotton operations remain under the control of state-owned cotton companies (Dioné 1989). Although this integrated model for cotton sector management is often attributed to the French, Fok (1997) notes that most other European colonial powers—including Belgium, Great Britain, and Portugal—likewise instituted vertically integrated, publicly owned cotton management systems in their African colonies.

After they achieved independence, most countries in the franc zone established state cotton companies, with the French-owned CFDT as a minority shareholder. The integrated approach used to manage cotton production in the franc zone begins with a regional breeding and agronomic research program managed by national agricultural research systems in a network of franc zone countries. In Mali, the Institut d'Économie Rurale (IER) manages cotton research activities. During the colonial era, the IRCT managed these research programs. In the postindependence years, France's international agricultural research center, the Centre de Coopération Internationale en Recherche Agronomique pour le Développement (CIRAD), has coordinated these research efforts throughout francophone Africa.

Across the franc zone, monopsonistic state cotton companies have provided inputs to farmers while at the same time guaranteeing the purchase of farmers' seed cotton at panterritorial and panseasonal prices. This system ensures input supply and output prices for farmers while at the same time ensuring credit reimbursement to the pool of banks that finance loans for fertilizer and seeds. In addition to supplying inputs such as seeds, fertilizer, and pesticides on credit and facilitating the acquisition of animal traction equipment, cotton companies have employed an extensive network of field agents to closely monitor all phases of production. As a result, they have traditionally controlled input supply, extension support, cotton collection, ginning, baling, and export. During the postindependence years, continued partnership with the CFDT allowed national cotton companies to retain this international technical expertise to support management of their production, ginning, and marketing operations.

The cotton companies of the franc zone export over 95 percent of cotton lint while selling the remaining 5 percent domestically to local textile manufacturers. Cottonseed, separated from the cotton lint during ginning, accounts for roughly 60 percent by weight and 10 percent by value of total seed cotton production. Typically, the franc zone cotton companies sell their cottonseed byproduct locally to subsidiary oil processing firms that manufacture soap, edible oil, and animal feed. The more valuable cotton lint produced in the franc zone attains a middling grade of $1^1/_{32}$ inch, thereby commanding a 9.3 percent quality price premium above the Cotlook A Index (Gillson et al. 2004).[4] Compagnie Cotonnière (COPACO), a CFDT marketing subsidiary and major international trading company, has historically sold the majority of CFA zone cotton on the international market to spinning mills. As cotton production has grown in francophone Africa, COPACO's share of the world market has grown too, reaching roughly 15 percent of world trade by the mid-2000s. Owned partly by the CMDT (Compagnie Malienne pour le Développement des Textiles) and other franc zone cotton companies, COPACO has benefited from the resulting scale economies, and this has enabled it to establish a market identity for franc zone cotton (Bingen, Dembélé, and Camey 1995; ICAC 1996). National cotton companies' association with this French multinational has also facilitated their access to development assistance from France's bilateral agencies as well as to formal international credit markets.

World Market and Price Incentives

Movements in world market prices have strongly influenced production incentives among African cotton producers over the past 45 years. As Figure 4.2 shows,

---

4. The price premium is due in part to the low percentage of knotted and short-fiber content and the low levels of contamination.

FIGURE 4.2 World market price of cotton fiber, 1960–2006

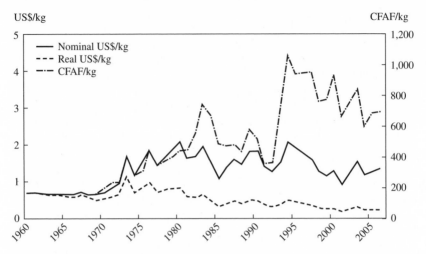

SOURCES: Oanda database; Cotlook database.
NOTE: CFAF, Communauté Financière Africaine franc.

the world market for cotton fiber (Cotlook Index A in US$) has fluctuated widely since about 1970.[5] Expressed in real terms, international cotton prices have trended downward since the 1960s as a result of slowing demand for cotton relative to synthetic fibers. By 2006, the real price of 1 kilogram of fiber stood at 37 percent of its 1960 level.

Cotton prices have also become more volatile. After a period of relative price stability during the 1960s and early 1970s, cotton prices began to fluctuate widely. Compared to 1960–72, world cotton prices became 4.5 times more volatile between 1973 and 1984. Although price fluctuations moderated somewhat in subsequent years, price volatility between 1985 and 2002 remained 2.5 times higher than in 1960–72 (Baffes 2004).

The effect of the 50 percent franc devaluation in January 1994 on the price of cotton fiber is clearly evident when Index A is expressed in CFA francs (CFAF) (see Figure 4.2). This macroeconomic shock coincided with a large upturn in international prices, and together they pushed the cotton fiber sales price to over 1,000 CFAF per kilogram.

The administered price system used by the CFDT and CMDT has attempted to shield Malian cotton farmers from this international price volatility. During the relatively rare period of stability on the world market between 1960 and 1972, Malian farmers consistently received 30 percent of the world market

---

5. Cotlook Index A is an "average of the cheapest five quotations from a selection of the principal upland cottons traded internationally" (Cotlook 1999).

FIGURE 4.3 Effect of world market price on farmers' price share, 1960–2005

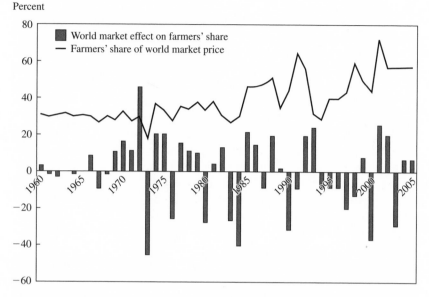

SOURCES: Cotlook database; CMDT (Compagnie Malienne pour le Développement des Textiles) database; Oanda database.

price (Figure 4.3).[6] But during periods of falling world prices—for example, in 1985, 1992, 1995, and 1999—farmers' share of world prices jumped rapidly because the CMDT did not feel it could decrease producer prices. In combination with the relatively high cost of maintaining an integrated system, this producer price rigidity exacerbated operating losses incurred by the CMDT. In these instances, French development agencies together with the Malian government and the European Union provided financing to cover these deficits. Conversely, during upturns in the world price, administered producer prices have not immediately adjusted upward, thus providing a window of opportunity for the French and Malian governments to generate profits and recover their losses (Dorey 1999). Over time, Mali has largely succeeded in growing its cotton production and share in these highly competitive and highly variable international markets. The following discussion examines how.

---

6. As recent studies have shown, this level is low relative to those of other producing countries (Pursell and Diop 1998). Seed cotton prices received by farmers in Zimbabwe and India were, respectively, 37 and 60 percent higher than farm-level prices in West Africa for similar types of seed cotton between 1983 and 1995. Since 1994, their prices have been 80 to 100 percent higher (Baffes 2004).

Key Phases and Turning Points in Mali's Cotton Production

Malian cotton production has grown rapidly over the past four and a half decades (Figure 4.4). In 1960, Malian farmers planted 28,000 hectares and produced 6,400 tons of seed cotton. Over the next 45 years, yields grew at a 2.8 percent annual rate while the area planted expanded annually by 5.9 percent. As a result, overall production grew at a compound rate of 8.7 percent per year for more than four decades. By the middle of the 2000s, Mali was producing roughly 500,000 tons of seed cotton annually, an increase of over 70-fold since independence. Average seed cotton yields rose appreciably over this period, growing from 225 kilograms per hectare in 1960 to roughly 1 ton per hectare in 2006. Growth in ginning outturn, the percentage of fiber derived from seed cotton during the ginning process, has likewise improved, from 35 to 42 percent over the past 45 years, a 0.5 percent annual growth rate.

Yet growth rates have varied over time, surging in some eras and subsiding in others. A look behind the aggregate trends reveals two periods of stellar growth when cotton production increased at 20 percent annually (Table 4.2). Subsequent periods of consolidation and adjustment have punctuated these periods of rapid growth. To explore the reasons for these differences in performance, the following discussion divides the postindependence years into four major phases:

- Phase 1: Early growth years, 1960–73
- Phase 2: Nationalization, growth, and crisis management, 1974–93
- Phase 3: Devaluation, 1994–98
- Phase 4: Growing pains, 1999–2006

FIGURE 4.4 Cotton area and production in Mali, 1961–2006

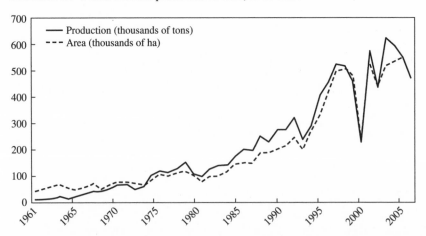

SOURCE: CMDT (Compagnie Malienne pour le Développement des Textiles) database.

TABLE 4.2 Annual growth rates in Malian cotton, by period (percent)

	Phase 1: 1960–73	Phase 2: 1974–93	Phase 3: 1994–98	Phase 4: 1999–2006	Total: 1960–2006
Area growth	5.5	5.5	22.2	3.1	5.9
Yield growth	15.0	2.1	–2.5	–0.1	2.8
Output growth	20.0	7.7	19.9	2.9	8.7

SOURCE: CMDT (Compagnie Malienne pour le Développement des Textiles) database.

The following presentation takes a detailed look at the performance of Mali's cotton sector during each of these periods in an attempt to identify the key forces driving change, the key responses by farmers and other sector stakeholders, and their impact on overall sector performance.

Phase 1: Early Growth Years, 1960–73

Institutional Backbone: The CFDT

Unlike other countries in francophone West Africa that created state-owned cotton companies at independence, Mali did not nationalize its cotton production and marketing company in 1960. Instead, the Malian government maintained the colonial cotton production system throughout the first decade and a half following independence. Building on the experience and expertise developed by the CFDT in the 1950s, the Malian government signed a 10-year formal contract with the CFDT to manage the country's cotton sector beginning in 1964 (Bingen, Dembélé, and Camey 1995; Kergna and Kébé 2001). During the first five years of this agreement, the CFDT doubled the cotton acreage to 56,000 hectares and increased average seed cotton yields from 225 to 322 kilograms per hectare.

The CFDT retained the vertically coordinated input supply, research, extension, and marketing model developed during the colonial era. The company announced input and output prices prior to harvest and supported farm production with a network of extension officers. Because of the reliability and predictability of the cotton contracts, Mali's cotton farmers quickly became the preferred borrowers of the formal banking system in rural areas, enabling them to finance inputs for other crops as well as the acquisition of farm equipment and even consumer goods.

During the early years of independence, the scope of the CFDT's interventions progressively broadened to include many elements of an integrated rural development program. To complement its cotton development efforts, the CFDT initiated programs in livestock production (1969), rural functional literacy (1971), and the manufacture of animal traction equipment (1970) (Dioné 1989).

This broader mandate did not, however, appear to distract the CFDT management from its primary objective of raising cotton production. The CFDT succeeded in increasing cotton production and productivity through the development and adoption of high-yielding varieties, promotion of mineral fertilizer and pesticides, extension of improved cultivation techniques, and helping farmers acquire and use animal traction equipment (Table 4.3). The following discussion examines each of these components of the CFDT promotional model in turn.

Improved Seeds

Mali's success in developing a continuous stream of new cotton production technology over the past four and a half decades stems directly from the effective collaboration among French and Malian agricultural research institutes (IRCT, CIRAD, and IER) and cotton companies (CFDT/Dagris and CMDT) coupled with strong regional cooperation among sister research institutions in neighboring franc zone countries. These partnerships resulted in the production, multiplication, and widespread adoption of a series of new cotton varieties, each with a lifespan of roughly 4.4 years (Fok 1997). Figure 4.5 details characteristics of the six most widely adopted cotton varieties released in Mali, each achieving over 80 percent adoption during their reign. Each new generation of seed technology achieved progressively higher agronomic and ginning yields as well as improved fiber quality (length, fineness, color, strength, maturity, and impurity content) desired by the textile industry (Dembélé 1996; Follin and Deat 1999; Kergna and Kébé 2001). This steady progression reflects the consistent effort by breeders to develop higher-yielding varieties that respond to both agronomic concerns of Malian farmers and ginning and quality concerns critical to overall sector profitability and export sales.

Of the six major cotton varieties adopted by Malian farmers as their principal variety, only one was initially bred by the Malian research system (NTA 88-6) (Dembélé 1996; Kergna and Kébé 2001). The five others originated from research stations in Chad, the Central African Republic, and Côte d'Ivoire. This highly effective record of regional research collaboration among franc zone cotton breeders underlines the important synergies that can be gained both from regional research collaboration and from partnerships among national and international research organizations.

Pesticide Use

In addition to improved cotton varieties, the increased use of pesticides, widespread farmer adoption of ultra-low-volume (ULV) pesticide equipment, and the introduction of pyrethroid pesticides have all further contributed to higher cotton yields. The introduction of the ULV method in the early 1970s freed farmers from transporting large quantities of water to the fields to apply pesticides, providing them with an additional incentive to expand their cotton acreage and improve yields. The introduction of pyrethroid pesticides in the late 1970s also contributed to improvements in yield. Over time, cotton specialists estimate that improved pesticides and pest control equipment have accounted

TABLE 4.3 Dynamics and drivers of change in Malian cotton, by period

	Phase 1: Early growth	Phase 2: Nationalization and growth under crisis management	Phase 3: Devaluation	Phase 4: Growing pains
Timing	1960–73	1974–93	1994–98	1999–2006
Key actors	Compagnie Française de Développement des Textiles (CFDT) Institut de Recherche Cotonnière et des Fibres Textiles Exotiques (IRCT) Smallholders	Compagnie Malienne pour le Développement des Textiles (CMDT) Smallholders Farmer organizations	West African central bank	CMDT Farmer organizations Government Donors
Motors of change	New varieties Increased use of fertilizer, pesticides, and animal traction Integrated development	Nationalization of cotton company World price slump in the mid-1980s Subsidy reductions Farmers complain of dishonest cotton grading and weighing, forcing reform	Communauté Financière Africaine (CFA) franc devaluation, January 1994	Mismanagement and losses at CMDT Farmers strike Donors insist on reforms in return for financial support
Beneficiaries	Smallholders CFDT		Smallholders	
Production growth	Area grows at 5% per year Yield grows at 15% per year Production grows at 20% per year	Production growth uneven; averages 8% per year	Production grows at 20% per year All growth due to increased area	Production grows at 3% per year
Impact	Substantial gains in farmer incomes	Big losses at CMDT as they try to protect farmers from falling world prices	Farmer price doubles following devaluation	Uncertainty

FIGURE 4.5 Cotton yield by variety and year, 1960–2002

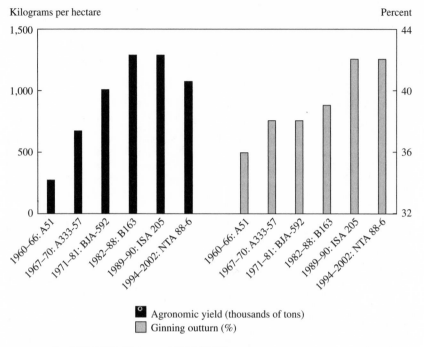

Agronomic yield (thousands of tons)
Ginning outturn (%)

SOURCES: Dembélé (1996); Kergna and Kébé (2001).

for 35–50 percent of the growth in seed cotton yield in francophone West and Central Africa (Follin and Deat 1999).

Fertilizer Promotion

The CFDT also focused heavily on fertilizer promotion during this period. Until 1976, the Société de Crédit Agricole et d'Equipement Rural (SCAER), the Malian government's agricultural credit and input distribution parastatal, managed short-term loans that allowed farmers to purchase subsidized seasonal inputs (at 20–50 percent discounts) (Dioné 1989). Following the bankruptcy and dismantling of the SCAER in 1980, the CMDT continued to offer some subsidies on the nitrogen, phosphorus, potassium, sulfur, and boron complex and urea fertilizers until 1984 (Dioné 1989).

Although detailed farm-level data are not available for the period between 1960 and 1974, research station cotton trials in Mali during the 1960s and 1970s recorded yield responses ranging from 2.6 to 11 kilograms of seed cotton per kilogram of fertilizer nutrients (N or $N + P_{205} + K_{20}$) (Pieri 1989; Henao et al. 1992). But more recent studies suggest that fertilizer response rates have declined over time. One study shows cotton yield gains per kilogram of fertilizer decreasing from 10 to 2.6 kilograms between 1969 and 1982 (Henao et al. 1992). The studies also note that on-station results may exaggerate the response obtained by a typical farmer who does not always use optimal cultural techniques. One illustrative study indicates that Malian farmers achieve roughly half the cotton yield response obtained on station (Guigou 1989).

Numerous analyses undertaken in Mali throughout the 1980s showed that the gross income attributable to fertilizer relative to its cost (value-cost ratio) is quite low. Value-cost ratios ranged from 0.5 to 1.9, levels that are inferior to the benchmark rate of 2 or more at which farmers' financial incentives are considered adequate (Yanggen et al. 1998). These results appear to be consistent with Malian farmers' practice of purchasing fertilizer on credit but applying less than the recommended level. Farmers have often preferred to sell part of it, use it on maize, or spread it over a larger area of cotton fields. The lack of data on farm-level fertilizer application rates makes it difficult to determine how much fertilizer use has contributed to the tremendous growth in yields during 1960–73.

Animal Traction

As in the case of fertilizer, the CFDT promoted the acquisition and use of draft oxen and equipment among cotton farmers through extension efforts, while the SCAER sold farm implements on credit to farmers at heavily subsidized prices. By the mid-1970s, locally manufactured equipment had gradually replaced the sale of imported machinery, which was available to farmers through two- to three-year loans. The certainty of a guaranteed market for seed cotton provided farmers a reliable income stream, thereby reducing their risks from investing in this new technology. Because few farmers had access to formal credit to finance their initial purchase of a plow and draft oxen, they invested in animal traction equipment and oxen gradually, typically over a period of four to five years. Once cotton farmers had begun to equip their farms with animal traction equipment, they became more attractive to lenders, because animal traction enabled them to expand their cultivated area, increase their cotton earnings, and more reliably service their loans (Dioné 1989).

Farmers' enthusiasm for animal traction arose in part because it allowed them to overcome peak-season labor bottlenecks, expand their cultivated area, and increase yields. Studies conducted in the 1980s suggest that well-equipped farms are able to manage cropped area per worker 40 percent greater than can nonequipped farms. Moreover, animal traction farms benefit from a 30 percent labor savings compared to those engaged in manual farming (Whitney 1981; Doumbia, Dramane, and Touya 1986; Cisse 1987; Dioné 1989). As a result, farms equipped for animal traction cultivate a larger area per worker and hence save on labor costs relative to nonequipped farms.

Animal traction farmers also achieve higher cotton yields. In part, this gain arises because the extensification effect of animal traction equipment is both "accompanied and restricted by a simultaneous intensification effect" in which

increasingly mechanized farms become familiar with and adopt other technological improvements (Dioné 1989, 239). Subsequent research has confirmed
that animal traction itself has a positive effect on yield. By facilitating more
timely and improved land preparation, as well as early planting and weeding,
ownership of animal traction equipment enables farmers to overcome peak-
season labor bottlenecks and optimally time key operations in the cropping calendar (Sargent et al. 1981; Follin and Deat 1999; Giraudy 1999).[7] The acquisition of draft oxen also provides a consistent source of manure, the application
of which the CFDT promoted as a means of further improving productivity and
soil fertility.

To encourage animal traction use by cotton farmers, the CFDT supplied
animal feeds—cottonseed cake, a by-product of cottonseed oil extraction—and
veterinary services to combat cattle disease and promote good animal nutrition.
The CFDT's animal husbandry programs emphasized good animal care and
management so farmers could perform at peak strength at the start of cropping
season. The CFDT programs for financing, equipping, and training blacksmiths
to manufacture spare parts, plows, and other equipment complemented its agricultural mechanization efforts.

Performance

The CFDT's efforts during this period proved highly successful in promoting
both higher yields and area expansion among Malian cotton farmers. By 1973,
56 percent of Malian cotton farmers were using animal traction, while 70 percent applied fertilizer and 84 percent used pesticides (Coopération Française
1991). As a result of the CFDT's efforts, between 1960 and 1973 seed cotton
yields grew at an annual rate of 15 percent, tripling average yields to 833 kilograms per hectare. At the same time, the cotton area expanded at an annual rate
of 5.5 percent, reaching 69,000 hectares in 1973 (see Table 4.2). The combined
effect of these large productivity gains and sustained rapid expansion in cultivated area resulted in 20 percent annual growth in seed cotton production. Improvements in ginning yields proved more modest, rising from 34 percent in
1960 to 36 percent in 1973, for a 0.75 percent annual growth rate. Consequently,
with cotton fiber production growing annually at 21 percent, Mali's cotton lint
exports jumped eightfold over 1960 levels.

Although the microdata required to assess on-farm profitability of cotton
production are not available from this early period, Malian farmers clearly considered cotton a profitable crop. In addition, cotton attracted farmer interest because of its guaranteed market and cash payment at harvest, as well as the access to credit and inputs available only to cotton farmers.

---

7. The discussion of conservation farming in Chapter 7 provides further evidence of the importance of early planting and timely weeding among cotton farmers.

Phase 2: Nationalization, Growth, and Crisis Management, 1974–93

Institutional Evolution: The Launching of the CMDT

Following the gradual development of Malian management capacity during the first 14 years after independence, the Malian government nationalized the cotton sector in 1974 by creating the CMDT. The French-owned CFDT retained a 40 percent stake in the new company, thus allowing the Malian cotton sector to benefit financially and technically from the continued involvement of the French private sector and government, with their access to external capital for rural development programs in the CMDT zone (Dioné 1989; Bingen, Dembélé, and Camey 1995).

This period marked the start of Mali's 1972 Rural Development Operation strategy, which envisioned CMDT implementation of certain integrated rural development programs financed by the World Bank, the International Fund for Agricultural Development, and French development agencies (Fonds d'Aide et de Cooperation and the French Development Agency) (Dioné 1989).[8] Under these projects, the CMDT stepped up its delivery of key public services as a complement to its cotton-specific activities. These services included the expansion of animal traction, blacksmith training, and animal health programs as well as new initiatives involving maize production, rural roads, health, potable water infrastructure, and support to farmer organizations (Deveze 1994; Bingen, Dembélé, and Camey 1995). These complementary public programs, while responding to many of their farmers' multiple needs, also served to strengthen the institutional and political position of the CMDT in Mali.

Three main developments occurred during this period: (1) the emergence and growing role of farmer organizations in the cotton sector, (2) the positive effect of cotton on coarse grain production and food security, and (3) the impact and response of the sector to increasing world market price variability. The following discussion reviews each in turn.[9]

Farmer Organizations

THE EMERGENCE OF THE *ASSOCIATIONS VILLAGEOUISES.* In 1974, a village-level CFDT agent organized local farmers to protest "dishonest cotton grading

---

8. Although most of the credit for France's contributions to the successful development of cotton production in francophone Africa is given to the CFDT, the French Ministry of Cooperation and particularly the French Development Agency—previously called Caisse Française de Développement—played equally important roles. Funding mechanisms managed by these two organizations financed the majority of France's cotton-specific and other development activities, a large percentage of which were concentrated in the cotton zone. The French Development Agency, in particular, after financing the French government's initial investment in the CFDT, continued to play a major role in directly funding a large share of France's cotton-related operations (e.g., ginning, transport, marketing, financing during crisis periods) (Alliot 1999).

9. The following section draws heavily on Bingen's long-term work on farmer organizations in Mali. See, in particular, Bingen (1994, 1996, 1998) and Bingen, Dembélé, and Camey (1995).

and weighing practices," triggering a chain of events that led to the formation of farmer groups in the cotton zone (Bingen, Dembélé, and Camey 1995). Farmer organizations participated in informal pilot efforts to manage village-level assembly, grading, and weighing of seed cotton. Several years later, the CMDT formalized this arrangement with farmer groups, or *associations villageoises* (AVs). The role of the AVs evolved to include responsibility for credit management and distribution of agricultural equipment and inputs among its members (Dioné 1989; Bingen, Dembélé, and Camey 1995).

Unlike previous top-down efforts aimed at organizing farmers through compulsory membership under expert management, the AVs grew out of grassroots farmer initiatives building on longstanding local traditions of farmer participation (Dioné 1989; Bingen, Dembélé, and Camey 1995). AVs' responsibility for these new functions lowered CMDT operating costs while at the same time raising credit recovery rates. They also spared the CMDT from having to tarnish its image through coercive recovery of production and input credit (Dioné 1989; Bingen, Dembélé, and Camey 1995). The fees earned by the AVs for these services, in turn, financed investment in schools, health centers, and wells, thereby generating substantial welfare and equity benefits within the cotton villages (Tefft, Staatz, and Dioné 1997). The CMDT supported this process and the growing role of farmer associations by providing literacy and management training for the farmer groups (Bingen, Dembélé, and Camey 1995). It also imposed standards and specific requirements for formal recognition by the CMDT.

The number of AVs expanded rapidly during this period, increasing from the first one in 1974 to 404 in 1981 and 950 in 1987. Their growth continued in later periods as well, so that by 2002 over 4,500 AVs operated in Mali's cotton zone.[10]

THE FARMER STRIKE OF 1991.   In May 1991, only months after the popular overthrow of President Moussa Traore at a time when Mali was experiencing a "wave of political freedom," a group of leading farmers presented the CMDT with a list of grievances and demands related to specific cotton pricing and marketing practices. When the CMDT refused to consider the demands, the farmers called a cotton strike. Through the direct intervention of the Ministry of Rural Development, the government quickly agreed to meet 9 of the 12 demands and to continue negotiations on the other 3 points. A roundtable discussion among farmers, the CMDT, the Malian and French governments, and other major donors took place in September 1991 in an effort to "restore a spirit of trust," certainty, and control to the sector. The roundtable resulted in several agreements on production quotas, preplanting announcement of cotton prices,

---

10. Although farmer organizations play an active and similar role in the cotton value chain in other cotton-producing countries of West Africa, particularly Benin and Burkina Faso, their involvement is arguably less political than that of their Malian counterparts.

farmer organization participation in cotton grading, and access to animal feed. The participants also approved the creation of a representative, legally binding farmers' organization that would become party to all "relevant CMDT decision-making units" (Bingen, Dembélé, and Camey 1995). This organization eventually became the Union of Cotton and Food Crop Producers (SYCOV).

FARMER INVOLVEMENT IN INPUT DELIVERY AND CREDIT REPAYMENT. The increasingly successful involvement of farmer associations in credit management and input distribution built on earlier systems developed by the CFDT and CMDT for managing the distribution of inputs and credit provided by the Malian banking system. Credit has been essential to the cotton companies' goal of promoting the adoption of technologies needed to improve productivity and increase the supply of seed cotton. By tying credit to the delivery of seed cotton at harvest, the interlocked credit, input, and output markets that are tied to the CFDT/CMDT's monopsony provided a direct way for banks to be reimbursed by farmers for input and equipment loans.

Due to the CFDT/CMDT's strict credit discipline, their outstanding solvency record, and the strategic importance of cotton in Mali, the sector has always received priority access to banking system credit. The lower risks created by a reliable output market, annually fixed seed cotton prices, and improved input productivity helped increase farmers' demand for inputs and credit. For most Malian farmers, cotton production has provided the primary vehicle for accessing farm input credit.

The CMDT's policy of prohibiting new input deliveries to farmers with unpaid credit (except in cases of crop failure) resulted in high loan repayment rates. Between 1980 and 1988, repayment rates on cotton loans never fell below 90 percent. And in 1987 and 1988, with the increasing involvement of farmers' associations in credit management, they reached over 97 percent (Dioné 1989).

Based on the principle of group solidarity with joint liability to guarantee loan repayment, farmer association revenues served as collateral to guarantee credit reimbursement. Because farmer associations were well positioned to determine the potential production capacity of individual farmers and to collectively bear the risk of sponsoring more households, they were able to guarantee formal credit to individual small farm households that otherwise would not have been eligible for loans. Village-based farmer organizations were also able to obtain bank credit for hunger relief and collective cereal marketing activities in their villages (Dioné 1989; Deveze 1994).

Cereal Production by Cotton Farmers

Contrary to popular fears that cash crops might have a negative effect on food crop production and household food security, cotton production has proven a boon to coarse grain production in Mali. Although the levels of cereal production for the country as a whole have varied widely since the 1960s, per capita coarse grain production has remained consistently highest in the cotton zone for a variety of reasons (Table 4.4).

Cotton-financed fertilizer and animal traction equipment permit area expansion as well as yield gains among cereal-growing cotton farmers. Indeed, Mali's cotton farmers traditionally cultivate cotton in rotation with coarse grains, particularly maize and sorghum. Unlike coarse grain produced outside the cotton zone, cereals grown by cotton farmers benefit from greater access to fertilizer as well as the residual effect of cotton fertilizers procured and financed through the cotton-based input credit system. Cereal fields also benefit from improved farming practices made possible through the use of animal traction equipment financed by cotton income. As a result, farmers equipped with animal traction equipment obtain higher yields in both cotton and coarse grains than the semiequipped and manual producers (Dioné 1989; Raymond and Fok 1994; Kébé, Diakité, and Diawara 1998). Well-equipped cotton farmers likewise prove best able to satisfy the demanding husbandry requirements of maize production, including timely planting and regular weeding (Boughton and de Frahan 1994). Extension support in the CMDT zones also contributed to higher cereal production, most notably by promoting access to early-maturing, disease-resistant maize varieties in the 1970s and 1980s. Although the total area planted to maize in the CMDT zone grew from 6,000 hectares in 1975 to 51,000 hectares in 1987, maize yields rose during the 1980s to 1.6 tons per hectare in 1985, double their 1960 level (Dioné 1989).

As a result, cotton farmers produce more coarse grain per capita than do non–cotton producers. During the late 1990s, per capita cereal production averaged roughly 70 percent higher in the cotton zone than in the surrounding regions (see Table 4.4). Similarly, in 1985/86 and 1986/87, a study of farmers in the CMDT zone found that cotton farmers produced two to three times more cereal per capita than did farmers outside the zone. Regression analysis estimated that a 10 percent increase in per capita cotton area was associated with a 12–13 percent increase in net coarse grain availability per capita (Dioné 1989).

TABLE 4.4 Cereal production, by zone, 1998 (kilograms per person per year)

Region	Regional average	CMDT (Compagnie Malienne pour le Développement des Textiles) zone
Kayes/Kita	133	223
Koulikoro/Fana	225	407
Sikasso	311.	241–454
Segou	306	132–314
National	184	314

SOURCES: CMDT (1999); DNSI (1999).

Cotton farmers tend to sell more grain to the markets, in part because of their access to animal traction and their consequently higher per capita production. In 1986/87, farmers owning animal traction equipment accounted for 67 percent of grain sales in the CMDT zone, with half of total grain sales coming from 6 percent of the farms (Dioné 1989). Because cotton farmers receive payment for their cotton crop at harvest time, they are able to meet their immediate cash needs (for school fees, taxes, and social functions), and they can time their cereal sales later in the cropping year, when prices are most favorable. The CMDT's construction and maintenance of regional feeder roads not only facilitates the collection and transport of seed cotton but simultaneously benefits food crop marketing by helping to lower marketing costs and enabling better integration of markets in the zone.

Coping with Price Variability and Cost Inflation

In the mid-1980s, the world price of cotton lint dropped precipitously following a structural shift in the United States' cotton support policy and China's move from net importer to the world's largest exporter (MacDonald 1997; Baffes 2004). The average market year price (Cotlook Index A) fell 21 percent between 1983/84 and 1984/85 and a further 29 percent in 1985/86 (ICAC 1996). With the sales price of cotton lint hitting a 30-year low in 1985/86 (49 cents per pound or 375 CFAF per kilogram) and the sector's total delivered unit cost of cotton fiber production averaging 505 CFAF per kilogram, the CMDT lost approximately 130 CFAF on every kilogram of cotton fiber.

Abruptly falling world prices and the resultant large losses at the CMDT provoked a series of major crises that revealed the growing frailty of the cotton sector. Financial and management audits at the CMDT exposed excessive costs arising from waste, overcharging, duplication of responsibilities, inadequate financial management, and a lack of incentives to control costs (Coopération Française 1991). These audits triggered discussions among the CMDT, the CFDT, and the Malian and French governments centering on several related issues: (1) the lack of management and financial rigor at CMDT, including a lack of cost-control incentives in the negotiated cost structure (*baremes*) needed to curb cost inflation; (2) the high cost of supporting cotton production in low-productivity or marginal areas; (3) a lack of commercial dynamism and less than optimal sales prices for cotton lint; and (4) the implications of financing the growing cost of CMDT rural development activities from the cotton budget. Largely ignored during periods of high world cotton prices, many of the cost-related issues that emerged during market downturns were intimately related to the structure of the CMDT-controlled cotton sector. Given recurring world price fluctuations, these issues continued to resurface over the next 20 years.

In 1985/86, several donors required the CMDT and the Malian government to undertake legal and economic reforms and cost-saving measures designed to restore financial viability as a condition for financing the CMDT's deficit of 9 billion CFAF. These actions included more rigorous financial management, subcontracting part of seed cotton and lint transport to the private sector, and giving CMDT direct control of lint exports by replacing the Société Malienne d'Import et d'Export, the state import-export agency. Perhaps most important for Mali's cotton producers, the CMDT modified farmers' incentive structure by freezing producer prices at 85 CFAF per kilogram and reducing input subsidies.[11] As a result, farmers' share of input costs increased from 75 to 94 percent of the actual unit cost (Coopération Française 1991). These initial cost-saving measures helped reduce Mali's total delivered unit cost of lint by 14 percent, to approximately 435 CFAF per kilogram, thereby allowing the CMDT to break even in the following two growing seasons (Coopération Française 1991).

In 1989, with an eye to further increasing sector efficiency and productivity, the CMDT and the Malian government signed a five-year performance agreement or "*contrat plan.*" In addition to separating the cotton-related production and marketing functions from the public service and rural development activities, this agreement included the following reform measures: (1) production and marketing quotas to maximize existing gin capacity, (2) price incentives to help meet the quotas, (3) a stabilization fund to maintain price incentives, and (4) a system for sector profit sharing with farmers.[12] Farmers, although not signatories to the agreement, were represented on the CMDT's board of directors.

The application of production quotas to limit cotton production during market downturns was not a new phenomenon; the sector had always operated as a meticulously planned supply chain. With available ginning capacity determining desired production levels, the CMDT planned every function in the vertically integrated supply chain a year in advance. Each season, the CMDT worked with farmer organizations to project the quantity of inputs needed for the upcoming planting season. They estimated the inputs needed for the planned number of hectares, which—at the expected yield—would result in a given quantity of seed cotton that could be collected, ginned, and baled before the start of the following rainy season. These figures determined farmers' input needs and dictated the volume and timing of their purchase, import, and delivery. The CMDT delivered inputs to villages in trucks designated for collecting seed cotton, thereby reducing transport costs and ensuring that farmers received inputs well in advance of the next planting season.

The brief respite provided by the *contrat plan,* however, did not last long. In 1992–93, world prices fell abruptly once again, at a time when the over-

---

11. The CMDT's 1986/87 producer price, 85 CFAF per kilogram, or 218 CFAF/kilogram in fiber equivalent, was the lowest level in the CFA zone, where the average fiber-equivalent price was 270 CFAF per kilogram.

12. The CMDT changed from a parastatal agency to a semipublic, limited-liability, industrial corporation (*société anonyme à caractère industriel*).

valuation of the CFAF had eroded the competitive position of the Malian cotton sector. As in previous crises, the CMDT depended heavily on financial support from the Malian and French governments, the European Union, and the World Bank to cover their losses (Bocchino 1999). Government and donors supplied deficit financing during these market downturns, knowing they could recuperate loans when world prices rose and the sector became profitable (Dorey 1999), as was the case after the 1994 CFAF devaluation.

Through the mid-1980s, most major stakeholders—the Malian and French governments, farmers, the CMDT/CFDT, and the World Bank—agreed that cotton could finance Mali's rural development. But when the financial crises that began in the second half of the 1980s forced a series of operational and financial reforms, this consensus began to unravel as the different actors sought to preserve their claims on a reduced pool of cotton sector profits (Deveze 1994). The growing power of the emergent farmers' movement and the "unprecedented political visibility" arising from the 1991 farmer strike and the subsequent establishment and growing role of the SYCOV were important factors contributing to this change (Bingen, Dembélé, and Camey 1995).

Sources of Growth

YIELD GROWTH.   Between 1974 and 1993, cotton yields increased at a 2.1 percent annual rate, considerably lower than the 15 percent annual yield growth during the first 15 years. By the late 1980s, average seed cotton yields averaged over 1,300 kilograms per hectare (546 kilograms per hectare of cotton lint), a cumulative increase of over 600 percent since independence.

This yield growth was driven by the combined efforts of the cotton sector's research and extension systems in maintaining the flow and adoption of improved technology. Three of the main factors contributing to Mali's yield growth included the widespread application of pesticides, fertilizer use, and continual improvements in seed varieties, with each factor accounting for approximately one-third of yield growth. Other indirect factors, such as growing access to animal traction and farmers' knowledge of the cropping calendar, including seeding dates, along with weeding and understanding of optimal planting density, allowed farmers to maximize the benefits of these technologies (Follin and Deat 1999).

By 1991, productivity growth appeared to hit a peak, after which yields began falling (Figure 4.6). Numerous factors contributed to this drop in farmer yields, including the genetic potential of existing seed varieties and growing pesticide resistance (Follin and Deat 1999). Although many people point to the deteriorating producer incentives (input and output prices) as determining factors influencing farmer decisionmaking and subsequently the decline in yields, the steady fall in the input-output ratio since the early 1990s would suggest that incentives have been improving (Figure 4.7). However, between 1950 and 2000, annual rainfall levels have exhibited a statistically significant downward

FIGURE 4.6 Trends in seed cotton yields in Mali, 1961–2006

SOURCE: CMDT (Compagnie Malienne pour le Développement des Textiles) database.

FIGURE 4.7 Input-output price ratios among Malian cotton farmers, 1980–2008

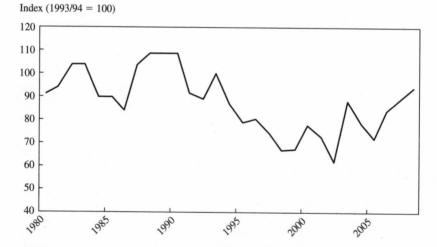

SOURCE: CMDT (Compagnie Malienne pour le Développement des Textiles) database.

trend, declining annually by 6 millimeters in southern Mali (Sikasso), possibly contributing to the plateauing of cotton yields.

FARMER INCENTIVES.   The CFDT and CMDT understood early on that the successful development of cotton production in Mali would require a positive incentive environment to guarantee farmers' commitment to growing cotton.

Their strategy, therefore, aimed to establish a productive relationship with farmers that would reward them for their membership in the "cotton club" (Deveze 1994). Cotton farmers' production decisions and cropping practices are strongly influenced by their concern for meeting their families' food needs and maintaining a certain standard of living while at the same time reducing risk (Tefft et al. 1998). Access to credit for inputs and equipment and a guaranteed market in which to sell their seed cotton at fixed prices have been major incentives for farmers to grow cotton, benefiting both cotton and food crop production.

In the mid-1980s, input costs relative to seed cotton output prices increased by 20 percent (see Figure 4.7). By lowering farmer incentives to use inputs, the rising input costs relative to output prices contributed to farmers' preference for extensification strategies over intensification efforts. Stagnant output prices and reduced profitability also placed a brake on the adoption of innovative new techniques, including equipment use, the use of cover crops, animal fattening, and the purchase of carts for manure transport and application.

GINNING PERFORMANCE.   Over the CMDT's first two decades of operation, the company's ginning outturn ratio advanced annually by 0.6 percent. This modest rate, however, masks important advances in cotton varietal breeding. In 1987, the CMDT began distribution of the ISA 205 variety, which eventually displaced B163 as the sector's main seed cotton variety in 1989/90. Ginning yields jumped immediately and averaged 42 percent over the next five years, a 9 percent rise from the 38.6 percent level recorded during the preceding seven years. These rates are among the highest in the world (Dembélé 1996).

Although average seed cotton yields for the two varieties remained constant, with B163 averaging 1,282 kilograms per hectare and ISA 205 averaging 1,274 kilograms per hectare, the higher ginning ratio of ISA 205 translated into higher profits for the CMDT. The 3.5 percent higher ginning ratio achieved with ISA 205 translated into increased lint production of 47,000 tons relative to the quantity of fiber that would have been produced by B163. When valued at the existing sales prices over the five-year period in which ISA 205 was used, this quantity amounts to an estimated gain of US$72 million, a 9 percent rise from what would have been earned had the CMDT continued to distribute the B163 variety (Dembélé 1996).

PRODUCTION GROWTH.   Despite the improvements in agronomic and ginning yields, the 7.7 percent annual growth in seed cotton production during this period was driven primarily by a 5.5 percent annual expansion in area planted. This represents a significant slowdown compared to the 20 percent annual production increases during the first phase of postindependence growth, when price incentives remained high (see Table 4.2).

During this consolidation and reorganizational phase, the sector's performance continued to be strongly affected by world market price variability, rising production costs, and the subsequent effect on farmer incentives. In the next phase of Mali's cotton development, a radical improvement in farmer incentives proved decisive in restoring rapid growth in cotton production and exports.

Phase 3: Devaluation, 1994–98

The 50 percent devaluation of the CFAF was a monumental event in franco-phone Africa. Since 1947, the CFAF had remained fixed at the exchange rate of 50 to 1 vis-à-vis the French franc. The January 1994 devaluation of the CFAF aimed to reduce francophone West Africa's heavy dependence on imports, stimulate export production and import substitution, and shift consumer demand toward more locally produced goods and services. The ultimate goal was to stimulate self-sustaining, broad-based economic growth (Dibley, Reardon, and Staatz 1996; Tefft, Staatz, and Dioné 1997). This section examines the impact of the devaluation on cotton sector performance in price transmission, farmer responses, and aggregate sector performance.

Price Transmission

The impact of the devaluation on Mali's cotton sector was immediate. Overnight, the CFAF sales price of cotton lint doubled, from 450 to 900 CFAF per kilogram of cotton lint. The devaluation coincided with a large upturn in world market prices, a 60 percent rise between 1993 and 1995, which together resulted in a 189 percent nominal increase in the CFA price of cotton fiber.

The transmission of this price increase to farmers, however, took place only slowly, over a period of years. Even though the CMDT realized a 463 CFAF net rise in the sales price per kilogram of cotton lint in 1994, given the rigidities in the producer price-setting formula, farmers received an increase of only 30 CFAF per kilogram of seed cotton.[13] And they received this price increment only after the seed cotton harvest of 1994/95, in 1995, a year and a half after the devaluation.

Over the next five years, the CMDT gradually raised the nominal base producer price for seed cotton by 65 percent, from 85 to 140 CFAF per kilogram, or 39 percent in real terms. When the farmers' share of sector profits (*ristourne*) is included, the total nominal producer prices increased 100 percent between 1993/94 and 1998/99. Although the long lag in transmitting the price increase to farmers resulted in a large decline in farmers' share of the world market price, to below 30 percent in 1993/94, the subsequent producer price rises and world market price pullback contributed to a gradual increase of their share to 58 percent in 1998/99 (see Figure 4.3).

The price of imported inputs also rose. In the first five years after the devaluation, input prices increased cumulatively by 35 percent, considerably lower than the overall inflation rate of 54 percent. The cost of fertilizer rose 65 percent during this period, but the nominal cost increase of the entire cotton input package was moderated by a change in the type and quantity of pesticides

---

13. This increment, the fiber equivalent of 12.5 CFAF per kilogram of seed cotton, represents the farmers' share of sector profits earned during the 1993/94 marketing year.

used by farmers. This generated downward pressure on the cost of farm inputs relative to the price of seed cotton. As a result, the input-output price ratio fell by 33 percent, thereby improving production incentives (see Figure 4.7). Farmers responded rapidly to these improved incentives.

The First Response to Devaluation: Extensification

Higher farm-level prices spurred large increases in the production of seed cotton and in the quantity of cotton ginned. Between 1994 and 1998, production grew annually by 20 percent. In the first four years after the devaluation, seed cotton and lint production increased 118 percent, tracking a similar trend witnessed throughout the region. The consequent increase in cotton lint exports quickly pushed francophone Africa's share of the world market from 8.8 percent in 1991/92 to 15 percent in 1997/98.

This expansion occurred primarily through increases in area cultivated. Over the entire cotton sector, the acreage planted in cotton grew annually by 22 percent between 1994 and 1998. Among cotton farmers, the CMDT observed that farmers had expanded the area planted in cotton by 85 percent and the area in coarse grains by 29 percent, resulting in a 45 percent average increase in total area cultivated among cotton farm households (Table 4.5). By 1998, the average cotton farm in the CMDT zone planted 2.4 hectares in seed cotton and 4.4 hectares in cereals, with a total planted area of 8 hectares (CMDT 1998).

Most farmers increased the acreage they cultivated by reducing fallow periods and clearing new land, with the latter behavior predominant in the relatively newer production zones (Diakité, Kébé, and Djouara 1996; Giraudy 1996b; CMDT 1999). The CMDT monitoring division observed that farmers began replacing the traditional 5- to 7-year fallow period on half of their holdings with almost continuous cropping while leaving the other half of their acreage in a 10- to 13-year fallow system (Giraudy 1999).[14]

The growing availability and use of animal traction equipment facilitated the rapid increase in total area planted (Table 4.6).[15] After the devaluation, the number of equipped and semiequipped farms (Types B and C) increased, respectively, by 6 percent and 11 percent, while the number of manual or nonequipped farms declined by 23 percent (CMDT 1998).

The CMDT's decision to open production in the Kita district in western Mali contributed to the large increase in area cultivated. With the addition of approximately 15,000 farm households beginning cotton production, the total

---

14. Kébé and Brons (1994) point out that in Mali's traditional cotton basin, with its growing demographic pressure from both human and animal populations, many farmers have begun putting fallow land into production out of fear of losing their customary rights to a given parcel.

15. The inability to replace aging equipment has resulted in a growing percentage of older, lower-performance equipment. This reduction in equipment quality is due to a number of factors, including a lack of income due to falling profitability for many farms and changes in equipment provisioning programs (Kébé, Diakité, and Diawara 1998).

TABLE 4.5 Change in area planted by Malian cotton producers

	1993/94	1997/98	Percent change
Cotton area planted (ha/household)	1.3	2.4	85
Cereal area planted (ha/ household)	3.4	4.4	29
Total farm size (ha/household)	5.5	8	45
Cotton as a percentage of total area	23	30	30
Cereal as a percentage of total area	61	55	−10
Average farm household size	12.7	15.1	19

SOURCES: Giraudy and Niang (1996); Doucouré and Healy (1999).

TABLE 4.6 Evolution of farm equipment levels and land holdings among Malian cotton farmers

	1985	1993	1998
Number of farms	93,000	135,000	182,000
Share of farms (percent), by equipment level			
Type A	46	30	30
Type B	0	42	44
Type C	32	13	14
Type D	22	15	12
Number of draft oxen	—	347,022	493,447
Number of plows	—	123,746	198,035
Cotton area cultivated (ha/farm)			
Type A	—	3.3	4.3
Type B	—	1.8	2.8
Type C	—	0.8	1.2
Type D	—	0.7	1.4

SOURCES: Dioné (1989); Giraudy and Niang (1996); Kébé, Diakité, and Diawara (1998).

NOTES: —, data not available. The 1985 results classify farms as follows: equipped farms own a plow, weeding and transportation equipment, and animals; semiequipped farms lack part of the draft equipment and/or animals; and nonequipped farms own no draft equipment (Dioné 1989). Since the early 1980s, the CMDT (Compagnie Malienne pour le Développement des Textiles) has stratified farm households into four groups based on the following: Type A—own at least two traction teams (a team consists of two oxen and a plow or multicultvateur) and at least six head of cattle; Type B—own 1 traction team without any cattle; Type C—own an incomplete traction team with animal traction experience; Type D—a nonequipped farm with no animal traction experience (Kébé, Diakité, and Diawara 1998).

number of cotton households increased substantially. Despite this massive influx, the CMDT successfully integrated the new farmers into their production support system. In 1998, 93 percent of the farm households in the CMDT zone grew cotton and benefited from the organization's services, up from 84 percent in 1993. By 2000, over 200,000 farm households grew cotton in Mali, a 50 percent increase compared to 1993.

It is important to underline that the supply response after the devaluation was made possible by the improved industry profitability that convinced the CMDT to invest in increased ginning capacity. The construction of 4 new cotton gins and upgrades to existing gins (a total of 17 gins with a capacity of approximately 600,000 tons) subsequently allowed the CMDT to lift strict production quotas and unleash farmers' pent-up demand for expanding cotton production.

The large supply response was not limited to cotton. The average per capita cereal production of CMDT farm households increased cumulatively by 14 percent in the four years following the devaluation, reaching 314 kilograms per capita in 1998 (see Table 4.4).

Yield Growth and Input Levels

Although the area planted increased substantially, average seed cotton yields continued their downward slide between 1994 and 1998, dropping 10 percent during the period. Average maize yields, in contrast, increased annually by 5 percent over these four years. With an improved incentive environment after devaluation, the percentage of cotton and maize acreage receiving inputs increased from 32 to 43 percent between 1994/95 and 1997/98. Although 98 percent of cotton fields received some fertilizer before and after the devaluation, the percentage of maize fields receiving fertilizer increased from 50 to 67 percent (Doucouré and Healy 1999). Farm level surveys show relatively little change in the quantity of NPK fertilizer applied to cotton fields between 1993 and 1998, with levels remaining at 75 percent of the CMDT-recommended quantity (CMDT 1998; Kébé, Diakité, and H. Diawara 1998). Urea fertilizer use on cotton fields increased by 15 percent after the devaluation, with average quantities slightly higher than the CMDT's recommendation of 50 kilograms per hectare (Kébé, Diakité, and Diawara 1998).

The total number of maize and cotton fields receiving manure increased from 22 to 29 percent after the devaluation. Cotton farmers also increased the quantity of manure applied to their cotton fields by 20–100 percent, with rates varying by zone and farms' equipment level (Doucouré and Healy 1999). Even so, the levels still remained at half of the recommended dosage of 5 tons per hectare. Greater use of manure was made possible partly by an increase in the total number of carts owned by cotton farmers (an 11 percent increase between 1993/94 and 1997/98) as well as the increased manure production spurred by cotton farmers' increased investment in cattle.

Pesticide use also rose following the devaluation. Mali's cotton farmers increased the pesticide quantities used from 3.6 liters per hectare in 1994/95 to 7.5 liters per hectare in 1998.[16] In addition to the doubling of insecticide use, the concentration of pyrethroids in the cotton insecticide formulations increased by 20 percent (Ajayi et al. 2002).

---

16. This takes account of the switch in 1994 from ULV formulations to emulsifiable concentrates.

The Impact on Farmer Incentives

The profitability of cotton farming increased after the devaluation of the CFAF. Between 1992/93 and 1997/98, nominal returns in CFAF more than doubled, while real returns to family labor increased by about 70 percent for both non-equipped and equipped farmers. These results are understandably sensitive to the methods used to estimate production costs and farm income, particularly the number of family labor days required. Using high-end estimates of 203 and 162 days of family labor per hectare, respectively, for nonequipped and equipped farms, it is important to note that 1997/98 returns of 516 and 677 CFAF are less than the 750 CFAF opportunity cost of family labor (Table 4.7).[17] However, under middle- to low-range estimates of labor use, animal traction cotton farming consistently generated returns to labor in excess of the 750 CFAF opportunity cost of labor after the devaluation. For hand-hoe cotton farmers, returns to labor remained below the opportunity cost of labor under all but the lowest estimate of family labor requirements. On average, animal traction cotton farming proves more profitable, generating returns to labor 50 percent higher than under hand-hoe farming.

For certain groups of Malian farmers, postdevaluation surveys suggest that maize and lowland rice are more profitable than cotton. Returns to labor in cotton production exceed those in maize for only the most mechanized farmers, those with at least two complete animal traction teams (Kébé, Diakité, and Diawara 1998; Doucouré and Healy 1999). For semiequipped and nonequipped farms, returns to maize are equal or superior to those for cotton. Similar research in the cotton zone in 1995/96 found that lowland valley (*bas-fonds*) rice production generated significantly higher returns per day of family labor than maize, sorghum/millet, and especially cotton (Dimithe et al. 2000).

Consumption and Indebtedness

Expenditure surveys conducted after the devaluation showed that farms reporting higher incomes generally spent cotton revenues on consumer goods such as radios, televisions, cement and roofing for houses, bicycles, motorcycles, sewing machines, and generators (Kébé, Diakité, and Diawara 1998). Between 1996 and 1998, many farmers also took advantage of less-than-rigorous banking practices and internal management procedures within village associations to gain access to bank loans to finance consumer purchases. These practices led to overleveraged farmer associations that, under the principle of joint liability, or *caution solidaire,* had to assume the unpaid debt of their members (Kébé and Kébé-Sidibé 1997; de la Croix 2001).

---

17. The high-end estimates of 203 person-days of family labor for nonequipped farms and 162 days for equipped farms come from studies by IER's Sikasso farming system research unit in 1989 and are similar to 1975 figures from Côte d'Ivoire (Peltre-Wurtz and Steck 1979, cited in Pieri 1989; Dimithe et al. 2000). A range of other labor estimates, from 2003, comes from cotton farmer associations, a later IER study, and the CMDT (MAEP 2003).

TABLE 4.7 Costs and returns to cotton production in Mali

Item	Nonequipped farm (CMDT Type D)		Equipped farm (CMDT Type B)				
	1992/93	1997/98	1991/92	1997/98	2002/03	2003/04	
Yield minus estimated losses (kg/ha)	932	906	1,083	1,030	824	1,080	
Cotton price (CFAF/kg)	85	170	85	170	180	180	
Variable costs (CFAF/ha)	33,545	42,836	36,165	48,524	63,660	90,950	
Hired laborers	5,000	6,500	5,000	6,500	17,000	0	
Fixed costs (CFAF/ha)	0	0	20,595	10,331	39,802	31,938	
Net returns (CFAF/ha)	40,675	104,684	40,495	109,745	27,858	71,512	
Total production costs (CFAF/kg), excluding family labor	37	49	51	57	132	102	
Incorporating labor into the analysis							
Family labor requirements (days/ha)							
High estimate (IER, 1989)	203	203	162	162	162	162	
Middle estimate (cotton farmer groups)	191	191	134	134	134	134	
Low estimate (IER, 2003)	151	151	106	106	106	106	
Lowest labor estimate (CMDT)	113	113	79	79	79	79	

(continued)

TABLE 4.7 Continued

Item	Nonequipped farm (CMDT Type D)		Equipped farm (CMDT Type B)			
	1992/93	1997/98	1991/92	1997/98	2002/03	2003/04
Returns to family labor (CFAF/day)						
High labor estimate	200	516	250	677	172	441
Middle labor estimate	213	548	302	819	208	534
Low labor estimate	269	693	382	1,035	263	675
Lowest labor estimate	360	928	513	1,389	353	905
Opportunity cost of family labor (CFAF/day)	500	750	500	750	825	1,000
Returns in U.S. dollars (constant 2005 US$)						
Exchange rate (CFAF/US$)	276	602	259	602	625	522
Net returns per hectare (US$/ha)	148	174	156	182	45	137
Returns to family labor (US$/day)						
High labor estimate	0.98	1.03	1.34	1.35	0.29	0.87
Middle labor estimate	1.04	1.09	1.62	1.63	0.35	1.06
Low labor estimate	1.32	1.38	2.05	2.06	0.45	1.34
Lowest labor estimate	1.77	1.85	2.75	2.76	0.60	1.79

SOURCES: Constructed using Giraudy and Niang (1994, 1996); Giraudy et al. (1994a,b); Giraudy (1996a); Kébé, Diakité, and Diawara (1998); Doucouré and Healy (1999); Dimithe et al. (2000); MAEP (2003).

NOTES: CFAF, Communauté Financière Africaine (CFA) francs; CMDT, Compagnie Malienne pour le Développement des Textiles; IER, Institut d'Économie Rurale. Farm budgets from the two IER studies, in 1989 and 2003, are available in Dimithe et al. (2000) and MAEP (2003), respectively.

Malian banks have generally used farmer organization bank accounts and their future stream of communally earned cotton revenues (*caution solidaire*) as the collateral to grant consumers loans (Fournier, Ichanju, and Lapenu 2002). Banks have, however, focused on the creditworthiness of the AV as a whole, with little consideration for the individual members' solvency. In many AVs, the total value of the groups' loans soon reached 60 percent of the value of cotton revenues, double the 33 percent threshold traditionally used by banks and AVs (de la Croix 2001). The high level of AV indebtedness and the tension created by these practices within the AVs led to reimbursement problems and internal social divisions within farmer associations that often led to their breaking up into smaller units.

This relatively recent problem of AV indebtedness should not detract from the positive role that village associations (farmer organizations) have played in the cotton zone. The investment of revenues earned from marketing and seed cotton assembly fees has generated a large impact in the cotton sector, perhaps most importantly in providing social infrastructure, such as new schools and community health centers. The cotton funds have enabled villages in the cotton zone to successfully participate in the government's push to increase schooling rates and improve access to medical care.

Phase 4: Growing Pains, 1999–2006

Mali's cotton sector has been many things to its various stakeholders. It provides an important source of fiscal revenues and export earnings as well as a development platform for the Malian government. As Mali's largest employer, it has provided highly sought-after and well-paid jobs. Cotton provides raw material for the small but influential textile and cottonseed industries producing vegetable oil, soap, and animal feed. The French government, as a minority shareholder in the CMDT and as the most important bilateral development partner, holds diverse financial and political interests in the sector. For farmers and farmer organizations, the income and access to resources provided by growing cotton have contributed to the capitalization of the rural economy and improved rural livelihoods. Although the interests of these various actors have occasionally conflicted over the past four and a half decades, it is important to note that they have more or less shared a common goal of maintaining the status quo, that is, the CMDT-controlled, integrated sector.

In the first half of the 2000s, however, this consensus has increasingly eroded as the sector has faced two major shocks: (1) rapid cost inflation, corporate mismanagement, and the resulting farmer boycott in 2000/01 and (2) the huge downturn in international prices in 2001/02 and subsequent government actions aimed at reducing the deleterious effects of international cotton subsidies on African producers. This section examines these events, the responses of different actors, and their implications for the performance of Mali's largest employer.

Cost Inflation and Mismanagement

Surveys of the comparative cost of production have shown that Malian farmers (along with their West African neighbors in the other producing countries) are among the lowest-cost cotton producers in the world (ICAC 2001). In part, this efficiency at the farm level has compensated for the inefficiencies and high cost of overall CMDT management.

The inflationary effects of the CFAF devaluation placed further pressure on CMDT's already bloated cost structure by increasing ginning costs. The average total delivered unit cost of producing cotton increased from 384 CFAF per kilogram in 1992/93 to 670 CFAF per kilogram in 1996/97, a 17 percent increase in real terms.[18] While the seed cotton purchase cost (that is, the producer price) dropped 1 percent in real terms, the "non–seed cotton costs to gin"— which include CMDT assembly, marketing, extension, roads, and overhead costs —rose 57 percent in real terms.

Within the postfarm segment of the supply chain, the costs of the CMDT's overhead and "public" development activity grew, respectively, by 30 percent and 94 percent (Waddell 1997). Between 1994/95 and 1996/97, an audit revealed that overhead costs had jumped 112 percent in two years, a large increase compared to the 17 percent rise in total unit cost (Waddell 1997; SEC-Diarra/ BAC+ 1998). Among the many expenditures that contribute to higher overhead costs, the average CMDT employee salary increased over 82 percent in real terms between 1993/94 and 1997/98 compared to a 3 percent real fall in government civil servants' wages (Tefft, Staatz, and Dioné 1997; SEC-Diarra/ BAC+ 1998). Budget audits also revealed numerous instances in which CMDT-operated functions, compared with comparable private sector services, significantly inflated the CMDT cost structure. For example, the CMDT outsourced only 20 percent of its transport operations to the private sector, even though private transport rates are half the cost of the CMDT's truck fleet. Likewise, CMDT cotton gins powered by CMDT generators are two times as costly as those powered by the Malian energy company.

More alarming still, the audits discovered gross mismanagement, fraud, and embezzlement in the CMDT (Waddell 1997, 1998; SEC-Diarra/BAC+ 1998). Coming at a period when the Malian government was making a concerted effort to reduce public sector corruption, the audit and subsequent investigation eventually led to the arrest and prosecution of numerous senior CMDT officials. Interviews with private sector partners of the CMDT undertaken in the context of an anticorruption campaign exposed a widespread belief that the CMDT was one of the most corrupt organizations in Mali. The minimal use of subcontracting, tenders, and auctions for the majority of its procure-

---

18. These include all costs required to produce, gin, and transport 1 kilogram of cotton to a European port. Costs are based on CIF prices in Rotterdam.

ment contracts provided vast opportunities for rent seeking while at the same time raising operating costs, generally to the disadvantage of farmers (Banque Mondiale 2002a). In addition to the heavy cost pressure arising from mismanagement and inefficient operation of critical industry functions, the CMDT faced tremendous financial pressure arising from its decision to invest in the construction of four new cotton gins.

The Financial Crisis at CMDT

In the four years following the devaluation, the total cost of producing, ginning, and exporting 1 kilogram of cotton lint had risen 94 percent, reaching 743 CFAF in 1998/99. Then, in the late 1990s, world prices turned unfavorable as the Asian economies entered a recession. After reaching a peak of 1,264 CFAF per kilogram in May 1995 and remaining above 900 CFAF per kilogram in the following three years, the average annual marketing year price of cotton lint fell 25 percent between 1997/98 and 1998/99, to 766 CFAF per kilogram.[19] This decline resulted from excess world production, weak Asian demand during the 1997 financial crisis, low synthetic fiber prices, and a stronger U.S. dollar (Baffes 2004).

The combined effect of high cost inflation and lower world prices placed unbearable pressure on CMDT profits (Figure 4.8). At the end of 1999, only five years after the devaluation, Mali's cotton sector confronted a major financial crisis. In five years, gross sales revenues had increased 365 percent, from 43 billion CFAF in 1992/93 to over 200 billion CFAF in 1997/98 and 1998/99. Yet by the end of the 1999/2000 period, the CMDT had generated cumulative losses totaling 58 billion CFAF (over US$100 million) (Banque Mondiale 2002b).

Despite these severe financial constraints, at the start of the 1999/2000 marketing year, the CMDT and the farmers' union (the SYCOV) agreed that farmers would receive a base price of 150 CFAF per kilogram plus a profit rebate of 35 CFAF per kilogram, essentially the same terms as the 1998/99 season. However, at harvest time the CMDT reneged on this agreement and paid farmers only 155 CFAF per kilogram (145 base price + 10 profit-sharing CFAF per kilogram). This lower payout created major financial problems for many village associations in paying farmers and reimbursing the costs of inputs. Long delays in collecting and paying farmers for seed cotton further soured relations between farmers and the CMDT. Compounding this tension, the reserve of 18 billion CFAF (US$36 million) that had built up in the years following the devaluation "disappeared" (Ministère du Développement Rural 2000; Sinaba 2000; Banque Mondiale 2002b).

---

19. This price represents the average price of the Cotlook Index A over the 12-month marketing year of August to July. The actual sales price depends on the timing of the sales and use of forward contracts.

FIGURE 4.8 Estimated total unit cost of cotton fiber production in Mali, 1986–2002

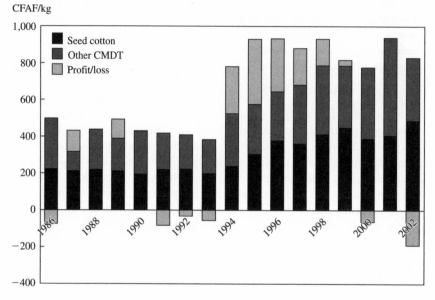

CFAF/kg

SOURCES: CMDT (Compagnie Malienne pour le Développement des Textiles) database; IMF (2001).
NOTE: CFAF, Communauté Financière Africaine franc.

The Farmer Boycott of 2000/01

In previous crisis periods, Malian cotton producers, the least powerful of the sector stakeholders, often had little choice but to accept the conditions and share of the pie offered to them. But by 1999, after almost a decade of increasing involvement in sector management, farmers had become increasingly knowledgeable about CMDT operations and consequently about the prevalence of rent-seeking activity within the cotton company. As a result, the farmers were prepared to act.

When the CMDT announced a price of 160 CFAF per kilogram for the 2000/01 growing season, the farmers' union called a boycott (Grain de sel 2000; Ministère du Développement Rural et de l'Environnement 2002).[20] When a large number of cotton farmers refused to plant cotton, the total area planted dropped 53 percent, from 482,000 hectares in 1999/2000 to 228,000 hectares in 2000/01, resulting in a 47 percent fall in seed cotton production, from 460,000 to 245,000 tons.

---

20. The price was eventually increased to 170 CFAF per kilogram.

The resulting CMDT losses were enormous. During a period of high international prices and an appreciating dollar, Mali's cotton sector lost at least 20 billion CFAF (US$29 million) in potential revenues.

Farmer Incentives

Mali's cotton farmers shared in the pain. Between 1997/98 and 2002/03, real returns to family labor for equipped farms declined by 77 percent.[21] Falling yields lowered revenue, while increased input prices in 2002/03, following the removal of the fertilizer subsidies, contributed to a large increase in variable costs (HORUS Enterprises 2003). The following season, 2003/04, real returns to family labor rebounded, though they remained 50 percent below the real, postdevaluation level. Indeed, under all estimates of labor input requirements, the returns to family labor under animal traction cotton farming remained below its opportunity cost in 2003/04 (see Table 4.7).[22]

Just how low remains a sensitive political issue. Estimated labor requirements affect cost of production estimates and hence affect price negotiations between farmers and the CMDT over what constitutes a "fair return" or "fair price" for seed cotton (Ministère de l'Agriculture de l'Elévage et de la Pêche 2003). Not surprisingly, the CMDT's estimate of 79 labor days for family labor is about 40 percent below the 134 days projected by cotton farmer associations for equipped farms (see Table 4.7). Taking an intermediate figure of 106 days of family labor for animal traction cotton farming leads to estimated returns of 675 CFAF per day in 2003/04, about 30 percent below the opportunity cost of labor. These results show that profitability is just one of the many factors influencing farmers' decisions to grow cotton. They also explain why farmers were so unhappy with the CMDT. The CMDT's desultory management had destroyed farmer incentives and shattered their confidence in the CMDT.

Reforms

In prior crises, the CMDT/CFDT's strategy had consisted of procuring deficit financing from the Malian and French governments and other donors in order to weather the market downturn as they made small adjustments to improve their finances and shore up a few underperforming areas. But they had never before considered changing the overall CMDT-led system.

The management audits and farmer boycott of 2000/2001, to a much greater degree than other crises, revealed the structural weaknesses of the system. Together they contributed to the growing realization that more serious re-

---

21. The 2002/03 data are based on a CMDT survey of 192 farms.

22. Though postdevaluation farm survey data are not available for hand-hoe cotton farmers, projections based on earlier production coefficients suggest that returns to family labor in hand-hoe cotton farming likewise remained 20 to 50 percent below the opportunity cost of labor in 2003/04.

forms were needed. The cotton sector was no longer serving as a dynamic motor of economic development in rural Mali.

These revelations helped to establish some common ground in the ongoing debate, started in the 1990s, between the World Bank, the French government, and CFA zone cotton companies on the most appropriate model for future development of the cotton sector. To simplify very complex and multifaceted positions, the French government, the CFDT, and the CMDT advocated maintaining the status quo, arguing to keep an integrated sector that had proven successful. The World Bank, in contrast, while recognizing the important achievements recorded by the CMDT and CFDT over the prior decades, argued for privatization of the cotton companies and liberalization of the sector. They posited that greater competition would lead to higher producer prices and farmer incomes, cost efficiencies, greater competitiveness, more rapid growth, increased rural and urban employment, and larger tax and foreign exchange earnings (CFDT 1998).

Faced with financial difficulties arising from world market events, the CFDT underwent an internal reorganization in 2002 aimed at reducing risks and improving its financial system and information technology (Peltier 2003).

In 2001, cotton sector stakeholders agreed to an emergency plan aimed at reducing deficits and reestablishing farmer confidence. The plan involved changing the CMDT leadership, freezing the cotton gin investment program, creating an independent reform commission, and conducting a series of further financial audits and diagnostic studies. After a series of technical discussions and a general assembly of cotton sector actors in April 2001, the Malian government signed the *Lettre de Politique de Développement du Secteur Coton*. This cotton sector development policy letter established an 18-month action plan (timed to coincide with Mali's electoral calendar) that changed seed cotton price-setting mechanisms, privatized the cottonseed oil–processing subsidiary, and reduced the CMDT's labor force by 27 percent. Perhaps most significantly, the letter committed the government to liberalize the sector and privatize the CMDT by 2005. While the immediate measures reduced fixed costs and non–seed cotton variable costs by 40 percent and 15 percent, respectively, resulting in a savings of 9 billion CFAF in 2001/02, the sector still lost 20 billion CFAF in 2002 (Ministère du Développement Rural 2001).

As in previous crisis periods over the past 45 years, the Malian government has moved slowly and cautiously to implement reforms.[23] In July 2004, it reneged on its original commitment to the reform calendar, opting to assess restructuring efforts in Benin and Burkina Faso. In January 2005, the government created an interim seed cotton pricing mechanism and in November increased the government's share in the capital of the CMDT from 60 to 70 percent. It for-

---

23. The discussion of cotton sector reforms since 2005 benefits substantially from information and discussion with Sarah Gavian.

mally announced that further reforms would be delayed until 2007 and that it would privatize the CMDT in 2008, establishing four cotton companies in which private actors (61 percent), the Malian state (17 percent), and a newly created cotton producers' association (20 percent) would retain shares (Gavian 2008).

With an eye to completing the cotton sector reforms in 2010, the government has been working to establish some of the elements of a new system, including the creation of a price support fund (controlled either by banks or by the Union Nationale des Sociétés Coopératives de Producteurs de Coton), a cotton commodity exchange, and a cotton grading service. The government has also conducted an evaluation of its pricing mechanism, assessed the value of CMDT assets, and developed a human resource reassignment plan for CMDT personnel and intends to create an interprofessional association once the CMDT has been privatized (Gavian 2008). According to the latest government timetable, privatization will occur during the course of 2010 (Coulibaly 2009).

World Prices and Subsidies

Between January and October 2001, world market prices fell 42 percent, dropping below 40 cents per pound for the first time in over 30 years. Because the CMDT was producing a kilogram of cotton lint for 822 CFAF, the drop in prices to 667 CFAF per kilogram (the average price in the 2001/02 marketing year) was ruinous for Mali's cotton sector. Many structural factors contributed to the steep drop in cotton prices, including the Chinese trade balance, the price of polyester, and the world economy.

Yet worldwide attention has focused on the role of the production and marketing subsidies of major exporting countries. In October 2001, the International Cotton Advisory Council (ICAC) released a study of the price-depressing effect of production and export subsidies in the United States, the European Union, and China. The ICAC estimated that the removal of U.S. cotton subsidies would raise world prices by 11 cents a pound in 2001/02, an increase of 26 percent.[24] If all producing countries eliminated their cotton subsidies, average prices would rise 31 cents per pound higher than the actual prices in 2001/02 (ICAC 2002a).

More recent analyses using alternative methods and assumptions about the structure of the cotton markets and supply elasticities estimate more modest price increases of 6–14 percent following the removal of U.S. subsidies and subsequent response and readjustments of production and stock levels (FAPRI 2002; Quirke 2002; Gillson et al. 2004; Alston, Sumner, and Brunke 2007).

How would the removal of U.S. cotton subsidies affect Malian cotton farmers? Using 10-year average figures for world prices, the exchange rate,

---

24. It is interesting to note that total direct assistance to 25,000 U.S. cotton producers in 2003/04 totaled $3.4 billion, a figure that, the popular press has informed us, equals Mali's 2002 gross domestic product (GDP) (ICAC 2005).

Malian seed cotton production, and the share of the world price paid out to farm households, a 6–14 percent rise in world prices would translate into a farmgate price increase of 11 to 26 CFAF per kilogram.[25] For a typical Malian cotton farm family planting 2.4 hectares of rainfed cotton and producing 1,044 kilograms per hectare, the estimated seed cotton price increases of 11–26 CFAF per kilogram, holding all other factors constant, would increase gross cotton revenues between US$19 and US$45 per hectare or US$45 to US$107 per farm. For a typical equipped cotton farm earning net returns of 71,512 CFAF per hectare or 171,629 CFAF per farm (US$159 per hectare or US$381 per farm) (see Table 4.7), these estimated price increases translate into a 12–28 percent boost in revenues. Nationally, for Mali's 200,000 farm households, these changes would represent a gain of US$9 to US$22 million in annual farm income. Associated income gains farther up the marketing chain would raise total national income by a further US$7 to US$15 million annually. So, in total, a 6–14 percent increase in the world price of cotton lint following the removal of U.S. cotton subsidies would result in a US$16 to US$37 million aggregate annual gain for Mali's cotton sector.[26]

It is important to note that even a complete removal of the subsidies would not necessarily have brought Mali's cotton sector out of the red in 2001/02. In 2001/02, the CMDT's total unit cost of producing and delivering 1 kilogram of fiber (CIF) was 822 CFAF per kilogram (62 cents per pound), 2 CFAF per kilogram higher than under the lower 6 percent price increase estimated without U.S. subsidies.

Although there is little argument that the removal of subsidies would generate gains for Malian farmers, the CMDT, and the Malian economy, their elimination is not the panacea that many make it out to be. One Malian newspaper argues that Malian cotton farmers suffer more from the CMDT's bad management than from the effects of American agricultural subsidies (Bolly 2004). Improving productivity and reducing operating costs remain essential to the competitiveness and profitability of Mali's cotton sector.

---

25. These calculations use the following 10-year averages: world price (Index A)—58 cents per pound; US$/CFAF exchange rate—607 CFAF per US$; world price (Index A)—767 CFAF per kilogram; cotton lint production—210,000 tons; seed cotton production—500,000 tons; ginning ratio—42 percent; farmer share of world price—58 percent; average farm size—2.4 hectares; average yield—1,044 kilograms per hectare.

26. These estimates, based on 10-year average prices, imply a world price increase of 3 to 8 cents per pound. Because world cotton prices vary substantially over time, actual losses from U.S. cotton subsidies in any one year may differ substantially from these 10-year averages. In 2003, for example, Mali's President Amadou Toumani Toure estimated a US$55 million total loss to Mali from U.S. cotton subsidies. Given a world price of 69 cents per pound that year, a 14 percent price rise—the high end of Alston, Sumner, and Brunke's (2007) estimate of the price impact of U.S. cotton subsidy withdrawal—would have increased world prices by 9.7 cents per pound. With Malian lint production of roughly 260 thousand tons, or 572 million pounds that year, losses to Mali could indeed have totaled US$55 million in 2003.

Mali and the WTO

In 2003, in response to the profound effect of the steep fall in world cotton prices on their economies and following Brazil's formal complaint about U.S. subsidies under the World Trade Organization (WTO) dispute mechanism, the Malian government joined with Benin, Burkina Faso, and Chad to launch a new initiative titled *Poverty Reduction: Sectoral Initiative in Favour of Cotton,* which was discussed in the run-up to the WTO's ministerial meeting in Cancún, Mexico. In this petition the four countries asked for the removal of all subsidies and requested financial compensation for export revenues lost due to U.S. subsidies (WTO 2003). Although the WTO ruled on Brazil's complaint that the United States had violated WTO obligations "by granting excessive subsidies to its growers between 1999 and 2002, depressing prices at the expense of Brazilian growers," the West African proposal failed, along with the rest of the Cancún agenda (Gillson et al. 2004, 21). The United States and four West African countries subsequently agreed in 2004 to pursue the issue in a cotton subcommittee during future agriculture negotiations (WTO 2004a,b). In December 2005, a WTO meeting in Hong Kong once again rejected the West African proposal for compensation (Fok 2006; UNCTAD 2007).

In August 2006, in response to the WTO ruling on behalf of Brazil's petition, the United States terminated export subsidies (Step 2 program) (WTO 2005; USDA 2007). Despite this action, in July 2007 the WTO ruled that the United States had failed to reform its cotton subsidy programs enough to comply with this earlier decision, "potentially opening the door to billions of dollars worth of sanctions from Brazil" (International Centre for Trade and Sustainable Development 2007, 1).

Although these actions have not yet resulted in the direct compensation desired by Mali and other cotton-producing countries, the West African petition, in combination with the Brazilian action, has helped to focus WTO attention on the subsidy issue. It has also set an important precedent for African countries in international trade negotiations, underscoring the type of action and regional collaboration that will increasingly be required by small countries to promote their common interests in global markets.

Sector Performance

Between 1999 and 2006, seed cotton production grew at 2.9 percent per year, all from area increases, while yield levels remained flat.[27] These figures mask large fluctuations in area planted and seed cotton production occurring over this period, falling approximately 50 percent during the boycott, increasing 133 percent the following year, dropping 17 percent in 2002, and jumping 30 percent in 2003/04 (see Figure 4.4).

---

27. Given the wide fluctuations during this period, these estimated trend lines did not differ significantly from zero.

Results

Income

In 2006, roughly 200,000 Malian smallholder farmers produced cotton for sale on the international market. Over the prior 45 years, cotton production had grown at 8.7 percent per year, providing an average income of US$375 per household for over 25 percent of Malian rural households.

This phenomenal long-term growth in cotton production has had a significant impact on Mali's economy. Cotton exports ranged from 40 percent of total national exports in the early 1990s to over 70 percent after the devaluation of the CFAF in the mid-1990s. In the first half of the 2000s, that share averaged roughly 25 percent as gold production and exports rose substantially. Cotton's share of GDP rose in real terms, from 4 percent in 1980 to 8 percent in 1999 (DNP 2003). Taxes paid directly and indirectly by the cotton sector have been one of the largest contributors to the national budget. In 1998, the cotton sector contributed 15 percent of the government's total fiscal revenues (PAMORI 2000).[28] Cotton's historically large share of national income, export earnings, and fiscal revenues underline its strategic importance to the Malian economy.[29]

Equity

Smallholder farmers produce all of Mali's seed cotton. The average cotton farming household farms 2.4 hectares of cotton and 8 hectares overall.

Because cotton enables farm households to acquire animal traction equipment and complementary purchased inputs, these households have proven able to expand their production, incomes, and asset holdings over time. As a result, the concentration of income among cotton households has become more pronounced than in other production systems, such as that of rice (Tefft and Kelly 2002).

In the cotton zone, the senior male head of a large extended family traditionally manages cotton and coarse grain production, controlling access to resources and the income earned from production. Young adult men and women, who remain part of a large extended family in the cotton zone and contribute labor to production activities, do not necessarily have access to or control of cotton resources. Incomes of young men and women in the cotton zone who are not heads of extended families are, in fact, lower than those in the rice zone, a likely contributor to high levels of child malnutrition in the cotton zone (Tefft and Kelly 2004). This unequal control and the consequently unequal distribu-

---

28. The combined effect of low world prices, high unit costs of fiber production, and delays in reforming the sector contributed to a cumulative debt of roughly US$200 million as of April 2007 (Camara 2007).

29. The cotton sector has played a similarly important role in the economies of several other West and Central African countries, including Benin, Burkina Faso, Chad, and Togo, with the economic reliance less important in the more diversified economies of Cameroon, Côte d'Ivoire, and Senegal.

tion of household profits among family members has contributed to the breakup of large extended production units into smaller autonomous units, many of which no longer have sufficient animal teams and farm equipment (Kébé and Kébé-Sidibé 1997).

Sustainability

FINANCIAL SUSTAINABILITY.   For two and a half decades, through the mid-1980s, Mali's cotton sector remained highly profitable and sufficiently productive that its surplus helped to finance general rural development programs, both directly through provision of rural infrastructure and services and indirectly through its substantial tax contributions. Over time, complacency, poor corporate governance, poor management, and outright corruption crept into the CMDT at a time when world market prices were becoming increasingly volatile. The collision of these two opposing forces triggered a series of financial crises beginning in the late 1980s and peaking in the early 2000s. The financial crises, in turn, have revealed a series of structural weaknesses in the sector and provoked a series of reform efforts. These remain ongoing as the Malian government, the CMDT, the farmers' union, and supporting donors seek adjustments that will result in a more viable, competitive production and marketing system.

ENVIRONMENTAL SUSTAINABILITY.   Soil fertility and soil mining remain concerns in the cotton zone. Mali's cotton farmers apply chemical fertilizers at roughly 75 percent of recommended input levels, and they apply manure and other organic soil amendments at half of recommended levels (CMDT 1998; Kébé, Diakité, and Diawara 1998). Given the variability of crop yields and fertilizer responsiveness under rainfed conditions, farmers have adopted these strategies to minimize credit risks and cash expenditures on increasingly expensive inputs (Follin and Deat 1999; Giraudy 1999). While understandable, these input application levels lead to negative soil nutrient balances and fears of soil mining (Pieri 1992; Smaling 1993).

Several studies of soil fertility have attempted to measure rates of soil nutrient loss in the CMDT zone. In 1992, one study estimated an average nitrogen nutrient deficit balance of 25 kilograms per hectare over the entire CMDT zone, suggesting that soil nutrient reserves in southern Mali could be sustained for only 30 years at this rate of soil nutrient depletion (van der Pol 1992). Subsequent studies, however, obtained less alarming results, with a nitrogen deficit of 8.2 kilograms per hectare and a predicted soil fertility lifetime of 95 years (Ramisch 1999). This later study also underlined the complex methodological issues involved in making these estimates. It highlighted the variability of soil nutrient balances across village locations; plots close to villages generated nutrient losses of 11.9 kilograms per hectare, parcels in distant hamlets deficits of 4.7 kilograms per hectare, and livestock herder plots nutrient surpluses of 23.3 kilograms per hectare. Although most researchers agree that soil mining remains a threat to the sustainability of cotton production in Mali, they also recognize that declining rainfall and other factors that affect farmer and herder behavior—including land tenure, livestock management, and watering rights— also influence soil fertility outcomes (Ramisch 1999).

In addition to the lower-than-recommended levels of fertilizer and manure application, environmental concerns have been amplified by farmers' minimal use of antierosion techniques. Despite many successful projects implemented in the 1980s and 1990s to address environmental problems, the CMDT estimates that only 28 percent of cotton farm households use antierosion techniques (CMDT 1998). In their efforts to ensure their households' food and income security in the least risky way possible, farmers tend to focus on the potential short-term benefit of using the recommended technologies while discounting the long-term financial returns to soil recapitalization stemming from current investments in fertilizer and conservation work (Tefft 2000).

With well-tested technical solutions available, such as those described in Chapter 7, there is little argument about the need to improve farmer incentives (through lower input and higher output prices) in order to stimulate greater use of intensification practices and investment in long-term soil conservation measures.[30] Sustainable solutions to environmental problems will inevitably need to go beyond the cotton sector to consider livestock–crop interactions, land tenure systems, wood collection and deforestation, crop diversification, and the establishment of viable credit and input markets for all crops. Mali's recently elected rural communes are well positioned to play a central role in working with communities and farmer organizations to address problems of land management and environmental degradation.

Policy Implications

Key Drivers of Past Success

Mali's long-term efforts to promote cotton production underline the difficulties and discipline required to remain competitive in international cotton markets. Two long periods of success punctuated by two periods of reversal suggest several critical issues that have remained at the forefront of Mali's efforts to retain its competitive edge. These key drivers of cotton sector performance have included (1) research; (2) links among credit, input, and output markets; (3) strong partnerships among farmers, private firms, and the public sector; and (4) product quality.

---

30. Declining yields are not due to nonperforming seed varieties. Yields obtained in on-farm trials and by the most productive farmers are 20–50 percent higher than average yields (Dembélé 1996; CMDT/Sikasso 1998).

RESEARCH AND EXTENSION. Investment in the human and institutional research capacity for developing and testing new technologies has proven critical to Mali's past efforts at increasing productivity, particularly at the farm level. Malian researchers, together with their colleagues at sister institutions across the region and in France, have succeeded in generating a steady stream of new cotton varieties, innovative pest management technologies, and agronomic practices that have raised cotton yields from 225 kilograms per hectare in the 1960s to over 1 ton per hectare in the 2000s. Growing problems of pesticide resistance and plateauing yields will require renewed research efforts in the future.

INTERLINKED CREDIT, INPUT, AND OUTPUT MARKETS. The CMDT has invested heavily to establish a viable and solvent system linking banks to farmer organizations and, more recently, involving private input dealers and transporters in order to provide farmers with timely delivery of quality inputs on credit and to ensure their reimbursement. The strength of this credit system hinges on interlocking input and output markets that have been instrumental in reducing credit defaults. Experiences from other countries that have liberalized their cotton marketing systems may prove instructive as Mali addresses this critical issue in the future (Tschirley, Poulton, and Labaste 2009).

PUBLIC–PRIVATE PARTNERSHIPS. Strong and effective partnerships have remained one of the hallmarks of Mali's cotton sector and a key ingredient of its long-term success. Private input and marketing management under the CFDT gave way to direct public investment in service delivery under the jointly owned CMDT. The government has remained responsible throughout for funding agricultural research, orchestrating credit links with the banks, and providing the intermittent financing necessary to insulate farmers from rapid swings in international prices. Farmer organizations have emerged to provide growers with a voice in industry governance. In an effort to help reduce costs, they have also taken over some input delivery services. As reform efforts proceed, the formation of innovative partnerships will be particularly important in order to ensure the smooth coordination of sector functions.

PRODUCT QUALITY. Cotton lint quality has remained central to Mali's long-term efforts to maintain its competitive position with spinning mills. Cotton breeders have therefore paid careful attention to fiber characteristics in developing improved varieties through their breeding programs. Likewise, meticulous execution and coordination of functions throughout the supply chain, from crop management to postharvest practices and ginning, have proven essential to producing excellent lint fiber. This has required the establishment of technically accurate, transparent procedures for grading seed cotton, classifying cotton lint, and linking price premiums to higher quality in order to strengthen farmers' confidence in the system and provide incentives for them to improve quality. The future involvement of multiple ginners in different regions may require quality coordination if the sector is to preserve the distinctive reputation of Malian cotton.

Future Challenges

IMPROVING INCENTIVES THROUGH INCREASED PRODUCTIVITY.   Improving farmers' incentives through lower input prices and higher seed cotton prices are prerequisites for motivating intensification and soil recapitalization. Actions to increase world market prices through subsidy elimination will offer temporary relief. Sustained gains in farm prices will require productivity gains in both the on-farm and the postfarm segments of the supply chain, particularly in ginning, transport, and CMDT's fixed costs. High costs at the CMDT present an obstacle to raising farm prices to the levels needed to stimulate intensification and soil conservation practices that, in turn, are needed to ensure the long-term sustainability of cotton production in Mali.

Reestablishing the competitiveness and profitability of Malian cotton will depend largely on how Mali restructures the sector to provide the necessary incentives to farmers and other sector actors. A liberalized cotton sector offers the potential to improve internal operating efficiencies and decrease rent seeking, both of which are needed to reduce the unit cost of cotton lint and increase processing and farm-level profits. At the same time, these reforms pose considerable challenges in finding ways to successfully coordinate many of the critical functions that have been effectively performed in the past by the CMDT's vertically and regionally integrated system.

OVERCOMING PESTICIDE RESISTANCE.   Effective pest management has played a predominant role in the CFDT/CMDT's efforts to increase cotton productivity over the past 45 years. The CFDT/CMDT has followed a coordinated approach to pest management through the uniform use of low-cost pesticide "cocktails" in the cotton zone. These efforts have effectively slowed the onset of pest resistance in a crop that is generally considered highly sensitive to pests and diseases. Numerous studies in Mali over the past 30 years have estimated potential crop losses due to pests at between 20 and 35 percent, far lower than the 60–65 percent average loss rates documented elsewhere in Africa (Delattre and Le Gall 1982; Oerke et al. 1995; Michel et al. 2000).

Looking forward, however, cotton specialists express growing concern that resistance may be developing in certain areas and that current pesticides are becoming ineffective. The increasing resistance to pyrethroid pesticides in the population of the American boll worm (*Helicoverpa armigera*) raises particular concern (Ochou and Martin 2000). Secondary pests such as the white fly (*Bemisia tabaci*) have also resurged following widespread insecticide use against other insects. Growing pest resistance is often cited as the main determinant of decreasing seed cotton yields. This situation has developed despite a doubling in the quantity of pesticide used on cotton over the 1990s. Many fear that if pesticide resistance persists and Mali continues on the pesticide "treadmill," it will be necessary to use increasingly more powerful and expensive pesticides whose cost can be supported only by a commensurate increase in productivity (Van der Valk, pers. comm., 1999). Potential solutions include greater extension of the "targeted staggered application" of pesticides, integrated pest management, the use of genetically modified organisms (GMOs), and the production of organic cotton without synthetic pesticides.

Since 1994, the CMDT has promoted a scheme of reduced insecticide use known as targeted staggered application (*lutte etagée ciblée*) that has proven an effective alternative to current methods. Pesticide applications follow the usual calendar method but at reduced dosages, with additional complementary sprayings dependent on the type and magnitude of insect infestation. Even though this method has produced similar yields but with 40 percent less pesticide application, it has been used on only 2 percent of the total cotton area in Mali. Adoption has been limited by the need for extensive farmer training, the considerable amount of farmer time needed to monitor cotton fields, and a lack of publicity (Michel et al. 2000; CIRAD 2004; GRAIN 2004).

Initial experiences with integrated pest management (IPM) techniques have shown promising results. A recent Food and Agriculture Organization of the United Nations (FAO) farmer field school project in Mali to strengthen integrated pest management practices reported a 70 percent reduction in pesticide applications, a 25 percent jump in yields, and a 49 percent increase in farm revenues (FAO 2004; GRAIN 2004). By reducing use of the most harmful products, IPM also improved biodiversity in cotton fields by increasing the number and diversity of natural enemies and increasing the predator-pest ratio. Reduced exposure to pesticides (during mixing, spraying, and cotton harvesting) in both the targeted staggered application and IPM methods also helps to limit pesticide poisoning, farmers' medical expenditures, and the number of lost workdays (FAO 2004).

ASSESSING GENETICALLY MODIFIED ORGANISMS.   Future productivity improvements may depend on access to a variety of performance-enhancing genetics recently developed by multinational agrochemical pharmaceutical firms. Initial results from studies of *Bacillus thuringiensis* (*Bt*) cotton in China, South Africa, and India show increases in yields, reduced pesticide levels, labor savings, lower production costs, and higher net income (Pray et al. 2001; Sahai and Rahman 2003; Thirtle et al. 2003; AC Nielsen 2004; Baffes 2004; GRAIN 2004; Pschorn-Strauss 2004; Russell 2004). Nonetheless, numerous critics have contested the validity of these studies, claiming a lack of methodological rigor, selective reporting of results, and limited duration of the studies on *Bt* cotton.

These debates underscore the importance of developing national capacity and processes to assess the new technology's effectiveness in crop protection as well as its productivity benefits, profitability, and risks (including environmental, health, and biodiversity concerns) before it is used commercially. Biotechnology research presents a scientific challenge to Mali's research system and regulatory agencies as they seek to gain a fuller understanding of the impacts of GMO technology. Developing the most appropriate organizational structure and institutional relationships—international partnerships or contractual mechanisms—may prove an important prerequisite to gaining access to this technology (Tefft et al. 1998).

ENCOURAGING DIVERSIFICATION.   Although cotton production will continue to be a major source of growth in southern and central Mali, Malians recognize the dangers of overdependence on a single crop. Almost all households grow cotton because it is the most reliable cash crop available. Many farmers would undoubtedly plant more maize or grow other crops if the input, credit, and output markets for these crops functioned more effectively.

The need for greater diversification in the cotton zone may also be justified by the concentration and control of cotton revenues by male household heads. The lack of access to productive resources and income by dependent adult household members (i.e., those who are dependents of the household head) has contributed to the breakup of large extended families into smaller, nuclear units. Greater opportunities for younger men and women in the cotton zone to gain control of resources and access to productive inputs may result in greater specialization of cotton production among those who intensify production and use more environmentally sound practices.

ENHANCING COORDINATION.   Current discussions indicate that the Government of Mali intends to replace a national ginning monopsony (i.e., the CMDT) with several regional ones and rely more on private sector actors throughout the supply chain.[31] Having several alternative outlets (three or four companies) through which farmers can sell seed cotton may not necessarily result in the desired efficiency and performance gains if the new structure does not improve services and increase producer prices. These issues are under discussion as part of the reform efforts.[32] Although the CFDT/CMDT's ownership and internalization of the majority of transactions between the vertically adjacent stages of production of cotton lint may have initially contributed to a reduction of transaction costs and risks and to greater assurance of consistent supplies of quality lint, the efficiency gains from the vertically integrated sector have been eroded by internal management difficulties and cost inflation.

An alternative way of organizing the sector may reduce internal inefficiencies and rent seeking, but the sector will need to pay attention to the effect of the new structure on transaction costs arising from exchanges between a larger number of actors in the system. Even if coordination is not controlled in-

---

31. See HORUS (2003) for a detailed discussion of different options for reforming the sector, including privatizing the CMDT and making farmers shareholders in the CMDT (as in the Burkina model).

32. See Goreux and Macrae (2002) for a detailed discussion of alternative pricing mechanisms that effectively transmit world prices to farmers while minimizing the negative effect of large price fluctuations and price rigidity.

ternally through ownership integration (i.e., within the control of the CMDT), alternative mechanisms to coordinate the sequence of sector stages must be established. Effective harmonization of the critical functions in the supply chain can be ensured through various types of contracting arrangements and diverse forms of association such as cooperatives, alliances, joint ventures, or networks. The fundamental challenge comes down to finding the best way of organizing individual and collective action to improve the productivity of the different levels of the sector and the coordination among those levels while taking into account economies of scale and trying to avoid rent-seeking behavior (Tefft et al. 1998).

IMPROVING GOVERNANCE. Whether or not restructuring disrupts the coordination between various levels of a sector depends on the capacity of new actors to carry out new functions, the efficiency of economic governance systems, and the mechanisms for the enforcement of contracts (Tefft et al. 1998). As the events of the past 10 years have shown, Mali's efforts to put the sector on more solid footing and in a more resilient competitive position in international markets will need to focus on improving governance and strict management rigor in order to reduce costs at all levels of the supply chain.

STRENGTHENING FARMER ORGANIZATIONS. To smooth the transition from CMDT-managed interlocked markets to a competitive system, farmer associations must improve their management skills and their ability to reduce strategic default. An expanded role for farmer organizations will also require successful resolution of several internal problems, including generational conflicts; increased economic differentiation in villages, leading to smaller associations grouped around smaller family units; diminished confidence in extension agents; and indebtedness resulting from unreimbursed individual credit secured by communal collateral (Kébé and Kébé-Sidibé 1997). To become more effective, farmer organizations will need to secure complete legal status as well as increase their numbers of functionally literate and numerate members and improve their financial management, transparency, and accountability. Difficulties incurred by the farmers' union in its first experience managing the import and distribution of fertilizer for maize grown in the cotton zone underlines the important challenges that lie ahead in training new actors.

DEFINING NEW PUBLIC ROLES. Although commodity sector reforms naturally focus attention on the development of private sector capacity to take over functions formerly executed by state agencies like the CMDT, one cannot underestimate the importance of developing the capacity of government agencies or an industry stakeholder group to provide key oversight and regulatory functions. Numerous areas will require public involvement, even as specific functions become privatized:

- Additional public investment in infrastructure (such as roads and electricity), strengthening of the legal system and mechanisms for contract enforcement and dispute resolution between industry actors, and provision of market information systems are all public services necessary to encourage private investment.

- Regulation and oversight of the import and use of pesticides, fertilizer, and biotechnology will be necessary to protect public safety and health.
- The government's initiative to petition the WTO offers a good example of the need for regional cooperation and increased involvement in international negotiations.
- The government will need to monitor the equity implications of reforms, particularly impacts on farmers in remote areas that private sector actors may not serve.
- Local governments will need to play a stronger role in finding sustainable solutions to land and environmental degradation.
- Government at all levels is responsible for promoting transparency throughout the system at both the corporate and farmer organization levels in order to minimize corrupt practices and rent-seeking behavior.
- It is important for the cotton sector to develop an independent capacity to analyze, monitor, and modify the complex and dynamic interactions among policies, institutional reform, technological change, and human capital development. As reform experiences in other countries have shown, restructuring commodity sectors is a dynamic, iterative process that often proceeds by trial and error, requiring continuous monitoring and adjustment.

Policy Lessons for African Agriculture

This review of Mali's experience growing rainfed cotton for the international market highlights several important lessons for future agricultural development in Sub-Saharan Africa. First is the importance of sustained government commitment. More than 50 years ago, the French government identified a market for cotton lint and systematically worked to develop a strategy that would enable African smallholders to compete in international markets. Decades of sustained investment in key institutions by the Malian and French governments succeeded in generating a stream of new technologies that expanded the productivity, production, and competitiveness of Malian cotton lint. Over the long term, growth in Malian cotton production has relied on unstinting government commitment to the kinds of public investments required to maintain competitive opportunities for farmers.

Long-term growth and competitiveness, in turn, require a steady stream of technological innovation. Over more than four decades, Malian researchers and their regional colleagues have developed and delivered a flow of new seeds, pest control methods, and agronomic practices to cotton farmers. When these efforts lapsed, as in the late 1990s, Mali lost its competitive edge. Given constant adjustments and adaptation by cotton's many natural pests and human competitors, the country's competitive position requires continuous technological innovation. Mali's long-term, innovative search for breeding break-throughs, low-cost pest management strategies, and more effective agronomic practices has provided the foundation for a highly competitive cotton sector.

This long-term commitment to technical innovation demonstrates the power of regional and international partnerships. In a succession of six major cotton varietal releases, only one emanated from Malian research stations; the other five came from sister institutes across West and Central Africa. Where small countries straddle common agroecological zones, regional sharing and technological exchange offer prospects for scale economies and cross-country spillovers. The importance of this regional technology collaboration mirrors the findings from the cassava and maize studies seen in Chapters 2 and 3.

Similarly, the cotton case study emphasizes the importance of collective action in the international arena. Cotton subsidies by the United States, the European Union, and China have clearly penalized Malian cotton farmers. U.S. subsidies alone—estimated in 2004/05 at US$4.7 billion in direct payments, countercyclical payments, and marketing loan benefits for U.S. cotton farmers (ICAC 2005)—reduce the income of Mali's 200,000 cotton farmers by about US$9 to US$22 million annually. Income forgone by the CMDT and other cotton sector firms raise losses by an additional US$7 to US$15 million per year. Therefore, over the entire value chain, Mali loses US$16 to US$37 million annually. Increasingly forceful presentations by Brazil and African cotton producers at the Doha Round WTO negotiations have resulted in elevated international awareness of the damages inflicted on African farmers by cotton subsidies abroad. The 2005 and 2007 WTO rulings led to the subsequent dismantling of a portion of U.S. cotton subsidies. Continued WTO review and appeal of these rulings will require persistence and collective action by the African cotton-producing countries.

The Malian cotton study likewise highlights the importance of efficient vertical coordination between smallholder farmers and international markets. Effective supply chains require timely input delivery, credit, processing, and marketing of final output. Although Mali began with a fully integrated state-controlled system, in recent years it has moved toward a more private sector–oriented model such as those common in many anglophone African countries (see Tschirley, Poulton, and Labaste 2009). While input credit remains a critical constraint throughout much of rural Africa, the Malian cotton-backed system offers a possible model for linking the formal banking sector with a strong cash crop. In Mali, the regular cash flow secured through cotton farming forms the backbone of a rural credit and input supply system that provides cotton farmers with access to fertilizer, equipment, and other inputs that are frequently unavailable to households that do not grow cotton.

Farmer organizations have played a critical role in the management and reform of Mali's cotton sector. Decades of rural education and farmer involvement in cotton extension, input distribution, and marketing have resulted in a growing network of capable, engaged, and assertive farmer organizations. Through a sequence of organized strikes and ultimately a seat on the CMDT board, farmer organizations have become key vehicles for representing farmers' interests and bringing about change in the system. Given the importance of governance and government commitment to agriculture, farmer organizations offer a potentially powerful tool for holding governments accountable to the majority of their citizens who work in agriculture.

5 Are Horticultural Exports a Replicable Success Story? Evidence from Kenya and Côte d'Ivoire

NICHOLAS MINOT AND MARGARET NGIGI

Scope of the Case Study

It is not difficult to see why African agricultural specialists consider export horticulture a success story, particularly in Kenya (see Chapter 1, Table 1.3). First, the sector has grown significantly over the past several decades. Fruit and vegetable exports from Kenya have increased fivefold in constant dollar terms since 1975, reaching over US$320 million in 2005. In the process, horticulture has become the third-largest source of foreign exchange after tourism and tea.[1] Second, small farmers have participated significantly in the growth of the sector. It is estimated that over half of Kenyan horticultural exports are produced by smallholders. Although less well documented, fruit and vegetable exports from Côte d'Ivoire have also expanded rapidly during certain periods. During the 1990s, for example, Ivorian horticultural exports grew 4.4 percent annually. Smallholders have also played an important role in exports from Côte d'Ivoire. After South Africa, Kenya and Côte d'Ivoire are the largest fruit and vegetable exporters in Sub-Saharan African.

This chapter examines the cases of Kenya and Côte d'Ivoire to assess whether horticultural exports represent a replicable success story. This inquiry addresses the following three questions examining the impact, driving forces, and policy implications of these cases, respectively:

- Do the horticultural sectors of Kenya and Côte d'Ivoire constitute valid success stories in terms of their impact on rural incomes, poverty, and sustainability?
- What factors have contributed to success (or lack thereof) in the horticultural sector?
- To what degree can lessons from these two horticultural sectors be replicated in other African countries?

---

1. Coffee and tea have been the main export commodities of Kenya for decades. However, as a result of recent declines in world coffee prices, the export revenue from horticulture surpassed that of coffee in 2000 (FAOSTAT 2008).

In spite of the rapid growth of the horticultural sector in Kenya, the answer to the first question is not obvious. First, some observers see a trend toward consolidation, with small farmers gradually being squeezed out of the lucrative export market for horticulture. The argument is that increasing concentration in European retail markets and rising concern over the environmental and labor conditions at the farm level are pushing exporters to work with larger farmers, who can more easily document their production practices (Dolan, Humphrey, and Harris-Pascal 1999). Second, it is not clear whether trade liberalization under the World Trade Organization will benefit African horticultural exporters, by further opening European markets, or hurt them, by eroding some of the preferential access to the European markets that they currently enjoy (Stevens and Kennan 1999; Oluoch 2008). And third, the fact that most of the exported fruits and vegetables are produced by small farmers certainly suggests a poverty-reducing impact, but it is difficult to make any definitive statement without better information on the number of beneficiaries, the characteristics of the growers, and the size of the gains.

Even if we assume, for the moment, that the horticultural sectors in Kenya and Côte d'Ivoire are success stories in terms of growth, poverty impact, and sustainability, an important question is whether there are lessons that can be applied to other African countries interested in helping small farmers participate in profitable export markets for horticultural goods. In other words, are the factors behind their success related to public policy and investment that other countries can emulate? Or is their success based on historical, climatic, and geographic factors that cannot be replicated elsewhere? To answer these questions, it is necessary to understand the historical development of horticulture. We are particularly interested in the role of policy, the regulatory environment, and public investment in facilitating the growth of the sector over time.

In conducting this review, analysis will focus only on fruit and vegetables, a subset of overall horticultural production. Broader definitions of horticulture typically include flowers and ornamental plants as well. Although cut-flower exports account for about half of Kenyan horticultural exports and are growing rapidly in Côte d'Ivoire, the cut-flower sector is dominated by large-scale capital-intensive operations.[2] Thus, the fruit and vegetable sector is a more promising topic for understanding the challenges of involving (and keeping) smallholders in an expanding export sector.

This chapter begins by discussing the case of Kenya in some detail because it is the most widely recognized success story in horticulture, because the growth of Kenya's horticultural sector is well documented, and because we have access to recent household data that shed light on the characteristics of horticultural growers there. Following this review, the chapter provides a briefer discussion

---

2. Kimenye (1995) reports that just 10 percent of Kenyan flower production for export is carried out by smallholders.

of the experience in Côte d'Ivoire, mainly to provide a basis for comparison with the Kenyan case. Similarities between the two countries help reinforce the assessment of factors underlying success, while contrasts demonstrate the diversity of experience across countries. Based on these comparisons, the chapter concludes by summing up evidence related to the three key questions posed above concerning impact, driving forces, and policy implications.

Dynamics in Kenyan Horticulture

The growth of the Kenyan fruit and vegetable sector has not been a smooth, continuous process. Rather, the sector has expanded in fits and starts, with numerous changes in the commodity mix, the role of the state, types of marketing institutions, and characteristics of participating farmers. Any division of this complex process is somewhat arbitrary, but for the purposes of presentation it is useful to divide the evolution of the sector into four periods: (1) the colonial period, from 1895 to 1962; (2) the early independence period, from 1963 to 1974; (3) the take-off phase, from 1975 to 1990; and (4) a consolidation phase, from 1991 to the present (Table 5.1).

Phase 1: Colonial Period, 1895–1962

Kenya's commercial horticultural production took root during the early years of the British-established protectorate, in 1895, and the colonization of Kenya, which began formally in 1920. The Imperial British East African Company began experimenting with temperate fruits and vegetables as early as 1893 (Hills 1956). In 1901, colonial white settler farmers founded the East African Agricultural and Horticultural Society (presently the Agricultural Society of Kenya). At the same time, Indians recruited to construct the Kenya–Uganda railway had introduced Asian vegetables, which today account for about 10 percent of the total volume of the country's fresh horticultural exports.[3]

The beginnings of Kenya's formal horticultural research activity can also be traced to this period. By 1911, the colonial government was experimenting with tropical fruits at Matuga along the Indian coast (M'Ribu, Neel, and Fretz 1993).[4] Later, in 1920, the colonial authorities established a second experimental site for tropical fruits close to where the National Agricultural Laboratories are currently located. In 1931, the Department of Agriculture embarked on a plant introduction service to facilitate the adoption and expansion of area planted with crops developed at the experimental stations.

Trade in small quantities of vegetables and tropical fruits already existed along the coast, with Arab and Indian traders exporting produce to Zanzibar

---

3. "Asian vegetables" include eggplant, chilis, *dudhi, karela,* okra, and other vegetables used widely in South Asian cooking.

4. This later became the site of the Matuga Agricultural Research Station.

TABLE 5.1 Dynamics and drivers of change in Kenyan horticulture, 1895–present

	Phase 1: Colonial period	Phase 2: Early independence	Phase 3: Take-off	Phase 4: New challenges
Timing	1895–1962	1963–74	1975–90	1991–present
Key actors	Commercial farmers Colonial research stations	Del Monte Corporation and large foreign firms Horticulture Crops Development Authority (HCDA)	Private traders Del Monte Corporation	Private traders
Motors of change	World War II Local research on tropical fruits	Foreign private investment HCDA plays a facilitating role; no market controls	Del Monte investments (by 1977, pineapple accounts for 65% of fruit and vegetable exports) Demand for Asian vegetables in the United Kingdom Rapidly growing tourism industry increases local demand and airfreight capacity Inexpensive smallholder irrigation technology	Increasing competition in export markets Food safety concerns in EU countries Rise of supermarkets

	Commercial farmers	Private exporters	Commercial farmers Exporters	Commercial producers
Beneficiaries	Commercial farmers Early outgrower schemes for smallholders	Private exporters Smallholder outgrowers have little access, accounting for only 10–20% of production	Commercial farmers Exporters Smallholder outgrowers increase their share to 50%	Commercial producers
Production gains	Limited exports of passion fruit juice Dehydrated vegetables exported to Allied armies in World War II Pineapple canning plants develop outgrower schemes By 1962, real exports reach US$25 million per year	Del Monte develops a 9,000-ha pineapple plantation Kenya Fruit Processing exports passion fruit juice Exports increase 60% to US$40 million per year (in real 2005 US$) Annual growth rate of 4.5%	Exports quadruple in real terms to US$159 million (in real 2005 US$) Annual growth rate of 9%	Export growth tapers off during the 1990s, to under 1% per year Diversification leads to recovery and 4.8% real growth over the period Total horticultural exports reach US$323 million in 2005
Impact			100,000–200,000 smallholders participate as regular export producers Regular suppliers sell $500–$1,000 per year	Smallholders disadvantaged by food safety regulations and increasing concentration among buyers

(Martin 1973, cited in Jaffee 1995). In the 1930s, low commodity prices motivated some European farmers to grow passion fruit. Private investors constructed four small factories to produce passion fruit juice for export to South
Africa and Australia, while colonial authorities created a Passion Fruit Board
to provide technical assistance and regulate trade. However, the quantities were
modest, and both production and processing collapsed with the disruption of
trade during World War II (Jaffee 1994).

Thus, a combination of private and public investments during this period
established the roots of Kenya's commercial horticultural sector. However,
given the limited domestic market, limited public interest, and the high costs of
transportation to external markets, the quantities actually marketed remained
modest.

World War II stimulated the development of horticultural production and
processing in two ways. First, regular trade flows were disrupted by hostilities,
reducing the availability of imported horticultural goods. Wartime regulations
meant tight controls on imports, particularly on commodities not considered essential to the economy. As a result, domestic producers and processors benefited from a larger domestic market, even if consumers were paying higher
prices for the goods.

Second, faced with high wartime demands, especially for provisions to the
Allied forces in North Africa and the Middle East, the authorities launched a
project to produce dehydrated vegetables. As part of this project, the Department of Agriculture constructed dehydration factories in Karatina and Keru-
goya. Some of the raw materials were supplied by large "nucleus estates" managed by the processors. However, the factories sourced much of their raw
material supplies from small-scale African farmers in the surrounding areas. To
boost production, the department established irrigation schemes in swampy areas for collective farming by African farmers. It organized farmers to supply
potatoes, cabbage, carrots, and other vegetables to the factories. The department
provided the farmers with improved seed, technical assistance, and a guaranteed market for their output. In spite of initial problems, the project eventually
expanded to process 22,000 tons of produce sourced from 13,500 small-scale
farmers. After the war, the demand for dehydrated vegetables by the military
dried up. By 1947, both plants were dismantled.

As Jaffee (1995) notes, the scheme was relatively short lived, but it was a
pioneering effort in several ways. It demonstrated that African farmers could
be mobilized for commercial agricultural production of new crops if inputs,
technical assistance, and a stable market could be provided. This model was
later adopted in various cash-crop programs such as the one implemented by
the Kenya Tea Development Authority.

This period also saw the expansion of experimental works started in the
previous period. By 1946, experimentation with tropical zone fruits had expanded to Kitale, Molo, and Tigoni agricultural research stations (the latter now

the location of the Potato Research Centre), and in 1955 the Perkerra Irrigation Research Station started work on hot-season fruits and vegetables. The National Horticultural Research Center was started in 1957 at Thika.

In the late 1940s, two British companies built pineapple-canning factories in Kenya to supply the United Kingdom. When they started operations, both factories sourced their raw material from large-scale settler farms. In 1954, the Swynnerton Plan called for government assistance to increase the participation of smallholders in the production of cash crops such as coffee and tea. Part of this plan was to increase the role of smallholders in supplying raw materials to the pineapple processing plants. Smallholders were subsequently provided with planting materials, technical assistance, and a guaranteed market. Early efforts suffered a number of serious problems, including understaffing, production in inappropriate zones, and violence associated with the independence movement. In spite of these problems, smallholders accounted for 75 percent of the supply of pineapples to these factories by the early 1960s (Jaffee 1994; Kimenye 1995; Winter-Nelson 1995).

Thus, during the postwar colonial period, horticultural development remained very limited. At the time of Kenya's independence, in 1963, fruit and vegetable exports were just US$3.8 million (US$25 million in 2005 dollars), representing less than 3 percent of agricultural exports (Figure 5.1). Nonetheless, the wartime dehydrated vegetable scheme demonstrated the feasibility of engaging smallholders in commercial horticultural production, given the right institutional support.

Phase 2: Early Independence, 1963–74

Independence brought three significant changes to the horticultural sector in Kenya. First, the new government came into power giving higher priority to improving conditions for the African majority. In short order, the new authorities launched a land reform program in which they purchased most of the land farmed by Europeans (particularly in the western highlands) and distributed it to tens of thousands of African smallholders. Because of the relatively good soils and location of this region, this program expanded the opportunities for smallholders to become involved in horticulture and other forms of commercial agriculture.

In a second important change, the new government created the Horticultural Crops Development Authority (HCDA) in 1967. Although the marketing boards for other crops generally played a direct role in buying and selling agricultural commodities, often with a legal monopoly on marketing, the HCDA played a more facilitative role, attempting to coordinate various participants in the industry.[5] This was partly a matter of practical necessity, because the HCDA

---

5. Initially, the HCDA was given a legal monopoly on onion exports, but this proved unsuccessful and was abandoned in 1986.

FIGURE 5.1 Value of Kenyan fruit and vegetable exports (left scale) and share of agricultural export revenue (right scale), 1961–2006

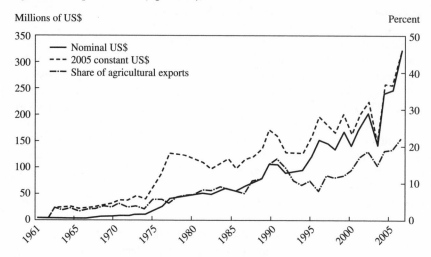

SOURCES: FAOSTAT (export data); U.S. Department of Labor (U.S. consumer price index).

had limited staff and resources. Even with a larger budget and staff, however, state enterprises rarely have the agility and skills necessary to deal with the diversity of the sector and the perishability of the product. Several researchers have noted that the HCDA's decision not to attempt direct management and control of the horticultural trade probably allowed the sector to develop more rapidly (Kimenye 1995; Djikstra 1997; Harris et al. 2001).

The third change in the postindependence period was the growth of international investment in the Kenyan horticultural sector. The most important example of this was the entry of the Del Monte Corporation into the Kenyan pineapple sector. In 1965, one of the two pineapple factories, Kenya Packers, came under the control of Del Monte (then called the California Packing Corporation), the largest fruit processor in the world. Although Del Monte invested in the factory and applied its technical and marketing expertise, the sector grew slowly and remained only marginally viable. According to Del Monte:

> In spite of a Government-sponsored drive to encourage quality pineapple production by smallholders, it soon became clear that these smallholders could not provide the necessary quantities on a regular basis to keep the canning plant consistently and profitably in operation. Many outgrowers chose instead to sell their crop to the local fresh fruit market where they could fetch better prices, while much of the locally grown fruit was not of a quality suited to the demands of Del Monte's stringent standards. (Del Monte 1988, 3)

In 1968, Del Monte arranged to lease 9,000 hectares of land from the government to develop a nucleus estate to produce pineapple for the factory. This would insulate Del Monte from changes in pineapple supply due to farmers' selling on the fresh market or switching to coffee when coffee prices rose. Furthermore, mechanization and hormone applications allowed the estate to spread production over much of the year, keeping the plant in operation longer. Del Monte managers expanded the capacity of the processing plant and the nucleus estate over time, and by 1974 they discontinued purchases from smallholder outgrowers.

In addition to Del Monte, other international companies came to invest in Kenya. A joint venture was formed between Cottees, an Australian firm, and a government parastatal. Kenya Fruit Processing (KFP) developed processing facilities and tried to stimulate local production. The HCDA assisted by providing seedlings, sprayers, chemicals, and other inputs on credit. By the early 1970s, KFP was one of the largest exporters of passion fruit juice in the world (Jaffee 1995).

Not all of the foreign investment projects succeeded. A joint venture between a British company and a Kenyan parastatal established a vegetable dehydration plant in Kinangop, a cool highland area with a new smallholder settlement scheme but relatively low agricultural potential. The government's interest in the scheme was to provide a marketing outlet for resettlement farmers in Kinangop, while the foreign partners were attempting to develop a viable commercial operation. Conflicts between these two objectives occurred often, and by 1968 the company was close to bankruptcy. The government purchased the plant and paid off its debts to protect the interests of smallholders in the area, but the factory continue to incur losses. In 1973, the Kenyan government adopted a more commercial orientation, implementing a new joint venture with a German firm. The scheme did well in the mid-1970s but eventually closed in 1982. The international market for dehydrated vegetables had contracted, while the local market for fresh vegetables had expanded, resulting in significant "leakage" that the company could not control.

Thus, the early independence period was characterized by more active support for the incorporation of smallholders in commercial agriculture, the formation of the HCDA, and increasing investment in horticulture, including joint ventures between foreign companies and state enterprises in processing. Between 1963 and 1974, although fruit and vegetable exports grew from US$3.8 million to US$10 million, their contribution to total agricultural exports remained at slightly less than 3 percent because other agricultural exports grew at a similar rate (see Figure 5.1).

Phase 3: Take-Off, 1975–90

Starting around 1975, Kenyan fruit and vegetable production and exports began to grow more rapidly. Overall, fruit and vegetable exports rose 9 percent per year in real terms over 1975–90. The importance of fruit and vegetable exports in overall agricultural exports increased dramatically during this period. Whereas fruits and vegetables had accounted for about 3 percent of agricultural export earnings in the 1960s and early 1970s, by 1990 their contribution had reached 17 percent (see Figure 5.1).

In the mid-1970s, private sector investments to increase capacity in the Kenyan pineapple processing industry, led by Del Monte, drove aggregate growth in Kenyan export horticulture. Between 1974 and 1977, pineapple product exports grew more than sixfold, and by 1977 they accounted for 65 percent of Kenyan fruit and vegetable exports. In contrast, during the late 1970s and 1980s, exports of fresh vegetables and, to a lesser degree, fresh fruit took over as the primary drivers of horticultural export growth in Kenya (Figure 5.2). Shifting world commodity prices, in part, motivated this diversification into fruits and vegetables. After peaking in 1977, coffee and tea prices fell sharply in the following years, forcing many farmers to look for alternative income-generating crops.

At the same time, export demand for vegetables grew during the 1970s as an indirect effect of the expulsion of the South Asian community from Uganda under the regime of Idi Amin. Many of these refugees resettled in the United Kingdom, contributing to a growing demand for Asian vegetables there. Kenya offered several advantages as a source of supply for this growing export market in Asian vegetables. It could supply Asian vegetables throughout the year instead of on a seasonal basis. In addition, Kenyan smallholders already had experience growing Asian vegetables for the local Asian community. In fact, traders exported small quantities of Asian vegetables to the United Kingdom as early as 1952 (Kimenye 1995). As a further stimulus to growth, the presence of an Asian community in Kenya translated into family and social ties between Asian traders in London and those in Nairobi, reducing the risk and transaction costs in expanding this trade (Djikstra 1997). The rapid growth in Asian vegetable exports led the surge in Kenya's horticultural exports during this period. Although the numbers are difficult to document precisely, trade sources believe that Asian vegetables accounted for the bulk of "other fresh vegetable" exports. The value of these other fresh vegetable exports ranged between US$10 and $20 million per year during the 1980s (see Figure 5.2).

Rapid growth in the Kenyan tourism industry provided further incentives for increasing fresh fruit and vegetable production. By 1980, 372,000 international tourists were visiting Kenya annually, second only to South Africa among African countries (World Bank 2002). Although canned goods can be transported by ship from Africa to Europe, fresh produce generally requires air freight.[6] When export volumes were too small to justify a charter cargo jet, the

---

6. Major exceptions are bananas and pineapple. As discussed later, Côte d'Ivoire exports bananas and fresh pineapple to Europe on specially designed refrigerated ships. In fact, bananas are transported from Latin America to Europe by ship.

FIGURE 5.2 Trends in the composition of Kenyan fruit and vegetable exports, 1961–2006

Millions of 2005 US$

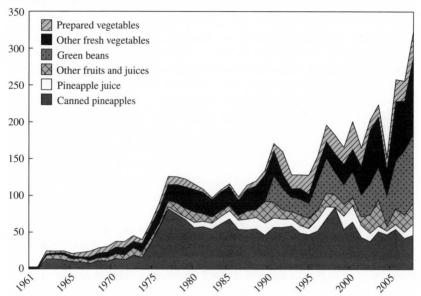

SOURCES: FAOSTAT (export data); U.S. Department of Labor (U.S. consumer price index).

cargo capacity of passenger jets provided a means of air-freighting Kenyan produce to Europe. Later, as volumes increased, full cargo jets became more widely available. In addition, the tourism industry increased the demand for high-quality fruits and vegetables by hotels and restaurants, giving Kenyan farmers more experience in horticultural production and an outlet for produce not meeting export standards. Thus, the horticultural sector in Kenya has benefited from the development of Nairobi as a regional air transport hub and as an important tourism destination.

The growth in Kenyan horticultural exports is also linked to the increasing involvement of smallholders in the sector. In the early 1970s, no more than several hundred smallholders were producing for the fresh fruit and vegetable export market, accounting for just 10–20 percent of the total volume. Later, during the late 1970s, low international prices for coffee and tea made it economical to involve smallholders in export horticulture. Although coffee prices boomed again in the 1980s, by then many smallholders had acquired skills in horticultural production. At least as important, exporters began to recognize the potential of smallholders in helping to meet the growing European demand. By the mid-1980s, Jaffee (1995) estimates that 13,000–16,000 thousand smallholders were involved in growing fresh produce for export. They accounted for 40–65 percent of the supplies of French beans, Asian vegetables, mangoes, avocados, and passion fruit for export.

Smallholders also play an important role in growing French beans for export. Fresh and canned French beans have become one of the most important horticultural exports from Kenya. Starting in the 1970s and accelerating at the end of the 1980s, Kenya's export diversification into French beans provided a major boost to Kenyan horticulture, helping to sustain horticultural export growth in the face of pressure in other fresh vegetable export markets. Initially, exports were limited to the winter–spring months, when European producers cannot supply these beans. However, the advantages of lower labor and land costs, combined with the rising need for suppliers who can provide produce throughout the year, resulted in a shift toward year-round sourcing of French beans and other vegetables from North Africa and Sub-Saharan Africa. By 1990, French beans accounted for $20 million in annual export earnings (see Figure 5.2). This growth resulted from continuous experimentation with alternative institutional arrangements by farmers and traders. Jaffee (1995) describes the tumultuous history of Hortiequip and Njoro Canners as they tried alternative institutional arrangements to provide inputs on credit, obtain reliable high-quality supplies, and ensure repayment of loans. At its peak, in 1990, these companies contracted with 24,000 smallholder farmers to grow French beans and other vegetables.

Not all fruits and vegetables produced for export are grown by smallholders, however. As mentioned earlier, Del Monte stopped purchasing pineapples from smallholders in 1974 and began relying entirely on its own production. Technological change in production and increasing international competition encouraged larger-scale operations and vertically integrated producer-processors. According to Jaffee (1994), the trend toward large-scale production of pineapples also emerged in other exporting countries such as the Philippines, Taiwan, and Thailand. Del Monte's canned pineapple exports increased by a factor of five between 1974 and 1977, reaching 45 thousand metric tons. By 1990, Kenya was exporting US$38 million in canned pineapple, making it the most important horticultural export. In addition, pineapple juice exports were in the range of US$7 million per year.

Overall, impressive growth in the production and export of pineapples, Asian vegetables, and French beans fueled horticultural export growth during this period. By 1988, Kenya had become established as the main supplier of fresh and chilled vegetables to the 12 countries then in the European Union (Dolan, Humphrey, and Harris-Pascal 1999).

Phase 4: New Challenges, 1991–Present

Available data suggest that the growth of Kenyan fruit and vegetable exports slowed during the first part of the 1990s before recovering their upward trajectory toward the end of the decade and into the early 2000s (see Figure 5.1). Horticultural export values rose from US$107 million in 1990 to US$141 million in 1999, representing an annual growth rate of under 1 percent in real terms over the decade. The horticultural share in overall agricultural exports remained in the range of 10–14 percent (see Figure 5.1).

Although export growth slowed during the 1990s, fruit and vegetable exports became more diversified, setting the stage for a later rebound in the mid-2000s. The importance of canned pineapple in fruit and vegetable export revenue fell from 40 percent in 1990 to 27 percent in 1999 (see Figure 5.2). This was partly due to the decline in canned pineapple exports (under pressure from Thailand and other exporters) and partly due to the expansion in fresh fruit and vegetable exports over this period. Although French beans, Asian vegetables, canned pineapple, and avocados dominate exports, Kenya now exports 30 different fruits and 27 vegetables (Thiru 2000). In spite of increased competition from Cameroon, Côte d'Ivoire, Morocco, South Africa, and Zimbabwe, Kenya remains the most important supplier of vegetables to the European Union.

To maintain these export markets, Kenya and other horticultural exporters face new challenges related to changes in the structure of consumer demand and to the transformation of the food retail market in Europe. Kenya's ability to maintain and strengthen its role in horticultural exports will continue to depend on its ability to adapt constructively to these changes.

THE RISE OF SUPERMARKETS. In 1989, supermarkets sold 33 percent of the fresh fruits and vegetables in the United Kingdom. By 1997, this share had increased to around 70 percent (Evans 1999). Furthermore, among supermarkets, chains have increased their market share. According to Dolan, Humphrey, and Harris-Pascal (1999), U.K. supermarket chains increased their market share in fresh fruits and vegetables from 63 percent in 1994 to 76 percent in 1997. This trend is also occurring in continental Europe. Increasingly, these supermarket chains are bypassing wholesalers to negotiate directly with exporters in Kenya and other countries. This creates a more direct link between consumer demand in the importing countries and producers in the exporting countries (Asfaw, Mithöfer, and Waibel 2007). In the interest of protecting their reputation, these supermarket chains are imposing new restrictions and even organizing production in developing countries. According to the managing director of Homegrown (Kenya) Ltd., one of the country's largest horticultural exporters, Homegrown rarely grows anything unless a supermarket has programmed it (Evans 1999).

INCREASING CONCERN OVER FOOD SAFETY. European consumers are increasingly aware of the health consequences of pesticide residues. Even consumers who are not part of the growing "organic food" movement (which is stronger in Europe than in the United States) are increasingly wary of agricultural chemicals. In 1990, the United Kingdom passed the Food Safety Act, which obliged food retailers to demonstrate "due diligence" to ensure that the food they sell is safe. In practice, this means that supermarkets have become much more involved in imposing requirements on how food is produced throughout the commodity supply chain, even to the degree of monitoring and controlling horticultural production in developing countries (Dolan, Humphrey, and Harris-Pascal 1999). Minimum residue levels of pesticides have become a focal point for their concern. The Fresh Produce Exporters Association (FPEAK) has produced a 31-page Code of Practice for growers (FPEAK 1999). The code covers employment practices, agrochemical application procedures, land use guidelines, and so on. The last two pages provide a 14-step documentation procedure for ensuring the traceability of produce being handled by the exporter. This is an important step in establishing a common set of standards regarding safe handling of fresh fruits and vegetables and disseminating the information. However, some aspects of the code imply significant costs, and there are currently no enforcement mechanisms.

INCREASING DEMAND FOR CONVENIENCE.   European consumers, like those in other industrialized countries, are demanding some forms of prepared fresh fruits and vegetables. This preparation can include washing, peeling, cutting, packaging in small units, premixing of vegetables, and so on. Because these activities are labor intensive, they provide an opportunity for adding value in the exporting country.

COMPETITION FROM OTHER SUPPLIERS.   Kenyan horticulture enjoyed duty-free access to European markets as a result of preferential treatment of selected African, Caribbean, and Pacific (ACP) countries under the Lomé Agreement. Because these unilateral preferences were considered discriminatory under the World Trade Organization (WTO) rules, they have been replaced by Economic Partnership Agreements (EPAs) that involve reciprocal trade concessions. The EPA with Kenya, signed in November 2007, was controversial because it involved phased liberalization in Kenya with little gain in Kenyan access to European markets. Without the EPA, however, horticultural exports would have been subject to 5–15 percent import tariffs, threatening an estimated 1.5 million jobs in Kenya that depend on horticulture and fisheries (Oluoch 2008). An analysis by Stevens and Kennan (1999) indicates that Kenya will face greater competition from Brazil, Chile, Egypt, South Africa, and Thailand as the European Union eliminates ACP preferential access.

Even without European trade liberalization, world horticultural markets remain highly competitive and subject to rapid shifts in competitive position. Jaffee (1995) describes the turbulent history of Kenya's attempts to expand its exports of dehydrated vegetables, passion fruit juice, and pineapple products, including several bankruptcies and government buy-outs. Kenya lost the European fresh pineapple market to Côte d'Ivoire in the 1980s, was squeezed out of avocado exports to Europe by the higher quality of Israeli and South African products, and lost the European market for courgettes, sweet peppers, and other temperate vegetables to European and Mediterranean suppliers.

Yet Kenyan exporters have shown resilience in finding new markets and expanding Kenya's exports of French beans, Asian vegetables, and cut flowers. During the mid-2000s, these efforts contributed to strong growth in Kenyan exports of French beans, green peas, and prepared vegetables (see Figure 5.2). Growth in these crops succeeded in raising horticultural exports to US$323 million in 2005 (Table 5.2), for a growth rate of 4.8 percent per year in real terms over the period.

Drivers of Change

PRIVATE INVESTMENT AND TRADE. The growth of Kenya's fruit and vegetable export sector rests largely on the efficiency and flexibility of the country's horticultural marketing system. Because a large share of the overall demand for fruits and vegetables is in urban areas and foreign markets, the volume of horticultural production critically depends on smoothly functioning markets links between producers and consumers. The perishability of fruits and vegetables makes prices volatile and production risky, thus increasing the potential

TABLE 5.2 Composition of Kenyan exports of fruits and vegetables, 2005

Product	Export value (millions of US$)
Fruits	
Pineapples, canned	46,394
Avocados	18,135
Pineapple juice	15,243
Mangoes and guavas[a]	3,986
Other fruit juices	734
Pineapples[a]	518
Other fresh fruit	4,450
Total fruit and fruit juices	89,460
Vegetables	
French beans	93,794
Fresh vegetables[a]	59,086
Green peas	45,584
Prepared vegetables	27,711
Onions	883
Other	6,528
Total vegetables	233,584
Total fruit and vegetables	323,044

SOURCE: FAOSTAT (2007), available at <http://faostat.fao.org/site/343/default.aspx>.

[a]2004 figures.

gain from the exchange of marketing information between producers and traders. Because fruit and vegetable production requires more labor, more purchased inputs, and more skill than does that of grains and legumes, the transmission of credit, inputs, and technical assistance is often necessary. Together, these characteristics of horticultural production suggest that vertical coordination between producers and traders is important in fruit and vegetable marketing, particularly when the producers are smallholders. Indeed, Kenyan private trade has experimented over many years with a wide range of initiatives to develop viable, financially sustainable production and marketing systems.

Substantial early investments by international firms helped to launch the pineapple and passion fruit export industries in Kenya. Firms from America, Australia, and Europe participated in the effort, investing in processing and canning facilities as well as large plantations. Together they spearheaded the first major surge of horticultural export products from Kenya and have served as the mainstay of the export trade since the 1960s (see Figure 5.2).

Private traders, particularly among the local Asian community, launched the second great wave of Kenyan horticultural exports. Profiting from family and community ties to the Asian expatriate community in Europe, they developed a growing market for Asian vegetables in Europe. During the 1970s and 1980s, Asian vegetables constituted roughly one-fourth of Kenya's fruit and vegetable exports.

SUPPORTIVE, NONINTRUSIVE GOVERNMENT POLICY.   Unlike other major agricultural subsectors, in which the Kenyan government has imposed controls on both external and domestic trade, the marketing of horticultural products has generally remained free of direct government intervention. With the exception of onions, the government has not been directly involved in the pricing, marketing, or storage of horticultural products. Government's role has been minimal, confined for the most part to regulatory and facilitative functions (Kimweli 1991). Through research support and modest capital injections into selected export ventures, the Kenyan government has provided intermittent, strategic support for private sector initiatives. Many traders attribute the remarkable performance of the industry to this largely laissez-faire government policy, which has engendered autonomy in production and marketing decisions, thus fostering significant local private initiatives and dynamism within the industry.

TOURISM.   The rise of tourism in Kenya contributed to the growth of horticulture marketing and export trade in two major ways. First, the growing domestic demand for high-quality fruits and vegetables in tourist hotels and safari camps stimulated a large local market for horticultural products. This offered farmers and traders an alternate market outlet, a means of diversifying risks, and an outlet for products graded below export standards. Second, and probably more critical, the regular flow of air traffic in and out of Nairobi provided regular air connections with major European and Middle Eastern cities. In the early days of the export trade, before the volumes were sufficient to justify full cargo loads, the prospects for sending small cargo shipments aboard passenger planes enabled Kenyan traders to establish market shares and develop the quality control systems and reputation required to grow their share of the export trade.

IRRIGATION. Growth in horticultural exports has advanced hand in hand with the growing use of irrigation. Without reliable water control, farmers cannot produce a steady supply of vegetables throughout the year, making them less interesting to full-time exporters. Producers reliant on rainfed production, therefore, must typically sell their output to traders for domestic sales or seasonally to small-scale "briefcase" exporters (Figure 5.3). As a result, export horticulture producers depend heavily on irrigation systems of various types (Boxes 5.1–5.3). Although only 12 percent of Kenyan farm households own any irrigation equipment, fully half of smallholder farmers growing French beans own such equipment according to a nationwide rural household survey conducted in 2000 (see Minot and Ngigi 2003). Similarly, a much smaller survey of 120 farmers along the Nairobi–Meru road (an area of very good market access) found that 90 percent of smallholder growers of horticultural export crops had irrigation compared to 36 percent of nonhorticultural producers (McCulloch and Ota 2002).

The development of new irrigation technologies has helped to spur the rapid growth of smallholder irrigation. Small-scale drip irrigation systems have been introduced by missionaries, improved by the Kenya Agricultural Research Institute, and disseminated by local nongovernmental organizations (NGOs), including FPEAK. These range from a bucket system that covers 15 square meters to a drum system irrigating 75 square meters to an "8-acre" system that can irrigate 450 square meters. In addition, several types of treadle irrigation pumps costing less than US$80 have been introduced. ApproTEC, a local NGO, reports that 24,000 of these pumps are being used by smallholders in Kenya and Tanzania, mainly for the production of vegetables and other high-value crops (Sijali and Okumu 2002; ApproTEC 2003).

SEEDS. Access to high-quality seed is important to horticultural producers, particularly those aiming at the export market. Over a dozen seed companies operate in Kenya, including both local and international companies. Among the international seed companies represented in Kenya are Monsanto, Panaar, Pioneer, and Seminis. The Kenya Seed Company is one of the largest and best-known African seed companies, having fostered the dissemination of hybrid maize seed in Kenya in the 1960s and 1970s. Formed as a private company in 1956, it became partly government owned after independence, though it operates much like a private company. In 1979 the company purchased an-

FIGURE 5.3 Export marketing channels for Kenya's French beans, 2001

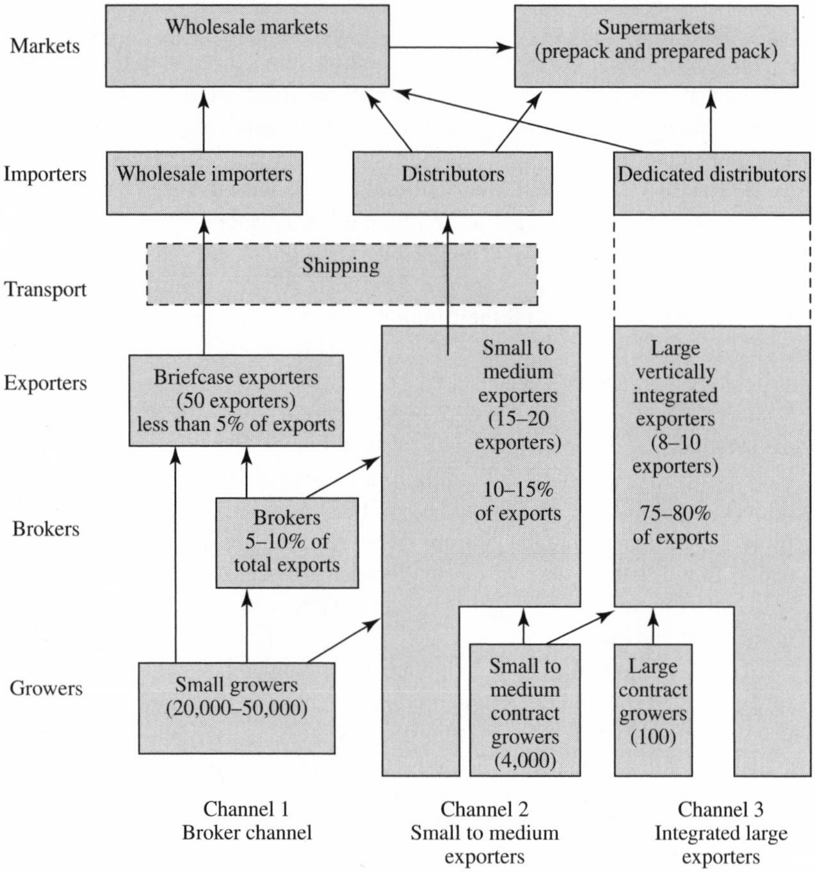

SOURCE: Ebony Consulting International (2001).

other seed company specializing in horticultural and flower seed. Today it sells over 100 varieties of vegetables, legumes, and root crops under the name Simlaw (Kenya Seed Company 2003). The largest vendor of French bean seed is Regina Seeds, a subsidiary of Seminis, the largest supplier of fruit and vegetable seed in the world. Regina distributes imported French bean seed and does not produce any locally. Trade sources estimate that 70 percent of the vegetable seed sold in Kenya is imported, with the remaining 30 percent produced locally (Regina Seeds 2003). This reinforces the imperative for close links among seed suppliers, exporters, and farmers in order to ensure the quality control necessary to maintain export standards.

BOX 5.1 An accounts clerk turns to passion fruit

Karimi is in his mid-30s and started engaging in commercial horticulture in 1999. Before then, he was an accounts clerk with the city council of Nairobi. His major motivation came from the observation that a friend who had resigned from Unilever–Kenya to grow passion fruit commercially had improved his lot greatly. Karimi resigned his job and uprooted his 0.25 acres of tea to plant passion fruit trees. There was a strong market demand in both the local and export markets. The export market offers a higher price, but it is very demanding in terms of quality, and only about 50 percent of his output is of export quality.

Karimi had a bad start: after only one season, his first crop of passion fruit was completely destroyed by counterfeit fungicides. The production of passion fruit is constrained by *muthu* birds, and protecting the fruit is very labor intensive. Since then, the crop has done better, and the well-being of Karimi's family has greatly improved. With the savings from passion fruit production, he bought an eighth-of-an-acre plot in Kirinyaga town, where he plans to put up a residential rental house. He has also been able to move his son to a better school.

Karimi cited lack of irrigation as the major factor constraining other farmers in his area from growing fruits and vegetables as a commercial activity. During dry spells he has to pay casual laborers to manually carry water from a bolehole on the farm. With regard to passion fruit growing, which is a fairly new activity in the area, he cited lack of knowledge about production methods, high costs of fruit tree planting, the long waiting period before the first harvest (about 6 to 9 months), and labor intensity as the major constraints. When asked how the government could assist horticultural producers, Karimi said that greater effort was needed to control the quality of agricultural chemicals and regulate input stockists. He does not have any other agricultural enterprise.

The Current Production and Marketing System

PRODUCTION. The rapid growth of Kenya's export and domestic horticultural markets has resulted in broad opportunities for Kenyan farmers as well as the development of a variety of input supply and marketing systems. The national Rural Household Survey of 2000 indicates that 98 percent of Kenyan farmers grow fruits and vegetables. On average, they grow 3.5 different types of fruit and 3.3 types of vegetables. The most important of these, in value terms, are avocados (16 percent of the fruit and vegetable value), bananas (12 percent), Irish potatoes (11 percent), and mangoes (10 percent). Tomatoes, *sukuma wiki,* cabbage, and pawpaws are also important, each representing at least 5 percent of the total value of fruit and vegetable production (Table 5.3). Horticultural producers indicate that success in horticultural production involves a continu-

TABLE 5.3 Summary measures of the importance of each crop, 2000 (percentage of production)

	Share of farms growing	Share of value of fruit and vegetable production	Share of value of fruit and vegetable sales	Share of production that is sold
Bananas	69	12	15	51
Avocados	35	16	5	12
Mangoes	31	10	2	8
Pawpaws	30	5	2	20
Guavas	27	1	0	11
Lemons	15	1	0	12
Oranges	15	2	1	33
Passion fruit	14	1	0	22
Lugard	14	1	0	5
Matomoko	6	1	0	9
Pineapples	5	0	0	42
Mero	3	0	0	27
Other fruit	6	1	3	85
Fruit subtotal	89	48	30	24
Sukuma wiki	63	9	6	29
Irish potatoes	38	11	13	48
Onions	35	4	5	48
Pumpkins	31	1	0	18
Tomatoes	30	9	16	74
Indigenous vegetables	29	2	0	10
Cabbage	23	8	17	79
Spinach	11	1	0	7
Carrots	10	2	2	51
Peppers	10	0	0	15
Green peas	8	0	0	25
Green grams	7	1	0	8
Pumpkin leaves	7	0	0	4
French beans	4	1	4	94
Capsicum	4	1	1	77
Other vegetables	7	2	4	61
Vegetable subtotal	90	52	70	53
Fruit and vegetable total	98	100	100	39

SOURCE: Egerton/Tegemeo/Michigan State University Rural Household Survey, 2000.

ous series of experiments and adjustments. Rarely do farmers "get it right" the first time, and often they try a succession of crops before identifying a competitive niche (Box 5.2).

The median Kenyan farmer produces fruit and vegetables worth Ksh 49,000 per year (US$658), on average. This amounts to slightly less than one quarter of the value of crop production. Farmers sell more than one-third (35 percent) of fruit and vegetable production on the market, though the share is higher for vegetables (49 percent) than for fruit (20 percent). A comparison of Food and Agriculture Organization of the United Nations statistics for horticultural production and exports suggests that about 96 percent of the volume of fruits and vegetables produced is marketed domestically, with just 4 percent destined for the export market.

Most growers sell relatively small volumes of fruits and vegetables, but a few farms generate quite sizable sales. Tables 5.4 and 5.5 show the distribution of farmers according to their fruit and vegetable sales. The average value of sales is relatively high, Ksh 17,000 (US$226) per year. Yet more than half the

---

**BOX 5.2 A long-time horticultural grower
adjusts to changing conditions**

Joyce Wambui and her husband have been growing commercial horticultural crops since they started a family in 1981. They started by selling tomatoes. Last season they cultivated a crop of French beans. At the time they were interviewed for this book, they were harvesting a crop of sweet corn. In their own assessment, they feel that their horticultural activity has afforded their family a relatively good livelihood. From the proceeds of this activity, they are able to pay their children's school fees. In addition, they have bought a dairy cow and a pair of oxen, and they have a brick house under construction.

One major concern of the Wambuis, which they explained is shared by many horticultural growers in the area, is that they have started observing problems with the soils. They explained that tomatoes and some varieties of French beans and even the traditional varieties of bananas have been affected by a wilting disease. To deal with this, they shifted from French beans and tomatoes to sweet corn.

Another problem experienced in the area is poor water-use management. During dry spells, farmers downsteam do not get sufficient water. To solve this problem the farmers in the areas have formed the Kutus–Kiriti Water Furrow Farmers' Group. However, although the group has designed a system of water use shifts, it has not been able to enforce the new system. The group is also encouraging farmers to use pipes to extract water from the main furrow instead of using lateral furrows. This effort has been more successful, mainly because the pipes help control the water seepage.

TABLE 5.4 Fruit and vegetable production by income category, 2000

	Income quintile					
	Poorest	2	3	4	Richest	Total
Percentage of farmers growing fruits and vegetables	92	99	100	100	100	98
Average number of fruit and vegetable crops grown	4.9	6.0	6.8	8.0	8.4	6.8
Average value of fruit and vegetable production (Ksh/household)	7,805	17,188	22,848	50,615	148,689	49,383
Value of fruit and vegetable production as a percentage of total crop value	25	26	21	25	22	23
Value of fruit and vegetable sales (Ksh/household)	2,178	5,163	6,874	15,962	55,123	17,043
Sales of fruit and vegetables						
Percentage of total crop sales	23	24	14	18	27	23
Sales of fruits and vegetables as a percentage of production	28	30	30	32	37	35
Value of fruit and vegetable production as a percentage of income	21	18	14	18	18	18

SOURCE: Egerton/Tegemeo/Michigan State University Rural Household Survey, 2000.

TABLE 5.5 Fruit and vegetable production by farm size, 2000

	Farm size (ha)					
	<1	1–2	2–5	5–10	>10	Total
Percentage of farmers growing fruits and vegetables	97	98	99	100	100	98
Average number of fruit and vegetable crops grown	6	6.8	7.4	8.6	8.3	6.8
Average value of fruit and vegetable production (Ksh/household)	35,039	43,139	69,407	80,531	70,047	49,383
Value of fruit and vegetable production as a percentage of total crop value	26	24	22	22	10	23
Value of fruit and vegetable sales (Ksh/household)	8,159	13,230	27,448	49,199	30,094	17,043
Sales of fruit and vegetables						
As a percentage of total crop sales	35	22	25	26	6	23
As a percentage of production	23	31	40	61	43	35
Value of fruit and vegetable production as a percentage of income	20	18	18	18	9	18

SOURCE: Egerton/Tegemeo/Michigan State University Rural Household Survey, 2000.

farmers have sales of less than Ksh 2,500. About 7 percent of them have sales of more than Ksh 50,000 (US$667). This group includes some quite large horticultural producers. Although they are a small proportion of the growers, they account for 72 percent of the sales (Minot and Ngigi 2004).

The sizes of the farms producing fruits and vegetables vary across crops depending partly on the economies of scale in production and processing. The Del Monte Corporation grows pineapples for canning on vertically integrated pineapple plantations covering 4,000 hectares (Del Monte 1988). This vertical integration allows the company to stagger production using plant hormones, thus providing a steady year-round supply of pineapples for processing. In contrast, smallholder farmers dominate the production of mangoes and avocados for export markets. Large-scale commercial growers of mangoes and avocados have not been able to compete with smallholders, who have lower labor costs and greater motivation to provide careful husbandry (Jaffee 2003).

French beans are grown on both small and large farms (Ebony Consulting International 2001). Large commercial farms of 50–100 hectares grow various types of vegetables for export using hired labor and modern technology. They are either owned by exporters or have formal contracts with large exporters. Small- and medium-scale contract growers may plant as little as 0.25 hectares of French beans, with the exporter providing seed and sometimes chemicals on credit. They hire about 15 laborers per hectare of French beans planted. Independent smallholders with 1–5 hectares plant only a fraction of this with French beans. Without a contract, they use fewer purchased inputs, often recycle seed, and sell at lower prices due to differences in quality and/or variety (see Figure 5.3).

MARKETING.   Horticultural producers supply rural consumers through direct marketing channels involving sales at the farmgate or at rural market centers. The smallest rural markets are informal and periodic, with one or two market days per week. These markets are located close enough to production areas so that the produce is transported to market by head-load and by bicycle. At these markets, farmers often sell directly to final consumers.

Urban markets, however, rely on a chain of intermediaries that may include assemblers, brokers, wholesalers, and retailers. Independent assemblers or wholesale agents bring produce to the urban markets after purchasing it directly from farmers or from rural markets. Transportation involves minibuses (for small quantities) or trucks (for larger quantities). Because of the widely ranging agroecological zones and the associated geographical distribution of production, long-distance traders and transporters play a very crucial role in moving fruits and vegetables to the urban markets. For the same reason, and because of the small size of many farms, commission brokers, acting on behalf of large and long-distance traders, play an important role in searching for supplies and organizing procurement into economical loads (Dijkstra 1999). Fruit and vegetable retailers, the final link in domestic supply chains, are typically small-scale traders operating in makeshift sheds in high-density residential areas, on the pavement, in busy urban streets, or hawking produce door to door in the residential areas.

Export channels likewise vary widely, but they can be roughly classified according to the degree of vertical integration. At one extreme is the vertically integrated Del Monte Corporation, which produces pineapples on its own plantation in Thika, processes the pineapples, arranges shipping to Europe or other destinations, and even distributes the goods to supermarkets and wholesalers in foreign markets. The four largest fruit and vegetable exporters indicate that 40 percent of production came from their own farms (Dolan and Humphrey 2000).[7]

A second channel involves exporters who contract farmers to produce fruits and vegetables for export. Dijkstra (1997) reports that almost all horticultural exporters rely to some degree on contract farmers. The agreements between exporters and farmers are often unwritten and are subject to frequent disputes. If the market price falls, exporters may fail to pick up the produce and try to source elsewhere. If the market price rises, farmers may sell elsewhere and default on the agreements (Jaffee 1995; Kimenye 1995). When exporters contract directly with farmers, they are often large- or medium-scale farmers. The four largest fruit and vegetable exporters obtain about 40 percent of their supplies from large-scale commercial farms and only 18 percent from smallholders (Dolan and Humphrey 2000).

A third channel involves various types of intermediaries between the farmer and the exporter. Small farmers and those who do not live in the main production zones often rely on traders or brokers to assemble produce for resale. Sometimes a large farmer who has a contract with an exporter will coordinate the production and marketing of the produce by smallholders living nearby. These are more likely to be spot market transactions. Exporters likewise use spot market purchases to fill in gaps between their regular supply (from their own production and contracts) and their commitments to distributors and supermarkets overseas (Jaffee 1995; Ebony Consulting International 2001). Alternatively, some farmers join marketing groups to ensure a minimum level of production to attract exporters or traders (Box 5.3). These farmer groups play an important role in reducing the transaction costs between small farmers and exporters. Through self-selection and peer monitoring, these groups also provide some assurance of quality and commitment. The groups allow exporters to distribute inputs on credit, assemble the output, and recover loan repayments with many small farmers. Brokers sometimes play this role, but many growers feel they are better off working through a farmer group.

About 200 licensed fresh produce exporters operated in Kenya in the early 1990s, but only 50 were full-time dedicated exporters. The other 150 were traders

---

7. As noted earlier, however, exporters may wish to exaggerate their own-farm production to reassure importers.

BOX 5.3 Diversification from staples to vegetables

Asha Muthori is a middle-aged woman who owns a 5-acre piece of land on the banks of the Thiba river, a permanent river. She started growing horticultural crops in 1996 after observing that her neighbors who grew horticultural crops were better off than those who did not. She also learned from the growers that returns from horticulture were generally higher than those from intercropping maize and beans, as she had been doing until then.

Asha started with a crop of tomatoes, which she sold to traders who resold them in the main wholesale market in Nairobi. Later she started growing French beans and selling them to brokers buying for major exporters. Last year she joined the Kimuri Farmers' Self-Help Group and sold her French beans to an exporter through the group. She explained that sale through the group has a number of advantages. First, her output is too small to attract direct deals with a major exporter. On her own, therefore, she is constrained to sell to brokers at a price that is lower than that offered by major exporters. As a group, however, members pool their produce to achieve volumes that attract direct negotiations with major exporters. Asha says that exporters offer a more reliable market outlet than do brokers. In addition, the group deposits each farmer's payments directly into his or her personal savings account, thus offering better security than cash transactions. This also saves the farmers the cost of traveling to the banks, which are usually located in major urban centers, to deposit the money.

At the same time, Asha points out a major weakness of selling through the group. The pooling of produce from member farmers for presentation to the buyer reduces the incentive to maintain quality control in production and handling. Some members do not strictly follow the recommended production practices, and the low quality of their output reduces the quality and price of the entire lot.

Asha stated that the well-being of her family has greatly improved since she started growing commercial horticultural crops. In particular, she said that she used to have difficulties paying her children's school fees, so her children were frequently sent away from school. Since she started horticultural production, this has no longer been a problem, and her children have been able to attend school without interruption. In addition, she said that she had once been forced to sell all her maize and beans at harvest to generate cash for school fees. This meant it was necessary to engage in casual wage labor to raise money for food. Now she is able to save some of her maize and bean harvest for her family's own consumption. Finally, she noted that she had used some of the proceeds of the horticulture farming to buy a plot of land in Mombassa, which she plans to develop.

When asked why other farmers in her area did not grow fruits and vegetables as a commercial activity, Asha cited lack of capital, especially the money required to acquire a water pump. Currently, her only other crop is a 3-acre intercrop of maize and beans. She also owns a dairy cow and two plough oxen. She ranks horticulture as her most important source of income, followed by dairy production.

who entered the market as opportunities arose (Jaffee 1995). Now, as then, the smallest and most transient of these are called "briefcase exporters." One-third of the export traders are Kenyans of South Asian origin, who make use of kin connections to export produce, particularly Asian vegetables, to the United Kingdom (Dijkstra 1997).

Several observers have noted that the export sector has become more concentrated since the early 1990s. A recent study of French bean export marketing channels indicates that 8–10 large-scale exporters with foreign distribution capacity account for 75–80 percent of the total export volume (see Figure 5.3). This concentration is a response to the increasing role of supermarkets as importers and the premium they give for reliability of supply, consistency of quality, and documentation of production conditions. Exporters are being required to monitor and document production practices affecting food safety (such as chemical use) and, increasingly, worker conditions and environmental impact. Furthermore, the trend toward prepackaging and labeling exports so they are ready for retail distribution increases the economies of scale in exporting (see Dolan and Humphrey 2000; Kamau 2000; Ebony Consulting International 2001; Jaffee 2003).

The Impact of Horticultural Export Growth

PARTICIPATION.   Over 98 percent of Kenyan farmers grow fruits and vegetables. Geographically, export growers remain clustered in locations with reliable access to water and close proximity to transport arteries and the major airports. Kenya's nationwide rural household survey of 2000 found over 70 percent of smallholder French bean growers in just three districts. Overall horticultural production for both domestic and export markets also varies geographically, with farmers in Eastern, Central, and Coast provinces producing fruits and vegetables valued at two to three times as much as those raised in Rift Valley and Western provinces.

Estimates of the number of smallholders supplying horticultural export markets vary widely, as does the intensity of their participation. Jaffee (1995) estimates that 13,000–16,000 smallholders were involved in fresh produce export, while Swanberg (1995) cites a figure of 500,000. In its study of French bean marketing, Ebony Consulting International (2001) indicates that 20,000–50,000 small growers participate in French bean exports alone. Though the rural household survey of 2000 does not distinguish between production for domestic and export markets, it indicates that 4 percent of smallholders—or 200,000 households—produce French beans, the most common export crop (see Table 5.3). That same survey indicates that 8 percent of Kenyan farm households earn over half of their income from horticultural products. These amount to 400,000 households, although this figure includes both domestic and export producers. If the smallholder French bean exporters in the small-sample survey by Kamau (2000) are typical of smallholder exporters, this would imply that there are about 200,000 smallholders in the horticultural export sector.[8] Although this figure must be considered tentative, it represents a plausible order of magnitude of the number farmers who regularly supply produce for export horticulture markets.

INCOME.   On average, Kenyan farmers produce fruit and vegetables valued at about Ksh 52,000 (US$693) (Minot and Ngigi 2003). But a small number of large growers heavily influence this figure. The median value of fruit and vegetable production is just Ksh 14,096 (US$188).

How much does fruit and vegetable production contribute to the incomes of growers? The national survey data reported in Table 5.5 suggest that fruits and vegetables provide merely supplemental income for most farmers. Yet a significant minority of farmers rely on fruits and vegetables for a major share of their income. For over two-thirds of the farmers in the survey, fruit and vegetable production provides less than 20 percent of household income.[9] At the other extreme, 8 percent of the farmers earn over half their income from fruit and vegetable production (Minot and Ngigi 2004).

Both anecdotal and survey data suggest that smallholders producing horticultural export crops are significantly better off than nonhorticultural smallholders. One study of 141 rural households in selected zones near Mount Kenya suggests that horticultural farmers earn significantly more than farmers who do not grow horticultural products, even after controlling for household characteristics such as age, education, ethnicity, and ownership of land (McCulloch and Ota 2002). The authors find that these farmers benefit directly from the higher income as well as indirectly through greater access to credit and extension services. Larger sample sizes from the national rural household survey of 2000 permit some inferences based on the income levels among producers of French beans, Kenya's single largest export crop. These results indicate that households growing French beans earn per capita incomes roughly double those of households that do not (Table 5.6).

Indeed, gross margin analysis comparing the most common export crop (French beans) with the most common domestic food crop (intercropped maize and beans) suggests that gross margins per hectare per year are between 6 and 20 times greater for French beans (Table 5.7). These results should be interpreted with some caution, however, for they exclude the investment costs required for horticultural production, interest costs on the cash required to pur-

---

8. Given US$320 million in exports, if we assume that 50 percent is supplied by smallholders with a ratio of 0.6 for the farmgate to freight on board price, this implies US$96 million in smallholder income from horticultural exports. If we also assume average smallholder horticultural sales of about US$450, this implies that more than 200 thousand farmers are supplying horticultural products for export.

9. Because it is difficult to attribute all production costs to different crops, these figures compare the *gross* value of fruit and vegetable production and *net* income, defined as gross revenue minus the cash costs of production.

TABLE 5.6 Comparison of French bean growers and other farmers, 2000

	French bean growers	Other farmers
Farm size (percent in each)		
<1 ha	35	35
1–2 ha	32	30
2–5 ha	26	28
5–10 ha	4	2
>10 ha	2	5
Average farm size (sown area) (ha)	2.57	2.15
Income quintile (percent in each)		
Poorest	8	21
2	15	20
3	13	20
4	25	20
Richest	38	19
Average per capita income (Ksh)	99,617	48,568
Province (percent in each)		
East/Central/Coast	30	58
Rift Valley	35	15
Western provinces	35	27
Distance to paved road (percent)		
Less than 1 km	17	12
1–5 km	30	33
5–10 km	24	45
10–20 km	22	8
More than 20 km	6	2
Average value of assets (Ksh)	110,692	139,019
Percentage owning irrigation equipment	50	10
Number of households	62	1548

SOURCE: Egerton/Tegemeo/Michigan State University Rural Household Survey, 2000.

chase inputs, and implicit costs of using unpaid family labor. Results likewise vary considerably by location. The gross margin analysis suggests that when the right conditions are present in terms of rainfall, markets, family labor, and households' ability to bear risk, French bean production can be much more profitable than maize–bean intercropping.

Anecdotal evidence from individual farmers indicates that most, though not all, believe commercial horticultural production has made a significant contribution to the well-being of their families. In many cases, they use the additional income to buy land or to pay school fees (see Boxes 5.1–5.3).

GENDER ISSUES.   Available information suggests that women play a major role in horticultural production and marketing in Kenya. According to a sur-

TABLE 5.7 Gross margins in Kenyan horticulture and staple food crop production, 2005

	Maize–bean intercropping	French beans
Value of output (2005 US$/ha)	688	7,505
Costs (2005 US$/ha)		
Land preparation	63	0
Seed	70	467
Fungicides	0	1,730
Fertilizer	82	496
Hired labor	253	2,154
Total variable cost	467	4,848
Gross margin (2005 US$/ha)	221	2,657

SOURCE: Minot and Ngigi (2004).

vey carried out by Dolan and Sutherland (2003), women represent 60 percent of the farm labor in horticultural production in Kenya, and half of the horticultural producer households are headed by women. Furthermore, women account for 66 percent of the employment in horticultural packhouses. Although horticulture represents an important source of employment for women, the study also found that women are disproportionately in the part-time, lower-level, unskilled positions in the packhouses and that they earn less than their male coworkers at the same level. Given these findings, it is somewhat surprising that women are more likely than men to say that they have been better off since they started working in the horticultural sector. This may be a reflection of the limited employment opportunities for women outside the sector.

EQUITY.   In the early 2000s, smallholder farmers produced 40 percent of exported fruit and 70 percent of exported vegetables, according to estimates provided by the HCDA (Harris et al. 2001). Given the greater importance of vegetable exports, this implies that 55–60 percent of fruit and vegetable exports are produced by smallholders. Similar estimates from the early 1990s likewise suggest that over half of the export fruit and vegetable production was supplied by smallholders (see Jaffee 1995; Kimenye 1995).

In the future, how will the expanding role of supermarkets and the increasing importance of food safety certification affect the participation of smallholders in Kenya's fruit and vegetable export sector? Dolan and Humphrey (2000) argue that smallholders are being squeezed out of export production because of the difficulty of ensuring compliance with food safety and quality requirements imposed by supermarkets and other buyers. They maintain that these requirements are leading exporters to grow their own produce or purchase from large-scale commercial farms. According to their interviews with four leading exporters, just 18 percent of vegetables for export come from smallholders. However, these four large exporters are probably not typical. Furthermore, exporters may wish to underreport the share of their production that comes from smallholders to satisfy European buyers who are suspicious of smallholder quality control (Harris et al. 2001). Jaffee (2003) interviewed several dozen exporters and estimates that smallholders account for 27 percent of exported fresh vegetables and 85 percent of exported fresh fruit, for an average of 47 percent of fresh fruit and vegetable exports.[10] He points out that, although the dominance of U.K. supermarkets has increased, about 60 percent of the Kenyan fresh fruit and vegetable exports are sold to U.K. wholesalers and other European countries that have much less strict food safety and quality requirements.

How do farmers supplying the fruit and vegetable export market differ from other farmers in Kenya? Available evidence suggests that growers of horticultural export crops have above-average farm sizes. One survey of farmers on a main road near Nairobi found that growers of horticultural export crops owned an average of 2.7 hectares, compared to 1.2 hectares for other farmers in the vicinity (McCulloch and Ota 2002). Similarly, national survey data on growers of French beans, the most commercialized and export-oriented smallholder crop, indicate that these growers operate slightly larger farms than other smallholders, 2.6 hectares versus 2.2 hectares (see Table 5.7). Incomes, however, differ sharply, with French bean growers earning more than twice as much as other farmers. As a result, only 8 percent of French bean growers are in the poorest income quintile, while 38 percent are in the richest quintile (see Table 5.6). Taken together, these results suggest a significant income impact on farm households able to access these lucrative export markets.

Looking across income quintiles reveals that virtually all farmers, rich and poor, participate in some form of horticultural production (see Table 5.4).[11] Better-off farmers seem to grow a wider variety of fruits and vegetables, and this leads to their more extensive portfolio of most horticultural products (Table 5.8). Poor households are equally likely to produce pawpaws, guavas, and citrus fruits as well as indigenous vegetables. But rich households dominate in most other categories (Table 5.8). Yet the value of fruit and vegetable production as a percentage of total crop production does not vary appreciably across income categories (22–25 percent). Nor does the importance of fruit and vegetable production in overall income show a trend across income classes, remaining in the range of 18–21 percent (see Table 5.4). Higher-income farmers, however, market a larger share of their fruit and vegetable production than do

---

10. Neither Dolan and Humphrey (2000) nor Jaffee (2003) provides the definitions used to classify farms as small, medium, or large, but Ngigi (2002) defines smallholders as those farming 1–2 acres (0.2–0.4 hectare) in high-rainfall zones and 5–10 acres (2–4 hectares) in semiarid zones.

11. Income per capita is calculated by combining estimates of crop income, livestock sales, animal product sales, household enterprise income, and income from wages and salaries. In the case of crop income, we include the imputed value of home production as well as the value of crop sales. In the case of both farm size and income per capita, the categories are quintiles. In each case (except for wages and salaries), the costs of production are subtracted from the gross sales.

low-income groups. The percentage rises from 28 percent among the poorest quintile to 37 percent among the richest quintile. In fact, it is somewhat surprising that the share does not rise faster across income quintiles. Similar trends emerge when comparing horticultural production and sales by farm size (see Tables 5.5 and 5.9).

SUSTAINABILITY.   Private traders, processors, and farmers have sustained a large and growing export horticulture industry in Kenya over the past 30 years. The system is clearly commercially viable, even highly profitable, for individual participants (see Table 5.7). Unlike the case of maize, which depended on

TABLE 5.8 Percentage of farms growing selected fruits and vegetables by income category, 2000

Crop	Income quintile					Total
	Poorest	2	3	4	Richest	
Bananas	49	67	72	78	84	70
Avocados	17	25	36	44	58	36
Mangoes	21	32	34	39	33	32
Pawpaws	22	32	35	37	25	30
Sukuma wiki	45	55	66	71	79	63
Irish potatoes	22	28	38	44	59	38
Onions	22	28	33	42	51	35
Pumpkin	25	28	30	36	35	31
Indigenous vegetables	27	34	33	30	23	30

SOURCE: Egerton / Tegemeo / Michigan State University Rural Household Survey, 2000.

NOTE: The table only covers fruits and vegetables grown by at least 30% of the farm households.

TABLE 5.9 Percentage of farms growing each crop by farm size, 2000

Crop	Farm size (ha)					Total
	<1	1–2	2–5	5–10	>10	
Bananas	70	69	71	73	64	70
Avocados	39	33	36	22	30	36
Mangoes	26	32	35	53	33	32
Pawpaws	28	29	33	31	33	30
Sukuma wiki	56	63	71	67	73	63
Irish potatoes	38	39	37	42	27	38
Onions	32	34	37	56	52	35
Pumpkins	27	26	35	55	64	31
Indigenous vegetables	27	29	32	35	39	30

SOURCE: Egerton / Tegemeo / Michigan State University Rural Household Survey, 2000.

NOTE: The table only covers fruits and vegetables grown by at least 30% of the farm households.

heavy subsidies (see Chapter 3), export horticulture remains largely privately financed and commercially viable. To maintain their competitive position, traders have had to make a series of adjustments over time in their product portfolio and in market outlets. Unsheltered from commercial pressures and imperatives, they have had to experiment and innovate to maintain their large and growing market share.

Contrasting Horticultural Dynamics in Côte d'Ivoire

The Evolution of the Ivorian Horticultural Sector

As of 2005, Côte d'Ivoire was the main horticultural exporter in West Africa, exporting US$146 million of fruits and vegetables (Figure 5.4). This placed Côte d'Ivoire at roughly half the level of Kenya and third only to South Africa among Sub-Saharan African countries (FAOSTAT 2008). This section examines the development of the horticultural sector in Côte d'Ivoire and the factors that contributed to the growth in this sector. The goal is not to provide a comprehensive analysis of horticultural exports but rather to highlight the variety of experiences in horticultural development across African countries, as well as to identify some similarities with the Kenyan case.

Unlike in Kenya, where horticultural exports are relatively diversified, in Côte d'Ivoire the horticultural exports are based largely on two commodities, pineapples and bananas, each of which has a long history in the country. Bananas and plantains have been grown in West Africa for centuries, and banana production for export in Côte d'Ivoire began in 1933, when European settlers adopted the crop in response to low cocoa prices. Exports were quite modest, however, and Guinea was the dominant supplier of bananas to France at the time (Sawadogo 1977, 119). During the 1950s, production of export crops by African smallholders expanded in spite of policies favoring European growers. In coffee and cocoa, African smallholders came to represent the bulk of production. The banana and pineapple sectors, however, evolved toward a dualistic structure, with both large-scale and small-scale production. Because of the cost of transportation and the perishability of the product, banana production for export was (and remains) concentrated along paved roads near Abidjan. By the time the country achieved independence, in 1960, banana exports were about 90,000 tons, representing about 5 percent of the value of agricultural exports.

Banana exports have benefited from the highly regulated European banana market. France, the United Kingdom, and other European countries gave preferential access to exports from ACP countries, most of which were former colonies.[12] In the case of bananas, this policy has given favorable treatment to

---

12. The 1957 Treaty of Rome established preferential access to markets in France, Greece, Italy, Portugal, Spain, and the United Kingdom for exporters from ACP countries. Exports from

FIGURE 5.4 Value of Ivorian fruit and vegetable exports (left scale) and share of agricultural export revenue (right scale), 1961–2006

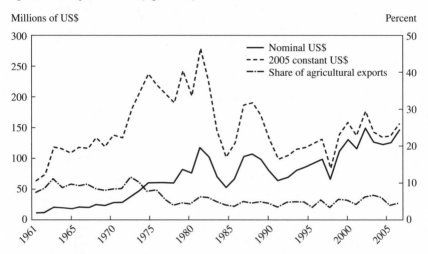

SOURCES: FAOSTAT (agricultural statistics); U.S. Department of Labor (U.S. consumer price index).

exports from Côte d'Ivoire, Cameroon, other African exporters, and a few Caribbean exporters at the expense of lower-cost producers in Latin America. The restrictions on European imports made banana exports quite remunerative, because European prices were significantly higher than world market prices, but import quotas limited the volume. In spite of a peak in 1980, banana exports from Côte d'Ivoire over 1961–89 averaged 120,000 tons per year, no greater than the level in the early 1960s.

The export of pineapple products also began during the colonial period, when foreign investors established two processing plants. At the time of independence, the export of pineapple products was less than half the value of banana exports (2 percent of agricultural exports). However, these exports grew steadily through the 1960s and 1970s so that, by the early 1970s, the export value of pineapples had surpassed that of bananas. At this time, most of the pineapple exports were in the forms of canned pineapple and single-strength pineapple juice. In the 1980s, however, Thailand expanded its exports threefold, increasing its share of the canned pineapple market to over 50 percent and pushing world prices down (Loeillet 1997). Also during the 1980s, economic reforms in Côte d'Ivoire reduced subsidies for many state enterprises and closed others, including Coopérative de Producteurs pour la Commercialization des Fruits

---

other countries, most notably in Latin American, were subject to a quota and 20 percent duty. Germany maintained a duty-free import policy. The other five member states maintained a 20 percent duty on banana exports from non-ACP countries. These disparate policies continued until 1993, as discussed later (Guyomard, Laroche, and Le Mouel 1999).

et Légumes de la Côte d'Ivoire (CORFRUITEL), the parastatal in charge of marketing fruit (Rougé and N'Goan 1997). As a result, Côte d'Ivoire's exports of canned pineapple and pineapple juice had practically disappeared by the late 1980s.

Much of the Ivorian pineapple production, however, switched over to fresh pineapple export to Europe by sea freight, using the same refrigerated freighters ("reefers") used to transport bananas. This move took advantage of Côte d'Ivoire's proximity to Europe, a factor much more important in the fresh pineapple trade than in the market for canned pineapple. This market is not without its problems, however. In the late 1980s, Côte d'Ivoire began to lose market share to Caribbean and Central American fresh pineapple exporters. After supplying close to 90 percent of the European market for fresh pineapple in the mid-1980s, its market share fell to two-thirds in 1990 (Rougé and N'Goan 1997).

The 1990s brought several changes favorable to Ivorian fruit and vegetable exports. First, in the 1990s the Office Centrale des Producteurs-Exportateurs d'Ananas et de Bananes (OCAB) was formed to represent the interests of exporters, set quality standards, and facilitate communication. OCAB has reduced the number of "approved" exporters of fruit in an attempt to maintain quality standards. It also organizes the charter of refrigerated ships to transport bananas and pineapples to Europe.

Second, in 1993, after much debate, Europe harmonized its banana import policies to make way for the single European market. Although the Latin American and U.S. exporters pushed for a more liberalized system, such as the one that existed in Germany, the European Union maintained the system of preferences for ACP countries, extending it to all members of the European Union. This expanded the size of the market to which Côte d'Ivoire and other ACP producers had preferential access.[13]

Third, the 50 percent devaluation of the Communauté Financière Africaine franc (CFAF) in January 1994 helped stimulate the economy, particularly the export sectors. The net effect of these three factors has been to reanimate fruit and vegetable exports from Côte d'Ivoire. Banana exports grew from 95,000 tons in 1990 to 235,000 tons in 2004, while fresh pineapple exports expanded

---

13. Under the regime announced in 1993, EU and ACP exporters were entitled to duty-free access to European markets for up to 858 thousand tons, with each exporter receiving a quota. Other imports were subject to a limit of 2.0 million tons and a duty of 100 European currency units (ECUs) per ton tariff that applied to non-ACP exporters only. Above 2 million tons, banana imports were subject to duties of 750 ECUs per ton for ACP bananas and 850 ECUs per ton for other bananas. A fund was established to assist ACP exporters in the transition. There were two challenges to the new rules under the General Agreement on Trade and Tariffs (GATT). In both cases, GATT panels ruled against the European Union, but adoption of the panel decision was blocked by the EU and ACP countries. To appease Latin American nations, the European Union negotiated concession to four of the five Latin American complainants. This "Framework Agreement" expanded the quota to 2.2 million tons, increased the country-specific quotas of these countries, reduced the non-ACP duty, and allowed these countries to issue export licenses, effectively transferring the quota rents to the exporting country governments (see Guyomard, Laroche, and Le Mouel 1999; Dickson 2002).

from 120,000 tons to 147,000 tons over the same period (FAOSTAT 2008). Côte d'Ivoire became the second-largest fresh pineapple exporter in the world after Costa Rica (Ti 2000). In addition, the export of mangoes has grown rapidly, increasing sevenfold over the 1990s to reach US$4 million. As of 2005, the total value of fruit and vegetable exports was US$146 million, of which 59 percent was bananas, 34 percent fresh pineapples, and 6 percent mangoes (Figure 5.5).

In the early 2000s, two international agreements have been signed that will affect Côte d'Ivoire's horticultural exports. Under the "Everything but Arms" policy, implemented by the European Union in March 2001, duties and quotas on almost all goods from the poorest 48 countries (including almost all of Sub-Saharan Africa) have been eliminated. Although the policy excludes bananas, it will facilitate exports of other fruits and vegetables from Côte d'Ivoire and other African countries. Yet quality and sanitary and phytosanitary barriers remain a key constraint to horticultural exports.

Under pressure from the United States and Latin America, supported by WTO rulings, Europe has reduced the preferential treatment of ACP countries in its banana imports. In 2006, the European Union changed from a quota–tariff system to a tariff-only system (€ 176 per ton), but it still allows duty-free ac-

FIGURE 5.5 Trends in the composition of Ivorian fruit and vegetable exports, 1961–2007

Value of exports (millions of 2005 US$)

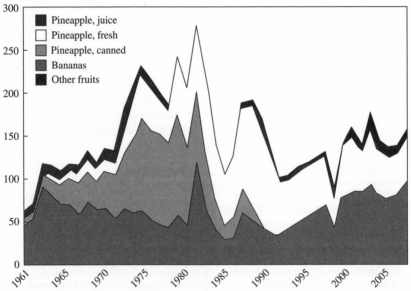

SOURCES: FAOSTAT (agricultural statistics); U.S. Department of Labor (U.S. consumer price index).

cess for ACP countries. Since 1996, the Latin American and U.S. exporters have filed a series of complaints with the WTO, which has consistently ruled in their favor. Thus, Côte d'Ivoire and other ACP producers will come under increasing competitive pressure from Ecuador and other low-cost Latin American exporters (Dickson 2002; Lambert 2002; AP 2007).

Drivers of Change

The success of the Ivorian fruit and vegetable sector is a qualified one. Fruit and vegetable exports from Côte d'Ivoire have not grown as fast as those from Kenya, and the role of smallholders is less important than in Kenya. On the other hand, Côte d'Ivoire is one of the three largest exporters of fruits and vegetables in Sub-Saharan Africa, and it maintained solid growth in the 1990s. Although smallholders play a less important role there than in Kenya, tens of thousands of rural households depend on the sector for their livelihoods as either farmers or agricultural laborers.

Several factors lie behind the qualified success of fruit and vegetable exports from Côte d'Ivoire. First, through the 1990s Côte d'Ivoire was known for its political stability. Until the past few years, Côte d'Ivoire had a reputation for being the most politically stable country in West Africa. Félix Houphouët-Boigny served as president from 1960 until his death in 1993. He was successful in promoting economic growth and minimizing political turmoil until the 1980s, when commodity prices fell. The advent of multiparty democracy in 1990 is said to have created (or perhaps just exposed) ethnic and religious divisions that deepened significantly during the mid-2000s.

Second, President Houphouët-Boigny, for the most part, supported agriculture-led growth. He came to prominence representing the interests of African cocoa growers during the colonial period. As president, he drew his support from the rural areas and maintained a cocoa farm himself. Although agriculture was taxed directly through the policies of the marketing boards and indirectly through overvalued exchange rates, investment in rural infrastructure and agricultural research reflected the priority given to agriculture.

Third, Côte d'Ivoire has benefited from its proximity to European markets. Côte d'Ivoire is just 8–10 days by sea freighter from Marseilles. Although it also benefits from frequent air connections with Paris, these are less important, because most of the Ivorian fruit and vegetable exports have been by sea freight.

Fourth, the government has had relatively limited involvement in production and marketing, particularly in the horticultural sector. Although the Ivorian agricultural policy was more interventionist than that of Kenya, President Houphouët-Boigny gave the country a more pro-market orientation than most of its West African neighbors. In particular, Côte d'Ivoire maintained close ties to France, while many of its neighbors rejected European involvement and experimented with different variants of socialism.

The Impact of Ivorian Horticultural Exports

Who benefits from fruit and vegetable exports from Côte d'Ivoire? According to Lambert (2002), the small-scale rainfed banana farms that used to dominate the sector have given way to medium- and large-scale irrigated farms of 100–1,000 hectares, mostly owned by Europeans and selling directly to French importers. In addition, exporters such as Chiquita and the Compagnie Fruitière are vertically integrated, with their own plantations. One factor behind this consolidation is the competitive pressure from non-ACP countries to reduce the cost of production. Another factor is the increasingly strict marketing requirements by European importers regarding the size, quality, and consistency of the fruit and the use of pesticides and other chemicals in production. The implication is that the greater part of any positive impact in terms of poverty reduction would be through the employment of workers on the plantations. It is estimated that 35,000 people are employed by the banana and pineapple plantations.

In pineapple production, on the other hand, smallholders continue to dominate. According to Rougé and N'Goan (1997), 70 percent of Ivorian pineapple exports are produced by smallholders with 0.5–10 hectares. The remaining 30 percent are produced by large plantations, including some owned by the vertically integrated banana companies such as Chiquita and Compagnie Fruitière. One reason for the greater involvement of smallholders in pineapple production compared to banana production is that the initial investment cost of establishing a plot is estimated to be three to four times as great for bananas (Rougé and N'Goan 1997).

Mangoes are the third most important horticultural export. They are produced by smallholders in the north of the country, as well as by farmers in Burkina Faso and Mali who export via Côte d'Ivoire (Lambert 2002). Thus, it is likely that a high proportion of the mangoes are produced by poor households. Given the cost of getting mangoes to the coast and then to Europe, the farm-gate price may be low, so it is not clear whether mango sales are an important component of the income of growers.

Policy Implications

This chapter began by posing three questions about the development of export horticulture in Kenya and Côte d'Ivoire. Returning to them now provides a way to summarize what these case studies reveal about the impact of horticultural exports, the key driving forces, and policy implications for other countries.

Is Kenyan and Ivorian Horticulture a Success Story?

Certainly horticulture in Kenya can be considered a success in terms of export growth. Fruit and vegetable exports have grown from US$2 to $3 million at independence to over US$320 million in 2005. The sector has even grown as a percentage of agricultural exports, rising from 3 percent of the total at independence to 17 percent in 2005. Although coffee and tea continue to dominate agricultural exports in Kenya, the growth of tourism and horticulture has reduced the vulnerability of the Kenyan economy to price swings in those two commodity markets.

It is more useful, though more difficult, to evaluate success in terms of the impact on the lives of Kenyan families, particularly the poor. Available evidence suggesting that smallholders provide between 47 and 60 percent of the exported fruits and vegetables lends strong support for the belief that horticultural development has been good for the rural poor. Survey evidence corroborates this notion, indicating that small farmers involved in export horticultural production earn substantially higher incomes than those who are not. However, estimates of the numbers of smallholder farmers involved vary widely, from 13,000 to 500,000. This variation most likely arises because many smallholders participate only intermittently or seasonally, while a much smaller core of larger smallholders accounts for the bulk of marketed sales. Our rough estimate is that about 200,000 Kenyan smallholder farmers regularly sell horticultural produce through export channels.

What is the direct impact of horticultural exports on Kenyan smallholders? Assuming that smallholders account for about 50 percent of fresh produce exports and that the farmgate price is 60 percent of the freight on board price, Kenya's horticultural exports contribute about US$96 million in revenue for Kenyan smallholders.

Although less visible, it is likely that the indirect benefits associated with horticultural exports are greater than the direct benefits. First, the multiplier effect of injecting US$96 million annually into the rural sector generates benefits for other households and businesses that produce goods purchased by export producers. Second, this analysis has focused on smallholders producing for export, but it is important to recognize that the employment effects of horticultural exports extend beyond this. Del Monte alone employs several thousand workers in its processing plants and on its estates. Third, the skills and institutional development stimulated by the horticultural export sector also serve to promote the domestic horticultural market. Given that 96 percent of fruit and vegetable production is consumed domestically, even small improvements in yield, postharvest methods, and marketing efficiency in the domestic supply chain could have benefits to the economy that are large relative to the direct benefits of horticultural exports.

It is less clear whether we can consider the Ivorian horticultural sector a success story. First, the sector has not grown consistently. In real terms, the value of fruit and vegetable exports in 2005 was US$146 million, marginally higher than in the late 1960s but significantly lower, in real terms, than in the mid-1970s and the mid-1980s. Second, the role of smallholders in the Ivorian fruit and vegetable sector is more limited. Bananas, the largest horticultural export, are produced mainly on large-scale farms and by vertically integrated multinational companies. Certainly there are thousands of farm workers whose livelihoods are supported by the banana sector, but it is likely that the benefits are less widely distributed among Ivorian households than they would be if banana production were based on smallholder production. Third, it is not clear to what degree the success of the Ivorian banana sector is based on European trade policies that discriminate against Latin American producers. Nor, in terms of sustainability, is it clear whether current levels of banana exports can be maintained when Europe removes these preferential policies, a change that is not imminent but may be inevitable under WTO commitments.

Nonetheless, the Ivorian horticultural sector does offer some positive signs. First, the sector was able to adjust to the loss of the canned pineapple exports by developing fresh pineapple exports to Europe.[14] In addition, Ivorian horticultural exports showed healthy growth (4.4 percent) over the 1990s, including expansion of smallholder crops such as pineapples, mangoes, and papayas for export. Although it is difficult to foresee the impact of the ongoing political tensions in Côte d'Ivoire, it seems inevitable that the institutional and commercial development necessary to expand horticultural exports will be set back by more than a few years.

What Factors Have Contributed to Success?

Several factors have contributed to the success of the horticultural sector in Kenya and, in a more limited way, in Côte d'Ivoire.

GEOGRAPHY AND CLIMATE.   Kenya is favored with an equatorial latitude and bimodal rainfall that reduce seasonality, combined with a range of altitudes, allowing the production of tropical fruits such as mangoes, pineapples, and avocados, as well as temperate vegetables such as French beans. Furthermore, Nairobi and its airport are located in the western highlands, an area endowed with good soils and a suitable climate for vegetable production. Similarly, the areas of Côte d'Ivoire most appropriate for banana production are along the coast, near the port of Abidjan. Among countries with a humid tropical climate, Côte d'Ivoire is one of the closest by sea to major European ports.

TRANSPORTATION INFRASTRUCTURE.   The cost and duration of transportation to major markets in Europe is a critical factor in the success of the horticultural sector. Both Kenya and Côte d'Ivoire serve as regional hubs for air traffic. The growth of the Kenyan tourism industry and the consequent frequency of air connections to Europe have facilitated the development of fresh produce exports to Europe via air freight. In Côte d'Ivoire, much of the horticultural export is by sea freight, so investment in and efficient management of the port in Abidjan are of critical importance. Domestic transportation infrastructure is also an important factor because horticultural exports do not toler-

---

14. Kenya, on the other hand, attempted to launch fresh pineapple exports to Europe, but it proved uneconomical.

ate delays in getting to the airport. The Kenyan horticultural sector benefits from an extensive road network in the highland areas. It is estimated that much of the export vegetable production in Kenya takes place within 100 kilometers of the airport. Similarly, banana production in Côte d'Ivoire is concentrated along paved roads near the port.

LIMITED DIRECT GOVERNMENT INTERVENTION IN HORTICULTURAL MARKETS. The Kenyan government has not intervened to any significant degree in horticultural markets to buy, sell, export, or set prices. In Kenya, the HCDA was originally given authority to fix prices, regulate trade, operate processing facilities, and market horticultural goods. Based on its unsuccessful experience, its functions were pared back to regulation, market information, and advisory services.[15] State enterprises were actively involved in various horticultural processing operations, often as part of joint ventures with foreign companies. Most of the growth in horticultural exports, however, has been in fresh produce. In any case, the horticultural sector was never as tightly controlled as were the maize, coffee, and tea sectors. In spite of the proliferation of state enterprises, the investment climate in Kenya was good, at least compared to those of many other African countries. This climate allowed investment in the horticultural sector by local and international firms, most notably by Del Monte in the 1960s.

Similarly, Côte d'Ivoire has largely followed an agriculture-led development strategy and kept direct intervention in agricultural markets to a modest level. Probably the area of greatest direct involvement in the horticultural sector was in pineapple processing, in which joint ventures between investors and various public institutions were the rule. When the export of processed pineapple products collapsed in the late 1980s, even this form of participation in horticulture disappeared.

POLICIES ALLOWING PRIVATE AND INTERNATIONAL INVESTMENT. Both Kenya and Côte d'Ivoire have had relatively liberal policies regarding foreign investment and investment by local businesses. In both countries, foreign investment has contributed to increasing the capacity of horticultural production, processing, and export. In Kenya, Del Monte is the largest example, but Dijkstra (1997) lists 20 other private processors of fruits and vegetables in the country as of 1990. Lambert (2002) also stresses the importance of Kenya's "open skies" policy, under which exporters and shipping companies may charter planes in their own name. In Côte d'Ivoire, Chiquita and Compagnie Fruitière have played a central role in banana and fresh pineapple production and export.

MACROECONOMIC STABILITY AND REALISTIC EXCHANGE RATES. In the 1960s and 1970s, both Kenya and Côte d'Ivoire earned reputations for politi-

---

15. The HCDA briefly maintained a monopoly on onion marketing and export and later competed with private onion traders. In 1986, the government required the HCDA to withdraw from direct marketing. It is probably not a coincidence that the only horticultural commodity that the HCDA attempted to market was one of the least perishable vegetables.

cal and macroeconomic stability, which is necessary to elicit long-term investments in productive capacity. Similarly, a realistic exchange rate, which gives exporters the full value of the foreign exchange they generate, is a critical factor in stimulating exports, including horticultural exports. Although both countries experienced economic problems in the 1980s, the level of inflation and the extent of exchange rate overvaluation were modest compared to those experienced by some of their neighbors, including Ghana, Tanzania, and Uganda. The 1994 devaluation of the CFAF provided an important stimulus to horticultural exports (among others) in Côte d'Ivoire, contributing to the healthy 4.4 percent growth rate in fruit and vegetable exports over 1990–99.

INSTITUTIONAL INNOVATION.   Horticultural development requires a continuous process of institutional innovation at two levels. First, institutions are needed to address sectorwide externalities and coordination problems. For example, the adoption of a common code of practice, the exchange of market information, and funding of research and extension are activities that benefit the sector as a whole but cannot easily be carried out by an individual firm. Second, marketing institutions are needed to improve vertical coordination among farmers, traders, and processors. These may include various types of contract farming, farmer credit groups, marketing cooperatives, or farmer associations.

The Kenyan government has allowed and (in some cases) promoted the development of a wide range of private marketing institutions such as FPEAK, local producer associations, self-help groups, and so on. In addition, it has allowed experimentation with a wide range of institutional arrangements between farmers and buyers. In spite of early attempts to oblige processors to work with smallholders, greater leeway is now given for the most economical arrangement to evolve in response to market signals. Over the decades, Kenyan participants in the horticultural sector have accumulated considerable experience in managing the relationships among growers and buyers. Today, contract farming may be more widely used in Kenya than anywhere else in Africa, though conflicts between farmers and buyers are an almost universal feature of these schemes. One source of conflict is the fact that after a buyer provides the assistance needed by smallholders (in the form of seed, inputs, and credit) he or she faces the risk that other buyers will come and "poach" the harvest and the loan will not be repaid. Alternatively, if the market price falls, the buyer may refuse to honor his or her commitment or use grading as a pretext for refusing shipment. Arbitrary and nontransparent grading procedures are a common complaint among contract growers.

In Côte d'Ivoire, the government has created a series of institutions to coordinate horticultural exports with varying levels of success. In the 1960s, small-scale horticultural producers formed an export cooperative. In 1976, this was replaced by a marketing board with a monopoly on horticultural exports. This approach failed due to high costs, bureaucratic procedures, and corruption. It was replaced in 1978 by CORFRUITEL, a producer organization with greater participation by exporters but without a legal export monopoly (Hörmann and Wietor 1980). More recently, the government created the OCAB to coordinate the sector and provide information and other public goods.

DOMESTIC DEMAND. In Kenya, tourism expanded the domestic demand for high-quality fruits and vegetables. As hotels and restaurants established supply chains to supply this produce, they gave Kenyan farmers more experience with horticultural production and indirectly strengthened the infrastructure and logistical skills of traders, all of which facilitated the development of the horticultural export sector. Similarly, the domestic demand for Asian vegetables gave Kenyans experience in growing and marketing these vegetables. These factors facilitated the development of market channels to supply fruits and vegetables to Asian and European consumers overseas. Although the idea is less well documented, the large French population in Côte d'Ivoire before and after independence may have facilitated the development of the export fruit sector there.

INTERNATIONAL COMMERCIAL LINKS. The presence of the Asian community in Kenya has undoubtedly contributed to horticultural crop development. Before the 1970s, the Asian community created a demand for Asian vegetables, providing smallholders with valuable experience in these crops that would later be useful in serving the U.K. market. In addition, the presence of the Asian community made it easier to penetrate the U.K. market, first with Asian vegetables and later with French beans and other fresh produce. In the case of Côte d'Ivoire, multinational corporations (Chiquita and Compagnie Fruitière) offer a different solution to the problem of coordinating African supply and European demand. By vertically integrating production, processing, and distribution, the flow of information and credit is facilitated.

What Policy Lessons Apply in Other African Countries?

Clearly, some of the factors mentioned in the previous section lie outside the control of public policy and investment. Little can be done to alter the geographic and climatic features of a country. Nor is it practical to alter the ethnic composition of a country to allow greater links with similar groups in Europe. On the other hand, most of the other factors carry lessons that are applicable to other countries.

STABILITY. Political and economic stability matter. Stability provides investors with the confidence that they will be able to reap the benefits of long-term investments. Although both Kenya and Côte d'Ivoire have had leaders whose tenure spanned decades, political stability should not be defined in terms of the duration of a given regime but rather in terms of the durability of policies and economic institutions over time.

NONINTERVENTION IN PRODUCTION AND MARKETING. The tendency of the Kenyan and Ivorian governments not to intervene directly in horticultural production and marketing is clearly an approach that can be (and is) emulated by other countries. The fresh fruit and vegetable sector is simply too diverse, too risky, and too fast-changing for state enterprises or marketing boards to play a constructive role. Kenya's earlier experience in promoting joint ventures between foreign companies and state enterprises was almost uniformly unsuccessful and serves as a counterexample. The most successful processed horticulture operation in Kenya has been Del Monte, which did not involve a partnership with a state enterprise.

AGRICULTURAL RESEARCH AND DISEASE CONTROL.   Both Kenya and Côte d'Ivoire have invested in horticultural research, developing institutions that have their roots in the colonial period. Disease control and postharvest processing are particularly important in the case of horticultural research. And new sanitary and phytosanitary requirements imposed by importing countries create a demand for research into ways to reduce or eliminate pesticide residues and prevent the spread of horticultural pests. Dealing with these externalities successfully will require collective action.

A MARKET EXCHANGE RATE.   Exchange rate policy is particularly important for horticultural exports. A market exchange rate provides greater incentives to produce exports (including horticultural exports). Furthermore, a liberalized market for foreign currency facilitates the purchase of imported equipment and inputs for production. This is more important for horticulture than for field crops because of the need for imported seed, agricultural chemicals, and specialized equipment. The positive response of Ivorian fruit exports to the 1994 devaluation of the CFAF demonstrates this point.

PROMOTION OF INSTITUTIONAL INNOVATION.   The Kenyan experience demonstrates the importance of allowing a variety of private institutions and marketing arrangements to develop. The early experience of Del Monte in Kenya shows that it takes more than experience and technical skills to survive in horticulture. It is necessary to continually experiment, innovate, and adapt to changing environments. The horticultural sector in Kenya is characterized by a wide array of institutional arrangements, including smallholders selling in spot markets, personalized relationships with traders, implicit contracts, explicit contracts, farmer organizations, medium- and large-scale farming, and vertically integrated producer-exporters. Many commodity channels involve various scales of production and several types of farmer–buyer linkages. The government can play a role in facilitating institutional innovation through the provision of market information and extension services, mediation of disputes, and the establishment of standards.

LINKING SMALLHOLDERS TO HIGH-VALUE URBAN AND EXPORT MARKETS. Linking small farmers to high-value urban and export markets is an important strategy for raising rural incomes and reducing poverty. Such a strategy may also be critical for maintaining export competitiveness, at least for some labor-intensive crops that require careful husbandry. How can the government promote smallholder involvement? First, it should avoid leasing land at concessionary rates, subsidizing credit for mechanization, and providing tax incentives for agricultural investment, all of which subsidize the formation of large-scale capital-intensive farms. Second, the government should avoid counterproductive attempts to impose cooperative production, contract farming, nucleus estate production, or any other specific marketing system. Efficient market institutions should evolve out of experiments with different forms. Third, contract farming shows some promise for delivering improved technology, credit, and information to farmers, but such schemes make sense only with a crop that involves new technology, an uncertain market, a large initial investment, and/or specialized husbandry. Even in these cases, contract farming schemes often collapse when other buyers come to "poach" at harvest, allowing farmers to avoid repaying loans. The government can, however, facilitate linkages between farmers and exporters or other buyers by helping to organize farmer groups, establishing ground rules for farmer–buyer contracts, disseminating lessons learned from successful contract schemes, establishing small claims courts to address contract disputes, and gathering and disseminating information about the past performance of buyers and farmers.

THE AIR TRANSPORT SECTOR. The importance of air freight costs in the competitiveness of export horticulture has implications for policy. The aviation industry is heavily protected in most parts of the world, with regulations controlling access by foreign carriers. Africa is no exception, with its plethora of small and uneconomic national airlines. Adopting an open skies policy might endanger some of these national airlines, but it would probably introduce greater competition and reduce the cost of air freight. This would have a positive impact on the export of fresh produce and other high-value commodities.

ETHNIC MINORITIES. The positive contribution of the Asian traders to Kenya's horticultural development has lessons for other developing countries. Ethnic minority trading communities are a common feature across the world, from the Chinese in Malaysia to the Lebanese in West Africa. Given the suspicion and resentment that inevitably occur on the part of the majority, special efforts are needed by the government to provide equal treatment under the law.

INVESTMENT IN IRRIGATION. Although public and private investment in irrigation has facilitated the growth of the horticultural sector, the implications must be drawn carefully. Large-scale public irrigation projects in Kenya and elsewhere in Africa have often proven uneconomic and unsustainable. Problems have arisen from the high cost of irrigation, the lack of adequate feasibility analysis, and problems in managing and maintaining the system after completion. In the past 10 years, most of the investment and increases in capacity in Kenyan irrigation have been carried out in the private sector by large-scale commercial farms and by groups of smallholders. The case studies discussed earlier provided several examples of farms that started horticultural production when they obtained a pump. This finding highlights the need for a competitive market for agricultural equipment, including water pumps. Given the externality issues associated with irrigation, the government has a role to play in facilitating the formation of water-user groups to regulate water use, organizing maintenance, and resolving disputes. In addition, the government can fund research and dissemination activities to stimulate innovation, particularly in microirrigation technology.

Clearly, the development of export horticulture depends in part on geography, historical accident, and agroclimatic factors. Because of these factors, some countries do not have the potential for large-scale horticultural development, even with the best policies and investment. However, many of the factors that have contributed to the success of the horticultural sectors in Kenya and Côte d'Ivoire are subject to influence through policy, regulation, and public investment. Furthermore, most of the lessons derived from the Kenyan and Ivorian examples make sense for the development of commercial agriculture in general, regardless of whether horticulture is involved.

6 Smallholder Dairying in Eastern Africa

MARGARET NGIGI, MOHAMED ABDELWAHAB AHMED,
SIMEON EHUI, AND YEMESRACH ASSEFA

Scope of the Study

Livestock have historically played multiple roles in the economic life and sociocultural traditions of African people. Africa's cattle-rearing societies value cattle not simply as a source of food (including milk, blood, and meat) and hides but also as a visible form of wealth and a source of social prestige.

The relative importance of cattle and the role they play, however, vary substantially across agroecological zones (Fitzhugh 1998; Freeland 1998). Throughout the tropical belt of Africa, endemic trypanosomiasis severely limits cattle rearing. Elsewhere, where the availability of water and forage permit, cattle provide draft power for both plowing and transport. In arid and semiarid zones, cattle offer valuable security against famine. Traditionally, cattle-rearing societies have valued cattle as payment of the bride price and beef as a food item in ceremonies. In arid and semiarid zones, people use cattle manure as fire fuel and building material, while in crop-farming areas they value it as a fertilizer.

In high-potential agricultural areas—where an abundance of cultivable soils, ample rains, and an absence of disease permit intensive agricultural production —the economic importance of cattle has increasingly shifted to commercial milk production. At the same time, cattle have retained their complementary role in sustaining soil fertility for crop production. In these favorable zones, increasing population pressure and the resulting need to sustain soil fertility have driven changes in production patterns. Typically these changes have involved more intensive crop–livestock interactions, with dairying becoming an important component of the agricultural production system.

The highland areas of Eastern Africa offer the most promising conditions for dairy production in Africa, a fact well recognized since the first livestock survey published by the Food and Agriculture Organization of the United Nations (FAO) in 1967 (FAO 1967). Moderate temperatures, good soils, two rainy seasons, and a low prevalence of livestock diseases make these tropical highlands ideal for cattle production. Because of these natural advantages, Eastern Africa accommodates over 40 percent of Africa's cattle herd of about 220 mil-

209

lion. The human population density there likewise remains among the highest in Africa (Figure 6.1). Predominantly rural, the region employs roughly 75 percent of its workforce primarily in agriculture (Table 6.1). Because livestock contribute to the livelihoods of a majority of farm families in the region, the identification of effective, broad-based strategies for increasing livestock pro-

FIGURE 6.1 Population density in the three study countries, 2005

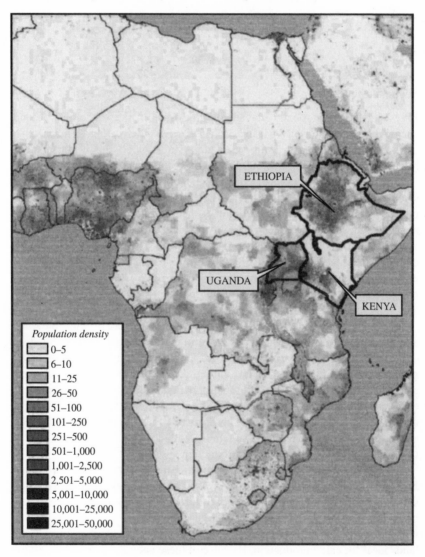

SOURCE: FAO GeoNetwork (<www.fao.org/geonetwork>).

TABLE 6.1 Selected indicators for the dairy sector in Kenya, Uganda, and
Ethiopia, 2006

	Kenya	Uganda	Ethiopia
Population[a]			
Total (millions)	33	29	76
Density (population/km^2)	57	119	69
Agriculture			
As a percentage of GDP[b]	28	32	48
Population dependent on agriculture[b]	73	76	80
Dairy			
Milk availability (kg per capita)[a]	99	26	22
Total milk production (millions of kg)[a]	3,500	760	1,575
Total cattle (millions)[a]	16.7	8.4	60.6
Total milk cows (millions)[a]	5.5	2.1	7.9
Milk cows as a percentage of total cattle[c]	33	25	13
Milk yield per cow (kg/year)[a]	636	361	200

NOTE: GDP, gross domestic product.
[a]FAOSTAT, data for 2006.
[b]*World Development Indicators,* data for 2006.
[c]Muriuki and Thorpe (2001), data for 1998.

ductivity offers a potentially powerful tool for raising incomes and improving
household welfare throughout the region.

This chapter compares the performance of the dairy industry in three East
African countries—Kenya, Uganda, and Ethiopia (see Figure 6.1). Kenya's
dairy development efforts, which began during the first decades of the 20th century, have proven so successful that Kenya's per capita dairy production now
ranks the highest in Sub-Saharan Africa, at more than double the African average (FAOSTAT 2008). Over 600,000 smallholder farmers participate in the
Kenyan dairy industry, accounting for over three-fourths of national milk production (Omore et al. 1999). Ethiopia and Uganda, on the other hand, have seen
only very limited dairy development. Despite favorable agroclimatic endowments, they have thus far failed to fully exploit their considerable potential for
dairy production.

In order to identify reasons for these widely differing outcomes, this study
reviews dairy development in each of these three countries in turn. As in the
other case studies reported in this volume, this chapter takes a historical look
at the dairy industry in each country. After identifying major development
periods and turning points, it examines the causes of differing performance over
time and across countries. The chapter aims to identify the forces and key actors that have driven change in these three dairy systems and to assess the resulting impact on overall dairy production, smallholder incomes, and the envi-

ronment. By comparing performance across countries and over time, the chapter also identifies the key ingredients necessary for achieving successful smallholder dairy growth elsewhere.

Smallholder Dairy Development in Kenya

Key Phases in Kenyan Dairy Development

Since the introduction of commercial dairying at the beginning of the 20th century, Kenya's dairy industry has evolved through a sequence of four distinct phases (Table 6.2). The first, running from about 1900 to 1953, coincided with the early integration of colonial Kenya into an expanding capitalist world. During this period, white settlers introduced hybrid dairy cattle and ultimately succeeded in obtaining the support of the colonial administration for dairy development in the colony.

The second phase, which extended from about 1954 to 1962, was triggered by the introduction of import-substituting industrialization in the colony. The resulting need to develop large and growing local markets to support industrial development benefited the fledgling Kenyan dairy industry. Furthermore, the changing needs and emphasis brought a growing government interest in smallholder dairy development, resulting in a rapid expansion of dairy production not only among settler farmers but also among indigenous farmers.

Kenya's independence, in 1963, launched a third phase in the country's dairy development. The early independence years brought with them strong interest in further expanding the benefits of dairy production to smallholder farmers. Running for roughly two and a half decades, through the late 1980s, this period saw explosive growth among smallholder dairy farmers and substantial increases in total milk production. These gains were driven by incremental modifications in dairy marketing policy as Kenya moved gradually from a farmer-controlled dairy industry to one tightly controlled by the government.

The fourth phase began in the late 1980s. The same forces of reform that led to the dismantling of costly maize marketing subsidies during this period (see Chapter 3) led to a similar liberalization in the dairy sector. The significant policy shocks introduced during this period initially led to slowing growth, a dip in the volume of milk marketed through formal channels, and growing importance of raw milk sales. The following discussion examines each of these periods in detail.

Phase 1: Emergence of Kenya's Dairy Institutions, 1900–53

During the colonial era, administrators and white settler farmers introduced a number of economically important crops and animal species, as well as a variety of improved farming methods and marketing institutions. In the dairy industry, several innovations proved particularly important. First was the introduction of artificial insemination (AI) reproductive technology. This made possible the improvement of milk yields by crossing low-yielding but disease-resistant local breeds of cattle (*Bos indicus*) with highly productive exotic breeds (*Bos taurus*). Second was the adoption of improved dairy management practices, including the use of acaricides in dips to control tick-borne diseases. Third, the colonial government launched a set of dairy marketing policies and institutions that have provided the foundation for postindependence dairy policy in Kenya. Although colonial authorities undertook these efforts for the benefit of the imperial country rather than the indigenous people, they nonetheless laid the foundation for Kenya's current dairy industry.

WHITE SETTLER FARMERS.   In 1901, the colonial government completed a railroad from the coastal seaport town of Mombasa to Nairobi, on across Kenya, and into the neighboring colony of Uganda. To ensure the profitability of the railway, the colonial administration encouraged white settlement along the vast expanse of land that straddled the rail line (Pandit and Thukur 1961; Leys 1975; Zwanenberg 1975; Bates 1989). They intended for settler agriculture to create freight for the railway as farm outputs and inputs were shipped to and from the coastal seaport by rail. This, in turn, would generate the revenues needed to underwrite the costs of administering the colony and financing the expansion of basic infrastructure.

Colonial agricultural policies, therefore, favored the establishment of the settler farmers. As Leys (1975), Zwanenberg (1975), and Bates (1989) have noted, the colonial administration enacted a series of legal measures designed to make land and cheap labor available to the white settlers. Under these laws, the settlers appropriated large tracts of land designated as "scheduled areas" and often referred to as the "white highlands."

BREEDING IMPROVEMENTS.   The low milk production potential of local cattle breeds limited the settlers' prospects for establishing a commercial dairy industry. Yet exotic breeds proved highly susceptible to endemic cattle diseases to which local breeds had acquired a degree of natural immunity over the years. The challenge, therefore, became one of producing breeds that combined the high milk yields of exotic breeds with the hardiness of the local breeds.

The first formal breeding work started in 1903 with the establishment of an experimental government dairy farm at Naivasha in Nakuru district—presently the Naivasha National Husbandry Research Centre of the Kenya Agricultural Research Institute. This work necessitated trials with numerous breeds, including Friesian, Guernsey, Ayrshire, and Jersey cattle. Nevertheless, government breeders made significant progress, and by 1909 they had developed a starter herd with moderate disease resistance for sale to settler farmers.

The introduction of AI began as a private initiative by a few settler dairy farmers, initially directed at curbing the spread of venereally transmitted cattle diseases. The practice soon caught on among other settler farmers, who quickly organized themselves into cattle breeders' associations. Over time, the major

TABLE 6.2 Dynamics and drivers of change in Kenya's dairy subsector, 1900–2006

	Phase 1: Emergence of Kenya's dairy institutions	Phase 2: Integration of smallholder producers	Phase 3: Acceleration of smallholder access	Phase 4: Liberalization
Timing	1900–53	1954–62	1963–86	1987–2006
Key actors	Commercial farmers Colonial government	Colonial government Kenya Cooperative Creameries (KCC)	Kenya Artificial Insemination Service (KAIS) Public extension and support services Kenya Dairy Board (KDB) KCC	Parliament Private processors Private raw milk marketing agents
Motors of change	Commercial farmers introduce improved breeds, artificial insemination (AI), tick control Commercial farmers lobby for government support Government complies by introducing quarantine laws, veterinary and AI services, and marketing and price controls	Political tension induces government to open dairying to smallholders AI services and extension support introduced for smallholders Milk market regulation begins through KCC	Land transferred to smallholders Expanded, subsidized AI offered through KAIS Public tick control, public veterinary services, and expanded dairy extension services offered Price controls modified to reduce discrimination against smallholders	Heavy subsidies dropped from AI and veterinary services Milk market liberalized: KCC and its formal milk monopoly abolished Raw milk sales decriminalized in urban areas

Beneficiaries	Commercial farmers	Commercial farmers Smallholders	Raw milk marketers Smallholders Private processors
Production gains		Smallholders, who received a 90% subsidy on AI services National milk production grows 3.7% annually between 1963 and 2006 Production growth accelerates to over 10% per year during the 1980s	Aggregate milk production stalls, then recovers In formal channels, private processors picked up market share ceded by KCC Raw milk sales increase as legal restrictions in urban areas abate
Impact	Smallholder share rises to 14% of marketed sales	Smallholders account for the majority of marketed milk volumes	Smallholders earn US$370 per year from dairy Smallholders' share of milk sales reaches 80% Producer prices rise with deregulation

objective of AI shifted to that of transferring high milk-yielding traits from exotic to local cattle breeds. As these efforts proceeded, the benefits of centralizing the production and distribution of bull semen became apparent. In accord with the prevailing development perspective of the period, which regarded state control of economic activities as crucial for economic development, the government assumed responsibility for centralizing semen production and distribution. In 1935, the colonial government established the Central Artificial Insemination Service (CAIS), which to date remains a Kenyan government parastatal. With the CAIS in place, semen production became the responsibility of the government, while farmers, through their cattle breeders' associations, retained responsibility for organizing and financing field insemination services. By the mid-1950s, Kenya boasted one of the best AI systems in the world (Conelly 1998).

The period also saw the beginnings of several complementary bodies, including the Kenya Stud Book (KSB) in 1920 and the Dairy Record Service of Kenya (DRSK) in 1949. Private initiatives with government support, both became instrumental in providing data for the country's livestock breeding programs. In the public arena, the colonial government established what would become the National Veterinary Laboratory at Kabete, near Nairobi, in 1910.

DISEASE CONTROL.   Settler dairy farmers perceived high risks from raising improved livestock alongside local breeds. Because the local breeds reared by indigenous people had built up strong immunities over the years against endemic diseases, local cattle could harbor disease-causing organisms without suffering serious clinical ills. Moreover, due to the substantial immunity of the local herds, indigenous farmers had little incentive to participate in tick control programs. For this reason, the settlers considered indigenous cattle a hazardous reservoir of disease-causing organisms, a serious source of negative externalities for the settler herd (Zwanenberg 1975).

In order to create a less dangerous environment for the settler dairy herd, the colonial administration enacted the Fencing Ordinance in 1928 and the Cattle Cleansing Ordinance in 1937. The former aimed, through the provision of favorable terms, to encourage settler dairy farmers to erect perimeter fences around their farms. The latter mandated that farmers dip or spray their animals weekly with acaricides as a measure to control tick-borne diseases (Hills 1956; Zwanenberg 1975; Conelly 1998). In addition, the government itself erected fences across various pastoralist livestock paths to control the movement of African herds.

The settler dairy farmers also successfully lobbied for the imposition of a quarantine against African stock (Zwanenberg 1975; Bates 1989). The quarantine, which entailed confining the African livestock herds within African Reserve (AR) areas, held far-reaching consequences for the indigenous people. It increased the already intense pressure on natural resources inside the ARs, leading to serious overgrazing. In response to the ensuing environmental degradation, the colonial administration initiated the African Land Development program in 1945, with specific reactive steps designed to curb land degradation.

MARKETING INSTITUTIONS.   Early in the second decade of the 1900s, with technological constraints to commercial milk production well on the way to being addressed, producer attention shifted to the issue of marketing. Organized milk marketing groups started in 1912 when settler dairy farmers in the Lumbwa area—presently, Kipkelion in Kericho district—formed the Lumbwa Cooperative Society, emulating the initiatives of dairy farmers in Australia and New Zealand (Kenya 1965). The cooperative society took charge of collecting members' milk for collective processing and marketing. Settler dairy farmers around Naivasha adopted the system in 1925 when they formed the Kenya Cooperative Creameries (KCC), and later, in 1928, so did farmers around Nanyuki, who formed the Nanyuki Cooperative Creamery.

The three cooperative creameries operated independently of each other and focused primarily on export markets. This orientation, however, changed following the economic downturn during the Great Depression of the 1930s. The collapse of international markets for dairy products forced the three creameries to turn their attention to the domestic market. However, the effective domestic market remained very small, limited by the low cash income available among the indigenous population. Given the narrowness of domestic outlets, the collapse of international markets gave rise to serious distributional conflicts among the three creameries over market share allocation. *The Dairy Commission of Inquiry Report* (Government of Kenya 1965, i) specifically enunciated these concerns, noting that "competition developed as to who should supply the home market with better returns and who should be left with the lower returns from export."

The need to resolve this conflict over domestic market share shaped the country's milk marketing institutions for over six decades. As Troup (1956, 3) observed, "Competition between the creameries, for a small market, became intense. This led to an agreement between the parties to merge and eventually amalgamation took place in 1931 to form the Kenya Cooperative Creameries Ltd." The KCC would decisively influence the evolution of the country's dairy marketing institutions for the next six decades. Indeed, from 1931 to 1992, the story of Kenya's milk marketing policy became the story of the KCC.

The merger enhanced the bargaining status of the member farmers. By establishing a clear hierarchy between the primary societies and an apex processing unit, the KCC became an obvious spokesperson for presenting farmers' collective problems to the administrative authority. In response to early KCC lobbying, the government enacted the Butter Levy Ordinance of 1931, which required all non-KCC members supplying butter to the local market to pay a levy (Hills 1956).

PRICE CONTROLS.   World War II provided the settler farmers with a unique opportunity to further press for statutory price controls. Faced with the need for large food supplies to feed its fighting forces, the British government directed the colonial states to contribute to provisioning forces positioned in North Africa and the Middle East (Bates 1989). This translated into pressure on the white settlers to increase their agricultural production to meet the state's needs. As a result, the bargaining power shifted in favor of the farmers, who success-fully demanded that the government insure them against price risks at least for the duration of the war. Wartime demands, coupled with high controlled prices and corresponding reductions in price uncertainties, served as major stimuli to the dairy industry, resulting in large expansions in primary production and in processing capacity (Troup 1956).

After the war, when the government withdrew as a major buyer, the con-tentious issue of how to share the domestic market reemerged with greater in-tensity. In response, the KCC found it necessary to alter its contract with its farmer-members. Rather than resume the prewar levy, the KCC designed a more complex system of quota-based contracts in 1954. The overall objective of the quota pricing system was to ensure seasonal capacity utilization at the KCC processing facilities. Producers contracting for a year-round quota—that is, those who could guarantee off-season supplies—received the highest price. Those contracting for a high-season quota received the next-best price, while those who could not guarantee any quota received the lowest price (Kenya 1965). This pricing system favored the best-capitalized dairies, those with in-tensive feeding operations that could ensure year-round milk supplies.

Phase 2: Integration of Smallholder Producers, 1954–62

Through the middle of the 20th century, colonial dairy policy focused on sup-porting the white settler farmers. But in 1954, priorities changed with the adop-tion of the Swynnerton Plan, which advocated the promotion of intensified agri-culture among indigenous Kenyans.

This radical change arose for several reasons. First, since the late 1940s, the colonial government had faced a mounting insurgency among the indige-nous people, culminating in the declaration of a state of emergency in 1952. Policy measures linked to the introduction of commercial dairying on the "white highlands" intensified the tensions underlying this insurgency. The adoption of commercial dairying by settler farmers resulted in the eviction of many squatters from the white highlands. Displaced and landless, they returned to the ARs, where the population density was already high. The resulting in-crease in land pressure inside the reserves aggravated deprivation among the indigenous people. At the same time, their prior experience on the settler farms sensitized them to the stark contrast between conditions in the reserves and in the white highlands. In time, these disparities prompted the indigenous people to exert sufficient political pressure to draw the attention of the colonial ad-ministration to their plight.

Second, it had become increasingly clear since the early 1930s that the domestic market could not adequately compensate for lack of export markets. With the end of the temporary export boom during World War II, Kenya's external markets once again receded, leaving colonial producers dependent on internal market demand. This led the imperial government to introduce a policy of import-substituting industrialization (ISI) in the colonies. In Kenya, the colonial authorities introduced ISI policies in the early 1950s, with a consequent need to promote a large and growing local cash market. Accordingly, a case was successfully advanced for intensification of the agricultural production of African smallholders (Swynnerton Plan 1954).

Following the Swynnerton Plan's recommendations, the colonial authorities began to encourage commercial dairy production among the indigenous people. They established specific programs to train smallholders in better methods of animal husbandry and to introduce exotic stock and AI schemes in the ARs. In medium-potential areas, agricultural staff upgraded smallholder herds with Indian Sahiwal breeds, while in the high-potential areas they introduced European breeds. In 1960, formal exclusion of indigenous Kenyans from the white highlands ended (von Haugwitz and Thorwart 1972).

As a result of these changes, smallholder milk production and marketed volumes rose significantly. Gross dairy revenues among smallholders increased at an average annual rate of 14.5 percent, from K£199,000 in 1957 to K£691,000 in 1964 (Figure 6.2). By 1964, smallholders accounted for 14 percent of total marketed dairy products, up from 4 percent in 1957, further splintering the small domestic market.

The integration of smallholder dairy farmers into the formal milk market posed a challenge to the KCC in managing the overall volumes sold and processed. The growing scale of smallholder supplies increased the susceptibility of milk processing plants operated by the KCC to seasonal fluctuations and market uncertainties. Further, the growing numbers and heterogeneity among dairy producers made it difficult to enforce rules informally. Uncontrolled marketing by the indigenous people likewise threatened to induce self-interested settler farmers to follow suit, diverting sales from the KCC to raw milk markets through their African farm hands (Troup 1956). With self-regulation increasingly difficult, the settler farmers came to see the need for a legitimate authority to facilitate problem resolution, to formulate market rules, and to monitor, sanction, and enforce compliance.

As a result, in 1956 the settler dairy farmers successfully lobbied the colonial government to institute statutory marketing controls. The outcome was enactment of the Kenya Dairy Industry Act—Chapter 336 of the Laws of Kenya—in 1958. As expected, the act accorded substantial protective powers to the KCC. It instituted a new regulatory agency, the Kenya Dairy Board (KDB), as the state agent in regulating the industry. Further, the act zoned the country into

FIGURE 6.2 Growth in Kenya's annual smallholder milk production, 1957–64

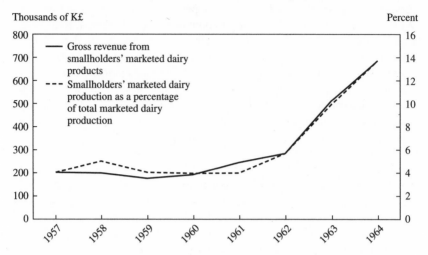

SOURCE: Authors' compilation on based data presented by Ruthenberg (1966).

"scheduled" and "unscheduled" areas. It also established regulations (the Dairy Industry Regulations, in Chapter 336 of the Laws of Kenya) expressly forbidding raw milk sales in scheduled (primarily urban) areas. According to the new act, households in scheduled areas would have legal access only to pasteurized milk from the formal marketing channels. Equally significant, the board appointed the KCC as its prescribed agent in managing milk processing, packaging, and sales in the scheduled areas.

As the colonial period drew to a close, Kenya had laid the foundations for a highly productive national dairy industry. The introduction of high-yielding breeds of cattle, coupled with systems for delivering artificial insemination, disease control, and veterinary care, enabled startling productivity gains and motivated large numbers of Kenyan farmers to enter dairy production. Equally important, the colonial authorities, in close collaboration with private dairy farmers, had developed a formal institutional framework for managing milk marketing as well as the production and delivery of curative and preventive services such as AI and tick control.

Phase 3: Acceleration of Smallholder Access, 1963–86

Implementation of the Swynnerton Plan in 1954 launched an agricultural transformation that gradually increased the role of smallholder agriculture in the Kenyan economy. This transformation accelerated rapidly after the country attained political independence in 1963.

LAND REALLOCATION. In their negotiations with the British government for political independence, Kenyan leaders insisted on a system for facilitating the acquisition of farms in the "white highlands" by indigenous farmers. Together with colonial administrators, they developed a plan intended to prevent a "cut-and-run" dilapidation of the settler farms with its consequent risks of slumping employment and commercial activity. Under the terms of these negotiations, the British agreed to provide funds to the incoming government, which they would in turn lend to landless Africans for the purchase of farms from the white settlers (von Haugwitz and Thorwart 1972; Leys 1975). Mortgaged ownership provided the principal mechanism through which the majority of landless Africans acquired land in the white highlands. A group of prospective buyers would form a land-buying company, identify a farm on sale, and arrange a mortgaged purchase with a bond that specified not to subdivide the land until full repayment of the mortgage. The company would then issue equity shares to prospective member-buyers and continue operating the farm as a limited company until the new owners fully repaid the mortgage. Because mortgage repayment extended over a number of years, it became feasible for low-income landless people to acquire land by making small payments over an extended period (Box 6.1).

The resulting land transfers brought remarkable changes in the structure of the country's agriculture. By 1990, smallholder agriculture dominated national production and marketed sales of most major crops. Presently, the country's agriculture consists principally of farm holdings of less than 2 hectares. Kenya's 3 million smallholder farm families supply an estimated 75 percent of national agricultural production and 50 percent of marketed surplus.

In addition to restructuring land ownership, the new government recognized that a combination of factors was crucial for enabling sustainable increases in milk production. These factors, discussed in the following paragraphs, include (1) enhanced milk production traits of smallholder dairy herds, (2) improved herd management on smallholder farms, and (3) improved milk market access.

ARTIFICIAL INSEMINATION SERVICES. The provision of efficient and affordable reproductive services has constituted a central plank in Kenya's dairy development strategy. Over the years, the Kenyan government has invested heavily in the delivery of AI services. At the time of the country's independence, CAIS, the government parastatal, operated mainly as a bull semen producing agent for the cattle breeders' associations, which in turn served mainly the large-scale dairy farmers.

To broaden CAIS coverage to include smallholder dairy farmers, the Kenyan government, with assistance from the Swedish International Development Cooperation Agency (SIDA), established Kenya National Artificial Insemination (KNAIS) in 1966 (FAO 1991; MoALDM 1997). The government mandated that KNAIS perform and coordinate actual field inseminations while

BOX 6.1 The tree that bears fruit every day

Mr. Ruto, a 70-year-old Kenyan dairy farmer, started his adult life working as a tractor driver on a white settler farm in Central Province. In 1968, he registered with a land-buying company, which bought a white settler's farm in Nakuru, in Rift Valley Province. In 1979, after repaying the mortgage, the company divided up the property among the shareholders according to each member's share contribution. Mr. Ruto received an 8-acre parcel. On top of the land share, the shareholders received one dairy cow each from the farm's dairy herd. In addition to that one cow, Mr. Ruto purchased additional cows from the farm's herd. In all, at the time the land was shared out, he owned four dairy cows. The four cows, all Friesian–Sahiwal crosses, constituted Mr. Ruto's foundation herd. Mr. Ruto maintained his herd at four cows by selling livestock each year to pay for his children's school fees. Then, in 1984, he allowed the herd to grow to six cows. But in 1986, he gave two cows as dowry for his son's wife.

Mr. Ruto sold his milk to the KCC up until 1997, when he sought other market outlets and began selling to hotels and restaurants in a shopping center 2 kilometers from his farm. In the past three years, he entered into an informal sales agreement with one of the hotels. He sells all his morning milk output to the hotel while retaining the evening milk for his family's consumption. His only regret about the liberalized market is that it has meant diminished opportunities for monthly contracts. As it is now, he sells his milk on a cash basis.

In addition to engaging in milk production, Mr. Ruto grows food crops, mainly maize, beans, and millet, for his family's consumption and sales. However, he rates his dairy enterprise highest in term of income earnings. He describes dairy as a "tree that bears fruit every day," unlike maize, which requires the family to wait for six months until harvest. Last season he harvested only 15 bags (1.35 metric tons) of maize from a 2-acre maize–bean intercrop. At the time he was interviewed for this book, the farmgate price of maize stood at Ksh 450 per bag. The gross value of his entire maize harvest, therefore, stood at Ksh 6,570. In comparison, his milk output averaged 20 kilograms per day. At the price of Ksh 19.60 per kilogram, his dairy milk was worth Ksh 392 per day, or Ksh 143,080 per year, over 20 times as much as his maize.

Mr. Ruto's land allocation reflects the importance dairy plays in maintaining his household's welfare. From his 8-acre farm he reserves 6 acres for his dairy enterprise, 4 planted with Rhode grass and 2 planted with napier and fodder sorghum. In addition, he has planted leguminous trees along the farm lines dividing the different farm plots. He explained that the leguminous trees were promoted by an agroforestry project implemented by the Kenya Forestry Research Institute in collaboration with the Japanese International Cooperation Assistance.

CAIS continued to maintain responsibility for recruiting Kenya-bred pedigree bulls and collecting, preserving, and distributing their semen. These efforts rely on the support services of a number of organizations including the KSB, the DRSK, and the Livestock Recording Centre (LRC).[1]

In order to serve large numbers of smallholder farmers, KNAIS designed a distribution system centered on the establishment of AI subcenters. They took over responsibility for receiving and maintaining stocks of semen and liquid nitrogen from the CAIS and providing the services to farmers. Provision of services operated through a system of designated service delivery points at roadside crushes, simple wooden enclosures erected along established routes to facilitate AI operations. Farmers drove their animals to the roadside crushes for services. Inseminators on motorized vehicles circuited the routes daily, servicing the cows delivered to the crushes. The heavy dependence on motorized transport, however, made these operations highly vulnerable to vehicle breakdowns (FAO 1991; MoALDM 1997). Furthermore, the system placed heavy demands on government expenditures and, as a consequence, provision of the services relied heavily on donor project funding. For two and a half decades, the government and donors invested heavily in the provision of AI services. Up until 1987, farmers met less than 20 percent of the cost of AI services (Table 6.3).

TICK CONTROL. The practice of cattle dipping in Kenya started in the early 1910s, when settler dairy farmers constructed the first effective dips as part of their personal initiatives to control tick-borne diseases (Hills 1956). The Veterinary Department facilitated these efforts by borrowing from the experiences of South Africa, where the practice was already developed. Tick control formally became a national concern with the enactment of the Cattle Cleansing Ordinance in 1937. Because of the externalities involved in tick control programs, groups of smallholder dairy farmers developed collectively managed communal dips. The farmer groups, however, proved inefficient. So in 1977 the government took over the management of the dips to enhance the effectiveness of the disease control. By 1987, the Government of Kenya operated 6,041 dips throughout the country.[2]

CLINICAL SERVICES. Clinical services began in 1974 when the Veterinary Department opened the first clinical center catering to smallholders. By 1978,

---

1. The KSB is specifically charged with the responsibility of recruiting animals into a voluntary upgrading scheme, monitoring the progeny upgrades, and maintaining a pedigree herd register. For its part, the DRSK is responsible for monitoring the milk performance of animals in the KSB register subject to farmers' voluntary participation. The third organization, the LRC, takes responsibility for evaluating the milk performance of the daughters of pedigreed bulls using the DRSK milk performance monitoring data.

2. Pegram et al. (1991) have questioned the basic assumption that indigenous cattle require as intensive a control regime as the exotic breeds. They argue that undue concern with the protection of a small herd of exotic breeds may have cost the country the loss of valuable tick resistance as well as the loss of enzootic stability. They recommend that a more efficient program vary with breed, type of cattle, and ecological conditions.

TABLE 6.3 Trends in artificial insemination charges, 1980–90

	1980–81	1984–85	1986–87	1988–89	1989–90
Actual cost (Ksh)	5.2	8.4	12.8	14.2	14.8
Producer charges (Ksh)	1.0	1.0	1.2	10.2	14.8
Producer charges/actual cost (percent)	19	12	9	72	100

SOURCE: Authors' computation from data presented by the FAO (1991).

18 clinical centers were operating nationwide, and by 1995 this number had expanded to about 284. Up until 1988, the services operated with strong state support, including government-employed veterinarians and nominal charges for drugs.

EXTENSION SERVICES.   Kenya's national extension program has placed a high priority on improving dairy husbandry practices. In addition, Kenya provides formal training at the university, diploma, and certificate levels. Donor agencies and local community organizations have contributed significantly to the efficiency of the livestock extension service (Box 6.2). Most notably, a bilateral Kenyan–Dutch collaborative effort launched the National Dairy Development Project in 1980 (MoALDM 1997). The project promoted intensive smallholder dairying in high-potential areas by introducing a zero-grazing package that included better napier grass management coupled with better cattle feeding practices (de Jong 1996). Later project staff introduced and promoted the production of leguminous fodder trees by farmers for use as an animal feed supplement (Kaitho, Tamminga, and van Bruchem 1993; Murethi, Tayler, and Thorpe 1995). In addition to the introduction of high-yielding fodder, the project promoted complementarities between dairy and crop production through better utilization of urine and manure.

MILK MARKETING.   Immediately following independence, the low market share supplied by smallholders in the formal milk market became an issue of political concern. Government policymakers interpreted the problem primarily as a conflict between the large- and small-scale producers over the smallholders' limited access to the formal milk market through the market gatekeeper, the KCC (Leys 1975; Bates 1989). They failed to consider the parallel problem of limited alternative market outlets, such as the informal raw milk markets emerging in urban areas in spite of legal sanctions against them. Instead, the government saw its task as one of redressing the inherited inequalities between the large- and small-scale dairy producers in the formal milk market. In July 1964, the authorities launched a commission of inquiry "to ensure that equitable price structure is established taking into account the interest of all dairy farmers" (Government of Kenya 1965, iii).

BOX 6.2 A Kenyan retiree turns to commercial dairy production

Mr. Wainaina retired from salaried employment in 1982 and used his benefits to buy a 3-acre piece of land on which he started rainfed horticulture, producing mainly tomatoes, onions and French beans. In 1983 he bought a dairy cow from the proceeds of the horticultural enterprise. By 1991 his dairy herd had expanded to four cows, but he had to gradually sell all of them to pay his children's school fees. In 1994 he received an in-calf heifer at a subsidized price of Ksh 2,800 credit from the Farming Systems Project, a church-based NGO with major objectives of helping poor households in high- and medium-potential areas of the country to start dairy enterprises. The organization operates a scheme that lends a "starter" in-calf heifer to an identified household. But first the organization offers training in dairy management to the identified households in a bid to enhance their capacities to manage dairy enterprises. On top of the subsidized monetary price, recipient households repay in-kind through the first in-calf heifer, which the organization lends to another farmer.

At the time of our interview, the cow, a Jersey breed, had calved eight times, producing twins twice. The offspring have been Jersey–Friesian crosses. Mr. Wainaina has maintained his herd at two milking cows.

Mr. Wainaina also serves as a milk-bulking commission agent for a milk trader. This entails assembling milk from neighboring farms up to the maximum quantity required by the trader. As he receives the milk, Mr. Wainaina screens each supplier's milk for adulteration. He keeps records of each supplier's accepted deliveries and transmits payment to the suppliers. To manage his own work effectively, Mr. Wainaina has designated his farm as a milk bulking point.

In addition to producing milk, Mr. Wainaina grows horticultural crops, mainly tomatoes, onions, French beans, sweet corn, kale, and oranges, under rainfed conditions. He rates his dairy enterprise highest in term of income earnings.

The inquiry judged that the existing institutional arrangements favored large-scale producers over small-scale dairy farmers (SDFs). Although the KCC had justified its three-tier pricing system, in use since 1954, as a way of minimizing seasonal supply and price fluctuations, the system resulted in price discrimination against SDFs because they could not achieve the quantity guarantees required to qualify for the premium price. Furthermore, because it was becoming increasingly difficult to qualify for a quota, the system conferred relative benefits on those already awarded quotas, primarily the large farmers.

To reduce the large-scale bias in accessing urban formal sector dairy markets, the inquiry recommended statutory price controls. As a result, in 1970 the pricing structure changed with the abolition of the quota pricing system. Then, in 1971, the KDB introduced a uniform panseasonal and panterritorial price for milk, mirroring the parastatal pricing systems in place for other major agricultural commodities, including maize (see Chapter 3), wheat, and beef.

Under the new system, the KCC became the administrative vehicle for implementing statutory control of milk prices and quantities marketed. The regulations required that all licensed milk processors procure raw milk supplies through the KCC, which then made arrangements for specific dairy farmers to deliver a specified amount of milk to the applicant. The resulting KCC control over input quantities and prices left other processors at a considerable competitive disadvantage compared to the KCC. As a result, in practice, private entrepreneurs were restricted to producing specialty dairy products such as cheese, yogurt, and ice cream. Thus, the pricing reforms of the early 1970s reaffirmed and reinforced the KCC's monopoly control of Kenya's milk market.

In order to guarantee a market outlet to all dairy farmers, the new regulations mandated that the KCC accept all milk delivered to its plants subject to minimum quality specifications and delivery schedules. Accordingly, the KCC expanded its capacity to achieve a national footprint commensurate with its new role. By 1991 it had an installed capacity of 1.2 million liters per day, including 11 milk chilling centers spread throughout the main dairy districts and 11 processing plants producing and packing a wide variety of dairy products, including low- and highfat fresh milk, condensed milk, ultra-heat-treated long-life milk, milk powder, butter, *ghee,* cheese, and fermented milk.

These postindependence changes brought several benefits to the small dairy farmers. First, the guaranteed market and guaranteed fixed price served to reduce risk to smallholder farmers, enabling them to secure market outlets for full lactation periods. Furthermore, the new marketing arrangements had the merit of allowing the establishment of routine operating procedures, a crucial feature given the highly repetitive nature of milk production and selling and the consequent need for regularity. The other obvious benefit was that of cushioning the farmer from seasonal price fluctuations.

As the power of the KCC increased, that of the KDB waned. In 1982, the KDB lost its dairy development section to the Ministry of Agriculture and its nutrition section to the KCC. Thus began a series of concessions that gradually limited the KDB's ability to regulate the industry while simultaneously increasing the KCC's privileges and monopoly rights. In particular, the KCC gained direct representation on the KDB's Licensing Committee, through which it exerted restrictive control over the issuance of licenses to potential entrants as well as placed limitations on the quantity of raw milk supplies to which other licensed processors had access (DANIDA and Ministry of Livestock Development 1990; Coughlin 1992).

Although settler dairy farmers had originally incorporated the KCC as a private sector organization to represent the interests of its members, the net result of these postindependence institutional changes was to transform it to a de facto parastatal. Indeed, the government entrusted the KCC with a variety of social roles, including (1) maintaining a strategic stock of milk; (2) serving as a buyer of last resort; and (3) implementing the School Milk Program as an agent for the Ministry of Education, beginning in 1979.

Performance of these social roles by the KCC inevitably meant that some of its operations were inconsistent with cost minimization strategies. It likewise shouldered the risks of milk supply fluctuations. The seasonal shortfalls in supplies that result in underrainfed natural and planted pastures (Figure 6.3) translated into low overall utilization of operating capacity. In the six years prior to milk market liberalization, between January 1986 and December 1991, monthly capacity utilization averaged about 0.92 million liters per day, or about 77 percent of the KCC's installed capacity of 1.2 million liters per day. Although plants were underutilized during the low supply periods, the KCC hired labor mainly on permanent terms and therefore could not flexibly manage hiring to prevent losses. Moreover, like many other public institutions, the KCC suffered from overstaffing coupled with a disproportionate share of nonessential staff. During the wet seasons, long queues of milk trucks built up at the processing plants' offloading bays, causing heavy congestion that in effect lengthened the time between milking and delivery (DANIDA and Ministry of Livestock Development 1990). This congestion resulted in high rates of milk spoilage, the cost of which the KCC passed on to producers through rejected milk.

FIGURE 6.3 Kenya's milk supply pattern, 1986–91

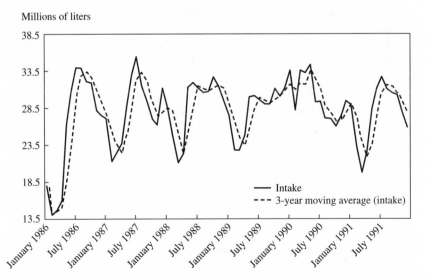

SOURCE: *Statistical Abstracts,* various issues.

Given the high cost of its operations, the KCC began accumulating trading losses as early as 1972. Initially, the government responded by allowing the KCC to retain 50 percent of the milk levy cess they collected on behalf of the KDB. Later, in 1984, the KCC was allowed to retain the total cess collected. Despite these concessions, mounting financial difficulties resulted in rising KCC indebtedness to both farmers and the government. Between 1985 and 1989, the KCC's operating costs, already high, increased by 121 percent and the KCC started falling into arrears with farmers' payments (FAO 1991). The problems culminated in persistent breaches of promissory obligations to pay for milk deliveries. Despite the many benefits this centralized, subsidized system conferred on dairy farmers of all sizes, the model proved financially unviable in the long run.

Phase 4: Liberalization, 1987–2006

At Kenya's independence, the new government as well as most Kenyans regarded state control of economic activities as crucial for successful social and economic development (Hewitt de Alca'ntara 1993).[3] The resulting highly interventionist strategy, while understandable as a means of increasing the economic participation of indigenous Kenyans during the transition period when the country was undergoing structural reform, was clearly not sustainable in the long run. As a result, with strong donor encouragement and support, from the mid-1980s on Kenya initiated a set of broad economic reforms aimed at reducing the role of the state while stimulating the growth of a more competitive and productive private sector (Republic of Kenya 1995).[4]

In the dairy industry, reforms began in 1987 with the launching of a process aimed at ending government provision of breeding services. This was followed, in 1988, by the initiation of a plan to divest the government of its role in the provision of clinical livestock services. Then, in 1989, the government liberalized the manufacture and sale of feeds, and in 1991 it began withdrawing from the management of cattle dips. The process culminated in 1992 with the liberalization of milk marketing.

BREEDING AND CLINICAL SERVICES.   Prior to these reforms, the government had supplied all AI and veterinary services and related supplies using salaried government employees. In order to ensure a smooth transition, devoid of gaps in the provision of these services, the government adopted a process of gradual divestiture. Starting in 1988, the government began to gradually increase the rate of cost recovery for breeding and veterinary services in order to encourage the establishment of private veterinarians. Policymakers presumed that veterinarians already in the government establishment would resign vol-

---

3. Chapter 3 describes the heavy government control of Kenyan maize markets during this period.

4. Kenya's liberalized dairy industry continued to adjust and adapt well into 2010. Data constraints, however, lead us to truncate this discussion of both policy and performance in 2006.

untarily to take up private practice, while newly qualified veterinarians would join in the competition. Farmer dairy cooperatives were also encouraged to compete in the provision of the services.

By the mid-2000s, nearly two decades after the institution of these changes, privatization had tended to flourish in high productivity areas that are easy to serve, while remote areas had seen service availability diminish. Some observers describe the result as market "skimming," whereby private suppliers serve primarily the most profitable areas. In the favorable zones, veterinarians venturing into practice have tended to set up integrated enterprises supplying feeds and retail drugs as well as offering on-call veterinary and AI services. Although no clear statistics are available, indications are that the majority of the private practices are run by veterinarians still in the government establishment, where their quasi-private status confers on them a competitive advantage over participants not affiliated with the government. This dual role may well hamper the development of a fully fledged private practice. Given that veterinarians in the government establishment can maintain a quasi-private status, they face no incentive to leave the establishment and become full-time private practitioners. More significantly, nonaffiliated veterinarians are obviously reluctant to invest, given their competitive disadvantage.

FORMAL SECTOR MILK PROCESSING AND MARKETING. In Kenya, "formal milk marketing channels" refers to channels that process milk in modern plants and then move the processed milk products to final consumers (Figure 6.4, Channels 1–3). Conversely, "informal milk marketing channels" refer to channels moving raw milk to final consumers (Figure 6.4, Channels 4–6). Because liberalization has resulted in partial decriminalization of raw milk sales in urban areas (the formally scheduled areas), the KDB has now licensed a number of businesses to sell raw milk in towns. Therefore, the terms "formal" and "informal" no longer connote a legal distinction. They simply distinguish between channels moving processed dairy products and those moving raw milk to final consumers.

Kenya's milk marketing reforms involved several related moves: abolition of the KCC monopoly on formal milk processing, liberalization of milk pricing, and decriminalization of raw milk sales in urban areas. Together these reforms spurred a series of private sector responses. Since removal of the KCC monopoly on formal milk processing in 1992, roughly 45 private dairies and over 150 cooperative milk processing plants have emerged. These developments first started with several large-scale dairy farms, including Brookside, Delamere, and Illara dairies. Using foundation supplies from their own herds to start production, they progressed quickly into taper integration—sourcing some fraction of their raw milk input from their own vertically integrated dairy farms and the balance from other farmers. Today all formal private processors depend heavily on raw milk supplies from farmers. By 2005, the processing capacity installed by the emerging processors had reached about 960,000 liters

FIGURE 6.4 Kenya's milk marketing channels, 2002

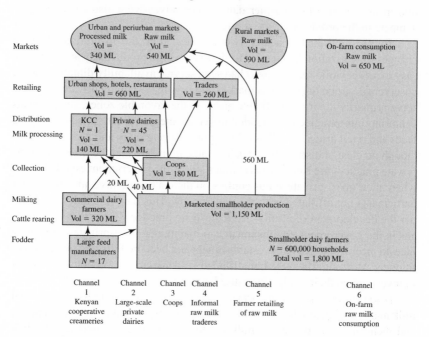

SOURCE: Ngigi (2005).
NOTE: coop, cooperative; KCC, Kenya Cooperative Creameries; *N,* number of producers; vol, volume in millions of liters (ML).

per day, while the KCC's installed capacity stood at 1.2 million liters per day (Ngigi et al. 2000).

Increases in private processing capacity and the attendant competition for supplies have challenged individual processors to actively cultivate suppliers in order to guard against underutilization of their installed capacity. Individual processors actively pursue regular procurement arrangements with farmers as part of their efforts to ensure a steady year-round milk supply. Already processors are formally contracting with collective farmer groups. Although the milk market has also attracted specialized traders who buy raw milk from the farmers to resell to processors, the processors prefer procuring milk directly from farmers through the Dairy Farmer Cooperative Societies (DFCS) or other collective milk assembly organizations because they are more reliable than the middlemen, who seek trade relationships only during times of high milk supplies.

RAW MILK MARKETING IN URBAN AREAS.   In rural "unscheduled" areas, the sale of raw milk has always been legal, even before dairy market liberalization in 1992. However, in the "scheduled" areas (which closely corresponded to the urban areas), raw milk sales became illegal under the Dairy Industry Act, with the KDB mandated to monitor compliance in urban areas.

Despite longstanding legal prohibitions, raw milk has always been traded actively in urban areas. Enforcement actions under the Dairy Industry Regulations failed to prevent the development of urban raw milk markets. Moreover, growing inefficiencies in the old single-channel formal system, coupled with the KDB's weakening position, permitted the illegal raw milk trade to thrive. By the early 1990s, the KDB's dwindling enforcement capacity could hardly cope. The sale of raw milk in urban areas is thus not a result of dairy market liberalization but rather a long-established practice that has always operated in parallel with the official processed milk marketing channels. Before Kenya's dairy market liberalization, the official KCC channel probably accounted for only about 38 percent of the nation's total marketed milk production (DANIDA/MoA 1995), a modest share and quite disproportional to the level of resources and official efforts devoted to developing the formal channel.

Legal issues involving raw milk sales remain murky and subject to various interpretations. In part, this ambiguity arises because the liberalization of the dairy industry in 1992 was not preceded by a formal review of the Dairy Industry Act. Instead, the change was communicated as an official government directive. Though explicit in encouraging potential processors to enter the market to open up the KCC to competition, the directive was not explicit on the question of raw milk sales in the scheduled areas. In general, the directive was understood as a move to encourage private sector participation in the dairy market. In practice, "over-the-fence" raw milk sales among neighbors are not considered to pose a significant public hazard. However, the legal status of larger volumes of marketed raw milk sales remains murky. The KDB's position has been characterized by ad hoc and reactive regulatory measures that have generally involved impromptu confiscation of milk supplies from raw milk traders (Ngigi et al. 2000). Nonetheless, given the competitiveness of the raw milk trade, available estimates suggest that formal processing channels still supply a relatively small share of the country's milk consumption, on the order of 15 percent (see Figure 6.4). Despite the legal ambiguity, dairy market liberalization has resulted in a visible increase in the activity of raw milk traders in urban areas. Indeed, market observers estimate that raw milk sales account for up to 70 percent of smallholder dairy cooperatives' total milk intakes. Overall, the raw milk supply channels dominate Kenyan dairy markets, accounting for 85 percent of the total volumes consumed and roughly 60 percent of the marketed volumes in urban areas.

Raw milk dominates Kenya's milk markets because of its low cost and because Kenyans habitually boil all fresh milk before consuming it in tea and coffee or as a hot drink (Omore et al. 2001; Staal, Nin Pratt, and Jabbar 2008). Thus, their milk does not require prior pasteurization and the cost it entails. The cost of processing and packaging pasteurized milk means that raw milk traders can operate competitively and profitably within the formal processor's price margins. As a result, raw milk traders procure milk from farmers at higher prices than those offered by formal processors and resell raw milk for a profit at a price far lower than that of packaged, pasteurized milk. Surveys conducted in 1999 and 2000 indicate that raw milk retailed for roughly half the price of packaged pasteurized milk, while farmers received a 15–50 percent premium when selling through the raw milk distributors (Table 6.4).

Despite the competitive advantage held by raw milk traders, critics point out that raw milk carries a risk of adulteration.[5] They also contend that the handling containers commonly used by a majority of raw milk traders are difficult to sterilize. Thus, the critics argue, raw milk sales pose a public health hazard due to sanitation and safety risks.

On the other hand, advocates of the raw milk trade feel that its continued dominance, despite official prejudice against it, implies a misallocation of efforts to develop a Western-model milk processing and distribution channel. They argue that giving legitimacy to the raw milk trade would give its participants a long-term view and, along with it, the confidence to scale up their businesses and engage in product and market development. Indeed, the persistence of raw milk sales may be an indication that participants have, to a large extent, devised ways of countering these problems. In fact, the highly perishable nature of raw fresh milk may itself partly mitigate the problem, demanding high standards of cleanliness to minimize spoilage losses. Repeat informal seller–buyer relationships, which are common in informal milk market channels, may contribute to enhanced monitoring and the accumulation of social capital, both of which help to mitigate moral hazard problems. Amid the ongoing debates, no one doubts that raw milk sales continue to dominate Kenya's dairy markets.

Drivers of Change

Improved production technology has resulted in significant productivity gains among Kenya's large- and small-scale dairy producers. The early import of improved breeds, AI services, and a multitude of in-kind loan programs have resulted in the widespread availability of cross-bred and grade dairy cattle (those with more than 87.5 percent exotic blood) (see Boxes 6.1 and 6.2). Early efforts at tick control and provision of veterinary services have further contributed to improved cattle health and productivity as well as to the profitability of dairy production. Extension support and development of a variety of improved fodder crops have underpinned growing efforts to intensify dairy production. Cumulatively, these efforts have enabled Kenyan dairy farmers to achieve the highest dairy productivity in the region, with milk yields per cow two to three times those attained in Uganda and Ethiopia (see Table 6.1).

---

5. A study by Omore et al. (2001) provides evidence that some traders indeed adulterate milk with water coupled with flour and margarine to increase the volume of sales while maintaining the specific gravity and butter fat content, especially during periods of low supply.

TABLE 6.4 Marketing margins in Kenya's formal and raw milk supply channels, 2000

	Milk prices (Ksh/liter)		Profitability	
	Farm purchase price	Retail price	As a percentage of retail price	US$/day
Pasteurized milk, formal supply channel	16	50	—	—
Raw milk, informal channels				
Nakuru town				
Milk bars	19	24	11	5.37
Hawkers	16	25	34	4.65
Nairobi				
Milk bars	25	31	5	3.76
Hawkers	21	27	11	2.83

SOURCE: Ngigi (2005).

NOTES: —, not available. Dollar figures are given in 2005 U.S. dollars.

Market development efforts have complemented these supply-side productivity-based interventions. Yet policy and promotional efforts have focused almost exclusively on Kenya's formal milk market. Bulking systems, often operated through dairy farmer cooperatives and marketing groups, enable smallholders to participate in formal milk markets. Investments in collection and cooling facilities have broadened the geographic reach of Kenya's peri-urban dairy industry.

In spite of the overwhelming attention given to urban formal milk markets, the informal raw milk markets remain dominant in both urban and rural areas as growing production surpluses have driven increases in milk availability. The low cost of raw milk (which retails at roughly half the price of pasteurized milk) and the Kenyan dietary habit of consuming raw milk primarily in boiled form translate into a compelling consumer preference for raw milk.

A broad array of support institutions has developed in Kenya over the past 100 years to support growth in both dairy productivity and marketing. On the production side, institutions such as the cattle breeders' associations, KSB, DRSK, KNAIS, LRC, National Animal Husbandry Research Service, and National Veterinary Lab have all contributed to the high productivity of Kenyan dairy farmers. The participants in the milk marketing and processing network, consisting of DFCS, private processors, the KCC, and the KDB, have all played key roles at various stages in Kenya's dairy development.

Finally, government regulation has driven many of the key changes in Kenya's dairy industry, for better and for worse. During the first half of the 20th century, regulations clearly favored dairy development on large farms while discriminating against small-scale producers through land allocation, grazing controls, and the imposed illegality of raw milk sales in urban areas. From 1954 onward, support efforts focused on helping smallholder dairy farmers gain access to formal processed milk markets. Though reversing the earlier bias in favor of large farmers, this new era nonetheless continued the legal harassment of raw milk markets. The broad deregulation of 1992 has broken the KCC processing monopoly and permitted the emergence of roughly 50 privately owned dairy processors. Though the legal status of raw milk marketing remains ambiguous and hotly contested, deregulation has clearly reduced the prior suppression of raw milk traders and favored the growth of urban raw milk markets over the past decade and a half.

Results

AGGREGATE OUTPUT.   Because of the difficulties in quantifying raw milk production, which accounts for roughly 85 percent of total milk consumption, aggregate figures offer only a rough approximation of actual output levels. Indeed, some studies suggest that official figures may significantly underestimate actual milk production in Kenya (Staal et al. 2002). Nonetheless, available aggregates offer the only general notions we have about total milk production trends over time (Figure 6.5). These figures suggest that over the 43-year period from 1963 to 2006, during the acceleration and liberalization phases of Kenyan dairy development, aggregate milk production in Kenya grew at a compound rate of about 3.7 percent per year (see Table 6.2). The most striking growth occurred during the 1980s when production grew at an average rate of over 10 percent per year.[6] During the early reform years, milk production appears to have declined initially as the formal milk processing sector adjusted to market liberalization and the rapid fall in KCC production during the first half of the 1990s. But output growth subsequently recovered as private processors and raw milk traders gained market share, from the late 1990s onward.

In formal milk markets, the KCC's own production figures provide a good indication of the country's performance in formal milk processing activities up to the early 1990s. These data show that between 1971 and 1984, the firm's milk intake remained roughly flat (Figure 6.6). However, in the final decade before market liberalization, intake grew at an average annual rate of 4.4 percent before peaking in 1990. Since then, the firm's participation in the industry has been decreasing at an average annual rate of 10 percent and amounted to only about 140 million liters in 2000. At these levels, KCC operated at about one-third of its capacity.

Since liberalization, the newly emerging private processors have almost fully taken over the formal market share ceded by the KCC. Estimates from the

6. These aggregate figures come from FAOSTAT data. Exponential trends have been computed from these data using ordinary least squares regression for each time period.

FIGURE 6.5 Trends in Kenya's annual milk production, 1961–2006

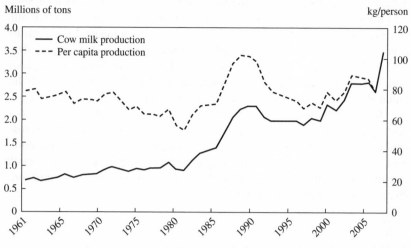

SOURCE: FAOSTAT.

FIGURE 6.6 Trends in Kenya Cooperative Creameries milk intake, 1971–2000

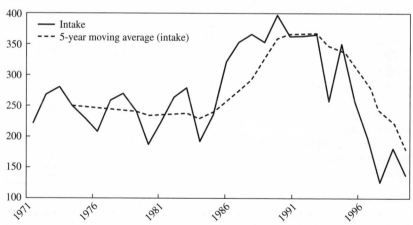

SOURCE: Author's compilation based on *Statistical Abstracts,* various issues.
NOTES: FAO climatic records suggest that Kenya experiences a drought every 5–7 years. Accordingly, because Kenya's dairy production is based mainly on rainfed natural and planted pastures, milk intake data have been deseasonalized using a 5-year moving average.

KDB's records show that in 2000 the emerging dairy firms processed about 0.6 million liters per day. This, combined with the KCC's production of about 0.37 million liters per day, brought the country's average daily volume of milk processed to about 0.97 million liters per day. This compares well with the country's preliberalization processed milk production, which averaged about 0.92 million liters per day. In absolute terms, Kenya's production of processed milk has not changed appreciably. Rather, as the KCC's installed capacity has fallen idle, that of other private entrepreneurs has increased.

In raw milk markets, the glimmers of available empirical evidence suggest a general upward trend since the 1960s. The growing availability of crossbred cows and rising milk production have largely fueled growth of the dominant raw milk markets, which currently account for 85 percent of Kenyan milk consumption. Estimates suggest that between 1980 and 2000, raw milk production roughly tripled (Table 6.5).

TABLE 6.5 Long-term trends in Kenyan dairy production, 1980–2000

	1980	1990	2000
Milk production (10^6 MT)			
Raw	0.73	1.92	1.91
Processed[a]	0.19	0.40	0.34[f]
Total[b]	0.92	2.32	2.25[f]
Per capita milk consumption (kg)[c]			
Raw	44.8	81.5	62.3
Processed	11.4	16.9	11.1
Total	56.2	98.4	73.4
National herd[d]			
Total cattle (million head)	10.0	13.8	13.8
Grade and crosses (%)	15.3	23.6	21.7
Local (%)	84.7	76.4	78.2
Grazing system[e]			
Stall feeding (zero grazing) (%)	—	32	29
Semizero grazing (%)	—	29	48
Open grazing (%)	—	39	23

NOTE: —, not available.

[a]Authors' compilation based on various issues of the Kenya Bureau of Statistics (KBS) Economic Survey and Kenya Dairy Board records.

[b]FAOSTAT.

[c]Authors' computation based on the milk production figures and national population statistics.

[d]Various Animal Production Reports, Ministry of Agriculture, unpublished data.

[e]Staal et al. (2002).

[f]Corrected for the amount processed by private processors (the KBS has not adjusted its recording to include this amount).

TABLE 6.6 Value of dairy production in Kenya as a percentage of total farm household income, 2000

Region	Mean
East–Central–Coast	33.1
North–Rift	25.0
Western	24.9
All	31.3

SOURCE: Egerton / Tegemeo / Michigan State University Rural Household Survey, 2000.

INCOME.   Across Kenya, dairying accounts for slightly over 30 percent of farm household income nationwide (Table 6.6). National farm household survey data from 2002/03 suggest that farm households earn about US$370 per year from dairying (Ngigi 2005). Two recent national farm-level surveys found that 72–75 percent of farm households engage in dairying. For over one-fourth of farm households, dairying contributes more than half of the households' income. This suggests that, for a large proportion of rural farm households in the country's high- and medium-potential areas, dairying is an important component of smallholder farm activities. It also underlines the importance of dairying as an integral component of smallholder farming systems.

EQUITY.   Smallholder milk production has expanded substantially in Kenya and now constitutes the major source of marketed milk. In 1975, smallholder dairy production accounted for only 35 percent of recorded milk sales (Minae 1981). Since then, smallholder dairy production has grown so rapidly that by the early 2000s smallholders accounted for roughly 80 percent of marketed milk supplies.

Among smallholder farmers, dairy income proves most important for the lower-income groups, where it accounts for 48 percent of total incomes. Among the richest quintile, the dairy income share falls to 28 percent of household income (Table 6.7). The composition of dairy earnings likewise varies across income groups. For high-income households, cash income from dairy operations is more likely to accrue from milk sales. Conversely, for low-income households, cash income from dairying is more likely to accrue from sales of animals. This suggests that low-income households keep dairy animals either as a source of on-farm consumption or as a form of security against lumpy cash needs.

On average, dairying households own three head of cattle with an average landholding of 2.6 hectares. The typical household includes six family members, with about 25 percent of households headed by women. Dairy households produce an average of 9 liters of milk daily. Of this, they consume about 2 liters and sell the remaining 7. Their dairy herds include mainly cross-

TABLE 6.7 Distributional impact of dairy income in Kenya, 2000

Income category	Dairy income as a percentage of total household income	Milk sales as a percentage of dairy cash income
Bottom quintile	48	32
2nd quintile	28	44
3rd quintile	29	56
4th quintile	36	59
Top quintile	28	71

SOURCE: Egerton/Tegemeo/Michigan State University Rural Household Survey, 2000.

breeds and indigenous breeds. Only about 20 percent of dairying households rear exclusively exotic breeds, while nearly 40 percent rear exclusively indigenous cattle (Ngigi 2005). This suggests that considerable scope remains for upgrading local herds through AI services to produce high-yielding cross-breeds and raise milk productivity.

Indeed, time-series data from Kenya suggest that dairy marketing contributes significantly to upward economic mobility for small and large farms alike. Using household panel survey data to track changes in asset poverty among Kenyan smallholder farmers between 1997 and 2004, a recent study finds that households participating in dairy markets increased their household wealth by about US$500 more than nondairy households did. Their analysis of poverty mobility concludes that "the importance of livestock production and marketing (especially milk) to the welfare of successful households shows up clearly, and this holds irrespective of farm size" (Burke et al. 2007, 33).

ECOLOGICAL SUSTAINABILITY.   Over 80 percent of the country's dairy cattle population is reared on mixed crop–livestock farms (Gitau et al. 1994; Republic of Kenya 1995). Indeed, some specialists argue that smallholder dairying is an inevitable result of tendencies to maximize land use, with cattle making a significant contribution to nutrient cycling (Lekasi et al. 1998). Currently in Kenya, dairy farming forms part of a complex animal–crop interaction in the smallholder systems, with strong interdependencies between crop and dairy enterprises. Draft power and manure from the livestock benefit plant production, while crop by-products such as maize stover, peelings from various crops, and crop stubble left on the farm after harvesting provide important sources of animal feed. Moreover, the sale milk provides farmers with a regular supply of cash, financing the purchase of crop inputs as well as other household cash costs. Under the mixed crop–livestock systems, animals and crops reinforce each other in a way that helps to sustain overall farm productivity.

Smallholder dairying operates under three different feeding regimes using varying levels of labor and land intensity. These include free grazing, semizero grazing, and zero grazing regimes. Given heavy land pressure, only about 25 percent of dairying households practice free grazing, while zero and semizero grazing account for slightly under 40 percent each (Table 6.8). Zero grazing predominates in high-potential areas where the human population density is high and landholdings are small. In these settings, confined livestock feeding releases land for crop production while at the same time facilitating the collection of manure for soil amendments to improve soil fertility and the carrying capacity of the land.

The farmers' choice of grazing systems is also strongly influenced by market access. Intensive dairy production has been promoted since the early 1980s in high-potential areas through a technical package of improved breeds, careful management, and use of high-yielding fodder. Compared to free grazing, intensive production requires both more capital and more labor (Table 6.9). Therefore, farmers will take the extra risk of investing their cash in intensive milk production only where they have access to an ensured market outlet. Table 6.10 reports the results of a multinomial logistic model estimated to assess the factors affecting farmers' choice of feed management systems. These results suggest that, all other things equal, the probability of using zero and semizero grazing systems compared to free grazing decreases significantly the farther away the farm is from an urban area. The probability also decreases significantly the farther away the farm is from a milk collection point. Reinforcing these spatial relationships, proximity to urban areas likewise raises land values, which in turn reinforce incentives to engage in intensive livestock production.

FINANCIAL SUSTAINABILITY.   Smallholder milk production and private trade in raw milk remain highly profitable enterprises. The advent of cross-bred cattle and more intensive dairy production technologies have increased both productivity and incomes (see Table 6.9). As a result, annual dairy income now averages US$370 per farm household, representing 30 percent of household income and one of the fastest-growing sources of small farmer income in Kenya (Ngigi 2005). Raw milk marketing likewise remains highly profitable, generating returns of roughly US$3 to $5 per day (see Table 6.4). Given the lack of processing costs, raw milk retails for about half the cost of pasteurized milk, leading to broad consumer preference for raw milk. Raw milk traders likewise

TABLE 6.8 Prevalence of the main dairy production systems in Kenya, 2000

Feed management system	Percentage of dairying households
Free grazing	25
Semizero grazing	38
Zero grazing	37
Total dairying households	100

SOURCE: Authors' computation from Smallholder Dairy Project survey data.

TABLE 6.9 Milk production costs in Kenya by feed management regime, 1999

Grazing system Location	Zero grazing Kiambu	Open grazing Nyandarua/Nakuru
Annual average yield per cow (liters)	2,215	1,633
Average farmgate price per liter (Ksh)	18	13
Milk sales (Ksh)	32,614	16,379
Home consumption (Ksh)	11,483	5,038
Sale of animals (Ksh)	3,843	3,306
Gross revenue per cow (Ksh)	47,940	24,722
Labor cost (Ksh)	15,970	3,204
Intermediate cost (Ksh)	13,357	5,588
Total cost per cow (Ksh)[a]	29,327	8,791
Gross margin (Ksh)	18,614	15,931

SOURCE: Ngigi (2005).
[a]Excludes cost of land.

pay slightly higher costs to farmers, leading both consumers and farmers to prefer raw milk markets.

While the private segments of the dairy market have generally proven financially viable, the heavily regulated KCC model did not. During the period of the de facto KCC monopoly, the imposition of social mandates and government-regulated panterritorial pricing proved financially unsustainable. Hemorrhaging costs at the KCC and other agricultural parastatals triggered the major reform of 1992, paving the way for the broad liberalization currently under way in the Kenyan dairy industry.

Dairy Development in Uganda

Phase 1: Colonial Period, 1894–1960

Despite sharing a common colonial experience with Kenya, as well as a generally favorable climate and soils, Uganda did not begin commercial milk production until the late 1950s. In part, this difference arose because of the varying success of settler agriculture in the two countries. Although in Kenya white settlers dominated commercial agriculture before the mid-1950s, this was not the case in Uganda, where white settler agriculture did not fully recover from the adverse conditions of World War I (Mamdani 1976; Southall 1988). Instead, Ugandan colonists left primary production largely to the indigenous people, while the Europeans and Asians concentrated on secondary production and on trade. During this period, settler farmers in neighboring Kenya were

TABLE 6.10 Factors influencing the choice of dairy feed management system in Kenya, 2000

| | Multinomial logistic estimates | | | |
Variable	Coefficient	Standard error	z	$P > |z|$
Zero grazing feed management system				
Size of landholding	−0.02	0.02	−1.08	0.28
Travel distance (in tens of km) to Nairobi	−0.04	0.02	−1.71	0.09
Travel distance (in km) to urban market	−0.01	0.01	−1.77	0.08
Travel distance (in km) to the nearest milk collection center	−0.04	0.01	−4.22	0.00
Head size (head)	−0.16	0.09	−1.76	0.08
Breed (1 if grade or cross, 0 if local)	1.31	0.24	5.49	0.00
Age of head of household	0.01	0.01	1.15	0.25
Sex of head of household (1 if male; 0 if female)	−0.16	0.27	−0.58	0.56
Number of years of school completed by head of household	0.05	0.03	1.42	0.15
Constant	0.80	0.84	0.95	0.34
Semizero grazing feed management system				
Size of landholding	−0.25	0.06	−4.31	0.00
Travel distance (in tens of km) to Nairobi	−0.22	0.03	−7.01	0.00
Travel distance (in km) to urban market	−0.04	0.01	−3.73	0.00
Travel distance (in km) to the nearest milk collection center	−0.02	0.01	−1.97	0.05
Herd size (head)	−0.46	0.14	−3.22	0.00
Breed (1 if grade or cross, 0 if local)	1.55	0.28	5.59	0.00
Age of head of household	0.02	0.01	1.54	0.12
Sex of head of household (1 if male, 0 if female)	−0.03	0.30	−0.09	0.93
Number of years of school completed by head of household	0.10	0.04	2.52	0.01
Constant	3.26	1.00	3.27	0.00

SOURCE: Authors' computation from Smallholder Dairy Project data.

NOTES: $N = 661$ smallholder dairy farm households (outcome-free grazing is the comparison category); LR χ^2 = 331.42; prob > χ^2 = 0.00; log likelihood = −551.09; pseudo R^2 = 0.23.

experimenting with commercial dairy production. Yet similar experimentation with high-yielding exotic and cross-bred cattle, by the government and settlers, did not begin in Uganda until 1928. Even these initial efforts were soon abandoned when the entire experimental herd was wiped out by diseases (Amann 1973).

The reasons for the quick abandonment of these initial forays into dairy production probably go beyond frustrations with disease. Attempts in neighboring Kenya in the early 1910s had faced similar problems. Yet the private farmers there persisted with their on-farm breeding experiments, leading to appreciable successes by the 1930s. Moreover, Uganda, starting later, should have benefited from the Kenyan experience, avoiding any mistakes made there and progressing more rapidly.

A more credible explanation probably lies in the economic circumstances prevailing at the time. The timing of these early attempts to introduce commercial dairying in Uganda proved unfortunate. Because Uganda's early efforts occurred during the early 1930s, they collided head-on with the collapse of international commodity prices during the Great Depression. Settler dairy farmers in neighboring Kenya, where dairy production had by then made appreciable advances, were forced to rely on an extremely limited East African market, which included regular exports to Kampala. Ugandan farmers, therefore, faced few incentives to enter into dairying.

Further attempts to develop commercial dairying in Uganda did not resume until the late 1950s (Amann 1973; Nsubuga 1973). Spearheaded by the colonial administration, this second round of efforts had to overcome obstacles similar to those faced by the white settler dairy farmers in Kenya during the early 1910s. These included dealing with the challenges posed by tick-borne diseases and the need to build a dairy herd with traits favoring high milk production. Fortunately, Kenyan farmers had made major advances in these two areas by the 1950s. Furthermore, high-yielding breeds were available across the border in Kenya, where dairy industry development had by then achieved an appreciable level. Experiences with the introduction of exotic and cross-bred cattle in Kenya pointed to tick control as the key starting point. Accordingly, the colonial administration advised prospective commercial dairy farmers that in order to prepare their farms for the introduction of exotic and cross-bred cattle they needed to create an environment less dangerous to the survival of the more productive breeds. To achieve this, they were instructed to use indigenous cattle as tick bait in an intense six-month tick control regime using acaricides. This practice proved quite successful, and the technological constraints to high-productivity dairy production were well on the way to resolution.

Phase 2: Seeking Milk Self-Sufficiency, 1960–70

The successful introduction of improved dairy breeds on large-scale farms led to a growing recognition that dairying presented a promising opportunity to diversify the country's agriculture. Furthermore, increases in domestic production could lead to a reduction in milk imports from Kenya, with valuable savings in foreign exchange. As a result, in the 1960s the Ugandan government started to pursue a policy of attaining self-sufficiency in milk. Government extension officers encouraged farmers in high-potential areas to integrate dairy and crop production so their farms could benefit from the complementarities, particularly the soil fertility amendments afforded by cattle manure.

The government launched a two-part strategy to expand dairy production. The first component involved expanding the number of high-yielding cattle, while the second facet revolved around enhancing dairy farmers' ability to manage the new breeds to their full potential. Efforts to expand the high-yielding herd included the import of high-yielding breeds, mainly from Kenya and later, when the supply from Kenya could not meet the demand, from the United Kingdom, the Netherlands, the United States, Denmark, and Canada. Subsequent local crossing aimed to build up local disease resistance. To realize the potential of exotic and cross-bred cattle, smallholder farmers had to adopt new management practices.

As a result of these efforts, national milk production increased and local supplies soon began to meet a significant proportion of the milk demands in Uganda's major consumption markets. Consequently, milk imports from Kenya fell steadily during the 1960s. Whereas imports supplied 75 percent of the total milk consumption in the Kampala market in 1961, by 1968 that share had fallen to 45 percent (Figure 6.7).

Given the growing success in increasing local milk production, the government shifted its focus to milk marketing. The country already had an organized milk collection and distribution system developed by a private company, Uganda Milk Processing Limited, which also imported fresh milk from Kenya for distribution in Kampala. However, the development perspective that guided not only Uganda but also many other countries at the time regarded state control of economic activities as crucial for social and economic development.

FIGURE 6.7 Change in sources of milk supply for greater Kampala, 1961–68

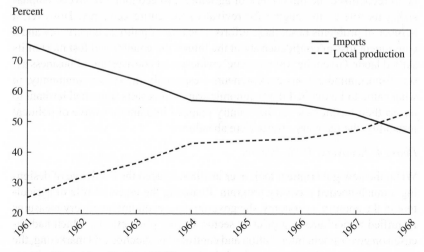

Percent

SOURCE: Adapted from Nsubuga (1973).

Accordingly, the Government of Uganda sought to foster further broadening of the country's growing dairy industry through a legal monopoly of the kind utilized in promoting the development of other important agricultural commodities. To this end, an act of parliament established a new government parastatal, the Dairy Corporation, in 1967. The act charged the Dairy Corporation with responsibilities comparable to those vested in the KCC by neighboring Kenya. These included the regulation of production, marketing, pricing, processing, manufacturing, and distribution of finished dairy products. By 1971, the Dairy Corporation had installed eight milk-chilling procurement centers across Uganda's major producing areas.

Phase 3: Civil Crisis, 1971–86

Growth in Uganda's dairy industry collapsed during the civil crisis that ravaged the country from 1971 to 1986. Unfortunately, this crisis coincided with the oil price shocks of the early 1970s and the collapse of the East African Community in 1977. These external shocks compounded the economic crisis gripping the country. Dairy production suffered further due to rustling, a decline in veterinary disease control following the disruptions in public services, and a resurgence of animal trypanosomiasis (Belshaw 1988). The public research and extension system also collapsed. Disruption of the marketing system further aggravated the fall in production and productivity as farmers retreated to subsistence farming.

When Idi Amin's military regime fell in 1979, the country appeared set to regain its composure. The new government launched a short-term stimulus program to promote economic and social recovery (World Bank 1982). The program recognized the importance of agriculture to economic recovery, emphasizing its role as the engine for revival of the entire economy. However, a number of problems beset these efforts. Because of political uncertainty and a consequent loss of confidence about the future, the country had lost most of its skilled labor. Given the Amin regime's widespread confiscation of business assets from nonindigenous entrepreneurs—especially the Asian community, in what came to be dubbed the "economic war"—investors remained hesitant to restart their businesses. As the country plunged into another wave of political instability, the recovery efforts were abandoned.

Phase 4: Recovery, 1986–Present

When the new government took over in 1986, it faced the challenge of designing a much-needed recovery program. Realizing the essential role of agriculture in the country's economy, the government's economic recovery measures identified agriculture as a priority sector. Unlike prior efforts, which had focused on government intervention and control of production and marketing, the new programs explicitly recognized the key role of the private sector in rebuilding the country's economy.

Empirical assessments confirmed the large potential for dairy production and marketing in Uganda. A collaborative study conducted in 1996 by the International Livestock Research Institute; Uganda's Ministry of Agriculture, Animal Industries and Fisheries; the National Agricultural Research Organisation; and Makerere University noted several factors underpinning the significant potential for dairy expansion in Uganda. To begin with, land per se is not yet a crucial limiting factor to the expansion of agricultural production there. The availability of high-potential agricultural land stands at about 2 hectares per person in Uganda compared to less than 0.4 hectares per person in Kenya.[7] Second, Uganda has a large cattle herd, though predominantly comprised of low-yielding indigenous breeds. Out of a total of 4.2 million cattle, only 3.4 percent are improved breeds (Okwenye 1994). Milk productivity of the indigenous breeds averages roughly 600 liters per lactation period compared to about 2,800 per lactation period for exotic breeds. Combined, these two facts suggest that improvement of the genetic productivity of the country's dairy herd offers significant potential for raising milk output and productivity. Third, milk production is predominantly based on natural pastures. Milk production is thus highly correlated with the rainfall variability. Improving the country's feed resources, therefore, holds great potential for increased milk production.

A market assessment undertaken during the same study demonstrated the substantial consumer potential for absorbing increased production. Although the country enjoys great potential for the expansion of dairy production, it experiences a milk shortfall estimated at 100–200 million liters of milk per annum. Furthermore, annual per capita consumption of milk stands at about 22 liters per person, well below the FAO's recommended 200 liters per person per year. Moreover, the urban population has been growing at a rate of 10 percent per annum. This rapid urbanization promises a growing milk market given that urbanization typically generates a growing market demand for food, particularly among commodities with a high income elasticity of demand, like milk. Regional exports may likewise prove feasible given the potential milk demand from neighboring countries such as Burundi and Rwanda.

Drivers of Change

Together, this evidence suggests great potential for increasing milk production and consumption in Uganda. The challenge appears to lie in designing and implementing initiatives that will enable dairy farmers to exploit that potential. Priorities clearly lie in measures to improve pastures and pasture management, improvement of dairy breeds and breeding programs that can gradually upgrade the productivity of indigenous cattle, and development of smallholder dairy technologies for milk processing and sale. In addressing these challenges, as

---

7. Nonetheless, the land fragmentation that coexists with large tracts of underutilized and unutilized land poses a tenurial challenge that must be overcome to facilitate dairy growth.

Fitzhugh (1998) has pointed out, the relevant technologies may already exist. What may be needed is an effective screening and promotion mechanism to enhance the transfer and adoption of appropriate technologies.

Improved farm productivity likewise depends on the efficiency of the marketing systems for production inputs as well as milk distribution and processing. Currently, two major supply channels link dairy farmers with urban consumers (Figure 6.8). Informal marketing of raw milk accounts for nearly 90 percent of milk sales, while formal marketing, through the Dairy Corporation, accounts for only about 10 percent of the marketed total. As in Kenya, promotional efforts that have historically focused on formal sector processing and packaging of milk may, in the future, benefit from recognizing the dominant importance of raw milk markets.

Dairy Development in Ethiopia

Like Kenya and Uganda, Ethiopia holds great potential for dairy development. The country currently manages the largest livestock population in Africa, estimated at 29 million cattle, 24 million sheep and goats, 18 million camels, 1 million equines, and 53 million fowl. Given its high population density and land pressure, Ethiopia faces a shortage of grazing as well as the lack of a well-developed feed industry. Nonetheless, a favorable climate throughout the country's high-

FIGURE 6.8 Uganda's milk marketing channels, 2002

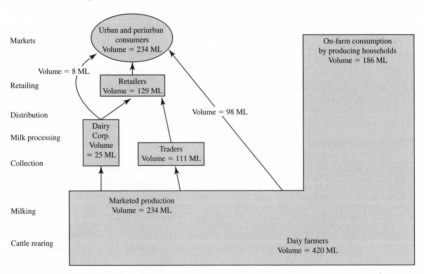

SOURCE: Adapted from the International Livestock Research Institute; Uganda's Ministry of Agriculture, Animal Industry, and Fisheries; the National Agricultural Research Organisation; and Makerere University.

lands supports the introduction of improved, high-yielding animal breeds and offers a relatively disease-free environment for livestock development.

Over the past decade and a half, following the political changes of 1993, Ethiopia's dairy industry has shown considerable progress. Its total milk production grew at an annual rate of 6.6 percent as compared to 2.1 percent during 1975–92, ending a three-decade trend of declining per capita production. The following discussion explores the reasons for this marked improvement as well as the prospects for further development of dairy production in Ethiopia.

Consumption Patterns and Production Systems

Unlike Kenya and Uganda, where raw milk dominates dairy consumption, Ethiopians consume primarily a traditional fermented butter. Traditional butter, which ferments slowly at room temperature, can keep for a year or longer, offering rural consumers a readily storable, long-lived dairy product. Overall, humans consume roughly two-thirds (68 percent) of the total milk produced in Ethiopia, while consumption by calves and wastage account for the remainder (Felleke and Geda 2001). Of the two-thirds destined for human consumption, traditional butter accounts for 40 percent, raw milk roughly 20 percent, and cheese slightly under 10 percent (Table 6.11). Because all farming systems in Ethiopia incorporate livestock, most households consume milk (Felleke and Geda 2001).

Milk marketing systems can be classified into two broad categories—the urban and periurban system and the rural milk production and marketing system (Figure 6.9). The urban and periurban milk system includes about 5,200 small, medium, and large dairy farmers who produce about 35 million liters of

TABLE 6.11 Structure of demand for milk products in Ethiopia, 2000

Milk products	Households			
	Rural	Periurban	Urban	Total
Raw milk consumed by calves (%)	32	13	9	32
Raw milk consumed by humans (%)				
Farm households	15	8	10	15
Marketed	2	59	61	4
Butter (%)	41	20[a]	8[a]	40
Cheese (%)	9			9
Pasteurized milk (%)	1	0	12	1
Total milk equivalent volume				
Percentage	100	100	100	100
Millions of liters	1,115	15	20	1,150

SOURCES: Gebre Wold et al. (2000), Felleke and Geda (2001), Redda (2001), Solomon et al. (2003).
[a]Sum of butter and cheese consumption.

FIGURE 6.9 Ethiopian dairy marketing channels, 2002

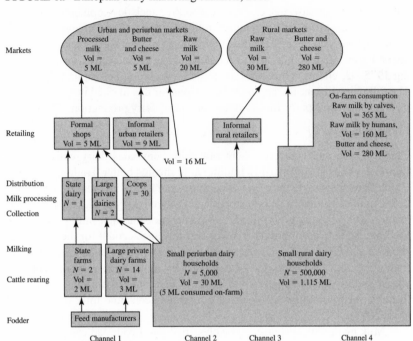

SOURCE: Ahmed, Ehui, and Assefa (2004).
NOTE: *N*, number of producers; vol, volume in millions of liters (ML).

milk annually. These smallholder and commercial dairy farmers, who operate in the proximity of Addis Ababa and other regional towns, control most of the country's improved dairy stock. The primarily subsistence rural dairy system includes pastoralist, agropastoralist, and mixed crop–livestock producers, mainly in the highland areas. The system is non–market oriented, with roughly two-thirds of the milk produced in this system retained for home consumption. Rural households process available surpluses using traditional technologies, and they market the processed butter, *ghee, ayib,* and sour milk through the informal market after satisfying their household needs (Redda 2001).

Three different types of dairy farmers supply these markets (Gebre Wold et al. 2000). The traditional smallholder system, roughly corresponding to the rural milk production system, produces 97 percent of the total national milk production and 75 percent of commercial milk production. This sector depends largely on indigenous breeds of low-productivity native zebu cattle, which produce about 400–680 kilograms of milk per cow during each lactation period.

State dairy farms, now in the process of privatization, use grade animals and are concentrated within a 100-kilometer radius around Addis Ababa. The third production system includes small and large private farms clustered around urban and periurban areas, primarily in the central highland plateaus (Felleke and Geda 2001). Commercially oriented, these farmers raise mainly grade and cross-bred animals that have the potential to produce 1,120–2,500 liters over a 279-day lactation period. This production system is now expanding in the highlands among mixed crop–livestock farmers, such as those found in Selale and Holetta, and serves as the major milk supplier to the urban market (Gebre Wold et al. 2000; Holloway et al. 2000).

Phases and Key Turning Points

The three phases of dairy development policy in Ethiopia coincide with three distinct political periods. They began with the imperial regime, from 1960 to 1974, characterized by an almost free market economic system during which modern commercial dairying first emerged. The socialist Derg regime that followed, from 1974 to 1991, instituted a centralized economic system and state dairy farms. The current phase, under the structural adjustment and market liberalization program, has continued from 1991 to the present. During each of these three phases, the country has followed a distinct political path leading to clear changes in development policies that have directly and indirectly influenced the dairy sector. Land and land tenure policy, macroeconomic policy, and the overall orientation of development efforts have all changed significantly.

Efforts to track performance with precision in each of these three periods are constrained by the fragile available data. Because over 95 percent of Ethiopia's milk production is rural and because trends on farm are understood only very generally, available aggregate data can be taken as only roughly indicative of general trends. Therefore, where possible, the following discussion supplements time series estimates with available microeconomic data sets.

Phase 1: The Emergence of Modern Dairying, 1960–74

Modern dairying began in the early 1950s when Ethiopia received a first batch of dairy cattle from the United Nations Relief and Rehabilitation Administration. With the introduction of these improved dairy cattle into the country, commercial liquid milk production started on large private farms in Addis Ababa and Asmera (Ketema 2000). The government intervened through the introduction of high-yielding dairy cattle in the highlands in and around major urban areas. The government also established modern milk processing and marketing facilities to complement these high-input production efforts. Most interventions during this phase focused on urban-based production and marketing, including the introduction of exotic dairy cattle, feeding with high-ratio dairy concentrated feeds, modern dairy infrastructure, and high-level management.

To facilitate the growth of the sector, the United Nations Children's Fund (UNICEF) established a public sector pilot processing plant at Shola, on the outskirts of Addis Ababa, in 1960. The plant started by processing milk produced by the large farms. The plant significantly expanded in a short period and started collecting milk from smallholder producers in addition to large farms. This led to the further expansion of large dairy farms. During the second half of the 1960s, dairy production in the Addis Ababa area began to develop rapidly. Large private dairy farms continued to expand, while the establishment of the milk collection centers facilitated growing participation by smallholder producers with indigenous cattle.

With the advent of modern dairying, the Government of Ethiopia established the Addis Ababa Dairy Industry (AADI) in 1966 to control and organize the collection, processing, and distribution of locally produced milk. Further, with the help of UNICEF, the Shola plant was expanded in 1969 and several government-owned dairy farms were established to supply the formal market and to serve as demonstration centers for the large commercial farms. In addition, the government introduced regular programs and projects for dairy development. The first effort, initiated by the governments of Ethiopia and Sweden, was the establishment of the Chilalo Agricultural Development Unit between 1970 and 1980. The unit produced and distributed cross-bred heifers, provided AI and animal health services, and assisted with forage production and marketing (Staal 1995).

To create an autonomous body responsible for dairy development, the Government of Ethiopia established the Dairy Development Agency (DDA) in 1971. The DDA took over the responsibilities of the AADI and assumed more tasks as well, including the provision of services for increasing milk production and the creation of formal milk markets in urban areas outside Addis Ababa. To support these efforts, the World Bank launched the Addis Ababa Dairy Development Project in 1971 with the objective of developing commercial dairy production and providing support for smallholder producers in the form of credit, imported cattle, and technical services. By 1972, the DDA was processing about 21,000 liters of milk per day, of which 57 percent came from 65 large farms (Staal 1995). In addition to collecting milk, the DDA sold milk and dairy products through its kiosks and shops as well as to large institutions. It also facilitated the creation of dairy cooperatives to assist with the provision of credit and technical extension services to dairy producers.

As a result of these efforts, milk production in Ethiopia grew steadily during the 1960s. Between 1961 and 1974, milk production increased at an average annual rate of 2 percent (Table 6.12). Factors underlying this growth included economies of scale in production and marketing, transport subsidies for the formal market, secured land tenure, and an active free market for feed and other inputs (Staal, Delgado, and Nicholson 1996). On a per capita basis, how-

TABLE 6.12 Trends in Ethiopian milk production, 1961–2006

| | Milk production (thousands of tons) | | Per capita production (kg/person/year) | |
Period	Annual average	Annual growth rate (%)[a]	Average	Annual growth rate (%)
1961–74	485	2.0	16.7	–0.6
1975–91	640	2.1[b]	15.1	–0.6
1992–2006[c]	1,155	6.6	19.1	3.9
1961–2006	761	2.7	16.0	0.2[d]

SOURCE: Calculations based on FAOSTAT data.

[a]Growth rates are estimated using an exponential function with a time trend.

[b]Statistically significant at the 10% level. Other trends are significant at the 1% level unless otherwise indicated.

[c]From 1993 onward, Eritrea has been independent of Ethiopia. Therefore, the 1992 base production was estimated at 94% of the preindependence total, an allocation proportional to population shares, in order to ensure the consistency of the trend estimates for this period.

[d]Not statistically different from zero.

ever, milk production declined during this period, at an average rate of 0.6 percent per annum.

Phase 2: Dairying during the Derge Regime, 1974–91

Following the 1974 revolution, economic policy in Ethiopia shifted toward socialism. The DDA continued to operate until 1979, when it was merged with numerous other nationalized dairy farms to establish the Dairy Development Enterprise (DDE). The DDE was established to operate the nationalized state farms, establish a milk collection network, process and market dairy products, provide advisory and limited technical services to farmers, and sell veterinary medicine and feed to farmers. At its inception, the DDE inherited facilities with a processing capacity of 60,000 liters of milk per day (Yigezu 1998).

During this phase, the government shifted some of its attention to rural producers. Although substantial resources remained devoted to establishing large-scale state farms to provide liquid milk for urban consumers, both the government and donors launched intensive efforts to develop the rural dairy sector through producer and service cooperatives.[8] Mostly input-oriented, these programs aimed to raise milk production and income through the introduction

8. The programs and projects implemented included the Minimum Package Program, Addis Ababa Dairy Rehabilitation and Development Project, Artificial Insemination Service, and Selale Peasant Dairy Development Pilot Project.

of improved feeding, breeding, and animal health programs while devoting less attention to marketing and processing.

As a result of these promotional efforts, Ethiopia's total milk production increased steadily during this phase, with the exception of the mid-1980s, when the country experienced a debilitating three-year drought (Figure 6.10). Despite the increase in aggregate milk production, per capita milk production continued to decline. This phase was characterized by low producer prices, which discouraged production; emphasis on cooperatives in rural areas; and neglect of most of the important private producers in urban areas. Dairy imports increased significantly beginning in 1978. This was partly due to increased food aid, World Food Programme milk powder imports, and a level of dairy production development that lagged far behind the demand (Redda 2001). Imports reached a peak of 315,000 metric tons in 1986, during the drought. Import dependency rose during this phase. Dairy imports as a percentage of total consumption increased from 4.1 to 12.8 percent between 1977 and 1989 (Redda 2001). Commercial imports likewise grew rapidly, at 24 percent per year. As a result, imported milk powder accounted for 23 percent of the Addis Ababa market (Felleke and Geda 2001).

Phase 3: Dairying during the Transition to a Market-Oriented Economy, 1991–2006

With the downfall of the Derg regime in 1991, Ethiopia embarked on policy reforms that aim to bring about a market-oriented economic system.[9] The new government implemented several macroeconomic policy changes. It altered the exchange rate policy from a fixed-rate system to a more market-determined system. A major devaluation of the currency took place in 1992, followed by a series of smaller devaluations thereafter. In general, these devaluations have discouraged milk and dairy imports while favoring domestic production. Similarly, the government introduced a new land policy that gave farmers long-term land use rights, including the authority to lease land out temporarily to other farmers and transfer it to their children, although not the authority to sell or mortgage it.

In addition to these major policy reforms, the new federal government launched a new national development strategy referred to as Agricultural Development-Led Industrialization. Although no explicit dairy development policy existed, it was envisaged that dairy policy would move increasingly toward private sector–led development. This implicit policy stance recognizes the potential of smallholder dairy production and accords due attention to small producers, although it also leaves room for the development of medium- and large-scale dairy farms in periurban areas.

---

9. Although this market liberalization continues, the lack of available data limits our ability to document performance past 2006.

FIGURE 6.10 Total and per capita annual milk production in Ethiopia, 1961–2006

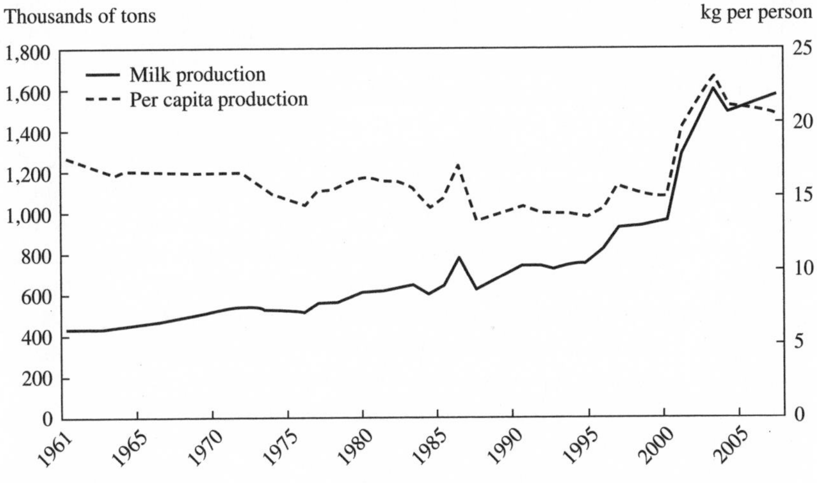

Thousands of tons   kg per person

SOURCE: FAOSTAT.

Within the dairy sector specifically, promotional activities have included improving health, breeding, and husbandry services; encouraging the participation of private investors through income tax incentives; improving the delivery of AI services; developing and expanding the marketing system in remote areas; and organizing farmers into milk producing, processing, and marketing cooperatives (Felleke and Geda 2001; Benin, Ehui, and Pender 2002). Two major donor-funded projects, the Smallholder Dairy Development Pilot Project and the Smallholder Dairy Development Project, focused exclusively on improving dairy production at the smallholder level. Unlike the promotional efforts implemented during the Derg regime, these two projects addressed the marketing problems of smallholder producers in addition to supply-side efforts at raising productivity and access to improved inputs.

In the post-Derg economy, the private sector has begun to enter the dairy market as an important actor. Several private investors have now established milk processing plants in Addis Ababa to supply fresh milk. Currently, privately held Sebeta Agroindustry competes with the government-owned DDE in supplying milk to urban consumers. Producer groups such as the Addis Ababa Dairy Producers Association have emerged, encompassing 90 percent of all urban dairy producers and a large proportion of periurban producers within a radius of 100 kilometers around Addis Ababa (Staal 1995). Given growing private enterprise competition, the DDE raised its producer price from 0.65 birr per liter to 1.00 birr and later to 1.25 birr. Meanwhile, the government has privatized inefficient state farms, reducing the number of state farms from 14 to only 2.

During the post-reform period, milk production has grown rapidly, at an annual rate of 6.6 percent (see Table 6.12). For the first time, growth in milk production has exceeded population growth, reversing the negative trend in per capita milk production during the two preceding phases. Most of the growth during the third phase has been concentrated in the periurban and rural production systems.[10]

In order to identify sources of growth during this period, we have attempted to disaggregate total milk consumption according to supply source. Rough estimates from the FAO database and available information from the DDE and Felleke and Geda (2001) suggest that the contribution of milk imports to total consumption declined radically, from 24 percent in 1985 to less than 1 percent in 2000. At the same time, the share of government-owned enterprises in total milk production decreased markedly. In contrast, the share of smallholder production in total national dairy consumption increased from 71 to 97 percent. Similarly, the contribution of large private farms increased from 21,750 tons in 1985 to 33,182 tons in 2000 (Table 6.13).

Driving Forces

MARKET INCENTIVES AND ACCESS.   The rapid growth in Ethiopian dairy production since 1993 has come largely from newly privatized dairies around Addis Ababa and other major urban centers. Clearly, the privatization of state enterprises and removal of input market controls have contributed to improved market incentives for private firms. The emergence of private processing industries and marketing units has stimulated producers in the periurban areas and rural production systems by offering producers an expanded market for their milk production.

Elsewhere, market access poses a key bottleneck to the expansion of smallholder milk production and processing, particularly in rural areas of Ethiopia. Although the cost of milk production in Ethiopia remains low, transaction costs are high, limiting dairy marketing for the moment.

HERD EXPANSION.   Over the past 45 years, roughly 60 percent of the growth in Ethiopian dairy production has been due to the increase in herd size (Ahmed, Ehui, and Assefa 2004). Only one-fourth has been due to increasing productivity per animal.

GENETIC IMPROVEMENTS.   Unlike in Kenya, the large cattle population of Ethiopia includes relatively limited numbers of exotic dairy cattle and crossbreeds. By the early 2000s, less than 1 percent of the 34.5 million cattle population of Ethiopia were exotic or cross-bred dairy cows (Muriuki and Thorpe 2001). Consequently, milk productivity in Ethiopia remains low (see Table 6.1).

To raise the productivity of the dairy herd, genetic improvement has featured heavily in the design of most dairy development efforts in Ethiopia over

---

10. Azage Tegene, personal communication.

TABLE 6.13 Changing structure of Ethiopian milk production and distribution systems, 1985 versus 2000

	1985	2000
Volume of milk supplied (tons)		
Imports of dairy products (milk equivalent)	279,651	8,290
Large producers	26,407	34,536
Government enterprises	4,657	1,354
Large private enterprises	21,750	33,182
Small producers	853,823	1,116,664
Improved cattle	—	13,585
Indigenous cattle	—	1,103,079
Total consumption	1,159,881	1,159,490
Herd size		
Indigenous breeds	—	34,903,496
Grade and pure dairy cattle		128,745
Large-scale private and public farms	—	96,541
Smallholder dairy farms	—	32,204
Total cattle herd	—	35,032,241

SOURCES: FAOSTAT; Dairy Development Enterprise; Felleke and Geda (2001).

NOTE: —, not available.

the past four and a half decades. Efforts have focused on production and distribution of cross-bred heifers and provision and strengthening of AI services and/or bull services. As a result, Ethiopia has built up a herd of 120,000 exotic cattle.

FEED CONSTRAINTS. An inadequate supply of quality feed and the low productivity of indigenous cattle breeds are the major factors limiting dairy productivity in Ethiopia. Feeds, usually based on fodder and grass, are either not available in sufficient quantities due to fluctuating weather conditions or, when available, are of poor nutritional quality. These constraints result in low milk and meat yields, high mortality of young stock, longer parturition intervals, and low animal weights (McIntire, Bourzat, and Pingali 1992). Improved nutrition through adoption of sown forage and better crop residue management can substantially raise livestock productivity. Despite these benefits, most dairy projects in Ethiopia have failed to address the genetic improvement and the feed shortage problem simultaneously.[11]

Empirical analysis of the adoption of dairy forage in mixed farming systems suggests that the potential for adoption of improved forage is highest

---

11. The only development project that addressed these issues simultaneously was the Smallholder Dairy Development Project implemented between 1995 and 1998 in 16 *weredas* in three regions.

where both livestock productivity and response to improved feed technology are high, as with cross-bred cows, and where production is market oriented, as in most periurban areas (Ahmed, Ehui, and Assefa 2004). In these settings, the potential for adoption is high because of the complementarities between regular cash income generation from dairy sales and the opportunity for intensification of crop production.

Results

INCOME.   In the typical mixed crop–livestock system of the highlands of Ethiopia, farming households produce milk using local zebu cows kept on communal pasture and fed crop residues. Milk productivity is low, and farmers retain most dairy products for home consumption. They process any available surplus into butter and cheese for consumption or sale. In contrast, improved dairy technology based on high-yielding cross-bred cows and production of improved forages has the potential of increasing the milk production of smallholder households for both home consumption and the market. Evidence from a smallholder dairy project conducted in the Holetta area of Ethiopia from 1993 to 1998 enables an empirical estimate of the impact of improved and traditional dairying on household income, consumption, and nutritional intake (Ahmed, Mohammed, and Ehui 2000; Ahmed, Ehui, and Assefa 2004).

Households with only local breeds of cattle generate, on average, about 15 percent of their income from livestock, mainly from live animal sales supplemented by sales of draft power and small volumes of dairy product sales. Each zebu increases household income by 0.12 percent, equivalent to about US$22 per person, much less than the estimated 0.51 percent, or US$91 per capita, income gain from cross-bred cows (Ahmed, Ehui, and Assefa 2004).

Cross-bred cows yield roughly twice as much milk per day as local breeds. Although they also require more inputs and higher variable costs, the gross margin per cow and the returns to labor are seven and three times higher, respectively, for the cross-bred cows (Table 6.14).[12]

As a result, the mean per capita income of an adopting household is 41 percent higher than that of a nonadopting household. This increase comes mainly from additional milk sales. The higher income from improved dairying allows adopting households to spend more on household consumer items as well as on farm inputs. In addition, the per capita intake of calories, protein, and iron is higher in adopting households (Table 6.15).

EQUITY.   Smallholder dairy farmers currently account for roughly 97 percent of Ethiopian dairy production and over 75 percent of marketed urban sales. Yet productivity continues to lag among smallholder dairy farmers, who own only about 25 percent of Ethiopia's grade dairy cattle (see Table 6.15). Although early dairy promotion efforts focused on large-scale private and state-owned

---

12. Ojala (1998) reaches a similar conclusion.

TABLE 6.14 Gross margin analysis for cross-bred and local cows in Ethiopia, 2003

Item	Unit	Local cows	Cross-bred cows
Gross revenue (per cow per year)			
Milk	Liters	134	784
Milk revenue (cash sales only)	Birr	141	823
Meat production	Birr	67	107
Heifer surplus	Birr	47	326
Value of manure	Birr	148	236
Gross revenue	Birr	403	1,492
Variable costs (per cow per year)			
Feeding of cows	Birr	135	217
Feeding of heifers	Birr	134	173
Purchased feed	Birr	12	154
Health care, artificial insemination service	Birr	1	11
Total variable cost	Birr	282	555
Gross margin (per cow per year)	Birr	121	937
Labor (per cow per year)			
Labor	Person-days	8	22
Value of labor per labor day	Birr	42	109
Returns to labor			
Gross margin per labor day	Birr	15	43
Gross margin per labor day	2005 US$	1.80	5.31
Returns to working capital (per year)			
Gross margin per unit of variable cost	Birr	0.4	1.7
Initial capital investment costs			
Birr	Birr	890	4,070
US$	2005 US$	110	504

SOURCES: Calculation by the authors and personal communication from Abebe Misinga.

farms, efforts over the past two decades have increasingly focused on small-holder dairy farmers.

Policy Implications

Similarities among Countries

In all three countries we have studied, smallholder dairying dominates national production. The resulting small batches of milk produced by dispersed individual households lead to high transaction costs in matching production surpluses with growing market demand in urban areas. Given the high perishability of raw milk, questions of aggregation and preservation loom large. For many years, all three countries addressed these issues by favoring large-scale modern dairy farms and processing facilities. Ultimately, on equity grounds,

TABLE 6.15 Profile of adopters and nonadopters of improved, market-oriented dairy cattle in Holetta, Ethiopia, 2002

Variable	Adopters (A)	Nonadopters (N)	(A–N)/N (%)
Per capita annual income (birr)	1,663***	1,178	41
Per capita annual cash expenditure on food (birr)	168	151	11
Per capita annual cash expenditure on nonfood (birr)	178	159	12
Household expenditure on farm inputs (birr)	1,382***	988	40
Proportion of cash income (birr)	0.4	0.3	28
Per capita nutritional intake			
Calories (kcal per person per day)	2,511***	2,177	15
Protein (g per person per day)	76***	67	13
Iron (mg per person per day)	131***	103	27
Farm area (ha)	3.3***	2.6	29
Area allocated to food crops (ha)	2.4*	2.2	13
Input use per hectare (birr)	379	369	3
Local breed herd size (tropical livestock unit)	5.6**	7.0	–21
Number of cross-bred cows	1.7***	0.0	
Labor units in adult equivalents	3.1	3.1	–2
Adult-equivalent size of household	5.7	5.9	–3
Age of household head	46	45	2
Age of mother or spouse	37	37	0
Dependency ratio	0.4	0.4	5
Ratio of women	0.5**	0.5	–12
Illiterate heads of household (%)	0.3	0.3	–19
Household heads with high school education (%)	0.2	0.1	7
Number of observations	78	69	

SOURCE: Ahmed, Ehui, and Assefa (2004).

NOTE: *, **, and *** indicate statistical significance at the 10 percent, 5 percent, and 1 percent confidence levels, respectively.

policymakers in all three countries changed their focus to favor the parallel integration of smallholder dairy producers into modern supply channels through higher on-farm productivity and collective marketing arrangements.

Raw milk (plus artisanal butter in Ethiopia) dominates dairy consumption in all three countries. Yet promotional efforts throughout the region have largely ignored raw milk marketing and instead have focused primarily on modern-sector pasteurized, packaged milk and dairy products. Indeed, up until 1992, Kenya actively suppressed raw milk sales in urban areas.

Formal and informal marketing channels continue to coexist in all three countries. In each, large legal monopolies have given way to liberalization and privatization of most production and processing. Although informal markets predominate everywhere, formal channels are most developed in Kenya, where they account for 15 percent of total human consumption of dairy products compared to only about 5 percent in Uganda and Ethiopia. Given lower processing and marketing costs in the informal channels, Kenyan evidence suggests that informal milk channels pay higher farmgate prices and charge lower prices to consumers, a win-win situation for consumers and farmers provided that public health can be ensured.

Increasing population and growing land pressure have led to an increasing recognition of the important role dairy farming can play in maintaining soil fertility under intensified mixed farming systems in the region. Under mixed farming, animals and crops reinforce each other in ways that can lead to substantial increases in per hectare productivity. Income from market-oriented dairying enables farm households to intensify their crop production through the purchase of high-yielding inputs coupled with the use of cattle manure. Crop intensification, in turn, frees up land for dairying, enabling farmers to grow specialized fodder crops that improve dairy productivity. As a result, raising the productivity of dairy herds and improving feeds and forages remain central to strategies for raising farm household income and sustaining soil fertility in this increasingly populous region.

Because of the positive impact of market-oriented dairying in raising smallholder incomes, effective market participation by smallholder dairy farmers has become a major public policy goal in all three countries. The predominance of smallholder agriculture in the region and the demonstrated complementarities between crop production and dairying mean that the promotion of high-productivity, market-oriented milk production can have a profound impact on farm incomes and on efforts at poverty reduction.

Contrasts

Kenya's superior dairy performance contrasts with slower growth and lower levels of dairy productivity in Ethiopia and Uganda. Grade and cross-bred dairy cows constitute 23 percent of the Kenyan herd compared to only 4 percent in Uganda and 1 percent in Ethiopia (Muriuki and Thorpe 2001). As a result, productivity per animal is two to three times higher in Kenya (see Table 6.1). In part, Kenya has benefited from less pressure on pastureland than in Ethiopia and more favorable timing and access to larger internal markets than in Uganda. In part, Kenya has invested more and over a longer time than the other two countries. Kenya's longstanding network of support institutions, many run by private farmer groups, continues to actively support AI services, livestock disease control, and improved feed and forage practices, all of which contribute to higher productivity, higher incomes, and stronger incentives for dairy farmers in Kenya.

The dominance of Ethiopia's artisanal long-life butter—which accounts for over half of human dairy consumption there—contrasts with the minimal share of processed dairy products consumed in Kenya and Uganda. The prevalence of fermented long-life butter in Ethiopia has emerged in response to seasonal production and poor transport networks that over the years have induced farmers to develop local preservation methods to minimize raw milk spoilage. Though driven by necessity, the predominance of Ethiopian long-life butter highlights the potential benefits of small-scale, labor-intensive processing technologies that serve to extend product shelf life and expand the market reach of small producers. In the future, as income grows, demand for processed dairy products such as yogurt, butter, and cheese is expected to grow as well. While past milk processing has focused almost exclusively on large-scale, formal sector processing methods, smaller-scale rural technologies may offer significant benefits to both producers and consumers, particularly given the continued prominence and seasonality of raw milk production.

Public Intervention

The three country experiences reviewed in this chapter suggest a strong rationale for public action to promote smallholder dairying. The predominance of smallholder agriculture in the region and the demonstrated complementarities between crop production and dairying mean that the promotion of market-oriented dairying, which significantly raises household incomes, can have a profound impact on poverty reduction. Indeed, this process appears to have already begun among Kenyan smallholders. Expansion of these benefits, in Kenya and elsewhere, will require effective, sustainable systems for product aggregation, disease control, infrastructure provision, research, and extension—all of which require some form of collective action. Clearly, public action remains crucial for smallholder dairy development.

Yet the heavily subsidized public input supply systems and publicly controlled output markets have proven unsustainable. So some balance is required between public and private action. Government provision of public goods must go hand in hand with incentives for private marketing, processing, and input supply services. Kenya's partially privatized veterinary services have left gaps in geographic coverage and mixed incentives for private input suppliers, suggesting that finding the right balance may require some fine tuning and adjustments.

Raising farm-level productivity quite clearly emerges as the first major element of successful dairy promotion efforts. Productivity gains generate highly lucrative opportunities for farm households while at the same time enabling them to produce growing milk surpluses for sale. The contrasting experiences from these three countries suggest that successful increases in smallholder dairy productivity will require several critical ingredients: (1) improved livestock breeds with enhanced milk production traits, (2) strong disease control and veterinary services, and (3) improved quality and quantity of feeds. Many of the relevant technologies already exist. Technology transfer and adoption, however, require strong extension support and training to promote better herd management. The most effective models rely on farmer involvement and participatory methods of extension. Given the small scale of many dairy producers, delivery of farm services will prove highly dependent on local institutions and capabilities. Farmer involvement, through emerging community-based organizations, offers one promising means of building effective service delivery channels.

Expanding market institutions and marketing facilities constitutes the second major element of past successful dairy development efforts. Taken together, the three case studies suggest several complementary market development strategies. One involves a continuation of longstanding efforts to improve smallholder access to existing formal markets through enhanced on-farm productivity coupled with bulking arrangements, expanded collection facilities, and collective organizational structures. At the same time, reorienting a portion of promotional resources to focus on raw milk, informal dairy markets, and low-cost processing technologies has gained increasing currency given the low cost, high profitability, and continued dominance of raw milk markets in all three countries.

7 Sustainable Soil Fertility Management Systems

STEVEN HAGGBLADE, GELSON TEMBO,
DANIEL KABORÉ, CHRIS REIJ, OLUYEDE C. AJAYI,
STEVEN FRANZEL, PARAMU MAFONGOYA,
AND FRANK PLACE

> The maintenance of the fertility of the soil is the first condition of any
> permanent system of agriculture.
>
> Sir Albert Howard, *An Agricultural Testament* (1940, 1)

Scope of the Case Studies

From the emergence of domesticated agriculture 7,000 years ago through about
the 1950s, African farmers maintained soil fertility primarily through shifting
cultivation (Raintree and Warner 1986). During this long period of land abundance, natural fallows of 10–30 years rejuvenated soils between cultivation cycles. Over time, rising demographic pressure has induced a series of changes.
First, African farmers expanded area under cultivation. Then, as suitable uncultivated land became increasingly scarce, they shortened fallow periods. Ultimately, as permanent cultivation has increasingly become the norm, farmers
have sought to maintain soil fertility through mixed farming, crop rotations, and
soil amendments.

In spite of ongoing efforts to maintain soil fertility, aggregate estimates suggest that nutrient balances in Africa have remained negative over many decades.
Pioneering work by Smaling and colleagues estimates that African soils have
sustained annual losses of 22 kilograms of nitrogen per hectare, 2.5 kilograms
of phosphorus, and 15 kilograms of potassium.[1] Given roughly 200 million
hectares under cultivation, these nutrient losses amount to about US$4 billion
per year (Drechsel and Gyiele 1999), a figure four times the value of donor assistance to African agriculture (see Chapter 9). Over time, current agricultural
practices are depleting Africa's soils, leading to growing concerns about agro-

---

Haggblade and Tembo have prepared the material on conservation farming, Kaboré and Reij have
written the section on Burkina Faso's *zaï,* and Ajayi, Franzel, Mafongoya, and Place have written
on improved fallows.

1. See Stoorvogel and Smaling (1990); Smaling, Stoorvogel, and Windmeijer (1993); and
Smaling, Nandwa, and Janssen (1997).

nomic and environmental sustainability (Cleaver and Schreiber 1994; Sanchez et al. 1997). On a continent where over two-thirds of the poor work in agriculture, declining soil fertility seriously constrains broad-based efforts to raise on-farm productivity, increase farm incomes, and reduce poverty.

This chapter traces the emergence of two pairs of soil fertility management systems developed in recent decades by African farmers and researchers in response to declining soil fertility, increasing land pressure, and rising mineral fertilizer costs.[2] The first pair, arising independently in Zambia and Burkina Faso, involve farmer-led development and dissemination of planting basins—minimum-tillage systems emphasizing water harvesting (in planting basins or along contoured rip lines), soil organic matter retention, crop rotations, and strategic additions of manure and mineral fertilizers. The second pair, a system of managed fallows using leguminous shrubs, emerged in Eastern Zambia and Western Kenya, initiated by agricultural researchers but designed and refined through extensive on-farm trials conducted in collaboration with farmers and nonprofit agencies.

The following discussion describes these technologies, the processes by which they emerged, and available evidence on their impact. Following presentation of the individual case studies, the chapter compares and contrasts these four soil fertility management systems. The discussion concludes with a summary of key policy implications.

Conservation Farming in Zambia

The Technology

Zambia's conservation farming (CF) system involves dry-season land preparation using minimum-tillage techniques, crop residue retention, crop rotations with nitrogen-fixing legumes, and reduced but precise mineral fertilizer applications. For hand-hoe farmers, CF revolves around dry-season preparation of a grid of 15,850 permanent planting basins per hectare, with each basin 20 centimeters deep, 30 centimeters long, and the width of a hoe blade. For farmers with access to animal traction, CF technology involves dry-season ripping, normally with the locally developed Magoye Ripper. For commercial farmers, mechanized minimum tillage with rotations of leguminous crops—such as soybeans, green gram, and sunhemp—completes the ladder of CF technologies.

Unlike the conventional hand-hoe and plowing technologies they replace, CF technologies require moving only about 15 percent of the soil where crops will be planted. By concentrating organic matter and fertilizer in fixed planting

---

2. Soil scientists employ the term "mineral fertilizer" when referring to petrochemical and other manufactured fertilizers (such as nitrogen, phosphorus, and potassium fertilizers) as well as mined fertilizers such as rock phosphate. This chapter likewise refers to these inorganic fertilizers as mineral fertilizer.

stations, CF focuses on improving the soil structure and fertility in these zones immediately proximate to the planted crops—in basins or along rip lines—where they will provide the greatest benefit. By breaking through preexisting hoe pan or plow pan layers, the CF technologies aim to improve water infiltration and root development while also harvesting water in years of sporadic rainfall. By reallocating land preparation to the dry season, in advance of the rains, CF redistributes heavy labor and draft power requirements outside the peak agricultural season. Early land preparation likewise enables farmers to sow with the first rains, when plants will benefit from the initial nitrogen flush in the soil. Over time, CF systems aim to improve soil structure, soil organic matter, and soil fertility in the fixed planting stations.

Development and promotion of CF have taken place in several key phases. Though any partitioning will necessarily prove arbitrary, it is useful to consider three main stages in the development and spread of CF in Zambia (Table 7.1).

Phase 1: Subsidized High-Input Maize Production, 1964–91

Three decades of heavy subsidies for maize, fertilizer, tractors, and plows ended in the early 1990s following the bankruptcy of Zambia's key agricultural parastatals and the collapse of world copper prices, which had financed the Zambian government for decades (see Chapter 3). Continuous high-input maize monocropping had left Zambian soils seriously degraded. "The underlying causes," according to a major review of Zambian agriculture, "relate to inappropriate farming practices, excessive erosion, increasing levels of fertilizer-induced acidity and soil compaction due to excessive and repeated cultivation" (INESOR 1999, 23).

In the early 1990s, a series of further shocks buffeted Zambian farmers. A serious drought rocked Zambian agriculture in 1992, while an outbreak of corridor disease during the 1990s reduced Zambia's cattle population significantly. Exchange rate devaluation, beginning in the second half of the 1980s, triggered soaring fuel and fertilizer prices.

Zambia's prior status quo—input-intensive ox-plowed maize cultivation—faltered in the face of these multiple shocks (see Chapter 3). As the price of imported fuel and fertilizer soared, farmers sought alternatives to the old regime of high-external-input technologies. The growing scale of Zambia's land quality problem further spurred efforts by farmers and researchers to find ways of improving soil structure and fertility.

Phase 2: Testing of Conservation Farming Technologies, 1985–2006

MECHANIZED COMMERCIAL FARMS. Influential commercial farmers in Zambia responded to these pressures by exploring low-tillage, low-external-input systems. In the mid-1980s, several members of the Zambia National Farmers Union (ZNFU) visited Zimbabwe, Australia, and the United States to investigate low-tillage systems (Vowles 1989). High fuel costs spurred interest

TABLE 7.1 Dynamics and drivers of change in Zambian conservation farming, 1964–present

	Period 1: Subsidizing high-input maize production	Period 2: Testing conservation farming (CF) technologies	Period 3: Scaling up extension
Timing	1964–91	1985–2006	1996–present
Key actors	National Agricultural Marketing Board	Zambia National Farmers Union; Conservation Farming Unit (CFU), established 1995 Golden Valley Agricultural Research Trust Dunavant Cotton Company	CFU Nongovernmental organizations (NGOs) Dunavant Cotton Company Government extension service
Motors of change	Subsidized fertilizer, seeds, tractors, and plows Guaranteed maize markets Population growth	Removal of fertilizer subsidy Drought Introduction and refinement of low-till technologies Testing of hand-hoe and animal draft power packages	Extension support (CFU, government, projects, Dunavant) Input supply (Dunavant and NGO projects)
Beneficiaries	850,000 smallholders (<5 ha) 20,000 medium holders (5–20 ha) 2,000 commercial farmers (>20 ha)	Some commercial farmers who began to adopt low-tillage practices	20,000–60,000 hand-hoe adopters in moderate- and low-rainfall regions 2,000–3,000 animal draft ripper adopters
Production gains	Maize production grows at 1.9% per year for 20 years	Maize area falls by 15% and production by about 25% during the 1990s	Maize yields increase by 1,150 kg/ha in a scattered-rainfall year Cotton yields increase by 370 kg/ha
Impact	Growth of maize yield and production, financed by large-scale subsidies Increased area under continuously cropped high-input maize Declining soil fertility due to acidification and plow pan buildup	Improved knowledge of low-tillage technologies	Rising yields under CF due to early planting and water harvesting Increased returns to land and peak season labor Variation of magnitudes by season and location

in these systems as Zambian farmers discovered that low-till cultivation enabled them to reduce their fuel consumption by 75 percent, from 120 to 30 liters per hectare, dramatically improving the profitability of mechanized maize production. Parallel benefits of reduced soil compaction and improved soil structure became apparent to early adopters (Hudson 1995; The Farmer 1995). Perhaps surprisingly, commercial farmers in the ZNFU subsequently became the prime movers in developing an appropriate minimum-tillage package not only for mechanized large-scale farmers but also for smallholder farmers tilling their land with hand hoes.

HAND-HOE MINIMUM-TILLAGE SYSTEMS.   In 1995, a Zimbabwean farm manager brought in by the ZNFU introduced a hand-hoe minimum-tillage system to Zambia. Engaged to help set up low-tillage farm trials at the newly established Golden Valley Agricultural Research Trust (GART), he related his experiences in developing a system of permanent planting basins for hand-hoe farmers in Zimbabwe (Oldrieve 1993). Inspired by examples from Zimbabwe of 6- to 8-ton maize yields under hand-hoe minimum-tillage cultivation (Oldrieve 1988), the ZNFU created a Conservation Farming Unit (CFU) to spearhead the development and extension of minimum-tillage technologies for smallholder farmers. Initially, the CFU focused on refining Oldrieve's system of planting basins for hand-hoe farmers while GART focused on draft-powered minimum tillage using an ox-drawn ripper.

Starting in the 1996/97 cropping season, the CFU began testing hand-hoe CF technology at the GART research stations as well as through a series of on-farm trials. With modest early funding from a variety of supporters—including the European Union, the Norwegian Agency for Development Cooperation, the Swedish International Development Cooperation Agency, Finland's Ministry of Foreign Affairs–Development Cooperation, and the Lonrho Cotton Company (subsequently bought out by Dunavant)—the CFU moved to develop guidelines appropriate for Zambia.[3] Because Oldrieve's basin system worked best in moderate- and low-rainfall zones, initial efforts focused on the semiarid regions of central, southern, and eastern Zambia.[4] Between 2001 and 2004, the CFU designed and supervised 400 farmer-managed on-farm trials annually (CFU 2006).

In these trials, the "emphasis has focused on testing 'additive' low-input technologies that provide further value/cost benefits to CF adopters and reduce reliance on mineral fertilizer" (CFU 2006, 12). The trials experimented with a

---

3. Similarly, in Zimbabwe the Zimbabwe Conservation Agriculture Task Force developed a closely related set of CF procedures for southern Zimbabwe and began actively promoting CF there in the mid-2000s (Twomlow and Hove 2006; Hove et al. 2007).

4. Although in later years the CFU did test and develop a minimum-tillage CF system for Zambia's high-rainfall zones (Agroecological Zone 3), it has opted to focus its initial extension efforts on the basin system developed for the semiarid zones. See CFU (2001) and Langmead (2002) for details on the high-rainfall CF technology.

range of crop rotations involving maize, cotton, and various legumes—as well as with liming and variable reductions in fertilizer application rates. The early CF trials likewise examined options for the size and spacing of planting basins that would best accommodate key crop rotations and ensure optimal plant populations in a single fixed basin. In the face of rising world oil prices, as Zambian fertilizer prices increased from US$290 to over $1,000 per ton between 2002 and 2008, GART and the CFU experimented with permanent low-cost sources of nitrogen. Their trials with the leguminous tree *Faidherbia albida* suggest that planting these trees on a 10-meter grid in farmers' fields can deliver a minimum of 75 kilograms of nitrogen per hectare to the farmers' fields each year.[5]

ANIMAL-DRAWN RIPPERS. Earlier efforts in agricultural engineering concentrated on the development of ox-drawn ripping equipment for animal draft low-tillage systems. In 1986, work began at the Ministry of Agriculture research station in Magoye under Dutch funding. This applied research resulted in the development of the Magoye Ripper, an ox-drawn ripping tool tested locally at GART and subsequently manufactured locally and exported in small quantities to surrounding countries in Southern and Eastern Africa (Bwalya 1999; Kaoma-Sprenkels, Stevens, and Wanders 1999; GART 2001; IMAG 2001). On-station trials gave way to on-farm field testing of the ripper in the early 2000s (Stevens et al. 2002).

In the early 2000s, after having refined its smallholder basin technology, the CFU increasingly coordinated efforts with GART to help field-test the ripper and promote its use among smallholder farmers. This alliance joined the traditional field orientation of the CFU with the more research station–based work of GART and has enabled extension officers to promote a full ladder of CF technologies to small and medium farmers.

Phase 3: Scaling Up Extension, 1996–Present

EARLY EXTENSION EFFORTS, 1996–2006. As part of its on-farm testing and technology development, the CFU has engaged in on-farm extension since its first full season of operation, in 1996/97. Given a small headquarters staff of two full-time professionals and an extension staff that varied as a function of available funding, the CFU has partnered with field agencies interested in agriculture. During the first decade of extension efforts, from 1996 through 2006,

---

5. Beginning in 2007/08, under its Conservation Agriculture (CA) program, the CFU team began a five-year program to distribute 26 million *Faidherbia* seedlings to 120,000 farm families. In addition to distributing the *Faidherbia* trees and encouraging the standard CF practices (crop residue retention, dry-season minimum-tillage land preparation, early planting, and crop rotations with 30 percent of land in legumes), the full CA program promotes small plots of cassava to ensure household food security, *jatropha* hedges to protect the cassava plots from cattle during the dry season, and fruit trees to provide extra vitamins (CFU 2006).

their approach relied heavily on farmer-managed demonstrations, which peaked at 1,000 per year in 2000/2001 (CFU 2006). Through these demonstrations, the CFU or its partner institutions supplied inputs to farmers in return for their co-operation in carefully measuring outcomes and hosting field days at which neighboring farmers could see CF in practice, interact with the lead farmers, and learn from them.

Over its first decade of operation, the CFU worked with a range of extension partners including the Catholic Diocese of Monze, Development Aid from People to People, World Vision, and Africare. They produced radio broadcasts and a series of field manuals in different local languages to facilitate CF extension by their staff and others (CFU 1997; GART 2004). Since 1999, the Ministry of Agriculture has formally adopted CF as its recommended extension practice (MAFF 2001). However, because of recurrent funding constraints and staffing shortages, support has, in practice, emerged through a series of donor-funded activities and projects (LCMF 2001; Burgess and Oscarsson 2002). Among this group, the CFU's two key field partners during its first decade of existence were the Dunavant Cotton Company and the Cooperative League of the USA (CLUSA), an agriculturally oriented nongovernmental organization (NGO) working in Zambia.

The Dunavant Cotton Company engaged the CFU to help run a series of training programs each cropping season for its group distributors (Arulussa 1997; CFU 2006). These distributors are lead farmers through whom Dunavant distributes inputs, credit, and information on key management practices to its 100,000-plus cotton farmers.[6] In addition, many of the Dunavant distributors serve as CF demonstration farmers, because the CF practices of early land preparation, early planting, early weeding, precise field layout, and careful input application coincide with best-practice management of cotton farms.

CLUSA's Rural Business Group Programme in Southern and Central provinces likewise emphasized CF planting basins in the field demonstrations and training sessions they ran for their 6,000–8,000 farmers. Following an appraisal of farmer performance in 1997, CLUSA concluded that farmers planting with CF basins consistently outperformed other group members and most reliably repaid their input credits. So from 1998 onward, CLUSA's managers in Central and Southern provinces required all of their farmers to adopt CF planting basins as a condition for receiving group loans and marketing support (Box 7.1). These efforts continued through 2004, when CLUSA's external funding for this work ended.

SCALING UP, 2007–PRESENT.   In 2007, after a decade of patchwork funding cobbled together from a series of small donor projects, the CFU and GART

---

6. Given growing cotton production in Zambia, the number of Dunavant distributor farmers increased from 1,400 in 2001/02 to 2,500 in 2005/06, while the number of cotton farmers they supported grew from 80,000 to over 180,000.

BOX 7.1 A recent convert to conservation farming basins

Wilson Mapiza of Mumbwa district in Central province saw the high yields achieved by his friends who practiced CF with a CLUSA-supported group nearby. Impressed by their results, he asked to join.

In his first season as a group member, Mapiza planted 2 limas (0.25 hectare) of maize and soybeans with inputs from CLUSA. In addition, he planted 2 limas of potholed maize with fertilizer and seed he had purchased using his own funds. He grows 1 lima of paprika on ridges and has ox-plowed 1 hectare of maize.

Because Mapiza prepared basins in the dry season, he planted his CF maize with the first planting rains on November 15. Due to a late start and sporadic early rains, he was unable to plow until December. He planted his 1-hectare plot of conventionally tilled maize on New Year's Day, fully six week later than his potholed maize. Mapiza reckons that he will harvest 3–4 tons per hectare from his CF basins. But from the plowed field he will be lucky to harvest even 1 ton. Mapiza says that about three farmers a day pass by to ask how he achieves such high yields.

---

together received a major five-year funding commitment from the Norwegian Agency for Development Cooperation to support full-scale extension of the CF hand-hoe and ripper systems to farmers in Zambia's moderate- and low-rainfall regions. To intensify its coverage in this phase, the CF team introduced a lead farmer training model. This funding has enabled, for the first time, an intensive, broad-based effort in support of CF. It has also provided resources to collect detailed baseline data and monitor adoption and soil fertility impacts over time, beginning with the 2007/08 season.

The Impact of Conservation Farming

Formal development and testing of CF practices in Zambia began only in the second half of the 1990s. Given the limited funding available before 2007, early extension efforts focused primarily on smallholder contract farmers growing cotton for the Dunavant Cotton Company and on a patchwork of donor-funded projects and NGOs. Empirical evidence therefore remains spatially fragmented and fragmentary, based primarily on small samples and single seasons.[7] This evidence nonetheless suggests several preliminary conclusions.

ADOPTION RATES. Available estimates of CF adoption remain subject to large margins of error. And currently available national sample surveys do not provide directly comparable information on CF practices over time. For 2001/02 and 2002/03, our national census of Dunavant cotton distributors enabled

---

7. See Keyser and Mwanza (1996); Arulussa (1997); ECAZ (1999); Langmead (2001, 2002); Stevens et al. (2002); Haggblade and Tembo (2003); and Kabwe, Donovan, and Samazaka (2007).

quantification of the single largest set of spontaneous unsponsored adopters, the cotton farmers. In addition, single-season large-scale surveys by Zambia's Central Statistical Office and the Land Management and Conservation Farming Project permit us to roughly bracket the scale of other spontaneous adopters. Cobbling together these various estimates suggests that in 2001/02 between 20,000 and 60,000 farmers practiced CF, the great majority using CF basins while 2,000–3,000 of them used rippers (Table 7.2). Of the hand-hoe farmers, roughly 11,000 were sponsored farmers who received inputs in return for planting CF trials and demonstration plots or as a condition for their participation in CLUSA groups.

Since then, adoption has likely increased as a result of scaled-up extension efforts and several erratic-rainfall years that showcased the water-harvesting benefits of CF. The CFU estimates that in 2006/07 between 125,000 and 175,000 farmers applied CF on a portion of their land (CFU 2006). However, firm data substantiating these estimates are currently lacking.[8] As a conservative order of magnitude, using the midpoint of the 2001/02 adoption figures as broadly indicative would suggest that roughly 40,000 farmers practiced CF on some portion of their land in the early 2000s. This represents about 9 percent of the 430,000 small- and medium-scale farmers operating in the moderate- and low-rainfall zones appropriate for CF.

The projections in Table 7.2 illustrate a key difficulty in accurately tracking adoption rates over time. Evidence indicates that the number of farmers practicing CF more than doubled between 2001/02 and 2002/3, with the bulk of this increase arising because, as a drought-relief measure, food aid donors offered food-for-work payments to 60,000 farmers on the condition that they dig CF basins prior to the 2002/03 season. Clearly, this one-time effort cannot be considered indicative of the number of continuing users, so the true numbers of farmers adopting CF since 2001/02 must await the results of the CF baseline study that began in 2007/08.

CHARACTERISTICS OF CONSERVATION FARMING ADOPTERS.   CF requires careful advance planning and meticulous, timely execution of key tasks. For this reason, cotton farmers constitute the single largest group of CF adopters, accounting for between 10 and 30 percent of total adopters (see Table 7.2). Because their cotton crop demands careful attention to planting date, regular weeding, and constant spraying and insect monitoring, as well as repeated careful hand harvesting, cotton farmers constitute a self-selected group of diligent, hardworking professional small farmers. A nationwide census of Dunavant cotton distributors in 2002 found that about 15 percent of cotton farmers in Zambia's moderate- to low-rainfall zones used CF basins (Haggblade and Tembo

---

8. The most recent survey estimates project CF adoption as between 5 percent (FSRP 2008) and 10 percent (Baudron et al. 2005) of smallholder farms.

TABLE 7.2 Adoption of conservation farming (CF) basins in Zambia, 2001/02 and 2002/03

	Number of farmers adopting CF basins	
Farmer categories	2001/02	2002/03
Sponsored farmers whose input supplies are tied to use of CF basins		
Cooperative League of the USA group members	6,000	28,000
CFU trials	1,000	450
Other nongovernmental organizations	4,000	32,500
Subtotal	11,000	60,950
Spontaneous adopters		
Dunavant farmers	6,000	10,200
Others	3,000–47,000	3,000–80,000
Subtotal	9,000–53,000	13,200–89,600
Total	20,000–60,000	74,000–150,000

SOURCE: Haggblade and Tembo (2003).

NOTE: CFU, Conservation Farming Unit.

2003). Field staff likewise suggest that retired schoolteachers, draftsmen, and accountants make good CF farmers.

Adoption rates vary by crop, gender, and length of experience with CF. Women, for example, apply CF to a greater proportion of their holdings than do men. The example set by lead cotton farmers, the Dunavant distributors, appears to influence the behavior of fellow group members. Tobit regression results suggest that when a distributor farms with CF basins, the prevalence of basins among the group members rises by 28 percent (Haggblade and Tembo 2003).

PARTIAL ADOPTION. Most farmers who adopt CF technologies do not apply them on all of their plots. On average, the farmers surveyed in Central and Southern provinces apply CF basins on about one-fourth of their cotton plots and about one-half of their maize plots. Because the hand-hoe fields are smaller than those tilled with a plow, CF plots account for 10–20 percent of area cultivated (Haggblade and Tembo 2003).

Over time, farmers who stick with CF gradually increase the proportion of their cropped area allotted to CF (Box 7.2). Although first-year cotton farmers experiment with basins on only 1 percent of their cotton area—often creating a few lines of basins as a test run—those with four or more years of experience apply basins to over 40 percent of their cotton holdings. Likewise with rippers, data covering four seasons indicate that contact farmers increased their ripped area from 1.3 to 2.4 hectares over that four-year period (Stevens et al. 2002).

BOX 7.2 A six-year conservation farming veteran

John Manchinchi and his wife retired from schoolteaching in 1994. They returned to their home village of Nangoma to begin cultivating their 3 hectares of land. In 1995, they planted cotton and maize in furrows, tilling with an ox-drawn plow.

Then, in 1996, they became CFU demonstration farmers and devoted 1 lima of land to a CF rotation of maize, soya, and green gram. Their 5 additional limas remained under conventional ox-plow tillage, planted, as before, with cotton and maize.

Because of the striking difference in output between his CF basins and plowed land, John Manchinchi planted an additional 2 limas in basins the following season, using his own resources to procure inputs. The remaining 2 limas remained under conventional tillage.

Each year, Manchinchi brought additional land under CF basins. By the 2001/02 season he was cultivating all 12 limas of land in basins under a variety of CF systems. On some plots he applies mineral fertilizer; on others he applies manure from his kraal. Plot samples taken from one of his self-financed maize plots, the one he fertilized with kraal manure, register a yield of 2.9 tons per hectare under CF with basins.

By 2007, after a decade of experience with CF, Manchinchi emphasizes that his land preparation and weeding time have diminished substantially. As we prepared to leave, he asked about a new variety of cassava called Bangweula, which he understands can yield over 20 tons per hectare. As it turns out, he is right.

DISADOPTION.   CF extension staff readily acknowledge that after a period of time, some farmers discontinue CF. In fact, during their early promotional efforts, agencies such as CLUSA and the CFU disqualified farmers who failed to rigorously maintain CF practices. These disqualifications amounted to as many as 20 percent of assisted farmers in a given year. Some farmers undoubtedly enter promotional programs purely to receive inputs on credit; with the demise of major farm credit agencies, they find it difficult to obtain these in any other way. Graduation of these farmers from reliance on project-supplied inputs will offer the only real proof of how significant their numbers are.

Disadoption has occurred at the institutional level as well. Several early NGO partners of the CFU stopped their CF promotion efforts after a number of early experimental years. Among institutions as well as individual farmers, CF is a management-intensive technology for which not all are well suited.

YIELD GAINS.   Most studies of CF document significant yield differences between CF and conventional tillage, usually in the range of 50–100 percent for maize and roughly half that for cotton (Table 7.3). The few available ripper

TABLE 7.3 Differences in output and inputs for cotton and maize under conservation farming (CF) and conventional tillage, central and southern Zambia, 2001/02

	Cotton					Maize		
	CF basins	Hoe	Ripper	Plow	CF basins	Hoe	Ripper	Plow
Number of sample plots	24	9	16	45	95	3	40	87
Yield (kg/ha)	1,278	986	557	818	3,054	—	1,727	1,339
Timing								
Field preparation before November 1 (percentage of plots)	84	22	5	2	92	—	3	0
Average planting date	Nov. 13	Nov. 20	Nov. 23	Nov. 28	Nov. 18	—	Nov. 27	Dec. 2
Input use								
High-yielding seeds (percent)	100	100	100	100	93	—	85	55
Mineral fertilizer (kg/ha)	27	0	0	7	236	—	168	45
Manure (kg/ha)	47	0	350	0	68	—	57	35
Pesticides (thousands of kwacha/ha)	212	186	156	151	0	—	0	0

SOURCE: Haggblade and Tembo (2003).

NOTE: —, insufficient sample size to produce a meaningful result.

studies suggest smaller yield differences between CF and conventional farmers, although maize gains still seem to outweigh those for cotton.[9]

At least part of the higher maize yields observed under CF stem from larger doses of fertilizer and high-yielding seeds that many CF maize farmers receive under input loans from their NGO sponsors. Likewise, because CF farmers prepare their basins and rip lines in the dry season, they are able to plant with the first rains, on average two weeks earlier than conventional hand-hoe and animal traction farmers, who must await the rains before they begin field preparation (Figure 7.1).

In order to separate the effects of planting date and differential input use from the water-harvesting and soil fertility build-up in CF basins, Table 7.4 presents regression results that attempt to measure the influence of each factor while controlling for the others. The results, together with data on input use by technology, suggest that greater input use accounts for roughly 500 kilograms of the observed higher maize yield in CF basins. Planting date (at 27 kilograms per day times 15 days) accounts for a further 400-kilogram gain.[10] About 750 kilograms of the yield difference stems from CF cultural practices themselves —the retention of crop residue, the buildup of soil organic material and the concentration of nutrients in the basins, and the water-harvesting effects of the basins during the sporadic rainfall of the 2001/02 season (Table 7.5).

Ripper farmers experience more variable results, with potential yield gains accruing from early planting, more uniform planting depth, better germination, and, in some seasons, water harvesting along contoured rip lines. A study of animal draft farmers in 2004/05 found that early-season land preparation by ripper farmers enabled them to plant maize and cotton three to four weeks earlier than plow farmers in Eastern Province. With the maize crop, this translated into an 18-kilogram gain for every day early they planted. Moreover, the ripped fields appeared to help harvest water along the rip lines, and this resulted in a doubling of yield gains for each kilogram of fertilizer applied (Kabwe, Donovan, and Samazaka 2007). In Southern Province, the same study found that although ripper farmers prepared land two weeks earlier than plow farmers, their planting dates did not differ significantly because of late rains. A separate study in central and southern Zambia during 2001/02 found that most ripper farmers failed to prepare their land earlier than farmers tilling with plows (Haggblade and Tembo 2003). Markedly expanded extension support for ripper farmers in

---

9. See, for example, Keyser and Mwanza (1996); Arulussa (1997); ECAZ (1999); Langmead (2001, 2002); Stevens et al. (2002); Haggblade and Tembo (2003); and Kabwe, Donovan, and Samazaka (2007).

10. This result is consistent with long-term agronomic data suggesting maize yield losses of 1 to 2 percent per day for each day a farmer delays planting after the first planting rains (Howard 1994; Keyser and Mwanza 1996; Nyagumbo 2008). Cotton experiences similar rates of yield loss under late planting (Arulussa Overseas 1997).

FIGURE 7.1 Timing of land preparation, by tillage method, Zambia, 2001

a. Percentage of cotton plots

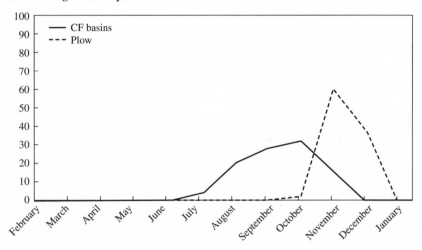

b. Percentage of maize plots

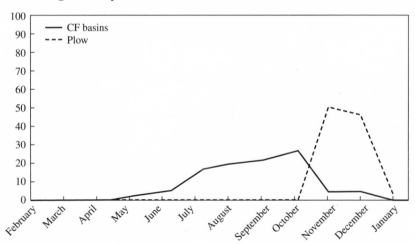

SOURCE: Haggblade and Tembo (2003).
NOTE: CF, conservation farming.

TABLE 7.4 Determinants of yield for cotton and maize under conservation farming in central and southern Zambia, 2001/02

Factors affecting yield	Cotton			Maize		
	1. Date only	2. Basic regression	3. Fertilizer interaction	1. Date only	2. Basic regression	3. Fertilizer interaction
Planting date, number of days after November 1	−9.0**	−3.7	−3.6	−41.4***	−27.0***	−28.0***
	(−2.2)	(1.1)	(−1.0)	(−6.2)	(−4.0)	(−4.0)
High-yielding seed (= 1, local = 0)					817***	836***
					(3.2)	(3.2)
Mineral fertilizer (kg/ha)		5.5***	6.7*		−0.6	−1.8
		(4.9)	(1.7)		(−0.7)	(−1.1)
Manure (kg/ha)		0.3	0.3		−0.1	0.4
		(0.5)	(0.5)		(−0.4)	(0.5)
Tillage method (plow = 0)						
CF basins		409***	417***		745**	772*
		(2.4)	(2.4)		(2.2)	(1.8)
Hand hoe		82	87			
		(0.5)	(0.6)			
Ripper		−88	−84		−192	−307
		(−0.5)	(−0.5)		(−0.5)	(−0.7)
Residue retention and no burning of residue		−81	−86		241	242
		(−0.9)	(−0.9)		(1.1)	(1.1)

	(1)	(2)	(3)	(4)	(5)	(6)
Years practicing CF		−51	−51		102	91
		(−1.4)	(−1.4)		(1.3)	(1.1)
Gender (male = 1, female = 0)		246***	245***		−209	−196
		(2.5)	(2.5)		(−0.9)	(−0.8)
Plot size (in hectares)		−192***	−192***		−107	−108
		(−3.0)	(−3.0)		(−1.6)	(−1.6)
Fertilizer interaction with CF						
Basins × chemical fertilizer			−1.3			1.0
			(−0.3)			(0.5)
Basins × manure						−0.3
						(−0.3)
Ripper × chemical fertilizer						2.2
						(1.1)
Ripper × manure						−1.6
						(−1.5)
Constant (kg/ha)	336***	139	135	1,545***	1,010***	1,035***
	(2.2)	(1.1)	(1.0)	(6.2)	(4.0)	(4.0)
Adjusted R-squared	0.04	0.45	0.44	0.16	0.33	0.34
Number of observations	95	95	95	200	200	200

SOURCES: IFPRI/FSRP survey; Haggblade and Tembo (2003).

NOTES: CF, conservation farming. t-ratios are listed in parentheses underneath the regression coefficients; *, **, and *** indicate significance at the 90 percent, 95 percent, and 99 percent confidence levels, respectively.

TABLE 7.5 Sources of yield gains in Zambian conservation farming of cotton and maize, 2001/02

	Yield (kg/ha)	
	Cotton	Maize
Conventional plowing	820	1,350
Conservation farming basins	1,280	3,000
Sources of difference		
Higher input use	90	500
Early planting[a]	40	400
Water harvesting in basins[a]	330	750
Total difference	460	1,650

SOURCES: IFPRI/FSRP survey; Haggblade and Tembo (2003).
[a]Gains attributable to conservation farming.

the intervening years may account for the improved timeliness of land preparation using rippers.

COSTS.   CF involves additional costs for farmers, particularly additional labor at weeding time given that farmers till only about 15 percent of the soil surface during field preparation, while plow farmers effectively begin weeding by soil inversion during land preparation. Dry-season land preparation under CF, though arduous in the early years, becomes easier over time. With CF basins, land preparation time falls by half after about five years (Figure 7.2). The redeployment of field preparation labor and draft power to the off season relieves peak-season labor bottlenecks, thus enabling early planting and early weeding.

INCOME.   Budget analyses that compare the value of increased output with the increased input and labor costs suggest that hand-hoe CF outperforms conventional tillage, generating higher returns to both land and peak-season labor. Results suggest that among hand-hoe cotton farmers CF technologies generate returns to land 65 percent higher and returns to peak-season labor over 100 percent higher than do their conventional-tillage counterparts (Table 7.6). The use of herbicides, which cuts peak-season weeding labor from 79 to 15 person-days per hectare, boosts returns to peak-season labor a further 100 percent.

For farmers with access to animal draft power, returns per hectare for those using rippers exceed returns to conventional plowing by 50 to over 100 percent. With cotton, the gains prove more modest, in the range of 10–30 percent higher for farmers using rippers (Table 7.7).

Among the 15 percent of smallholders in Zambia's moderate- and low-rainfall zones who possess adequate draft power of their own, properly executed ripping technology proves the most profitable CF technology. For the remaining 60 percent of smallholders who practice hand-hoe agriculture and the

FIGURE 7.2 Declining labor requirements over time for digging conservation
farming basins, 2003

Field preparation time (person-days per ha)

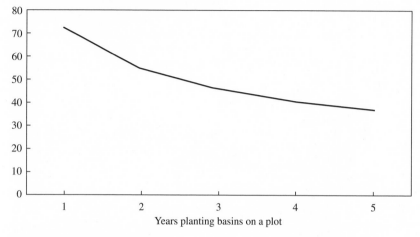

Years planting basins on a plot

SOURCE: Haggblade and Tembo (2003).

25 percent who plow with borrowed or rented oxen, basins or dry-season rental
of oxen and rippers remain the most attractive choices. Crop choice and ac-
companying practices, such as the use of cover crops, also influence the financial viability of CF (Breman and Tembo 2006).

Evidence from similar technologies in other parts of Africa suggests that
the effectiveness of CF varies not only across regions but also over time due to
variations in soil, weather, and rainfall (see Table 7.9 below).[11] In addition,
many of the benefits of CF—including improved soil structure, gains from
nitrogen-fixing crop rotations, and reduced field preparation labor—occur
gradually over time. Therefore, a definitive assessment will require long-term
monitoring of CF and control plots across a broad range of geographic settings,
crops, and seasons.

EQUITY. The ZNFU launched Zambia's CFU specifically to develop and
deliver low-till technologies to Zambia's smallholder farmers. Indeed, with its
focus on hand-hoe agriculture, the CFU has consistently targeted smallholders
since its inception. Not surprisingly, available evidence indicates that over 95
percent of hand-hoe CF farmers operate small farms of under 5 hectares. The

_____

11. Related evidence from Zimbabwe indicates that CF planting basins prove more profitable than conventional plow tillage during normal and drought years when early planting, better
water retention, and greater fertilizer responsiveness enable superior yields (Mazvimavi and Twomlow 2007).

TABLE 7.6 Returns to conservation farming (CF) and conventional farming

	Hand hoe tillage			Rented animal draft tillage			Owner-supplied animal draft		
	CF basins: First year		Conventional HYV seed	Ripper: HYV seed		Plow: HYV seed	Ripper: HYV seed		Plow: HYV seed
	Hand weeding	Weedwipe		Late preparation	Early preparation		Late preparation	Early preparation	
Maize farmers									
Output (kg/ha)[a]	3,000 (250,000 farmers)	3,000	—	1,499 (110,000 farmers)	2,255	1,499	2,066 (70,000 farmers)	2,255	2,066
Gross margin (US$/ha)									
Revenue	394	394	—	197	296	197	271	296	271
Input costs	109	130	—	121	121	121	121	121	121
Gross margin	285	264	—	75	175	75	150	175	150
Returns to labor (US$/person-day)									
Peak season labor	2.31	4.55	—	1.42	3.95	1.42	2.83	3.95	2.83
Total labor	1.36	1.83	—	1.20	2.79	1.20	2.39	2.79	2.39
Cotton farmers									
Output (kg/ha)[a]	1,280	1,280	871	871 (70,000 farmers)	871	871	871	871	871
Gross margin (US$/ha)									
Revenue	282	282	192	192	192	192	192	192	192
Input costs	56	78	56	85	85	85	85	85	85
Gross margin	226	205	136	107	107	107	136	136	136
Returns to labor (US$/person-day)									
Peak season labor	2.14	4.96	0.96	1.36	1.49	1.36	1.72	1.88	1.72
Total labor	1.02	1.29	0.83	0.98	0.92	0.98	1.24	1.16	1.24

SOURCE: Haggblade and Tembo (2003).

NOTE: HYV, high-yielding variety; —, insufficient sample size to produce a meaningful result.

[a]Estimated from the regression 2 coefficients in Table 7.4 assuming standard quantities of purchased inputs, plot size, and male gender. Yields therefore differ according to planting dates and tillage practices.

TABLE 7.7 Returns to animal draft technologies in maize and cotton plots, eastern and southern Zambia, 2004/05

	Eastern Province		Southern Province	
	Ripper	Plow	Ripper	Plow
Maize plots				
n	20	71	30	66
Yield (kg/ha)	2,350	1,479	1,224	1,122
Revenue (US$/ha)	386	243	199	183
Costs (US$/ha)	180	157	143	146
Income (US$/ha)	206	86	56	36
Cotton plots				
n	19	69	40	54
Yield (kg/ha)	1,015	880	780	697
Revenue (US$/ha)	254	220	195	174
Costs (US$/ha)	155	130	114	113
Income (US$/ha)	99	90	81	61

SOURCE: Kabwe, Donovan, and Samazaka (2007).

remaining 5 percent of hand-hoe CF farmers operate primarily on medium-scale farms (Haggblade and Tembo 2003). A handful of commercial farmers have likewise experimented with CF basins because of the ease of managing farm labor on a piece-work basis.

Rippers, on the other hand, are more commonly used by medium-scale farmers who own 5–20 hectares of land and who require animal traction to farm such large areas. Even so, because ripping technology, unlike plowing, enables dry-season rental, it can potentially enable even smallholders without animal draft power of their own to expand the area planted and enjoy the considerable yield gains afforded by early planting.

SUSTAINABILITY. Over time, farmers practicing CF aim to build a sustainable platform for long-term cropping by improving soil structure and soil organic matter and maintaining soil fertility. In areas where long-term plowing and repeated heavy doses of mineral fertilizer have damaged soil structure and fertility, investments in CF amount to reclaiming damaged farmland by restoring soil fertility.

Although soil-monitoring efforts have begun, detailed time-series analysis of fertility in individual CF and control plots is not yet available. Labor input data, which offer an imperfect window into these changes, point to rapidly declining labor demands on CF plots over time (see Figure 7.2). This trend is consistent with the hypothesis that improved soil structure over time results in reduced land preparation time as well as reduced weeding labor. A firm assessment, however, must await the results of long-term trials currently being conducted by GART, the CFU, and others involved in monitoring fertility profiles over time.

Burkina Faso's *Zaï*

The Technology

A technology similar to the CF hand-hoe basins, Burkina Faso's improved planting pits (or *zaï*) emerged independently in West Africa roughly a decade earlier.[12] To reclaim severely degraded land for agricultural use, farmers in central Burkina Faso dig a grid of planting pits across the affected plots and then add organic matter to the bottom of each basin. Although dimensions vary, the basins typically range between 20 and 30 centimeters in diameter and are about 20 centimeters deep. In the Yatenga region, farmers dig between 8,000 and 18,000 basins per hectare, with the upper bound roughly comparable to the density of planting basins under CF.[13] The quantity of organic material transferred to the planting pits also varies, with farmers normally applying between 3 and 5 tons per hectare (Hien and Ouédraogo 2001). As in CF, dry-season preparation of the *zaï* basins permits early planting, with the first rains, and helps to moderate peak-season labor bottlenecks. Some farmers also practice dry seeding just before the onset of the rainy season. In many instances, farmers also construct stone bunds in contours across their fields to slow run-off and complement the water harvesting in the basins.

The *zaï* planting pits concentrate water and nutrients in one spot in the same way as CF basins and rip lines. The organic material improves soil fertility and moisture retention. It likewise attracts termites to the basins. As they dig channels in the soil, the termites improve the soil architecture while at the same time digesting organic matter and making nutrients more easily available to the crops planted in the pits. Because the pits harvest water and conserve organic matter, they improve plants' responsiveness to mineral fertilizers as well.

Phase 1: Environmental Degradation, 1930–79

The Yatenga region of central Burkina Faso saw its population double from 250,000 inhabitants in 1930 to 530,000 in 1975 (Marchal 1977, 1979, 1985). This increasing population pressure, in turn, led to a significant expansion of cultivation on marginal soils, a steady reduction in fallow periods, increasing erosion, decreasing soil fertility, and a drop in agricultural productivity (Table 7.8).

---

12. Reij, Scoones, and Toulmin (1996) report the independent emergence of many similar soil and water conservation technologies across Africa.

13. Elsewhere in Burkina Faso, the *zaï* numbers range between 23,000 and 31,000 per hectare in the village of Donsin (Kaboré 2000) and between 46,000 and 51,000 per hectare in the Yako region (Slingerland and Stork 2000, 64).

TABLE 7.8 Dynamics and drivers of change in the *zaï* planting pits in Burkina Faso, 1930–2005

	Phase 1: Environmental degradation	Phase 2: Farmer innovation	Phase 3: Technology dissemination
Timing	1930–79	1980–84	1985–2005
Key actors		Innovative farmers, Sawadogo and Zorone	Private farmer extension networks Nongovernmental organizations (NGOs) Government extension staff
Motors of change	Recurrent drought Population pressure Soil fertility decline	Farmer experimentation and development of *zaï* technology	Private extension initiatives by farmers Spread of *zaï* technology by NGOs and government extension services
Beneficiaries			Medium and rich farmers, who reclaim land All villagers, who benefit from rising water tables
Impact	Environmental degradation (soil fertility loss; water table declines)		Land is reclaimed and soil fertility improves Yields rise by about 400 kg/ha Water tables rise, up to 5 meters in some locations Trees and shrubs regenerated in *zaï* fields

By the 1970s, farmers permanently cultivated sorghum and millet on 80 percent of all farmland in the central part of the Yatenga. Fallows largely disappeared as a means of restoring soil fertility, with farmers cultivating 70–85 percent of the village land area, about 40 percent of this marginal agricultural land (Marchal 1977, 1979).

In the early 1970s, a series of droughts rocked West Africa's Sahel, precipitating an acute environmental crisis in the densely populated northern part of the Central Plateau. Recurrent droughts led to frequent harvest failures. Between 1975 and 1985, the region witnessed substantial outmigration to less densely populated regions with better soils and higher rainfall. Between 1975 and 1985, some villages lost up to 25 percent of their families due to recurrent drought and the worsening economic and environmental situations (Reij, Tappan, and Belemvire 2005). Women had to walk longer distances to collect firewood. Farm families cut vegetation not only for firewood but also to expand their cultivated land. Groundwater levels fell by an estimated average of 1 meter per year, and many wells and boreholes went dry just after the end of the rainy season. Yields of sorghum and millet averaged only 400–500 kilograms per hectare, with substantial interannual variation depending on rainfall (Dugué 1989). Because of frequent droughts, cultivation of the upper and middle slopes became difficult, if not impossible. Those farmers with access to the lower slopes and valley bottoms concentrated their cultivation in these parts of the toposequence (Stoop and Vierich 1990). The surface of completely barren land increased dramatically. These trends were particularly pronounced in the central part of the Yatenga region, where the population density averaged as much as 100 people per square kilometer. By 1980, the Yatenga region had become the most environmentally degraded region of Burkina Faso.

Phase 2: Farmer Innovation, 1980–84

EARLY SOIL AND WATER CONSERVATION EFFORTS.   In this difficult environment, both farmers and NGO technicians started to experiment with soil and water conservation (SWC) techniques. In general, farmers concentrated on improving their traditional *zaï,* while NGO technicians concentrated primarily on contour stone bunds. This combination of techniques proved highly efficient in rehabilitating strongly degraded land. As a result, agricultural intensification in this region started in the early 1980s with the availability of SWC technologies, which were simple in that they could be mastered by all farmers and efficient in the sense that they immediately increased yields.

THE ORIGINS OF THE *ZAÏ.*   Around 1980, farmers in the village of Gourga, situated close to the regional capital Ouahigouya, started to experiment with *zaï.* Traditionally, farmers dug planting pits on a small scale to rehabilitate rock-hard, barren land (called *zipélé*) into which rainfall could no longer infiltrate. Some of these patches of barren land are formerly cultivated fields that degraded because of overcultivation. Most, however, are created by human destruction of the vegetative cover. After some experimentation, farmers in Gourga increased the dimensions of the pits from a diameter of 10–15 centimeters to 20–30 centimeters and a depth of about 20 centimeters. In a second innovation, they applied manure in the pits. In this way, the improved planting pits concentrated both water and nutrients in one spot. Farmers dug the pits during the dry season, a slack agricultural period when labor was readily available.[14] The organic material they use attracts termites, which play a crucial role in improving soil architecture as they dig channels in the soil. At the same time, the termites digest organic matter and make nutrients more readily available to crops planted or sown in the pits.

One farmer, Yacouba Sawadogo, stands out as a key innovator in the development and dissemination of the improved *zaï*. Although he may or may not have been the very first farmer to experiment with *zaï*, he has nonetheless clearly played a decisive role in improving and expanding the use of the improved planting pits. The questions we have are: What triggered him to start experimenting? Where did he get his ideas? His main motive appears to have been to combat the recurrent droughts and the associated food shortages, which made life very difficult for farm families in the region. Many families left the region to settle in better parts of Burkina Faso or in Côte d'Ivoire.[15] Yacouba preferred to stay on the land of his ancestors, but he realized that something had to be done to combat land degradation. As a result, he began experimenting with the traditional planting pits. Over time he found that increasing their size and depth, incorporating organic matter, and combining them with stone bunds led to markedly improved results.

Phase 3: Technology Dissemination, 1985–2005

Other farmers in Gourga quickly perceived the remarkable millet and sorghum yields obtained by Yacouba on land that used to produce nothing. So they started to copy him. The OXFAM-funded agroforestry project, which experimented in the Yatenga with different SWC techniques, immediately recognized the potential of the improved planting pits and started to promote the technology by bringing visitors to Gourga. Other NGOs, projects, and government agencies quickly became aware of the potential of this technique. In the first few years, the pits mainly spread within the Yatenga region, where they were often combined with contour stone bunds, which reduce the force of surface run-off and prevent destruction of the planting pits (Wright 1985).[16] After a few years, *zaï* started spreading to other parts of the Central Plateau.

---

14. As with CF, farmers dig *zaï* basins during the dry season, when the opportunity cost of labor is low. In contrast, the system of tied ridges, an alternate water-harvesting technology promoted in Burkina Faso during the first half of the 1980s, involves rainy-season land preparation using animal draft power to prepare basins between furrows after the first rains of the season, when most farmers begin land preparation (Sanders, Nagy, and Ramaswamy 1990). Unlike CF and the *zaï*, tied ridges compete for farm labor and animal draft power during the peak agricultural season.

15. Many farm households have strong links with small plantations in Côte d'Ivoire, which they own or are owned by relatives. The importance of these links and their impact on the allocation of labor resources and on the transfer of funds has not yet been adequately studied.

16. The contour stone bunds are the outcome of a process of on-farm experimentation by the OXFAM-funded agroforestry project and farmers during 1979–81. In 1982 this project designed an extension strategy for contour stone bunds (Reij 1983; Wright 1985). Contour stone bunds and *zaï* have become the most successful SWC techniques on the Central Plateau and are now widespread.

Two farmers played a key role in the dissemination and spread of *zaï* technology. The first, Yacouba Sawadogo, started an Association pour la Promotion des Zaï (Association for the Promotion of *Zaï*). He trained farmers in many villages in how to use this technique and several times organized a "*zaï* market" in which representatives from about 100 villages came to Gourga to share their experience.

The other key farmer, Ousseni Zorome, lives in Somyaga, another village close to the regional capital of Ouahigouya. In the early 1980s Ousseni was a small trader who borrowed a large piece of strongly degraded land on which only nine trees had survived. He gradually treated the land with *zaï*. Like many farmers, he started at the lowest point of his fields and worked upward.[17] While doing so, he systematically protected naturally regenerating trees and bushes. As a result, he now has about 2,000 trees on his fields. Ousseni created a "*zaï* school," a group of farmers who jointly learn how to rehabilitate a plot of degraded land. By the early 2000s, his district association of *zaï* schools had about 1,000 members (Sawadogo et al. 2001).

Both Yacouba and Ousseni, on their own initiative, set up private extension services. To some extent, these private efforts replaced the public extension service, which had become crippled by structural adjustment programs and increasingly concentrated their limited activities in Burkina Faso's cotton-growing regions.

SWC projects also played a key role in the spread of *zaï* outside the Yatenga region. They organized and funded study visits for their farmers, who upon their return adopted and sometimes adapted the *zaï* on their own fields. Neighboring farmers who observed what their neighbors had achieved subsequently followed their example. A good example of this spread effect comes from a visit to Yatenga organized in 1989 by an SWC project funded by the International Fund for Agricultural Development for 13 farmers from Illéla district in Niger. This visit produced an impressive spreading of *zaï* (in Haussa these are called *tassa*) in the Illéla region and subsequently also in other parts of Niger. By 1992, farmers in Illéla district were actively buying and selling strongly degraded land to rehabilitate with *tassa*. A survey in 1998 showed that 40 percent of the farm families there had bought or sold degraded land (Hassane, Martin, and Reij 2000).

In most instances, farmers rehabilitate degraded land by digging *zaï* without any external support. They do all the work themselves. The key contribution provided through public funding is in the form of study visits and support for the transport of stones for the construction of bunds.

---

17. The technical SWC manuals all advocate starting the treatment of land at the highest point of the catchment and to work downward. Farmers in the Yatenga and in many other semiarid regions prefer to start at the lowest point in order to catch run-off from upslope, without which it would be difficult to produce a harvest in drought years.

Results of the Zaï

ADOPTION.   For several reasons, it is difficult to precisely estimate the land area treated with *zaï,* both inside and outside the Yatenga region. First of all, farmers treat individual fields, often bush fields, which are spread over the village territory. This means that one generally does not find big blocks of treated land. Moreover, a considerable portion of land rehabilitated with *zaï* becomes normal farmland again after about 6–10 years. As existing pits become well established, farmers dig new *zaï* basins in between the existing basins until they have rehabilitated the entire field and can once again till it with a plow or a hand hoe.

Although precise area estimates are not available, our fieldwork suggests that farmers have treated tens of thousands of hectares of land with *zaï* on the northern part of the Central Plateau (Figure 7.3). Field visits in 2008 to Burkina Faso and Niger showed that farmers continue to use this technique to rehabilitate degraded land. Given a standard area of roughly 1 hectare per household, this implies an equal number of adopting households.[18]

YIELD GAINS.   When asked about the impact of *zaï* on yields, farmers in the northern part of the Central Plateau systematically state that they lead not only to higher yields but also to increased yield security, to more water in their wells, to a stronger growth of trees, and to a higher production of fruit (Reij and Thiombiano 2003). Surprisingly, the fragmentary available quantitative evidence on yield gains under *zaï* come primarily from outside the Yatenga region. Given the wide variation in annual rainfall, yields with and without *zaï* basins vary substantially from one year to the next. This necessitates multiyear monitoring to assess performance across rainfall regimes. Evidence from six consecutive seasons in Niger's Illéla district suggests that planting pits with manure (T1) produce sorghum yields 175–700 kilograms higher than do adjacent untreated fields (T0). On average, sorghum yields increase from 125 kilograms per hectare without *zaï* to 500 kilograms per hectare with *zaï* plus manure to over 750 kilograms per hectare with *zaï* plus manure plus mineral fertilizer (Table 7.9). Similarly, in Burkina Faso, evidence from the Yatenga region finds gains in sorghum yield of 630 kilograms per hectare under *zaï* with 3 tons of organic matter (Roose, Kaboré, and Guenat 1993). A similar study in Donsin village of Burkina Faso's Boulsa region used a multiple-regression analysis to estimate yield gains of 310 kilograms per hectare under *zaï.* Gains improved further, to 710 kilograms per hectare, under *zaï* plus contour stone bunds (Kaboré 2000).

INCOME.   Improved traditional planting pits make it possible to rehabilitate strongly degraded land. In the "without *zaï*" situation, yields on strongly de-

---

18. A survey undertaken in 1998 in five provinces covering the northern part of the Central Plateau showed that 123 households that had undertaken SWC had reclaimed, on average, 1.33 hectares per household using *zaï* and contour stone bunds (SAEC 2000, 45).

FIGURE 7.3 Distribution of *zaï* in Burkina Faso, 2002

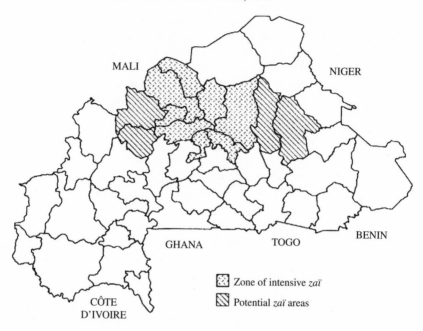

MALI

NIGER

GHANA   TOGO   BENIN

CÔTE
D'IVOIRE

Zone of intensive *zaï*

Potential *zaï* areas

SOURCE: Centre de Télédétection et Système d'Information Géographique/Institut de l'Environnement et de Recherches Agricoles.

TABLE 7.9 Impact of planting pits (*tassa*) on cereal yields in Niger's Illéla district, 1991–96

	1991	1992	1993	1994	1995	1996	Average 1991–96
Rainfall (mm)							
Badaguichiri district	726	423	369	613	415	439	498
Illéla district	581	440	233	581	404	440	447
Cereal yields (kg/ha)							
T0: Control	—	125	144	296	50	11	125
T1: *Tassa* plus manure	520	297	393	969	347	553	513
T2: *Tassa* plus manure plus fertilizer	764	494	659	1486	534	653	765
District average	386	241	270	362	267	282	301
T1 – T0	520	172	249	673	297	542	388
T2 – T0	764	369	515	1190	484	642	640

SOURCE: Hassane, Martin, and Reij (2000).

NOTE: —, no data.

graded land are 0 kilograms per hectare, and farmers clearly perceive that every kilogram of sorghum, millet, cowpeas, or maize harvested on this land represents a net output gain.[19]

The heavy labor inputs required to construct the *zaï* planting pits, however, impose an opportunity cost, albeit a low cost, during the dry season when the *zaï* land preparation takes place. The key economic question becomes how returns to labor deployed in land preparation under *zaï* compare with dry-season shadow wage rates. Table 7.10 examines this question by presenting a production budget for 1 hectare of *zaï* in a year of average rainfall. Variable costs include the amortization of tools used to produce the compost, the cost of maintenance of a compost pit, the cost of emptying the pit, and the costs of transporting the compost to the fields.[20]

Returns to labor under *zaï* cultivation reach an estimated 133 Communauté Financière Africaine francs (CFAF) per hour compared to notional estimates of the dry-season shadow wage rates of about 100 CFAF per hour. Assuming a 6-hour workday, this would mean a return to labor of 797 CFAF per person-day, or about US$1.35 per day. This figure will, of course, fluctuate from year to year depending on rainfall conditions.

In reality, the benefits of *zaï* are higher, because this budget does not take into account their many other benefits. Farmers on the northern part of the Central Plateau systematically report that *zaï* and other SWC techniques lead not only to higher yields but also to increased yield security, more water in their wells, stronger tree growth, and higher fruit production (Reij, Tappan, and Belemvire 2005).

FOOD SECURITY. During an impact assessment of SWC, agroforestry, and agricultural intensification in five villages on the northern part of the Central Plateau, farmers agreed unanimously that SWC, in particular *zaï,* had had a positive impact on their household food security (Reij and Thiombiano 2003). In years of good rainfall, many farmers produce a small surplus of grains that provides a buffer in years of low rainfall. This same picture also emerges in Niger, where farm families with SWC produce an estimated surplus of 70 percent in years of good rainfall but an estimated deficit of 28 percent in years with low rainfall (Hassane, Martin, and Reij 2000, 33).

EQUITY. Both rich and poor farmers can master the simple technology required to prepare improved traditional planting pits. Yet field experience suggests that the better-off rich and medium-scale farmers apply this technology more frequently than the poor, largely because they have access to more fam-

---

19. Researchers tend to underestimate the impacts of *zaï* when they use average yields obtained in a region as the "without" situation. Farmers correctly consider 0 kilograms per hectare the "without" situation, because almost all *zaï* are used to rehabilitate strongly degraded land.

20. According to Lowenberg-DeBoer et al. (1994), a compost of 10–11 cubic meters is needed to produce 2.5 tons of compost.

TABLE 7.10 Crop production budgets with *zaï* planting pits in Burkina Faso, 2003

	Unit	Quantity	Price	Value CFAF	Value US$
A. Gross revenue (per ha)					
Sorghum					
Grains	kg/ha	900	100	90,000	152
Stover	kg/ha	1,665	12	19,980	34
Cowpeas					
Grains	kg/ha	150	212	31,800	54
Fodder	kg/ha	248	15	3,720	6
Total revenue				145,500	246
B. Variable costs (per ha)					
Equipment amortization	CFAF/ha	9,566			
Pit maintenance	CFAF/ha	2,761			
Emptying pit	CFAF/ha	739			
Compost transportation	CFAF/ha	5,000			
Total variable costs	CFAF/ha			18,066	31
C. Gross margin (per ha)	CFAF/ha			127,434	216
D. Labor requirements					
Zaï					
Digging *zaï*	Hours/ha	450			
Putting compost into the pits	Hours/ha	150			
Compost pit[a]					
Digging	Hours/ha	96			
Filling	Hours/ha	78			
Planting[b]	Hours/ha	40			
Weeding[b]	Hours/ha	95			
Harvesting[c]	Hours/ha	50			
Total labor hours	Hours/ha	959			
E. Returns to labor	CFAF				
Per hour				133	0.22
Per 6-hour day				797	1.35

SOURCE: Kaboré and Reij (2004).

NOTE: CFAF, Communauté Financière Africaine franc.

[a]Based on Lowenberg-DeBoer al. (1994) and Roose et al. (1999).

[b]Based on International Crops Research Institute for the Semi-Arid Tropics (ICRISAT) crop production budgets and farmer estimates.

[c]Based on ICRISAT crop production budgets.

ily labor and the means to hire additional labor as required. Poor families are more likely to benefit from project-supported construction of stone bunds, which is usually done by groups of farmers on blocks of land that include fields of small farmers as well as fields cultivated by women.[21]

The broader question is whether *zaï* and other SWC techniques have contributed to reducing rural poverty. Some microlevel studies appear to support this claim. Using their own criteria to define wealth, which are mainly related to the level of food security, the villagers of Ranawa (Zondoma Province) estimated that the number of poor families decreased by 50 percent between 1980 and 2001 (Ouédraogo and Reij 2001, 35).[22] This was largely due to the wide range of SWC activities undertaken in this village after 1985, which has led to the progressive rehabilitation of about 600 hectares of degraded land, most of which had become unproductive. The environmental and socioeconomic situation in this village was dire in the early 1980s. Due to SWC, more land is cultivated and yields have increased. This has led to a substantial improvement in household food security and a systematic natural regeneration of important stands of trees that grow on what used to be barren land. The numbers of livestock have increased substantially, and livestock management (livestock fattening and use of external inputs) has changed from extensive to semi-intensive. Manure is collected systematically and used to fertilize the fields. These profound changes are not only due to SWC but have also been influenced by macroeconomic policies, such as the devaluation of the West African franc in January 1994, which increased the value of livestock and livestock products. Fuller disentangling these effects will require more detailed microeconomic evidence.

SUSTAINABILITY.   Land reclamation under *zaï* frequently leads to improved vegetative cover. The manure and compost used in *zaï* contain seeds of trees, shrubs, and grasses. As a result, pitted fields show substantial regeneration of woody and herbaceous species. Farmers selectively protect species regenerating naturally. The resulting natural regeneration on treated fields contributes more to tree cover than the planting of trees under village forestry projects. The species protected include *Adansonia digitata* (baobab), *Acacia albida, Sclerocarya birrea,* and *Piliostigma reticulatum.* After two years under *zaï,* an initially barren field was found to be growing 23 herbaceous species and 13 species of trees and shrubs (Roose, Kaboré, and Guenat 1999).

Groundwater levels similarly recover in areas where farmers build large clusters of *zaï* fields and undertake related SWC measures. In the early 1980s,

---

21. This is confirmed by preliminary data from the previously mentioned Central Plateau study, which show that poor farmers benefit equally from SWC.

22. This figure should be regarded with some caution. It is justified to say that the number of poor families in Ranawa has decreased substantially. As one farmer explained, "In 1985 only two families had livestock, but now all families have at least one head of cattle and most have more."

groundwater levels on the Central Plateau dropped an estimated 50–100 centimeters per year (Reij 1983, 10). Many wells went dry immediately after the end of the rainy season and had to be deepened regularly. This led to considerable extra work for women and girls, whose task it is to fetch water. In the village of Rissiam, in Bam Province, and in the village of Ranawa, in Zondoma Province, all wells went dry at the end of the rainy season, and women had to walk 5–6 kilometers to a lake and a well, respectively. By the early 2000s, all wells and boreholes in both villages had water during the entire dry season. In several villages included in a study of long-term economic and environmental change on the northern part of the Central Plateau, though not in all, the levels of water in wells have improved substantially during the past 10–15 years (Reij and Thiombiano 2003). Although higher rainfall during the 1990s likely contributed to these trends, comparisons of villages with and without broad *zaï* and related SWC measures suggest that these efforts generated additional benefits, including improved control of surface run-off and better water infiltration.

The *zaï* planting pits improve soil fertility by recapitalizing unproductive plots and converting them into usable farmland. A study comparing the soil fertility parameters of plots treated with *zaï* after 3 and 5 years found a systematic improvement in all parameters. The organic matter content increased from 1 to 1.40 percent, and nitrogen levels increased from 0.05 to 0.80 percent. The soil structure also improved considerably, with an increase in its clay content and a decrease in the sand fraction (Mando 2003).

Many agricultural development specialists have emphasized the need to recapitalize African soils (Sanchez et al. 1997). Some advocate low-external-input technologies (Pretty 2000), while others emphasize the use of mineral fertilizers (Borlaug 1996; Sachs 2006). Farmers on the Central Plateau of Burkina Faso have begun recapitalizing their soils through the construction of *zaï* and stone bunds, usually without the use of mineral fertilizers, which they consider both risky and expensive.

Improved Fallows in Eastern Zambia and Western Kenya

The Technology

An alternative technology for recapitalizing soils and reducing dependence on petroleum-based fertilizers has emerged in the improved fallows promoted by the World Agroforestry Centre (ICRAF). Improved fallows use fast-growing, nitrogen-fixing leguminous trees to rejuvenate soils for subsequent crops. Under improved fallows, leguminous trees fix nitrogen from the atmosphere, accumulate it in their root and leaf biomass, and recycle it into the soil, thereby increasing soil organic matter and improving soil physical and chemical properties (Juo and Lal 1977; Kwesiga and Coe 1994). During the fallow period, which typically lasts one to two seasons, the leguminous trees act as a break crop to smother weeds (De Rouw 1995). In some circumstances, other essential nutrients such as phosphorus may be cycled through deep root capture and returned to the soil during litter decomposition, thereby converting nutrients to more available forms (Sanchez and Palm 1996). Elsewhere, supplementation of phosphorus and potassium may be required to fully capitalize depleted soils (Sanchez et al. 1997).

The following discussion reviews two closely related experiences with improved fallows, one in Eastern Zambia and the other in Western Kenya (Table 7.11). Spearheaded by ICRAF researchers, together with national agricultural researchers in Zambia and Kenya, these efforts have emphasized technology development through close interaction with farmers and technology dissemination through a broad array of NGOs and government extension staff. The two parallel country efforts followed a similar sequence of diagnostic work, technology development, and dissemination. Because the efforts in Zambia preceded those in Kenya by several years, the following chronology refers to the Zambian case, while the discussion draws on evidence and experience from both.

The Settings

The plateau area of eastern Zambia is characterized by a flat to gently rolling landscape and altitudes ranging from 900 to 1,200 meters. Seasonally waterlogged, low-lying areas, known locally as *dambos,* are also common. The main soil types are loamy-sand and sand Alfisols, well drained and relatively fertile but with low water and nutrient-holding capacities (Government of Zambia/ICRAF 1988; Raussen, Daka, and Bangwe 1995). Rainfall averages about 1,000 millimeters per year, with about 85 percent falling in the four months from December through March. Rainfall is highly variable; the area received less than 600 millimeters in two of the eight years between 1990 and 1997. Population density varies between 25 and 40 persons per square kilometer. About one-third of the farmers own oxen, while most of the others cultivate by hand hoe. Average cropped area ranges from 1.1–1.6 hectares for hoe cultivators to 2.3–4.3 hectares for ox cultivators.

The research in western Kenya focused largely on medium- to high-potential highland areas with higher rainfall, higher altitudes, and higher population density than in Eastern Zambia. Altitudes range between 1,250 and 1,600 meters above sea level in Western Kenya, with undulating topography and moderate slopes. Rainfall ranges from 1,200 to 1,800 millimeters per year, with two cropping seasons annually. The long rains occur over five months, from March to July, while the more erratic, short rains arrive over a three- to four-month period from August to December. Soils are of generally good physical structure but low in nutrient stocks. In many parts of the region, phosphorus is the major limiting nutrient, but nitrogen and potassium limitations are also prevalent (Shepherd et al. 1996; Jama et al. 1998a). Moreover, heavy infestation with *Striga hermontica,* a parasitic weed that devastates the maize

TABLE 7.11 Dynamics and drivers of improved fallows in Eastern Zambia and Western Kenya, early 1960s–2006

	Period 1: Soil fertility decline	Period 2: Collaborative technology development	Period 3: Technology dissemination
Timing	Zambia: 1964–90 Kenya: 1960–90	Zambia: 1987–97 Kenya: 1991–2001	Zambia: 1998–2006 Kenya: 1998–2003
Key actors	Government input and crop marketing agencies	World Agroforestry Centre (ICRAF) Kenya Agricultural Research Institute, Kenya Forestry Research Institute, Zambia's Ministry of Agriculture Farmer researchers	Nongovernmental organizations Government extension staff ICRAF
Motors of change	Growing population pressure Declining soil fertility Fertilizer subsidies (Zambia only)	Technology development: in Zambia, on-station (1987–92) and on-farm (1992–97); in Kenya, on-farm (1991–2001)	Extension Seed multiplication
Beneficiaries			Zambia: middle-income groups, who are most likely to adopt IF Kenya: rich and poor, who adopt IF at equal rates Benefits are gender neutral in both countries
Impact	Population pressure Reduced fallow periods Soil fertility loss		Improved soil structure, soil organic matter, and fertility (N) Improved water infiltration and retention Risk reduction (no cash costs) compared to fertilizer Adoption: in Zambia, 66,000 (average IF plot size, 0.2 ha); in Kenya, 15,000 (average plot size, 0.04 ha)

NOTE: IF, improved fallows.

crops, is common (Oswald et al. 1996). High population densities, ranging from 500 to 1,200 per square kilometer, lead to small farm sizes of about 0.7 hectares per household. Because of these resource constraints, Western Kenya is considered the poorest region of the country, with 32 percent of households classified as hardcore poor, as opposed to 20 percent for all rural areas (Government of Kenya 2000).

Phase 1: Soil Fertility Decline, 1964–90

Zambia's postindependence agricultural strategy focused on increasing maize production through broad interventions in input and output markets, including subsidized fertilizer and credit, a parastatal monopoly on maize marketing, and a network of depots in rural areas to supply inputs and purchase maize (see Chapter 3). Fertilizer subsidies were introduced in 1971, and by 1982 they averaged 60 percent of landed costs. Fertilizer use expanded from 20,000 tons of nutrients per year in the mid-1970s to 85,000 tons annually in the mid-1980s (Howard and Mungoma 1996). Fertilizer use was common among farmers in Eastern Province during the 1980s, but the removal of subsidies and the collapse of the parastatal marketing system in the late 1980s and early 1990s had dramatic effects. Between 1986/87 and 1995/96, the price of nitrogen relative to maize increased from 3.1 to 11.3 percent, and fertilizer use in Zambia declined by 70 percent (Howard, Rubey, and Crawford 1997).

In this setting, an ICRAF diagnostic survey in Eastern Province revealed a serious breakdown of traditional strategies to sustain the production of food, fodder, and fuelwood (Ngugi, 1988). Farmers and researchers identified declining soil fertility as the major problem responsible for low yields of maize— the main staple food crop. Nitrogen deficiencies are widespread, and large responses to mineral fertilizers are common. (Kwesiga and Kamau 1989). The traditional fallows on which farmers relied to restore soil fertility have been shortened by land pressure and have become inadequate to restore soil fertility. In fact, most farmers continuously crop their fields, even if they have uncultivated land (Kwesiga and Chisumpa 1992; Peterson et al. 1999). Their reason, which researchers confirm, is that short-term natural fallows of 1–3 years do not increase yields. As a result of declining long fallow periods, both crop yields and household food security have declined.

The breakdown in subsidy and credit programs and the subsequent reduction in fertilizer use marked a key turning point in the farmers' socioeconomic environment. Farmers had "tasted fertilizer," but after the breakdown in support systems promoting its use, they were left with a huge "felt need" for more affordable soil fertility improvement practices. At the same time, most still had uncultivated land. Farmers thus found themselves in the intermediate stage of land intensification. They had begun to perceive a decline in soil fertility but still had some fallow land (Raintree and Warner 1986). The time appeared ripe for developing an improved fallow practice that, with relatively low inputs of labor, could increase the productivity of their farms.

Phase 2: Collaborative Technology Development, 1987–97

RESEARCH STATION TRIALS IN EASTERN ZAMBIA.   Because Zambian farmers do not traditionally plant trees to improve soil fertility, researchers themselves had to identify tree species that could increase soil fertility during a short fallow period. Such a tree must grow quickly and out of the reach of free-ranging livestock by the first dry season, be resistant to annual fires, and be tolerant of periodic droughts. The selected tree must grow and survive under the nitrogen-limiting conditions prevalent on most small-scale farms in Zambia. Using these criteria, ICRAF researchers identified *Sesbania sesban,* an indigenous tree, as a potential species because of its wide distribution in Zambia (Kwesiga 1990), its fast growth, its ease of propagation and removal, and because it nodulates easily, fixes nitrogen, and produces a high level of biomass (Evans and Rotar 1987). Soil from well-established stands of *Sesbania* serve to inoculate the newly planted seedlings.

Early on-station trials conducted from 1987 to 1991 indicated that *Sesbania*-improved fallows could increase maize yields significantly, with or without mineral fertilizers. The trials achieved maize grain yields of 5.0 and 6.0 tons per hectare in 1990 and 1991 following two- and three-year *Sesbania* fallows, respectively. This compared to 4.9 and 4.3 tons per hectare from continuously cropped maize with mineral fertilizer (112 kilograms of nitrogen per hectare) and 1.2 and 1.9 tons per hectare without fertilizer. The fallows generated strong residual effects on maize yields. The total yield in the four cropping seasons following the two-year fallow was 12.8 tons per hectare compared to 7.6 tons per hectare for six seasons of continuous unfertilized maize. In addition, the fallow plots produced 15 and 21 tons per hectare of fuelwood after two- and three-year fallows, respectively (Kwesiga and Coe 1994). As a result, the financial analyses of the on-station improved fallow results proved very encouraging.

Two important lessons emerged from the on-station trials. First, a three-year fallow appeared less attractive than the one- or two-year fallow. Therefore, subsequent work focused on the shorter fallows. Second, the cost of seedlings emerged as a major factor affecting overall profitability and the length of the payback period. This result suggested that future work would need to focus on finding cheaper methods of plant establishment. In fact, the farmers themselves helped to resolve this second problem during the course of the on-farm trials that followed.

TYPE 1 ON-FARM RESEARCH TRIALS: RESEARCHER-DESIGNED, RESEARCHER-MANAGED TRIALS.   Based on the favorable initial agronomic and financial results, in 1991 researchers in Eastern Zambia decided to experiment under farmers' field conditions (Kwesiga et al. 1999). The researchers initiated five researcher-managed on-farm trials beginning in the 1992/93 season in order to measure biological performance under farmers' soil conditions. Fallows established from bare-root and potted *Sesbania* seedlings resulted in remarkable maize yield increases compared with the yields achieved following continuous unfertilized maize and grass fallows. Moreover, maize yields following a two-year *Sesbania* fallow equaled those achieved under fully fertilized control plots. However, direct sowing of *Sesbania* proved distinctly less productive.

TYPE 2 TRIALS: RESEARCHER-DESIGNED, FARMER-MANAGED TRIALS. Researchers started farmer-managed trials on a small scale by selecting categories of farmers most likely to benefit from improved fallows. Between 1992 and 1994, the researchers worked with eight farmers to test *Sesbania*-improved fallows and methods of establishing these fallows. Establishment and tree growth were satisfactory, and bare-root seedlings emerged as farmers' preferred establishment method. In 1994, the team decided to greatly expand participatory on-farm research as a follow-up to the encouraging on-station results, the positive indications from the financial analysis, and the on-farm trials (Box 7.3).

In 1994/95, the team assisted four farmer training centers and six individual farmers to establish nurseries in various agricultural extension camps in Chadiza, Chipata, and Katete districts.[23] Using bare-root seedlings from these nurseries, and in some cases direct sowing, 158 farmers initiated researcher-designed, farmer-managed (Type 2) trials with plots of improved fallows measuring 400 square meters (Franzel, Phiri, and Kwesiga 2002).

These trials aimed to assess the biophysical response of trees and crops under farmers' management, measure the costs and returns of the technology, and obtain farmers' assessments. In these expanded trials the researchers made a distinct effort to involve farmers representing the range of different types found in the area—including high- and low-income, male and female, and oxen- and hoe-using farmers. In these expanded trials, each farmer selected one of six options from among the researchers' menu of improved fallow technologies. The options represented a factorial combination of three species (*Sesbania, Tephrosia,* and pigeon pea) and two methods of fallow management (pure stands and intercropping with maize during the first year of establishment and then allowing the legumes to grow into a pure stand fallow in the second year). As controls, the farmers compared these options with continuous cropping of fertilized and unfertilized maize. Farmers planted *Sesbania* fallows using bare-root seedlings while directly sowing *Tephrosia* and pigeon pea. Researchers helped farmers in laying out about half of the trials, while government extension staff helped farmers plant the rest. The project supplied *Sesbania* seeds, inoculum, maize seed, and fertilizer for the trials.

The Type 2 trials revealed a series of important findings. Given the low and sporadic rainfall during the 1994/95 season, farmers had to reseed or gap

---

23. In Zambia, a "camp" defines the area served by a single agricultural extension officer, who is designated as the "camp officer."

BOX 7.3   A pioneer experimenter with improved fallows

Jennifer Zulu is one of the early collaborators testing improved fallow in Eastern Zambia. At age 40, Ms. Zulu is the head of her household of eight, comprised of five males and three females. She has a modest education, having attained formal education up to primary grade 4. In addition to the staple food maize, Ms. Zulu also cultivates groundnuts, sunflowers, cowpeas, and beans.

Ms. Zulu established her first improved fallows when she planted fields of *Sesbania sesban* and *Tephrosia vogelii* on a trial basis in 1992/93. After seeing the benefits of the technology, Ms. Zulu has continued to plant improved fallows each year ever since. In addition to the species she started with, she has ventured into planting other improved fallow species including *Gliricidia sepium* and *Cajanus cajan*. She has conducted her own innovative research, exploring weeding frequency in fallow plots, intercropping versus growing trees in pure stands, and intercropping improved fallow species with other crops, including sunflowers and groundnuts.

Why does Ms. Zulu continue to plant improved fallows after almost a decade? She says it is due to "the high maize yield I get from improved fallow which helps me achieve food security in my house" and also because improved fallows are "cheap and very sustainable for me."

Over the years, Ms. Zulu has benefited from improved fallows in several ways: she has enough food to feed members of her household, she has been able to build a four-bedroom house with an iron roof, and she is able to sell the surplus produce from her fields, which enabled her to send all her children to school. In addition, she obtains abundant firewood from the improved fallow fields and so does not have to walk long distances to collect it.

Summarizing her experience with improved fallows, Ms. Zulu said: "Improved fallows are very beneficial, cheap, and very sustainable. They are especially useful for rural poor people, who are unable to buy fertilizer, to achieve food security."

---

trees in two-thirds of the trials, one to two times. From this experience, researchers concluded that 60 percent survival of the fallow species in the first three months is required for satisfactory biomass production at the end of two years. Aside from drought, the farmer-managed trials revealed problems of weed competition, animal browsing (for pigeon pea), and a leaf-defoliating beetle (for *Sesbania*). A paired comparison of survival rates at six months and one year after planting showed that *Sesbania* ranked highest in ability to withstand the long dry season (Kwesiga et al. 1999). Despite researchers' concerns about the potential adverse impacts of intercropping trees with maize during the first year, 17 percent of the farmers participating in the 1994/95 trials opted for this fallow management method to economize on land and labor (Keil 2001). In many ways, this farmer experimentation helped both researchers and farmers to understand the advantages and disadvantages of different improved fallow practices.

TYPE 3 TRIALS: FARMER-DESIGNED, FARMER-MANAGED TRIALS.   In order to understand how farmers adapt improved fallows to their existing farm practices and to enable farmer innovations to feed back into ongoing research and extension efforts, the researchers facilitated a series of farmer-designed, farmer-managed on-farm trials. They gave interested farmers seeds or seedlings as well as advice on available options governing fallow length, tree density, and planting methods. They then left the farmers to design their own trials, planting trees where they wished on their own farms. The number of farmers designing and managing Type 3 trials increased from 5 in 1993/94 to 37 in 1994/95 to 797 in 1995/96.

Initially, farmers planted fallows in areas ranging from about 0.04 to 0.09 hectare. Over time, these areas have increased steadily to an average of 0.2 hectares in 2003 (Ajayi et al. 2007). Many farmers who initially started off as Type 2 farmers also planted Type 3 trials after experiencing the benefits of improved fallows or after observing the experiences of others. Usually they used planting material from their own farms.

Surveys of Type 3 trials have allowed researchers to monitor the performance of improved fallows under farmers' own management and to assess how they use and modify the practice. Early surveys of the Type 3 trials revealed increasing interest in *Tephrosia* relative to *Sesbania* (Keil 2001). Likewise, farmer experimentation during the Type 3 trials yielded two key innovations that have subsequently altered research priorities as well as the menu of fallow systems offered by extension services. First was the use of bare-root seedlings instead of potted seedlings. In these Type 3 trials, farmers received potted seedlings grown at farmer training centers. But to reduce the cost of transporting them to her farm, one farmer removed the seedlings from the pots and carried them bare-root in basins. When farmers' plantings of these seedlings proved successful, researchers conducted Type 1 trials to compare the performance of bare-root seedlings grown in raised seedbeds with that of potted seedlings. They found no significant difference in performance. Moreover, bare-root seedlings are easy and cheap to produce and, with precaution, are also easy to transport in baskets or ox-drawn carts. The change to bare-root seedlings reduced costs from about US$100 per hectare to about US$37 per hectare. Because potted seedlings were much more costly to produce, the research team phased them out (Kwesiga et al. 1999).

The farmers' second major innovation involved intercropping during the year of tree establishment. The researchers therefore began formal testing of this practice during subsequent rounds of on-farm trials. The trials determined that intercropping reduces maize yields and tree growth during the year of establishment. Yet many farmers prefer intercropping because it reduces the number of seasons without a maize crop and economizes on weeding labor. Over time, intercropping became increasingly popular. The percentage of farmers intercropping rose from 17 percent during the 1994/95 to 49 percent in a survey conducted in the 2000/2001 planting season (Keil 2001).

Several other key farmer innovations include the following:

- The use of *Sesbania* regenerations as planting material for establishing new fallows. This innovation saves farmers from having to establish nurseries during the dry season.
- Planting seedlings into a bush fallow without preparing the land first.
- Planting *Sesbania* seedlings behind an ox plow; as the plow moves along an adjacent furrow, it covers the seedling roots with soil.
- Planting *Sesbania* at weeding time in parts of fields where maize is performing poorly.
- Testing the effect of improved fallows on crops other than maize, such as sunflowers and groundnuts.
- Removing *Sesbania* tips to stimulate lateral branching and thus biomass production.
- Using *Sesbania* wood for making granaries and tools, such as machetes and hoe handles.

DEVELOPING IMPROVED FALLOW TECHNOLOGY IN WESTERN KENYA. Diagnostic studies conducted by ICRAF in the early 1990s in Western Kenya, like those in Zambia, highlighted poor soil fertility as a major constraint to farm productivity. As a result, ICRAF conducted initial experiments with improved fallows in Western Kenya for several years, beginning in 1991, including research station and on-farm trials. These early tests focused only on *Sesbania sesban,* given its proven performance in Southern Africa (Kwesiga and Coe 1994) and its prolific biomass production under West Kenyan conditions (Onim, Otieno, and Dzowela 1990). However, the long-cycle *Sesbania* fallows proved uneconomic, so work on improved fallows ceased in Western Kenya during the mid-1990s (Hartemink et al. 1996; Swinkels et al. 1997; Jama, Buresh, and Place 1998b).

In 1996, inspired by promising early results from Eastern Zambia, ICRAF, the Kenya Agricultural Research Institute (KARI) and the Kenya Forestry Research Institute (KEFRI) decided to resume efforts to develop viable improved fallow technologies for Western Kenya. Because early economic analysis had shown that short-cycle fallows were the most promising (Swinkels et al. 1997), researchers conducted initial screening trials to identify suitable leguminous shrubs with a shorter life cycle than *Sesbania sesban,* the most promising of which proved to be *Crotalaria grahamiana* and *Tephrosia vogelii* (Niang et al. 1999). They evaluated the trees' impact on weeds and nematodes and experimented with alternative planting densities. Field surveys indicated that 20–60 percent of farmers in Western Kenya use traditional fallows and that 60 percent of these last for at least two seasons (Wangila, Rommelse, and De Wolf 1999; De Wolf and Rommelse 2000). From 1996 to 2001, the researchers conducted extensive on-farm experiments to assess the feasibility and profitability of various improved fallow management options, including supplementation with phosphorus fertilizer.

In the end, the Kenyan trials produced very different recommendations than those in Zambia. Given multiple rainy seasons and greater land constraints, the most promising improved fallow technologies in Kenya involved faster-growing, smaller species such as *Crotalaria* and *Tephrosia*. By intercropping these legumes during the long rains and leaving them in full fallow during the ensuing short rains, researchers and farmers developed a 9- to 10-month improved fallow system that prepared land for crop planting during the following long rains as opposed to the much longer 2-year fallows recommended in Eastern Zambia.

Phase 3: Technology Dissemination, 1998–2006

EASTERN ZAMBIA.   During the on-farm trials, researchers spent considerable time in the villages with farmers, NGO staff, and farmer groups, in the process learning more about land use and farmers' problems. By working directly with farmers, the researchers came to appreciate the need for low-input, low-cost technologies in the highly credit-constrained rural economy. In the process of working together, they developed mutual trust and genuine partnerships. These relationships helped enhance farmers' confidence and increased their experimentation and modification of the prototype.

The Zambia/ICRAF project facilitated the establishment of an informal network to conduct adaptive research and training, as well as the dissemination of improved fallows (Katanga et al. 2002). The network serves two functions: (1) providing coordinated analytical mechanisms for participatory monitoring and evaluation of on-farm research and (2) acting as a catalytic, action-oriented group for the widespread dissemination of the technology. The network began when the project started supplying planting material, training, and information to extension services, development projects, NGOs, and farmer groups that wanted to help their members test improved fallows. In exchange, these organizations provided the project with feedback on the performance of the technology.

The network is based on the principle that adaptive research and extension are really two sides of the same coin; once on-farm research has confirmed that a technology has adoption potential, dissemination is already beginning. Researchers need to maintain close involvement to obtain feedback from farmers and extension staff on problems and to identify researchable issues. Moreover, the more extension staff become involved in on-farm research, the more knowledgeable and enthusiastic they become in extending the practice. Their involvement helps save scarce research resources and improves farmers' feedback to the researchers.

The network thus generated several favorable impacts (Cooper 1999):

- It reduced the cost of conducting on-farm research as field-based extension officers and NGOs established and monitored on-farm trials.
- It enhanced the breadth of input into and the relevance of the research.
- It expanded the range of sites under experimentation at relatively little additional cost.
- The partners were increasingly well informed on key aspects of technology options and better placed to disseminate technologies and respond to farmer feedback.
- The partners have developed a sense of involvement in, enthusiasm for, and ownership of promising innovations.

Zambia's government extension service and several NGOs were full partners in the on-farm research during the 1990s. The managing of on-farm trials was seen as a normal duty of extension and NGO staff rather than a burden imposed on them from outside. Development projects provided some incentives to extension staff, including bicycles and lunch allowances. That only one researcher and one technician from the Zambia/ICRAF project were involved in the establishment and monitoring of the hundreds of on-farm trials in the mid-1990s attests to the strength of the network.

Through a second major funding source (the United States Agency for International Development, or USAID), the Zambia Integrated Agroforestry Project (ZIAP) was initiated in 1998 with the goal of improving household food security and incomes. The project promoted the adoption of low-cost, environmentally sustainable agricultural production techniques, including short-term fallows of leguminous trees and shrubs.

ZIAP targeted 12,000 rural households in five districts of Eastern Zambia to test the improved agricultural technologies over a five-year period. The project worked through lead farmers selected by the community together with government and project field officers. After receiving basic training in agroforestry, the lead farmers, with the help of extension staff, conducted community sensitization meetings and mobile courses. In order to meet the large demand for tree seed, the project contracted with seven farmers to manage eight large seed production stands. The project then bought the seed and distributed it to farmers on a loan basis: farmers were required to pay back twice the amount of seed they received.

WESTERN KENYA.   A collaborative project implemented by the KARI, KEFRI, and ICRAF began disseminating improved fallows in 1997, focusing on 17 pilot villages in two districts of Western Kenya. Project staff helped farmers to establish village committees to facilitate information flow between the community and research staff. In addition, project funding permitted the posting of field technicians to many of the villages for a period of about two years.

Building on the strong interest and uptake of farmers in the pilot villages, the project began wide-scale dissemination of improved fallows across western Kenya, starting in late 1998. To disseminate the technology more widely, the project developed partnerships with the Ministry of Agriculture; NGOs such as CARE–Kenya, Kenya Woodfuel Agroforestry Project–Busia, Hortiquip–Vihiga, Siaya Community Development Project–Siaya, VI–Agroforestry Project–Kitale, and Africa 2000–Vihiga; church groups; and many community-based organizations. The NGO partners integrated agroforestry technologies into their existing portfolios of options for communities and disseminated them using their own approaches, including training of contact farmers, field days, and exchange tours. In addition, the research team trained project and government extension staff in the establishment and management of improved fallows and provided germplasm for the new species. The extension staff, in turn, distributed promotional materials and conducted field days at researcher-managed sites and later in farmers' own fields. By 2000, these various partners were providing improved fallow extension services in 16 districts across Western Kenya.

Because the fallows constituted a highly visible new feature of the landscape, considerable informal dissemination of information took place—for example, when relatives came to visit or large groups gathered for a funeral. From 1999 onward, the research center at Maseno received visitors almost daily requesting information or germplasm for improved fallows or other agroforestry systems. In one particularly interesting instance, a subchief from West Kanyaluo, in Rachuonyo district, led a small group of farmers to Maseno to acquire information and seed for his community. As a result, over 100 farmers are practicing improved fallows in the community without ever having had any technical assistance from research or extension staff.

The Impact of Improved Fallows

ADOPTION.   By the 2005/06 season, about 66,500 farmers in Eastern Zambia had planted improved fallows (Zambezi Basin Agroforestry Project 2006). Following a dip of about 10,000 in 2002/03, as World Vision's ZIAP support ended, adoption recovered quickly following the launch of a new USAID-funded extension project (Figure 7.4). After five years of extension efforts, most of the continuing farmers had planted improved fallows for a second time and were considered to have graduated from testers to adopters. These accounted for 12–14 percent of farmers in the region. In Kenya, researchers estimated that between 10,000 and 20,000 farmers were using improved fallows by 2002. As in Zambia, the Kenyan experience suggests a distinct falloff in the use of the new technology following a reduction in project-funded extension support and promotional services. For example, the proportion of farmers using agro-

FIGURE 7.4 Number of farmers planting improved fallows in Zambia, 1995–2006

Number (thousands)

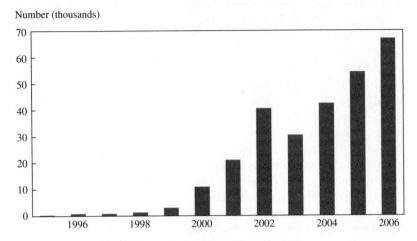

SOURCE: Zambia/ICRAF Agroforestry Project, Annual Report (2005).

forestry practices in project villages in western Kenya declined from 22 to 14 percent following the end of project support in 2000 (Place et al. 2005). Monitoring of the Kenyan program likewise underscores the importance of distinguishing between testers, who may or may not continue, and adopters, who voluntarily plant improved fallows a second time following initial favorable results. Kiptot et al. (2007) note that a substantial number of users were "pseudo-adopters," farmers who use a practice not for its intrinsic advantages (in this case, improved soil fertility) but to gain benefits from the projects promoting it. These benefits included credit, social prestige, and the availability of a seed market from projects promoting the practice.

Plot sizes under improved fallows are small, roughly 0.2 hectare in Zambia and 0.04 hectare in Kenya, representing about 10 percent of household cropped area in Zambia (Ajayi et al. 2007) and 6 percent in Kenya. Given the early stage of extension efforts in both countries, it is not clear whether these magnitudes represent farmer-determined optimum levels of adoption or simply early readings on an upward-sloping incremental adoption trajectory. Likewise, it should be recognized that "full" adoption of improved fallows would involve considerably less than total cultivated land area, so that food requirements could be met. In Zambia, improved fallows usually operate on four- to five-year cycles, two years in fallow followed by two to three years under maize, so a full adopter would plant about 0.3 hectare (one-fourth of the average of 1.2 hectares under maize) in improved fallows each year. A full adopter in Zambia would thus plant about 15 percent of cropped area in improved fallows each year. The figure for western Kenya is 12 percent.

Data from Western Kenya reinforce the field findings from Zambia, suggesting that farmer interest has grown not only in improved fallows but also in other practices for maintaining soil fertility. Five years of monitoring data from nonproject villages in Western Kenya document growing use of not only improved fallows but also animal manure, mineral fertilizer, and biomass transfers (Table 7.12).

YIELD GAINS.   Improved fallows clearly increase maize yields (Table 7.13). Compared to yields of just under 1 ton per hectare under continuously cropped but unfertilized maize (or 4.8 tons over five seasons), output following two-year improved fallows averaged 2.8 tons per hectare per season in Eastern Zambia (or 8.5 tons over three seasons following a two-year fallow). On the same farms, continuously cultivated maize plots treated with mineral fertilizer averaged 4.4 tons per hectare (or 21.9 tons over five seasons).

INCOME.   Using on-farm data from Eastern Zambia, Table 7.13 compares the financial profitability of improved fallows with continuously cropped maize, fertilized and unfertilized. The main benefits of improved fallows relative to continuously cropped maize are labor saved in years one and two because maize was not planted, fuelwood production in year two, increased maize yields in years three through five, and reduced land preparation and weeding costs in the first postfallow maize crop. Added costs include those for *Sesbania* seed and labor for establishing the nursery; transplanting, maintaining, and harvesting the fallow; and harvesting and threshing the increased maize produced. Given a five-year cycle of plot management, with two-year improved fallows followed by three years of crop production, the following figures discount cash flows at 30 percent per year to account for the different timing of benefits and costs under each system.

Returns to land consistently rank improved fallows higher than continuously unfertilized maize but lower than fertilized maize. In the 2002/03 season, continuously cropped unfertilized maize yielded US$156 per hectare per year, while a two-year *Sesbania* fallow followed by three years of maize cultivation yielded US$370 per hectare. At the then-prevailing input and output prices,

TABLE 7.12 Trends in soil fertility restoration systems in non–pilot project areas of Western Kenya, 1997–2001

Soil fertility replenishment system	Adoption rate (percentage of households)				
	1997	1998	1999	2000	2001
Improved fallows	4.1	7.2	13.7	13.0	12.4
Biomass transfer	0.1	8.0	14.7	19.9	21.6
Chemical fertilizer	10.8	14.4	19.1	24.1	28.0
Animal manure	30.5	36.0	43.5	49.0	50.1

SOURCE: Place et al. (2005).

TABLE 7.13 Returns to labor and land under alternative soil fertility restoration systems in Eastern Zambia, 1996–2002 (constant 2005 US$)

Option	Labor (days/ha)		Maize (tons/ha)		Returns to land: Net present value (US$/ha)			Returns to labor: Net returns (US$) per workday		
	1996	2002	5-year total	Average per cropped year	1996	1998	2002	1996	1998	2002
Continuous unfertilized maize	499	462	4.8	1.0	7	7	156	0.56	0.95	1.32
Improved 2-year *Sesbania* fallow	441	521	8.5	2.8	204	258	370	1.33	1.96	3.00
Continuous fertilized maize	645	532	21.9	4.4	274	652	597	1.25	2.61	3.83

SOURCES: Franzel et al. (2002); Ajayi (2007).

continuously cropped fertilized maize yielded the highest returns of all the soil fertility management options, about US$597 per hectare.

Returns to labor, however, tend to be more relevant to small farmers in Eastern Zambia, given that dependence on hand-hoe labor under rainfed cultivation translates into acute peak-season labor bottlenecks that typically constrain farm output and incomes. In terms of returns to labor, improved fallows outperformed continuously unfertilized maize by a wide margin (see Table 7.13). However, comparisons with fertilized maize vary across years, depending on rainfall, yield response, and relative maize and fertilizer prices. Using 1996 prices, improved fallows narrowly outperformed continuously fertilized maize. Using 2002 farmgate prices for mineral fertilizer and maize, the return to a person-day of labor for a mineral fertilizer land use system is US$3.83 at a 50 percent subsidy, but the figure falls to U$3.07 at nonsubsidized fertilizer prices. For the three agroforestry options, returns to labor were US$3.00, $2.88, and $2.28, respectively. These figures compare with US$1.32 in unfertilized maize fields with a daily agricultural wage of about 60 cents in eastern Zambia (Ajayi et al. 2007).[24] Not surprisingly, changes in fertilizer subsidy rates and in the relative prices of fertilizer and maize can alter the profitability ranking of the alternative soil fertility management systems.

Risk also affects farmer decisionmaking. Relative to continuous use of mineral fertilizer, improved fallows are likely to reduce farmers' risk. Although available data do not permit a formal testing of this proposition, several features of improved fallows make them likely to moderate risk. First, because improved fallows improve soil structure and build up soil organic matter, they enhance the soil's moisture retention capacity during drought years. Second, productivity gains from improved fallows are spread over a three-year period, whereas those from nitrogen fertilizer have relatively less effect after the first year. Thus, even if a farmer's crop fails in the first postfallow season, he or she will likely benefit from a substantial response the following year. Third, in the event of a complete crop failure, a farmer using fertilizer would lose his or her cash investment of US$185 per hectare, whereas the improved fallow costs of US$108 per hectare represent mostly in-kind costs. Finally, fertilizer supply has proven problematic in Eastern Zambia (though not in Kenya) due to vacillating public involvement and subsidies, which have tended to scare away private fertilizer traders and leave farmers vulnerable to late delivery of public supplies (Jayne et al. 2003).

EQUITY.   Although wealthy households in Eastern Zambia are more likely to test improved fallows, middle-income households are most likely to continue planting for a second cycle (Keil, Zeller, and Franzel 2005). Using voluntary

---

24. To enable comparability across chapters, these values have been converted to constant 2005 dollars.

planting for a second cycle as the definition of adoption, the available data suggest no correlation between wealth and adoption of improved fallows in Zambia (Figure 7.5). Likewise, in Kenya the landowning poor adopt improved fallows at about the same rate as the wealthy (Place et al. 2005). However, other soil fertility management options—such as the use of mineral fertilizer, manure, and composting—are all more likely to be adopted by wealthier households (Table 7.14).

GENDER ISSUES.   In both countries, the initial testing and early adoption of improved fallow technology appears to be gender neutral overall (Place et al. 2005; Ajayi et al. 2006). Several studies have found no statistically significant differences in the proportion of women and men planting improved fallows.[25] Women manage improved fallows as well as men (Franzel, Phiri, and Kwesiga 2002). However, in some areas women plant smaller improved fallow plots than men, possibly due to land and labor constraints or greater risk aversion (Franzel, Phiri, and Kwesiga 2002). Likewise, female participants tend to favor some improved fallow species over others. Pigeon pea fallows, in particular, have attracted the highest proportion of female participants in Zambia, probably because pigeon peas are edible and because women are responsible for feeding the family. Ajayi et al. (2006) pointed out that factors affecting the adoption of a given agroforestry technology at the initial "testing" phase may differ (or assume different importance) from those affecting the "expansion" phase. Although gender may not be important in the "testing" phase of improved fallows, over time, institutional factors such as fire and grazing, land tenure, control of production resources by the other gender, and government policies may assume more importance for the expansion phase of improved fallows than when farmers are testing the technology on a smaller scale (Ajayi and Kwesiga 2003).

FINANCIAL SUSTAINABILITY.   Because of its low cash costs, improved fallow technology represents a feasible and reliable means of improving soil fertility for many small-scale farmers. Many cash-poor farmers indicate that they have adopted improved fallows because of their low cash costs and because they offer a reliable means of enhancing soil productivity and household food production (Box 7.4).

ECOLOGICAL SUSTAINABILITY.   Agronomically, improved fallows aim to recapitalize deteriorated soils. Over time, the roots and biomass from leguminous fallows build up soil organic material, improve soil structure and water infiltration, and enhance water retention capacity (Table 7.15). Improved soil structure results in higher rainwater infiltration rates and increased groundwater storage in the improved fallow systems (Torquebiau and Kwesiga 1996).

---

25. See Franzel, Phiri, and Kwesiga (1999); Keil (2001); Gladwin et al. (2002); Phiri et al. (2004); Place et al. (2005); and Ajayi et al. (2006).

FIGURE 7.5 Adoption of improved fallows in Zambia, by wealth category, 2001

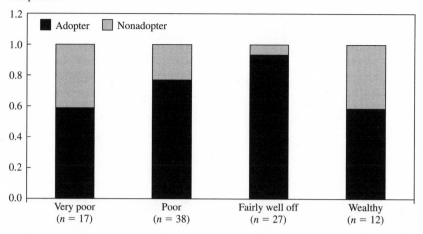

SOURCE: Keil (2001).

Details of the ecosystem impacts of improved fallows in eastern Zambia have been documented by Ajayi et al. (2007)

Nitrogen balances under improved fallows remain positive when two-year fallows are followed by two years of maize cultivation (Table 7.16). However, recent tests in Eastern Zambia suggest that gains in maize yields drop off during the second year of maize cultivation and turn negative during the third year. This has led ICRAF to recommend a two-year fallow followed by two years of cultivation in future testing and extension work.

Phosphorus balances likewise remain positive under improved fallows in Zamiba due to the low uptake of phosphorus in maize grain and stover and generally high levels of phosphorus in native soils. However, in areas of western Kenya where phosphorus availability is constraining, improved fallows alone do not increase maize yields and thus require phosphorus supplementation.

Most African cropping systems show negative balances of potassium. Improved fallows are no exception given the high potassium uptake by maize. At present, potassium stocks at the sites tested in Eastern Zambian remain high and do not limit maize production. However, at sites with low stocks of potassium in the soil, maize productivity may be adversely affected.

Overall, the available evidence suggests that leguminous fallows can effectively transfer sufficient nitrogen from the atmosphere to sustain maize cultivation at high yields. Thus, improved fallows can serve as a substitute for or complement to inorganic nitrogen fertilizers. But given negative potassium and sometimes negative phosphorus balances under improved fallows,

TABLE 7.14 Factors affecting the use of soil fertility replenishment systems in 17 villages in Western Kenya, 1997–2001

	Improved fallows		Other soil fertility management systems		
	Used early and dropped	Used throughout period	Chemical fertilizer	Animal manure	Compost
Wealth index	0.042	0.039	0.590***	0.337***	0.315***
	0.590	0.470	0.000	0.000	0.000
Land area owned	0.142**	0.231**	0.041	0.070*	0.088***
	0.024	0.000	0.256	0.090	0.010
Education level of household head					
Secondary	-0.855**	0.233	0.788***	-0.004	0.368*
	0.024	0.358	0.004	0.986	0.076
Upper primary	-0.231	0.176	0.633***	0.072	-0.377**
	0.399	0.407	0.008	0.692	0.029
Lower primary	-0.219	-0.069	0.198	0.338*	-0.057***
	0.434	0.754	0.431	0.060	0.000
Gender of household head					
Female; husband away	0.675**	0.046	-0.920***	-0.290	0.549***
	0.031	0.858	0.001	0.194	0.005
Female; no husband	0.107	0.026	-0.129	-0.237	-0.202
	0.691	0.893	0.533	0.150	0.198

Male, single or polygamous	0.663**	0.172	-0.069	-0.524***	0.083
	0.013	0.416	0.749	0.005	0.635
Number of adult household members	0.269***	0.094**	0.006	0.101***	0.024
	0.000	0.023	0.781	0.000	0.156
Luo household	1.351***	0.999**	1.560***	-0.798***	0.072
	0.000	0.000	0.000	0.000	0.523
Age of household head	-0.017***	-0.006	-0.011**	-0.0005	-0.021***
	0.039	0.307	0.037	0.909	0.000
Pilot village	0.655***	0.804**	n.a	n.a.	n.a.
	0.000	0.000			
Constant	0.656**	0.804**	-3.382***	-0.056	-0.162
	0.001	0.000	0.000	0.858	0.563
Number of observations	1,583	1,583	1,620	1,623	1,621
Percentage of cases observed	9.1	22.0	20.5	71.0	40.6

SOURCE: Place et al. (2005).

NOTES: *, **, and *** indicate significance at the 90 percent, 95 percent, and 99 percent confidence levels, respectively; n.a., not applicable.

**BOX 7.4 A farmer's comparison
of improved fallows and mineral fertilizer**

Tafadi Mbewe of Kapita village, in Chipata North district, has been planting improved fallows since 1997. Her first-year *Tephrosia* field is doing exceptionally well. She also hosts a "Type 2" researcher-designed, farmer-managed trial in which she is comparing mixed plots of *Gliricidia* and *Tephrosia* trees with separate plots of *Gliricidia* and *Tephrosia.*

Answering a question from visiting scientists about her preference between improved fallows and fertilizer, she answers by stating: "Unlike fertilizer, which is normally stolen by agricultural workers, improved fallow trees cannot be stolen once they are established on farm. For example, in 2001 most of the subsidized fertilizer meant for peasant farmers did not reach the intended beneficiaries because it was stolen. Most of my friends who had hoped to use the same fertilizer are now starving, but in my case I have enough maize from my pigeon pea improved fallow field that I harvested last year."

---

supplementation with rock phosphates or inorganic potassium and phosphorus fertilizers will be required to sustain food crop cultivation over time in most African settings.

Contrasts and Similarities among Countries

The four case studies reviewed in this chapter present four situation-specific responses to declining soil fertility. Each offers a slightly different strategy for improving farm productivity and maintaining soil fertility: (1) water harvesting under minimum tillage, crop residue management, leguminous crop rotations, and strategic doses of mineral fertilizer in Zambia's CF; (2) water harvesting and concentrated soil amendment with compost, manure, and fertilizer in Burkina Faso's *zaï;* (3) two-year improved leguminous fallows in Eastern Zambia; and (4) 10-month leguminous shrub fallows in Western Kenya (Table 7.17). All emphasize organic soil amendments and improved water retention. Yet they all likewise recognize the benefits of mineral fertilizer supplementation where key nutrients are lacking.

All four systems rely on careful agronomic management to economize on purchased inputs. They basically substitute management and either labor (dry-season labor in the case of CF and *zaï*) or land (in the case of improved fallows) for external purchased inputs, particularly nitrogen-based fertilizers. This trade-off reduces cash costs, though it imposes additional time and manpower costs in developing feasible, context-specific technologies. Knowledge-intensive, these technologies likewise require extra attention to dissemination.

TABLE 7.15 Effects of land use system on soil physical properties after eight years of improved fallow–crop rotations at Msekera, Chipata-Zambia, 1998

Land use system	Average infiltration rate (mm/min)	Average cumulative water intake after 3 hours (mm)	Average water stored in 70 cm root zone at 8 weeks after planting (mm)	Average penetrometer resistance at 40 cm soil depth (Mpa)	Average water stable aggregates >2.00 mm (%)
Sesbania sesban	4.4a	210.6ab	235.4a	2.2c	83.3a
Cajanus cajan	5.2a	235.8a	222.7b	2.9b	80.8a
Natural fallows	5.3a	247.9a	209.5c	2.9b	65.7b
Continuous M + F	3.1b	142.0bc	208.8c	3.9a	65.6b
Continuous M – F	2.1c	103.4c	217.3b	3.2b	61.2a
Mean	4.0	187.9	218.7	3.1	71.5
SED	0.5	36.0	7.9	0.2	3.1

SOURCE: Chirwa et al. (2004).

NOTES: Means in a column followed by the same letter or letters are not significantly different at $P \leq .05$ based on Duncan's multiple range test. M + F, maize plus fertilizer; M – F, maize without fertilizer; Mpa, megapascals; SED, standard error of the difference between sample means.

TABLE 7.16 Nutrient balances of improved fallows at Msekera Research Station, following eight years of fallow–crop rotation, 1998–2002 (kg/ha)

Soil management system	Nitrogen balance			Phosphorus balance			Potassium balance		
	1998	1999	2002	1998	1999	2002	1998	1999	2002
Cajanus[a]	44	17	84	21	8	33	37	9	27
Sesbania[a]	47	19	110	39	24	32	−20	−25	−20
Fertilized maize	70	54	48	14	12	12	−56	−52	−65
Unfertilized maize	−20	−17	−22	−2	−1	−2	−31	−30	−38

SOURCE: Mafongoya et al. (2005).
[a]Two-year fallows.

All four of the case studies relied on heavy farmer involvement in technology development and dissemination. Although large commercial farmers launched Zambia's CF initiative, small farmers initiated the technology development and extension of the Burkina Faso *zaï*. Although researchers initiated work on improved fallows, they developed the practices in close collaboration with farmers, starting with the initial diagnostic work. After short on-station trials, researchers moved quickly to on-farm testing, including farmer-managed and farmer-designed trials. From the discussion of improved fallow development in Zambia it is clear that farmer experimentation resulted in significant changes to the portfolio of recommended improved fallow practices.

All four efforts have proven vulnerable to irregular and episodic flows of external financial and technical support. In each case, entrepreneurial team leaders have cobbled together support from shifting coalitions of donors, NGOs, church groups, and government agencies. Although the improved fallow work carried out by ICRAF has enjoyed modest but relatively stable core funding over 15 years, even it has not been immune from the vagaries of project-supported NGO support. The wind-up of a key NGO agroforestry project in 2003 led to a 25 percent fall in the number of farmers planting improved fallows in Eastern Zambia (see Figure 7.4). Similarly, a large one-year infusion of food-for-work money led to a temporary spike in CF basins dug in Zambia during that same season (see Table 7.2). Not until 2007 did one of the four, Zambia's CF team, receive large-scale long-term funding. Meanwhile, the other three groups continue to operate under more modest, often piecemeal, financing. As a result of patchwork funding and scattered pockets of project activities, the long-term data required for monitoring adoption and fertility impacts over time remain meager.[26]

---

26. Perhaps because of the research orientation of their ICRAF promoters and because of their relatively stable core budget support, the improved fallows have been documented most carefully. See, for example, Chirwa et al. (2004), Mafongoya et al. (2005), and Ajayi et al. (2007).

TABLE 7.17 Contrasts and similarities in the four soil fertility case studies

	Zaï planting pits, Burkina Faso	*Conservation farming, Zambia*	*Improved fallows, Eastern Zambia*	*Improved fallows, Western Kenya*
Stimulus to action	Drought Deforestation Declining soil fertility	Declining soil fertility Rising fuel and mineral fertilizer prices	Declining soil fertility Rising mineral fertilizer prices	Declining soil fertility Population pressure
Initial innovators	Small farmers	Large farmers	Researchers	Researchers
Supporters	NGOs Government extension staff	Cotton companies NGOs Government extension staff	Farmer testers NGOs Government extension staff	NGOs Government extension staff
Strategy for improving soil fertility				
Increasing nitrogen	Manure Urea	Leguminous crop rotations Permanent leguminous trees Mineral fertilizer	Two-year leguminous shrub fallows	Three-month leguminous shrub fallows
Increasing phosphorous	Mineral fertilizer	Mineral fertilizer	Rock phosphates	Rock phosphates
Increasing potassium	Mineral fertilizer	Mineral fertilizer	Mineral fertilizer	Mineral fertilizer
Increasing SOM	Compost Manure	Crop residue retention in permanent planting basins and rip lines	Leaf litter	Leaf litter Biomass transfer
Increasing water infiltration and retention	Planting pits Root channels Termite tunnels SOM buildup	Planting basins and rip lines Root channels SOM buildup	Root channels SOM buildup	Root channels SOM buildup
Addressing peak-season labor constraints	Dry season land preparation	Dry season land preparation	None	None
Crops evaluated	Sorghum Millet	Maize Cotton Soybeans, cowpeas	Maize	Maize

NOTE: NGO, nongovernmental organization; SOM, soil organic matter.

Early indicators appear promising. Yet dissemination efforts for most of the technologies discussed in this chapter remain in their early stages. Only the developers of Burkina Faso's *zaï* have actively disseminated their technology for more than a decade. In spite of short timelines and modest budgets, each technology has attracted a core of spontaneous adopters. The most prominent of these are the farmer-innovators launching the Burkina Faso *zaï* and the Zambian cotton farmers, who have consistently paid for their own inputs but practice CF because it is agronomically well suited to their needs. Because many of the other early testers have benefited from project-supplied inputs and extension support, it is unclear how many project-supported adherents will continue these practices once external support is withdrawn. Given the short time spans to date and the long-term nature of soil fertility investments, each of these four activities will require ongoing monitoring to see how soil fertility profiles and adoption trajectories progress over time.

Policy Implications

Improving Agronomic Practices

These four case studies all highlight the significant gains available from improved agronomic practices. The CF and *zaï* technologies explicitly aim to capture available yield gains of 1–2 percent per day from early planting. Hence their focus is on relieving peak-season labor bottlenecks, common under rainfed hand-hoe agriculture, by redeploying land preparation work to the dry season. Optimal timing of planting and weeding, optimal plant spacing, and optimal placement of fertilizer in close proximity to the plant all increase output. In all four of the case studies, mulching and crop residue management help control weeds, minimize water run-off, and improve soil organic matter. Crop rotations and controlled fallows with nitrogen-fixing plants improve soil fertility. Supplementation with manure improves soil fertility and organic content. In various combinations, the technologies reviewed in this chapter have applied these agronomic tools to craft improved soil fertility management packages in four different settings.

In the past, most agricultural research in Africa has focused on developing and delivering yield-enhancing input packages such as new crop varieties, new seeds, fertilizer, and pesticides. The four case studies reviewed in this chapter suggest that increased attention to agronomic practices may offer equally high productivity gains. But achieving these gains will require increased attention to agronomic management in both research and extension.

Extension of Management-Intensive Technologies

All of the technologies described in this chapter offer ways of raising efficiency through improved farm management. The agronomic gains achieved by these four technologies rely on careful management both during the cropping season and in the dry season. As a result, they typically take longer to disseminate and assimilate, leading to slower adoption than input packages of improved seeds and fertilizer. The case studies uniformly suggest that knowledge-intensive technologies such as these require greater attention to extension than does the typical release of improved inputs and plant varieties.

The promotional efforts reviewed here make frequent use of lead farmers and farmer groups of various sorts to help lower contact costs and provide on-the-ground support for farmers. All of the case studies involved efforts to build institutional capacity for technology development, adaptation, and extension. In the face of rapidly eroding African extension services, future work will need to build on these lessons and continue to experiment with effective means of improving extension for management-intensive farming technologies (Franzel, Cooper, and Denning 2001; Barrett et al. 2002).

Farmer Involvement in Technology Development

Farmers led in developing the CF and *zaï* technologies. The improved fallow technology likewise depended heavily on farmer-designed innovations. Indeed, the Zambian improved fallow experience offers a good example of how scientific agricultural research can systematically involve farmers in technology development. Given the heterogeneity of agroecological conditions and household resource constraints prevailing among African agriculturalists, farmer involvement clearly improves prospects for developing effective, feasible technologies well adapted to farmers' local conditions (Katanga et al. 2007). Yet promoting farmer innovations—and ensuring that such innovations reach researchers, extension staff, and other farmers—poses a key challenge for development practitioners.

Given the diversity of farming conditions prevailing in rural Africa, the processes described here for involving farmers in technology development and testing may well prove more readily transferable than the individual technologies themselves. The process descriptions in these four case studies offer a range of strategies for successfully integrating farmers into technology development, testing, and dissemination.

Whole-Farm versus Commodity-Based Research

Most agricultural research systems organize technology development around specific commodities. Yet the case studies in this chapter suggest that cross-cutting research on fundamental issues, such as soil fertility, may provide a necessary complement to the more prevalent commodity-based research. Labor constraints affect the timing of key operations in all crop and livestock activities. Soil fertility depends on crop rotations, residue management, soil amendments, and crop–livestock interactions. Altering land or labor allocations in one crop or task affects allocations to other farming activities. Of the cases examined here, the CF team has adopted the most integrated whole-farm approach—including work on cash crops, marketed food crops, food security crops, legumes, and livestock. The diagnostic tools and close farmer involvement in development of the Zambian improved fallows likewise offer useful examples of ways to integrate a whole-farm perspective in technology design (Franzel, Phiri, and Kwesiga 2002).

Organic versus Mineral Fertilizers

Discussions of soil fertility in Africa frequently focus on mineral fertilizers (Borlaug 1996; McPherson and Rabbinge 2006; Sachs 2006; Yara International 2007). Yet proponents of a doubly green revolution highlight the virtues of organic nutrients (Conway 1999; Pretty 2000). Straddling both points of view, the African Union ministers of agriculture declared "fertilizer, from both inorganic and organic sources, a strategic commodity without borders" at the 2006 Africa Fertilizer Summit in Abuja (African Union 2006, 2). But in practice, most governments rely primarily on mineral fertilizers to address soil fertility constraints. Many favor fertilizer subsidies despite the heavy expense and generally poor performance of past programs (Morris et al. 2007). In Africa, high petrochemical prices, high transport costs, small markets, and poor fertilizer distribution networks translate into the highest fertilizer prices in the world, often double those found in Asia (Yanggen et al. 1998). Although fertilizer output gains in some African settings and for some crops (particularly maize and rice) are comparable to those achieved in Asia and Latin America, Africa's predominantly rainfed agriculture makes fertilizer application generally riskier there than elsewhere. As a result of higher fertilizer costs and more variable returns under rainfed conditions, optimal fertilizer application rates in most of Africa are lower than in irrigated Asian agriculture, where better water control and lower fertilizer prices make fertilizer use more profitable and less risky (Morris et al. 2007). Weak rural credit systems in Africa fuel further interest in organic and management-intensive alternatives to mineral fertilizers.

The case studies in this chapter explore a range of alternatives to petrochemical nitrogen fertilizer—alternatives including manure, leguminous crop rotations, leguminous fallows, and permanent nitrogen-fixing trees. The improved fallow teams point to rock phosphates as a potential alternative to chemical phosphates. None, however, offers an organic substitute for potassium fertilizer.

In spite of the often strident "either/or" tone of many fertilizer debates, the soil fertility work presented in this chapter highlights the complementarities between organic and inorganic fertilizer. CF proponents recommend a combination of leguminous nitrogen-fixing crop rotations, soil organic matter buildup, and water harvesting that together improve plant responsiveness to low but strategic doses of mineral fertilizer. Research on *zaï* planting pits highlights the gains from combining organic soil amendments such as compost and manure with mineral fertilizer. Technical research on improved fallows also emphasizes the benefits of combining organic and inorganic fertilizers. Biologically produced nitrogen—from leguminous fallows, crop rotations, or bulk transfer of organic matter—decreases the quantity of nitrogen fertilizer required. Organic soil amendments—which improve soil structure, soil organic matter, water retention, and cation exchange—simultaneously enhance the effectiveness of supplementary applications of nitrogen, phosphorus, and potassium fertilizers.[27] The message emerging from these case studies seems to be that a balanced approach to soil fertility management may prove most effective in many African settings.

Looking forward, future work on soil fertility management seems likely to benefit from an expanded focus on the complementarities between organic and inorganic fertilizers in improving and sustaining soil fertility over time (Ajayi et al. 2007). African governments and donors currently spend massive sums on fertilizer subsidies. Yet they rarely match these resources with the complementary efforts required to develop and disseminate agronomic practices that will improve soil structure, soil organic matter, water retention capacity, and soil biotic activity in ways that enhance the effectiveness of mineral fertilizers. To capture these synergies will require a more balanced future approach to soil fertility management and research.

---

27. See, for example, Padwick (1983); Bekunda, Bationo, and Ssali (1997); Kauffman, Koning, and Heerink (2000); Vanlauwe et al. (2001); Chirwa et al. (2004); Akinnifesi et al. (2007); Marenya and Barrett (2009); and Sauer and Tchale (2009).

PART III

Lessons for the Future

8 Lessons from Past Successes

STEVEN HAGGBLADE

Contrasting Cases

The case studies reviewed in Part II of this book offer a series of important contrasts. Motors of change and key actors differ across settings, even sometimes in the same country or for the same management practices being promoted. To help summarize from this diverse experience, it is helpful to classify the case studies into four broad groups.[1]

1. Comprehensive Public Support Packages: Maize and Cotton. The maize and cotton case studies (Chapters 3 and 4) chronicle progress in Africa's leading food staple and cash crop. In spite of obvious differences between export-oriented cotton production and domestically marketed maize, promoters of these two commodities have followed the same general model. Initially both relied on a comprehensive package of public support for technology development, input supply, and guaranteed markets. After several decades, both abandoned government marketing monopolies in favor of gradual market liberalization. Although intervention strategies and performance have wavered in recent years, both promotional efforts have propelled production surges lasting decades.

2. Publicly Funded Technology Research: Cassava. The multiple production surges across Africa's cassava belt constitute a second category unto themselves. All have emanated from the same initial impulse: the publicly funded breeding research started at the Amani Research Station in Tanganyika and completed at the International Institute of Tropical Agriculture (IITA) with the release of the Tropical Manioc Selection (TMS) cassava varieties beginning in the late 1970s (Chapter 2). Invigorating cassava breeding lines across Africa, the resulting productivity gains have triggered production surges in multiple locations across Africa's cassava belt. In contrast with the input-intensive cotton

---

1. This categorization and the ensuing case study synthesis draw on input received from agricultural stakeholders in a series of Africa consultations (see Chapter 1, Table 1.2). To give the reader a flavor of these workshop deliberations, Appendix 8A reproduces the final statement from the Pretoria Conference, the first of the Africa stakeholder consultations.

and maize technologies, Africa's smallholder cassava production has required no annual purchased inputs, only an initial supply of improved cuttings. Neither did it attract large-scale government marketing support until the early 2000s, when Nigeria's presidential cassava initiative focused continentwide attention on the potential for cassava processing and marketing. In spite of this high-profile government stance, commercial growth of cassava markets has depended primarily on private sector initiatives.

3. Regional Successes: Dairying and Horticulture. The smaller regional success stories in dairying and horticulture (Chapters 5 and 6) form a third logical grouping. The clearest successes in this category centered in Kenya, under identical ecosystems and under the same government. Yet the motors of growth differed completely. While advances in Kenya's dairy sector drew on heavy government involvement in technology development, regulation, and marketing, the export horticulture boom emerged largely through private initiatives undertaken with benign government neglect, offering a clear contrast for members of the analytical team to explore.

4. Alternate Responses to Common Natural Resource Pressures. The four sustainable soil fertility management case studies document two pairs of responses to growing pressure on soil fertility (Chapter 7). In each case, similar technologies emerged in different locations.

With the planting basins in Burkina Faso and Zambia, private rather than public sector actors led technology development efforts. In Burkina Faso, experimentation by small farmers led to on-farm technology development and even to early private sector extension efforts, although later nongovernmental organizations (NGOs) and the government also supported extension efforts. In Zambia, in contrast, progressive commercial farmers led the charge. Having explored the benefits of minimum tillage on their large-scale mechanized farms, they explicitly set out to develop comparably viable low-tillage methods for small-scale hand-hoe and animal traction farmers. As in Burkina Faso, after initial experimentation in the private sector, NGOs and the goverment began to support these extension efforts.

In contrast, public sector researchers initiated experimentation and extension efforts on the improved fallow technology. But they actively solicited farmer input and feedback. In fact, farmer-managed experiments led to two important changes in the technology package that researchers ultimately promoted. Together, researchers and farmers disseminated the technology through a series of on-farm trials and demonstrations conducted in collaboration with national extension systems and a network of NGOs.

The following discussion more fully explores the common themes emerging from these case studies. To summarize and organize the key findings, the discussion returns to the Decisionmaking Environment–Action–Results (DE-A-R) framework (see Chapter 1, Figure 1.4) to highlight the instruments, actors, and results that have proven critical in settings where Africa's agricultural systems have performed well.

Changes in the Farmers' Decisionmaking Environment (DE)

Levers driving change in all of these case studies have concentrated on the farmers' decisionmaking environment. Given that farmers must ultimately implement any change necessary to increase on-farm productivity and output, successful promotional efforts must induce farmers to change their behavior. Typically, promotional efforts influence farmers' conduct in one of two ways. Either they expand farmers' productive capacity—through improved technology, more productive assets, or better forms of organization—or they alter farmers' incentives. Sometimes they do both.

Expanded Productive Capacity

PRODUCTIVITY GAINS.   Overwhelmingly, the case studies reviewed in Part II of this book suggest that successful past efforts in African agriculture have relied on enhancing farm productivity through improved agricultural technology (Table 8.1). In all of the case studies under review, production and farm income growth have depended on the adoption of some form of new technology. Conventional breeding programs enabled long-term productivity surges in the maize, cassava, cotton, and dairy studies. Horticulture export growth required farmers to adopt specified varieties of seeds as well as certified pest and disease control systems. Access to complementary inputs such as fertilizer, pesticides, fungicides, and livestock health and breeding services played an important role in the maize, cotton, horticulture, and dairy case studies.

Improved agronomic practices can also effectively boost farm productivity. In several of the cases under review, improved farm management proved more important than new seeds and new packages of purchased inputs. Consider the planting basin systems in Zambia and Burkina Faso. Although both involve strategic application of mineral fertilizer, manure, and improved seeds, their centerpiece involves dry-season land preparation under minimum-tillage management systems that emphasize crop residue retention and soil organic matter buildup. The Zambian conservation farming system likewise incorporates crop rotations using soybeans, cowpeas, pigeon peas, velvet beans, and other legumes to build up soil nitrogen. Together, these dry-season minimum-tillage packages enable improved timing of key on-farm operations, better moisture retention, improved fertilizer responsiveness, and long-term soil fertility maintenance. Among Zambian smallholders, these management practices alone increase maize yields by 1.1 tons per hectare and cotton output by 400 kilograms per hectare (Chapter 7, Table 7.5). To achieve these agronomic gains, farmers must alter their agricultural calendar significantly by moving heavy

TABLE 8.1 Case study summaries

	Maize	Cotton	Cassava
Region	East and Southern Africa	West Africa	West Africa
Who initiated change?			
Key instigators	Commercial farmers Government breeders Government policymakers Parastatal marketing companies	Donor and national governments Parastatal marketing companies	IITA National agricultural research systems Rural artisans
Supporting actors	Private seed companies	Farmer organizations	Private oil companies NGOs
What interventions triggered change?			
Expanded productive capacity			
Technology	***	**	***
Input supply	***	***	*
Investments in asset base		*	
Improved incentives			
Political lobbying	***	*	
Output markets	***	***	
Market outlets	Domestic	Export	Domestic
Were large recurrent public subsidies involved in sustaining smallholder growth?	Yes	Yes	No

NOTES: ***, critical interventions; **, important activities; *, supporting activities. Blank cells indicate no significant interventions. ICRAF, World Agroforestry Centre; IITA, International Institute of Tropical Agriculture; NGO, nongovernmental organization.

Case studies

| | Cassava | Horticulture | Dairy | Sustainable soil fertility management | |
				Planting basins	Improved fallows
	Southern Africa	Kenya, Côte d'Ivoire	Kenya	Burkina Faso, Zambia	Kenya, Zambia
	National agricultural research systems IITA	Private traders	Commercial farmers Government policymakers Parastatals	Private farmers	ICRAF
	NGOs			Government extension NGOs Private cotton company	Farmer researchers NGOs Government extension
	*** *	* **	*** *** **	*** * ***	*** * ***
			***		
		***	**		
	Domestic No	Export No	Domestic Yes	Domestic No	Domestic No

land preparation to the slack season, thus freeing up labor for more timely planting and weeding during the peak agricultural season, at the start of the rains. In rainfed, hand-hoe agriculture, where peak-season labor constraints typically limit farmers' incomes, experience with maize and cotton farming suggests that farmers lose 1–2 percent in yield for each day they delay planting (Chapter 7). Hence the significant returns to improved management and timely planting.

The improved fallow systems likewise seek productivity gains through changes in farmers' agronomic practices. These involve managed fallows of up to two years followed by two to three seasons of maize or other staple food production. Using carefully selected varieties of leguminous shrubs during the managed fallow period, this special form of crop rotation enables farmers to supplement soil nitrogen levels biologically, thus reducing reliance on mineral fertilizers. In doing so, farmers achieve annual equivalent maize yields of 2.8 tons per hectare without purchased fertilizer (Chapter 7, Table 7.13). Essentially, this system enables farmers to substitute improved management for purchased fertilizer.

Work on cassava and cotton similarly indicates that improved agronomic practices can provide a powerful complement to new varietal development. Timely planting and weeding of cassava plots easily double yields of even the best new cassava varieties when compared with normal farming practices (Barratt et al. 2006). In cotton production, timely planting, weeding, and pest surveillance contribute to significant output gains (see Chapters 4 and 7). As these examples illustrate, improved farm management practices, although more expensive to disseminate than new packages of fertilizer and seeds, can generate significant on-farm productivity gains.

LONG-TERM RESEARCH COMMITMENTS.   Though powerful, new technology development and dissemination take time. Perhaps the most striking finding from these case studies is that timelines for effective research must be measured in decades rather than years. The original maize breeding programs that led to the development of the transformational Zimbabwean maize hybrid SR52 required 28 years (Chapter 3). Africa's highly successful cassava breeding programs, begun at the Amani Research Station in Tanganyika and completed by scientists at IITA, spanned 40 years and required 25 years of active breeding— 18 prior to World War II and 7 during the 1970s—to develop the breakthrough TMS varieties. Since their release in the late 1970s, TMS varieties have sparked breakthroughs in dozens of country breeding programs across the continent (Chapter 2). With a similarly long-term focus, cotton breeders at sister stations across West Africa have produced a steady stream of new cotton varieties over the past five decades (Chapter 4).

Because pests and diseases evolve continuously and rapidly, successful research programs cannot risk resting on their laurels. Worldwide, between one-third and one-half of all crop research focuses on maintenance breeding aimed at stabilizing yields in the face of ever-evolving pests and diseases (World Bank 2007a). Simply to keep pace with constantly mutating viruses, pests, and diseases and maintain yields at their current level requires substantial annual investments in research. To raise productivity in the face of rapidly evolving pests and diseases requires still greater research investments.

In Africa, recent problems with the cassava mosaic virus (CMV) illustrate these dangers most vividly. In the first half of the 1990s, a virulent mutation of the CMV destroyed 500 varieties of cassava and over half of Uganda's cassava crop in less than five years. Fortunately, in this instance the availability of alternative improved varieties, introduced through crash testing and seed multiplication programs, permitted the restoration of cassava production by the end of the decade. Only an ongoing, regionally coordinated breeding pipeline, developed and maintained over time, enabled this swift and effective response during the CMV crisis (Otim-Nape et al. 1997, 1998; University of Greenwich 2000).

This collective experience suggests that policymakers cannot consider ongoing funding for agricultural research an optional expenditure. Without a continuous stream of new technology available to farmers, plant and animal pests and diseases will evolve unchallenged and human agriculture will not simply stall but decline—sometimes spectacularly. Sustained agricultural research is therefore not a luxury but rather a necessity if human agricultural systems are to advance.

Improved Incentives

MARKETS.   In roughly half of the case studies reviewed, an explicit focus on market development played a critical role in enabling agricultural growth. The importance of market development emerges most clearly in the case of export crops, such as cotton and horticulture. In the case of francophone Africa's cotton exports, publicly supported marketing companies provided a guaranteed market for smallholder cotton farmers (Chapter 4). In contrast, private traders led the drive to develop and exploit lucrative export markets for horiticultural producers in Kenya and Côte d'Ivoire (Chapter 5). The increased frequency of airline flights and the consequently improved availability of air freight made possible by the rise of Kenya's tourist industry played an important role in making the export of fresh vegetables viable.

In domestic maize markets, publicly run marketing agencies played a key role in stimulating early production growth. The pervasive establishment of parastatal grain marketing companies—in Kenya, Malawi, Zambia, and Zimbabwe —enabled governments to guarantee maize prices, often at subsidized pan-territorial prices (Chapter 3). In the dairy industry, public marketing agencies have typically favored formal sector dairy processing while ignoring or even actively suppressing informal raw milk markets in urban areas (Chapter 6). In Kenya, for example, legal prohibitions restricted raw milk sales in urban areas. When government authorities lifted these restrictions, raw milk sales surged, and raw milk now accounts for 60 percent of the milk volumes marketed in urban areas.

In contrast, technology-led surges in cassava production throughout Africa's tropical belt have stimulated subsequent growth of local markets for cassava and cassava-derived products. In most cases, private processors and traders have spearheaded these developments. In West Africa, private sector development of mechanized grating and processing technology has been instrumental in reducing labor bottlenecks during processing as well as in developing convenience foods and increasing the shelf life of cassava-based products (Chapter 2). In Southern Africa, marketing has tended to focus either on fresh cassava, as in Malawi, or on trade in dried chips for use in composite flours and livestock feeds, as in Madagascar and Zambia. Unlike maize marketing, which has attracted highly interventionist public policies, cassava marketing has remained predominantly the province of the private sector. Not until the early 2000s, with the highly publicized work of Nigeria's presidential cassava initiative, did African governments begin to look at cassava markets seriously.

SUBSIDIES.   Some of the production surges examined in this book have depended on heavy government subsidies in both input and output markets. Particularly in their early phases, the comprehensive public support packages for maize, cotton, and dairy development involved significant subsidies (Chapters 3, 4, and 6). At their peak in the mid-1980s, Zambia's maize subsidies accounted for 17 percent of total government spending (Chapter 3). There, as elsewhere, these massive subsidies proved fiscally unsustainable. Under heavy financial and donor pressure, all four of the countries reviewed in Chapter 3 disbanded their maize marketing subsidies as part of sweeping structural adjustment programs. Subsequent liberalization efforts have proceeded in fits and starts, resulting in varying levels of private sector involvement in maize markets. Francophone Africa has likewise begun to modify and partially privatize its earlier public sector model of full-service support for cotton production and marketing (Chapter 4). Under similar pressure from mounting losses, the Kenyan government withdrew its subsidies for livestock services as well as its price controls on processed milk beginning in the late 1980s (Chapter 6).

In contrast, the case studies on cassava, horticulture, and sustainable soil fertility management involved no recurrent input or marketing subsidies. The cassava and improved fallow cases, however, did depend on public spending for technology development. Apart from these investment costs, the governments involved have largely refrained from recurrent subsidies on inputs or outputs in these sectors. Because the case studies on both cassava and the sustainable soil fertility management technologies reviewed in Chapters 2 and 7 revolve around low external input technologies, the question of input subsidies typically does not arise. In cassava output markets, governments have likewise largely resisted the highly interventionist tendencies that have characterized their involvement with maize (Chapter 2). High-value horticulture production, despite its high input costs, has avoided recurrent input subsidies to producers, largely because the private sector rather than the government has initiated and organized these efforts (Chapter 5).

In general, the case studies reviewed in Part II of this book suggest a clear role for government investment in *public goods* that the private sector will not supply. Research in open-pollinating crops, control of contagious animal diseases, and road construction and maintenance all constitute classic public goods requiring public support. However, the case for publicly financed recurrent subsidies on *private inputs*—such as seed, fertilizer, and artificial insemination services—is far less clear. Private fertilizer dealers, seed retailers, and veterinarians are willing to enter these markets where a minimum threshold of commercial demand permits. But they withdraw in the presence of government subsidies with which they cannot compete (Chapters 3 and 6).[2]

Subsidies, nonetheless, remain politically popular. On economic grounds, some agricultural specialists advocate temporary subsidies as a way of kick-starting fledgling input supply industries and enabling them to rapidly achieve minimum economies of scale. Others justify permanent subsidies on welfare grounds, for remote areas or low-income groups, or as a means of correcting for negative externalities associated with soil fertility depletion (see Morris et al. 2007; Yara International 2007).

Input subsidy programs of the type reviewed in this book have generally succeeded in expanding input use—though at a very high cost. On the ground, high administrative costs, mistargeting, late delivery, and rent seeking have plagued many of these programs. Given limited agricultural budgets and the high cost of subsidy programs, subsidies for private inputs risk squeezing public funds required to finance research, extension, roads, and other clearly public goods required to get agriculture moving. Thus, the opportunity cost of input subsidies may be very high.[3] Reviewing evidence through the early 2000s, a recent study of fertilizer subsidy programs in Africa has concluded that "the weight of empirical evidence now show(s) that fertilizer subsidies are likely to be inefficient, costly and fiscally unsustainable" (Morris et al. 2007, 3).

Looking back, the maize, cotton, and dairy case studies reviewed in this volume generally confirm the difficulties associated with the old-style para-

---

2. Studies of recent fertilizer subsidy programs in Malawi and Zambia estimate displacement of commercial fertilizer sales in the range of 30–40 percent of the volume of the subsidized fertilizer distributed (Dorward et al. 2008; Minde et al. 2008).

3. In recent years, fertilizer subsidies accounted for between one-third and one-half of government agricultural budget allocations in Malawi and Zambia (Govereh et al. 2006; Haggblade 2007; Dorward et al. 2008). Together, subsidies on fertilizer and crop marketing accounted for over 60 percent of government agricultural spending in the two countries (Minde et al. 2008).

statal input subsidy programs of the 1970s and 1980s.[4] In all of the instances reviewed, agricultural subsidies have proven politically difficult to phase out. At the same time, they have proven too expensive for governments to afford over long periods of time. In the cases reviewed in this book, only acute fiscal crises have enabled governments to muster the political will necessary to suspend their politically popular subsidy programs. In practice, subsidies on private goods such as fertilizer, seeds, and other purchased inputs have proven difficult to contain and to sustain.

The Two Together: New Technology and Market Outlets

The case studies in this volume demonstrate that farmers respond with alacrity when clearly superior new technology arrives together with financially attractive market outlets. But one without the other may not suffice, as the Nigerian cassava experience demonstates most clearly. Although the TMS cassava varieties became available in 1977, farmers did not adopt them in large numbers until seven years later, when the Nigerian government abandoned their policies favoring cheap cereal imports and allowed the value of the naira to fall from its previously overvalued level (Chapter 2). When the playing field leveled, from 1984 onward, cassava production became more commercially attractive and farmers rapidly expanded production of TMS varieties. Similarly, the 1994 CFAF devaluation triggered a major shift in incentives for cotton farmers in Mali. As farmgate cotton prices doubled, farmers rapidly scaled up their cotton production using the technology packages developed for smallholder export farmers (Chapter 4).

Kenya's raw milk markets similarly illustrate the results from synchronizing regulatory incentives and productivity gains. During the 1970s and 1980s, despite the widespread availability of highly productive new dairy breeds, the Kenyan government officially banned raw milk sales in urban areas. Once it suspended these restrictions, with the milk market liberalization of 1992, Kenya's productive small-scale raw milk producers flocked to urban raw milk markets, where the marketed volumes of raw milk increased significantly (Chapter 6).

The ebbs and flows of maize production in East and Southern Africa likewise demonstrate the impact of combining new technology with improved (albeit artificially inflated) market incentives. Under subsidized input and output prices, farmers expanded areas planted with hybrid maize packages, and national maize production surged. Yet when financially overstretched governments withdrew these subsidy packages, area planted and national maize production fell back to lower levels, often abruptly (Chapter 3).

---

4. In response to the inefficiencies of the parastatal subsidy systems, a new generation of input promotion programs—dubbed "smart" or "market-smart" subsidies—is currently being field tested. The forward-looking discussion in Chapter 9 summarizes early findings from these redesign efforts.

Key Actors (A)

The Government

The provision of key public goods, particularly government-financed agricultural research, has proven directly responsible for triggering growth in three-fourths of the case studies reviewed in this volume. Indirectly, the availability of public roads, communications, and transport facilities has contributed in all of them. Agricultural research on open-pollinating crops and vegetatively propagated plants is a classic public good. Because farmers can reproduce these seeds and planting materials free of charge year after year, the private sector is unable to charge farmers an annual fee for using these new, more productive technologies. As a result, private firms routinely underinvest in research on improved varieties of cassava, sweet potatoes, bananas, rice, and open-pollinating maize. Not surprisingly, African research on cassava and open-pollinating maize has all been publicly funded (Chapters 2 and 3). Likewise, control of contagious livestock diseases requires collective action, which is often most easily coordinated in the public arena.

A stable exchange rate and open trade policies have proven instrumental in the growth of export horticulture and cotton (Chapters 4 and 5). Fluidly functioning domestic markets require year-round passable roads, effective communications networks, and a stable policy environment. Private investors have proven willing to invest in national cell phone networks, where public policy permits. But roads and policies affecting business investments and behavior remain squarely in the public domain. As a result, active public involvement with and commitment to agricultural growth have proven central to Africa's past agricultural successes.

Farmers

PRODUCTION RESPONSES. These case studies suggest that farmers respond readily when improved technology coincides with readily accessible market outlets. They prove particularly responsive when both inputs and output markets are guaranteed, as in the cotton, maize, dairy, and horticulture examples (Chapters 3–6). In some instances, farmers participate directly in technology diffusion as well, as in the cases of the farmer extension under Burkina Faso's *zaï* system and the widespread farmer-to-farmer dissemination of TMS cassava varieties.

Agronomic changes, however, prove more difficult to effect. Conservation farming, the *zaï* planting basins, and improved fallows, in particular, require significant changes in farmer behavior (Chapter 7). To ensure timely planting, conservation farming and *zaï* require dry-season land preparation at a time when most hand-hoe farmers are used to resting or pursuing nonfarm occupations. Improved fallows require new crop rotations and long-term plot management over a four- to five-year cycle. Early data from both of these technologies suggest that adoption rates have proven slowest for these management-intensive production packages. Behavioral change likewise requires greater focus on extension support than does dissemination of new input packages, which raise productivity while maintaining conventional management practices. Nonetheless, the productivity gains from improved farm management frequently prove substantial, even for farmers using conventional technology. Under new input packages, improved agronomic practices boost productivity increments even further (Chapter 7).

POLITICAL LOBBYING.   In some instances, African farmers have successfully shaped their policy environment through political lobbying. Among the present case studies, effective lobbying by maize, dairy, and cotton farmers proved instrumental in influencing the design and development of government support programs. Dairy farmers in Kenya successfully lobbied for input subsidies and price controls through the Kenya Cooperative Creameries (Chapter 6). Similarly, early settler farmers in Northern and Southern Rhodesia successfully lobbied for price supports for white maize farmers. These supports persisted until independence, when they were extended to all farmers (Chapter 3). More recently, organized lobbying by Malian cotton farmers played a critical role in shaping reform efforts in cotton production and marketing during the 1990s (Chapter 4).

In a handful of instances, farmers have also successfully lobbied for publicly funded agricultural research. In two of the case studies investigated, powerful commercial farm lobbies laid claim to government resources—for maize breeding in Southern Rhodesia (now Zimbabwe) and among Kenyan dairy farmers. As these examples suggest, farm lobbies can, in some instances, prove highly effective. However, to do so they require effective organization and political access, ingredients not always present among the majority of today's African smallholder farmers.

RESEARCH.   Farmers innovate, as these studies and a large body of ongoing empirical work have emphasized (Sumberg and Okali 1997; Reij and Waters-Bayer 2001). Examples from this book emerge most clearly among the sustainable soil fertility management systems described in Chapter 7. Large commercial farmers spearheaded the development of conservation farming in Zambia. Small-scale farmers launched the *zaï* planting basins in Burkina Faso. And farmer-designed, farmer-managed trials of improved fallows contributed two major changes to the recommended research system package. These experiences underline the important potential gains to be achieved through farmers' involvement in agricultural research and extension.

Private Agribusiness

Private agribusiness has proven decisive in driving change in a number of these case studies. In the case of horticultural exports, private traders provided the driving force for market development, input supply, and market organization

(Chapter 5). Cassava processing in West Africa likewise remains the province of a broad array of private firms. These firms have contributed to the development and adaptation of various grating, milling, pressing, fermenting, and toasting processes, with periodic input from public research institutions (Chapter 2). Similarly, private seed companies have emerged in Southern and Eastern Africa to sell hybrid maize seeds (Chapter 3).

In maize markets, large private mills have dominated the liberalized era. Less appreciated but even more important for low-income consumers has been a flourishing cohort of small-scale, straight-run hammer mills, often operating as service millers (Jayne et al. 1999). Informal markets for raw milk have similarly dominated the Kenyan dairy industry since the liberalization of milk marketing in the early 1990s (Chapter 6).

Private firms have also supported research and extension efforts when they have seen direct benefits to their business. Because private seed companies can charge a premium for improved hybrid varieties, which farmers must purchase every season, most of the large private seed companies operating in Eastern and Southern Africa conduct their own research in an effort to expand their commercial repertoire of improved genetic material. In providing farmer extension support, Zambia's conservation farming offers a good example of private support for extension services (Chapter 7). Because conservation farming offers particular benefits to cotton farmers—enabling timely planting, weeding, and optimal plant populations—privately owned Dunavant Cotton contributed financial support to the Zambia National Farmers Union's Conservation Farming Unit for over a decade following its inception (Arulussa Overseas 1997; CFU 2006). However, in the case of many less valuable crops, for which private firms cannot capture the gains from their investments, farmers will continue to rely on public research and extension.

Pests and Diseases

Nonhuman actors have played key roles in many of these case studies. Over time, in Darwinian fashion, viruses and pests evolve in response to changing on-farm conditions. As farmers adopt new varieties, new pesticides, and new control measures, resistant strains of pests and viruses emerge. In response, human managers of domesticated agricultural systems must run ever faster just to keep up with the rapid mutation of agricultural pests and diseases.

Successful control of pests and diseases has formed an integral part of the long-term research programs in the cassava, maize, cotton, horticulture, and dairy studies. The cassava example vividly demonstrates the speed at which devastating diseases and pests can emerge. The accidental import of the cassava mealybug into Uganda in the late 1970s triggered a continental infestation and elicited a coordinated, highly successful Africa-wide response involving biological pest control methods (Chapter 2). With maize, gray leaf spot and other fungal diseases require the regular release of new seed varieties and fungicides.

Similarly, in the case of livestock, a key component of raising the productivity of dairy cattle revolved around developing effective tick control sytems (Chapter 6). With horticultural crops, fungal disease remains a perennial problem. Among cotton producers, the prevalence of a broad spectrum of plant pests and diseases demands labor-consuming monitoring and spraying throughout the season. For this reason, pest control has formed a central pillar of cotton promotion efforts in francophone West Africa over the past five decades (Chapter 4).

These case studies all suggest that sustainable growth in agricultural systems requires ongoing research on resistant varieties and on new pest and disease control methods. Thus, agricultural research is best viewed not as a one-time investment but rather as an ongoing process of institutionalized technology development and adaptation enabling farmers to overcome ever-evolving plant and animal pests and diseases.

Results (R)

Using the three criteria established by the analytical team to measure performance, some of the case studies proved unambiguously successful over long periods. Africa's cassava surge has expanded food availability and income for small farmers on a continental scale for over two decades without recurrent input subsidies (Chapter 2). Though more localized, Kenya's horticultural exports have likewise substantiallly boosted incomes for several hundred thousand smallholders over at least three decades (Chapter 5).

Other case studies have performed well along one or more dimensions of "success" but not along others. Africa's maize promotion efforts in East and Southern Africa succeeded in significantly raising smallholder farm productivity, output, and incomes. But because the support systems relied on massive infusions of recurrent input and output subsidies, governments proved unable to sustain them financially (Chapter 3). Table 8.2 and the following discussion summarize the case study results along all three designated dimensions of success.

Income

Output growth rates have proven impressive in many of the case studies, particularly for cassava, cotton, and Kenyan horticulture, in which production continued to grow at 6–20 percent annually for two decades or more. Despite recent dislocations and adjustments, Mali's cotton output has grown at a compound annual rate of over 8 percent per year for four and a half decades.

Likewise, all of the case studies document significant on-farm productivity gains. Whether in terms of output per cow or harvest per hectare, the physical productivity of the new crop varieties, cattle breeds, and input packages frequently exceeded 100 percent. As a result, returns to labor typically increased as well, often by 50–100 percent or more (Table 8.2).

The most lucrative activities appear to be dairy and horticulture production, judging from the available evidence on returns to land and labor. Cotton production, though widespread and highly sought after by smallholder farmers across much of Africa, generates much lower returns per person-day due to heavy labor demands at weeding, spraying, and harvesting times, coupled with depressed world prices.

These partial budgets, however, must be treated with some caution, because they fail to account for important interactions and spillovers across activities. Dairy production enhances soil fertility, improves family nutrition, and provides seasonal input financing for crop agriculture. Similarly, cotton farming finances the accumulation of productive assets that, in turn, permit significant expansion of area cropped in both cotton and food crops. The cash earnings and collateral provided by cotton contracts enable Malian cotton farmers to obtain financing for fertilizer and other inputs that, in turn, make them the most productive cereal farmers in the country.

In terms of scale, the cassava, maize, and cotton cases dominate. Both cassava and maize productivity gains have benefited over 5 million African farm households in the case study countries alone, probably double that in total, while in francophone Africa roughly 1 million farmers grow cotton each year.

Equity

Most of the case studies examined involved significant smallholder participation. Cassava promotion, improved soil fertility management, and cotton production have overwhelmingly focused on smallholders (Chapters 2, 4, and 7). Even opportunities less accessible to low-income groups, such as horticultural exports and hybrid maize packages, have seen significant rates of smallholder participation and adoption of improved input packages (Chapters 3 and 5). Detailed income distribution data from the Kenyan dairy study suggest that, proportionally, the bottom quintile of rural households benefit most from smallholder dairying income (Chapter 6, Table 6.7). Although dairy promotion efforts in pre-independence Kenya focused primarily on large-scale commercial farmers, governments since 1954 have successfully reoriented their efforts toward smallholder dairy farmers. As a result, studies of poverty dynamics in Kenya find that dairy income contributes to upward income mobility among farms of all size.

Gender outcomes suggest some common themes as well as some differences across the case studies. In terms of staple food production, the cassava and maize studies suggest that neither is primarily a woman's or a man's crop. But both suggest that as commercialization increases, so does men's involvement in production. Where cash and credit do not constrain technology adoption, women prove able to access new technology as readily as men. In the case of cassava, which requires no purchased inputs following an initial distribution

TABLE 8.2 Case study impact summary

	Income				
	Output growth during surge		Productivity gains (tons/ha)		
	Annual rate (%)	Duration (years)	New technology	Old technology	Percent change
Cassava					
Nigeria, 1984–94[c]	11	10	19.4	13.4	45
Ghana, 1986–2005	7	19	—	—	—
Malawi, 1995–2005	20	10	—	—	—
Zambia, 1987–2002	6	15	12.0	6.0	100
Maize					
Kenya, 1965–80	3.3	15	—	—	—
Malawi, 1983–93	3.1	15	2.8	0.7	272
Zambia, 1970–89	1.9	19	—	—	—
Zimbabwe, 1980–89	1.8	9	—	—	46
Cotton					
Mali, 1960–73	20.0	13	0.8	0.2	270
Mali, 1960–2006	8.7	46	1.0	0.2	332
Other francophone Africa	—	—	—	—	—
Horticulture[e]					
Kenya, 1975–90	9.0	15	2,657	221	1,102
Côte d'Ivoire, 1961–80	6.3	19	—	—	—
Dairy[f]					
Kenya, 1963–2006	3.7	43	2,215	600	269
Ethiopia, 1992–2006	6.6	14	784	134	485
Improved soil fertility management					
Burkina Faso: Zaï	n.a.	n.a.	0.5	0.1	310
Zambia: CF basins, maize	n.a.	n.a.	3.1	1.3	128
Zambia: CF ripper, maize	n.a.	n.a.	2.3	1.5	51
Zambia: Improved fallows	n.a.	n.a.	2.8	1.0	180
Kenya: Improved fallows	n.a.	n.a.	—	—	—

SOURCE: Chapters 2–7.

NOTES: —, information not available; CF, conservation farming; CFU, Conservation Farming Unit; n.a., not applicable.

[a]Valued in 2005 U.S. dollars.

[b]Maize: percentage of area planted to improved seed varieties. All other cases: percentage of beneficiaries who are smallholders.

[c]Dates indicate the years of the output surge evaluated in each case study.

Income			Equity		Sustainability	
Returns to labor (US$/day)[a]			Households participating			
New technology	Old technology	Percent change	Total (thousands)	Smallholder percentage[b]	Environmental?	Fiscal?
2.82	1.75	61	4,605	100	Yes	Yes
—	—	—	1,025	100	Yes	Yes
—	—	—	660	100	Yes	Yes
4.78	2.70	77	420	100	Yes	Yes
—	—	—	3,263	71	Uneven[d]	No
3.17	1.69	88	617	22	Uneven[d]	No
—	—	—	318	73	Uneven[d]	No
—	—	—	1,157	80	Uneven[d]	No
—	—	—	30	100	Uneven[d]	Yes, if
2.06	1.38	49	200	100	Uneven[d]	managed
—	—	—	800	100	Uneven[d]	efficiently
—	—	—	200	55	Yes	Yes
—	—	—	—	37	—	—
—	—	—	600	80	Yes	No
5.31	1.80	195	32	97	Yes	Yes
—	—	—	10	100	Yes	Yes
2.31	1.42	63	40[g]	100	Yes	Yes
3.95	1.42	178	2	100	Yes	Yes
3.00	1.32	127	66	100	Yes	Yes
—	—	—	15	100	Yes	Yes

[d]Sustainability possible with good soil management and input packages but often not under existing farming practices.

[e]Horticulture productivity measured as gross margin per hectare, valued in U.S. dollars.

[f]Dairy productivity measured in liters of milk per cow per year. Kenya figures compare stall feeding with open grazing. Ethiopia compares local with cross-bred cows.

[g]This estimate dates from 2002. By 2007, the CFU estimated that roughly 150,000 farmers practiced CF. However, independent monitoring data are not yet available to substantiate this later estimate.

of improved planting material, women have adopted TMS cassava varieties as readily as men in Nigeria, even though males account for 95 percent of the extension officers handling distribution of cassava cuttings (Chapter 2). Similarly, the improved fallow and conservation farming technologies, which emphasize careful labor management and minimize cash inputs, appear to attract women adopters as readily as men (Chapter 7). Even in cash-demanding maize input markets, when access to credit and cash are held constant, gender does not appear to affect access to seeds and fertilizer (Chapter 3). Where gender-linked differences in the adoption of improved maize packages arise, they appear to stem primarily from differences in access to complementary inputs such as credit, land, and labor (Gladwin 1992; Doss 2001). Among cash crop producers, the cotton case study suggests that in male-dominated polygamous families in Mali, men control access to cotton revenues (Chapter 4). Among horticultural growers in Kenya, women are well represented, although among wage laborers in the export packing houses, women predominate in the low-paying jobs (Chapter 5). Given an acute shortage of data on intrahousehold differences in labor allocation, income earnings, and consumption and given the heterogeneity among different categories of female-headed households (widows, single mothers, wives of long-term migrants), an in-depth assessment of gender differences in African agriculture will require additional detailed microeconomic data collection.

Sustainability

ECOLOGICAL SUSTAINABILITY.   Not surprisingly, the most ecologically sustainable of the case study technologies are the four improved soil fertility management technologies and the smallholder dairying technology, all of which emphasize the intentional buildup of soil organic matter and the return of nutrients to the soil (Chapters 6 and 7). Among the other case studies, cassava production has typically relied on the fewest external inputs, and long-term cassava trials suggest that the natural return of leaf litter to the soil can maintain soil fertility over long periods of time (Chapter 2).

Like all crops, cotton and maize extract nutrients from the soil, which therefore requires some amendment. Given the high nitrogen response of maize and the heavy fertilizer subsidies in some locations, maize has attracted the largest share of fertilizer use in Africa (Yanggen et al. 1998). This has led to problems of soil acidification in some locations and to a consequent need for liming (Chapter 7). Cotton farming has typically involved negative nutrient flows, which ultimately require soil recapitalization (Chapter 4). As land pressure increases and permanent cropping becomes more common, agricultural technology development in Africa will need to focus increasing attention on systems for replenishing and maintaining soil fertility.

FINANCIAL SUSTAINABILITY.   The technologies reviewed in Part II of this book have all proven profitable at the farm level, some highly so. This profitability, though, tends to fluctuate over time with variations in input and output prices. Cotton farmers, in particular, have faced acute pressure in recent years as falling world cotton prices and rising input prices have squeezed their incomes severely (Chapter 4).

In terms of fiscal sustainability, most of the case studies reviewed involve some public financing, particularly ongoing funding for public research and technology development. In addition, several of the promotional efforts have involved recurrent annual subsidies for private inputs such as seeds, fertilizer, and veterinary services and for producer price subsidies. In the maize and dairy value chains primarily, these recurrent subsidies have ultimately proven unsustainably expensive (Chapters 3 and 6). Without donor financing, African governments have had to suspend their large-scale recurrent input and output subsidy programs.

Implications

What Is Generalizable?

In some instances, the case studies suggest that technologies can be transferred directly from one location to another. SR52, the breakthrough hybrid maize first released by the Zimbabwean agricultural service in 1960, spread rapidly in Zimbabwe and also to the surrounding countries of Malawi and Zambia, where it remains important in breeding lines even today (Chapter 3). Five of the six improved cotton varieties instrumental to the steady rise of farm productivity in Mali came from outside Mali, from allied research institutes across the Sahel (Chapter 4). The Malawian cassava variety, Manyokola, has spread into Zambia and is now the most popular fresh variety sold on the Lusaka market. Given small countries and highly arbitrary political boundaries in Africa, significant prospects exist for technology sharing across neighboring countries that straddle common agroecological zones.

Yet in other instances, technologies prove location-specific. Cassava varieties imported directly from Nigeria to Zambia have not fared well because of differences in altitude, temperature, soils, and rainfall. Similarly, many varieties of hybrid maize developed for temperate zones will not flower in equatorial regions because differences in daylight hours trigger tasseling. Pests, soils, and policy environments vary across locations, making direct technology transplants uncertain.

In these cases, the process of change may prove more replicable than the individual technologies themselves. Therefore, the analytical team and expert reference groups convened to help generalize from these case studies paid particular attention to how the processes of change unfolded in each instance. They asked explicitly what institutions, investments, and interactions have proven key to enabling success in each of the cases under review.

Common Ingredients

Evidence from this roster of case studies suggests two fundamental prerequisites for sustained agricultural growth: (1) sustained increases in agricultural productivity and (2) favorable incentives for farmers and agribusinesses.

PRODUCTIVITY GAINS.   Virtually all of the case studies reviewed in this book involve some form of improved technology: biological, agronomic, mechanical, or organizational (Table 8.1). Frequently the resulting productivity gains have exceeded 100 percent (Table 8.2). Significantly, they have raised both land and labor productivity. Given the current low productivity in African agriculture (Chapter 1, Table 1.1), expanding the scope and scale of these productivity gains remains central for boosting farm income and output and for lowering consumer food prices.

Timelines for the research programs reviewed in these case studies suggest that agricultural research and development require sustained efforts over multiple decades. Breakthroughs in maize breeding in Southern Africa required nearly three decades, development of TMS cassava varieties took place over four decades, and West African cotton research has continued to produce improved technologies for well over five decades (Chapters 2–4).

Regional spillovers have amplified the impact of the agricultural technology and disease control efforts described in these case studies. The transcontinental spread of TMS cassava varieties and of cassava mealybug and CMV control efforts illustrate the powerful regional spread effects possible in agricultural technology development and diffusion (Chapter 2). Similarly, in maize and cotton breeding, regional research collaboration has yielded significant spillover benefits across countries in common agroecological zones (Chapters 3 and 4). The importance of cross-country research spillovers has led to increasing interest in regional research collaborations of the sort embodied in the Association for Strengthening Agricultural Research in Eastern and Central Africa and the West and Central African Council for Agricultural Research and Development (Abdulai, Diao, and Johnson 2005; IFPRI 2005).

FAVORABLE INCENTIVES.   Growing markets spurred increased farm production in the maize, cotton, horticulture, and dairy case studies. In the cassava case study, market-led growth over several generations spurred production in West Africa. In Southern Africa, the marketing of sweet cassava varieties has grown rapidly, while the expansion of bitter varieties has been spurred less by market incentives than by households' incentives to ensure their food security in a drought-prone environment where maize production and government maize subsidies have proven erratic (Chapter 2).

A stable set of favorable trade and macroeconomic policies has proven instrumental in enabling horticultural export growth in Kenya and cotton exports from West Africa (Chapters 4 and 5). Conversely, unpredictable or inimical policies limit private sector involvement in agricultural markets. The lifting of regulatory prohibitions on urban raw milk marketing in Kenya has resulted in a surge in raw milk markets, which now account for 85 percent of national (rural plus urban) and 60 percent of urban dairy consumption there (Chapter 6). Similarly, the partial liberalization of maize marketing in Eastern and Southern Africa has led to tepid responses by maize traders and input suppliers, particularly in the face of wide swings in trade, government marketing, and pricing policies (Chapter 3). The case studies, as a group, clearly indicate that where improved technology and favorable incentives coincide, agricultural production and marketing have grown rapidly.

Public versus Private Roles

What has to happen is clear. The case studies consistently suggest that the combination of improved productivity and favorable incentives will induce rapid growth in agricultural output and incomes. The question of *who* needs to intervene to supply these two critical ingredients suggests several general principles as well as some nuances.

AGRICULTURAL RESEARCH AND EXTENSION. Publicly funded agricultural research played a decisive role in driving productivity gains in the cassava, maize, cotton, and dairy case studies. Yet in Kenya's dairy industry, private breeding efforts have helped to accelerate these gains. For over 80 years, private dairy farmers have actively engaged in importing improved breeds, monitoring breeding records, and measuring the milk production performance of breed cattle (Chapter 6). Similarly, in maize breeding, after the initial public breakthroughs in maize hybridization, private seed companies have increasingly conducted research and development efforts of their own (Chapter 3). With hybrid maize seeds, private firms are able to charge an annual fee for any genetic improvements they produce through their seed sales. In contrast, with vegetatively propagated crops like casssava, farmers can reproduce exact clones from their own fields after an initial distribution of TMS planting material (Chapter 2). Private firms, therefore, have no incentive to invest in research on vegetatively propagated crops such as cassava, sweet potatoes, and bananas. Hence, for these crops, public research is essential.

Some agricultural research has fallen primarily in the private domain. Horticultural seed development and input production remain primarily in the private sector (Chapter 5). The development of *zaï* and conservation farming technology began among private farmers before moving into the public arena (Chapter 7). Cassava processing technology has remained primarily driven by private innovation, although public research institutes have also contributed (Chapter 2). In general, the private sector has become involved in breeding and processing technology when it can capture the gains to its research and development investments. In the case of low-value, vegetatively propagated or closed-pollinating crops, the private sector has declined to invest.

DISEASE CONTROL EFFORTS.   Containment of pests, viruses, and diseases has figured prominently in most of the case studies under review. In most instances, the externalities posed by these threats required collective, publicly coordinated interventions. The transcontinental battles against cassava mealybug, CMV, and various livestock diseases vividly illustrate the need for public coordination (Chapters 2 and 6). In the presence of these large externalities, public intervention has proven essential.

MARKETS.   In input markets, private firms have typically dominated in the supply of seeds, fertilizers, herbicides, and fungicides required by horticultural growers (Chapter 5). In contrast, public input supply systems initially dominated in the maize, cotton, and dairy case studies (Chapters 3, 4, and 6). But over time, in each of these three instances, the heavily subsidized parastatal systems bred inefficiency and ultimately unsustainably heavy costs. As the parastatal supply systems became unaffordable, governments restructured and privatized input markets to varying degrees. In response, private input suppliers (of hybrid maize seeds, fertilizer, and veterinary services) have creamed off the most profitable markets, typically those closest to transport and market facilities. Without subsidies, remote areas have seen input service delivery diminish (Chapters 3 and 6).

In agricultural output markets, private trade has dominated in cassava, horticulture, and raw milk sales (Chapters 2, 5, and 6). In contrast, formerly heavy public control of output marketing in the maize, cotton, and dairy industries has given way to varying degrees of privatization (Chapters 3, 4, and 6). As in the case of the input supply systems, output market privatization has tended to reduce marketing activity in remote areas, where real costs of input supply are highest and market prices lowest (Chapters 3 and 5). Following the withdrawal of panterritorial subsidized prices, incentives for both production and private marketing diminish in outlying zones.

Taken together, the case studies suggest that private traders offer the default option for most agricultural markets over the long term. However, private firms will not serve poor households or remote regions unless the financial incentives are adequate. Given small markets and limited competition in some situations, public regulation and monitoring will also be required. Indeed, some African governments remain reluctant to exit politically sensitive markets, such as maize and cotton, fearing collusion by private traders, particularly in small national markets with small numbers of major players (Chapters 3 and 4). In these situations, particularly in maize markets in much of Eastern and Southern Africa, governments retain tight regulatory controls as well as government marketing operations that serve as a counterweight to the private trade (Chapter 3). The resulting partial liberalization creates a slippery landscape, subjecting governments to conflicting pressures each season from farmers, millers, and traders and resulting in frequent policy backsliding and unpredictability. In these circumstances, many maize traders mistrust their governments. In the long run, to function efficiently, private traders require stable, predictable policies. Governments, in turn, require reliable, competitive, efficient markets. The mutual trust required to achieve both ends grows through dialogue, transparency, predictability, and market competition.

THE REGULATORY AND POLICY ENVIRONMENT.   Public policy has played a key role in regulating markets and in setting trade, foreign exchange rate, and credit policies. Apart from cell phone infrastructure, public investment has accounted for the lion's share of infrastructure investment—in roads, land-based telephone lines, ports, and railroad infrastructure. Although public agencies have likewise played a key role in setting grades and standards for many agricultural commodities, growth in export horticulture and domestic supermarkets has led to some private sector influence in establishing product and phytosanitary standards in horticulture and processed foods, even in domestic food chains. Overall, the case studies suggest that governments need not necessarily be highly interventionist, as the horticulture and cassava examples illustrate. But they must be supportive of agricultural growth, ensuring favorable, stable incentives and key public goods such as agricultural research and roads.

The Bottom Line

Collectively, the case studies affirm that it is indeed possible to create conditions under which African agriculture can flourish for protracted periods of time. Typically, episodes of strong agricultural performance emerge where technological improvements and favorable incentive systems converge. Stable, favorable incentives enable the "slow magic" of agricultural research to drive productivity and output growth over time.[5] This suggests that government commitment to enabling policies and to sustained investments in agricultural research will provide the crucial building blocks for future successes in African agriculture.

---

5. See Pardey and Beintema (2001) on the "slow magic" provided by agricultural research.

Appendix 8A: The Pretoria Statement on the Future of African Agriculture

Preamble

Significant poverty reduction will not be possible in Africa without rapid agricultural growth.[6] Only improved agricultural productivity can simultaneously improve welfare among the two-thirds of all Africans who work primarily in agriculture as well as the urban poor, who spend over 60% of their budget on food staples.

Regrettably, past performance has proven inadequate. Africa remains the only region of the developing world where per capita agricultural production has fallen over the past forty years. To stem deepening poverty, social inequity and political instability, African farmers, governments, international partners and the private sector must all do better in the future. Recognizing this imperative, African Heads of State and Government agreed, at the African Union Summit in July 2003, to make agriculture a top priority and to raise budget allocations for agriculture to a minimum of 10% of total public spending within five years.

Africa's sluggish aggregate performance, however, masks a rich historical record of substantial agricultural successes. Though these episodic and scattered booms have proven insufficient to sustain aggregate per capita growth in agriculture, they do prove informative in pointing to promising areas for effective intervention in the future. In a rapidly changing global environment—with increasingly concentrated market power and rapidly changing biological, information and communication technologies—and given increased pressures on the natural resource base, public budgets and the growing threat of HIV/AIDS, governments and their private sector partners must learn to apply the lessons from these past successes.

Evidence from a series of successful episodes in African agriculture suggests two fundamental pre-requisites for sustained agricultural growth as well as a number of promising specific opportunities:

Fundamental Pre-requisites

GOOD GOVERNANCE.   High-level political commitment has consistently proven essential to improving the welfare of farm households. It translates directly into favorable policy environments and budget allocations to agricultural support institutions and related infrastructure. Effective farmer organizations remain central to improving the communication and articulation of farm sector needs to government. Both farmers' organizations and governments must take responsibility for initiating overtures and organizational forms to make this pos-

---

6. For the full conference program and a complete list of participants, see <www.ifpri .org/event/successes-african-agriculture>.

sible. We call upon governments to work closely with the private sector, civil society and farmers' organizations in the allocation of increased public funding to agriculture. In consultation with the private sector, governments should create and facilitate an enabling environment for the private sector to perform.

SUSTAINED FUNDING FOR AGRICULTURAL RESEARCH AND EXTENSION. Raising productivity remains central to boosting farm output and lowering consumer food prices. Virtually all of the successes we have identified involve some form of improved technology: biological, agronomic, mechanical or organizational. Therefore, governments must elevate funding for agricultural research and extension. Furthermore, it is important that farmers' innovations be mainstreamed into the research agenda. Governments, together with donors, must ensure the training of staff capable of mastering new biological research technologies. Given the growing role of private research in biotechnology and hybrid breeding, governments must develop partnerships and protocols for making new technologies developed in the private sector available to smallholder farmers.

Promising Opportunities

SOIL AND WATER CONSERVATION. We have been impressed with the number and range of innovative efforts by farmers and researchers to sustain soil fertility and water resources in response to increasingly degraded natural environments. Therefore, further testing of these models across national borders merits additional examination and support with the aim of refining and scaling up successes in restoring and sustaining soil fertility. This will require interaction among formal researchers, farmers and their supporting institutions.

REPLICATION OF PROVEN COMMODITY-SPECIFIC BREEDING AND PROCESSING SUCCESSES. We are impressed with the importance of upscaling cassava breeding and processing research to meet food security, livestock feed and industrial uses. Strong complementarities across regions suggest regional cooperation and sharing of biological and mechanical technologies will magnify returns. Tissue-culture bananas and Nerica rice offer further examples of commodity-specific replication potential. NEPAD and leading centers of technology development should take the lead in initiating this exchange.

MARKETING AND INFORMATION SYSTEMS. Mechanisms for aggregating and improving the quality of the products of smallholder farmers and providing relevant and timely market information will enhance market efficiency. This will prove necessary in enabling them to compete in increasingly concentrated domestic, regional and global markets. A variety of models exist—contract farming among cotton and horticulture producers, dairy marketing groups and others —for grouping small farmers into economically viable market entities.

VERTICAL SUPPLY CHAINS. To improve efficiency, raise value-added in production and processing, and ensure improved coordination between producers and final markets will require increasing attention to supply chain management rather than an exclusively production orientation. Successes in cotton, horticulture, dairy and maize all reveal the importance of vertical farmer-to-market coordination.

REGIONAL COOPERATION IN TRADE AND AGRICULTURAL TECHNOLOGY. Regional trade offers significant potential for moderating food insecurity through cross-border exchange. Harmonization of trade regulations on a regional basis will prove necessary to facilitate these commodity flows. In research as well, countries along common agro ecological zones mean that regional technology and information exchange offer significant opportunities for sharing research and development overheads, expanding benefits and reducing costs. This cross-border technology exchange has proven vitally important in the cases of cassava, maize and natural resource management technologies. For this exchange, capacity-building is necessary. NEPAD and the regional economic organizations remain uniquely suited to facilitate such exchange.

We believe that with renewed commitment to building partnerships between governments, farmers' organizations, international partners and the private sector, significant gains are achievable in African agriculture. And achieve them we must, to ensure significant economic growth and poverty reduction in the decades ahead. We call upon the organizers of this conference and all participants to play their rightful role to ensure the realization of these recommendations.

Participants of the International Conference on
Successes in African Agriculture, Building for the Future

December 3, 2003
Pretoria, South Africa

9 Implications for the Future

STEVEN HAGGBLADE, PETER B. R. HAZELL,
AND WILBERFORCE KISAMBA-MUGERWA

This chapter returns to several key questions posed at the beginning of this book. Why has Africa not experienced agricultural success more frequently? How will recent changes in global markets and agricultural science affect future strategies for stimulating for agricultural growth? Looking forward, what needs to change to get African agriculture growing more rapidly?

The summary of case study evidence presented in Chapter 8 has identified two key determinants of superior agricultural performance: (1) a steady stream of productivity-enhancing agricultural technology and (2) favorable market incentives for farmers and agribusinesses. Successes have emerged when and where these two ingredients have converged. Where agriculture has performed poorly, one or both of these preconditions has been absent.

Achieving these two preconditions for success requires that several underlying drivers be in place. Given the long lead times required to develop most new agricultural technologies, their availability requires sustained investment in research and development (R&D) over time. Uptake at the farm level requires effective extension, input supply, and credit systems that enable farmers to access needed inputs such as improved seeds, planting materials, and fertilizers. Positive market incentives require macro-level, trade, and agricultural sector policies that do not discriminate against agriculture; sufficient infrastructure to enable timely, cost-effective access by farmers to markets and inputs; and marketing and pricing policies that encourage private trade, storage, and processing and that provide farmers with competitive prices and reasonable assurance of stable prices, at least on the down side. Finally, all these factors must come together in a coordinated way, a daunting challenge for agricultural policymakers. The availability of improved technologies will make little difference if farmers cannot access key inputs or if they do not have access to markets at prices that make adoption of the improved technology profitable. Effective public institutions are a prerequisite for coordinating agricultural development strategies and implementing key components.

As Africa faces the challenge of creating favorable conditions for more rapid agricultural growth, the environment in which it must do so is changing.

Population growth and past neglect of agriculture have resulted in serious degradation of the natural resource base underpinning agricultural growth. Climate change may compound these problems. World commodity markets are currently in some disarray, but there is every likelihood that the low and relatively stable prices of recent decades are now over. Fertilizer and energy prices also seem destined to remain high going forward. Possible changes in the agricultural policies of the Organisation for Economic Co-operation and Development (OECD) and in world trade agreements may affect commodity prices and agricultural trade options for Africa. Global integration in many agricultural supply chains places increasing control in the hands of supermarkets, large processors, and exporters, posing challenges for small farms. Advances in patentable biological innovations have led to growing involvement of private firms in agricultural technology development. Forward-looking agricultural strategies will need to adapt lessons from the past to these changing realities.

This chapter begins by examining Africa's past inability to achieve the preconditions necessary for more successful agricultural growth and assessing the requirements for reversing this situation. The discussion then turns to the changing environment in which African agricultural policymakers will operate in coming decades. In light of evolving ecological and market conditions, the chapter concludes by suggesting ways of moving forward, taking account of lessons learned from past experience as well as the changing environment in which African agriculture will operate in coming decades.

Missing Preconditions for More Widespread Success

Sustained Investment in Agricultural Research and Development

SPENDING LEVELS.   In recent decades, few African countries have invested sufficiently in agricultural R&D to meet the technology needs of their farmers. R&D spending grew at a modest 2 percent per year in the 1970s before falling to 1.3 percent per year in the 1980s and to a mere 0.8 percent per year in the 1990s. Outside of Nigeria and South Africa, R&D spending actually declined by 0.3 percent per year during the 1990s for the rest of Africa (Table 9.1), with a particularly sharp decline in West Africa. Compare these levels of investment with those achieved in Asia, where public spending on agricultural research grew by 6 percent per year during the 1970s, the heyday of the green revolution, before slowing to about 4 percent per year in the 1980s and 1990s. Even today, Asia invests more in agricultural R&D than does Africa (Beintema and Stads 2006; Pardey, Alston, and Piggott 2006).

Total donor funding for agricultural R&D has also declined since the mid-1990s (Beintema and Stads 2006). This declining growth in public agricultural R&D investments has not been offset by growth in private sector investment or by the international agricultural research centers. In fact, recent evidence sug-

TABLE 9.1 Trends in agricultural research and development spending in Sub-Saharan Africa, 1960s–2000

Annual growth rate in spending (percent)	1960s	1970s	1980s	1991–2000
All Sub-Saharan Africa	6.0	2.0	1.3	0.8
Nigeria	—	5.6	–6.7	6.3
South Africa	—	0.1	0.1	1.9
Sub-Saharan Africa excluding Nigeria and South Africa	—	2.5	3.3	–0.3

Spending per scientist (thousands of constant 2005 US$)[a]	1971	1981	1991	2000
All Sub-Saharan Africa	351	246	181	168
Nigeria	231	190	81	106
South Africa	573	503	404	480
Sub-Saharan Africa excluding Nigeria and South Africa	291	199	159	130

SOURCES: Beintema and Stads (2006); U.S. Department of Labor (2008).

NOTE: —, data breakdown not available.

[a]Converted from 1993 US$ using the U.S. Consumer Price Index.

gests that the private sector accounts for a mere 2 percent of total research investments in Africa (Beintema and Stads 2006).

Total public spending on R&D urgently needs to increase across Africa. After an extensive review of Africa's agricultural research systems, the Inter-Academy Council called for R&D investment to grow by at least 10 percent per year until 2015 (InterAcademy Council 2004).

INEFFICIENCIES IN SPENDING. Not only have African and donor governments spent too little on agricultural R&D across Africa, they have also deployed their modest resources inefficiently. The fragmentation and small size of many research programs pose a key problem. Nearly 400 public entities conduct agricultural research in Africa. Of these, nearly 200 are public research institutions and another 200 are universities. Many are very small. Forty percent employ fewer than 5 scientists, and 93 percent staff fewer than 50 full-time researchers (Beintema and Stads 2006). The small size of many African countries prevents them from maintaining comprehensive R&D programs for all of their important crops and livestock species.

Yet considerable scope exists for achieving efficiency gains and scale economies through more regionally coordinated research on problems of common interest—including shared crops, common agroecological zones, biotechnology research, biosafety regulation, and plant and animal disease control efforts. Among the case studies reviewed in Part II of this book, the maize, cotton, cassava, dairy, and improved fallow studies all involved significant cross-country collaboration and technology spillovers. Zimbabwe's blockbuster maize hybrid, SR52, released in 1960, has invigorated breeding lines throughout the region and remains used in regional breeding programs even today (Chapter 3). The cotton case study similarly illustrates the effectiveness of regional francophone research networks. Of the six cotton varieties released in Mali between 1960 and 2005, five came from outside of Mali, from sister research stations across the Sahel (Chapter 4). Ugandan dairy breeders have imported improved breeding stock from Kenya, building on over 80 years of regional experience crossing exotic and African cattle (Chapter 6). The pan-African cassava surge has demonstrated the value of cross-border exchange of agricultural technology in combating the transcontinental spread of the cassava mealybug. Likewise, the International Institute of Tropical Agriculture's (IITA) release of mosaic virus–resistant Tropical Manioc Selection (TMS) cassava varieties has fueled a highly productive subsequent stream of national cassava research, resulting in the release of a series of disease-resistant, high-yielding TMS progeny across the continent (Chapter 2).

To provide an institutional framework for regional agricultural technology coordination, agricultural scientists and policymakers have formed a series of regional research organizations: the West African and Central African Council for Agricultural Research and Development (WECARD/CORAF), founded in 1987; the Association for Strengthening Agricultural Research in Eastern and Central Africa (ASARECA), formed in 1994; and the Southern African Centre for Cooperation in Agricultural Research and Training (SACCAR), constituted in 1984. Although SACCAR has faced difficulties in navigating the highly politicized intergovernmental politics of its parent organization, both ASARECA and WECARD/CORAF have succeeded in initiating effective regional research networks (IFPRI 2005).

Because Africa's many small countries often straddle common agro-ecological zones, regional research collaboration can generate significant technology spillovers as well as potential economies of scale. A team from the International Food Policy Research Institute (IFPRI), working with researchers at ASARECA, has estimated the magnitude of these spillovers for specific commodity research programs in the East African Community (EAC) countries of Kenya, Tanzania, and Uganda. According to their estimates, every dollar of direct farmer income gains due to the release of improved agricultural technologies in these three EAC countries generates spillovers in neighboring ASARECA member countries ranging from 26 percent for maize to 50 percent for cassava and Irish potatoes and over 100 percent for sorghum and rice (Abdulai, Diao, and Johnson 2005).[1] To capture these gains, regional research net-

---

1. Worldwide, Alston (2002) suggests that roughly half of all gains from agricultural research and development come from spillovers.

works and the international research community will need to play larger and more effective roles in furthering regional agricultural research.

Rural Infrastructure

Today Africa has built only a fraction of the infrastructure that Asia had available in the 1950s. The road density in mainland Africa in 2000–2005 ranged from 3–4 kilometers per 1,000 square kilometers in Ethiopia and Mali to 50–70 kilometers per 1,000 square kilometers in Namibia and Botswana (World Bank 2007a). In contrast, India's average road density at the start of the green revolution stood at 388 kilometers per 1,000 square kilometers (Spencer 1994). Within countries, large differences exist in access to infrastructure. In Kenya, for example, road density ranges from 0.88 kilometers per square kilometer in the highlands to 0.12 kilometers per square kilometer in the lowlands (Thurlow, Kiringai, and Gautam 2007). In Burkina Faso, Uganda, and Zambia, walking affords the principal means of transportation for 87 percent of rural residents (Torero and Chowdhury 2005).

As the Asian experience amply demonstrates, investments in rural infrastructure can lead to high rates of return and favorable poverty impacts. In India, for example, every rupee spent on rural roads in the 1990s increased agricultural gross domestic product (GDP) by 3.2 rupees, while every 1 million rupees spent lifted 335 poor people above the poverty line (Fan, Gulati, and Thorat 2007).

Likewise, in Africa investments in roads serve to reduce marketing costs, lower input prices, and raise output prices received by farmers, thus raising their incomes. In Uganda during the late 1990s, investments in feeder roads generated a benefit-cost ratio of 7, and every million shillings spent on feeder roads lifted 34 people out of poverty (Fan, Zhang, and Rao 2004). Moreover, investing in roads can generate positive spillover benefits between neighboring countries. For example, estimates suggest that improvements in Mozambique's road and transport infrastructure, which increase total factor productivity in the transport sector by 50 percent, not only lead to a 6 percent increase in agricultural productivity in Mozambique but to a spillover increase of 2.6 percent in the agricultural productivity of neighboring Malawi (Abdulai, Johnson, and Diao 2006). Comparable improvements in transport efficiency across Africa could lead to a continent-wide increase in agricultural production of 7.6 percent, in agricultural real income of 9.6 percent, in total agricultural exports of 28 percent, and in intraregional trade of 22 percent (Abdulai, Johnson, and Diao 2006).

African countries urgently need to increase their public expenditures on rural infrastructure if they are to launch more rapid agricultural growth. Yet over the past two and a half decades, spending on transport and communications has fallen significantly in Sub-Saharan Africa (Fan and Saurkar 2008). Based on estimates of the likely demand for roads, railroads, telecommunications, electricity, water, and sanitation in Africa, policymakers will need to invest an additional US$93 billion annually between 2006 and 2015 (Foster and Briceño-Garmendia 2010). Of that annual sum, two-thirds would be devoted to investment in new infrastructure, with the remaining one-third for operations and maintenance. Overall, this will require increased annual spending equal to 15 percent of African GDP.

Enabling Policies

POLICY REFORMS.   Prior to the 1980s, most African countries pursued macroeconomic, trade, and pricing policies that heavily discriminated against agriculture, reduced the profitability of new investments and technologies, and discouraged agricultural growth (Krueger, Schiff, and Valdes 1991). The structural adjustment programs (SAPs) initiated in the 1980s by the World Bank and the International Monetary Fund helped correct the worst of these distortions and potentially opened the way for more productive investments in agriculture. In 14 African countries for which data are available, the net rate of taxation on agriculture fell from 21 percent in 1980–84 to 8 percent in 2000–2004 (Anderson and Masters 2009, Table 1.10).[2] But the reforms have also introduced some problems of their own. At the macro level, while SAPs improved economic incentives for agriculture, they also slashed the public spending that was needed to enable the sector to respond to these improved incentives. At sectoral and local levels, they produced mixed effects on farmers' access to key inputs and markets.

As part of the reforms, governments have withdrawn support for parastatal marketing companies, reduced subsidies on agricultural inputs and outputs, and relaxed regulatory restrictions on private trade (Jones 1987; van der Laan, Dijkstra, and van Tillburg 1999; Kherallah et al. 2002). Heavy financial losses by agricultural parastatals, and the consequent extreme budgetary pressure these losses imposed, forced many of these changes. The maize, cotton, and dairy case studies reviewed in Part II of this book document these budgetary pressures and the resulting policy changes (Chapters 3, 4, and 6).

In general, these changes have resulted in a declining public role in agricultural markets and a corresponding increase in private sector trade. Following the liberalization of the Ugandan coffee market, for example, over 120 private companies emerged to replace the coffee marketing board. Subsequently, however, most of them collapsed, leaving three international companies and two local companies operating with international partners. The same scenario has played out in the Ugandan horticulture industry. As the public sector has withdrawn, both weak and strong private sector players have emerged, assuming an increasingly vital role in both research and marketing.

However, individual reform efforts have varied widely. Countries such as Mali and Mozambique have maintained generally liberalized trade policies and

---

2. This is a simple average of all Sub-Saharan countries excluding South Africa.

open borders (Dioné 2000; Tschirley et al. 2006; Tschirley and Jayne 2008). But policy hesitation and significant slippage has occurred in Malawi, Zambia, and many other places. Uncertainties remain, and backsliding has occurred in many cases, making private traders nervous and slowing the development of efficient post-reform marketing systems (Jayne et al. 2002a; Mwanaumo et al. 2005).

As a result of these policy changes, government parastatals no longer directly manage the preponderance of Africa's agricultural input and output markets. Although privatization has proceeded at varying rates and with variable degrees of backsliding across countries and commodities, most African governments now rely more on private agents than they have in the past. This means that future marketing strategies will revolve less around direct government control and more around the establishment of consistent policies that ensure incentives for private sector participation and competition.

To the extent that agricultural input and output markets have become privatized, market services to remote areas and to many small farms have declined (see Chapters 3 and 5). Growing evidence suggests that small farmers growing food staples now have less access to markets and credit, pay high prices for modern inputs, and are more fully exposed to the vagaries of market price and production risks. This has led to a significant reduction in the adoption of modern crop varieties and fertilizers. According to a recent study, fertilizer use per hectare actually declined in about one-half of all African countries during the 1990s (Morris et al. 2007, 22).

INPUT SUBSIDIES.   Following the SAP reforms, many African governments have stopped financing input subsidies, though this remains controversial given the subsequent reduction in fertilizer use and worries about future high fertilizer prices. Today, in response, a new generation of input subsidy programs is currently being field tested in Africa. Dubbed "smart" subsidies, these new programs favor market-friendly delivery systems that promote private sector involvement and competition through a variety of instruments, including targeted vouchers and competitive procurement systems. The results of early evaluations vary. A study of Malawi's 2006/07 Targeted Input Program estimates an economic benefit-cost ratio of between 0.76 and 1.36, depending on assumptions about rainfall, displacement of commercial fertilizer sales, and projected fertilizer and maize prices (Dorward et al. 2008). These estimates suggest that, under good management, the new-generation fertilizer subsidy programs can generate positive returns. Better targeting, to poor households and underserved areas, would reduce commercial displacement and incline results toward the high end of this projected range.[3] Nonetheless, the high cost of

---

3. Early assessments of fertilizer subsidy programs from Malawi and Zambia estimate displacement of commercial fertilizer sales in the range of 30–40 percent of the volumes of subsidized fertilizer distributed (Dorward et al. 2008; Minde et al. 2008).

petroleum-based fertilizer makes these subsidy programs expensive. In Malawi and Zambia, fertilizer subsidies consumed 33–50 percent of government budget allocations for agriculture in 2006 (Govereh et al. 2006; Haggblade 2007; Dorward et al. 2008). The inclusion of maize marketing subsidies raises that share to over 60 percent (Minde et al. 2008). At these levels, input subsidies risk diverting significant budgetary and manpower resources away from other promotional activities, such as agricultural research and extension, where rates of return have historically proven high. A review of over 180 impact evaluation studies in Africa estimated a 34 percent median rate of return to public investment in agricultural research (Alston et al. 2000). So the opportunity cost of input subsidies may be very high indeed.

In contrast, Kenya has witnessed a near-doubling of fertilizer use over the past decade and a half without recourse to subsidies. The liberalization of fertilizer marketing through the removal of retail price controls and import licensing began in 1990. Since then, an increasingly dense network of fertilizer retailers has emerged in Kenya, along with intense competition in importing and wholesaling, which together have resulted in a 45 percent decline in fertilizer transport and marketing costs from Mombassa to Western Kenya. As a result, total fertilizer use increased from 250,000 tons per year in the early 1990s to over 450,000 tons in 2007 (Minde et al. 2008). Thus, the evidence of the past few years suggests a general renunciation of the parastatal subsidy distribution model but widespread differences in successor approaches, from "smart" subsidies to largely free-market solutions.

CREDIT.   Agricultural credit markets, despite liberalization, have largely failed to develop successfully in Sub-Saharan Africa (Chigunta, Herbert, and Mkandawire 2003). Steep transaction costs, highly variable returns to input use under rainfed conditions, and uncertainty over government price controls make agricultural lending risky. Given high inflation and high returns on government bonds, many banks have opted to place their cash in government securities rather than risking depositor funds on agricultural lending. While the formal banking system has largely failed to deliver credit to the small farm sector, microfinance has fared little better. Despite highly touted successes in microfinance lending in urban areas and in densely settled parts of rural Asia, microfinance institutions have thus far failed to develop a commercially viable model for lending to African farmers (Meyer and Nagarajan 2000).

Across this generally difficult landscape, the most reliable models of agricultural credit delivery in Africa have emerged among the cash crop outgrower schemes. The cotton program and some of the horticultural programs discussed in Chapters 4 and 5 offer classic examples of this direct, in-kind input provision on credit followed by loan recovery during crop purchasing at harvest time. In some cases, these programs have enabled finance to move beyond cash crops as well, as in the cotton case study from Mali, where rural bank lenders use cotton contracts as security in lending for input purchases for cereals and other noncotton crops (Chapter 4). Among cash crop outgrower schemes in Kenya, similar extension of credit has enabled rural lending for the fertilizer, seeds, and other inputs used in nonexport crops, contributing to the highest smallholder fertilizer use in Sub-Saharan Africa (Ariga, Jayne, and Nyoro 2006; Ariga et al. 2008). Currently, the financing of African farm inputs depends largely on cash crop credit schemes and associated spillovers as well as on farm households' nonfarm earnings and remittances.[4]

INTRAREGIONAL TRADE. Intraregional trade barriers remain an important constraint to the development of Africa's agricultural markets. Because Africa's highly arbitrary political borders—rendered by colonial negotiators in Berlin in 1885—cut across population groups and natural trade corridors, many times surplus zones and the deficit areas they serve emerge on the opposite sides of international borders. Cattle from Mali and Burkina Faso supply beef markets in Côte d'Ivoire and Ghana. Eastern parts of the Democratic Republic of Congo (DRC) connect most naturally with Burundi and Rwanda, while foods surpluses from northern Zambia offer close proximity to the mining towns in Katanga province of the DRC. Farmers in northern Mozambique export significant volumes of maize, often informally and in small lots, across the border to neighboring Malawi during drought years (Whiteside 2003; Tschirley et al. 2006; Haggblade, Longabaugh, and Tschirley 2009).

As a result of these natural complementarities, more open intraregional trade among African countries offers important opportunities for exploiting differences in comparative advantage, achieving greater scale economies in marketing, and helping stabilize food supplies in the face of adverse weather. Expanding regional markets can serve as a vent for surplus production. They can help to increase the volumes traded in thin domestic markets and diminish the likelihood of price collapses following significant gains in agricultural productivity. Behind closed borders, domestic prices may fluctuate dramatically from one year to the next in response to rainfall variability and consequently volatile cereal production. Open borders introduce import and export parity prices that place upper and lower bounds on price movements, thus moderating price volatility over time (Figure 9.1). A recent study estimated that if Africa were to double its cereal production over the next five years, average farmgate prices would fall by 40 percent if current intraregional trade barriers and transport costs prevail. But under full regional trade liberalization and expanded infrastructural investments to bring transport costs down, prices would fall by only 10 percent (Diao et al. 2006). These open- and closed-border scenarios translate into very different outcomes for farmers. Under open borders, farm incomes increase when prices fall 10 percent because their unit production costs fall by more than 10 percent, but they are net losers under closed borders when

---

4. On the links between nonfarm earnings and agricultural input finance, see, for example, Francis and Hoddinott (1993); Reardon et al. (1993); and Barrett, Reardon, and Webb (2001).

FIGURE 9.1 Domestic and border wholesale prices for white maize, Randfontein, South Africa, 1996–2006

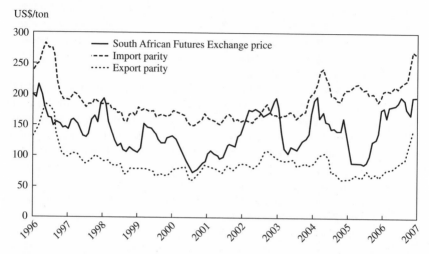

SOURCE: Traub (2008).
NOTE: Domestic prices are those on the South African Futures Exchange.

prices fall by 40 percent. As a result, more fluid cross-border flows of food staples will play a critical role in maintaining production incentives for producers in high-potential areas while at the same time ensuring low-cost food supplies in deficit zones. Yet many African governments in Eastern and Southern Africa continue to restrict cross-border trade in food staples (Whiteside 2003; Mwanaumo et al. 2005; Tschirley and Jayne 2008).

Over time, the political fragmentation that followed African independence, during the 1960s, generally disrupted earlier colonial efforts toward economic integration. However, since the 1990s, intra-African regional trading blocs have reinforced earlier efforts, and cross-border trade flows have generally increased. With the demise of apartheid and the advent of majority rule in South Africa, in 1994, neighboring African countries lifted their economic sanctions. As a result, by the end of the decade intraregional trade in Southern Africa had tripled (Pratt and Diao 2006). In 1994, 21 states in Eastern and Southern Africa signed the Common Market for Eastern and Southern Africa (COMESA) treaty committing to the establishment of a free trade area and a common external tariff (COMESA 2007). As a result, between 2000 and 2008, internal trade within the COMESA Free Trade Area increased fivefold, to US$15 billion (Times of Zambia 2009). In 1993, the 15 members of the Economic Association of West African States signed a revised treaty aimed at accelerating economic integration among the member states. In 2007, Burundi and Rwanda joined the newly expanded EAC in order to facilitate trade linkages with Kenya, Tanzania, and Uganda, natural trading partners with links to key ports on the Indian Ocean. Initiatives since 2003 by the African Union's New Partnership for Africa's Development (NEPAD) have likewise promoted regional strategies in agriculture, science, and infrastructure using the regional economic commissions as their basic building blocks (AU/NEPAD 2003b).

Intra-African agricultural trade has further responded to growing opportunities emanating from South Africa. The liberalization of domestic maize marketing by the South African government during the late 1990s launched a wave of trader consolidation as the major farmer cooperatives developed and merged, forming a series of large private grain trading companies (Essinger, Hill, and Laubscher 1998; Bayley 2002; Traub and Jayne 2004). The parallel emergence of grain trading on the South African Futures Exchange, including transparent spot markets and forward pricing, have all favored the rise of cross-border trade in agricultural commodities. Taking advantage of these new opportunities, the World Food Programme (WFP) has increasingly moved to procure food aid commodities destined for Africa from within the continent through local and regional food aid procurement. Between 1995/96 and 2004/05, the WFP scaled up the share of food aid it procured within Africa from 13 to 22 percent (Tschirley and del Castillo 2007). Medium-term projections suggest that a complete removal of internal trade barriers would result in a 50 percent increase in intra-African trade (Abdulai, Diao, and Johnson 2005). Improvements in transport facilities would accelerate this growth further.

An Effective Public Sector

Agricultural growth takes off when the preconditions for growth come together in a coordinated way. Achieving these preconditions requires critical accumulated levels of investment in agricultural R&D and infrastructure; working markets for inputs, credit, and outputs; and an enabling policy environment. Coordinating agricultural development strategies and implementing key components of those strategies require effective public institutions.[5]

In theory, the primary role of the public sector should be to provide (or at least finance) key public goods such as rural roads and some types of agricultural research that the private sector has limited incentive to supply, as well as to implement policies, laws, and regulations that create an enabling economic and institutional environment in which private and civil society agents, including farmers, can flourish. These are important roles that many African countries have yet to manage successfully.

Following the SAP reforms, Africa's public sector has generally reduced its direct involvement in the supply of agricultural input and marketing services and has refocused on regulating markets and trade. Yet post-liberalization

---

5. See Hazell et al. (2007) and Poulton and Dorward (2008) for good discussions of these issues.

performance has remained mixed, in part because of past neglect of many of the public institutions that serve agriculture and their consequent loss of morale and key staff (Eicher 1999, 2009).

The post-SAP era has seen many African countries struggle in coordinating the components of their agricultural strategies. Asia managed its coordination problem through a heavy state-led role, with state agencies actually controlling and subsidizing most of the research, input supply, credit, and marketing services. This heavy state role is less feasible in Africa today, where many of the public institutions that serve agriculture are weak and disempowered. Moreover, NGOs, community-based organizations, and some types of private firms have come to play important roles, larger than was the case in Asia at a comparable stage of development. Rather than the strong state-led role adopted in Asia, Africa may need to take a more flexible and opportunistic approach that builds strategic partnerships between key actors at local, meso, and macro levels. The process of the African Union's (AU's)/NEPAD's Comprehensive African Agricultural Development Programme (CAADP), though initiated by African heads of state, has involved dialogue with private sector partners as well as a strong emphasis on implementation through regional economic organizations. Alternative approaches, such as those under consideration by the Alliance for a Green Revolution in Africa, may center around national think tanks that lead through evidence-based policy analysis and dialogue (Ngoni 2009).

Political Commitment

Accelerating agricultural growth in Africa will require a significant change of attitude among governments and donors. Agricultural prosperity will require expanded and sustained financial and policy support for the sector. These changes in government attitudes and support turned Asian agriculture around in the 1960s, but in the past they have been missing in Africa. Can these changes happen today?

AFRICAN GOVERNMENTS.   African government commitment to agriculture has varied substantially across countries and over time. Taking public spending as a proxy for government commitment, broad fiscal aggregates suggest that over the past two and a half decades African government spending on agriculture has fallen, slipping from 6 percent of total budget authorizations in 1980 to 5.3 percent in 2004.[6] Spending on transport and communications has fallen even more abruptly during this period (Fan and Rao 2003; Fan and Saurkar 2008).

Several factors account for this reduction in agricultural spending. As African governments disbanded their pervasive agricultural parastatals and heavy

---

6. As a share of agricultural GDP, government spending has also fallen, from 7.5 percent in 1980 to about 6 percent in 2004. Over that same period, government spending in developing Asia fell from 10 percent to about 8 percent.

agricultural subsidy programs, spending on agriculture fell. At the same time, during the structural adjustment period of the 1980s and 1990s, governments faced pressure to raise spending on social sectors. Weak farmer organizations in many countries translated into limited political lobbying for agricultural priorities.[7] As a result, by 2005, Sub-Saharan Africa's governments ranked education, defense, and health as their top three spending priorities (Fan and Saurkar 2008).

By the early 2000s, key African leaders began to express concerns that they had marginalized agriculture for too long. In the words of Nigeria's former president, Olusegun Obasanjo, one of the architects of the AU/NEPAD's CAADP, "NEPAD believes that agriculture will provide the engine for growth in Africa. Improving agricultural performance is at the heart of improved economic development and growth, and its role in poverty eradication and in the restoration of human dignity can never be over-emphasised" (AU/NEPAD 2003a, iii). In recognition of this priority, at the AU Summit in Maputo in July 2003, the African heads of state committed their governments to allocate at least 10 percent of their national budgets to agriculture within a period of five years. This commitment represented a near-doubling from the then-prevailing level of roughly 5 percent (Fan and Rao 2003).

Skeptics will note that the AU leaders have committed to agriculture before, most notably under the Lagos Plan of Action (LPA) in 1980 (OAU 1980). Following on the heels of the food crises of the 1970s, the LPA adopted a goal of food self-sufficiency for Africa, with a target of 4 percent annual agricultural growth. Like the current NEPAD leadership, those formulating the LPA concluded that African governments had neglected agriculture: "At the root of the food problem in Africa is the fact that Member States have not usually accorded the necessary priority to agriculture, both in the allocation of resources and in giving sufficient attention to policies for the promotion of productivity and improvement of rural life" (OAU 1980, para. 17, 8). The LPA projected a cost of US$21 billion for agricultural programs over the first five years, from 1980 to 1985, or US$10 billion per year in 2002 dollars—roughly half of the US$18 billion per year proposed in the CAADP plan (AU/NEPAD 2003a). Under the LPA, African heads of state pledged to finance at least half of this internally, although individual country contributions remained unspecified, unmonitored, and unfulfilled. Like the LPA, NEPAD's CAADP plan appears to rely heavily on donor contributions.[8] Yet, unlike the LPA, which relied on self-monitoring

---

7. Conversely, where strong farmer groups exist, they can successfully lobby for resources and policy support. See, for example, Bingen (2000), Birner and Resnick (2005), Palaniswamy and Birner (2006), and the examples of farmer lobbying in Chapters 3, 4, and 5.

8. Of the US$18 billion in annual spending for African agriculture, the CAADP document proposes 39 percent from African governments, 35 percent from donors, and 26 percent from private investment and commercial loans.

of funding and achievements, NEPAD's CAADP plan has set up a centralized system for monitoring budgetary commitments as well as an African Peer Review Mechanism of eminent persons to monitor targets and implementation progress (AU/NEPAD 2006; Mwape 2006).

By 2004, data from 32 African countries indicated that the majority (62.5 percent) of African governments allocated less than 5 percent of their budgets to agriculture, while 25 percent allocated between 5 and 10 percent.[9] Only a small minority, four of the reporting countries (or 12.5 percent), exceeded the 10 percent budget target (Table 9.2). A recent simulation study suggests that these few are the countries most likely to reach the first of the United Nations Millennium Development Goals (MDGs), cutting poverty in half by 2015. Others, who remain far from the 10 percent target, will need to increase their agricultural spending between 20 and 30 percent annually to achieve the MDG target on poverty reduction (Fan et al. 2008). The CAADP commitments appear critical to reaching this goal.

DONORS.   Following a period of strong commitment to rural development during the 1970s and early 1980s, donors entered a subsequent period of acute agro- and Afro-pessimism (Eicher 2003; Binswanger-Mkhize and McCalla 2008). Like their African government counterparts, donors began to reduce their funding for agriculture. As a result, aid flows for African agriculture fell roughly by half, from over US$2 billion to $1 billion per year between the mid-1980s and the early 2000s (Figure 9.2).

Pendulums swing back, however. In recent years, agriculture has returned to favor, led largely by the growing chorus of support for efforts to meet the MDG of halving poverty by 2015. Donors, like African governments, increasingly believe that they must commit greater financial resources to agriculture, where the majority of poor Africans earn their livelihoods, if they are to help Africa achieve broad-based poverty reduction. As donors gear up to increase their aid to African agriculture, past reviews of donor experience in African agriculture (Lele 1991; Eicher 2003) suggest the following lessons:

- *Favorable macro and sectoral policies.* Donor aid clearly works best when deployed in a macroeconomic and sectoral policy setting that is favorable to agricultural producers. In inhospitable policy environments, the resources become largely ineffective.
- *Long-term commitments.* Successful institution building is an accretionary process requiring a multigenerational time span. Therefore, the public investments required to sustain agricultural growth require long-term commitments, measured in decades rather than in three- to five-year project

---

9. Using a smaller sample of 19 countries reporting under the CAADP budget monitoring program, Mwape (2006) computed very similar shares: 63 percent of countries under 5 percent, 21 percent between 5 and 10 percent, and 16 percent over 10 percent.

TABLE 9.2 African government budget allocations for agriculture, 2004

	Share of government budget allocated to agriculture
Benin	3.9
Botswana	4.5
Burkina Faso	15.9
Burundi	4.4
Cameroon	3.6
Central African Republic	2.7
Chad	9.7
Côte d'Ivoire	4.4
Democratic Republic of Congo	1.5
Ethiopia	13.6
Gabon	0.8
Gambia	8.5
Ghana	0.8
Guinea	14.0
Guinea Bissau	0.5
Kenya	4.2
Lesotho	3.0
Madagascar	8.0
Malawi	7.0
Mali	14.5
Mauritania	5.5
Mauritius	2.9
Mozambique	9.1
Namibia	5.3
Niger	0.9
Nigeria	3.2
Rwanda	4.0
Senegal	4.4
Sudan	5.4
Swaziland	3.3
Tanzania	5.5
Togo	2.3
Uganda	5.0
Zambia	4.0
Zimbabwe	6.6
Average	5.5

SOURCE: Fan and Saurkar (2008).

FIGURE 9.2 Trends in donor aid for African agriculture, 1975–2007

Millions of constant 2005 US$

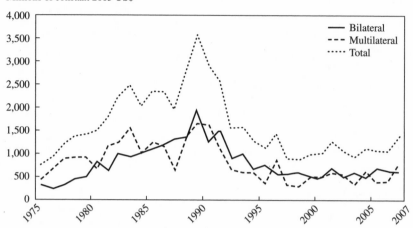

SOURCE: OECD Donor Reporting Service.

cycles. Donors and major foundations will need to adjust their funding cycles accordingly.

- *A return to regionalism.* Regional collaboration offers prospects for capturing potentially large cross-country spillovers as well as benefits from economies of scale in agricultural research, trade, infrastructure, and policy work (Abdulai, Diao, and Johnson 2005). Donors have, in fact, played a key role in supporting regional efforts by Comité permanent Inter-Etats de Lutte contre la Sécheresse dans le Sahel, ASARECA, WECARD/ CORAF, and a series of regional commodity networks. Yet most donor support remains tied to bilateral programs. The recent mobilization of donor consortia in support of COMESA and other regional CAADP programs offers one sign of increased willingness to support regional agricultural efforts. Because most regional efforts to date have relied on donor funding during their initial phases, the question becomes one of how to ensure the financial sustainability of these initiatives over the long run.

- *Reconciliation of contradictory donor policy stances.* What the donors give out with one hand, through their funding of agricultural support programs in Africa, they take away with the other, through the price-depressing effect of their domestic farm subsidies. In recent years, donors' domestic farm subsidies have reduced African farm incomes by roughly double the amount of annual aid flows to African agriculture. Meanwhile, donor food aid offers quick fixes that reduce incentives for African farmers and policymakers to develop long-run solutions for ensuring food security. As a result, in many settings African policymakers find it easier to entice food aid from donors than to extract domestic budget allocations for agricultural research, extension, and roads. Together, African governments and donors must confront and reconcile these conflicting incentives.

Fulfilling the Preconditions

In broad terms, past agricultural performance in Africa has failed because the two fundamental ingredients for growth—increased productivity and favorable farmer incentives—have not coincided frequently enough. During the 1970s and 1980s, donors and African governments provided extensive public resources for agricultural research, extension, and roads. But the policy environment in which they operated was often unfavorable to agriculture, with high rates of agricultural taxation, overvalued exchange rates, and heavy restrictions on private sector trading in key agricultural markets.

In contrast, during the 1990s and early 2000s, the macro policy environment for agriculture has improved in Africa. Although ambiguities and uncertainties remain in specific agricultural markets, rates of agricultural taxation have generally fallen and agricultural markets have become more open to private processors and traders (World Bank 2007a; Anderson and Masters 2009). But during this period, the engine of agricultural productivity growth has stalled as government and donor resources for agriculture fell and agricultural research, extension, and rural road systems generally deteriorated (see Table 9.1, Figure 9.2). As the flow of new agricultural technology dwindled, productivity gains faltered in many parts of the agricultural system.

In 2010, at the beginning of the second decade of the 2000s, restored public interest in agriculture stands poised to coincide with an improving incentive environment. For the first time in a generation, growing public resources and growing interest in agriculture may enable the two preconditions for agricultural growth to coincide across a broad swath of African agriculture.

The Changing Environment

Can African policymakers seize this opportunity? In order to do so, they must apply the lessons from past agricultural successes in an evolving environment where a series of major changes is currently under way.

Africa's Eroding Resource Base

Until quite recently, African farmers enjoyed abundant land resources, and agricultural growth resulted mainly from area expansion rather than from higher yields. But demographic pressures have exhausted the land frontier in many locations, so this pattern of extensive growth cannot continue. Average farm sizes in Africa are already falling (Figure 9.3), and small farms of less than 5 hectares increasingly dominate farm size distributions (Jayne, Mather, and Mghenyi 2006; Valdés et al. 2009).

FIGURE 9.3 Mean farm size by continent, 1930–90

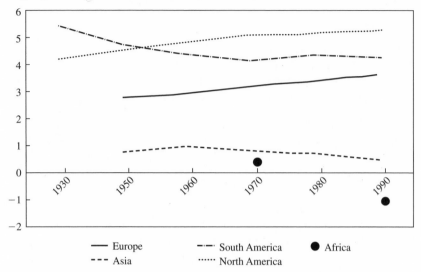

Log ha per farm

SOURCE: Eastwood, Lipton, and Newell (2010).

Resource degradation has accompanied this increasing land scarcity. Yields have not grown fast enough to keep up with growing populations. Meanwhile, crop expansion into fragile areas, shorter fallows, and low fertilizer application rates have all contributed to widespread erosion and soil mining (Cleaver and Schreiber 1994; Sanchez et al. 1997). Farmers in Sub-Saharan Africa apply only about 8 kilograms of mineral fertilizers per hectare compared to an average of 100 kilograms in all developing countries (Morris et al. 2007). Given crop nutrient uptakes and soil erosion, net nitrogen flows are negative on average, with net annual losses of 22 kilograms per hectare per year (Smaling, Nandwa, and Janssen 1997). In some areas, losses range as high as 40–60 kilograms per hectare of nitrogen, phosphorus, and potassium nutrients each year (Wood, Sebastian, and Scherr 2000). The combination of increasing resource scarcity and degradation threatens future prospects for Africa's farmers, a majority of whom are already poor. Climate change seems likely to compound many of these problems, particularly in more marginal agricultural areas.

Increasingly, future breakthroughs in Africa will need to include improved natural resource management (NRM) practices, a complex and site-specific undertaking. Given the heterogeneity within African agriculture, these efforts will require participatory research involving scientists and farmers in order to identify practices suitable for specific conditions. They will also require strong links to grassroots organizations with the capacity to help farmers and communities introduce and manage improved NRM practices.

Because many NRM investments involve action at landscape levels, they require cooperation by groups of farmers or even entire communities (Knox, Meinzen-Dick, and Hazell 2002). Because investments in better NRM yield payoffs over the long term, they require secure long-term property rights over resources. Because much of rural Africa bases land rights on customary tenure implemented and enforced at community and tribal levels, the provision of secure property rights depends in large part on effective local leadership (Place and Hazell 1993; Bruce and Migot-Adholla 1994).

Changes in Agricultural Science

Advances in the biological sciences are changing the ways in which some agricultural research is undertaken. The new research technologies require greater access to highly specialized staff and laboratories as well as development of effective biosafety regulations and protocols to protect human health and the environment. Molecular biology and genetic engineering offer considerable promise for developing new crop varieties that can prosper in Africa's drought- and pest-prone environments and for overcoming many entrenched livestock diseases.

But few of Africa's public research systems can marshal the human and financial resources needed to undertake this kind of research and regulate its use; Kenya and South Africa are two exceptions. Therefore, African research organizations must forge links with research partners, in Africa and outside, that can provide this expertise (Eicher 1999, 2009). Similarly, regionally coordinated research and biosafety networks within Africa offer scope for concentrating some of the scarce human resources that do exist. Regional research networks (such as ASARECA and CORAF), together with the Forum for Agricultural Research in Africa and NEPAD, are already beginning to play this role in support of national research systems.

Market liberalization policies and proprietary modern research products have also opened the door for rapid expansion of private agricultural research around the world (Pardey and Beintema 2001; InterAcademy Council 2004). Although privatization of agricultural R&D is still small in Africa (less than 2 percent of total spending), it is likely to grow more rapidly in the future, and public research systems must recognize that some lines of research—such as the improvement of major food crops and many high-value cash crops— will become increasingly privatized. Rather than competing or duplicating private sector research efforts, public agricultural researchers should see this as an opportunity for the public research sector to focus on those kinds of research that the private sector has less incentive to undertake. These include research on the improvement of many orphan crops (such as secondary food staples), the problems of most small subsistence-oriented farmers, and most NRM research.

Greater privatization has given rise to intellectual property (IP) rights over many of the products of agricultural research. Moreover, given changing tastes and growing food processing industries, even the processing and fortification of traditional staples such as sweet potatoes and bananas may be subject to IP rights. With the growing use of patents and licensing arrangements in industrial countries, African countries face pressure to adopt international agreements on IP rights that protect such rights around the world—for example, the World Trade Organization (WTO) agreement on Trade-Related Aspects of Intellectual Property Rights. Countries can still use protected materials and methods for research on commodities that are not traded internationally. But obtaining access to protected materials remains difficult.[10] African countries need to develop their own IP legislation that balances their international obligations to respect the IP of other countries with their own national needs, including protection of their own indigenous plant genetic materials, farmers' rights, and research products (Omamo and von Grebmer 2005).

Agribusiness Consolidation

Since the early 1990s, relaxation of restrictions on foreign direct investment, foreign exchange markets, and international trade have launched rapid consolidation in food retailing and export agriculture worldwide. In Africa, two major South African supermarket chains, Shoprite and Pick N Pay, have expanded into 13 other African countries as well as into Australia, India, and the Philippines. In Kenya, four home-grown supermarket chains have emerged in recent decades, and they now operate over 200 urban retail outlets (Weatherspoon and Reardon 2003).

Over time, growing concentration in food retailing and agricultural export triggers a parallel consolidation in wholesaling, processing, and distribution (Reardon 2007). Therefore, growing concentration in food retailing, agricultural export, and agroprocessing implies changing marketing requirements upstream for African farmers. Large retailers, processors, and exporters require large lots, consistent quality, standard packaging, food safety compliance, and guaranteed timing of delivery—things most smallholders find difficult to achieve without some sort of collective action, investments, or support. This implies a growing public role in helping to enable collective smallholder action by facilitating institutional innovation, establishing standards, providing market information, enforcing contracts, and mediating disputes (see Chapter 5 for examples).

Commodity Prices

Commodity prices for Africa's traditional bulk export commodities—cotton, cocoa, coffee, and tea—generally trended downward during the 25 years from the late 1970s to the middle of the first decade of the 2000s (World Bank 2007a). During this period, the composition of world agricultural trade shifted from bulk commodities to processed agricultural goods. In 1980, the value of bulk farm com-

---

10. The African Agricultural Technology Foundation was formed in 2002 to facilitate partnerships that will remove the constraints on agricultural technology transfer and use by African farmers.

modity exports worldwide amounted to double the value of processed agricultural products. But by 2000, the rankings had reversed (Regmi and Gehlhar 2003). World markets for processed agricultural products demand strict attention to health and food safety issues, product quality, and sanitary standards, as do nontraditional exports such as fresh fruits and vegetables. For many potential African suppliers, these stringent requirements act as nontariff barriers. Given falling commodity prices and the general shift to processed agricultural goods, Africa's share of world agricultural trade fell steadily, from about 7.5 percent in the 1960s to under 2.5 percent in the early 2000s (Johnson, Temu, and Hazell 2003).

With the world commodity price boom of 2007 and 2008, food prices have moved sharply higher during the second half of the decade. These price increases have arisen, at least in part, from the introduction of biofuel subsidies in the United States and other major agricultural countries. Forecasts through the year 2020, from a 1997 base, project an increase of 20–40 percent in the world price of maize, Africa's most important staple food (Rosegrant et al. 2006). Combined with rising oil prices and consequently increased costs for fuel and petroleum-based mineral fertilizer, these forces will tend to raise maize production costs in Africa (World Bank 2007a). In the face of rising petrochemical prices, improvements in the efficiency of fertilizer use and development of alternative management practices for maintaining soil fertility assume increasing urgency (see Chapter 7). More broadly, these trends amplify the calls by African leaders for greater attention to agriculture and to expanded research and regional trade in food staples (AU/NEPAD 2008).

World Trade and OECD Farm Subsidies

In 2005, OECD countries spent roughly US$1 billion every working day, or about US$280 billion a year, on agricultural subsidies for their farmers (OECD 2005). These substantial subsidies artificially boost production and depress world prices for key supported commodities. Global simulations using world trade models suggest that OECD farm subsidies cost farmers in Sub-Saharan Africa US$1.8–$1.9 billion per year in lost agricultural income (Beghin, Roland-Holst, and van der Mensbrugghe 2002; Diao, Diaz-Bonilla, and Robinson 2003). Meanwhile, aid agencies mandated to assist African farmers deploy only about half that amount, roughly US$1 billion per year, for African agriculture (see Figure 9.2). Ironically, as a result, "taxpayers in OECD countries are paying twice for development assistance: once to reduce the incomes of poor farmers and again to alleviate the same poverty" (Beghin, Roland-Holst, and van der Mensbrugghe 2002, 27). These pressures and donor policy inconsistencies surface most clearly in this volume in the discussion of Mali's cotton sector (Chapter 4).

Trade liberalization may likewise penalize African farmers. Many models of Doha Round trade liberalization suggest that African farmers may lose out as access to protected European agricultural markets opens up to competition from Brazil, India, Indonesia, and Thailand, particularly under partial liberalization scenarios (Achterbosch et al. 2004; Yang 2005; Badiane 2006). Already in sugar markets, reductions in internal EU supports have resulted in falling export prices for developing-country suppliers, including several in Africa.

Together, these trade and subsidy concerns suggest that in coming years African leaders will need to renew their engagement in WTO and donor discussions on trade, aid, and farm subsidy issues. At a minimum, efforts will need to focus on finding alternative subsidy instruments that would enable rich countries to court favor with their domestic farm lobbies but in ways that do not lower world prices and, in turn, harm African farmers. As François Traore, president of Burkina Faso's national Cotton Producers Union, notes, "If the United States can go to the moon, which is rather complicated, one would think it could figure out a way, if it wanted, to help its cotton producers, without hurting us farmers in Africa" (New York Times 2003, A18). Clearly, African farmers have a stake in ongoing WTO negotiations. So African political leaders will need to support their farmers, not only at home but also abroad, in international negotiations.

The Way Forward

Changes

As in the past, African farmers face a changing environment going forward. Population growth, diminished fallow periods, and increasing pressure on the land will continue to motivate the search for alternate means of sustaining soil fertility over time. New agricultural technologies—such as biotechnology and tissue culture—involve proprietary private sector technology development. In agricultural marketing, the demise of parastatals and public marketing agencies during the 1990s has opened up economic space now filled by private firms.

Many of these changes represent a continuation of earlier trends. This continuity is particularly evident in Africa's growing land and natural resource pressure, which has been apparent in many regions for some time; in private sector technology development, which began over a generation ago with the introduction of hybrid maize; in smallholder participation in concentrated international markets, which began with export crops during the colonial era; and in the growing importance of regional trade and regional research, for which recent initiatives represent a return to earlier regional models.

These changes suggest an evolving partnership between public and private sector actors. Private firms seem poised to play an increasingly important role in the technology development, marketing, and processing systems crucial to successful agricultural growth. For this reason, in the future more than ever, governments will need to adopt transparent, predictable policies conducive to private sector investment in farming and agribusiness.

Yet public agencies will still play an essential role in providing public goods such as roads, water, education, health, and power. Government's role likewise remains unchallenged in research and technology development for self-pollinating and vegetatively propagated crops and in the development and management of systems for controlling contagious livestock and plant diseases. Particularly for low-value but critical food security crops—such as cassava, sweet potatoes, and yams—the absence of pecuniary incentives for private sector innovators will leave agricultural technology development squarely in the public domain. Continuously evolving plant and animal viruses, pests, and diseases demand collective action and coordination both within and across international borders, giving rise to further public responsibilities in helping to maintain agricultural productivity.

Constants

In the face of continually evolving natural environments, global economic systems, and agricultural technologies, two bedrock principles remain firm. Our review of the processes that drive agricultural growth has covered a broad spectrum of commodities and geographic settings over intervals of 25–100 years each. This long-term perspective suggests two recurring requirements for agricultural growth: (1) long-term investment in agricultural productivity and (2) favorable incentive systems for farmers and agribusinesses (Chapter 8).

To deliver these two key prerequisites in the presence of ongoing incremental changes in the scientific, global, and natural environments will require subtle shifts of emphasis going forward. In research, given growing private sector involvement in agricultural technology development, governments will need to concentrate more than in the past on protocols that will facilitate private research initiatives while at the same time ensuring public safety and farmer access at reasonable prices. Direct public provision of new genetic material will nonetheless remain critical in areas where the private sector cannot capture economic gains, particularly in low-value crops with closed-pollinating or vegetatively propagated crops.

Similarly, growing pressure on land and water resources will require an increasing focus on developing input packages and management systems that maintain soil fertility over time. Improved agronomic practices will form a key part of these efforts, and these require a sound understanding of farmer constraints and priorities in order to develop feasible higher-productivity management systems. This understanding will likely require an increasing emphasis on early interaction between researchers and farmers in technology development as well as increased focus on building and maintaining effective extension systems. The research processes described in Chapter 7 offer insights into possible means of managing these interactions among farmers, researchers, and extension staff.

Finally, a regional perspective will become increasingly important in getting African agriculture moving more rapidly and efficiently. Regional flows of agricultural products and technologies are on the rise, for good reason. Cross-border investments by large agribusiness firms, rising population densities, and falling communication costs are leading to increasing opportunities for agricultural commodity trade and technology diffusion. The expansion of regional research partnerships and agricultural training institutions offer opportunities for developing and capturing the gains from cross-border technology spillovers. Given growing opportunities for cross-border trade, Africa's regional economic organizations stand positioned to play an increasingly important role in maintaining incentives and ensuring policy coordination across borders.

Patience and Perseverance

Policymakers seeking quick fixes are destined for disappointment. In the future, as in the past, patience and long-term commitment will be essential for sustaining agricultural growth.[11] The Zimbabweans invested in maize research for 28 years before coming out with SR52, their blockbuster hybrid that boosted productive capacity throughout the region (Chapter 3). IITA built on 18 years of colonial research and invested for a further 7 before releasing the TMS cassava varieties that have transformed farm opportunities across Africa (Chapter 2). Cotton researchers across the Sahel have produced a steady stream of new varieties over the past 45 years (Chapter 4). Dairy breeding and AI services in Kenya have involved long-term institutional development and close private–public collaboration for the past 80 years (Chapter 6). Clearly, slogans and election-year input subsidies will not suffice. These case studies suggest that agricultural R&D programs, like strong families, require careful nurturing and steadfast commitment over decades and across generations.

Because animal and plant diseases evolve continuously, research systems must produce a continuous stream of agricultural innovations. Without a steady flow of improved technology, mutation by pests and diseases will gradually erode past technological gains, and farm productivity will fall over time. As a result, sustained investment in agricultural research is necessary simply to maintain constant productivity in the face of evolving natural competitors. Still greater efforts are required to raise productivity over time.

Success is clearly possible in African agriculture. The case studies reviewed in this book suggest that agricultural growth can occur across a broad range of African settings provided technological improvements and favorable incentive systems converge. To improve agricultural incentives in coming decades, African leaders will need to build on the generally improved macro policy environment for agriculture and further improve incentives by bringing policy transparency and predictability to major agricultural markets. To increase productivity, they will need to raise additional resources for agriculture, as pledged in Maputo, and deploy these increased funds to supply the public goods—agricultural research, rural infrastructure, extension services, and support institutions—necessary for sustaining agricultural productivity gains over time.

---

11. See, for example, De Wilde (1967); Lele (1975, 1991); Eicher (1989, 1999, 2009); Pardey and Beintema (2002); and InterAcademy Council (2004).

References

Abdulai, A., X. Diao, and M. Johnson. 2005. Achieving regional growth dynamics in African agriculture. Development Strategy and Governance Division Discussion Paper 17. Washington, D.C.: International Food Policy Research Institute.

Abdulai, A., M. Johnson, and X. Diao. 2006. Leveraging regional growth dynamics in African Agriculture. *African Journal of Agricultural and Resource Economics* 1 (1): 49–66.

Achterbosch, T. J., H. B. Hammouda, P. N. Osakwe, and F. W. van Tongeren. 2004. *Trade liberalisation under the Doha Development Agenda: Options and consequences for Africa.* Report 6.04.09. The Hague: Agricultural Economics Research Institute.

AC Nielsen. 2004. *Nationwide survey by AC Nielsen ORG-MARG underscores benefits of Bollgard™ cotton.* AC Nielsen/Mahyco Monsanto Press release, March 26.

Adegboye, R. O., and J. A. Akinwumi. 1990. Cassava processing innovations in Nigeria. In *Tinker, tiller and technical change,* ed. H. Appleton and N. Carter, pp. 64–79. London: Intermediate Technology Publications; New York: Bootstrap Press.

Adjebeng-Asem, S. 1990. The Nigerian cassava grater. In *Tinker, tiller and technical change,* ed. H. Appleton and N. Carter, pp. 80–96. London: Intermediate Technology Publications, and New York: Bootstrap Press.

Africa Research Bulletin. 2006. Cassava: Nigeria. *Africa Research Bulletin: Economic, Financial and Technical Series* 43 (5): 16982A–16982B.

African Union. 2006. *Declaration on fertilizer for the African Green Revolution.* Abuja, Nigeria: African Union, June 13. Available at <www.africafertilizersummit.org>.

Agboola, S. A. 1968. The introduction and spread of cassava in Western Nigeria. *Nigerian Journal of Economics and Social Studies* 10 (13): 369–385.

AGRA (Alliance for a Green Revolution in Africa). 2009. *AGRA annual report, 2007.* Nairobi, Kenya: AGRA.

Agricultural Committee of the National Liberation Council. 1966. *Report of the Agricultural Committee of the National Liberation Council.* Accra, Ghana: Agricultural Committee of the National Liberation Council.

Ahmed, M. A. M., S. Ehui, and Y. Assefa. 2004. Dairy development in Ethiopia. Environment and Production Technology Division Discussion Paper 123. Washington, D.C.: International Food Policy Research Institute.

Ahmed, M., J. Mohammed, and S. Ehui, 2000. Household level economic and nutritional impacts of market-oriented dairy production in the Ethiopian highlands. *Food and Nutrition Bulletin* 21 (4): 460–465.

Ajayi, O. C., and F. Kwesiga. 2003. Implications of local policies and institutions on the adoption of improved fallows in Eastern Zambia. *Agroforestry Systems* 59 (3): 327–336.

Ajayi, O. C., M. Camara, G. Fleisher, F. Haidara, M. Sow, A. Troare, and H. van de Valk. 2002. *Socio-economic assessment of pesticide use in Mali.* Special Issue Publication Series 6. Hanover, Germany: Pesticide Policy Project, University of Hanover.

Ajayi, O. C., C. Massi, R. Katanga, and G. Kabwe. 2006. Typology and characteristics of farmers planting improved fallows in Eastern Zambia. *Zambian Journal of Agricultural Sciences* 8 (2): 1–5.

Ajayi, O.C., F. K. Akinnifesi, G. Sileshi, and S. Chakeredza. 2007. Adoption of renewable soil fertility replenishment technologies in Southern African region: Lessons learnt and the way forward. *Natural Resource Forum* 31 (4): 306–317.

Akande, S. O. 2000. *Price and trade policy in Nigeria: Agricultural trade review.* Washington, D.C.: World Bank.

Akinnifesi, F. K., W. Makumba, G. Sileshi, O. C. Ajayi, and D. Mweta. 2007. Synergistic effect of inorganic N and P fertilizers and organic inputs from Gliricidia sepium on productivity of intercropped maize in Southern Malawi. *Plant Soil* 294: 203–217.

Akoroda, M. O. 1999. *Study of the contribution of cassava and sweetpotato to total food availability in Malawi.* Lilongwe, Malawi: Southern Africa Root Crops Research Network.

Akoroda, M. O., and M. L. Mwabumba. 2000. *Sweet success: Cassava in Lilongwe East RDP.* Lilongwe, Malawi: Southern Africa Root Crops Research Network.

Alderman, H. 1990. *Nutritional status in Ghana and its determinants:* Social dimensions of adjustment in Sub-Saharan Africa. Policy Analysis Working Paper 3. Washington, D.C.: World Bank.

Alliot, J. 1999. Interventions de l'Agence française de développement en faveur des filières cotonnières. In *Coton et développement (1999): Cinquante ans d'action cotonière au service du développement,* Hors série, septembre.

Alston, J. M. 2002. Spillovers. *Australian Journal of Agricultural and Resource Economics* 46 (3): 315–346.

Alston, J. M., C. Chan-Kang, M. C. Marra, P. G. Pardey, and T. J. Wyatt. 2000. A meta-analysis of rates of return to agricultural R&D. Research Report 113. Washington, D.C.: International Food Policy Research Institute.

Alston, J. M., D. A. Sumner, and H. Brunke. 2007. *Impacts of reductions in U.S. cotton subsidies on West African cotton producers.* Boston: Oxfam America. Available at <www.oxfamamerica.org>.

Amani, H. K. R., and W. Maro. 1992. Policy to promote an effective private trading system in farm products and farm inputs in Tanzania. In *Food security research in southern Africa: Policy implications,* ed. J. Wyckoff and M. Rukuni. Harare: University of Zimbabwe.

Amann, V. F. 1973. Exprience in smallholder dairy production in Uganda as a basis for setting production policy objectives. In *Agricultural policy issues in East Africa,* ed. V. F. Amann, pp. 154–178. Kampala, Uganda: Makerere University.

Anderson, K., and W. A. Masters, eds. 2009. *Distortions to agricultural incentives in Africa.* Washington, D.C.: World Bank.

Anga, B. 2003a. The Nigerian international trade mission to South America on cassava commercialization. Mission Report, August 31–September 12. Lagos, Nigeria: Presidential Initiative on Cassava Production and Export.

———. 2003b. The Nigerian international trade mission to Europe on cassava export and investment promotion. Mission Report, October 4–23. Lagos, Nigeria: Presidential Initiative on Cassava Production and Export.

Anthony, C. G. 1988. *Mechanization and maize: Agriculture and the politics of technology transfer in East Africa.* New York: Columbia University Press.

AP (Associated Press). 2007. Banana trade dispute returns to the fore. *International Herald Tribune,* March 8. Available at <www.iht.com/articles/2007/03/08/business/wto.php>.

ApproTEC. 2003. *Micro-irrigation technologies.* Available at <www.approtec.org/ tech _irrigate.shtml>.

Argwings-Kodhek, G., T. S. Jayne, G. Nyambane, T. Awuor, and T. Yamano. 1999. *How can micro-level household information make a difference for agricultural policy making?* Nairobi, Kenya: Tegemeo Institute of Agricultural Policy and Development and Kenya Agricultural Research Institute; East Lansing: Michigan State University. Mimeo.

Ariga, J., T. S. Jayne, and J. Nyoro. 2006. Factors driving the growth in fertilizer consumption in Kenya, 1990–2005: Sustaining the momentum in Kenya and lessons for broader replicability in Sub-Saharan Africa. Working Paper 24. Nairobi, Kenya: Egerton University, Tegemeo Institute.

Ariga, J., T. S. Jayne, B. Kibaara, and J. K. Nyoro. 2008. Trends and patterns in fertilizer use by smallholder farmers in Kenya, 1997–2007. Working Paper 28. Nairobi, Kenya: Egerton University, Tegemeo Institute of Agricultural Policy and Development.

Arulussa Overseas. 1997. *The Implications of minimum tillage as practiced by cotton producers: Final report of the cotton production and management systems survey.* Lusaka, Zambia: Lonrho.

Asfaw, S., D. Mithöfer, and H. Waibel. 2007. What impact are EU supermarket standards having on developing country export of high-value horticultural products? Evidence from Kenya. Paper prepared for presentation at the 105th EAAE seminar, International Marketing and International Trade of Quality Food Products, Bologna, Italy, March 8–10. Available at <http://ageconsearch.umn.edu/bitstream/7870/1/cp070006.pdf>.

AU/NEPAD (African Union/New Partnership for Africa's Development). 2003a. *Comprehensive Africa agricultural development programme.* Midrand: NEPAD Secretariat.

———. 2003b. *NEPAD agricultural program: Action plan 2003–2004.* Pretoria: New Partnership for Africa's Development.

———. 2006. Agricultural expenditure tracking system in African countries. Conference Paper 18, presented at the New Partnership for Africa's Development conference Championing Agricultural Successes for Africa's Future: A Parliamentarians' Dialogue on NEPAD, Somerset West, South Africa, May 15–18.

———. 2008. *Framework for African food security (FAFS).* Addis Ababa, Ethiopia: NEPAD.

Badiane, O. 2006. Agricultural trade liberalization under Doha: The risk facing African countries. Discussion Paper 39, Development Strategies and Governance Division. Washington, D.C.: International Food Policy Research Institute.

Baffes, J. 2004. *Cotton market setting, trade policies, and issues.* Washington, D.C.: Development Prospects Group, World Bank.

Bagachwa, M. S. D. 1992. Choice of technology in small and large firms: Grain milling in Tanzania. *World Development* 20 (1): 97–107.

Balagopalan, C., G. Padmaja, S. K. Nanda, and S. N. Moorthy. 1988. *Cassava in food, feed, and industry.* Boca Raton, Fla., U.S.A.: CRC Press.

Bamikole, O. T., and M. Bokanga. 2000. The ethanol industry in Nigeria growing on a new crop. Paper presented at the International Fuel Ethanol Workshop, Windsor, Ontario, Canada, June 20–23.

Bangwe, L. M. 1998. Will the dominance of maize ever diminish? Constraints to crop diversification in Zambia. Occasional Working Paper 2. Prepared for presentation at the Sixth SAAFSR-E Regional Conference, Mulungushi International Conference Centre, Lusaka, Zambia, February 2–4.

Banque Mondiale. 2002a. Recommandations visant à renforcer le programme anti-corruption: La Réforme du secteur public et renforcement des capacités. Washington, D.C.: Région Afrique, Banque Mondiale. Mimeo.

———. 2002b. Réformes du secteur cotton au Mali. Washington, D.C.: Banque Mondiale. Mimeo AFTR2, 11 décembre.

Barratt, N., D. Chitundu, O. Dover, J. Elsinga, S. Eriksson, L. Guma, M. Haggblade, S. Haggblade, T. O. Henn, F. R. Locka, C. O'Donnell, C. Smith, and T. Stevens. 2006. Cassava as drought insurance: Food security implications of cassava trials in central Zambia. *Agrekon* 45 (1): 106–123.

Barrett, C. B., T. Reardon, and P. Webb. 2001. Nonfarm income diversification and household livelihood strategies in rural Africa: Concepts, dynamics and policy implications. *Food Policy* 26: 315–331.

Barrett, C. B., F. Place, A. Aboud, and D. R. Brown. 2002. The challenge of stimulating adoption of improved natural resource management practices in African Agriculture. In *Natural resources management in African agriculture: Understanding and improving current practices,* ed. C. B. Barrett, F. Place, and A. A. Aboud, pp. 1–22. Wallingford, U.K.: CAB International.

Bates, R. H. 1981. *Markets and states in tropical Africa: The political basis of agricultural policies.* Berkeley: University of California Press.

———. 1989. *Beyond the miracle of the market: The political economy of agrarian development in Kenya.* Cambridge: Cambridge University Press.

Baudron, F., H. M. Mwanza, B. Triompe, M. Bwalya, and D. Gumbo. 2005. Challenges for the adoption of conservation agriculture by smallholders in semi-arid Zambia. Harare, Zimbabwe: Centre de Coopération International en Recherche Agronomique pour le Développement.

Bayley, B. 2002. *A revolution in the market: The deregulation of South African agriculture.* Oxford Policy Management Report 6. Oxford: Oxford Policy Management.

Beghin, J. C., D. Roland-Holst, and D. van der Mensbrugghe. 2002. Global agricultural trade and the Doha Round: What are the implications for North and South? Working Paper 02-Wp 308. Ames: Center for Agricultural and Rural Development, Iowa State University.

Beintema, N., and G.-J. Stads. 2006. *Agricultural R&D in Sub-Saharan Africa: An era of stagnation.* Agricultural Science and Technology Indicators Initiative Background Report. Washington, D.C.: International Food Policy Research Institute.

Bekunda, M. A., A. Bationo, and H. Ssali. 1997. Soil fertility management in Africa: A review of selected research trials. In *Replenishing soil fertility in Africa,* ed. R. J. Buresh, P. A. Sanchez, and F. Calhoun, pp. 63–79. SSSA Special Publication 51. Madison, Wis., U.S.A.: Soil Science Society of America.

Belshaw, D. G. R. 1988. Roles and performance of financial markets and institutions. In *Agricultural development in Africa. Farm finance and agriculture development.* Tokyo: Asian Productivity Organization.

Benesi, I. R. M., C. C. Moyo, N. M. Mahungu, J. Mkumbira, M. M. Soko, R. F. N. Sauti, and V. S. Sandifolo. 1999. Progress in developing improved cassava varieties in Malawi. In *Food security and crop diversification in SADC countries: The role of cassava and sweetpotato,* ed. M. O. Akoroda and J. M. Teri. Ibadan, Nigeria: International Institute of Tropical Agriculture.

Benin, S., S. Ehui, and J. Pender. 2002. Policies for livestock development in the Ethiopian highlands. Socio-economic and Policy Research Working Paper. Addis Ababa, Ethiopia: Livestock Policy Analysis Program, International Livestock Research Institute.

Benson, T. 1997. *The 1995/96 fertilizer verification trial—Malawi: Economic analysis of results for policy discussion.* Lilongwe, Malawi: Action Group I, Maize Productivity Task Force, Chitedze Agricultural Research Station.

———. 1999. *Validating and strengthening the area-specific fertilizer recommendations for hybrid maize grown by Malawian smallholders.* Lilongwe, Malawi: Maize Commodity Team, Chitedze Agricultural Research Station.

Berg, E. 1981. *Accelerated development in Sub-Saharan Africa: An agenda for action.* Washington, D.C.: World Bank.

Béroud, F. 1999. Les filières partenaires. In *Coton et développement (1999): Cinquante ans d'action cotonière au service du développement,* Hors série, septembre.

Bienen, H. 1988. Nigeria: From windfall gains to welfare losses? In *Oil windfalls: Blessing or curse?* ed. Alan Gelb et al., pp. 227–260. New York: Oxford University Press.

Bingen, R. J. 1994. Agricultural development policy and grassroots democracy in Mali —the emergence of Mali's farmer movement. *African Rural and Urban Studies* 1 (1): 57–72.

———. 1996. Leaders, leadership, and democratization in West Africa: Observations from the cotton farmers movement in Mali. *Agriculture and Human Values* 13 (2).

———. 1998. Cotton, democracy and development in Mali. *Journal of Modern African Studies* 36 (2): 265–285.

———. 2000. Prospects for development and democracy in West Africa: Agrarian politics in Mali. In *Democracy and development in Mali,* ed. R. J. Bingen, D. Robinson, and J. Staatz. East Lansing: Michigan State University Press.

Bingen, R. J., E. Dembélé, and D. Camey. 1995. *The Malian union of cotton and food crop producers: Its current and potential role in technology development and transfer.* London: Agricultural Research and Extension Network, Overseas Development Institute.

Binswanger, H. P., and J. McIntyre. 1987. Behavioral and material determinants of production relations in land-abundant tropical agriculture. *Economic Development and Cultural Change* 36 (1): 75–99.

Binswanger, H. P., and V. W. Ruttan. 1978. *Induced innovation: Technology, institutions, and development.* Baltimore, Md., U.S.A.: Johns Hopkins University Press.

Binswanger-Mkhize, H., and A. F. McCalla. 2008. *The changing context and prospects for agricultural and rural development in Africa.* Rome: International Fund for African Development.

Birner, R., and D. Resnick. 2005. Policy and politics for smallholder agriculture. Paper presented at The Future of Small Farms Research Workshop, Wye College, Wye, U.K., June 26–29.

Blackie, M. J. 1990. Maize, food self-sufficiency and policy in East and Southern Africa. *Food Policy* 15: 383–394.

Bloom, D. E., and J. D. Sachs. 1998. Geography, demography and economic growth in Africa. *Brookings Papers on Economic Activity* 2. Washington, D.C.: Brookings Institution.

Bocchino, F. 1999. Les modifications du panorama cotonnier de 1949 à 1999. In *Coton et développement (1999): Cinquante ans d'action cotonière au service du développement,* Hors série, septembre.

Bolly, M. 2004. *Mauvaise gestion à la CMDT: Le mirage du mieux-être des paysans.* Available at <www.maliweb.net>.

Borlaug, N. E. 1996. Mobilizing science and technology for a green revolution in African agriculture. In *Achieving greater impact from research investments in Africa,* ed. S. A. Breth, pp. 209–213. Mexico City: Sasakawa Africa Association.

Boserup, E. 1965. *The conditions of agricultural growth: The economics of agrarian change under population pressure.* Chicago: Aldine.

Boughton, D., and B. H. de Frahan. 1994. Agricultural research impact assessment: The case of maize technology adoption in Southern Mali. International Development Working Paper 41. East Lansing: Department of Agricultural Economics, Michigan State University.

Bourdillon, M., P. Hebinck, J. Hoddinott, B. Kinsey, J. Marondo, N. Mudege, and T. Owens. 2002. Impact of agricultural research on poverty reduction: Assessing the impact of HYV maize in resettlement areas of Zimbabwe. Systemwide Poverty Impact Draft Report. Washington, D.C.: International Food Policy Research Institute.

Breman, H., and G. Tembo. 2006. *An assessment of the Golden Valley Agricultural Research Trust (GART) activity research and development of innovative commercial farming systems.* RNE Activity 1244. Muscle Shoals, Ala., U.S.A.: International Center for Soil Fertility.

Bridges Weekly Trade News Digest. 2007. US cotton subsidies still not WTO-compliant: Interim ruling. *Bridges Weekly Trade News Digest* 11 (28).

Brimer, L. 2000. Cyanogenic glycosides—occurrence, analysis and removal from food and feed: Comparison to other classes of toxic and antinutritional glycosides. Ph.D. dissertation, Royal Danish School of Pharmacy, Copenhagen.

Brock, J. E. 1955. Nutrition. *Annual Review of Biochemistry* 24: 523–542.

Bruce, J. W., and S. E. Migot-Adholla. 1994. *Searching for land tenure security in Africa.* Dubuque, Iowa, U.S.A.: Kendall/Hunt.

Bryceson, D. 1993. Urban bias revisited: Staple food pricing in Tanzania. In *Real markets: Social and political issues of food policy reform,* ed. C. Hewitt de Alcantara. London: Frank Cass.

Buccola, S., and C. Sukume. 1988. Optimal grain pricing and storage policy in controlled agricultural economies: Application to Zimbabwe. *World Development* 16 (3): 361–371.

Burgess, S., and P. Oscarsson. 2002. *Living soils: Conservation farming handbook no. 1.* Lusaka, Zambia: Land Management and Conservation Farming Programme.

Burke, W. J., T. S. Jayne, H. A. Freeman, and P. Kristjanson. 2007. *Factors associated with farm households' movement into and out of poverty in Kenya: The rising importance of livestock.* MSU International Development Working Paper 90. East Lansing: Department of Agricultural Economics, Michigan State University.

Bwalya, M. 1999. Conservation farming with animal traction in smallholder farming systems: Palabana experiences. In *Conservation tillage with animal traction: A resource book of animal traction network for Eastern and Southern Africa (ATNESA),* ed. P. G. Kaumbutho and T. E. Simalenga. Harare, Zimbabwe: ATNESA. Available at <www.fao.org/ag/ags/agse/3ero/namibia1/c17.htm>.

Byerlee, D., and C. K. Eicher, eds. 1997. *Africa's emerging maize revolution.* Boulder, Colo., U.S.A.: Lynne Rienner.

Byerlee, D., and P. W. Heisey. 1996. Past and potential impact of maize research in Sub-Saharan Africa. *Food Policy* 21 (3): 255–277.

———. 1997. Evolution of the African maize economy. In *Africa's emerging maize revolution,* ed. C. K. Eicher and D. Byerlee. Boulder, Colo., U.S.A.: Lynne Rienner.

Camara, Y. 2007. Privatisation de la CMDT: Un passif de 20 milliards de FCFA à éponger avant la filialisation en 2008. *L'Indépendent,* May 5, 2007. Available at <www.maliweb.net>.

Carr, S. 2001. Changes in African smallholder agriculture in the twentieth century and the challenges for the twenty-first. *African Crop Science Journal* 9 (1): 331–338.

Carter, S. E., L. O. Fresco, P. G. Jones, and J. N. Fairbairn. 1992. *An atlas of cassava in Africa: Historical, agroecological and demographic aspects of crop distribution.* Cali, Colombia: International Center for Tropical Agriculture.

CFDT (Compagnie Française pour le Développement des Fibres Textiles). 1998. Contresens et contre-vérités sur les filières cotonnières africaines éléments de réponse à un document provisoire abondamment diffusé. *Coton et développement* 26 (avril–juin): 2.

CFU (Conservation Farming Unit). 1997. *Conservation farming handbook for small holders in regions I and II.* Lusaka, Zambia: Zambia National Farmers Union CFU.

———. 2001. *Low cost environmentally sustainable CF maize production systems for agro-ecological regions I, II and III based on the use of lime.* Technical Release 8. Lusaka, Zambia: Zambia National Farmers Union CFU.

———. 2006. *Reversing food insecurity and environmental degradation in Zambia through conservation agriculture.* Lusaka, Zambia: Zambia National Farmers Union CFU.

Chigunta, F., R. Herbert, and R. Mkandawire. 2003. National environments for agricultural policy. Conference Background Paper 15, prepared for the Internationale Weiterbildung und Entwicklung, International Food Policy Research Institute,

New Partnership for Africa's Development, and Technical Center for Agricultural and Rural Cooperation conference Successes in African Agriculture, Pretoria, December 1–3. Available at <www.ifpri.org/event/successes-african-agriculture>. Accessed November 2009.

Chimedza, R. 1994. Rural financial markets. In *Zimbabwe's agricultural evolution,* ed. M. Rukuni and C. Eicher, pp. 139–152. Harare: University of Zimbabwe Press.

Chirwa, T. S., P. S. Mafongoya, D. N. M. Mbewe, and B. H. Chishala. 2004. Changes in soil properties and their effects on maize productivity following Sesbania sesban and Cajanus cajan improved fallow systems in eastern Zambia. *Biology and Fertility of Soils* 40: 28–35.

Chitundu, D., and R. Soenarjo. 1997. *Cassava field production guide.* Mansa, Zambia: Luapula Livelihood and Food Security Programme.

Chitundu, D. C. 1999. Accelerated multiplication and distribution of cassava and sweetpotato planting materials in Luapula province of Zambia. In *Food security and crop diversification in SADC countries: The role of cassava and sweetpotato,* ed. M. O. Akoroda and J. M. Teri. Ibadan, Nigeria: International Institute of Tropical Agriculture.

Chitundu, M., K. Droppelmann, and S. Haggblade. 2009. Intervening in value chains: Lessons from Zambia's task force on acceleration of cassava utilisation. *Journal of Development Studies* 45 (4): 593–620.

Chiwona-Karltun, L. 2001. A reason to be bitter: Cassava classification from the farmers' perspective. Ph.D. dissertation, Karolinska Institutet, Stockholm.

Chiwona-Karltun, L., L. Brimer, J. D. K. Saka, A. R. Mhone, J. Mkumbira, L. Johansson, M. Bokanga, N. M. Mahungu, and H. Rosling. 2004. Bitter taste in cassava roots correlates with cyanogenic glucoside levels. *Journal of the Science of Food and Agriculture* 84: 581–590.

Christiansen, R. E., and V. R. Southworth. 1988. Agricultural pricing and marketing policy in Malawi: Implications for a development strategy. Paper presented at the Symposium on Agricultural Policies for Growth and Development, sponsored by the Government of Malawi, Mangochi, Malawi, October 31–November 4.

CIRAD (Centre de Coopération Internationale en Recherche Agronomique pour le Développement). 2004. *Développement des nouveaux programmes de protection en Afrique de l'Ouest: Les problémes parasitaires.* Paris: CIRAD.

Cisse, Y. 1987. Resource use and productiveness: A comparative study of intensive and non-intensive farming systems in Mali-Sud rural development project. M.S. thesis, Department of Agricultural Economics and Rural Sociology, Ahmadu Bello University, Zaria, Nigeria.

Cleaver, K. M., and G. A. Schreiber. 1994. *Reversing the spiral: The population, agriculture and environment nexus in Sub-Saharan Africa.* Washington, D.C.: World Bank.

CMDT (Compagnie Malienne pour le Développement des Textiles). 1998. *Annuaire statistique 97/98: Résultats de l'enquête agricole permanente.* Bamako, Mali: Direction de la Production Contrôle et Gestion.

———. 1999. *Rapport annuel de la CMDT Campagne 1997–98: Annexes.* Bamako, Mali.

CMDT/Sikasso. 1998. *Eléments d'analyse de l'évolution des rendements du coton de la campagne 1994/96 à la campagne 1997/98.* Sikasso, Mali: Direction Régionale de Sikasso.

Collier, P. 2007. *The bottom billion: Why the poorest countries are failing and what can be done about it.* Oxford: Oxford University Press.

———. 2009. Africa's organic peasantry: Beyond romanticism. *Harvard International Review* (Summer): 62–65.

Collier, P., and J. W. Gunning. 1999. Why has Africa grown slowly? *Journal of Economic Perspectives* 12 (3): 3–22.

COMESA (Common Market for Eastern and Southern Africa). 2007. *Report of the Secretary General to the 12th COMESA summit in Nairobi.* Lusaka, Zambia: COMESA Secretariat.

Conelly, W. T. 1998. Colonial era livestock development policy: Introduction of improved dairy cattle in high-potential farming areas of Kenya. *World Development* 26 (9): 1733–1748.

Conroy, A. 1997. Examination of policy options facing government in the event of a shortfall in national maize production. Discussion paper. Lilongwe, Malawi: Ministry of Finance.

Conway, G. 1999. *The doubly green revolution: Food for all in the twenty-first century.* Ithaca, N.Y., U.S.A.: Cornell University Press.

Cooper, P. J. M. 1999. Agroforestry: Learning as we go in Africa. In *Cultivating forests: The evolution of agroforestry systems,* ed. G. Martin, A. Agama, and R. Leakey, pp. 30–33. *People and Plants Handbook,* Issue 5. Available at <http://159.226.69.10/whatweproduce/Handbooks/handbook5/index.html>.

Coopération Française, Groupe de Travail. 1991. *Le coton en Afrique de l'Ouest et du Centre: Situation et perspectives.* Paris: Ministère de la Coopération et du Développement.

Cotlook Limited Services. 1999. Database. Available at <www.cotlook.com/>.

Coughlin, P. 1992. Development policy and inappropriate product technology: The Kenyan case. In *Industrialization in Kenya: In search of a strategy,* ed. P. Coughlin and G. K. Ikiara, p. 143. London: East African Education Publishers.

Coulibaly, T. 2009. L'avenir de la filière coton sera assuré. April 16. Primature, Mali. Available at <www.primature.gov.ml/index.php?option=com_content&task=view&id=2109&Itemid=2>.

Cromwell, E. 1996. *Governments, farmers and seeds in a changing Africa.* London: CAB International and Overseas Development Institute.

Cromwell, E., and B. T. Zambezi. 1993. *The performance of the seed sector in Malawi.* London: Overseas Development Institute.

CSM (Christian Science Monitor). 1996. Grain scandal could hurt Zimbabwe's food exporting efforts, *CSM,* April 30, 1996, 11.

Cuddy, J. D. A., and P. A. Della Valle. 1978. Measuring instability of time series data. *Oxford Bulletin of Economics and Statistics* 40: 79–85.

Daily Graphic. 2001. President launches export initiative. *Daily Graphic* (Accra, Ghana), August 17.

DANIDA (Danish International Development Agency)/MoA (Ministry of Agriculture). 1995. *Agricultural sector review: The role and functions of agricultural cooperatives in a competitive market economy.* Nairobi, Kenya: MoA.

DANIDA (Danish International Development Agency) and Ministry of Livestock Development. 1990. Kenya dairy master plan. Nairobi, Kenya: Ministry of Livestock Development.

De Carbon Ferrière, J. 1999. Le développement de la CFDT. Speech given at the Cercle France Outre-Mer dinner, May 20, 1969. In *Coton et développement (1999): Cinquante ans d'action cotonière au service du développement,* Hors série, septembre.

de Jager, A., S. M. Nandwa, and P. F. Okoth. 1998. Monitoring nutrient flows and economic performance in African farming systems (NUTMON), I: Concepts and methodologies. *Agriculture, Ecosystems and the Environment* 71 (1–3): 37–48.

de Jong, R. 1996. Dairy stock development and milk production with smallholders. Ph.D. thesis, Department of Animal Production Systems, Wageningen Agricultural University, Wageningen, the Netherlands.

de la Croix, D. 2001. Un point de vue du syndicalistes maliens, compte-rendu: Débat sur les filières cotton. *Grain de Sel* 19 (novembre).

de Langhe, E., R. Swennen, and D. Vuysteke. 1996. Plantain in the early Bantu world. In *The growth of farming communities in Africa from the equator southwards,* ed. J. E. G. Sutton. *Azania* (Nairobi, Kenya) 29–30: 147–160.

Delattre, R., and J. Le Gall. 1982. Réseau de parcelles d'observations à différents niveaux de protection phytosanitaire en culture cotonnière. *BioControl. Springer* 27: Supplement 1 (March).

Del Monte. 1988. *The Del Monte story in Kenya.* Nairobi, Kenya: Del Monte.

Dembélé, S. 1996. Recherche cotonnière au Mali. Presentation Sommaire de quelques Resultats Saillants. Sikasso, Mali: Institut d'Economie Rurale, Direction Scientifique Programme Coton.

Department of Agriculture. 1992. *Review of agronomic work on cassava: 1970 to 1990.* Chilanga, Zambia: Mt. Makulu Research Station.

Dequecker, J. 1999. Des origines de la recherche cotonnière française a l'IRCT. Extract of a speech given at the Academie Sciences d'outre-mer on February 20, 1998. In *Coton et développement (1999): Cinquante ans d'action cotonière au service du développement,* Hors série, septembre.

De Rouw, A. 1995. The fallow period as a weed-break in shifting cultivation (tropical wet forests). *Agriculture, Ecosystems and Environment* 54: 31–43.

Deveze, J.-C. 1994. *Les zones Cotonnières entre Développement, Ajustement et Dévaluation: Réflexions sur le rôle du coton en Afrique Francophone de l'ouest et du Centre.* Paris: Division du développement rural Département Afrique centrale et australe, Caisse française de développement.

DeVries, J., and G. Toenniessen. 2001. *Securing the harvest: Biotechnology, breeding and seed systems for African crops.* New York: CABI Publishing.

De Wilde, J. C. 1967. *Experiences with agricultural development in tropical Africa.* 2 vols. Baltimore, Md., U.S.A.: Johns Hopkins University Press.

De Wolf, J., and R. Rommelse. 2000. *Improved fallow technology in Western Kenya: Potential and reception by farmers.* Nairobi, Kenya: International Centre for Research in Agroforestry.

Diagne, A., and M. Zeller. 2001. *Access to credit and its impact on welfare in Malawi.* IFPRI Research Report 116. Washington, D.C.: International Food Policy Research Institute.

Diakité, L., D. Kébé, and H. Djouara. 1996. *Incidence de la dévaluation du franc CFA sur le Comportement des producteurs de coton dans les régions CMDT de Sikasso et de Koutiala.* Bamako, Mali: Programme Economie des filières, Institut de l'Economie Rurale, and Programme Régionale de Renforcement Institutionnel en Matière de Recherche sur la Sécurité Alimentaire au Sahel.

Diamond, J. 1998. *Guns, germs and steel.* New York: W. W. Norton.

Diao, X., E. Diaz-Bonilla, and S. Robinson. 2003. *How much does it hurt? The impact of agricultural trade policies on developing countries.* Washington, D.C.: International Food Policy Research Institute.

Diao, X., P. Hazell, D. Resnick, and J. Thurlow. 2006. The role of agriculture in development: Implications for Sub-Saharan Africa. DSGD Discussion Paper 29. Washington, D.C.: International Food Policy Research Institute.

Diarra, S. B., J. M. Staatz, J. R. Bingen, and N. N. Dembélé. 2000. The reform of rice milling and marketing in the Office du Niger: Catalysts for an agricultural success story in Mali. In *Democracy and development in Mali,* ed. R. J. Bingen, D. Robinson, and J. M. Staatz. East Lansing: Michigan State University.

Dibley, D., T. Reardon, and J. Staatz. 1996. How does a devaluation affect an economy? Lessons from Africa, Asia and Latin America. Staff Paper 96-105. East Lansing: Department of Agricultural Economics, Michigan State University.

Dickson, A. 2002. *The EU banana regime: History and interests.* Report commissioned by Banana Link for Euroban. Available at <www.bananalink.org.uk/trade_war/trade_war_main3.htm>.

Dijkstra, T. 1997. *Trading the fruits of the land: Horticultural marketing channels in Kenya.* Aldershot, U.K.: Ashgate.

———. 1999. Horticultural marketing in Kenya: Why potato farmers need collecting wholesalers. In *Agricultural marketing in tropical Africa—contributions from the Netherlands,* ed. H. L. van der Laan, T. Dijkstra, and A. van Tilburg. African Studies Centre Research Series 15/1999. Aldershot, U.K.: Ashgate.

Dimithe, G., R. Bernsten, J. M. Staatz, B. S. Coulibaly, D. Mariko, and A. O. Kergna. 2000. Financial profitability of Mali-Sud bas-fond rice production systems. Department of Agricultural Economics Staff Paper 2000-12, Michigan State University, East Lansing.

Dioné, J. 1989. Informing food security policy in Mali: Interactions between technology, institutions and market reforms. Ph.D. dissertation, Department of Agricultural Economics, Michigan State University, East Lansing.

———. 2000. Food security policy reform in Mali and the Sahel. In *Democracy and development in Mali,* ed. R. J. Bingen, D. Robinson, and J. M. Staatz, pp. 119–144. East Lansing: Michigan State University Press.

DNP (Direction Nationale de Planification). 2003. Macroeconomic database. Bamako, Mali: Ministry of Planning and Territorial Development.

DNSI (Direction Nationale de la Statistique et de l'Informatique). 1999. Base de données de l'enquête agricole. Bamako, Mali.

Dolan, C., and J. Humphrey. 2000. Governance and trade in fresh vegetables: The impact of UK supermarkets on the African horticultural industry. *Journal of Development Studies* 37 (2): 147–176.

Dolan, C., and K. Sutherland. 2003. Gender and employment in the Kenyan horticultural value chain. Globalisation and Poverty Discussion Paper 8. Norwich, U.K.: University of East Anglia. Available at <www.gapresearch.org/production/Final Draft.pdf>.

Dolan, C., J. Humphrey, and C. Harris-Pascal. 1999. Horticultural commodity chains: The impact of the UK market on the African fresh vegetable industry. IDS Working Paper 96. Sussex, U.K.: Institute for Development Studies.

Dorey, G. 1999. Les effets induits de la filière cotonnière. In *Coton et développement (1999): Cinquante ans d'action cotonière au service du développement,* Hors série, septembre.

Dorward, A., E. Chirwa, V. Kelly, and T. Jayne. 2008. *Evaluation of the 2006/7 agricultural input supply programme, Malawi.* Final Report. East Lansing: School of Oriental and African Studies, Wadonda Consult, Michigan State University, and London: Overseas Development Institute; undertaken for the Ministry of Agriculture and Food Security, Government of Malawi, March.

Dorward, A., J. Kydd, and C. Poulton. 1998. *Smallholder cash crop production under market liberalisation: A new institutional economics perspective.* Wallingford, U.K.: CAB International.

Doss, C. R. 2001. Designing agricultural technology for African women farmers: Lessons from 25 years of experience. *World Development* 29 (12): 2075–2092.

Doss, C. R., and M. L. Morris. 2001. How does gender affect the adoption of agricultural innovations? The case of improved maize technology in Ghana. *Agricultural Economics* 25 (2001): 27–39.

Doucouré, C. O., and S. Healy. 1999. *Evolution des systèmes de production de 94/95 à 97/98: Impact sur les revenus paysans.* Siskasso, Mali: Compagnie Malienne pour le Développement des Textiles and Bamako, Mali: Direction de la Production Contrôle et Gestion.

Doumbia, K., M. Dramane, and J.-C. Touya. 1986. *Étude sur les coûts de production des principales cultures maliennes.* Bamako, Mali: Division de Planification et d'Evaluation/Institut de l'Economie Rurale, Ministère de l'Agriculture, République du Mali.

Drechsel, P., and L. A. Gyiele. 1999. *The economic assessment of soil nutrient depletion: Analytical issues for framework development.* Bangkok: International Board for Soil Research and Management.

Dugué, P. 1989. *Possibilités et limites des systèmes de culture vivriers en zone Soudano-Sahelienne: Les cas du Yatenga (Burkina Faso).* Montpellier, France: Direction des Statistiques Agricoles/Centre International de Recherche Agronomique pour le Développement.

Eastwood, R., M. Lipton, and A. Newell. 2010. Farm size. In *Handbook of agricultural economics,* Vol. 4, ed. P. Pingali and R. Evenson, pp. 3323–3400. Amsterdam: Elsevier.

Ebony Consulting International. 2001. *The Kenyan green bean subsector.* Report prepared for the Department for International Development, Nairobi, Kenya. Johannesburg: Ebony Consulting International.

ECAZ (Environmental Conservation Association of Zambia). 1999. *Evaluation and impact monitoring of the development and adoption of conservation farming practices in Zambia,* Vol. 1, *Main evaluation and impact monitoring.* Lusaka, Zambia: U.S. Agency for International Development.

Eicher, C. K. 1989. Sustainable institutions for African agricultural development. Working Paper 19. The Hague: International Service for National Agricultural Research.

———. 1995. Zimbabwe's maize-based green revolution: preconditions for replication. *World Development* 23 (5): 805–818.

————. 1999. *Institutions and the African farmer.* Distinguished Economist Lecture. Mexico City: Centro Internacional de Mejoramiento de Maíz y Trigo.

————. 2003. Flashback: Fifty years of donor aid to African agriculture. Conference Background Paper 16, prepared for the Internationale Weiterbildung und Entwicklung, International Food Policy Research Institute, New Partnership for Africa's Development, Technical Center for Agricultural and Rural Cooperation conference Successes in African Agriculture; Pretoria, December 1–3.

————. 2009. Building African scientific capacity in food and agriculture. *Review of Business and Economics* 54 (3): 238–257.

Eicher, C. K., and B. Kupfuma. 1997. Zimbabwe's emerging maize revolution. In *Africa's emerging maize revolution,* ed. D. Byerlee and C. K. Eicher. Boulder, Colo., U.S.A.: Lynne Rienner.

Ellis, F. 2000. *Rural livelihoods and diversity in developing countries.* London: Oxford University Press.

————. 2005. Small farms, livelihood diversification and rural-urban transitions: Strategic issues in Sub-Saharan Africa. Paper presented at the conference The Future of Small Farms, organized by the International Food Policy Research Institute, Overseas Development Institute, and Imperial College, London, Withersdane Conference Centre, Wye, U.K., June 26–29. Available at <www.ifpri.org/events/seminars/2005/smallfarms/sfproc.asp>.

Ellis, R. T. 1954. An investigation into the types and relationships of the maize in Nyasaland (1954) occurring in peasant cultivation. Ph.D. thesis, University of London, London.

————. 1962. The food properties of flint and dent maize. *East African Journal* 24: 251–253.

Engelmeyer, C. 1987. *Cassava experiments in Zambia: 1941–1986.* Research Memorandum 30. Chingala, Zambia: Mt. Makulu Research Station.

Essinger, S., L. D. Hill, and J. M. Laubscher. 1998. Privatization progress in the South African maize industry. Staff Paper AE-4723. Urbana-Champaign: University of Illinois.

Evans, D. O., and P. P. Rotar. 1987. Productivity of sesbania species. *Tropical Agriculture* (Trinidad) 64: 193–200.

Evans, L. T. 1996. *Crop evolution, adaptation and yield.* Cambridge: Cambridge University Press.

Evans, R. K. 1999. *From small farms to supermarkets.* Nairobi, Kenya: Homegrown Ltd. Partnership for Rural Development in Sub-Saharan Africa.

Fan, S., and N. Rao. 2003. Public spending in developing countries: Trends, determination and impact. EPTD Discussion Paper 99. Washington, D.C.: International Food Policy Research Institute.

Fan, S., and A. Saurkar. 2008. *Tracking agricultural spending for agricultural growth and poverty reduction in Africa.* Regional Strategic Analysis and Knowledge Support System. Available at <www.resakss.org/publications/Expenditure%20trends%20brief.pdf>.

Fan, S., A. Gulati, and S. Thorat. 2007. Investment, subsidies, and pro-poor growth in rural India. Discussion Paper 716. Washington, D.C.: International Food Policy Research Institute.

Fan, S., X. Zhang, and N. Rao. 2004. Public expenditure, growth and poverty reduction in rural Uganda. Development Strategy and Governance Division Discussion Paper 4. Washington, D.C.: International Food Policy Research Institute.

Fan, S., M. Johnson, A. Saurkar, and T. Makombe. 2008. Investing in African agriculture to halve poverty by 2015. Discussion Paper 751. Washington, D.C.: International Food Policy Research Institute.

FAO (Food and Agriculture Organization of the United Nations). 1951–1960. *Production yearbook.* Rome: FAO.

————. 1967. *East African livestock survey,* Vol. II. Rome: FAO.

————. 1991. Kenya Dairy Development Project. Nairobi, Kenya: FAO and World Bank.

————. 2004. Benefits from farmer education, impact of IPM-FFS in cotton in Asia. *Cotton IPM Newsletter* 5, August.

————. 2005. *Food security and agricultural development in Sub-Saharan Africa: Building a case for more public support.* Rome: FAO, New Partnership for Africa's Development, Republic of France.

————. Various years. *Production yearbook.* Rome: FAO.

FAOSTAT. 2008. Food and Agriculture Organization statistical database. Available at <http://apps.fao.org>.

FAPRI (Food and Agricultural Policy Research Institute). 2002. The Doha Round of the World Trade Organization: Liberalization of agricultural markets and its impact on developing economies. Paper presented at the International Agricultural Trade Research Consortium Winter Meetings, San Diego, Calif.

Farmer, The. 1995. Conservation tillage helps in a drought year. *The Farmer,* June 15, supplement.

Felleke, G., and G. Geda. 2001. *The Ethiopian dairy development policy: A draft policy document.* Addis Ababa, Ethiopia: Ministry of Agriculture/Animal and Fisheries Resources Development and Regulatory Department/Animal and Fisheries Resources Development Team/Food and Agriculture Organization of the United Nations/Swedish Society for Photogrammetry and Remote Sensing.

Fitzhugh, H. A. 1998. *Global agenda for livestock research.* Occasional Publication. Midlothian, Scotland: British Society of Animal Science.

Fok, A. C. M. 1997. Etat, production et exportation cotonnières, industrie textile et développement économique: Une histoire économique du coton/textile dans le monde. Doctorat en Economie, Université Montpellier I, Montpellier, France.

————. 2006. Libéralisation, distorsion de concurrence et évolution technologique: Portée et limites du succès du coton en Afrique Zone Franc. Paper presented at the New Partnership for Africa's Development conference Championing Agricultural Successes for Africa's Future: A Parliamentarians' Dialogue on NEPAD, Somerset West, South Africa, May 15–18.

Follin, J.-C., and M. Deat. 1999. Le rôle des facteurs techniques dans l'accroissement des rendements en culture cotonière. *Coton et développement (1999): Cinquante ans d'action cotonière au service du développement,* Hors série (septembre): 14–23.

Foster, J., and C. Briceño-Garmendia. 2010. *Africa's infrastructure: A time for transformation.* Washington, D.C.: World Bank.

Fournier, Y., P. Ichanju, and C. Lapenu. 2002. Potentialités et limites de la caution solidaire. Bulletin d'information du Mardi 34-16 et 22 (octobre). Nogent-sur-Marne:

Groupe de recherche et d'échanges technologiques, l'espace d'echanges francophones sur la microfinance.

FPEAK (Fresh Produce Exporters Association of Kenya). 1999. *Code of practice.* 2nd ed. Nairobi, Kenya: FPEAK.

Francis, E., and J. Hoddinott. 1993. Migration and differentiation in western Kenya: A tale of two sub-locations. *Journal of Development Studies* 30 (1): 115–145.

Franzel, S., P. Cooper, and G. L. Denning. 2001. Scaling up the benefits of agroforestry research: Lessons learned and research challenges. *Development in Practice* 11 (4): 524–534.

Franzel, S., D. Phiri, and F. R. Kwesiga. 1999. Assessing the adoption potential of improved tree fallows in Eastern Zambia. Afghanistan Research and Educational Network Association Working Paper 124. Nairobi, Kenya: World Agroforestry Centre.

———. 2002. Assessing the adoption potential of improved tree fallows in Eastern Zambia. In *Trees on the farm: Assessing the adoption potential of agroforestry practices in Africa,* ed. S. Franzel and S. J. Scherr, pp. 37–64. Wallingford, U.K.: CAB International.

Freeland, G. 1998. *Setting donor research agenda.* Occasional Publication. Midlothian, Scotland: British Society of Animal Science.

FSRP (Food Security Research Project). 2008. *Patterns of maize farming behavior and performance among small and medium-scale smallholders in Zambia: A review of statistical data from the CSO/MACO crop forecast survey 2000/2001 to 2007/08 production seasons.* Lusaka, Zambia: FSRP.

Gabre-Madhin, E., and S. Haggblade. 2003. Successes in African agriculture: Results of an expert survey. Markets and Structural Studies Division Working Paper 53. Washington, D.C.: International Food Policy Research Institute.

———. 2004. Successes in African agriculture: Results of an expert survey. *World Development* 32 (5): 745–766.

Garrett, J. 2004. *Living life: Overlooked aspects of urban employment.* FCND Discussion Paper 171. Washington, D.C.: International Food Policy Research Institute.

GART (Golden Valley Agricultural Research Trust). 2001. *Conservation farming.* GART Yearbook, pp. 50–65. Lusaka, Zambia: GART.

———. 2004. *How to use the Magoye Ripper: Operator's manual.* 2nd ed. Chisamba, Zambia: GART.

Gebre Wold, A., M. Alemayehu, S. Demeke, S. Dediye, and A. Tadesse. 2000. Status of dairy research in Ethiopia. In *The role of village dairy co-operatives in dairy development.* Proceedings of a conference sponsored by the Smallholder Dairy Development Project. Addis Ababa, Ethiopia: Ministry of Agriculture.

Gerhart, J. 1975. The diffusion of hybrid maize in Western Kenya. Ph.D. dissertation, Princeton University, Princeton, N.J. Abridged by Centro Internacional de Mejoramiento de Maíz y Trigo (CIMMYT). Mexico City: CIMMYT.

Ghana, Ministry of Food and Agriculture. 2005. Cassava development in Ghana. In *Proceedings of the Validation Forum on the Global Cassava Development Strategy.* Vol. 2, *A review of cassava in Africa with country case studies on Nigeria, Ghana, the United Republic of Tanzania, Uganda and Benin.* Rome: International Fund for Agricultural Development and Food and Agriculture Organization of the United Nations.

Gigou, J. 1989. Optimisation de la fertilisation des cultures dans la région Mali-Sud: Rapport d' une mission de consultation auprès de la CMDT, 25 juin au 13 juillet 1989. Montpellier, France: Institut de recherches agronomiques tropicales et des cultures vivrières.

Gilbert, E., L. C. Phillips, W. Roberts, M. T. Sarch, M. Smale, and A. Stroud. 1993. *Maize research impact in Africa: The obscured revolution.* Washington, D.C.: Division of Food, Agriculture and Resources Analysis, Office of Analysis, Research and Technical Support, Bureau for Africa, U.S. Agency for International Development.

Gillson, I., C. Poulton, K. Balcombe, and S. Page. 2004. *Understanding the impact of cotton subsidies on developing countries.* ODI Background Report. London: Overseas Development Institute, May.

Giraudy, F. 1996a. *Prix des intrants et marges sur coton.* Suivi-Evaluation. Bamako, Mali: Direction de la Production Contrôle et Gestion.

———. 1996b. *Evaluation des systèmes de production dans la zone Mali-Sud: Quelques faits.* Suivi-Evaluation. Bamako, Mali: Direction de la Production Contrôle et Gestion.

———. 1999. Culture attelée, culture cotonnière, crédit et intensification de l'agriculture. *Coton et développement* 29 (janvier–mars): 20–24.

Giraudy, F., and M. Niang. 1994. *Revenus paysans en zone Mali-Sud,* Première partie, *Revenus et dépenses des individus et des exploitations.* Suivi Evaluation. Siskasso, Mali: Compagnie Malienne pour le Développement des Textiles.

———. 1996. *Impact de la dévaluation sur les systèmes de production et les revenus paysans en zone Mali-Sud.* Siskasso, Mali: Compagnie Malienne pour le Développement des Textiles.

Giraudy, F., K. M. Outtara, M. Niang, and J. Macrae. 1994a. *Revenus paysans en zone Mali-Sud,* Deuxième partie, *Comptes d'exploitation paysans et impact de la dévaluation.* Annexes. Suivi Evaluation. Siskasso, Mali: Compagnie Malienne pour le Développement des Textiles.

———. 1994b. *Revenus paysans en zone Mali-Sud,* Deuxième partie, *Comptes d'exploitation.* Siskasso, Mali: Compagnie Malienne pour le Développement des Textiles.

Gitau, G. K., C. J. O'Callaghan, O. McDermott, A. O. Omore, P. A. Odima, C. Mulei, and J. K. Kilungo. 1994. Descriptions of smallholder farms in Kiambu District, Kenya. *Preventive Veterinary Medicine* 21: 155–166.

Gladwin, C. H. 1992. Gendered impacts of fertilizer subsidy removal programs in Malawi and Cameroon. *Agricultural Economics* 7 (2): 141–153.

Gladwin, C. H., J. S. Peterson, D. Phiri, and R. Uttaro. 2002. Agroforestry adoption decisions, structural adjustment, and gender in Africa. In *Natural resources management in African agriculture: Understanding and improving current practices,* ed. C. B. Barrett, F. Place, and A. Aboud, pp. 115–128. Wallingford, U.K.: CAB International.

GMB (Grain Marketing Board). 1991. *Response from the management of the grain marketing board to the structural adjustment programme.* Harare, Zimbabwe: Planning Unit, GMB.

Goreux, L., and J. Macrae. 2002. Liberalizing the cotton sector in SSA, Part 1, Main issues. Washington, D.C.: World Bank, mimeo.

————. 2003. Reforming the cotton sector in Sub-Saharan Africa (SSA). Africa Region Working Paper Series 47. Washington, D.C.: World Bank.

Govereh, J., T. S. Jayne, and A. Chapoto. 2008. Assessment of alternative maize trade and market policy interventions in Zambia. Working Paper 33. Lusaka, Zambia: Michigan State University Food Security Research Project.

Govereh, J., J. J. Shawa, E. Malawo, and T. S. Jayne. 2006. Raising the productivity of public investments in Zambia's agricultural sector. Working Paper 20. Lusaka: Zambia Food Security Research Project. Available at <www.aec.msu.edu/ agecon/ fs2/zambia/index.htm>.

Government of Kenya. 1965. *The dairy commission of inquiry report: Government of Kenya.* DAIRY/INQ/A/64. Nairobi, Kenya: Government of Kenya, Ministry of Agriculture.

Government of Zambia/ICRAF (World Agroforestry Centre). 1988. *Agroforestry research project for the maize-livestock system in the unimodal upland plateau in Eastern Province, Zambia.* ARENA Report 10. Nairobi, Kenya: ICRAF.

Graffham, A. J., J. T. Ababio, N. Dziedozoava, G. Day, A. Andah, G. S. Ayernor, S. Gallat, and A. Westby. 1998. Market potential for cassava flours and starches in Africa: A case study in Ghana. *Tropical Agriculture* 75: 267–270.

GRAIN. 2004. GM cotton set to invade West Africa: Time to act! Briefing paper. Available at <www.grain.org/briefings/?id=184>. Accessed November 2009.

Guyomard, H., C. Laroche, and C. Le Mouel. 1999. An economic assessment of the Common Market Organization for bananas in the European Union. *Agricultural Economics* 20 (2): 105–120.

Haggblade, S., ed. 2004. *Successes in African agriculture: Building for the future.* Findings of an international conference, Pretoria, South Africa, December 1–3, 2003. Feldafing, Germany: Internationale Weiterbildung und Entwicklung.

————. 2005. Conference summary: Agricultural Successes for the Greater Horn of Africa. Findings of an international conference, Nairobi, Kenya, November 22–25, 2004. Available at <www.ifpri.org/event/nepadigad-regional-conference-agricultural-su>.

————. 2007. Returns to investment in agriculture. Policy Synthesis 19. Lusaka, Zambia: Food Security Research Project. Available at <www.aec.msu.edu/fs2/zambia/ ps19.pdf>.

Haggblade, S., and M. Nyembe. 2007. Commercial dynamics in Zambia's cassava value chain. Food Security Research Project Working Paper 32 and Cassava Transformation in Southern Africa Task 3 Report. Lusaka, Zambia: Michigan State University.

Haggblade, S., and G. Tembo. 2003. Conservation farming in Zambia. Environment and Production Technology Division Working Paper 108. Washington, D.C.: International Food Policy Research Institute.

Haggblade, S., and B. Zulu. 2003. The cassava surge in Zambia and Malawi. Conference Background Paper 9. Prepared for the Internationale Weiterbildung und Entwicklung, International Food Policy Research Institute, New Partnership for Africa's Development, Technical Center for Agricultural and Rural Cooperation conference Successes in African Agriculture, Pretoria, December 1–3.

Haggblade, S., P. Hazell, and J. Brown. 1989. Farm–nonfarm linkages in rural Sub-Saharan Africa. *World Development* 17 (8): 1173–1201.

Haggblade, S., P. Hazell, and P. Dorosh. 2007. Sectoral growth linkages between agriculture and the rural nonfarm economy. In *Transforming the rural nonfarm economy: Opportunities and threats in the developing world,* ed. S. Haggblade, P. Hazell, and T. Reardon, pp. 141–182. Baltimore, Md., U.S.A.: Johns Hopkins University Press.

Haggblade, S., S. Longabaugh, and D. Tschirley. 2009. Spatial patterns of food staple production and marketing in southeast Africa: Implications for trade policy and emergency response. MSU International Development Working Paper 100. East Lansing: Department of Agriculture, Food, and Resource Economics, Michigan State University.

Hahn, S. K., A. K. Howland, and E. R. Terry. 1980. Correlated resistance of cassava to mosaic and bacterial blight diseases. *Euphytica* 29: 305–311.

Harlan, J. R. 1992. *Crops and man.* 2nd ed. Madison, Wis., U.S.A.: American Society of Agronomy.

———. 1995. *The living fields, our agricultural heritage.* Cambridge: Cambridge University Press.

Harrigan, J. 2003. Turns and full circles: Two decades of agricultural reform in Malawi, 1981–2000. *World Development* 31 (5): 847–863.

Harris, C., P. V. Hegarty, M. Kherallah, C. Mukindia, J. Ngige, P. Sterns, and J. Tatter. 2001. *The impacts of standards on the food sector of Kenya.* Report prepared by the Institute for Food and Agricultural Standards, Michigan State University, East Lansing, for the U.S. Agency for International Development.

Harrison, M. N. 1970. Maize improvement in East Africa. In *Crop improvement in East Africa,* ed. C. L. A. Leakey, pp. 21–59. Farnham Royal, U.K.: Commonwealth Agricultural Bureau.

Hartemink, A. E., R. J. Buresh, B. Jama, and B. H. Janssen. 1996. Soil nitrate and water dynamics in Sesbania fallows, weed fallows and maize. *Soil Science Society of America Journal* 60: 568–574.

Hassan, R. M. 1998. *Maize technology development and transfer: A GIS application for research planning in Kenya.* Wallingford, U.K.: CAB International.

Hassan, R. M., and D. D. Karanja. 1997. Increasing maize production in Kenya: Technology, institutions and policy. In *Africa's emerging maize revolution,* ed. D. Byerlee and C. K. Eicher. Boulder, Colo., U.S.A.: Lynne Rienner.

Hassan, R. M., M. Mekuria, and W. Mwangi. 2001. *Maize breeding research in Eastern and Southern Africa: Current status and impacts of past investments made by the public and private sectors, 1966–1997.* Mexico City: Centro Internacional de Mejoramiento de Maíz y Trigo.

Hassan, R. M., K. Njoroge, M. Njore, R. Otsyula, and A. Laboso. 1998. Adoption patterns and performance of improved maize in Kenya. In *Maize technology development and transfer: A GIS application for research planning in Kenya,* ed. R. M. Hassan, pp. 107–136. Wallingford, U.K.: CAB International.

Hassane, A., P. Martin, and C. Reij. 2000. *Water harvesting, land rehabilitation and household food security in Niger: IFAD's soil and water conservation project in Illéla district.* Rome and Amsterdam: International Fund for Agricultural Development and Vrije Universiteit.

Hayami, Y., and K. Otsuka. 1993. *The economics of contract choice: An agrarian perspective.* Oxford: Oxford University Press.

Hazell, P. B. R., and S. Wood. 2008. Drivers of change in global agriculture. *Philosophical Transactions of the Royal Society B* 363 (1491): 495–515.

Hazell, P. B. R., A. Dorward, C. Poulton, and S. Wiggins. 2007. The future of small farms for poverty reduction and growth. 2020 Discussion Paper 42. Washington, D.C.: International Food Policy Research Institute.

Heisey, P. W., and W. Mwangi. 1996. Fertilizer use and maize production in Sub-Saharan Africa. CIMMYT Economics Working Paper 96-01. Mexico City: Centro Internacional de Mejoramiento de Maíz y Trigo.

Heisey, P. W., and M. Smale. 1995. Maize technology in Malawi: A green revolution in the making? CIMMYT Research Report 4. Mexico City: Centro Internacional de Mejoramiento de Maíz y Trigo.

Henao, J., J. Brink, B. Coulibaly, and A. Traore. 1992. *Fertilizer policy research program for tropical Africa: Agronomic potential of fertilizer use in Mali.* Muscle Shoals, Ala., U.S.A.: International Fertilizer Development Center and Bamako, Mali: Institut d'Economie Rurale.

Herren, H. R. 1981. Biological control of the cassava mealybug. In *Tropical root crops research strategies for the 1980s,* ed. E. R. Terry, K. O. Oduro, and F. Caveness, pp. 79–80. Proceedings of the First Triennial Symposium of the International Society for Tropical Root Crops Africa Branch, September 8–12, 1980. Ottawa: International Development Research Center.

Herren, H. R., and P. Neuenschwander. 1991. Biological control of cassava pests in Africa. *Annual Review of Entomology* 36: 257–283.

Herren, H. R., P. Neuenschwander, R. D. Hennessey, and W. N. O. Hammond. 1987. Introduction and dispersal of *Epidinocarisi lopezi* (Hym. Encytidae), an exotic parasitoid of cassava mealybug, *Phenococcus manihoti* (Hom. Pseudococcidae) in Africa. *Agriculture, Ecosystems, and Environments* 19: 131–144.

Hewitt de Alca'ntara, C. 1993. Introduction: Marketing in principles and practice. In *Real markets: Social and political issues of food policy reforms,* ed. C. Hewitt de Alca'ntara. Geneva: Frank Cass.

Hichaambwa, M. 2005. *Commercialization of cassava for increased food security: Indicative trends and patterns towards commercialization.* Lusaka, Zambia: Food and Agriculture Organization of the United Nations.

Hien, F., and A. Ouédraogo. 2001. Joint analysis of the sustainability of a local SWC technique in Burkina Faso. In *Farmer innovation in Africa: A source of inspiration for agricultural development,* ed. C. Reij and A. Waters-Bayer, pp. 256–266. London: Earthscan.

Hill, P. 1963. *Migrant cocoa farmers of southern Ghana: A study in rural capitalism.* Cambridge: Cambridge University Press.

Hills, M. F. 1956. *Cream country: The story of the Kenya Co-operative Creameries Limited.* Nairobi: Kenya Co-operative Creameries.

Holloway, G., C. Nicholson, C. Delgado, S. Staal, and S. Ehui. 2000. How to make a milk market: A case study from the Ethiopian highlands. Socio-economic and Policy Research Working Paper 28. Addis Ababa, Ethiopia: International Livestock Research Institute.

Hörmann, D., and L. Wietor. 1980. Export-oriented horticulture in developing countries–Ivory Coast. Working Paper 26. Hannover, Germany: Institute for Horticultural Economics, University of Hannover.

HORUS Enterprises. 2003. *Étude sur les étapes et les options de la libéralisation du secteur coton au Mali.* Primature. Bamako, Mali: Mission de Restructuration du Secteur Coton.

Hove, L., S. J. Twomlow, D. Rohrbach, N. Mashingaidze, M. Moyo, P. Maphosa, and W. Mupangwa. 2007. Planting basins increase maize yields for smallholder farmers in the semi-arid areas of southern and western Zimbabwe. Paper presented at the Southern African Development Community Land and Water Management meeting, Gaborone, Botswana, February.

Howard, A. 1940. *An agricultural testament.* New Delhi: Other India Press.

Howard, J. A. 1994. The economic impact of improved maize varieties in Zambia. Ph.D. thesis, Department of Agricultural Economics, Michigan State University, East Lansing.

Howard, J. A., and C. Mungoma. 1996. Zambia's stop-and-go revolution: The impact of policies and organizations on the development and spread of maize technology. MSU International Development Working Paper 161. East Lansing: Department of Agricultural Economics, Michican State University.

Howard, J. A, L. Rubey, and E. W. Crawford. 1997. Getting technology and the technology environment right: Lessons from maize development in southern Africa. Paper presented at the Meeting of the International Association of Agricultural Economics, Sacramento, Calif., August 10–16.

Hudson, J. 1995. Conservation tillage. *Profit,* April.

Hyami, Y., and J. P. Platteau. 1997. Resource endowments and agricultural development: Africa vs. Asia. *Cahiers Série Recherche (Belgium)* 192 (juin). Facultés Universitaires Notre-Dame de la Paix, Namur, and Faculté des Sciences Economiques et Sociales.

Hyami, Y., and V. Ruttan. 1971. *Agricultural development: An international perspective.* Baltimore, Md., U.S.A.: Johns Hopkins University Press.

ICAC (International Cotton Advisory Committee). 1996. Marketing cotton in francophone Africa. *Cotton: Review of the World Situation* 49 (March–April): 9–14.

———. 2001. *Survey of the costs of production of raw cotton.* Washington, D.C.: ICAC.

———. 2002a. *Production and trade policies affecting the cotton industry.* Washington, D.C.: ICAC.

———. 2002b. Update to government measures affecting cotton production, ginning and trade. Standing Committee document. Attachment II to SC-N-459, Revised. Washington, D.C.: ICAC, April 23.

———. 2005. Minutes. Second plenary session, 64th plenary meeting, September 27.

IFPRI (International Food Policy Research Institute). 2003. Analyzing successes in African agriculture: The DE-A-R framework. Conference Background Paper 18. Prepared for the Internationale Weiterbildung und Entwicklung, IFPRI, New Partnership for Africa's Development, Technical Center for Agricultural and Rural Cooperation conference Successes in African Agriculture, Pretoria, December 1–3.

———. 2004. Ending hunger in Africa: Prospects for the small farmer. Policy Brief. Washington, D.C.: IFPRI.

———. 2005. *Africa without borders: Building blocks for regional growth.* Washington, D.C.: IFPRI.

IITA (International Institute of Tropical Agriculture). 1992. Plant health management.

In *Sustainable food production in Sub-Saharan Africa: IITA's contributions,* pp. 139–169. Ibadan, Nigeria: IITA.

IMAG (Institute of Agricultural and Environmental Engineering). 2001. *Smallholder agricultural mechanization: Research development and promotion.* Wageningen, the Netherlands: IMAG.

IMF (International Monetary Fund). 2001. Cotton sector: Crisis and reform. Washington, D.C.: IMF. Mimeo.

INESOR (Institute of Economic and Social Research). 1999. *Agricultural sector performance analysis, 1997–99.* Lusaka, Zambia: Ministry of Agriculture, Food and Fisheries.

InterAcademy Council. 2004. *Realilzing the promise and potential of African agriculture: Science and technology strategies for improving agricultural productivity and food security in Africa.* Amsterdam: InterAcademy Council Secretariat.

International Centre for Trade and Sustainable Development. 2007. WTO panel: US has failed to comply with cotton ruling in dispute with Brazil. *Bridges Weekly Trade News Digest* 11 (35). Available at <http://ictsd.org/i/news/bridgesweekly/6571/>. Accessed November 2009.

Jabara, C. 1984. Agricultural pricing policy in Kenya. *World Development* 13 (5): 611–626.

Jaeger, W. K. 1992. The causes of Africa's food crisis. *World Development* 20 (11): 1631–1645.

Jaffee, S. 1994. Contract farming in the shadow of competitive markets: The experience of Kenyan horticulture. In *Living under contract: Contract farming and agrarian transformation in Sub-Saharan Africa,* ed. P. Little and M. Watts. Madison: University of Wisconsin Press.

———. 1995. The many faces of success: The development of Kenyan horticultural exports. In *Marketing Africa's high-value foods: Comparative experiences of an emergent private sector,* ed. S. Jaffee and J. Morton. Dubuque, Iowa, U.S.A.: Kendall/Hunt.

———. 2003. *From challenge to opportunity: The transformation of the Kenyan fresh vegetable trade in the context of emerging food safety and other standards.* Washington, D.C.: PREM Trade Unit, World Bank.

Jama, B., R. J. Buresh, and F. Place. 1998b. Sesbania tree fallows on phosphorus-deficient sites: Maize yield and financial benefit. *Agronomy Journal* 90 (6): 717–726.

Jama, B., A. Niang, J. De Wolf, B. Amadalo, and M. R. Rao. 1998a. Sources of nutrients in nutrient depleted soils of Western Kenya. Proceedings of Centro Internacional de Mejoramiento de Maíz y Trigo's Sixth Regional Maize Conference for Eastern and Southern Africa, Addis Ababa, Ethiopia, September 21–25.

Jansen, D. 1977. *Agricultural policy and performance in Zambia: History, prospects and proposals for change.* Berkeley: Institute of International Studies, University of California.

Jansen, D., and K. Muir. 1994. Trade, exchange rate policy and agriculture in the 1980s. In *Zimbabwe's agricultural revolution,* ed. M. Rukuni and C. Eicher. Harare: University of Zimbabwe Press.

Jayne, T. S. 2008. Forces of change affecting African food systems: Implications for public policy. In *The transformation of agri-food systems: Globalization, supply chains, and smallholder farmers,* ed. E. B. McCullough, P. L. Pingali, and K. G. Stamoulis. London: Earthscan.

Jayne, T. S., and G. Argwings-Kodhek. 1997. Consumer response to maize market liberalization in urban Kenya. *Food Policy* 22 (5): 447–458.

Jayne, T. S., and M. Chisvo. 1991. Unravelling Zimbabwe's food insecurity paradox. *Food Policy* 16 (5): 319–329.

Jayne, T. S., and S. Jones. 1997. Food marketing and pricing policy in Eastern and Southern Africa: A survey. *World Development* 25 (9): 1505–1527.

Jayne, T. S., and M. Rukuni. 1993. Distributional effects of maize self-sufficiency in Zimbabwe: Implications for pricing and trade policy. *Food Policy* 18 (4): 334–341.

Jayne, T. S., D. Mather, and E. Mghenyi. 2006. Smallholder farming under increasingly difficult circumstances: Policy and public investment priorities for Africa. MSU International Development Working Paper 86. East Lansing: Department of Agricultural Economics, Michigan State University.

Jayne, T. S., L. Rubey, D. Tschirley, M. Mukumbu, M. Chisvo, A. P. Santos, M. T. Weber, and P. Diskin. 1995. Effects of market reform on access to food by low-income households: Evidence from four countries in Eastern and Southern Africa. International Development Paper 19. East Lansing: Department of Agricultural Economics, Michigan State University.

Jayne, T. S., M. Mukumbu, M. Chisvo, D. Tschirley, M. T. Weber, B. Zulu, R. Johansson, P. Santos, and D. Soroko. 1999. Successes and challenges of food market reform: Experiences from Kenya, Mozambique, Zambia, and Zimbabwe. International Development Working Paper 72. East Lansing: Michigan State University.

Jayne, T. S., J. Govereh, A. Mwanaumo, and J. K. Nyoro. 2002a. False promise or false premise? The experience of food and input market reform in Eastern and Southern Africa. *World Development* 30 (11): 1967–1985.

Jayne, T. S., T. Yamano, J. Nyoro, and T. Awuor. 2002b. Do farmers really benefit from higher maize prices? Balancing rural interests in Kenya's maize pricing and trade policy. Tegemeo Working Paper 3. Nairobi, Kenya: Tegemeo Institute of Agricultural Policy and Development, Egerton University.

Jayne, T. S., J. Govereh, M. Wanzala, and M. Demeke. 2003. Fertilizer market development: A comparative analysis of Ethiopia, Kenya, and Zambia. *Food Policy* 28: 293–316.

Jayne, T. S., J. Govereh, P. Chilonda, N. Mason, A. Chapoto, and H. Haantuba. 2007. Trends in agricultural and rural development indicators in Zambia. Working Paper 24. Lusaka, Zambia: Food Security Research Project.

Jenkins, C. 1997. The politics of economic policy-making in Zimbabwe. *Journal of Modern African Economies* 35 (4): 575–602.

Jennings, D. L. 1976. Breeding for resistance to African cassava mosaic disease: Progress and prospects. In *African cassava mosaic,* ed. B. L. Nestel, pp. 39–44. Report of an interdisciplinary workshop held at Muguga, Kenya, February 19–22. Ottawa: International Development Research Center.

Johnson, M., A. Temu, and P. Hazell. 2003. Global environment for African agriculture. Conference Paper 17. Presented at the Internationale Weiterbildung und Entwicklung, International Food Policy Research Institute, New Partnership for Africa's Development, Technical Center for Agricultural and Rural Cooperation conference Successes in African Agriculture, Pretoria, December 1–3.

Johnson, M. E., and W. A. Masters. 2004. Complementarity and sequencing of innovations: New varieties and mechanized processing for cassava in West Africa. *Economic Innovation and New Technology* 13 (1): 19–31.

Jones, S. P. 1994. *Privatization and policy reform: Agricultural marketing in Africa.* Oxford: Food Studies Group, University of Oxford.

Jones, W. O. 1957. Manioc: An example of innovation in African economies. *Economic Development and Cultural Change* 5 (2): 97–117.

————. 1959. *Manioc in Africa.* Stanford, Calif., U.S.A.: Food Research Institute, Stanford University.

————. 1987. Food-crop marketing boards in tropical Africa. *Journal of Modern African Studies* 25 (3): 375–402.

Juo, A. S., and R. Lal. 1977. The effect of fallow and continuous cultivation on the chemical and physical properties of an Alfisol in Western Nigeria. *Plant and Soil* 47: 567–584.

Kaboré, D., and C. Reij. 2004. The emergence and spreading of an improved traditional soil and water conservation practice in Burkina Faso. Environment and Production Technology Division Working Paper 114. Washington, D.C.: International Food Policy Research Institute.

Kaboré, P. D. 2000. Performance des technologies de conservation des eaux et du sol en champs paysans à Donsin, Burkina Faso. *Annales de l'Université de Ouagadougou,* série A, 13: 109–129.

Kabwe, S., C. Donovan, and D. Samazaka. 2007. Assessment of the farm-level financial profitability of the Magoye ripper in maize and cotton production in southern and eastern provinces. Working Paper 23. Lusaka, Zambia: Food Security Research Project.

Kähkönen, S., and H. Leathers. 1999. *Transaction costs analysis of maize and cotton marketing in Zambia and Tanzania.* Technical Report 105, SD Publication Series. Washington, D.C.: Office of Sustainable Development for Africa, United States Agency for International Development.

Kaitho, R. J., S. Tamminga, and J. van Bruchem. 1993. Rumen degradation and in vivo digestibility of dried *Calliandra calothyrsus* leaves. *Animal Feed Science Technology* 43 (1–2): 23–45.

Kaluwa, B. 1992. Malawi food marketing: Private trader operation and state intervention. In *Food security research in Southern Africa,* ed. J. Wyckoff and M. Rukuni. Harare: University of Zimbabwe.

Kamau, M. 2000. The way forward in export oriented small-holder horticulture. Background paper for a stakeholder consultation meeting, Norfolk Hotel, Nairobi, Kenya, February 8.

Kambewa, P., and M. Nyembe. 2008. *Structure and dynamics of Malawi's cassava markets.* Cassava Transformation in Southern Africa Task 3 Report. Lund, Sweden: Lund University. Available at <www.aec.msu.edu/fs2/catisa/Dynamics_Malawi_Cassava_Market.pdf>.

Kandoole, B. F., and L. Msukwa. 1992. Household food and income security under market liberalization: Experience from Malawi. In *Food security research in Southern Africa: Policy implications,* ed. J. Wyckoff and M. Rukuni. Harare: University of Zimbabwe.

Kaoma-Sprenkels, C., P. A. Stevens, and A. A. Wanders. 1999. IMAG-DLO and conservation tillage: Activities and experiences. In *Conservation tillage with animal traction,* ed. P. G. Kaumbutho and T. E. Simalenga. Harare, Zimbabwe: Animal Traction Network for Eastern and Southern Africa.

Karanja, D. D. 1990. The rate of return to maize research in Kenya: 1955–88. M.S. thesis, Department of Agricultural Economics, Michigan State University, East Lansing.

————. 1996. An economic and institutional analysis of maize research in Kenya. International Development Working Paper 57. Department of Agricultural Economics, Michigan State University, East Lansing.

Katanga, R., D. Phiri, A. Böhringer, and P. Mafongoya. 2002. The adaptive research and dissemination network for agroforestry: A synthesis of the adaptive workshops. In *Proceedings of the 14th Southern Africa Regional Review and Planning Workshop, 3–7 September 2001, Harare,* ed. F. Kwesiga, E. Ayuk, and A. Agumya, pp. 93–99. Harare, Zimbabwe: International Centre for Research in Agroforestry.

Katanga, R., G. Kabwe, E. Kuntashula, P. L. Mafongoya, and S. Phiri. 2007. Assessing farmer innovations in agroforestry in Eastern Zambia. *Journal of Agricultural Education and Extension* 13 (2): 117–129.

Kauffman, S., N. Koning, and N. Heerink. 2000. Integrated soil management and agricultural development in West Africa, 1, Potentials and constraints. *The Land* 4 (2): 73–92.

Kébé, D., and J. Brons. 1994. Quand le rythme du tam-tam change. Document 94/25. Bamako, Mali: Institut d'Economie Rurale/Equipe Système de Production et de Gestion des Ressources Naturelles.

Kébé, D., and M.-C. Kébé-Sidibé. 1997. *Étude diagnostique de la crise des associations villageoises en zone.* Siskasso, Mali: Compagnie Malienne pour le Développement des Textiles.

Kébé, D., L. Diakité, and H. Diawara. 1998. *Impact de la dévaluation du FCFA sur la productivité, la rentabilité et les performances de la filière coton (Cas du Mali).* Bamako, Mali: Programme Régionale de Renforcement Institutionnel en Matière de Recherche sur la Sécurité Alimentaire au Sahel/Institut Sahel–Economie des filières/Institut de l'Economie Rurale.

Keil, A. 2001. Improved fallows using leguminous trees in eastern Zambia: Do initial testers adopt the technology? M.Sc. thesis, University of Goettingen, Goettingen, Germany.

Keil, A., M. Zeller, and S. Franzel. 2005. Improved tree fallows in smallholder maize production in Zambia: Do initial testers adopt the technology? *Agroforestry Systems* 64: 225–236.

Kenya Seed Company. 2003. *About us.* Available at <www.kenyaseed.com/profile.htm>. Accessed April 2003.

Kergna, A. O., and D. Kébé. 2001. *Evaluation economique de l'impact de la recherche sur le coton au Mali.* Rapport Provisoire. Bamako, Mali: Programme Economie des Filières, Institut d'Economie Rurale, Direction Scientifique, Ministère du Développement Rural.

Ketema, J. 2000. *Dairy development in Ethiopia.* The role of village dairy cooperatives in dairy development. Smallholder Dairy Development Project Proceeding. Addis Ababa, Ethiopia: Ministry of Agriculture.

Keyser, J., and M. H. Mwanza. 1996. *Conservation tillage.* Lusaka, Zambia: Institute of Africa Studies, University of Zambia.

Keyter, C. 1975. *Maize control in Southern Rhodesia: 1931–1941; The African contribution toward white survival.* Local Series 34. Harare, Zimbabwe: Central African Historical Association.

Kherallah, M., C. Delgado, E. Gabre-Madhin, N. Minot, and M. Johnson. 2002. *Reforming agricultural markets in Africa.* Baltimore, Md., U.S.A.: Johns Hopkins University Press.

Kimenye, L. 1995. Kenya's experience in promoting smallholder production of flowers and vegetables for European markets. *African Rural and Urban Studies* 2 (2–3): 121–141.

Kimweli, P. K. 1991. Exporting of horticultural produce in Kenya. In *Marketing management in the horticultural industry,* ed. S. Carter, pp. 131–151. Proceedings of a conference, Nairobi, Kenya, November 11–15. Nairobi, Kenya: Food and Agriculture Organization of the United Nations Network and Centre for Agricultural Marketing in Eastern and Southern Africa.

Kiptot, E., P. Hebinck, S. Franzel, and P. Richards. 2007. Adopters, testers or pseudo-adopters: Dynamics of the use of improved tree fallows by farmers in western Kenya. *Agricultural Systems* 94 (2): 509–519.

Knox, A., R. Meinzen-Dick, and P. Hazell. 2002. Property rights, collective action and technologies for natural resource management. Paper presented at The Commons in an Age of Globalisation, the ninth conference of the International Association for the Study of Common Property, Victoria Falls, Zimbabwe, June 17–21.

Kokwe, G. M. 1997. *Maize, markets and livelihoods: State intervention and agrarian change in Luapula Provice Zambia, 1950 to 1995.* Helsinki: Institute of Development Studies, University of Helsinki.

Krueger, A. O., M. Schiff, and A. Valdes. 1991. *The political economy of agricultural pricing policy.* Baltimore, Md., U.S.A.: Johns Hopkins University Press.

Kupfuma, B. 1994. The payoffs to hybrid maize research and extension in Zimbabwe: An economic and institutional analysis. M.S. thesis, Michigan State University, East Lansing.

Kwesiga, F. 1990. The potential of *Sesbania sesban* in the traditional land use systems in Zambia. In *Perennial Sesbania species in agroforestry systems,* ed. B. Macklin and D. O. Evans, pp. 131–138. Waimanalo, Hawaii: Nitrogen Fixing Tree Association.

Kwesiga, F., and R. Coe. 1994. The effect of short rotation *Sesbania sesban* planted fallows on maize yield. *Forest Ecology and Management* 64: 199–208.

Kwesiga, F., and I. Kamau. 1989. *Agroforestry potential in the unimodal upland plateau of Zambia.* Afghanistan Research and Educational Network Association Report 7. Nairobi, Kenya: World Agroforestry Centre.

Kwesiga, F. R., and S. Chisumpa. 1992. *Ethnobotanical survey in Eastern Province, Zambia.* Afghanistan Research and Educational Network Association Report 49. Nairobi, Kenya: World Agroforestry Centre.

Kwesiga, F. R., S. Franzel, F. Place, D. Phiri, and C. P. Simwanza. 1999. *Sesbania sesban* improved fallows in eastern Zambia: Their inception, development, and farmer enthusiasm. *Agroforestry Systems* 47: 49–66.

Kydd, J. 1989. Maize research in Malawi: Lessons from failure. *Journal of International Development* 1 (1): 112–144.

Kydd, J., and R. D. Christiansen. 1982. Structural change in Malawi since independence: Consequences of a development strategy based on large-scale agriculture. *World Development* 10 (5): 377–396.

Lambert, A. M. 2002. *A scoping study for detailed case-studies of trade facilitation/export promotion projects for non-traditional agricultural products in Sub-Saharan Africa.* Report prepared for the Africa Region (AFTR2). Washington, D.C.: World Bank.

Langmead, P. 2001. Does conservation farming really benefit farmers? In *GART Yearbook 2001,* pp. 58–64. Lusaka, Zambia: Golden Valley Agricultural Research Trust.

———. 2002. *Conservation farming technologies in agro-ecological region III: Results 2001/2002.* Lusaka, Zambia: Conservation Farming Unit.

Langmead, P., and J. Baker. 2003. *Cassava: A market research study.* Lusaka, Zambia: Shallholder Enterprise and Marketing Programme.

Langyintuo, A. S., M. Banziger, A. O. Diallo, J. Dixon, J. MacRobert, and W. Mwangi. 2008. *An analysis of the bottlenecks affecting the production and deployment of maize seeds in eastern and southern Africa.* Harare, Zimbabwe: Centro Internacional de Mejoramiento de Maíz y Trigo.

Latham, M. C. 1979. *Human nutrition in tropical Africa.* Rome: Food and Agriculture Organization of the United Nations.

Laws of Northern Rhodesia. 1952. Lusaka, Zambia: Government Printer.

Legg, J. P., P. Sseruwagi, J. Kamau, J., S. Ajanga, S. C. Jeremiah, V. Aritua, G. W. Otim-Nape, A. Muimba-Kankolongo, R. W. Bigson, and J. M. Thresh. 1999. The pandemic of severe cassava mosaic disease in East Africa: Current status and future threats. In *Food security and crop diversification in SADC Countries: The role of cassava and sweetpotato,* ed. M. O. Akoroda and J. M. Teri. Ibadan, Nigeria: International Institute of Tropical Agriculture.

Lekasi, J. K., J. C. Tanner, S. K. Kimani, and P. J. C. Harris. 1998. *Manure management in the Kenya highlands: Practices and potential.* Kenilworth, U.K.: Emmerson Press.

Lele, U. 1975. *The design of rural development: Lessons from Africa.* Baltimore, Md., U.S.A.: Johns Hopkins University Press.

———. 1990. Structural adjustment, agricultural development and the poor: Some lessons from the Malawian experience. *World Development* 18 (9): 1207–1219.

———. 1991. *Aid to African agriculture: Lessons from two decades of donors' experience.* Baltimore, Md., U.S.A.: Johns Hopkins University Press.

Leonard, D. K. 1991. *African successes: Four public managers of Kenyan rural development.* Berkeley: University of California Press.

Levy, S., ed. 2005. *Starter packs: A strategy to fight hunger in developing countries?* Wallingford, U.K.: CAB International.

Levy, S., and C. Barahona. 2001. *Main report of the monitoring and evaluation programme: 2000–2001 targeted inputs programme.* Reading, U.K.: Calibre Consultants and Statistical Services Centre, University of Reading.

Levy, S., C. Barahona, and I. Wilson. 2000. *1999–2000 starter pack evaluation programme main report.* Reading, U.K.: Statistical Services Centre, University of Reading.

Leys, C. 1975. *Underdevelopment in Kenya: The political economy of neo-colonialism.* Berkeley and Los Angeles: University of California Press.

Loeillet, D. 1997. Panorama du marché mondial de l'ananas: L'importance de l'Europe. Proceedings of the 2nd International Pineapple Symposium. *Acta Horticulturae* 425.

López-Pereira, M. A., and M. L. Morris. 1994. *Impacts of international maize breeding research in the developing world, 1966–1990.* Mexico City: Centro Internacional de Mejoramiento de Maíz y Trigo.

Low, A. 1986. *Agricultural development in Southern Africa: Farm household economics and the food crisis.* London: James Curry.

Lowe, R. G. 1986. *Agricultural revolution in Africa?* London: Macmillan.

Lowenberg-DeBoer, J., J. M. Boffa, J. Dickey, and E. Robins, eds. 1994. *Recherche integrée en production agricole et gestion des ressources naturelles.* West Lafayette, Ind., U.S.A.: ARTS Project, Purdue University.

Lynam, J. K., and R. M. Hassan. 1998. A new approach to securing sustained growth in Kenya's maize sector. In *Maize technology development and transfer: A GIS application for research planning in Kenya,* ed. R. M. Hassan, pp. 3–14. Wallingford, U.K.: CAB International.

MacDonald, S. A. 1997. Forecasting world cotton prices. In *Federal forecasters conference—1997, papers and proceedings,* ed. D. E. Gerald. Washington, D.C.: National Center for Education Statistics.

MAEP (Ministère de l'agriculture de l'élevage et de la pêche). 2003. *Commission d'application du mécanisme de détermination du prix du coton graine.* Rapport. Atelier sur le mécanisme de détermination du prix du coton graine aux producteurs. Mali: Ségou.

MAFF (Ministry of Agriculture, Food and Fisheries). 2000. *Impact assessment of root and tuber research in Northern Zambia.* Soils and Crops Research Branch, Farming Systems and Social Sciences Division. Chilanga, Zambia: Mt. Makulu Central Research Station.

———. 2001. *Conservation farming and land use: 5 year programme proposal for ASIP successor programme.* Lusaka, Zambia: MAFF.

Mafongoya, P. L., T. S. Chirwa, P. Gondwe, R. Chintu, and J. Matibini. 2005. The effects of mixed planted fallows of tree species and herbaceous legumes on soil properties and maize yields in Eastern Zambia. Msekera Research Station, Chipata, Zambia. Mimeo.

Mahungu, N. M. 1999. Cassava germplasm enhancement in Southern Africa. In *Food security and crop diversification in SADC Countries: The role of cassava and sweetpotato,* ed. M. O. Akoroda and J. M. Teri. Ibadan, Nigeria: International Institute of Tropical Agriculture.

Malambo, C., J. Chakupurakal, M. K. Sakala, S. Kunda, and M. Meelo. 1999. Biological control as an integrated pest management strategy against cassava mealybug and cassava green mite in Zambia. In *Food security and crop diversification in SADC countries: The role of cassava and sweetpotato,* ed. M. O. Akoroda and J. M. Teri. Ibadan, Nigeria: International Institute of Tropical Agriculture.

Mamdani, M. 1976. *Politics and class formation in Uganda.* London: Monthly Review Press.

Mando, A. 2003. Gestion des sols et évolution de la fertilité des sols dans la partie nord du Plateau Central du Burkina Faso. Étude Plateau Central. Rapport de travail 16. Ouagadougou, Burkina Faso: Conseil National pour la Gestion de l'Environnement.

Mann, C. 1998. Higher yields for all smallholders through best bet technology: The surest way to restart economic growth in Malawi. Soil Fertility Network Research Results Working Paper 3. Harare, Zimbabwe: Centro Internacional de Mejoramiento de Maíz y Trigo.

Manyong, V. M., A. G. O. Dixon, K. O. Makinde, M. Bokanga, and J. Whyte. 2000. *The contribution of IITA-improved cassava to food security in Sub-Saharan Africa.* IITA Impact Study. Ibadan, Nigeria: International Institute of Tropical Agriculture.

Manyong, V. M., J. G. Kling, K. O. Makinde, S. L. Ajala, and A. Menkir. 2003. Improvement of IITA germplasm improvement on maize production in West and Central Africa. In *Crop variety improvement and its effect on productivity: The impact of international agricultural research,* ed. R. E. Evenson and D. Gollin, pp. 159–183. Wallingford, U.K.: CAB International.

Marchal, J. Y. 1977. Système agraire et évolution de l'occupation de l'espace au Yatenga (Haute Volta). In *Cahiers ORSTOM, série Sciences Humaines,* vol. 14, no. 2, pp. 141–149. Paris: Office de la Recherche Scientifique et Technique d'Outre-Mer.

———. 1979. L'espace des techniciens et celui des paysans: Histoire d'un périmètre anti-érosif en Haute Volta. In *Maitrise de l'espace agraire et développement en Afrique tropicale,* pp. 245–252. Paris: Office de la Recherche Scientifique et Technique d'Outre-Mer.

———. 1985. La déroute d'un système vivrier au Burkina: Agriculture extensive et baisse de production. *Economie des Vivres* (juillet–décembre): 265–280.

Marenya, P. P., and C. B. Barrett. 2009. State-conditional fertilizer yield response on Western Kenyan farms. *American Journal of Agricultural Economics* 91 (4): 991–1006.

Marter, A. 1978. *Cassava or maize: A comparative study of the economics of production and market potential of cassava and maize in Zambia.* Lusaka: University of Zambia.

Martin, E. 1973. *The history of Malindi.* Nairobi, Kenya: East African Literature Bureau.

Martin, S. M. 1988. *Palm oil and protest.* Cambridge: Cambridge University Press.

Masters, W. A. 1994. *Government and agriculture in Zimbabwe.* Westport, Conn., U.S.A.: Praeger.

Masters, W. A., and M. S. McMillan. 2001. Climate and scale in economic growth. *Journal of Economic Growth* 6 (3): 167–186.

Maxwell, S. 2003. Six characters (and a few more) in search of an author: How to rescue rural development before it's too late. Paper presented at the 25th International Conference of Agricultural Economists, Durban, South Africa, August 16–23.

Maxwell, S., I. Urey, and C. Ashley. 2001. Emerging issues in rural development: An issues paper. London: Overseas Development Institute.

Mazvimavi, K., and S. Twomlow. 2007. Conservation farming for agricultural relief and development in Zimbabwe. Paper presented to the African Association of Agricultural Economists Meeting, Accra, Ghana, August.

Mba, R. E. C., and A. G. O. Dixon. 1998. Genotype x environment interaction, phenotypic stability of cassava yields and heritability estimates for production and pests resistance traits in Nigeria. In *Root crops and poverty alleviation,* ed. M. O. Akoroda and I. J. Ekanayake, pp. 255–261. Ibadan, Nigeria: International Institute of Tropical Agriculture.

McCann, J. C. 2005. *Maize and grace: Africa's encounter with a New World crop, 1500–2000.* Cambridge, Mass., U.S.A.: Harvard University Press.

McCulloch, N., and M. Ota. 2002. Export horticulture and poverty in Kenya. Working Paper 174. Sussex, U.K.: Institute for Development Studies.

McIntire, J., D. Bourzat, and P. Pingali. 1992. *Crop–livestock interaction in Sub-Saharan Africa.* Washington, D.C.: World Bank.

McPherson, P., and R. Rabbinge. 2006. *Fertilizer subsidies without basic infrastructure, technology, and training will leave Africa just one step away from the next food crisis.* Abuja, Nigeria: Africa Fertilizer Summit.

Mellor, J. W. 1976. *The new economics of growth.* Ithaca, N.Y., U.S.A.: Cornell University Press.

Meyer, R. L., and G. Nagarajan. 2000. *Rural financial markets in Asia: Policies, paradigms and performance.* Manila: Oxford University Press and Asian Development Bank.

Michel, B., M. Togola, I. Tereta, and N. N. Traore. 2000. La lutte contre les ravageurs du cotonnier au Mali: Problématique et évolution recente. *Cahiers d'études et de recherches francophones Agricultures* 9 (2 mars–avril): 109–115.

Minae, S. 1981. Evaluating the performance of the marketing boards: The small farmer milk marketing system in Kenya. Ph.D. thesis, Department of Agricultural and Resource Economics, Cornell University, Ithaca, N.Y., U.S.A.

Minde, I., T. S. Jayne, E. W. Crawford, J. Ariga, and J. Govereh. 2008. Promoting fertilizer use in Africa: Current issues and empirical evidence from Malawi, Zambia, and Kenya. ReSAKSS Working Paper 20. Pretoria: Regional Strategic Agricultural Knowledge Support System for Southern Africa.

Minde, I. J., P. T. Ewell, and J. M. Teri. 1999. Contributions of cassava and sweetpotato to food security and poverty alleviation in the SADC counties: Current status and future prospects. In *Food security and crop diversification in SADC countries: The role of cassava and sweetpotato,* ed. M. O. Akoroda and J. M. Teri. Ibadan, Nigeria: International Institute of Tropical Agriculture.

Ministère du Développement Rural. 2000. *Rapport de synthèse des travaux de la commission technique de sortie de crise de la filière cotonnière au Mali.* Bamako, Mali, août.

———. 2001. *Lettre de politique de développement du secteur coton.* Calendrier Amendé par le Conseil des Ministres en sa Session du 03 Octobre. Bamako, Mali: Ministère du Développement Rural.

Ministère du Développement Rural et de l'Environnement. 2002. *Note d'information sur la problématique de l'approvisionnement des producteurs en intrants agricoles et propositions de solutions d'amélioration.* Bamako, Mali: Secrétariat Général, août.

Ministry of Agriculture. 1989. *National biological control programme for the control of cassava mealybug and cassava green mites in Zambia: Progress report for the period July 1986 to December 1989.* Lusaka, Zambia: Ministry of Agriculture.

Ministry of Health. 1999. *HIV/AIDS in Zambia: Baseline projections and impact interventions.* Lusaka, Zambia: Ministry of Health.

Minot, N., and M. Ngigi. 2004. Are horticultural exports a replicable success story? Evidence from Kenya and Côte d'Ivoire. Environment and Production Technology Division Working Paper 120. Washington, D.C.: International Food Policy Research Institute.

Minot, N., M. Kherallah, and P. Berry. 2000. Fertilizer market report and the determinants of fertilizer use in Benin and Malawi. MSSD Discussion Paper 40. Washington, D.C.: International Food Policy Research Institute.

Miracle, M. P. 1966. *Maize in tropical Africa.* Madison: University of Wisconsin Press.

Mkumbira, J. 2002. Cassava development for small-scale farmers: Approaches to breeding in Malawi. Ph.D. dissertation, Swedish University of Agricultural Sciences, Uppsala.

MoALDM (Ministry of Agriculture, Livestock Development and Marketing). 1997. *National dairy development project–pilot privatization project: Foundation knowledge on community based private AI service.* Nairobi, Kenya: MoALDM.

Moore, H., and M. Vaughan. 1994. *Cutting down trees: Gender, nutrition and agricultural change in Northern Province of Zambia, 1890–1990.* Portsmouth, N.H., U.S.A.: Heinemann.

Morris, M., V. A. Kelly, R. J. Kopicki, and D. Byerlee. 2007. *Fertilizer use in African agriculture: Lessons learned and good practice guidelines.* Washington, D.C.: World Bank.

Morris, M. L. 1998. Maize in the developing world: Waiting for a Green Revolution. In *Maize seed industries in developing countries,* ed. M. L. Morris. Boulder, Colo., U.S.A.: Lynne Rienner.

———. 2001. *Assessing the benefits of international maize breeding research: An overview of the global maize impacts study.* Part II of the CIMMYT 1999–2000 World Maize Facts and Trends. Mexico City: Centro Internacional de Mejoramiento de Maíz y Trigo.

Morris, M. L., J. Risopolous, and D. Beck. 1999. Genetic change in farmer-recycled maize seed: A review of the evidence. Economics Working Paper 99-07. Mexico City: Centro Internacional de Mejoramiento de Maíz y Trigo.

Morris, M. L., R. Tripp, and A. A. Dankyi. 1999. Adoption and impacts of improved maize production technology: A case study of the Ghana grains development project. Economics Program Paper 99-01. Mexico City: Centro Internacional de Mejoramiento de Maíz y Trigo.

Mosley, P. 1975. Maize control in Kenya, 1920–1970. Bath, U.K.: Center for Development Studies, University of Bath.

———. 1983. *The settler economies: Studies in the economic history of Kenya and Southern Rhodesia, 1900–63.* Cambridge: Cambridge University Press.

Moyo, C. C., I. R. M. Benesi, and V. S. Sandifolo. 1998. *Current status of cassava and sweetpotato production and utilization in Malawi.* Lilongwe, Malawi: Ministry of Agriculture and Irrigation.

M'Ribu, H. K., P. L. Neel, and T. A. Fretz. 1993. Horticulture in Kenya. *Horticultural Science* 28 (6): 779–781.

Murethi, J. G., R. S. Tayler, and W. Thorpe. 1995. Productivity of alley farming with leucaena (*Leucaena leucocephala* Lam. de Wit) and Napier grass (*Pennisetum purpureum* K. Schum) in coastal lowland Kenya. *Agroforestry Systems* 3: 59–78.

Muriuki, H. G., and W. Thorpe. 2001. Smallholder dairy production and marketing in Eastern and Southern Africa. In *Proceedings of the South–South Workshop on Smallholder Dairy Production and Marketing—Constraints and Opportunities, March 12th–16th, 2001, Annand, India.* Addis Ababa, Ethiopia: International Livestock Research Institute.

Muthee, A. M. 1995. The adjustment gap. Constraints on development of private sector delivery systems for animal health services and inputs in Kenya's dairy production districts. MRAS/Technical Paper 1. Nairobi, Kenya: Ministry of Agriculture and Rural Development.

Mwanaumo, A., T. S. Jayne, B. Zulu, J. J. Shawa, G. Green, S. Haggblade, and M. Nyembe. 2005. *Zambia's 2005 maize import and marketing experience: Lessons and implications.* Policy Synthesis 11. Lusaka, Zambia: Lusaka Food Security Research Project.

Mwape, F. 2006. Implementing the agricultural expenditure tracking system in Africa. Presentation 18 at the New Partnership for Africa's Development conference Championing Agricultural Successes for Africa's Future: A Parliamentarians' Dialogue on NEPAD, Somerset West, South Africa, May 15–18.

Nabli, M. K., and J. B. Nugent. 1989. *The new institutional economics and development: Theory and applications to Tunisia.* Amsterdam: North-Holland.

Nakhumwa, C. 2002. *Assessment of marketing and utilisation of improved maize seed in Malawi: Cases of Lilongwe and Salima ADDs.* Lilongwe, Malawi: Southern African Drought and Low Fertility Project.

Nartey, F. 1977. *Manihot esculenta* (cassava): Cyanogenesis, ultra-structure and seed germination. Ph.D. dissertation, University of Copenhagen, Munksgaard, Copenhagen, Denmark.

NEPAD (New Partnership for Africa's Development). 2010. *Championing agricultural successes for Africa's future in support of the Comprehensive Africa Agriculture Development Programme: Synthesis report of a parliamentary dialogue.* Midrand, South Africa: NEPAD.

New York Times. 2003. The long reach of King Cotton. *New York Times,* August 5, A18.

Ngigi, M. W. 2005. The case of smallholder dairying in Eastern Africa. Environment and Production Technology Division Working Paper 131. Washington, D.C.: International Food Policy Research Institute.

Ngigi, M. W., C. Delgado, S. J. Staal, and S. Mbogoh. 2000. Role of market outlet in determining terms for milk sales by smallholders in Kenya. Paper presented at the Symposium on Expanding Market Participation in the Developing World, Annual meeting of the American Agricultural Economics Association, Tampa, Fla., U.S.A., July 31–August 3.

Ngigi, S. 2002. Review of irrigation development in Kenya. In *The changing face of irrigation in Kenya: Opportunities for anticipating change in eastern and southern Africa,* ed. H. G. Blank, C. M. Mutero, and H. Murray-Rust. Colombo, Sri Lanka: International Water Management Institute.

Ngoliya, A. 1999. *Comparative advantage of growing cassava and maize.* Nchelenge, Zambia: Ministry of Agriculture and Cooperatives.

Ngoma, H. W., F. Miti, and M. Mbunji. 1999. Multiplication and distribution of improved cassava and sweetpotato planting materials in Zambia. In *Food security and crop diversification in SADC countries: The role of cassava and sweetpotato,* ed. M. O. Akoroda and J. M. Teri. Ibadan, Nigeria: International Institute of Tropical Agriculture.

Ngoni, N. 2009. Green Revolution alliance to form agriculture policy hubs. October 15. Available at <http://allafrica.com/stories/200910150019.html>.

Niang, A., J. De Wolf, S. Gathumbi, and B. Amadalo. 1999. The potential of short duration improved fallow with selected trees and shrubs for crop productivity enhancement in the densely populated highlands of Western Kenya. In *La jachère en Afrique tropicale,* ed. C. Floret and R. Pontanier. Dakar, Senegal: West and Central African Council for Agricultural Research and Development; Marseille, France: Institut de Recherche pour le Développement; and Montrouge, France: John Libbey Eurotext.

Nichols, R. F. W. 1947. Breeding cassava for virus resistance. *East African Agricultural Journal* 12: 184–194.

Nicol, B. M. 1954. A report of the nutritional work which has been carried out in Nigeria since 1920, with a summary of what is known of the present nutritional state of the Nigerian peasants. Ministry of Health, Eastern Region, Enugu, Nigeria. Mimeo.

Nigeriafirst.org. 2005. *Cassava initiatives in Nigeria.* June 24. Available at <www .nigeriafirst.org/printer_4301.shtml>. Accessed January 2007.

Noble, A. D., J. Pretty, F. Penning de Vries, and D. Bossio. 2004. Development of bright spots in Africa: Cause for cautious optimism? Conference Paper 18. Presented at the New Partnership for Africa's Development/Intergovernmental Authority on Development Regional Conference on Agricultural Successes in the Greater Horn of Africa, Nairobi, Kenya, November 22–25.

Norgaard, R. B. 1988. The biological control of the cassava mealybug in Africa. *American Journal of Agricultural Economics* 70: 366–371.

North, D. C. 1990. *Institutions, institutional change and economic performance.* Cambridge: Cambridge University Press.

Nsubuga, H. S. K. 1973. Dairy developpment in Uganda: Policy and institution matters. In *Agricultural policy issues in East Africa,* ed. V. F. Amann, pp. 135–153. Kampala, Uganda: Makere University.

Nthonyiwa, A., A. Mhone, H. Kazembe, C. Moyo, V. Sandifolo, S. Jumbo, D. Siyene, N. M. Mahungu, V. Rweyendela, and J. Abaka-Whyte. 2005. Cassava starch pilot factory, the first of its kind in Malawi. *Roots* 9 (2): 20–22.

Nweke, F. I. 1978a. Irrigation development in Ghana. *Oxford Agrarian Studies* 7: 38–53.

———. 1978b. Agricultural credit in Ghana: Priorities and needs for domestic food production. *Canadian Journal of Agricultural Economics* 26 (3): 37–46.

———. 1979. Farm mechanization and farm labor in Ghana: An analysis of efficiency and policy issues. *Quarterly Journal of International Agriculture* 18: 171–184.

———. 2004. New challenges in the cassava transformation in Nigeria and Ghana. EPTD Discussion Paper 118. Washington, D.C.: International Food Policy Research Institute.

Nweke, F. I., S. K. Hahn, and B. O. Ugwu. 1994. Circumstances of rapid spread of cultivation of improved cassava varieties in Nigeria. *Journal for Farming Systems Research and Extension* 4 (3): 93–119.

Nweke, F. I., D. C. Spencer, and J. K. Lynam. 2002. *The cassava transformation: Africa's best-kept secret.* East Lansing: Michigan State University Press.

Nweke, F. I., A. G. O. Dixon, R. Asiedu, and S. A. Folayan. 1994. Cassava varietal needs of farmers and potentials for production growth in Africa. COSCA Working Paper 10. Ibadan, Nigeria: Collaborative Study of Cassava in Africa, International Institute of Tropical Agriculture.

Nweke, F. I., J. Haleegoah, A. G. O. Dixon, O. Ajobo, B. O. Ugwu, and R. Al-Hassan.

1999a. Cassava production in Ghana: A function of market demand and farmer access to improved production and processing technologies. Collaborative Study of Cassava in Africa Working Paper 21. Ibadan, Nigeria: International Institute of Tropical Agriculture.

Nweke, F. I., B. O. Ugwu, A. G. O. Dixon, C. L. A. Asadu, and O. Ajobo. 1999b. Cassava production in Nigeria: A function of farmer access to markets and to improved production and processing technologies. Collaborative Study of Cassava in Africa Working Paper 20. Ibadan, Nigeria: International Institute of Tropical Agriculture.

Nyagumbo, I. 2008. A review of experiences and developments towards conservation agriculture and related systems in Zimbabwe. In *No-till farming systems,* ed. T. Goddard, M. Zoebisch, Y. Gan, W. Ellis, A. Watson, and S. Sombatpanit, pp. 345–372. Special Publication 3. Bangkok: World Association of Soil and Water Conservation.

Nyoro, J., M. Kiiru, and T. S. Jayne. 1999. Maize market liberalization in Kenya. Paper presented at the Third Workshop on Agricultural Transformation in Africa, Tegemeo Institute of Agricultural Policy and Development, Egerton University, Nairobi, Kenya, June 27–30.

OAU (Organization of African Unity). 1980. *Lagos plan af action for the development of Africa, 1980–2000.* Addis Ababa, Ethiopia: OAU.

Ochou, O. G., and T. Martin. 2000. *Prévention et gestion de la résistance de Helicoverparmigera (Hübner) aux pyréthrinoïdes en Côte d'Ivoire.* 2ème rapport d'exécution technique du Projet régional de prévention et de gestion de la résistance de Helicoverpa armegira aux pyréthrinoïdes en Afrique de l'Ouest. Paris: Centre de coopération internationale en recherche agronomique pour le développement.

Odhiambo, M., and D. Wilcock. 1990. Reform of maize marketing in Kenya. In *Food security policies in the SADCC region,* ed. M. Rukuni, G. Mudimu, and T. Jayne. Harare: University of Zimbabwe.

OECD (Organisation for Economic Cooperation and Development). 2005. *Agricultural policies in OECD countries: Monitoring and evaluation, 2005.* Paris: OECD.

Oerke, E. C., H. W. Dehne, F. Schonbeck, and A. Weber. 1995. *Crop production and protection: Estimated losses in major food and cash crops.* Amsterdam: Elsevier.

Ohadike, D. C. 1981. The influenza pandemic of 1918–19 and the spread of cassava cultivation on the Lower Niger: A study in historical linkages. *Journal of African History* 22: 379–391.

Ojala, R. 1998. *Gross margin and production cost calculations of milk production at different production and management levels.* Addis Ababa, Ethiopia: Smallholder Dairy Development Project.

Okigbo, B. N. 1980. Nutritional implications of projects giving high priority to the production of staples of low nutritive quality: The case of cassava in the humid tropics of West Africa. *Food and Nutrition Bulletin* (United Nations University, Tokyo) 2 (4).

Okwenye, A. 1994. Rehabilitation of the dairy industry in Uganda. *World Animal Review* 99 (2): 2–7.

Oldrieve, B. 1993. *Conservation farming for communal, small-scale, resettlement and cooperative farmers of Zimbabwe: A farm management handbook.* Harare, Zimbabwe: Rio Tinto Foundation.

Oluoch, A. 2008. Kenya: How country's economy survived the EPA threat. *East African Business Week* (Kampala), March 24.

Omamo, S. W., and K. von Grebmer. 2005. *Biotechnology, agriculture and food security in Africa*. Washington, D.C.: International Food Policy Research Institute.

Omore, A., H. Muriuku, M. Kenyanjui, M. Wango, and S. Staal. 1999. *The Kenya dairy sub-sector: A rapid appraisal*. Nairobi, Kenya: International Livestock Research Institute.

Omore, A., S. Arimi, E. Kange'the, J. McDermott, S. Staal, E. Ouma, J. Odhiambo, A. Mwangi, G. Aboge, E. Koroti, and R. Koech. 2001. Assessing and managing milk-borne health risks for the benefit of consumers in Kenya. Nairobi, Kenya: International Livestock Research Institute.

Osuntokun, B. O. 1973. Ataxic neuropathy associated with high cassava diets in West Africa. In *Chronic cassava toxicity*, ed. B. Nestel and R. MacIntyre, pp. 27–36. Proceedings of an Interdisciplinary Workshop, London, January 29–30. Ottawa, Canada: International Development Research Centre.

———. 1981. Cassava diet, chronic cyanide intoxication and neuropathy in Nigerian Africans. *World Review of Nutrition and Diet* 36: 141–173.

Oswald, A., H. Frost, J. K. Ransom, J. Kroschel, K. Shepherd, and J. Sauerborn. 1996. *Studies on potential for improved fallow using trees and shrubs to reduce striga infestations in Kenya*. Proceedings of the Sixth Parasitic Weed Symposium, Cordoba, Spain. Seville: Dirección General de Investigación Agraria.

Otim-Nape, G. W., A. Bua, Y. Baguma, and J. M. Thresh. 1997. Epidemic of severe cassava mosaic disease in Uganda and efforts to control it. *African Journal of Root and Tuber Crops* 2: 42. Abstract.

Otim-Nape, G. W., A. Bua, G. N. Ssemakula, Y. K. Baguma, R. Van Der Grift, C. Omongo, G. Acola, S. Ogwal, W. Sserubombwe, T. Alicai, and S. Tumwesigye. 1998. Impact of a century of cassava research and development on the economy and well being of the people of Uganda. Paper presented at the Centenary of Agricultural Research in Uganda, Entebbe, Uganda, October 11–13.

Otoo, J. A., A. G. O. Dixon, R. Asiedu, J. E. Okeke, G. N. Maroya, K. Tougnon, O. O. Okoli, J. P. Tette, and S. K. Hahn. 1994. Genotype x environment interaction studies with cassava. In *Tropical root crops in developing countries*, ed. F. Ofori and S. K. Hahn, pp. 146–148. Proceedings of the International Society for Tropical Root Crops, Accra, Ghana, October 20–26, 1991.

Oyejide, T. A. 1986. *The effects of trade and exchange rate policies on agriculture in Nigeria*. Research Report 55. Washington, D.C.: International Food Policy Research Institute.

Pachai, B. 1973. Land policies in Malawi: An examination of the colonial legacy. *Journal of Modern African History* 14 (4): 681–689.

Padwick, G. W. 1983. Fifty years of experimental agriculture II. The maintenance of soil fertility in tropical Africa: A review. *Experimental Agriculture* 19 (4): 293–310.

Page, S. L. J., and P. Chonyera. 1994. The promotion of maize fertilizer packages: A cause of household food insecurity and peasant impoverishment in high rainfall areas of Zimbabwe. *Development of Southern Africa* 11 (3): 301–320.

Palaniswamy, N., and R. Birner. 2006. Financing agricultural development: The political economy of public spending on agriculture in Sub-Saharan Africa. Paper 4. Presented at the German Development Economics Conference, Berlin Research Committee Development Economics. Available at <http://econpapers.repec.org/paper/zbwgdec06/4727.htm>.

PAMORI (Projet d'Appui à la Mobilisation des Ressources Internes). 2000. *La filière coton et son potentiel fiscal.* Rapport définitif. Agence Canadienne de Développement International, Ministère des Finances du Mali. Bamako, Mali: Société de Gestion des Marches Autonomes.

Pandey, S. 1998. Varietal development. In *Maize seed industries in developing countries,* ed. M. L. Morris. Boulder, Colo., U.S.A.: Lynne Rienner.

Pandit, S., and N. S. Thukur. 1961. *A brief history of the development of Indian settlement in Eastern Africa.* Nairobi, Kenya: Panco.

Pardey, P., J. James, J. Alston, S. Wood, B. Koo, E. Binebaum, T. Hurley, and P. Glewwe. 2007. Science, technology and skills report. Commissioned by the CGIAR Science Council and prepared as a background paper for the 2008 World Development Report of the World Bank and the CGIAR Science Council's 2007 bi-annual report. Washington, D.C.: International Food Policy Research Institute.

Pardey, P. G., and N. M. Beintema. 2001. *Slow magic: Agricultural R&D a century after Mendel.* Washington, D.C.: International Food Policy Research Institute.

Pardey, P. G., J. M. Alston, and R. R. Piggott. 2006. *Agricultural R&D in the developing world: Too little too late?* Washington, D.C.: International Food Policy Research Institute.

Pardey, P. G., J. Roseboom, and N. M. Beintema. 1997. Investments in African agricultural research. *World Development* 25 (3): 409–423.

Partnership to Cut Hunger and Poverty in Africa. 2002. *Now is the time: A plan to cut hunger and poverty in Africa.* Washington, D.C.: Partnership to Cut Hunger and Poverty in Africa.

Pegram, R. G., A. D. James, G. P. M. Oosterwijk, K. J. Killorn, J. Lemche, M. Ghirotti, Z. Tekle, H. G. B. Chizyuka, E. T. Mwase, and F. Chizhyka. 1991. Studies on the economic impact of ticks in Zambia. *Experimental and Applied Acarology* 12: 9–26.

Pelletier, D. L., and L. A. H. Msukwa. 1990. *Intervention planning in response to disasters: A case study of the mealy bug disaster in Malawi.* Cornell Food and Nutrition Policy Program Monograph 6. Ithaca, N.Y., U.S.A.: Cornell University.

Peltier, G. 2003. *Message du Président Directeur Général.* Dagris Web site. Available at <www.dagris.fr>.

Peltre-Wurtz, J., and B. Steck. 1979. *Influence d'une société de développement sur le milieu paysan: Coton et culture attelée dans la région de la Bagoé (Côte d'Ivoire).* Abidjan, Côte d'Ivoire: Office de la Recherche Scientifique et Technique d'Outre-Mer.

Pender, J., S. Scherr, and G. Duron. 2001. Pathways of development in the hillsides of Honduras: Causes and implications for agricultural production, poverty, and sustainable resource use. In *Tradeoffs or synergies? Agricultural intensification, economic development and the environment,* ed. D. R. Lee and C. B. Barrett. Wallingford, U.K.: CAB International.

Pender, J., P. Jagger, E. Nkonya, and D. Sserunkuuma. 2004. Development pathways and land management in Uganda. *World Development* 32 (5): 767–792.

Peters, P. E. 1995. Uses and abuses of the concept of female-headed households in research on agrarian transformation and policy. In *Women wielding the hoe: Lessons from rural Africa for feminist theory and development practice,* ed. D. F. Bryceson. Washington, D.C.: Berg.

Peters, P. E. 1996. Failed magic or social context? Market liberalization and the rural poor in Malawi. Development Discussion Paper 562. Cambridge, Mass., U.S.A.: Harvard Institute of International Development.

Peterson, J. S., L. Tembo, C. Kawimbe, and E. Mwangamba. 1999. *The Zambia integrated agroforestry project baseline survey: Lessons learned in Chadiza, Chipata, Katete, and Mambwe Districts, Eastern Province, Zambia.* Lusaka, Zambia/Gainesville, Fla., U.S.A.: World Vision/Ministry of Agriculture/University of Florida.

Phillips, T. P., D. S. Taylor, L. Sanni, and M. O. Akoroda. 2004. *A cassava industrial revolution in Nigeria: The potential for a new industrial crop.* Rome: International Fund for Agricultural Development and Food and Agriculture Organization of the United Nations.

Phiri, A. R., E. Chapasuka, J. Phiri, R. Chirambo, C. Ndamala, and C. Mataya. 2001. *Applying a sub-sector analysis approach to studying the marketing of cassava in Malawi: A qualitative assessment of the subsector.* Lilongwe, Malawi: Southern African Root Crops Research Network.

Phiri, D., S. Franzel, P. Mafongoya, I. Jere, R. Katanga, and S. Phiri. 2004. Who is using the new technology? A case study of the association of wealth status and gender with the planting of improved tree fallows in Eastern Province, Zambia. *Agricultural Systems* 79 (2): 131–144.

Pieri, C. 1989. *Fertilité des terres de savane: Bilan de trente ans de recherche et de développement agricole au sud du Sahara.* Paris: Ministère de la Coopération, Centre de Coopération Internationale en Recherche Agronomique pour le Développement/Institut de Recherches Agronomiques Tropicales.

Pieri, C. J. M. G. 1992. *Fertility of soils: A future for farming in the West African savannas.* Berlin: Springer.

Pinckney, T. C. 1993. Is market liberalization compatible with food security? *Food Policy* 18 (4): 325–333.

Place, F., and P. Hazell. 1993. Productivity effects of indigenous land tenure systems in sub-Saharan Africa. *American Journal of Agricultural Economics* 74 (3): 360–373.

Place, F., M. Adato, P. Hebinck, and M. Omosa. 2005. *The impact of agroforestry-based soil fertility replenishment practices on the poor in Western Kenya.* Research Report 142. Washington, D.C.: International Food Policy Research Institute and World Agroforestry Centre.

Pongolani, C., and S. M. Kalonge. 1999. Re-introducing crop diversity in Zambia: The case of cassava. In *Food security and crop diversification in SADC countries: The role of cassava and sweet potato,* ed. M. O. Akoroda and J. M Teri, pp. 207–211. Ibadan, Nigeria: International Institute of Tropical Agriculture.

Poulton, C., and A. Dorward. 2008. Getting agriculture moving: Role of the state in increasing staple food crop productivity with special reference to coordination, input subsidies, credit and price stabilization. Paper presented at the Alliance for a Green Revolution in Africa policy convening, Nairobi, Kenya, June 23–25.

Pratt, A. N., and X. Diao. 2006. Exploring growth linkages and market opportunities for agriculture in Southern Africa. Development Strategy and Governance Division Working Paper 42. Washington, D.C.: International Food Policy Research Institute.

Pray, C. E., J. Huang, D. Ma, and F. Qiao. 2001. Impact of Bt cotton in China. *World Development* 29: 813–825.

Pretty, J. 2000. Can sustainable agriculture feed Africa? New evidence on progress, process and impacts. *Environment, Development and Sustainability* 1: 253–274.

————. 2005. *Sustainable agriculture.* London: Earthscan.

Pretty, J., and R. Hine. 2001. *Reducing food poverty with sustainable agriculture: A summary of new evidence.* Final Report from the SAFE-World Research Project. Colchester, U.K.: Essex University.

Price, T. D., and A. B. Gebauer. 1995. *Last hunters first farmers.* Santa Fe, N.M., U.S.A.: School of American Research Press.

Pschorn-Strauss, E. 2004. *Bt cotton and small-scale farmers in Markhathini: A story of debt, dependency, and dicey economics.* Cape Town: Biowatch South Africa.

Pursell, G., and M. Diop. 1998. Cotton policies in francophone Africa. Why and how the "filières" should be liberalized. Washington, D.C.: World Bank.

Quirke, D. 2002. *Trade distortions and cotton markets: Implications for global cotton producers.* Canberra: Cotton Research and Development Corporation, Centre for International Economics.

Raintree, J., and K. Warner. 1986. Agroforestry pathways for the intensification of shifting cultivation. *Agroforestry Systems* 4: 39–54.

Ramisch, J. 1999. In the balance? Evaluation of soil nutrition budgets for an agro-pastoral village of southern Mali. Managing Africa's Soil 9. London: Drylands Programme, International Institute for Environment and Development.

Raussen, T., A. E. Daka, and L. Bangwe. 1995. *Dambos in Eastern Province.* Chipata, Zambia: Ministry of Agriculture, Food, and Fisheries.

Ravallion, M., S. Chen, and P. Sangraula. 2007. New evidence on the urbanization of global poverty. World Bank Policy Research Working Paper 4199. Washington, D.C.: World Bank.

Raymond, G., and M. Fok. 1994. Relations entre coton et vivrier en Afrique de l'Ouest et du Centre, Le coton affame les populations? Une fausse affirmation. Centre de Coopération Internationale en Recherche Agronomique pour le Développement, Paris.

Reader, J. 1997. *Africa: A biography of the continent.* New York: Vintage Books.

Reardon, T. 2007. Global food industry consolidation and rural agroindustrialization in developing economies. In *Transforming the rural nonfarm economy,* ed. S. Haggblade, P. Hazell, and T. Reardon, pp. 199–215. Baltimore, Md., U.S.A.: Johns Hopkins University Press.

Reardon, T., A. A. Fall, V. Kelly, C. Delgado, P. Matlon, J. Hopkins, and O. Badiane. 1993. Agriculture-led income diversification in the West African semi-arid tropics: Nature, distribution and importance of production-linkage activities. In *African economic issues,* ed. A. Atsain, S. Wangwe, and A. G. Drabek. Nairobi, Kenya: African Economic Research Consortium.

Redda, T. 2001. Small-scale milk marketing and processing in Ethiopia. Proceedings of the South–South Workshop on Smallholder Dairy Production and Marketing—Constraints and Opportunities, Anand, India, March 12–16.

Regmi, A., and M. Gehlhar. 2003. Consumer preferences and concerns shape global food trade. *Food Review* (USDA) 24 (3): 2–8.

Reij, C. 1983. *L'évolution de la lutte anti-érosive en Haute Volta depuis l'indépendence: Vers une plus grande participation de la population.* Amsterdam: Institute for Environmental Studies, Vrije Universiteit.

Reij, C., and T. Thiombiano. 2003. *Développement rural et environnement au Burkina Faso: La réhabilitation de la capacité productive des terroirs sur la partie nord du Plateau Central entre 1980 et 2001 ; Rapport de synthèse.* Ouagadougou, Burkina Faso: Ambassade des Pays-Bas, GTZ–PATECORE, and U.S. Agency for International Development.

Reij, C., and A. Waters-Bayer. 2001. *Farmer innovation in Africa: A source of inspiration for agricultural development.* London: Earthscan.

Reij, C., I. Scoones, and C. Toulmin, eds. 1996. *Sustaining the soil: Indigenous soil and water conservation in Africa.* London: Earthscan.

Reij, C., G. Tappan, and A. Belemvire. 2005. Changing land management practices and vegetation on the Central Plateau of Burkina Faso (1968–2002). *Journal of Arid Environments* 63: 642–659.

Reij, C. P., and E. M. A. Smaling. 2007. Analyzing successes in agriculture and land management in Sub-Saharan Africa: Is macro-level gloom obscuring positive micro-level change? *Land Use Policy* 25 (3): 410–420.

Republic of Kenya. 1995. *Agricultural sector review.* Nairobi, Kenya: Ministry of Agriculture, Livestock Development and Marketing; Agricultural Sector Investment Programme Secretariat.

Rindos, D. 1980. Symbiosis, instability and the origins and spread of agriculture: A new model. *Current Anthropology* 21 (6): 751–772.

———. 1984. *The origins of agriculture: An evolutionary perspective.* Orlando, Fla., U.S.A.: Academic Press.

Rodney, W. 1974. *How Europe underdeveloped Africa.* Washington, D.C.: Howard University.

Rohrbach, D. D. 1988. The growth of smallholder maize production in Zimbabwe: Causes and implications for food security. Ph.D. dissertation, Michigan State University, East Lansing.

Rohrbach, D. D., I. J. Minde, and J. Howard. 2003. Looking beyond national boundaries: Regional harmonization of seed policies, laws and regulations. *Food Policy* 28: 317–333.

Roose, E., V. Kabore, and C. Guenat. 1993. Le zaï: Fonctionnement, limites et amélioration d'une pratique traditionnelle africaine de réhabilitation de la végétation et de la productivité des terres dégradées en région soudano-sahelienne (Burkina Faso). *Cahiers Orstom, série Pédiologie* 2: 159–173. Paris: Office de la Recherche Scientifique et Technique d'Outre-Mer.

———. 1999. Zaï practice: A West African traditional rehabilitation system for semiarid degraded lands; A case study in Burkina Faso. *Arid Soil Research and Rehabilitation* 13: 343–355.

Rosegrant, M. W., M. S. Paisner, S. Meijer, and J. Witcover. 2001. *Global food projections to 2020: Emerging trends and alternative futures.* Washington, D.C.: International Food Policy Research Institute.

Rosegrant, M. W., S. A. Cline, W. Li, T. B. Sulser, and R. A. Valmonte-Santos. 2005. Looking ahead: Long-term prospects for Africa's agricultural development and security. 2020 Discussion Paper 41. Washington, D.C.: International Food Policy Research Institute.

Rosegrant, M. W., W. Msangi, T. Sulser, and R. Valmonte-Santos. 2006. Bioenergy and agriculture: Promises and challenges. IFPRI 2020 Vision Focus 14, Brief 3. Washington, D.C.: International Food Policy Research Institute.

Rougé, B., and M. N. N'Goan. 1997. L'anana en Afrique de l'ouest et du centre. *Acta Horticulturae* 425: 75–82.

Rubey, L. 1995. Maize market reform in Zimbabwe: Linkages between consumer preferences, small enterprise development and alternative market channels. Ph.D. dissertation, Michigan State University, East Lansing.

Rusike, J. 1995. An institutional analysis of the maize seed industry in Southern Africa. Ph.D. thesis, Department of Agricultural Economics, Michigan State University, East Lansing.

————. 1998. Zimbabwe. In *Maize seed industries in developing countries,* ed. M. L. Morris. Boulder, Colo., U.S.A.: Lynne Rienner.

Rusike, J., and C. K. Eicher. 1997. Institutional innovations in the maize seed industry. In *Africa's emerging maize revolution,* ed. D. Byerlee and C. K. Eicher, pp. 173–192. Boulder, Colo., U.S.A.: Lynne Rienner.

Russell, D. 2004. *Farmers experience with Bt cotton in China.* PowerPoint presentation to the second Conference on Biotechnology for Asian Development, New Delhi, April 7–8. London: National Resources Institute, University of Greenwish, July.

Ruthenberg, H. 1966. *African agricultural production development policy in Kenya 1952–65.* Berlin: Information und Forschung–Institut für Wirtschaftsforschung Studienstele.

Ruttan, V. 2001. *Technology, growth, and development: An induced innovation perspective.* New York: Oxford University Press.

Sachs, J. D. 2001. Tropical underdevelopment. NBER Working Paper 8119. Cambridge, Mass., U.S.A.: National Bureau of Economic Research, February.

————. 2006. *Keynote address to the African fertilizer summit, Abuja, Nigeria.* Available at <www.africangreenrevolution.com/en/green_revolution /africas_predicament/ fertilizer_summit/sacs_says/index.html>.

SAEC (Société Africaine d'Études et Conseils). 2000. *Rapport d'évaluation d'impact socio-économique de la première phase du Programme Spécial CES/AGF sur les ménages agricoles.* 2 vols. Ouagadougou, Burkina Faso: SAEC.

Sahai, S., and S. Rahman. 2003. Performance of Bt Cotton: Data from first commercial crop. *Economic and Political Weekly* 38 (30): 37–39.

Sahn, D., and J. Arulpragasam. 1991. The stagnation of smallholder agriculture in Malawi. *Food Policy* 16 (3): 219–234.

Sahn, D. E., P. A. Dorosh, and S. D. Younger, eds. 1997. *Structural adjustment reconsidered—Economic policy and poverty in Africa.* Cambridge: Cambridge University Press.

Sanchez, P. A. 1999. Improved fallows come of age in the tropics. *Agroforestry Systems* 47: 3–12.

Sanchez , P. A., and C. A. Palm. 1996. Nutrient cycling and agroforestry in Africa. *Unasylva* 185 (47): 24–28.

Sanchez, P. A., K. D. Shepherd, M. J. Soule, F. M. Place, R. J. Buresh, A. N. Izac, A. U. Mokwunye, F. R. Kwesiga, C. G. Ndiritu, and P. L. Woomer. 1997. Soil fertility replenishment in Africa: An investment in natural resource capital. In *Replenishing soil fertility in Africa,* ed. R. Buresh, P. A. Sanchez, and F. Calhoun, pp. 1–46. SSSA Special Publication 51. Madison, Wis., U.S.A.: Soil Science Society of America.

Sanders, J. H., J. G. Nagy, and S. Ramaswamy. 1990. Developing new agricultural technologies for the Sahelian countries: The Burkina Faso case. *Economic Development and Cultural Change* 39 (1): 1–22.

Sargent, M. W., J. A. Lichte, P. J. Matlon, and R. Bloom. 1981. An assessment of animal traction in francophone West Africa. MSU Agricultural Economics Working Paper 34. East Lansing: Department of Agricultural Economics, Michigan State University, March.

SARRNET (Southern African Root Crops Research Network). 1994. *Progress of multiplication and distribution of cassava and sweetpotato planting material in Malawi: Progress report no. 5.* Lilongwe, Malawi: SARRNET.

Sauer, J., and H. Tchale. 2009. The economics of soil fertility management in Malawi. *Review of Agricultural Economics* 31 (3): 535–560.

Sauti, R. F. N., E. M. H. Khonje, G. Thaulo, M. Chibambo, and G. M. Bulla. 1994. The importance of cassava and production constraints in Malawi. In *Root crops for food security in Africa,* ed. M. O. Akoroda. Proceedings of the Fifth Triennial Symposium of the International Society for Tropical Root Crops–Africa Branch, Kampala, Uganda, November 22–28, 1992.

Sawadogo, A. 1977. *L'agriculture en Côte d'Ivoire.* Paris: Presse Universitaire de France.

Sawadogo, H., F. Hien, A. Sohoro, and F. Kambou. 2001. Pits for trees: How farmers in semi-arid Burkina Faso increase and diversify plant biomass. In *Farmer Innovation in Africa: A source of inspiration for agricultural development,* ed. C. Reij and A. Waters-Bayer, pp. 35–46. London: Earthscan.

Schoenbrun, D. L. 1993. Cattle herds and banana gardens. *African Archaeological Review* 2: 39–72.

Scott, G. 1995. Agricultural transformation in Zambia: Past experience and future prospects. Paper presented at the Agricultural Transformation Workshop, Abidjan. East Lansing: Michigan State University.

SEC-Diarra/BAC+. 1998. *Evaluation technique de la filière coton.* Dans le cadre de l'exécution du contrat-plan Etat–Compagnie Malienne pour le Développement des Textiles–Exploitants Agricoles (1994–1998), 2e phase de l'Étude, Bilan Diagnostic du secteur cotonnier, Perspectives d'évolution à moyen terme, Recommandations, Rapport Provisoire. Bamako, Mali: Cellule d'Appui à la Mise en Oeuvre du Plan d'Action, Ministère du Développement Rural et de l'Eau.

Shepherd, K. D., E. Ohlsson, J. R. Okalebo, and J. K. Ndufa. 1996. Potential impact of agroforestry on soil nutrient balances at the farm scale in the East African Highlands. *Fertilizer Research* 44: 87–99.

Shopo, T. 1985. The political economy of hunger in Zimbabwe. Working Paper 2. Harare: Zimbabwe Institute of Development Studies.

Siandwazi, C., S. Bhattarai, and S. K. Kumar. 1991. The effects of technological change on food consumption and nutritional status in Eastern Province. In *Adopting improved farm technology: A study of smallholder farmers in Eastern Province, Zambia,* ed. R. Celis, J. T. Milimo, and S. Wanmali. Washington, D.C.: International Food Policy Research Institute.

Sibale, P. K., A. M. Chirembo, A. R. Saka, and V. O. Lungu. 2001. *Food production and security: Module 1 of the 2000–2001 targeted inputs programme.* Calibre Consultants, Reading, U.K.: Calibre Consultants and Statistical Services Centre, University of Reading.

Sijali, I., and R. Okumu. 2002. New irrigation technologies. In *The changing face of irrigation in Kenya: Opportunities for anticipating change in eastern and southern Africa,* ed. H. G. Blank, C. M. Mutero, and H. Murray-Rust. Colombo, Sri Lanka: International Water Management Institute.

Sinaba, F. 2000. Au Mali, la grève du coton désamorée. *Grain de sel* 15 (juillet).

Siyeni, D., N. M. Mahungu, A. Mhone, C. C. Moyo, V. Sandifolo, A. Nthonyiwa, and S. Jumbo. 2005. Use of high quality cassava flour by bakery industries in Malawi. *Roots* 9 (2): 7–10.

Slingerland, M. A., and V. E. Stork. 2000. Determinants of zai and mulching in north Burkina Faso. *Journal of Sustainable Agriculture* 16 (2): 53–76.

Smale, M. 1992. Risk, disaster avoidance, and farmer experimentation: The microeconomics of HYV adoption in Malawi. Ph.D. thesis, Department of Agricultural and Resource Economics, University of Maryland, College Park.

———. 1995. Maize is life: Malawi's delayed green revolution. *World Development* 23 (5): 819–831.

Smale, M., and P. W. Heisey. 1994. Maize research in Malawi revisited: An emerging success story? *Journal of International Development* 6 (November–December): 689–706.

Smale, M., and T. S. Jayne. 2003. Maize in Eastern and Southern Africa: "Seeds of success in retrospect." Environment and Production Technology Division Working Paper 97. Washington, D.C.: International Food Policy Research Institute.

Smale, M., with Z. H. W. Kaunda, H. L. Makina, M. M. M. K. Mkandawire, M. N. S. Msowoya, D. J. E. K. Mwale, and P. W. Heisey. 1991. Chimanga cha makolo, hybrids and composites: An analysis of farmer adoption of maize technology in Malawi. CIMMYT Economics Working Paper 91/04. Mexico City: Centro Internacional de Mejoramiento de Maíz y Trigo.

Smale, M., Z. H. W. Kaunda, H. L. Makina, and M. M. M. K. Mkandawire. 1993. *Farmers' evaluation of newly released maize cultivars in Malawi: A comparison of local maize, semi-flint and dent hybrids.* Harare, Zimbabwe: Centro Internacional de Mejoramiento de Maíz y Trigo.

Smale, M., and A. Phiri, with contributions from G. A. Chikafa, P. Heisey, F. Mahatta, M. N. S. Msowoya, E. B. K. Mwanyongo, H. G. Sagawa, and H. A. C. Selemani. 1998. Institutional change and discontinuities in farmers' use of hybrid maize and fertilizer in Malawi: Findings from the 1996–7 CIMMYT/MOA survey. Economics Working Paper 98-01. Mexico City: Centro Internacional de Mejoramiento de Maíz y Trigo.

Smaling, E. M. A. 1993. An agroecological framework for integrating nutrient management, with special reference to Kenya. Ph.D. thesis, Agricultural University, Wageningen, the Netherlands.

Smaling, E. M. A., S. M. Nandwa, and B. H. Janssen. 1997. Soil fertility in Africa is at stake. *Replenishing soil fertility in Africa.* SSSA Special Publication 51. Madison, Wis., U.S.A.: Soil Science Society of America.

Smaling, E. M. A., J. J. Stoorvogel, and P. N. Windmeijer. 1993. Calculating soil nutrient balances in Africa at different scales, Part 2, District scale. *Fertilizer Research* 35: 237–250.

Smith, B. D. 1995. *The emergence of agriculture.* New York: Scientific American Library.

Soenarjo, R. 1993. *Research review of root and tuber, 1983 to 1992.* Mansa, Mali: Luapula Regional Research Station.

Solomon, A., A. Workalemahu, M. A. Jabbar, M. M. Ahmed, and B. Hurissa. 2003. Livestock marketing in Ethiopia: A review of structure, performance and development initiatives. ILRI Socio-economics and Policy Research Working Paper 52. Addis Ababa, Ethiopia and Nairobi, Kenya: Livestock Marketing Authority and International Livestock Research Institute.

Southall, A. 1988. The recent political economy of Uganda. In *Uganda now: Between decay and development,* ed. H. B. Hansen and M. Twaddle, pp. 54–69. London: James Currey.

Spencer, D. 1994. Infrastructure and technology constraints to agricultural development in the humid and subhumid tropics of Africa. EPTD Discussion Paper 3. Washington, D.C.: International Food Policy Research Institute.

Staal, S. J. 1995. Peri urban dairying and public policies in Ethiopia and Kenya: A comparative economic and institutional analysis. Ph.D. dissertation, Department of Food and Resource Economics, University of Florida, Gainesville.

Staal, S. J., C. Delgado, and C. Nicholson. 1996. Smallholder dairying under transactions costs in East Africa. *World Development* 25: 779–794.

Staal, S. J., A. Nin Pratt, and M. Jabbar. 2008. Dairy development for the resource poor. Part 2: Kenya and Ethiopia dairy development case studies. Pro-Poor Livestock Policy Initiative Working Paper 44-2. Nairobi, Kenya: International Livestock Research Institute.

Staal, S. J., G. A. Waithaka, G. A. Owour, and M. Herrero. 2002. *Demand and supply changes in the livestock sector and their impact on smallholders: The case of dairy in Kenya; A summary.* Nairobi, Kenya: International Livestock Research Institute.

Stevens, C., and J. Kennan. 1999. Will Africa's participation in horticultural chains survive liberalization? IDS Working Paper 106. Sussex, U.K.: Institute for Development Studies.

Stevens, P., D. Samazaka, A. Wanders, and D. Moono. 2002. *A starting point for conservation farming: Impact study on the acceptance of the Magoye ripper.* Chisamba, Zambia: Institute of Agricultural and Environmental Engineering / Golden Valley Agricultural Research Trust.

Stoop, W. A., and H. I. D. Vierich. 1990. Changes in West African savanna agriculture in response to growing population and continuing low rainfall. *Agriculture, Ecosystems and Environment* 31: 115–132.

Stoorvogel, J. J., and E. M. A. Smaling. 1990. *Assessment of soil nutrient depletion in Sub-Saharan Africa: 1983–2000.* Report 28, Vols. 1–4. Wageningen, the Netherlands: Winand Staring Center.

Storey, H. H., and R. F. W. Nichols. 1938. Studies of the mosaic diseases of cassava. *Annals of Applied Biology* 25 (4): 790–806.

Sumberg, J., and C. Okali. 1997. *Farmers' experiments: Creating local knowledge.* Boulder, Colo., U.S.A.: Lynne Reinner.

Swanberg, K. 1995. Horticultural exports from Kenya. *Horticultural Trade Journal* 3: 3–5.

Swinkels, R., S. Franzel, K. D. Shepherd, E. Ohlsson, and J. K. Ndufa. 1997. The economics of short rotation improved fallows: Evidence from areas of high population density in Western Kenya. *Agricultural Systems* 55: 99–121.

Swynnerton, R. J. M. 1954. *A plan to intensify the development of African agriculture in Kenya.* Nairobi, Kenya: Government Printer.

Tefft, J. 2000. Cotton in Mali: The "white revolution" and development. In *Democracy and development in Mali,* ed. R. J. Bingen, J. M. Staatz, and D. Robinson, pp. 211–242. East Lansing: Michigan State University Press.

————. 2003. Mali's white revolution: Smallholder cotton from 1960 to 2003. Conference Background Paper 4, prepared for the Internationale Weiterbildung und Entwicklung, International Food Policy Research Institute, New Partnership for Africa's Development, and Technical Center for Agricultural and Rural Cooperation conference Successes in African Agriculture, Pretoria, December 1–3.

Tefft, J., and V. Kelly. 2004. Understanding and reducing child malnutrition in Mali: Interim research findings for the project on linkages between child nutrition and agricultural growth (LICNAG). Staff Paper 2004-27. East Lansing: Department of Agricultural Economics, Michigan State University.

Tefft, J., and V. Kelly, in collaboration with the LICNAG Research Team. 2002. *Understanding and reducing child malnutrition in Mali: Interim research findings for the project on linkages between child nutrition and agricultural growth (LICNAG).* Staff Paper 2004-27. East Lansing: Department of Agricultural Economics, Michigan State University.

Tefft, J., J. Staatz, and J. Dioné. 1997. Impact of the CFA devaluation on sustainable growth for poverty alleviation: Preliminary results. Paper presented at World Bank Conference on Poverty Alleviation, Stockholm, October.

Tefft, J., J. Staatz, J. Dioné, and V. Kelly. 1998. *Food security and agricultural subsectors in West Africa: Future prospects and key issues four years after the devaluation of the CFA franc, cotton subsector.* Bamako, Mali: Sahel Institut/Comité permanent Inter-Etats de Lutte contre la Sécheresse dans le Sahel.

Tembo, S. P. M., and D. C. Chitundu. 2001. *Applying a subsector analysis approach to studying the marketing of cassava and sweet potato in Southern Africa: The case of Zambia.* Lusaka, Zambia: Southern African Root Crops Research Network.

Terri, J. M., V. S. Sandifolo, E. H. Kapeya, C. C. Moyo, F. P. Chipungu, and I. R. M. Benesi. 2000. *Root crops revolution in Malawi: Lessons learned.* Lilongwe, Malawi: Southern African Root Crops Research Network.

Thirtle, C., L. Beyers, Y. Ismaël, and J. Piesse. 2003. Can GM technologies help the poor? The impact of Bt cotton in the Makhathini Flats of KwaZulu-Natal. *World Development* 31 (4): 717–732.

Thiru, A. 2000. International trade in fruits and vegetables: Opportunities and constraints for Kenya. Paper presented at the Technical Workshop on Fruit and Vegetable Standards and Grades, Naro Moro River Lodge, Kenya, August 15–17.

Thresh, J. M., G. W. Otim-Nape, J. P. Legg, and D. Fargette. 1997. African cassava mosaic virus disease: The magnitude of the problem. *African Journal of Root and Tuber Crops* 2 (1–2): 13–19. Ibadan, Nigeria: International Society of Tropical Root Crops–African Branch/International Institute of Tropical Agriculture.

Thurlow, J., J. Kiringai, and M. Gautam. 2007. Rural investments to accelerate growth and poverty reduction in Kenya. IFPRI Discussion Paper 723. Washington, D.C.: International Food Policy Research Institute.

Ti, T. C. 2000. The global pineapple economy. *Acta Horticulturae* 529: 49–50.

Times of Zambia. 2009. COMESA trade jumps to US$15.2 billion. Lusaka, Zambia:

Times of Zambia, June 2. Available at <http://www.lusakatimes.com/?p=13341>. Accessed February 2010.

Tindall, P. E. N. 1968. *History of Central Africa.* London: Longman Green.

Torday, E., and Joyce, T. A. 1911. Notes ethnographiques sur les peuples communément appelés Bakuba, ainsi que sur les peuplades apparantées—Les Bushongo. Belgium Ministère des Colonies, *Annales du Musée du Congo Belge, Ethnographie, Anthropologie, Series 3, Documents ethnographiques concernant les populations du Congo Belge,* Tome II, Fascicule 1, fevrier. Brussels, Belgium: Ministere des Colonies.

Torero, M., and S. Chowdhury. 2005. Increasing access to infrastructure for Africa's rural poor. Issue Brief 2. Washington, D.C.: International Food Policy Research Institute.

Torquebiau, E. F., and F. Kwesiga. 1996. Root development in *Sesbania sesban* fallow-maize system in eastern Zambia. *Agroforestry Systems* 34: 193–211.

Toye, J. 1992. Interest group politics and the implementation of adjustment in Sub-Saharan Africa. *Journal of International Development* 4 (2): 183–198.

Traub, L. N. 2008. Maize trade profile: Country-level assessment of South Africa. Strengthening Food Security through Regional Trade Liberalization Background Paper 1. East Lansing: Michigan State University

Traub, L. N., and Jayne, T. S. 2004. The effect of market reform on maize marketing margins in South Africa. MSU International Development Working Paper 83. East Lansing: Department of Agricultural Economics, Michigan State University.

Tripp, R. 2001. *Seed provision and agricultural development.* London: Overseas Development Institute; Oxford: James Currey.

Troup, L. G. 1956. *A report of the committee of inquiry into the dairy industry.* Nairobi, Kenya: Government Printer.

Tschirley, D., and A. M. del Castillo. 2007. Local and regional food aid procurement: An assessment of experience in Africa and elements of good donor practice. International Development Working Paper 91. East Lansing: Michigan State University.

Tschirley, D., and T. S. Jayne. 2008. Food crises and food markets: Implications for emergency response in Southern Africa. International Development Working Paper 94. East Lansing: Department of Agriculture, Food, and Resource Economics, Michigan State University.

Tschirley, D., C. Poulton, and P. Labaste. 2009. *Organization and performance of cotton sectors in Africa: Learning from reform experience.* Washington, D.C.: World Bank.

Tschirley, D., J. J. Nijhoff, P. Arlindo, B. Mwinga, M. T. Weber, and T. S. Jayne. 2006. Anticipating and responding to drought emergencies in Southern Africa: Lessons from the 2002–3 experience. International Development Working Paper 89. East Lansing: Michigan State University.

Twomlow, S., and L. Hove. 2006. Is conservation agriculture an option for vulnerable households? Briefing Note 4. Bulawayo, Zimbabwe: International Center for Research in the Semi-Arid Tropics, September.

UNCTAD (United Nations Conference on Trade and Development). 2007. Cotton and the WTO. *Information Note* press release, April 27.

University of Greenwich. 2000. An application nominating the National Agricultural Research Organization of Uganda (NARO) for the King Baudouin International Development Prize. Greenwich, U.K., University of Greenwich, January 19.

USDA (United States Department of Agriculture). 2007. *Cotton and wool situation and outlook yearbook.* CWS-2007. Washington, D.C.: Market and Trade Economics Division, Economic Research Service, USDA.

U.S. Department of Labor. 2008. Consumer price index. Washington, D.C.: Bureau of Labor Statistics.

Valdés, A., and W. Foster. 2005. Reflections on the role of agriculture in pro-poor growth. Paper presented at The Future of Small Farms Research Workshop, Wye, U.K., June 26–29.

Valdés, A., W. Foster, G. Anríquez, C. Azzarri, K. Covarrubias, B. Davis, S. DiGiuseppe, T. Essam, T. Hertz, A. P. de la O, E. Quiñones, K. Stamoulis, P. Winters, and A. Zezza. 2009. A profile of the rural poor. Background paper for Chapter 1: "Setting the Scene," IFAD Rural Poverty Report 2009. Rome: International Fund for Agricultural Development.

Van den Bosch, H., A. de Jager, and J. Vlaming. 1998. Monitoring nutrient flows and economic performance in African farming systems (NUTMON), Part 2, Tool development. *Agriculture, Ecosystems and Environment* 71: 54–64.

Van der Laan, H. L., T. Dijkstra, and A. van Tillburg, eds. 1999. *Agricultural marketing in tropical Africa: Contributions from the Netherlands.* Aldershot, U.K.: Ashgate.

Van der Pol, F. 1992. *Soil mining: An unseen contributor to farm income in southern Mali.* Bulletin 325. Amsterdam: Royal Tropical Institute.

Vanlauwe, B., K. Aihou, S. Aman, E. N. O. Iwuafor, B. K. Tossah, J. Diels, N. Sanginga, O. Lyasse, R. Merckx, and J. Deckers. 2001. Maize yield as affected by organic inputs and urea in the West African moist savanna. *Agronomy Journal* 93: 1191–1199.

van Otterdijk, R. 1996. *Baseline survey: Production and field management, post harvest and marketing of root crops in Zambia.* Mutanda Regional Research Station, Zambia: Root and Tuber Improvement Programme.

von Haugwitz, H., and H. Thorwart. 1972. *Some experiences with smallholder settlement in Kenya 1963/64 to 1966/67.* Munich: Weltforum Verlag.

Vowles, M. 1989. *Conservation tillage: A handbook for commercial farmers in Zimbabwe.* Harare, Zimbabwe: Desktop Publishing.

Waddell, A. 1997. Rapport financier: Application des mécanismes de rémunération et de stabilisation de la filière coton; Étude realisée à la demande du Comité de Suivi et de Gestion du Contrat–Plan État/Mali Textile Development Society/Producteurs, Novembre.

———. 1998. *Étude concernant la contribution de la CMDT aux recettes fiscales de l'État: Rapport principal,* vol. 1. Bamako, Mali: Ministère des Finances, République du Mali.

Wangila, J., R. Rommelse, and J. De Wolf. 1999. *An insight into the socioeconomics of agroforestry client-farmers in western Kenya.* Pilot Project Report 12. Nairobi, Kenya: International Centre for Research in Agroforestry.

Weatherspoon, D. D., and T. Reardon. 2003. The rise of supermarkets in Africa: Implications for agrifood systems and the rural poor. *Development Policy Review* 21 (3): 333–355.

Weinmann, H. 1972. Agricultural research and development in Southern Rhodesia, 1890–1923. Department of Agriculture Occasional Paper 4. Harare: University of Zimbabwe.

Whiteside, M. 2003. *Enhancing the role of informal maize imports in Malawian food security.* Lilongwe, Malawi: Department for International Development.

Whitney, T. 1981. *Changing patterns of labor utilization, productivity and income: The effects of draft animal technology on small farms in southeastern Mali.* M.S. thesis, Department of Agricultural Economics, Purdue University, West Lafayette, Ind., U.S.A.

Wiggins, S. 2000. Interpreting changes from the 1970s to the 1990s in African agriculture through village studies. *World Development* 28 (4): 631–662.

———. 2007. Is there a Green Revolution taking place in West Africa? Discussion paper presented at the Agricultural Economics Society Conference, Reading, April 2–4.

Williams, L. B., and J. H. Allgood. 1990. *Fertilizer situation and markets in Malawi.* Muscle Shoals, Ala., U.S.A.: International Fertilizer Development Center.

Williamson, J. 1956. *Useful plants of Malawi.* Zomba, Malawi: Government Printer.

Winter-Nelson, A. 1995. A history of agricultural policy in Kenya. In *Agricultural policy in Kenya: Applications of the policy analysis matrix,* ed. S. R. Pearson, E. Monke, G. Argwings-Kodhek, A. Winter-Nelson, S. Pagiola, and F. Avillez, pp. 31–48. Ithaca, N.Y., U.S.A.: Cornell University.

Wood, A. P., S. A. Kean, J. T. Milimo, and D. M. Warren, eds. 1990. *The dynamics of agricultural policy reform in Zambia.* Ames: Iowa State University Press.

Wood, S., K. Sebastian, and S. J. Scherr. 2000. Pilot analysis of global ecosystems: Agroecosystems. Washington, D.C.: International Food Policy Research Institute and World Resources Institute.

World Bank. 1982. *World development report.* Washington, D.C.: World Bank.

———. 1989. *Sub-Saharan Africa: From crisis to sustainable growth.* Washington, D.C.: World Bank.

———. 2000. *Can Africa claim the 21st century?* Washington, D.C.: World Bank.

———. 2002. *From action to impact: The Africa region's rural strategy.* Washington, D.C.: World Bank.

———. 2007a. *Agriculture for development: World development report 2008.* Washington, D.C.: World Bank.

———. 2007b. *World development indicators.* Washington, D.C.: World Bank.

———. 2009. *Awakening Africa's sleeping giant: Prospects for commercial agriculture in the Guinea Savannah Zone and beyond.* Directions in Development— Agriculture and Rural Development. Washington, D.C.: World Bank.

Wright, P. 1985. *La gestion des eaux de ruissellement.* Province du Yatenga, Burkina Faso: OXFAM, Projet Agro-Forestier.

WTO (World Trade Organization). 2003. *Poverty reduction: Sectoral initiative in favour of cotton.* Joint Proposal by Benin, Burkina Faso, Chad and Mali. Ministerial Conference Fifth Session, Cancun, September 10–14. Washington, D.C.: World Bank.

———. 2004a. Doha work programme. Draft General Council Decision of July 31. Washington, D.C.: World Bank.

———. 2004b. Agriculture negotiations: Backgrounder. The Cotton Initiative. Updated April 20. Washington, D.C.: World Bank.

———. 2005. United States—subsidies on upland cotton. AB-2004-5. WT/DS267/AB/R. Washington, D.C.: World Bank, March 3.

Yang, Y. 2005. Africa in the Doha Round: Dealing with preference erosion and beyond. IMF Policy Discussion Paper PPD/05/8. Washington, D.C.: International Monetary Fund.

Yanggen, D., V. Kelly, T. Reardon, and A. Naseem. 1998. Incentives for fertilizer use in Sub-Saharan Africa: A review of empirical evidence on fertilizer response and profitability. MSU International Development Working Paper 70. East Lansing: Michigan State University.

Yara International. 2007. *African Green Revolution conference summary: Productivity.* Available at <www.africangreenrevolution.com/en/conferences/2007/documentation/summaries/index.html>.

Yigezu, Z. 1998. DDE's experience in milk collection, processing and marketing. In *Proceedings of a conference on the role of village dairy co-operatives in dairy development,* pp. 52–68. Addis Ababa, Ethiopia: Ministry of Agriculture.

———. 2000. DDE's experience in milk collection, processing and marketing: The role of village dairy co-operatives. In *Dairy development: Smallholder Dairy Development Project (SDDP) Proceeding.* Addis Ababa, Ethiopia: Ministry of Agriculture.

Zachary, G. P. 2008. The coming revolution in Africa. *Wilson Quarterly* (Winter): 50–66.

Zambezi, B. T., F. K. Nyondo, G. Nkhono, G. F. Mbingwani, and T. R. Chakuta. 1997. Evaluation of recycled maize hybrids at three levels of nitrogen in Malawi. In *Proceedings of the 5th Eastern and Southern Africa Regional Maize Conference, June 3–7, Arusha, Tanzania.* Nairobi, Kenya: Centro Internacional de Mejoramiento de Maíz y Trigo.

Zambezi Basin Agroforestry Project. 2006. *Annual report, 2005/2006 season.* Harare, Zimbabwe: World Agroforestry Centre Regional Office.

Zambia/ICRAF (World Agroforestry Centre). 2005. *Annual report: Zambia/ICRAF Agroforestry Project.* Nairobi, Kenya: ICRAF.

Zambia, Department of Agriculture. 1992. *Review of agronomic work on cassava: 1970 to 1990.* Chilanga, Zambia: Mt. Makulu Research Station.

Zimbabwe, Ministry of Agriculture. 1995. Unpublished data files, Ministry of Agriculture, Harare, Zimbabwe.

Zulu, B., J. J. Nijhoff, T. S. Jayne, and A. Negassa. 2000. Is the glass half-empty or half-full? An analysis of agricultural production trends in Zambia. Working Paper 3. Lusaka, Zambia: Food Security Research Project.

Zwanenberg, R. M. A. 1975. *Colonial capitalism and labor in Kenya, 1919–1939.* Kampala, Uganda; Nairobi, Kenya; and Dar es Salaam, Tanzania: East African Literature Bureau.

Contributors

Mohamed Abdelwahab Ahmed is an agricultural policy specialist with the International Center for Agricultural Research in the Dry Areas, Aleppo, Syria.

Oluyede C. Ajayi works as a senior agricultural economist with the World Agroforestry Centre (ICRAF), Nairobi, Kenya. He is based in Lilongwe, Malawi.

Yemesrach Assefa was formerly a research assistant at the International Livestock Research Institute, Addis Ababa, Ethiopia.

Simeon Ehui is sector manager for agriculture and rural development for the South Asia region at the World Bank.

Steven Franzel works as an agricultural economist with the World Agroforestry Centre (ICRAF), Nairobi, Kenya. He is based in the United States.

Eleni Gabre-Madhin is chief executive officer of the Ethiopia Commodity Exchange, Addis Ababa, Ethiopia. She was previously a senior research fellow in the Development Strategy and Governance Division of the International Food Policy Research Institute, Washington, D.C.

Steven Haggblade is a professor of international development in the Department of Agriculture, Food, and Resource Economics at Michigan State University, prior to which he was a senior research fellow in the Development Strategy and Governance Division of the International Food Policy Research Institute, Washington, D.C.

Peter B. R. Hazell was formerly director of the Development Strategy and Governance Division of the International Food Policy Research Institute, Washington, D.C.

Thomas S. Jayne is a professor of international development in the Department of Agriculture, Food, and Resource Economics at Michigan State University, East Lansing, Michigan, U.S.A.

Daniel Kaboré is an economist at the Centre d'Analyse des Politiques Economiques et Sociales (CAPES), Ouagadougou, Burkina Faso.

Wilberforce Kisamba-Mugerwa is chairman of Uganda's National Planning Authority, Kampala, Uganda. He previously served as visiting professor at Williams College, Williamstown, Massachusetts, U.S.A.; division director of the International Service for National Agricultural Research Division of the International Food Policy Research Institute, Washington, D.C.; and Uganda's Minister of Agriculture.

Paramu Mafongoya is a lecturer at the University of Zimbabwe, Harare, Zimbabwe, prior to which he was a scientist with the World Agroforestry Center (ICRAF), Nairobi, Kenya.

Nicholas Minot is a senior research fellow in the Markets, Trade and Institutions Division of the International Food Policy Research Institute, Washington, D.C.

Margaret Ngigi is a senior lecturer with the Department of Agricultural Economics and Agribusiness Management, Egerton University, Njoro, Kenya.

Felix Nweke is a visiting professor at Michigan State University, East Lansing, Michigan, U.S.A., prior to which he was an agricultural economist with the International Institute of Tropical Agriculture, Ibadan, Nigeria.

Frank Place is an economist with the World Agroforestry Centre (ICRAF), Nairobi, Kenya.

Chris Reij is a natural resource management specialist at the Centre for International Cooperation of the VU University Amsterdam, Amsterdam Netherlands.

Melinda Smale is a senior researcher, Agriculture and Trade, at Oxfam America. At the time this work was conducted, she was a senior research fellow in the Environment and Production Technology Division of the International Food Policy Research Institute, Washington, D.C.

James Tefft is an economist in the Agricultural Development Economics Division of the Food and Agriculture Organization of the United Nations, Rome.

Gelson Tembo is a lecturer in the Department of Agricultural Economics and Extension Education of the University of Zambia, Lusaka, Zambia.

Index

Page numbers for entries occurring in boxes are suffixed by *b,* those for entries occurring in figures by *f,* those for entries occurring in notes by *n,* and those for entries occurring in tables by *t.*

423